Opening and Operating a Successful Child Care Center

Early Childhood Education

providing lessons for life

www.EarlyChildEd.delmar.com

Opening and Operating a Successful Child Care Center

Dorothy June Sciarra Ed.D. (Emerita)
University of Cincinnati

Anne G. Dorsey
University of Cincinnati

DELMAR

™

THOMSON LEARNING

Australia Canada Mexico Singapore Spain United Kingdom United States

Opening and Operating a Successful Child Care Center
by Dorothy June Sciarra, Anne G. Dorsey

Business Unit Director:
Susan L. Simpfenderfer

Executive Editor:
Marlene McHugh Pratt

Acquisitions Editor:
Erin O'Connor Traylor

Developmental Editor:
Melissa Riveglia

Editorial Assistant:
Alexis Ferraro

Executive Production Manager:
Wendy A. Troeger

Production Editor:
J. P. Henkel

Technology Project Manager:
James Considine

Executive Marketing Manager:
Donna J. Lewis

Channel Manager:
Wendy E. Mapstone

Cover Design:
Tom Cicero

For permission to use material from this text or product, contact us by
Tel   (800) 730-2214
Fax   (800) 730-2215
www.thomsonrights.com

Library of Congress Cataloging-in-Publication Data
Sciarra, Dorothy June
   Opening and operating a successful child care center / Dorothy June Sciarra, Anne G. Dorsey.
      p. cm.
   Includes bibliographical references and index.
   ISBN 0-7668-3598-7
   1. Day care centers--United States. 2. Day care centers--United States--Administration. I. Dorsey, Anne G. II. Title.
HQ778.63.5355 2001
362.71'2'068--dc21   2001023482

NOTICE TO THE READER

Publisher does not warrant or guarantee any of the products described herein or perform any independent analysis in connection with any of the product information contained herein. Publisher does not assume, and expressly disclaims, any obligation to obtain and include information other than that provided to it by the manufacturer.

The reader is expressly warned to consider and adopt all safety precautions that might be indicated by the activities herein and to avoid all potential hazards. By following the instructions contained herein, the reader willingly assumes all risks in connections with such instructions.

The publisher makes no representation or warranties of any kind, including but not limited to, the warranties of fitness for particular purpose or merchantability, nor are any such representations implied with respect to the material set forth herein, and the publisher takes no responsibility with respect to such material. The publisher shall not be liable for any special, consequential, or exemplary damages resulting, in whole or part, from the readers' use of, or reliance upon, this material.

Contents

Preface

This book was written primarily for directors and owners of child care centers. The authors are early childhood education specialists with many years of experience in teaching at the preschool and college levels. Both authors have administered programs, and Professor Dorsey has taught graduate and undergraduate courses in child care administration for the past two decades. Since the book covers the director's responsibilities for starting a new center and for maintaining an ongoing program, readers are introduced to the total range of administrative demands in different types of early childhood education centers.

A unique feature of this book is its focus on interpersonal relationships, combined with emphasis on developing sound fiscal and program management skills. Funding and budgeting skills, evaluating, hiring, collecting fees, and writing reports are essential for program survival; however, we are convinced that these skills are not sufficient for effective program operation unless they are combined with good interpersonal communication skills. Therefore, the book presents administration information in an interpersonal framework.

Director's Resources and a Director's Library are featured in this book. The Director's Resources include sample letters, job descriptions, personnel policies, parent handbook, and many other forms directors may need. An expanded annotated bibliography of resource books supplementing this comprehensive administration text can be found in the Director's Library. The Working Papers at the end of each chapter include applicable information about what was covered in the chapter. The accompanying CD-ROM includes all the Working Papers and Director's Resources, and select figures from the book. These forms can be easily downloaded or printed from the CD-ROM for use in an early childhood program.

Material for the Director's Corner came from interviews with experienced practicing child care directors and/or special educators. We gratefully acknowledge the directors who participated in these informative interviews. They are: Debbie Gleason, Sandy Hoover, Chris Kelly, Pam Mitchell, Barbara Pearson, Annette Quallen, Eila Roark, Diane Rocketenetz, Tracey Rowe, Sally Wehby and others we interviewed. These interviews gave us insight into the "real world" of the working director, and inspired us to make a special place in the book for sharing their words and comments with our readers.

This book addresses a number of timely issues for the year 2000 and beyond. Among these are: 1) use of computers for handling administrative matters including payroll, budgeting, scheduling, and the like; 2) information on funding; 3) a section on the Child Development Associate credential; 4) ideas for dealing with unusual emergencies including allegations of child abuse at the center, or unexpected use of weapons or force by irate visitors; and 5) health and nutrition information that includes a detailed chart on communicable diseases as well as information on policies for exclusion of sick children.

We hope we have been successful in presenting the technical information needed to operate a viable program, and in conveying the challenge and personal satisfaction derived from creating and implementing an excellent educational program for young children and their families.

D.J.S. and A.G.D.

DIRECTOR'S CORNER

To Do

_____ Call plumber 555-1234

_____ Talk to building inspector ✔ left message

~~_____ Call Red Cross—1st Aid Training dates~~

~~_____ Need detergent~~

_____ Do statistics for YMCA committee

_____ Send bills to parents who haven't paid tuition

_____ Rewrite snack menu

_____ Check coverage for classroom for Monday—teachers have parent conference
✔ OK-Susie will do

_____ Meet with Toddler teachers 1:45

_____ Appointment 5:00—parents to see center

_____ Call job applicant for interview for part-time

_____ Place ad for full-time job—deadline Friday for Sunday paper

_____ Order supplies
tissues
paper plates
plastic gloves

John
555-2345

"Making a 'To Do List' is the only way I can come close to keeping track of the many things I must do each day. I recommend it to your readers who hope to become directors. By the way, I also recommend they learn something about plumbing!"

—Director, community agency center

CHAPTER 1

The Working Director

A ny person who is doing a good job as the director of an early childhood education center is involved in all the jobs that will be described in this text, from enrolling children to evaluating staff, from budgeting to taking inventory, and from maintaining a physical plant to bandaging a child's scraped knee. The director's job includes all aspects of program and people maintenance. To do any one of these tasks, a director must have skills and knowledge; to do all of them requires stamina, understanding, and organization; and to do all of them effectively demands exceptional interpersonal skills. These skills enable the director to bring the best to parents, children, staff members, board members, and the community. In turn, serving as a model of these skills encourages those same people to give their best to the center. The effective director realizes that an early childhood education center can never be a one-person operation. There is a network of caring that transcends the day-to-day chores and makes being a part of a center worthwhile.

ADMINISTRATIVE STYLES AND ROLES

Although all directors are responsible for administering a program, their administrative styles are unique and the outcomes of their programs are markedly different. Some of the differences are based on the roles that are assigned to the directors whereas others are based on the personalities of the directors.

Roles

If all the directors of centers in one state or county were to gather and discuss their roles, the job descriptions would undoubtedly cover a very wide range of categories. Some directors teach, perhaps spending half of every day in their own classrooms. Others never teach but are responsible for several centers and travel between them, keeping aware of two or more sets of circumstances, staff members, children, equipment lists, and so forth. Some may be responsible to an industry, to a corporate system, to a public school principal, or to a parent co-operative association; others are proprietors and owners.

Some directors make all the policy and procedure decisions; others are in settings where some policy is set by a school system or corporate managing team. In other situations, every procedural detail is administered by the board. A director in a large center may have an assistant director, secretary, receptionist, and a cook; however, a director of a small center often does all the record keeping, supervising, telephone answering, and meal preparation. Directors work with half-day programs, full-day programs, or even twenty-four-hour care programs. The programs may offer care for infants and toddlers or for older children, both before and after school. Sick child care or care of children with special needs also may be provided.

The financial plan may involve proprietary or agency operation, and may or may not be organized to make a profit. Program goals range from providing a safe place where children are cared for to furnishing total developmental services for children including medical and dental care, social services, screening and therapy, and activities that promote intellectual, motor, emotional, social, and moral development.

The expectations of the clients served by the program and those of the community will affect the center director's role. Some communities appreciate a director who is active in participating in the affairs of their community council, in lobbying for legislative reform, and in seeing that the cultural backgrounds of the children are preserved. Others prefer a director who focuses strictly on center business or on preparing children to deal with the demands of the elementary school. Directors must blend their personal philosophies with those of the community to achieve a balance. This blending can occur only if a potential director and a board explore each others' philosophies before agreeing on the responsibility for administering a particular program. If the philosophies of the director and those of the center are truly incompatible, one or the other must be changed.

Sometimes, the director is confronted with a conflict between the two roles. The job description

DIRECTOR'S CORNER

I had no idea how complex my role as director would be. Such a wide variety of people seem to need me immediately for such a wide variety of reasons. Meeting them all would probably be impossible (and maybe not even wise) but at the end of the day—most days—I know the challenges have been worthwhile. All it takes is one little pairs of arms hugging me or one teacher smiling on her way out. "See you tomorrow, Chris!"

—Director, large suburban preschool

and the expectations of the people connected with the center may dictate that the director be present to greet teachers, parents, and children each day, and to bid them good-bye each evening. In between, the director may be expected to be present in case an emergency arises. Simultaneously, however, there are obligations to the profession and to the community that must be met. The director may be asked to speak to a luncheon meeting of a community group that is ready to make a contribution to the center, to attend a board meeting of a local professional association, or to provide information at a session called by the diagnostic clinic to plan for one of the children with special needs who attends the early childhood education center.

Directors, especially those with experience, also have a responsibility to serve as child advocates. Although the National Association for the Education of Young Children (NAEYC) Code of Ethical Conduct calls on all who work with young children to "acknowledge an obligation to serve as a voice for children everywhere,"[1] directors are more likely to have opportunities to see the broader picture of events in the community and beyond. They can keep informed about important legislative issues and conditions affecting children and families by reading professional journals and newsletters, and by being knowledgeable about local and national news. For example, NAEYC publishes Alert, an up-to-the-minute report of legislative proposals and calls to action. Because directors are leaders and models, not only in their own centers, but throughout the community, staff, parents, and others often look to them for information about advocacy issues. Some directors may post information for staff and parents, and others may make a concerted effort to involve people in an action plan. Some may write letters to the editors or to legislators, and others may testify before various governmental groups. In determining participation in advocacy efforts, each director must weigh the responsibility to be an advocate against the responsibility to the center, as well as considering personal time.

Although most directors work more than a forty-hour week, it is unreasonable and unwise to

[1]Feeney, S., & Kipnis, K. (1990). Code of Ethical Conduct & Statement of Commitment: Guidelines for Responsible Behavior in Early Childhood Education. Washington, D.C.: National Association for the Education of Young Children.

expect them to devote evening and weekend hours to their jobs on a regular basis. Directors who spend too much time on the job may become physically and emotionally exhausted, leading to ineffectiveness. As models for staff members, directors must demonstrate they can balance meeting personal and center needs.

Personal Qualities

Directors may become enmeshed in unreasonable workloads because they have become personally involved in the center's work. An effective director should be closely involved with the activities of the center while maintaining distance, a difficult combination to attain. The primary reason for the difficulty in achieving this balance is that good directors assume their role largely because they care about people, yet at times, find that there are overwhelming numbers of people who require care. This caring is exemplified in their willingness to do the mundane such as changing a diaper when a teacher is dealing with a crisis or mopping up the kitchen when the dishwasher overflows just before lunch. Caring is apparent when the director assumes the role of learner as well as teacher, and keeps abreast of current research while providing this information to staff when it is relevant. Caring is demonstrated by paying attention to detail: spelling an unusual name correctly, ordering the special food a teacher would like for a project, and seeing that each board and staff member is notified of an early childhood lecture that is being held in the community. Caring is regarding the operation of the center in a serious manner, yet maintaining a sense of humor.

For some people, caring is shown in an exuberant manner with lots of enthusiastic conversation, hugging, and facial animation. Others, who are just as caring, are quiet, seem somewhat reserved, and perhaps move into a relationship more slowly. Directors may have other combinations of personal qualities, but the genuine and essential ability to care is the one that makes the difference.

An interesting aspect of caring is that it may be misunderstood. Because they are concerned for others, directors may sometimes have to adjust the style in which they relate to people. For example, some individuals may be uncomfortable being touched. If the director unknowingly puts an arm around people who feel this way, they may be annoyed or insulted and be unable to accept the care and concern that is intended.

Being a caring person in the face of all the responsibilities of directing a center can be difficult. The caring director is constantly helping others by listening and providing emotional support for both children and adults, and may well need people to respond in kind. Those individuals who become effective directors usually enjoy giving to others; they seem to thrive on it. However, because they are seen at the center as the source of so much giving, they must seek sustenance from either the caring network at the center or a relative or friend outside the center. Even those people who freely and happily give of themselves need, at times, to receive support and encouragement through recognition and understanding.

Directing can be stressful because the director, although surrounded by people, is in a very real sense an isolate. He or she has no peers in the center, and no matter how loved and respected, is "the boss." It would be inappropriate for the director to confide in one particular staff member because some of the information with which the director works cannot be shared with anyone at the center. Some directors have established a network of directors. They meet, perhaps monthly, for a relaxing lunch and conversation. There is reassurance in knowing that other directors have to report child abuse, experience staff turnover, have too many forms to fill out, and have considered quitting. As a group, directors can create ways to solve problems, to support one another, and to heighten community awareness regarding the needs of young children and their caregivers.

In order to be effective leaders, directors must ensure that their own needs are met. Being a martyr, even a cheerful martyr, who never takes vacation or sick days may, in fact, lead staff to feel somewhat guilty when they recognize and meet their own needs. Competent directors serve as models of balance.

PROGRAM MAINTENANCE

Although a broad range of roles may be assigned to directors, and although they may bring a variety of personal qualities to these roles, every director is responsible for program maintenance. This task, whatever its parameters, is possible only when the director is skilled and knowledgeable. Throughout this book, the information essential to doing the work of a center director will be discussed. This information, when combined with some teaching and administrative experience, should help you perform the tasks that are necessary for efficient program maintenance. The tasks are to:

1. develop goals and objectives in relation to the center's philosophy, placing emphasis on the needs of clients
2. work with staff to plan a curriculum to meet the objectives of the center
3. develop a positive working relationship with the board of directors and its committees, placing emphasis on communicating the center's accomplishments and needs
4. establish policies for center operation or become familiar with policies established by the center board, parent corporation, board of education, or other sponsor
5. draw up procedures for implementation of policies
6. prepare and maintain a manual for board and staff members
7. work with licensing agents to meet applicable licensing regulations
8. provide adequate insurance coverage
9. comply with all local, state, and federal laws relating to the center's operation
10. establish and operate within a workable budget
11. keep accurate financial records
12. pay bills and prepare payroll
13. collect tuition
14. write proposals and seek other funds for operation of the center
15. locate and maintain suitable physical facilities for the center's program
16. order and maintain equipment
17. publicize the center
18. enroll and group the children
19. employ appropriate staff
20. evaluate the program, the staff members, and the children's progress
21. develop effective communication among staff members through regular staff meetings, conferences, and informal conversations
22. provide in-service training for both staff and volunteers
23. fill roles of other staff members in emergency situations
24. plan and implement a parent program that is responsive to parents' needs and interests
25. explain the center's program to members of the community
26. participate in professional organizations
27. continue professional development through reading and attending pertinent courses, workshops, conferences, and lectures

PEOPLE MAINTENANCE

Directors sometimes acquire their program-maintenance skills and stop there, failing to realize the importance of people-maintenance skills. Centers can and do run, at least for a while, without people maintenance; however, centers that lack program maintenance quickly close their doors. Yet people maintenance is at the very heart of a worthwhile early childhood education program.

Directors can enhance their people maintenance effectiveness by developing an understanding of their own interpersonal styles. They also will benefit from studying various approaches to management, analyzing their own managerial styles, and determining their strengths and weaknesses in these areas. Most directors have had limited opportunities to acquire this information because they often move into administrative roles because they were effective teachers.

Fortunately, many seminars, books, and video and audio cassettes are available to enable directors to learn about interpersonal styles and management approaches. The center board of directors may be willing to fund some training opportunities for the director, particularly if board members themselves understand and use this type of information. Possibly, a board member could furnish training or related materials.

Another option is to provide total staff or joint board/staff training in an approach such as Total Quality Management (TQM). This training, if well done, should lead to confirming the director's role as leader while establishing the responsibility of each staff member for the success of the center's program in addition to the responsibility of the director to see that staff are involved in decision-making and that their ideas are valued and accepted.

The staff and board members who agree to commit to a total quality type of philosophy use as a starting point the concept that their customers (children and families) are their first priority. By extension, a priority of directors must be staff satisfaction, and a priority of the board must be director and staff satisfaction. This approach works well when everyone understands it and accepts this basic principle.

Directors who are quite comfortable with a very authoritarian role may find it difficult or impossible to relinquish that role, just as teachers who are convinced that a teacher-directed approach is the only appropriate way to work with children may be unable to provide choices for children. Directors who are willing to invest time and effort in learning about management will usually find they are far more able to lead the staff and clients in ways that are more satisfying to everyone, and that the responsibility for the smooth running of the center will no longer rest primarily with one person.

The staff-oriented director plans time each day to visit each classroom, to greet each staff member, and to acknowledge their efforts and successes. He or she coaches and supports them as they develop new understandings and skills, and provides honest, sensitive feedback. The staff-oriented director remembers and relates to events and incidents that are significant to staff, children, and families. It may be commenting to a teacher about how well she managed a frightened child during a thunderstorm by describing specifically the effective approach the teacher used. Perhaps the director stops to greet a child who is proudly bringing his rabbit to school for a visit. Maybe the director telephones a father to thank him for organizing a book fair to benefit the center.

Tending to the personal and professional development of the people associated with a center's program is seminal to the success of the program. The manner in which the director carries out people-maintenance tasks is a major contributing factor in program maintenance, and vice versa. There is a delicate balance between successfully dealing with the mechanics of efficient program operation and simultaneously creating a caring environment for adults and children.

A director can have human relations skills, care for others, ask for their ideas and opinions, encourage them to try new methods, and provide them with positive feedback. But if that same director does not have the skills and knowledge to accomplish the huge amount of work required of an administrator, the program cannot succeed. The director who is task oriented, skilled, and knowledgeable may conduct a center that provides services but never really addresses or satisfies peoples' needs. Obviously, the director must combine work orientation skills with communication skills. If skills in either area are lacking, precious time will be wasted doing jobs or rebuilding relationships. Meanwhile, the children will not receive the excellent care they deserve.

MANAGEMENT TOOLS

Every director has a limited amount of time in which to do numerous tasks and develop many relationships. This work can be accomplished most effectively if the director is well-organized. Then, when the inevitable unexpected event occurs, the director will be in a position stable enough to withstand the demands of the crisis. For example, the director whose financial records are in order may not have extra cash available to replace a broken water heater but is better prepared to adjust other budget categories to provide the funds. The disorganized director may not even know what funds and expenses will occur within the next few months in order to adjust the budget to meet the financial crisis. An efficient director comfortably can take time to listen to a group of excited children who burst into the office describing all the worms they found on the sidewalk, but a disorganized administrator may be too busy planning menus that are already overdue. It is obvious that administration will not always run smoothly for any director; however, the director who knows about appropriate techniques and uses them is certainly better prepared to cope effectively with the hubbub that is often evident in a child care center.

The use of several management tools can enable directors to administer programs effectively.

These tools include policies and procedures manuals and time-use skills.

Policies and Procedures Manual

A manual containing all the center's policies and procedures facilitates the administrator's job. Generally, the board members make policies and the director develops procedures for implementation. For example, the board may establish a policy to admit any child between the ages of three and five who can profit from the center's program. The director then establishes the procedures that are necessary to accomplish the children's enrollment such as plans for informing the community, distributing and receiving enrollment forms, and notifying parents that their child has been accepted or that the center is full. The director also designs the necessary forms and includes copies in the manual.

When procedures are overly detailed or cover self-explanatory material, they become burdensome, and even may be neglected or circumvented by staff members. For example, teachers may be required to fill out a lengthy form to request permission to purchase something for which they will be reimbursed from petty cash; they might also be required to fill out another form after having purchased the item. At this point, some teachers may decide not to bother with purchasing needed items for their classrooms; they can carry their reaction one step further by disregarding the otherwise accepted procedures for using materials from the central storeroom. It is natural to anticipate that some established procedures will be unpopular with the staff, but if directors are open about why the procedures are important, and if they are careful about limiting the number of procedures to be followed, they will find that staff members are willing to comply.

Staff input prior to the establishment of procedures is usual, although the director may still need to make some independent decisions. When directors focus on their own need for power instead of on the establishment of procedures that will ensure the smooth running of an operation, it becomes impossible for the staff to feel respected. Staff members for whom every procedure is spelled out have no freedom. How then can they be expected to offer freedom to the children with whom they work?

Other Contents.   In addition to policies and procedures, the manual contains the center's bylaws, job descriptions, salary schedules, and information about the center such as philosophy, goals, sponsorship, funding, and perhaps a brief history. If the manual is large, a table of contents and an index are helpful. Placing all materials in a loose-leaf binder enables staff members to add and delete pages as necessary. Each staff and board member receives a manual on initial affiliation with the center, and it is the holder's responsibility to keep the manual up to date and to return it to the center when vacating the board or staff position.

Time-Use Skills

Some directors study time management as a tool to use in allocating available time wisely. The board may provide tuition or released time for a director to attend a time management course or seminar. Several time management techniques can be acquired easily and put to immediate use.

Analyzing Use of Time.   As a beginning, directors can analyze how they spend their time by writing down in detail everything they do for several days. The next step is to make a judgement about which of the activities have not been enjoyed, have not been done well, or have not been related either to the personal goals of the director or the goals of the center. When time is frittered away on such activities, less time is available to invest in other more productive activities. The individual alone can decide which activity should take priority. In some businesses, listening to a client discuss an emotional problem would be considered a waste of the administrator's time. In early childhood education, with its focus on children and families, time that the director spends listening may be the most effective use of the available administrative time.

Voice mail, e-mail, and other computer communication approaches help the director keep in touch while controlling the use of time. However, directors must be careful to avoid communicating with families and staff solely through technology. The sensitive director is alert to the need for live human contact and a hand-written note in some situations.

Although some of the director's tasks may not be appealing, they may need to be done. A director can, at least, recognize how much time must be devoted to undesirable tasks, then this amount of time can be put into perspective. If the majority of tasks seem undesirable, the director may choose to change jobs.

Grouping and Assigning Tasks.   The director who needs to economize on time may also decide to make an effort to read and answer all mail, place outgoing telephone calls, and record financial transactions at a specified time each day. Directors who allocate time for these types of chores and establish the policy that they are not to be disturbed during that time, will probably have more time for meeting people's needs during the rest of the day.

Directors also should consider which jobs they must do and which jobs they can delegate to someone else. For example, could the janitor inform the director of supplies that are needed on a regularly scheduled basis instead of having the director do this? Perhaps the receptionist could be trained to respond to the general calls for information about the center rather than involving the director in a routine conversation about when the center is open and the ages of children who are served.

Once the center's operation is reasonably under control, additional staff people can be trained to fill the director's role in his or her absence, thereby allowing the director to move out into the wider community on occasion. It is not appropriate to insist that other staff people do the director's work, but it is appropriate to begin to train them to assume the role of director temporarily. In this way, both parties can benefit professionally.

Planning a Time Line.   One of the ways a director develops efficiency is through the development of a time line. Jobs that must be done on a regular basis are scheduled. Then the director does them according to the schedule. This simple concept curtails procrastination by helping the director recognize that when a job that is scheduled this week is postponed because it is distasteful, time and energy are going to be spent thinking about it anyway. Since the job must be completed eventually, no time is saved by waiting until next week; nor does the job become easier.

Reflections

Imagine that at 3:00 P.M., you are greeted by a teacher who is leaving for the day and who wants to talk about her husband who has just lost his job. You had planned to spend the rest of the afternoon working on the major equipment order needed for a board committee report the following morning. You may choose:

1. to listen to the teacher.

2. to tell the teacher that you do not have time to listen because of the report you must prepare.

3. to schedule time the following afternoon to listen to the teacher.

4. some other plan.

Any of these choices could be appropriate; the director must make the best choice. The director who always finds himself or herself too busy to listen, or one who spends too much time listening must analyze why their scheduling problems recur. Think about your own reaction to this situation.

A suggested time line for a working director appears in Director's Resource 1–1 on page 13. Each director must develop a time line based on the personal responsibilities unique to the type of program and the client's needs. No matter which jobs and time frames are included, writing a time line gives the director and others a clear picture of the work to be done. The time line can be flexible when circumstances warrant, but the goal is to adhere to the plan so that regularly scheduled tasks will be completed and time for working with people will be made available.

In Chapter 2, you will learn about the importance of the director's interpersonal relationships and that they set the tone for the center. Directors who know what is involved in the job, who work to acquire the necessary knowledge and skills, and who use a managerial approach that reflects an understanding of the needs of staff and clients, are found in nearly every community.

These competent and successful directors know that being a director is exhausting, frequently challenging, sometimes frightening, never boring, sometimes lonely, many times hectic, and, yes, even fun.

They know that being a director, a really good director, means being a leader, a manager, a model, a coach, and a supporter. Although being a good director is hard work and time consuming, it is deeply satisfying, exhilarating, and richly rewarding!

SUMMARY

An effective director is a person who combines skills, knowledge, and caring. Although directors fill a variety of roles in countless styles, no effective director can let either the management and operation of the center or the care of and communication with people occupy an inappropriate proportion of time. For each director in each situation, personal decisions must be made about the style of directing.

Two tools that enable the director to blend program maintenance and people maintenance are the policies and procedures manual and time-management techniques. Each director must develop an appropriate balance so that the program maintenance does not override the people maintenance. Because people maintenance can readily be overlooked by directors who find themselves in the throes of program maintenance, directors must develop skills that enable them to excel at program maintenance. Only then will they have the time and energy to devote to people maintenance which is the very essence of a quality child care program.

Working Paper 1–1

Director's Time Form

How much time is spent on keeping financial records?_____

How much time is spent on communicating with parents, staff, board members, or children?

_____

How much time is spent handling emergencies?_____

Other information: _____

_____

Make a computer graph or diagram to depict these relationships.

Working Paper 1–2

Policy on Holiday Celebrations

1. Meeting the child's needs appropriately will be our first priority.

2. We will be sensitive to the interests and wishes of other school staff, parents, and community.

3. We will inform parents, principals, and staff of our plans and of our rationale and welcome dialogue on these issues.

In the space below, practice writing some procedures for the above policy.

Working Paper 1–3

Policy Statement for Outdoor Play

Do you agree with the procedure for Implementation of the Outdoor Policy? What would you add and/or delete from the procedures? Comments below.

The NAEYC policy statement on Developmentally Appropriate Practice states that outdoor experiences should be provided for all young children through age eight, on a daily basis. Because their physical development is occurring so rapidly, young children should go outside daily to practice large muscle skills, learn about outdoor environments, and experience freedom not always possible indoors. Outdoor time is an integral part of the curriculum and should be planned.[2]

Procedures for Implementation of Outdoor Policy

1. All children will go outdoors daily for at least 20 minutes. This time may be spent on the playground and/or on a walk. The outside time is to be viewed as an integral part of the curriculum. Therefore, planning for and discussion of that experience will be included in the Friday processing and lesson planning.

2. Parents will be informed that all children will be going out each day. Children not well enough to go outdoors are probably not well enough to be in school.

3. Plans will be made to provide caps, mittens, sweaters, etc. if needed.

4. Circumstances which might preclude daily outdoor play are:

   a. chill factor below freezing (32° F) at the time the children go outdoors
   b. steady rain or downpour. Length of stay outdoors will be adjusted on drizzly or snowy days
   c. during tornado watch or tornado warning period

5. On days when circumstances do preclude going outdoors, opportunity for large motor activity and/or walks within the building will be provided. Therefore, alternative plans will be discussed during the Friday processing and lesson planning.

[2]Bredekamp, S. (Ed.). (1987). *Developmentally appropriate practice in early childhood programs serving children from birth through age 8. Expanded edition*. Washington, D.C.: National Association for the Education of Young Children.

Working Paper 1–4

Policy Statement Form

Choose a topic such as job requirements, job responsibilities, or the like. In the space provided, write the policy or policies on the topic you have chosen.

Now write the procedures for implementation of the above policy.

Director's Resource 1–1

Sample Director's Time Line

Annual Tasks

Early Spring

Prepare budget and get board approval.
Determine salaries for following year.
Get staff contracts for following year.
Make arrangements for special summer activities for children.
Conduct open house for families of potential students.

Late Spring

Advertise for, interview, and hire replacement or additional staff.
Enroll children for autumn.
Conduct election of parent advisory committee.
Participate in election of new board members (if director has voting rights).
Set up calendar for following year.

End of School Year

Evaluate all staff.
Hold staff conferences.
Do self-evaluation.
Evaluate operation of the program.
Hold final parent meeting.
Assist teachers in evaluating children's progress and in holding conferences with parents.
Recognize volunteers.
Evaluate the center's goals (may be done biannually).
Clean, repair, and inventory equipment.
Order equipment and supplies for Autumn.
Thoroughly check building for needed maintenance and arrange to have this work done.

Summer

Assign teachers and children to groups and classrooms for September.
Apply for license renewal.
Check insurance coverage.
Arrange for medical, dental, and social services.

Autumn

Orient new staff.
Recruit and orient volunteers.
Distribute keys and supplies.
Place new equipment and supplies.
Arrange with colleges for student teachers.
Orient new children.
Conduct opening parent meeting.

Director's Resource 1–1 (continued)

Interview substitutes and draw up new substitute list.
Check on children's and staff medical records.
Establish individual work plans and evaluate procedures with staff.
Plan supervision schedule.

Winter
Write proposals for following year.
Evaluate policies, make suggestions for changes to board.
Evaluate procedures. Plan changes for following year.

Monthly Tasks
Prepare financial report.
Check budget; make report to board.
Attend and participate in board meetings.
Plan menus.
Order non-perishable food.
Order supplies.
Check building and grounds and equipment; provide for required maintenance.
Review teachers' classroom plans (may be done weekly).
Send bills.
Receive tuition.
Pay bills.
Complete forms for funding and governmental agencies.
Attend professional meetings.
Prepare parent newsletter.
Collect attendance records.
Conduct fire drill.

Weekly tasks
Prepare payroll (may be bi-weekly or monthly).
Supervise teachers (observe and confer).
Order fresh food.
Conduct staff meetings (may be bi-weekly).
Maintain bulletin board.

Daily Tasks
Greet each staff member at least briefly.
Talk with children and parents.
Record financial transactions.
Answer mail and phone calls.
Deal with crises.
Deal with the mundane.
Teach, including planning, implementing, and cleaning up (if included in job description).

Director's Resource 1–1 (continued)

Periodically
Fill roles of absent staff.
Participate in fund raising.
Attend fund-raising events.
Conduct visitors' tours.
Arrange for in-service training.
Confer with college supervisor about student teachers.
Conduct meetings to discuss individual child.
Contact other agencies to develop rapport.
Participate in community activities, such as the opening of a neighborhood recreation center.
Obtain and disseminate information on legislation.
Inform legislators of your opinion on issues related to early childhood education.
Attend courses, professional conferences, and workshops.
Give workshops.
Lead parent groups.
Attend parent advisory meetings.
Recommend termination of employment of staff member, as necessary.
Do any weekly, monthly, or annual job as need arises (for example, interview potential staff member or enroll new child as openings for staff or children occur.

CHAPTER 2

Developing Interpersonal Relationships

T he following quote is from the director of a community nonprofit child care center. "In order to be successful as a director of a child care center, I think, above all else, you have to be a people person. You have to realize that this job goes far beyond administrative policy and doing paperwork; that being the boss here is not really being a boss in the traditional sense. Being the boss here has to do with forming trusting relationships with your staff, respecting their individuality, being firm when you need to be firm and being gentle when they need a gentle hand. It's important to remember that you won't get respect if you don't show respect. Also, remember that others can do the paperwork, but you are the one who must build the relationships with your staff. Of course, you are also responsible for building relationships with parents and the community."

Clearly, the interpersonal issues and the time it takes to work them out are at the very core of every management position. Much of what follows in this book deals with budgets, boards, licensing, and record keeping, but the real task of the director as a manager[1] is to work effectively with, and provide support to, those who will implement the program. The manager must relate to these people and motivate them to do the tasks delegated to them. Members of the staff implement the total program, but the director, acting in the capacity of leader and motivator, orchestrates.

The reader may then legitimately ask, "Why learn about boards and budgets? Why not focus on interpersonal skills?" These questions are legitimate, but books about interpersonal skills and management strategies have been written by others with particular expertise in both management and communication. The Director's Library on page 479 includes helpful suggested readings in the section entitled "Leading People." Familiarize yourself with some of those books so that as you read about budgeting and buying equipment, developing personnel policies, or planning a facility you will be able to use that information in concert with effective interpersonal strategies.

The discussion in this chapter focuses on the importance of first developing good management skills, then using these skills, coupled with good communication skills, as the basis for functioning as an administrator of a child care center or any other type of child care program. Obviously, the person in charge must have knowledge of how to draw up a budget, write policy and job descriptions, decide about equipment, and so forth. However, writing policy, hiring staff, making budgets, and ordering equipment will

---

[1]The terms *manager*, *director*, and *administrator* will be used interchangeably. All these terms refer to the person who is in charge of, and responsible for, the total program.

all be wasted efforts unless the manager has those special interpersonal and communication skills necessary to select, motivate, and relate to the people who are to carry out the program within the framework set by the program philosophy, the budget, and the personnel policies.

Once the policies are established, the members hired, and the children enrolled, the function of the administrator parallels that of a classroom teacher. The administrator or director makes the total center program "go" much as the teacher makes the classroom "go" after the learning environment has been set up. Evans suggests, "It is like leaping from one to another of a dozen different merry-go-rounds, each traveling at a different speed, each playing a different tune, and each blaring a separate cadence. Yet the administrator must land gracefully, never missing a beat, always in perfect time with the music."[2] Once the program is going, the function of the director becomes catalytic or facilitative. The total task of the director is then accomplished by creating an environment in which others may grow. Through the growth and development of staff members, the program is implemented and the program goals are reached. The process unfolds in much the same way as in the classroom where the teacher attains the program goals through the growth and development of the children and their families.

CREATING A POSITIVE CLIMATE

As a leader, the director has the major responsibility for creating a climate of care, trust, and respect. This climate can best be achieved by demonstrating caring behavior, by taking steps to build a feeling of community or partnership, and by creating a climate for good communication among and between all members of the center community. The goal is to optimize the developmental potential of children, families, and staff.

Modeling

The emotional tone at the center is set by the way the director feels about others and by the success with which those feelings are communicated to others in the setting. The director creates a climate of warmth, caring, and acceptance by relating to staff members, parents, and children with honesty and openness. Mutual trust and respect will grow in an environment in which respect is earned, and the best way to earn respect is to show respect for others.

Emotional stability, maturity, and a positive sense of self are the basic characteristics of a leader who has the potential for assuming responsibility and leading people in a caring manner. This leadership style creates a climate that, in turn, motivates others to imitate the pattern of acceptance and warmth in their interactions; the caring behaviors become contagious. Most of you have read about and observed "modeling" in young children. One child who is perceived as the leader displays a pattern of behavior, and others imitate it. Johnny says, "Yuk! Spinach!" and soon everyone at the table is saying such things as "Yuk, spinach!" "Slimy spinach!" However, if Johnny says, "Yummm, spinach!" other children are more likely to respond positively to the vegetable being served. Although this example is clearly an oversimplification of what typically happens in a group, behavior is contagious, and there is evidence that a leader who serves as the model does indeed control the behavioral climate of the setting.

Modeling begins with the very first encounter the director has with the new staff members as they come into the center for interviews, or when a newly hired director is introduced to the staff for the first time. The basic trust and mutual respect that are communicated and felt during this initial meeting are the building blocks for the relationships that will develop among the people in the center. The pattern established during these first meetings will set the stage for future meetings, and will influence the ways in which staff members will interact with one another and with the families and children who come to the center.

Although warmth, acceptance, and mutual respect are clearly fundamental to creating a favorable environment for the growth and development of the people involved in the center program, other behaviors demonstrated by successful directors

---

[2]Evans, E. B. *Day care administration.* Cambridge, MA: Educational Day Care Services Association, n.d., p.2.

also facilitate personal and professional growth, and lead to more favorable environments for children. The director who shows intellectual curiosity and is always seeking more information to do a better job can inspire others to do the same. A leader who does not serve as a model of professional commitment and enthusiasm for learning more about children, families, human relationships, trends, and issues in early childhood cannot expect staff members to invest energy in these areas. The leader's responsibility is to show interest and enthusiasm for what is going on in the program and the profession, and to serve as a resource for staff members and parents. They, in turn, will be stimulated to improve themselves as people and as caregivers[3] of children.

Community Building

The director is responsible for developing and maintaining a sense of community among staff, parents, and children. Morale will be higher and the environment more conducive to growth for all involved if there is a "we" feeling, a feeling of belonging. As the feeling of belonging increases, anxiety, self-doubt, hostility, and feelings of rejection decrease.

Staff members who feel that it is *their* center and *their* program, who feel a sense of ownership about the program, will be more self-assured and enthusiastic about assuming responsibility. They will not only perform the tasks they are competent to perform, but also will be willing to invest energy into learning more so they can extend their area of responsibility. The total task of serving children and families becomes *our* task, and *we* provide the richest and best service we can given our human and material resources.

The "we" feeling radiates beyond staff to families and children. It becomes *our* center or *our* program, and children begin to talk about "my" school. The feeling of community permeates the entire environment; all who participate in the many aspects of the center program feel they play an important part in the total program. All participants feel that they own a piece of the program and contribute to its success or failure. Parents and children alike recognize that they are valued,

DIRECTOR'S CORNER

"I often think back on my own experiences in the classroom when I was there eight hours a day. I remember that I was expected to be nurturing and giving of myself all day long—it helps me remember how much I, in turn, needed to be nurtured. That's why I have an "open door" policy for my staff—I take time to actively listen, to problem-solve with them, to listen to them. I often have to put my paperwork aside because I know that a staff person needs to talk right now! This job goes beyond, 'I'm the boss and you're the staff person' relationship."
—Director, independent not-for-profit center

and that their contribution to the program is important. They come to understand that they are the very reason for the center's existence. There would be no reason for the center to continue if there were no families and children to serve.

All the discussion about a feeling of community or partnership in a child care environment produces questions about what a director can do to create and maintain that atmosphere. Some of it will grow out of the trust and mutual respect that result from the modeling behavior described previously. Community feeling also stems from good interpersonal communication.

Reflections

Take a moment to reflect on your own practicum experiences. Think through whether or not there was a sense of community in the center in which you gained experience. Consider whether or not you were made to feel that you were an important member of the community. If you recall feeling positive about the experience, who was most instrumental in creating that accepting environment for you? Did you sense the children also felt this was *their* place? Who was responsible for creating the "we" feeling in the classroom?

---

[3]Caregiver is defined as "one who is responsive to the needs of children."

Communicating

Every director will engage in a certain amount of written communication. When there is a need to communicate in writing, the first question to ask is, Who needs to know? Interpersonal relationships often are damaged inadvertently because some members of the group do not receive information that they feel should be relayed to them. For example, although a change in next week's menu may, on the surface, affect only the cook in a child care center, a teacher who has planned a special science experiment around one of the foods to be served on a given day may be very annoyed to learn about the change in menu after implementing the special lesson. The message itself, including the exact wording, can be more easily drafted once the audience for the message has been determined. Therefore, the audience receiving the message will determine both the content and the wording.

Although some communication will be in writing, much of it will be face-to-face communication, verbal or nonverbal. To be an effective leader, the director must be a competent communicator and take responsibility for helping the entire staff develop communication skills.

Verbal communication skills can be learned. The director can learn to send effective messages, to become a good listener, and to engage in effective problem-solving. It is possible to define specific behaviors, both verbal and nonverbal, that block communication. It is possible to improve communication skills and, as a result, enhance interpersonal relationships. Note that we have said this is possible, but it is not easy. Unless directors believe wholeheartedly in the importance of open communication for good interpersonal relationships, they are unlikely to invest the energy necessary to develop the skills and to practice them until they become totally integrated into a personal communication style. However, once this integration has come about, the director's communication style will inevitably serve as a model for others. The model will set the pattern for all the other people in the center and create an atmosphere more conducive to open communication.

It is important that verbal and nonverbal messages be congruent. Sensitive leaders will take care to convey the real message with their words and body postures. "Some communications researchers believe that fully 60 percent of all communication between people is based on body language."[4] Words that convey approval or acceptance but are accompanied by a frown and a closed body posture conveying rejection and hostility send a "mixed message" that is confusing to the receiver. Supportive, positive words and actions will help build trusting relationships among the people in the center. In a trusting relationship, criticism or negative reactions can be handled without destroying the relationship, provided they are given discretely and are carefully timed. For the director to criticize a teacher in front of the receptionist when the teacher is on the way to the classroom to help a crying child is the epitome of poor communication, and it will have a negative impact on future attempts at open communication. Other, more subtle blocks to communication that will set the stage for a defensive response, hostility, or feelings of inadequacy include demanding and controlling messages, put-downs, use of sarcasm or threats, or flip, humorous responses to serious concerns. It is important to consider what needs to be said, how to say it, and when to say it.

A sensitive leader is well-advised to consider carefully whether a situation calls for *telling* or *listening*. Telling often comes more easily than listening; however, in many situations, listening is a better vehicle for maintaining open communication and strengthening a relationship. Dealing with the personal problems of families or staff members often requires listening rather than telling. Such communication is energy draining and time consuming, but when done well, has a powerful and positive influence on the entire network of interpersonal relationships. It is time and energy well-spent.

In spite of all the caring and planning that go into creating a supportive atmosphere, conflict will arise. This is human and does not necessarily mean poor management; also, it does not imply weakness in the network. It does, however, re-

[4]Child Care Information Exchange: *The Director's Magazine*, January 1993, p. 5.

quire attention, and there are communication skills that can be learned by the director and the staff to facilitate conflict resolution. It is beyond the scope of this book to train the reader in basic communication and problem-solving skills, but there are a number of excellent resources that provide both basic information about effective communication and training exercises for practice purposes. Several suggested readings are included in the Director's Library in the "Leading People" section on page 479.

MOTIVATING THE STAFF

The director does the orchestrating, but programs are effected through the efforts of other people. The staff of a center must be motivated to plan and implement the total program. Just as communication skills can be learned, so can the skills for guiding mental and physical energies toward defined goals. Without training in how to guide and motivate human energy toward shared goals, the director will follow some rules of thumb that may leave the role of director-as-motivator to chance. This practice may be compared to designing a program for young children based on knowledge gained from having been a child, having parented a child, or having been through a public school system. Although these experiences may be useful, they cannot substitute for theoretical knowledge and sound educational background in the field.

As directors begin to think about ways to motivate employees, they usually think about salary increases, a better building, new equipment, more help in the center, and a number of other items that are related to money and budget. Certainly, low salaries and poor working conditions can lead to dissatisfaction, but the promise of more money, or the threat of less, will probably not have far-reaching or long-lasting effects on individual or group performance levels. However, if a leader is using dollars to control and motivate perfor-

mance, it becomes increasingly more difficult to find the necessary supply to meet the demand. In addition, extrinsic motivators or rewards motivate employees to get the rewards and do not alter the emotional or intellectual commitments that underlie behaviors.[5]

There are a number of useful strategies for motivating people to commit themselves to a task and to actualize their potential. Two of the strategies that seem particularly applicable to the child care setting are use of encouragement and provision of job enrichment.

Use of Encouragement

Encouragement is a positive acknowledgment focused on a specific attribute of some action or piece of work completed.[6] Rewards or reinforcements may motivate the staff, but as with teaching, they tend to increase dependency on the one who controls the source of the rewards and they also heighten competition, thereby defeating the overarching goal of developing a sense of a cooperative community. Encouragement, on the other hand, tends to build self-confidence and a sense of intrinsic job satisfaction.

The classroom teacher makes sure that encouragement is specific, focused on process, usually given in private, and is not judgmental or evaluative. The director keeps these same principles in mind when working with staff. To encourage a teacher who has just helped a screaming toddler, you might say, "I noticed how calm you managed to be with Tommy while he was having such a hard time in the bathroom. It worked out well." These words of encouragement are more specific and process-oriented than, "I like the way you work with toddlers." Telling the teacher of four-year-olds, "You must have done some detailed planning for the graphing activity you did today to make it go so smoothly. It's surely fun for you to watch their progress" is more specific and less evaluative than, "That was a nice graphing activity."

[5]ERIC/EECE Newsletter, (1993). Vol. 6, No. 2. ERIC Clearinghouse on Elementary and Early Education, 805 W. Pennsylvania Ave., Urbana, IL 61801-4897.
[6]Hitz, R., & Driscoll, A. (1988). Praise or encouragement? New insights into praise: Implications for early childhood teachers. *Young Children*. Vol. 43, NO 5. Although the focus of the article is on teacher-child interactions, the principles also apply to director-staff relationships.

DIRECTOR'S CORNER

"Encouraging staff is so important. The little words of praise, "good job" or "how nice" do not mean the same as when you take ten minutes of conversation with a staff person to say, 'Look at the changes in your room! What happened that made you think about changing the dramatic play area to a ballet studio? The aesthetics of the area and the detailed thought you've given to the choice of props is surely a delight for the children.'"

—Director, independent not-for-profit center

Job Enrichment

Job enrichment is a management strategy that enhances job satisfaction by presenting more challenges and increasing responsibility which, in turn, produce a sense of personal achievement and on-the-job satisfaction.

It is possible to design a job enrichment program for a child care center so that staff members are motivated to higher levels of commitment. As a result, they will experience greater intrinsic rewards. The job enrichment principles particularly applicable to child care centers are as follows:

1. Give new and added responsibilities to staff members so they are constantly challenged and empowered to control aspects of their work setting.
2. Provide opportunities for ongoing training that will contribute to quality of performance and to personal and professional growth.
3. Give staff members special assignments, including occasional delegation of coworkers' or supervisor's jobs, to broaden each person's understanding of the total operation of the organization. This procedure can bring more recognition from other staff members and open up greater opportunities for advancement.

Obviously, there is some overlap among the three stated principles, both in terms of the method used and the outcome expected. There also are other ways to enrich staff members' jobs that will broaden their experience and bring them intrinsic and extrinsic rewards. The many possibilities are limited solely by the creativity and imagination of the person in charge.

At first glance, it may seem that added responsibility will lead to dissatisfaction and demands for more money or other material rewards. However, there is evidence to suggest that, more often than not, the person who is challenged and who "stretches" to assume more responsibility will feel a sense of pride and achievement. For example, the classroom aide who, at midyear, is given the added responsibility of meeting and greeting parents and children at arrival time, will find that job intrinsically satisfying. The aide will develop better skills for helping children make that first daily break from a trusted caregiver, and acquire new skills for accomplishing the added responsibility. Assigning added duties can best be accomplished in an atmosphere of mutual trust, and it must be done through the use of positive communication skills.

The training needed to develop the skills necessary for managing a new task effectively often can be offered informally by other members of the staff and by exposure to resources such as books, pamphlets, videos, or opportunities to observe. Ongoing training can be expanded to include more formalized in-service sessions on curriculum, child abuse, communication skills, working with children with disabilities and their families, or other topics selected to serve a specific need within the center program. Release time or financial support for workshops, seminars, and additional coursework are still other ways to provide job enrichment opportunities for the personal and professional growth of staff members.

Delegating special assignments to staff members usually evokes a sense of achievement and recognition even though it means extra work. A cook who is consulted about menu planning and buying, and who is later asked to help evaluate the total food service program when the center is undergoing a self-study for accreditation, gains an understanding of what is involved in the total food planning and preparation program and developing a greater potential for advancement, whether in the present job or in another work setting.

SUMMARY

In this chapter, the intent is to point out the importance of good interpersonal relationships and trust within a center. Only through a feeling of community and a spirit of cooperation can a director create a supportive environment where both adults and children can grow to their fullest potential. There must be a strong element of acceptance and positive regard in the surrounding climate to establish a mutually helping relationship for staff, families, and children. It is the responsibility of the director, as a leader, to serve as a model of caring and respect for others to build a strong sense of community among all the people involved in the center program. Effective interpersonal communication among the staff members, children, and families is also an important basic element in creating a supportive, comfortable environment at a center, and it is up to the director to be the model of good communication in order to create an atmosphere of openness, warmth, and acceptance.

The director uses encouragement and job enrichment to motivate staff members. Neither of these motivational means requires money; however, both require special interpersonal skills a director can acquire. Effective use of these support tools will facilitate personal growth and a feeling of positive self-worth, and help move the center program forward.

Working Paper 2–1

Job Enrichment Strategies

1. Based on your understanding of the use of encouragement as a motivator, write an appropriately phrased positive acknowledgment for:

   The secretary

   The cook

   The custodian

2. Describe a way you could use the job enrichment strategy with:

   The assistant infant teacher

   The van driver

   The student teacher

CHAPTER 3

Providing for Personal and Professional Staff Development

The center director is responsible for the personal and professional development of the staff. In large centers or in corporate systems, the business and fiscal maintenance functions may be separated from the educational program maintenance, in which case the education director is accountable for the educational program and the accompanying staff development programs. However, in most centers, one person is responsible for both the business and educational program components.

A basic assumption underlying staff development programs is that adults have the capacity to change and grow; this capacity is, in a sense, similar to that manifested by children in their growth processes. Likewise, the director's responsibility, as it relates to the center staff, parallels that of the classroom teacher, namely, to create a favorable environment for optimum growth and development of all the people in the environment. Having the director serve as a model of professionalism in handling staff meetings, staff training programs, staff supervision, and assessing staff problems facilitates and enhances the personal and professional development of the center staff. The specific content or the specific strategy employed in any aspect of the staff development program depends on group composition. In the same way that classroom teachers assess the needs of children in planning appropriate learning environments, directors evaluate staff needs and plan staff development programs. In addition, the director establishes expectations for teachers which represent the bottom line and which are to be followed.[1]

STAFF MEETINGS

The director is responsible for planning and conducting staff meetings. Although conducting a staff meeting may seem to be a routine and relatively easy task, holding meetings which are satisfying and worthwhile for both the director and the staff require careful planning and preparation. Effective implementation of the planned agenda is largely dependent on the director's ability to maintain open communication among those attending the meeting.

Purpose of Staff Meetings

Communication is the main purpose of staff meetings. Although much can be communicated through memorandums and newsletters, posting bulletin board notices, and exchanging information on a casual,

[1]Jones, E. (1993). *Growing teachers: Partnerships in staff development.* National Association for the Education of Young Children, p. xv.

one-to-one basis, many issues and problems are resolved more effectively in a meeting.

Two-way communication in a meeting permits an interchange of ideas and feelings, and provides a forum for thoughtful discussion and clarification of problems and issues. The final outcome for each individual should be a better understanding, not only of problems and issues, but also of self and others. When staff members are involved in discussing program issues or problems, when their opinions have been heard, and when they have had some voice in decision-making, they feel a greater sense of self-worth and consider themselves to be a more integral part of the total center community. To be successful, staff meetings must provide a safe environment where staff members can ask questions, challenge others by presenting alternative ideas, and share feelings with the group.[2]

To prevent the meeting from deteriorating into a "gripe session," the director must take an active role in channeling the complaints and concerns toward improvement strategies. Open communication during staff meetings is one way to develop cooperation and harmony, and to encourage the "we" feeling among staff members. The sense of community is fundamental for the creation of a favorable environment for the personal growth of staff members, children, and families who participate in the center program.

When the director becomes aware there is an undercurrent of discontent among the staff, a staff meeting discussion focused on concerns and issues may be useful, but only after talking informally with several staff to see if the problem can be remedied, thus leaving staff meeting time for other agenda items. If, however, staff unrest persists, it may be necessary to assess staff morale through the use of a *climate survey*. A well-designed survey tool that includes items related to motivation, commitment, satisfaction or dissatisfaction, and other concerns can yield useful information directors then can use to provide a framework for a staff meeting discussion. The climate *survey* becomes a means to an end because it

helps staff focus on their most urgent issues, and it helps the director bring the staff meeting discussion toward problem resolution. Although both director and staff can have input into the design of the survey tool, calling in an expert to help design the questions is often the best way to proceed.[3]

Staff meeting discussions may involve specific questions such as which piece of outdoor equipment to buy, or whether to buy tricycles or books with the equipment money available at the end of the year. Sometimes, discussions focus on the use of available building or outdoor space, or on the appropriateness of timing the meal service or the monthly fire drill. The director may decide to use staff meeting time to discuss more general philosophical or educational program issues such as "what changes should we consider in our program planning in order to focus more attention on emerging literacy?" A question that logically follows is, "How do we, as a staff, learn more about the application of a whole language approach in the classroom?" Discussions about educational programs and general program philosophy often lead to group decisions about the focus and content of future in-service training sessions. If the group makes decisions about the training needs of the teaching staff, there undoubtedly will be a greater commitment to the training program than if the director makes those decisions without group input.

Directors and teachers sometimes decide to use part of each staff meeting to discuss individual children and their needs. These discussions, which are confidential among those involved, are particularly productive for the total staff when the center program is open and free-flowing, and the children regularly interact with different staff members. Although it may seem less productive to involve the total staff in a discussion of one child when that child is in a self-contained classroom, if others feel free to contribute they often can lend a degree of objectivity to the discussion.

Nonetheless, when staff meeting discussions are not of particular relevance to those in attendance, boredom and restlessness become appar-

[2]Teamwork terminators and some sure cures by Hawaii retreat attendees. *Child Care Information Exchange: The Director's Magazine,* July 1992, p. 7.
[3]Werner, S. (1996). Need a barometer for assessing the climate of your center. *Child Care Information Exchange: The Director's Magazine,* 109, May/June, p. 29.

ent, and members feel that the time is wasted. To maintain interest and open communication, try to select agenda items that are of concern to most of the staff members who are expected to attend the regular staff meetings. The agenda items that pertain only to the work of a few can be reserved for special meetings or assigned to small committees for discussion and subsequent decision-making.

DIRECTOR'S CORNER

"Our staff scheduling problems are so complex, there is no way I can plan a staff meeting during the day. We have evening meetings and everyone is expected to attend. Each new employee is advised of that expectation and assured that she will receive comp time or overtime pay."
—Director, employer-sponsored child care center in hospital

Timing of Staff Meetings

The frequency and timing of staff meetings vary, depending on the amount of business typically transacted and the amount of time devoted to each meeting. Weekly or biweekly meetings that are well-planned and brief may be more productive than long sessions that are held less frequently. Although staff members usually prefer daytime meetings because they need evenings and weekends to rest and take care of personal matters, evenings may be the only time everyone can meet together.

In half-day programs, staff meetings can be scheduled after the children leave at noon, or in centers with double sessions, early in the morning or late in the afternoon. However, full-day child care programs present special problems because the centers are open from early morning until very late afternoon, and the center staff usually works a staggered schedule. Naptime is often the time set aside for meetings because most staff members are present in the middle of the day; however, sleeping children must be supervised. Use of volunteers or parents for naptime supervision is an alternative, but one which licensing disallows in some places. In smaller centers, hiring substitutes to cover nap rooms may be a better solution.

The center staff and the director must decide which staff members, in addition to classroom staff, should be encouraged to attend staff meetings. It may be beneficial to have the bus driver, cook, or the receptionist at staff meetings because the kind of contact these staff members have with the children and families enables them to make a unique contribution to staff meeting discussions. Directors also may find it useful to ask the consulting psychologist, the special education resource teacher, or other professionals involved in the program to attend staff meetings. Anyone who can profit from, or contribute to, the discussions should be encouraged to come to the meetings.

DIRECTOR'S CORNER

"I reserve one half hour at the end of each monthly staff meeting, and have one staff member take over the meeting. Last month a teacher talked about a workshop she had attended on dealing with stress. It was great! We all participated in some of the stress relieving exercises she had learned."
—Director, employer-sponsored child care center

Preparation for Staff Meetings

Both the director and the staff members must prepare for a staff meeting so that the meeting will be productive for everyone. The director is responsible for preparing and posting the agenda, and for distributing any material that should be read by the staff before the meeting. Even though the director holds final responsibility for planning the agenda, all staff members should be invited to suggest agenda items before or after it is posted. The posted agenda should include a brief description of each item and the action to be taken. For example, if the agenda item about the use of outdoor space is to cover the timing for its use, the responsibility for setting up and cleaning up, and the equipment needs, all these subjects for discussion should be listed. The agenda should also clearly state which items are open for discussion and group decision, and which items are open only for discussion. In the latter case, the director hears the discussion, considers the ideas and feelings of the staff, and subsequently makes the decision. In the case of the outdoor space questions, the classroom staff probably should decide about the timing for the use of outdoor space; the total staff, including the janitor or housekeeper should be involved in the discussion and decision about setting up and cleaning up the space; the final decision about equipment purchase should be made by the director after hearing the preferences of the entire staff. When all these expectations are clearly spelled out on the posted agenda, there is little room for confusion or misunderstanding about what will occur during the meeting.

Each item on the posted agenda should include the name of the person responsible for presenting the item and leading the discussion, and a rough time estimate for adequate coverage of the item. This procedure notifies staff members about their responsibility during the meeting and ensures coverage of the entire agenda within a specified period of time. Giving staff members responsibility for selected agenda items is an excellent way to encourage interest in center operations. Reserving part of each meeting to have a staff member present on a topic of interest also contributes to the feeling of collegiality.

The director should distribute copies of minutes from previous staff or board meetings and any other information that will provide a common basis for discussion to enhance the quality of the dialogue during the meeting. For example, if there is to be a discussion about curriculum planning as it relates to emerging literacy, research studies and program ideas on this topic should be duplicated and given to staff members several days before the meeting. Individual staff members also should be encouraged to search out additional information on the topic so the time spent during the meeting is productive and informative for everyone. Occasionally, a specialist from the community can be invited to a staff meeting to contribute to a discussion that requires particular expertise such as services provided by the local children's protective agency or new information on infectious diseases in child care centers. When the director prepares the agenda carefully, and both the director and the staff members come well-informed, the outcome can be satisfying for everyone.

Staff Meeting Procedure

The director usually serves as the convener and assumes the responsibility for moving the group through the agenda by facilitating, but not dominating, the discussion, and helping the group maintain a balance between dealing with tasks and dealing with interpersonal processes.

At the outset, it is important that the meeting begin at the stated time and end on schedule. When the convener does not call the meeting to order on time and moves immediately to the first agenda item, group members are inclined to come late because they assume the meeting will not start on time. When the discussion of an agenda item extends beyond the time assigned, the convener should call attention to that fact and have the group decide whether or not more time should be spent on that item.

Perhaps all this emphasis on time seems unimportant, but time management is important. Time is finite, and you and your staff must develop good time-management skills to accomplish as much as you can within a specified time frame. The staff meeting is an excellent place for you, as a director, to demonstrate good time management.

Clearly, conducting an effective staff meeting takes careful planning and requires special skills on the part of the director. However, when meetings are satisfying and productive for the staff, they not only serve as a vehicle for communication, but also promote cooperation and good feeling among staff. Furthermore, staff meetings give the director a chance to model good interpersonal communication skills that serve as the basis for all interactions with children, parents, and other staff members.

Reflections

Think about your own schedule and the routine responsibilities you must face on a daily basis. Then suppose a parent arrives two hours late to pick up her child from school. For the next two hours, you will have to placate a frightened child and keep him or her entertained until a family member arrives. Now, you are two hours late for dinner and probably will miss the first act of that play you were looking forward to seeing. Remember, the only way you will be able to manage your time well is to have others with whom you interact regularly maintain their time commitments to you.

STAFF TRAINING

The staff training program begins with the orientation of new staff members and includes all aspects of in-service training. Planning the total staff training program depends on the composition of the center staff. Just as the classroom teacher individualizes approaches to children, so the director should recognize the developmental level of each teacher and plan training accordingly. The training must be adjusted to the experience level and career stage, as well as to the specific concerns, capabilities, and perspectives of each person, and should focus on long-term growth and change in individuals' thinking skills.[4]

Fully trained and qualified classroom teaching staff members should have basic child development information, and should be able to plan curriculum and classroom management strategies with a minimum of additional training. However, they may be ready for some help on working with the special education resource teacher who comes to consult with them about the children with disabilities in the center. Because special classroom strategies must be employed in order to truly include children with disabilities into a noncategorical classroom, training in techniques and strategies to accomplish that integration can be helpful to even the experienced teacher. The interdisciplinary classroom team of early childhood and special educators must work together to provide quality programming for all children in an inclusive environment. An interdisciplinary team-building and staff development approach for both the special educators and the early childhood staff is to provide mutual training so these professionals develop their own professional skills together, as well as come to appreciate more fully the knowledge and skills of other members of the team. As team members come to accept and extend the skills and knowledge of fellow professionals, mutual respect and camaraderie are reinforced. Further, with more preschools in public schools, where program expectations and philosophies are often incongruent with early childhood principles, team-building and staff development programs for both preschool and public school personnel in these settings is clearly indicated.

On the other hand, paraprofessional classroom staff may need training to prepare classroom materials, understand growth and development, or develop basic management skills. Custodians, food service staff, or clerical staff may need different levels and types of assistance. When planning a staff training program, the director has to assess the training needs of everyone, and then make decisions about time, content, and training methods for the sessions. An experienced director can assess training needs by observing staff as they carry out their job responsibilities, and by having conferences with them to discover more about their own analysis of training needs and their interest in professional advancement. Assessment of training needs is an ongoing process, and, as personal and professional development proceeds, the director's task is to present more challenging training opportunities.

Time and Place for Training

Finding a suitable time for training meetings is even more difficult than finding a suitable time for staff meetings. In the case of regularly scheduled staff meetings, the staff can plan ahead for the full year, and schedule their other duties and commitments around the meeting times. However, training sessions usually occur with less regularity, often require a larger block of time than a staff meeting, and have to be planned to coincide with the schedules of consultants or outside experts whose services are needed. If the director and center staff members are the only people involved in the training, scheduling difficulties are somewhat alleviated. Nonetheless, the problems of late afternoon or evening fatigue, and the inability of the staff to leave the classroom during the day create special problems for the training of child care staff unless the training can be planned for naptime, or can be incorporated into the staff meetings. Since most training requires larger time blocks, it may be necessary to discuss the possibility of a Saturday meeting. Half-day preschool programs that usually meet during the public school academic

[4]Jorde-Bloom, P., Sheerer, M., & Britz, J. (1991). *Blueprint for action.* Horizons, p. 95.

year often have training meetings in the early autumn before school begins or in the spring after school closes. In any case, if in-service training attendance is mandatory, this point must be included in the employee's job description and spelled out during orientation of new employees.

Whether or not attendance at training sessions should be mandatory or optional is a question that must be decided by the director or by the group. In some places where licensing requires a given number of clock hours of training each year, the planned training could be mandatory for some staff and not for others. If attendance is mandatory, the feelings of resentment may negate the possible benefits. On the other hand, if attendance is not mandatory, those who attend may feel resentment toward those who have decided not to attend. As a director, you will have to work closely with your staff to get a feel for their commitment to the training program, and their possible reactions to mandatory or voluntary attendance.

Reflections

Think about your personal feelings when you were told that you had to attend some function, such as a meeting, a party, or a class, as opposed to the times when you were given a choice. When it was a matter of choice, what were the factors that motivated you to attend? Was it curiosity about who would be there or what would take place? Was it interest in what you expected would take place? Was it to please the person who requested you attend or who told you about the event? Can you analyze your feelings and reactions when you went someplace to please someone else as opposed to the times when you went because you were intrinsically motivated?

When there is a comfortable lounge or conference room at the center, the staff may prefer to stay in the building for the training sessions. The comfort and familiarity of the center helps create a feeling of openness which could be very important if the success of the training is dependent on dialogue and exchanging ideas among staff members. If the training is a cooperative effort and several centers are involved, a space in a centrally located community building may be more convenient for the trainees.

Training Methods and Resources

The methods or strategies employed in the in-service training program will depend on the amount of time and resources available, and the nature of the content selected. For example, if one hour of a staff meeting is set aside for a refresher course in first aid, the best way to present that information may be in a lecture given by a representative from the health department or with a film presentation. If, on the other hand, there is more time to spend on the topic of first aid, it may be desirable to plan a full day session with a Red Cross specialist. Enrolling some staff members who do not have first aid certificates in a Red Cross course that extends over several weeks but is available evenings or on Saturday is yet another alternative. First aid training can be expanded to include health, nutrition, and safety. The expansion of the program creates new training strategy possibilities. Group discussions led by the director would be an appropriate method to use in making the staff more aware of safety issues in the center. The program could include discussions about safety when using outdoor equipment, planning cooking experiences, or organizing field trips. The health or nutrition questions might be handled best by a nurse, physician, or a dietitian who would attend a seminar. A special educator might come to discuss health and safety issues when these relate to special needs children. When outside consultants are brought in, the director's role is to sit in on the training in order to enable follow-up with the staff, thus extending the new information to specific situations each teacher encounters in the classroom. There are any number of possible methods from which to choose; each one requires different amounts of time and different resources, and all are individualized to meet the needs of the trainee.

On-site workshops are useful mechanisms for encouraging direct involvement of the staff in a special content area. Implicit in the workshop concept is the idea that those who attend participate actively in the program. Frequently, workshops are planned for a staff that expresses a need to know more about curriculum areas such as developing writing centers, math or science experiences for young children, or music in the classroom. Other areas, such as building skills for more effective conferences with parents or for ways to interact with volunteers, also can be handled in a workshop format that involves participants in a series of role play or simulation games. Workshops require active involvement from the participants and are more suitable for some training needs than are lectures, films, or seminars.

DIRECTOR'S CORNER

"One of the most helpful things we did in my administration class at college was role playing. I especially remember role playing a parent conference. Now I use that technique all the time with my staff. In staff training sessions, when we are discussing an issue like dealing with a difficult parent, I ask for a specific example, and immediately turn it into a role play. 'OK—now I'm the parent and here is my concern—you are the teacher,' and we play it out. Then we often reverse roles so I take the role of the teacher. It works very well for me as a director."

—Director, YMCA-sponsored center

Visits to other centers are encouraged by some directors and comprise part of the total staff training program. Watching other teachers and children is refreshing and interesting for some staff members. After such visits, they bring back program ideas, new and different ways to set up the physical environment, and sometimes a renewed interest in developing classroom materials such as math games or interactive charts. Some teachers who are able to move beyond the more obvious things like equipment or curriculum ideas may begin to compare and contrast classroom environments and teaching strategies, relating these differences to those in the stated philosophies of the programs. Follow-up group discussions will help teachers refine their understanding of how theory relates to practice. Why are the children in one program encouraged to negotiate with one another about dividing up the play dough, while the teacher controls amounts for each child in another center? The two strategies clearly reflect different program goals. Group discussions also may en-

courage teachers to reexamine the theoretical basis for the center program in which they work and reevaluate the curriculum to ascertain how closely it reflects the stated philosophy of the center, as well as their own philosophy of early childhood education.

Professional conferences and workshops provide excellent training opportunities for staff. Directors who commit to a personal program of professional development by attending professional meetings set a standard of excellence for their teachers to emulate. It is important to encourage staff to take advantage of these training opportunities, and facilitate their attending conferences by allowing time off from work and subsidizing their travel and registration expenses if at all possible. Some child care programs not only subsidize conference attendance but also pay for teachers' memberships in professional organizations such as the National Association for the Education of Young Children (NAEYC) which includes membership in local affiliates, or the Association for Childhood Education International (ACEI).

Staff members who express an interest in professional advancement should be commended for their ambitious goals and encouraged to take courses toward a college degree in child development or early childhood education, or the Child Development Associate (CDA) certificate in communities where these types of training programs are available. Some centers will help pay tuition for relevant courses as well as adjust work schedules to allow staff to attend daytime classes. Directors can lend further support to part-time staff by showing interest in what they are learning and guiding them to helpful resources available at the center.

In order to provide on-site materials to support and enhance all aspects of the staff training program, it is the job of the director to establish a professional library and a teachers' resource center. The library books should cover information on child development, curriculum, classroom management, special needs children, and working with other professionals and with families. Books on specific curriculum areas such as literacy, math, science, cooking, or music will help the staff plan for the children. Recent copies of professional journals and newsletters should be available in the teachers' library, along with a collection of audio-visual materials including tapes, slides, videotapes, and film strips which provide a rich source of information on curriculum development and classroom management.

The teachers' resource center should be a space where teachers can make math games, charts, big books, and other teacher-made classroom materials. Supplies like paper, tag board, paper cutter, scissors, glue, tape, plain die, marking pens, and so forth must be available, in addition to a large working surface. When teachers have materials and space to work, they are more likely to develop individualized teacher-made classroom materials.

Training Content

A number of program ideas for a staff training program have already been mentioned in the previous discussions on methods of training. Training needs will vary according to the previous training and experience of the center staff. Many teachers are constantly seeking new curriculum ideas and resource materials for the classroom; consequently, training in curriculum areas is usually welcomed. There is always interest in strategies for dealing with the difficult, disruptive child or the withdrawn child. Furthermore, most teachers are interested in learning more about community resources where they can get advice about how to handle children with special needs, or about where to refer children and families for additional help.

The director should determine if staff members need special coaching in conducting a home visit or a parent conference. These duties are taxing, produce anxiety, and require very special communication skills suitable for the particular parent population being served. It is important to know that some families may be slow to accept a stranger and will draw back from a person whom they perceive as too intrusive. Attitudes about accepting newcomers, education, and child rearing vary among cultural, ethnic, and socioeconomic groups, and it is essential for staff to know what those differences are when they work with children and families. Staff members also find it helpful to have special guidance from the director in effective interpersonal communications.

There is a pressing need to assist staff with dealing with diversity in the classroom. Including children with disabilities, and children from diverse cultural and ethnic groups into early childhood education programs means there must be training programs that focus on providing information about ways to meet the individual needs of children from these groups. Other timely issues where teachers often need help include children of divorce, single-parent families, hospitalization of a parent or the child, victims of child abuse, and so forth.

When the staff is experienced and fully capable of dealing with the day-to-day, here-and-now events in the classroom, training can move on to the question of early childhood education in the next century. What do children need to know to survive in the twenty-first century? How will life change in the next fifty years, and what personality characteristics and thinking dispositions will be essential to function competently during those fifty years? The job of staff training is never completed because there are always new challenges.

STAFF SUPERVISION AND COACHING

The director, or educational director in the case of large centers or corporate chains, is responsible for supervision of classroom staff. (The director will be referred to as *supervisor* for the purposes of this discussion.) By observing, coaching one-to-one, and working in the classroom with the children and the staff, the supervisor gives support and guidance to each staff member, and establishes a trusting relationship with each one. The trust and mutual respect that develop provide the basis for building a teaching-learning relationship that parallels the relationship between adult and child. Then the supervisor is able to create a favorable environment in which each staff member can gain new understandings of children, of self, and of his or her expectations.

An experienced supervisor knows that sometimes growth and change take place slowly. Working together, talking together, and planning together will promote personal and professional competence on the part of classroom staff members, provided the supervisor is supportive and encouraging, and is not perceived as being critical or threatening.

Principles of Supervision

A number of basic principles or assumptions should be kept in mind as you think about the director as staff supervisor. The same principles apply to the supervisory role whether you are working with a new, inexperienced staff member or a mature, qualified, experienced teacher, or are a new director moving into a fully staffed center.

- Supervision is a dynamic, evolutionary process that is based on trust.
- Supervision is individualized and adapted to the personality and teaching style of each staff member.
- Supervision provides a support system for each staff member.
- Supervision provides a framework within which the supervisor demonstrates professional skills for the entire staff.

However, an individualized model of staff development means you must use a developmental approach to supervision, and teachers who are at different stages in their careers will require qualitatively different supervisory strategies.[5]

Supervisory Process

As classroom staff members grow and change, the thrust and focus of the supervisory process shifts accordingly. The process begins by providing support and guidance for a new staff member who is actively integrating past learning experiences into a personal teaching style that is compatible with the center philosophy. The process changes as the staff member adjusts and develops into an accomplished teacher who will in turn, supervise assistants, aides, student teachers, or be paired with a new teacher and become a mentor. If you think of this supervisory process on a continuum, it moves from a very directive approach for new teachers where the control is in the hands of the supervisor, to a collaborative model where an accomplished teacher and the supervisor share control of the process.

One-to-one coaching is the essential ingredient of the supervisory process whether working with the beginning teacher or the accomplished professional who, in turn, will coach others in the center. Coaching includes modeling, observing, and giving specific feedback. Communicating with staff after an observation is usually handled in a conference, but when time is short, a brief note with some specific feedback may have to suffice.

The method and intensity of supervision varies from actually teaching in the classroom with the classroom teacher in order to coach and model exemplary practice, to frequently scheduled classroom observations and conferences, or occasional observations and conferences. In addition to this ongoing supervisory process, there must also be a regularly scheduled, more formal review of all teaching staff. After the notes or checklists from supervisory classroom observations are shared with the staff member, they become part of that teacher's file and are subsequently utilized as a basis for the regularly scheduled teacher evaluation and review process. (See Chapter 11, Director's Resource 11–8 for a sample teacher evaluation, Director's Resource 3–1 at end of this chapter for a sample checklist for supervisory classroom observations, and Chapter 15 for additional discussions of teacher evaluation.) When staff have been effectively supervised and coached through ongoing observations and conferences, they usually know what to expect from their more formal evaluation review.

Supervising New Teachers. New teachers need daily or even hourly support; therefore, the supervisor must plan to spend some time each day not only observing but also teaching with the new teacher. If a new teacher is also recently trained, that teacher will be developing a personal teaching style and will profit from the example that is set by an experienced supervisor. It is very important for a supervisor to work beside a new teacher with the children in the classroom. This supervisory procedure creates a rich learning environment for the new teacher, and often provides a more favorable transition for the children and families who know the supervisor but are not yet acquainted with the new teacher. As a supervisor,

[5]Ibid., p. 98.

you must remove yourself gradually so that the new teacher can build a relationship with the children and families, and begin to manage the classroom without your constant support. What you are doing, in effect, is providing hourly or daily support during the initial trust-building period but stepping back when the new teacher is able to function autonomously. However, staying nearby is important because your ongoing support is still needed when things do not go well.

DIRECTOR'S CORNER

"Since I am new here I haven't developed a schedule for regular observations as yet, but I make the rounds at least twice a day, if only to let my teachers know I am available. Of course, I have a chance to catch things going on in each room—maybe a new chart or a teacher reading a book to a sleepy child. I make sure I leave a short note in each teacher's box, mentioning some little thing I noticed when I came by. If I see an activity or a procedure which concerns me, I mention it. 'I noticed you had the toddlers fingerpainting with chocolate pudding today. Drop by when you have a chance—I have some ideas about that which I would like to share with you.' It seems to work well for me."

—Director, community-agency-sponsored center

Supervising Experienced Teachers. As teachers develop their skills and become more competent, they continue to profit from the supervisor's support. Positive reinforcement and constructive criticism from supervisors are excellent motivating factors, but experienced teachers are also ready for expansion and growth in new directions. They are still integrating and reorganizing what they have learned in the past, but they are now able to reach out for new learning opportunities. These teachers are now comfortable with their teaching style and can direct more attention to curriculum development. They are ready for the intellectual stimulation; they can draw from taking course work, reading new publications, and attending professional meetings. Therefore, although the supervisor continues to observe these teachers and have conferences with them on a regular basis, emphasis is now placed on the supervisor as a resource person. The supervisor should supply new program ideas, new theoretical information, articles from professional journals, research materials, and as many opportunities as possible to participate actively in professional organizations and conferences.

While experienced teachers are perfecting their teaching skills under the guidance of the supervisor, they should also be developing self-evaluation skills. With encouragement and help from a supervisor, experienced teachers feel secure enough to step back and evaluate their teaching. They can begin to ask themselves some of the questions a supervisor has been asking them and engage in some self-searching about their methodology. For example, one teacher might make the inquiry, "How could I have handled the situation better between those two children who had a conflict over the sand bucket? What I did was really not productive. I must find alternative ways of handling those two children." Another teacher might ask, "How can I adjust my questioning techniques for all the children in order to help them become better problem solvers? I heard you mention Rheta deVries. Maybe you could give me something she has written on that topic that will help me."

Supervising Accomplished Teachers. The accomplished, long-term teacher is still perfecting teaching and self-evaluation skills, and revising curriculum. However, having reached a new level of mastery, this teacher is ready to develop supervisory skills. While working with the teachers, the supervisor has not only exemplified teaching and self-evaluation skills, but supervisory skills as well. In working with accomplished teachers, the supervisor now turns to coaching them in supervisory skills. This teacher is preparing to assume responsibility for the supervision of assistants, aides, and, in some situations, student teachers. To serve in this capacity, the teacher will need instruction and support to develop the necessary skills for fulfilling supervisory responsibilities. The supervisor is still observing and having conferences on a regular basis, giving attention to teaching strategies and self-evaluation. However, the new thrust is directed to this teacher's interaction with, and supervision of, other adults in the classroom.

Supervision is one of the most difficult and anxiety-producing aspects of the director's job. It draws on every bit of professional skill the director has because it demands expertise in interpersonal communication, children's programming, teaching strategies, and self-evaluation. It also helps the director focus on the importance of being a model for the staff by making positive suggestions to coach and motivate by using supportive, caring gestures, and voice tone. This sets the tone for staff who, in turn, are more likely to follow a similar pattern in their interactions with children and families.

Reflections

Think about the supervisor who guided your practicum. Did you receive support and constructive criticism? Did that person serve as a model of good supervisory skills for you? Think about how he or she might have been more helpful. What do you feel you need before you can become a supervisor of a center classroom staff?

ASSESSING STAFF PROBLEMS

Assessing what staff members view as work-related problems provides the basis for designing the staff development program and focusing individualized supervision activities. Once you have identified what teachers feel are their major problems, you can take the first steps toward helping them solve those problems.[6] The expressed needs of staff can be addressed directly. If a teacher has problems handling the aggressive behaviors of a child, the director can respond in various direct ways, including offering relevant readings, observing or participating in the classroom, discussing various management strategies, calling in a consultant to observe and conference with the classroom staff, or discussing the general problems of dealing with aggression in a staff meeting. This direct response to an expressed need is certain to motivate the staff member to become involved in a training plan offered by the director. On the other hand, when the selection of staff development activities is based on those issues the director views as problems, motivating staff in-

terest will be more difficult. For example, if a new director finds the long-term staff is using punitive and age-inappropriate techniques in response to unacceptable classroom behaviors, but the teachers are comfortable with their management methods, those teachers will resist making a commitment to any training designed to encourage them to use more positive management strategies. The new director will have to spend time establishing a trusting, working relationship with the professional staff before training related to the classroom management question will be accepted. Because the use of punitive management techniques can be hard on children, the new director may choose to bring in a consultant to work with individual staff members or may even consider making staff changes. A new director is well advised to design the initial staff development activities in response to the teachers' expressed needs.

Expressed Teacher Concerns

Expressed teacher concerns cluster around a number of problem areas.[7]

The director's task is to identify and then respond to these concerns. The areas of greatest concern include the following.

Dealing with Subordinate Staff.   Teachers have a problem getting their assistants to follow through on assigned responsibilities and to work as a member of a cooperative team. In response to this problem, effective directing, evaluating and giving feedback to subordinate staff would be appropriate areas to address in the staff training program. The best way for the director to help teachers with this problem is to model exemplary supervisory skills.

Managing the Classroom.   Teachers report problems with controlling children's unacceptable behaviors. Included in their list are items such as aggression, not picking up, not sharing, and not cooperating. In addressing this problem, the director might first focus on developmental expectations for the specific age group in question, followed by ways to encourage prosocial behaviors. This is a sensitive problem area because the perceived problems sometimes result from

[6]Ibid., p. 250.
[7]Ibid., p. 256.

teachers' unrealistic expectations. Directors must model developmentally appropriate responses to children's behaviors whenever they have encounters with children in the center.

Helping Children with Special Needs and Their Families.   Teachers report that they do not know enough about how to deal appropriately with atypical children. This becomes a serious problem when children with previously unidentified social or emotional problems join the group. Teachers suddenly realize that this child is, indeed, disturbed and in need of special help, but they are not prepared for the disruption and management challenges this new child presents. They want help on how to provide rich environments for these children as well as ways to work effectively with the family. Providing reading materials and planning special meetings on this topic will be helpful to teachers who are searching for better ways to help these special children. Directors also must watch for upcoming conferences and meetings on the topic, and encourage staff to attend.

Relating to Supervisors.   Directors must face the reality that they are often perceived as a major problem by staff members. Teachers complain about not being treated fairly and not being respected as professionals. The response to this problem is clearly in the director's hands. Directors must work on their own professional development to enable them to become better staff managers.

Maintaining Parent Cooperation.   Teachers have problems with parents who send a sick child to school, who are not prompt about picking up their child from school, or those who do not cooperate with the teachers' efforts to encourage the use of "messy" materials. Here, the director can reinforce center policies by reviewing the Parent Handbook material with the parent and participating in parent conferences, when necessary, to mediate and give support to both the teacher and parent. In-service training focused on working with parents and becoming sensitive to their needs may help teachers feel more secure about handling difficult situations with them.

Managing Time.   Time to deal with nonteaching tasks such as cleaning, planning, making materials, or doing other paperwork is a problem for teachers. Since time management is also a major problem for directors, it is something they have in common. Time management seminars under the guidance of an experienced trainer can be part of the staff development program. It is especially important for the director to be a part of this training and to model good time management.

Although staff concerns are always situation-specific, there is a common core of recurring problems that fall into the categories listed here. It can be reassuring to you, as a director, to know that your teachers' expressed needs are much like those of most teaching staffs.

SUMMARY

The staff development program contributes to both the personal and professional growth of the center staff. Through the planning and implementation of effective staff meetings, staff training programs, and staff supervision, the director creates an enriched learning environment for the staff. Given the benefits of an enriched environment and a director who demonstrates good interpersonal and professional skills, the staff members have the opportunity to enjoy the inevitable personal satisfaction and excitement that result from positive, individualized, professional growth experiences.

Working Paper 3–1

Staff Meeting Questions

Based on your experience at a recent staff meeting, answer the following questions.

1. Did you fulfill the role of keeping the group focused on the agenda items? How?

2. Was there any attempt to follow a time line? If not, what effect do you suspect it had on the feelings of the staff?

3. Were there any notable incidents where staff members seemed not to be heard? Describe them, and indicate the behaviors that you observed in those staff members after the incidents.

Working Paper 3–2

Expressed Teacher Problems

1. Based on your experiences in your professional career, rank in order the expressed teacher problems listed below from most difficult (1) to least difficult (10).
   ____ Finding time to relax and do paperwork.
   ____ Getting the supervisor to respect my opinion.
   ____ Knowing how to handle aggressive children.
   ____ Handling a child with a physically disabling condition.
   ____ Handling a demanding child without neglecting the other children.
   ____ Handling a parent who is very punitive with her child when she picks him up.
   ____ Getting the other adults in the room to do their share of cleanup and "dirty" work.
   ____ Keeping children's attention during group time.
   ____ Motivating myself to be involved with professional organizations
   ____ Dealing with criticism from my supervisor.

2. Select problem 1, 2, or 3 from your ranking, above, and complete a staff-training plan to addresses that problem by listing the relevant material you would provide in the staff library for the staff to read.
   • Books

   • Journals (give name of articles and authors)

   • Audio-visuals

3. Develop an agenda for a staff meeting to address the problem you chose for Question #2. Include:
   • Format (panel, speaker, role playing, and the like)

   • Outline of content

   • Discussion of the direct steps you would take, as a director, to support the staff as they deal with this problem on a day-to-day basis.

Director's Resource 3–1

Sample Checklist for Supervisory Classroom Observations

Ratings:

5   Consistently exceeds performance standard
4   Consistently meets and often exceeds performance standard
3   Consistently meets performance standard
2   Usually meets performance standard
1   Seldom meets performance standard
0   Does not meet performance standard
N/O Not Observed
N/A Not Applicable

The staff person:_____ Performance Standard	Date			
I. PROVIDES A PROGRAM TO MEET THE DEVELOPMENTAL NEEDS OF THE CHILDREN IN A SAFE, HEALTHY, AND EDUCATIONALLY CHALLENGING ENVIRONMENT.				
• shows awareness of the importance of safety in the environment				
• adjusts the space to ensure safety of children				
• positions self in the environment to optimize and maintain total group awareness				
• arranges space with clear pathways so children can move about without disturbing others				
• provides open space for crawling infants				
• provides protected play space for infants				
• washes hands carefully before handling food and/or after toileting or changing a child				
• washes tables and toys regularly with sanitizing solution				
• is alert to sharp edges or splinters on toys and equipment				
• provides only objects that could not be swallowed by infants or toddlers				
• provides toddlers and/or preschoolers spaces for a variety of individual and small group activities including block building, dramatic play, art, music, science, math, quiet book reading, and writing				
• provides water and other sensory activities both indoors and outside on a regular basis				

Director's Resource 3–1 (continued)

The staff person:_____ Performance Standard	Date				
• provides private areas where a child can play alone or with a friend					
• provides soft, cozy places where children can relax on rugs, cushions, in a rocking chair with an adult, and the like					
• keeps floor spaces relatively free of clutter to maintain safety for all children					
• makes certain that children are NEVER left alone: school-age children may be out of sight, but the teacher knows where they are and checks on them regularly					
• takes cues from other adults in the room and moves to those areas where needed					
II. PLANS ACTIVITIES THAT WILL PROVIDE OPPORTUNITIES FOR CHILDREN TO CREATE, EXPLORE THE ENVIRONMENT, SOLVE PROBLEMS, AND HAVE HANDS-ON EXPERIENCES WITH AGE-APPROPRIATE MATERIALS. (For assistants, evaluate in terms of how well he or she works with the teacher to carry out the program plans)					
• plans experiences that reflect awareness of developmental skills of the age group					
• plans experiences that reflect awareness of previous experiences in the same area					
• plans experiences relevant to the children's life experiences					
• plans experiences that have children focus on experimentation and exploration					
• plans experiences that focus on process as opposed to product (as in art activities)					
• carefully sets up the spaces for each planned experience, making all supplies and materials accessible to children and staff					
• plans for backup materials for activities in order to be able to increase complexity of tasks as needed					
• utilizes multiracial, nonsexist, and nonstereotyping pictures, dolls, books, and materials in the room					

Director's Resource 3–1 (continued)

The staff person:_____ **Performance Standard**	**Date**			
• provides developmentally appropriate materials for: *infants:* rattles, squeak toys, music, cuddly toys, teething toys, mobiles, mirrors, books, sturdy places to pull-self-up objects for reaching and grasping *toddlers:* push and pull toys, stacking toys, large wooden beads/spools/cubes, picture books, music, pounding bench, telephones, dolls, pretend props, large paper and crayons or markers, sand and water toys, sturdy furniture to hold onto while walking, active play equipment for climbing *preschool:* active play equipment for climbing and balancing, unit blocks and accessories, puzzles and manipulatives, books, records, musical instruments, art materials such as paint, glue, scissors, tape, staplers, paper, dramatic play materials including dolls, dress-ups, props, child-sized furniture, water and sensory materials such as homemade playdough, clay, silly putty, materials for writing *school-age:* active play equipment such as balls and bats, basketballs, construction materials such as blocks, woodworking, materials for hobbies such as art, science or sewing projects, materials for creative drama and cooking, books, records, musical instruments, board and card games				
III. PROVIDES PLAY OPPORTUNITIES FOR CHILDREN TO INITIATE THE SELECTION AND EXPLORATION OF MATERIALS IN ORDER TO PROMOTE INDEPENDENCE, AUTONOMY, SELF-ESTEEM, AND A SENSE OF MASTERY.				
• provides choices for the child for most of the day and carries through on the choices the child makes				
• uses questioning and encouragement to guide children toward success experiences				
• encourages self-help by having children set tables, clean up place at table, dress or undress (depending on age of child)				
• respects the rights of a child NOT to participate in some activities				
• has school-age children help prepare, plan, and choose their own activities most of the time				
• prepares space so children can independently wash hands, put on smocks for painting, hang paintings to dry, hang up clothes				
• tells children about transitions that are about to occur				

Director's Resource 3–1 (continued)

The staff person:_____ Performance Standard		Date			
• does not require that children always move as a group from one place to another (inside to outside, large motor room, room to bathroom)					
• prepares the new activity or the space (room, outside, large motor room) BEFORE the transition from the previous space takes place					
• allows school-age children to help plan and prepare for transitions					
• allows school-age children a block of time to adjust to the transition from school to the center					
• uses age-appropriate transition strategies (songs, chants, poems) and/or quiet, individual directions to the children who are involved in the transition					
IV. SERVES AS A POSITIVE ROLE MODEL AND PROVIDES CARE THAT IS SUPPORTIVE, NURTURING, WARM, AND RESPONSIVE TO INDIVIDUAL CHILDREN'S AND PARENT'S NEEDS.					
• uses correct grammar when speaking to the children and parents					
• uses a soft, effective teaching voice					
• when talking to a child, stoops down, gets eye contact, and speaks clearly and quietly to the child					
• uses appropriate manuscript printing for all labels, charts, and messages in the classroom					
• checks spelling on all written materials used in the classroom to ensure that all writing samples are spelled correctly					
• talks with children of all ages and encourages them to talk					
• listens carefully to what children of all ages say (repeats sounds that infants make)					
• communicates acceptance of children of all ages nonverbally by smiling, touching, holding					
• quickly comforts distressed children of all ages by reassuring, comforting, listening to concerns, and reflecting feelings the child seems to have (sad, lonely, angry, fearful)					
• uses positive methods for controlling and redirecting unacceptable behavior					
• individualizes responses to unacceptable behavior based on the context of the situation and the particular child involved					

Director's Resource 3–1 (continued)

The staff person:_____ Performance Standard	Date			
• plans ahead to avoid problems				
• encourages prosocial behavior by modeling turn-taking, and cooperation				
• helps children negotiate with each other in conflict situations rather than using adult power to solve the situation for them				
• uses feeding time and changing times with infants for affectionate chatting, singing, peek-a-boo games				
• sits with children at snack and meals, and converses with them to model vocabulary, conversational turn-taking, good grammar				
• builds trust with children and with parents by being friendly, sincere, respectful of individual interests and needs, and by being a good listener				
V. SHOWS PROFESSIONALISM				
• understands the importance of confidentiality regarding ALL events, conversations, and interactions that take place at the work site				
• focuses on the classroom and does not allow personal problems to affect the work with children and parents				
• shows a willingness to go beyond the minimum requirements set out in the job description				
• is interested and enthusiastic about learning new things in the field of early childhood education				
• understands the importance of being a good role model for children and parents (in social interactions at the center, correct grammar and spelling, use of correct printing, interest in learning, and attitudes toward schooling				
• comes to work dressed appropriately for full classroom and indoor/outdoor participation in the planned program				
• is rarely absent or tardy, and always notifies director when absence or tardiness is unavoidable				
• completes all written tasks (lesson plans, child evaluations, notes on parent conferences) in a neat and timely fashion				
• is able to self-evaluate realistically in order to plan for future goals as a growing professional				
• shows self-control in the educational environment				

Director's Resource 3–1 (continued)

The staff person:_____ **Performance Standard**		Date			
• takes the initiative to develop materials for the classroom					
• establishes positive working relationships with other staff members, but avoids becoming a part of cliques or groups within the group that could lead to divisiveness among staff or to undermining the position of the administrator or others responsible for the total operation					
ADDITIONAL COMMENTS:					

CHAPTER 4

Assessing Community Need and Establishing a Program

Creating a new institution is an exciting challenge that requires abundant creativity and energy, and is overwhelmingly complex. The amount of activity inevitably taking place simultaneously during the early thinking and planning stages for establishing a center makes it impossible to outline a set pattern of sequential steps to be followed. Clearly, there must be a need for the program and some driving force in the community, whether an individual or a group, that will generate the creative energy to

1. examine the need.
2. develop the program philosophy.
3. decide about the type of program that will fit the need and the resources..

These three major activities will be taking place simultaneously, and each will influence the type of program and the program philosophy. On the other hand, the type of program that is realistic to offer will influence the question of the ability to respond to the need.

The driving force might be an early childhood educator with a desire to open a center or a group of parents who have an interest in providing child care services for their children. Sometimes, community agencies choose to expand their services to include child care, and there is an expansion of both employer- and public-school-sponsored child care programs.

The nucleus of the driving force, whether an individual, agency, or corporation, must be prepared to carry out all preliminary tasks until a director is hired. They may have to deal with funding issues, undertake public relations campaigns, and carry out the needs assessment.

Program sponsors must examine what services can be delivered realistically without diluting the quality of the program. Usually, it is unrealistic to try to set up a program that will be responsive to every demand and meet all needs. It also is unrealistic to expect to start a new program and have it fully enrolled immediately. It can take several years to bring a new program up to full enrollment. It is better to begin on a small scale, carefully weighing the assured need against the services that can be delivered under the existing financial and resource constraints. It is dangerous to overextend by trying to meet everyone's needs or by providing a large-scale operation that overtaxes the resources. Problems also arise when the need is overestimated and a program is set up that is underenrolled. In either case, program quality diminishes and children become the victims of impoverished environments. Then families do not trust the program to deliver the promised services and it is doomed to failure.

ASSESSING THE NEED

To ensure that the planned program is properly scaled to meet the size and nature of the community need, it is important to do a needs assessment during the preliminary planning period. The needs assessment can begin before or after a director is designated or hired, but it must be completed before any financial or program planning begins. The purpose of the needs assessment is to determine the number of families and children that will use a child care service, and the type of service desired by those who will use it.

What You Must Know about Need

The first step in the needs assessment process is to determine what you need to know. Once that has been decided, procedures for collecting the data can be worked out.

Number of Families and Children.   First, you must find out how many families are interested in having their children participate in an early childhood education program and the number of eligible children in each family. It is useless to go beyond the earliest thinking or planning stage unless there are families available who will use the service. Simply assessing the number of children is not sufficient because number alone does not determine interest or need. If you currently are running a program for preschool children but get many calls for infant/toddler or school-aged child care, you are alerted to a need to expand your program offerings. However, between the time you assemble your waiting lists and accomplish the program expansion, many of

those families on your list will have made other child care arrangements. One quick and informal way to decide whether or not to proceed with a needs assessment is to find out if other centers in the vicinity have waiting lists.

Planners sometimes overestimate the number of families who need child care and fail to consider how many of those families will use or pay for center-based care if it is provided. Although the numbers of preschoolers in child care whose mothers work outside the home has increased threefold since the 1970s, almost one-third of preschoolers from working families are cared for by relatives.[1]

Socioeconomic Level of Families.   Many families may be interested in child care services but are unable to pay enough to cover the cost of the services they choose or need. When families are unable to pay the high cost of quality child care outside the home, operators cannot depend on tuition but must seek outside sources of funding if planned programs are to succeed. When families are able to pay, it is important to determine what they are willing to pay for center-based or home-based care. It is reasonable to expect that most families can afford to pay up to 10 percent of their total income for child care. However, low-income families may pay as much as 28 percent of their income for child care whereas this figure may be under 5 percent for those in higher-income brackets.[2]

Ages of Children to be Served.   The ages of participating children affect all the program planning considerations and can make a considerable difference in the cost of delivering the service. Determine the number of families who expect to have infants or toddlers participate in the group care program outside the home. Although early childhood education programs traditionally served three- and four-year-old children, the increase in the number of one-parent families and the number of working mothers has increased the demand for care before and after school, as well as the need for year-round programs for school-aged children. Therefore, when doing the needs assessment, inquire not only about three- and four-year-

[1]*The State of America's Children—Yearbook 1996.* Children's Defense Fund, 25 E Street NW, Washington D.C., 20001, p. 27.
[2]Ibid, p. 26.

olds who may need care, but also about older children as well as those under age three.

Type of Service the Families Prefer. In assessing the need for a program, one of the first things you must find out is whether families prefer full-day child care or a half-day program. Working families must have full-day care, and they often need full-day care for children ranging in age from birth through school-age.

Families that choose half-day programs may use a program for toddlers and three- and four-year-olds (sometimes called preschoolers), but may prefer to keep infants at home. These families might select a five-day program for preschoolers but often prefer a two-day or three-day program for toddlers. Parents who wish to become involved in the program may choose to place their children in a cooperative child care program. Other parents may not have the time or interest to become directly involved in the school program.

In some situations, family child care homes may be more suitable than a center-based program because they can serve a broad range of needs, are available for emergency care, and can provide evening and weekend care. The family child care home involves parents taking their children to someone else's home and paying for child care on an hourly, daily, or weekly basis. These arrangements are usually made individually although there is often some regulation on the number of children for whom care can be provided in a given home. In a few cases, satellite programs are set up involving the coordination of family child care homes by a child care center staff or an employer. Parents make arrangements through the child care center or the employer referral service for placement of their children in an affiliated family child care home, and make payments to the center or make use of this employer benefit. The center or employer, in turn, pays the caregiver and provides the parents with some assurance that the home and the caregiver have been evaluated, and that placement for the child will be found if the caregiver becomes unable to provide the service because of illness or for other reasons. When the need for care is immediate and critical, it may be useful to locate and organize a few child care homes while the planning and financing of a center-based program is underway.

How Do You Find Out about Need?

Once you have determined the kind of data necessary to substantiate the need for a program, you are ready to decide how to collect the data. Some information for long-range planning can be obtained from census figures, Chambers of Commerce, or data on births from the Health Department. However, detailed information needed for decision-making is best obtained through other means. The data must be collected, recorded, compiled, and analyzed so that the need for the program can be explained to anyone who is involved in initial planning, including members of a sponsoring group or funding agency. The data-collection process might be formal and wide in scope to cover a broad potential population, or it can be informal and confined to a very small group of parents and community representatives. Mailed questionnaires, telephone surveys, or informal small-group meetings are other methods of collecting needs assessment data.

Use of Questionnaires. When a large group of potential clients must be sampled, it is wise to develop a questionnaire that can be returned in an enclosed, self-addressed, stamped envelope. Returned questionnaires provide specific data that can be recorded, compiled, and analyzed. These data are usually quite accurate; however, it is possible that some families will indicate interest in child care and then no longer need it or decide not to use it when it becomes available.

The major problems encountered with questionnaires used for data collection are the low percentage of returns and the task of developing a good questionnaire. Enclosing a self-addressed, stamped envelope increases the number of returns, but it does not eliminate the problem of lack of response. Unreturned questionnaires create more questions because it isn't clear whether the families are not interested in the service, or are interested but have neglected to return the questionnaire.

Good questionnaires are very difficult to develop. Not only must the questionnaire be brief and understandable by the recipient, but also items included must be carefully selected to provide precisely the data that are important to the needs assessment for any given program.

Therefore, if you are involved in drafting a questionnaire, it is imperative to analyze the potential audience first so that items are covered in terms that the audience understands; then you must be sure to include inquiries about all the information you need while keeping the form brief.

Review the sample needs assessment questionnaire in Director's Resource 4–1 on page 59 to see what types of questions are asked for assessing need. Before planning location, type and size of program, and ages of children to be served, it is helpful to ask about the following:

- number of adults in the household
- number of those adults employed
- number and ages of all children in the household
- number of children currently cared for outside the home
- number and ages of children with special needs
- estimate of family income
- estimate of how much is or could be spent on child care
- days and hours child care is needed
- preferred location of child care
- will the family use the proposed child care center when it becomes available?

Use of Telephone Surveys. Since the percentage of returns on mailed questionnaires is unpredictable, a telephone survey of potential users of a program may be a more accurate procedure for collecting needs assessment data. Telephone surveys are time consuming and costly if you expect to survey a large number of families. However, you can sample a large potential population and obtain fairly accurate information about the total group without calling each family. If you are involved in an extensive needs assessment program, you should consult a marketing specialist about appropriate sampling techniques. On the other hand, if you have access to a group of volunteers who can do some telephone calling and the population to be contacted is small, telephoning prospective families may yield accurate data, provided the questioning is conducted uniformly and the data collected are what you need to know.

To ensure uniformity, telephone surveys must also utilize a questionnaire. The survey caller verbally asks the questions and fills in the questionnaire. The same considerations that apply to mailed questionnaires apply to those used in telephone surveys:

1. understandable wording
2. complete coverage of data
3. brevity

Small Group Meetings. Holding informal group discussions with parents who express interest in having their children participate in a program is a good way to obtain information about need. It is practical where the potential client population is defined (for example, church members, apartment complex dwellers, employees of a particular company) or where the size of the community or neighborhood limits the number of families who might use the center. Informal meetings have the advantage of establishing a basis of trust and open communication between the providers of the service and the families who will use it. Without the constraints of a specific questionnaire, parents are free to discuss their values and goals for their children, their unique needs and desires in terms of their family situation, and their feelings about different types of programs that might become available. However, this informal data collection process yields information that is often less valid and reliable, as well as more difficult to tabulate and analyze than questionnaire data. You may find that it is beneficial to work out a combination of the informal discussion and formal questionnaire procedures by holding a series of small-group meetings in which parents fill out a brief questionnaire at the close of the meeting. Needs assessment data that are collected through formal and informal channels not only provide the basis for the decision about whether or not to open a program but also furnish information about family values and goals that will enter into formulating the program philosophy. Of course, the values and the educational interests of the program planners and the director also will have a significant impact on the philosophy.

Reflections

Think, for a moment, about being called by someone doing a telephone survey. What was your reaction to the call? Was the call at a convenient time, or did it interrupt your free time or dinner? Did the caller get to the point quickly or waste your time inquiring about your health or if you were having a good day? What led you to agree to participate in the survey, decline, or hang up? Recalling your reaction to a telephone survey can help you gain insights into how parents might respond to a needs assessment telephone survey.

PROGRAM PHILOSOPHY

The characteristics of an early childhood education program are based on the philosophy of the program. Program philosophy guides directors' decisions about hiring new staff and selecting appropriate staff training because they want to ensure that all staff are prepared to implement a program consistent with the adopted philosophy. The program goals that determine what the curriculum and teaching strategies will be also are based on the program philosophy. If, for example, the program philosophy is based on the theoretical assumption that it is through the process of inventing ideas and developing hypotheses that children come to understand about things and people in their world, then the overarching program goal should be to have children become autonomous problem-solvers. Therefore, in the child care classroom, rather than planned activities set up to teach letters or numbers, the adult would provide a print-rich environment which would include books, charts, and a writing center, and children would enjoy the use of math games, measuring tools, and simple machines such as pulleys and pendulums. The two major questions to be answered in connection with the program philosophy are: Who decides about the philosophy? and What is the basis for deciding what the philosophy should be?

Who Decides about Philosophy?

During the early planning stages, the individuals who make up the nucleus of the driving force must discuss and finally formulate a program philosophy. Occasionally, this discussion will be delayed until a director is hired because it is important that the director feel comfortable with the adopted philosophy. However, when the planners have specific ideas about program philosophy or a new director is hired for an ongoing program, the philosophy is written and a director is hired who can operate within the adopted philosophical framework. Frustrations over incompatible philosophies can create unworkable teaching situations for dedicated staff who need the support of the new director.[3] If the adopted position is based on the assumption that the child is born *a tabula rasa* (the mind at birth is a blank tablet to be written on by experience and the stated goal of education is to fill that tablet with experiences), it is imperative that the program director be committed to that same philosophy. A director with a cognitive-developmental or constructivist point of view who does not accept the *a tabula rasa* premise could not develop or direct an educational program that would reflect the stated program philosophy.[4]

The need for a philosophical position as a base for program design seems clear.[5] Other factors such as cultural values and the knowledge base we agree children should have also influence program design, but the program philosophy underlies most programmatic decisions. The program philosophy should reflect the values, beliefs, and training of the director, as well as the wishes and interests of the program planners and families who will participate in the program. When administrators carry out programs for which they are unable to state a philosophy, and substantiate that the curriculum and accompanying pedagogical

---

[3]Kuykendall, J. (1990). Child development: Directors shouldn't leave home without it. *Young Children*, NAEYC, July, p. 49.
[4]DeVries, R., & Kohlberg, L. (1988). *Programs of early education: The constructivist view*. Longman has a good discussion of constructivism and a comparison of programs sharing the cognitive-developmental orientation.
[5]Decker, C. A., &. Decker, J. R. (1997). *Planning and administering early childhood programs* (6th ed.), Merrill/ Prentice-Hall, p. 33.

strategies can be explained in terms of that philosophy, they risk internal confusion, lack of unity, and loss of teamwork plus an inability to help parents understand their true purpose.

What Is the Basis for Choosing a Philosophy?

When programs are planned and implemented, the curriculum content and teaching strategies either consciously or unconsciously reflect a philosophy that is based on assumptions about how children learn, values of the program planners and the families involved, and views of the planners regarding basic issues in education. Although the three areas that influence the philosophy of the program can be discussed separately, they interact with one another and, in reality, are almost impossible to identify and delineate.

Assumptions about How Children Learn. In the very broadest sense and in the most simplistic terms, assumptions about how children learn fall into three major categories: environmental, maturational, and interactional. The environmental position assumes that the child's learning is dependent on extrinsic motivators in the form of tokens, compliments, smiles, gold stars, and so forth. What the child is to learn is decided by the adult who plans lessons designed to teach content and skills. One of the basic assumptions of this position is that anything worth teaching is also observable and measurable. Attempts to relate this particular assumption about learning to some theoretical base usually lead to the mention of Thorndike, Watson, and Skinner.

The maturational position assumes that there is an internal driving force that leads to the emergence of cognitive and affective systems, which, in turn, determine the child's readiness for mastery of developmental tasks. Mastery of the task is itself rewarding, so the reinforcement is based on intrinsic satisfactions derived from accomplishment and task mastery. Learning is controlled by an internal growth force and the child selects from various offerings, thereby learning what he or she is ready to learn. The theorists associated with the extreme maturational position are Freud and Gesell.

The interactional position assumes that learning results from the dynamic interaction between the emerging cognitive and affective systems and the environment. The interaction with both the material and the human environment is not driven solely by an internal force but also is nurtured, facilitated, and intensified by the timely intervention of significant adults in the environment. The child intrinsically is motivated to select appropriately from the environment, but the adult is responsible for preparing the environment, and for timely and appropriate questions and ideas to alert the child to the learning opportunities in each situation. The adult facilitates the development of intellectual competence. The impetus for the interactional approach came from Piaget's work. Rheta DeVries says, " . . . (the) theory of Piaget is . . . the most advanced theory we have of mental development."[6] Additional insights into the interactive theoretical perspective come from Vygotsky's work. He emphasized the important connection between a child's social and psychological worlds for cognitive development.[7]

Reflections

Think about a program in which you have taught or observed. Carefully analyze the time and energy the children and the adults invested in different activities offered in the daily program. Would you judge that cognitive development was valued over social/emotional development, or vice versa? What evidence could you present to support your judgment? Think about activities you may have planned for children or behaviors you encourage, and try to determine the area of development you most value.

Values of the Program Planners and the Parents. The program philosophy is influenced by the priorities parents and planners set for the children. When questioned, most administrators state that they value the optimum development of the whole child (social, emotional, physical, and

[6]DeVries, R., & Kohlberg, L. (1988). p. ix (Preface).
[7]Berk, L. E., & Winsler, A. (1995). *Scaffolding children's learning: Vygotsky and early childhood education.* NAEYC. p. VII.

cognitive). However, when the philosophy of the ongoing program is analyzed, it may become clear that priorities do indeed exist. Concern for the development of the whole child is the stated position, but careful analysis reveals that cognitive outcomes are given priority over social or emotional goals, or vice versa.

Views on Basic Issues in Education.   A number of basic issues in education are implied, if not directly addressed, in the philosophy. One of these issues is the content versus process issue, sometimes interpreted as school orientation versus human orientation. Those who subscribe to content orientation support the notion that the goal of education is to provide children with content that enables them to succeed in school as it exists. Their focus is on preparation for the next step in schooling, and achievement is evaluated by relating each child's progress to norms or grade level. The goal of education for those who support human orientation is the upward movement of the child as an independent learner to higher levels of intellectual competence. The process of learning and the development of problem-solving skills are more important than content mastery. Autonomy, collaboration, and cooperation are valued, and the years in school are considered an integral part of life itself. The major goal is for children to become autonomous problem-solvers.[8] Schooling is not viewed as either preparation for later school or preparation for life. Achievement is not dependent on reaching a norm or the next grade level, but on the ability to cope with the here and now.

The philosophy dictates what the role of the teacher will be. If the focus is on content, the adult is expected to "teach" the children letters, numbers, shoe tying, manners, and the like. On the other hand, in a process-oriented environment, the adult, as an interactor, is a questioner, role model, reflector, observer, and evaluator.

At first glance, this discussion about program philosophy may seem unrelated to the problems of starting a center or taking over as director of an ongoing program. However, it is impossible to make program decisions without a commitment to an agreed-upon philosophy. Once that is in place, subsequent program decisions can be checked against the philosophy to ensure consistency with the stated position. The sample philosophies in Figure 4.1 will serve as a guide for writing a program philosophy.

The third major item to be determined, after the need has been assessed and the program philosophy written, is the type of program to be offered. After deciding on the type of program in terms of sponsoring agency and funding, the decision about ages of children to be served must be made before making arrangements for site selection, licensing, budgeting, staffing and equipping the center, and enrolling the children.

TYPES OF PROGRAMS

The type of program that will be set up is certainly related to the assessed need and stated philosophy, but it also depends on the sources of available funds and the origin of the impetus for the program. Not-for-profit programs receive financial support through government funding or subsidies from sponsoring agencies whereas proprietary programs are supported by capital investments of individuals or corporations. A wide range of program philosophies, including Waldorf and those based on Montessori's teachings, can operate under any of the program types discussed in the following section.

Not-for-Profit Programs

There are public and private not-for-profit programs (sometimes called nonprofit) that range in size and scope from the small cooperative nursery school to the large complex agency-sponsored child care center. Although not-for-profit and nonprofit may be differentiated for legal reasons in some states, in most places the terms are used interchangeably.

Individual Cooperative Programs.   Cooperative programs, often called parent co-ops, are owned and operated by a group. Since parents are expected to help in the classroom, the small co-op usually functions with one or two paid staff

[8]Kamii, C. (1982). Number in preschool and kindergarten: Educational implications of Piaget's theory. National Association for Education of Young Children. pp. 73–86.

Program Philosophy #1

The program is based on the philosophy that most children can learn the skills necessary to succeed in school, that each child learns at his or her own rate, and that success in learning will develop the child's self-image.

Program Philosophy #2

The educational philosophy of the child development center is based on meeting the developmental needs of children. The work of Erikson and Piaget provides the theoretical framework around which programs are planned to meet each child's emotional, social, cognitive, and physical needs.

This developmental program is based on the assumption that growth is a sequential and orderly process, and that children do indeed pass through stages of development that occur in a predictable sequence in their physical, emotional, social, and cognitive growth. The adult's responsibility in a developmental program is to assist the child in growing to his or her fullest potential by recognizing each stage of development and fashioning a curriculum that will nurture and facilitate growth during that stage.

Program Philosophy #3

The program is designed to meet the developmental needs of young children (3 to 5 years). It provides experiences that enrich and enhance each child's cognitive, language, social, emotional, physical, and creative development. Within the center's daily schedule, each child has opportunities to create, explore the environment, learn problem-solving and personal interaction skills, and learn concepts through first-hand experiences. Children develop a positive self-concept through a balance of self- and teacher-directed activities. Opportunities for solitary play as well as group activities are provided. Staff serve as positive role models and provide care that is supportive, nurturing, warm, and responsive to each child's individual needs. We respect parents as the primary and most important provider of care and nurturing, and we believe parents and teachers are partners in children's care and education.

Figure 4–1   Program Philosophies

members, one of whom is usually a teacher/director. Costs are kept at a minimum and tuition is lower than in other centers. Most co-ops are half-day programs because they require parent participation; however, there are co-ops organized as child care centers.

Agency-Sponsored Programs.   Many not-for-profit early childhood education programs are sponsored by community agencies such as church groups, labor unions, service agencies, neighborhood houses, and United Way organizations. These programs may be set up as full-day care centers for working families or as half-day enrichment programs. Such programs are found in both rural and urban areas, and can serve both lower-income and middle-income families, depending on how much support is provided by the sponsoring agency. Agency-sponsored programs sometimes receive partial support from a sponsor such as United Way, and obtain the remaining support from tuition, government funds, and/or grants.

Government-Sponsored Programs.   Head Start is perhaps the best known of the federal government-sponsored, early childhood education programs. Head Start is a comprehensive compensatory program that serves children of low-income families. That is, it is a program in-

tended to compensate for experiences the children from impoverished families may have missed. In addition to educational services, Head Start also provides comprehensive health and social services to children and families.[9] The funding for Head Start programs is allocated by the federal government from the U.S. Department of Health and Human Services, Administration for Children, Youth and Families (ACYF), Head Start Bureau (HSB). These funds are usually distributed through and monitored by the local Community Action Agency. Funding for Head Start programs may go to public school systems, universities, and public or private not-for-profit agencies. The programs may be center-based or home-based, may provide child care on a full-time or half-time basis, and usually serve four-year-olds. Those who receive funds from Head Start (grantees), are mandated to serve children with disabilities (10 percent of enrollment opportunities) who must be mainstreamed and receive a total care package through direct services from the grantee or other resources in the community. Innovative programs for younger children are funded through special Head Start grants. The Department of Defense and the Veteran's Administration also sponsor child care programs in some regions of the country, as do some state governments.

---

[9]*The State of America's Children—Yearbook 1996.* Children's Defense Fund, pp. 32–33.

Public School-Sponsored Programs. More states are mandating that local school boards provide preschool programs. These programs are usually funded through local or state tax monies, or other public funds. Full-day or half-day public school programs are staffed by people hired through public school personnel offices, and the programs are housed in public school buildings. Local school boards, public school administrators, and teacher unions typically have a voice in making policy as well as in both teacher and program evaluation. The building principal is the appointed instructional leader, and at the state level, these programs fall under the jurisdiction of the superintendent of public instruction or the commissioner of education.

Practices in public preschools still tend to focus on academic success, school readiness, and standardized testing but advocates for developmentally appropriate practice in preschools are challenging this academic readiness position of some public school instructional leaders. These philosophical differences are at the forefront of educational reform.[10] The 1988 report of a task force of the National Association of State Boards of Education (NASBE), which advocates early childhood units in public schools, will affect how young children are served in public schools in the next decade.[11]

Before- and after-school programs for school-aged children are often housed in public schools. Some are public school-sponsored whereas others are run by community agencies or service groups such as the Salvation Army and YMCA. The public school-sponsored programs may be staffed by teachers in the building or by high school or college students who are free during early morning and late afternoon hours. Often, the person in the school system responsible for the preschool programs also oversees these programs, and the building principal is the on-site administrator-in-charge.

Campus Child Care Programs. Laboratory schools and child care programs for children of students, faculty, and staff are two types of programs that can be found on college campuses. The programs may be sponsored and subsidized by the college or university, or by government funds. These programs often provide facilities for research, observation, and teacher training. They may be full-day or half-day, and may charge full, or in some cases, partial, tuition for those affiliated with the university. In some places where student groups as well as the university itself offer support for the care of students' children, the students pay minimum tuition for their children, and the program hours are flexible to accommodate the students' course schedules.

Privately Sponsored Not-for-Profit Programs. Many large industries, hospitals, and apartment complexes are including child care centers in their facilities, and are offering services for the children of their employees and residents. These not-for-profit centers are set up for the comfort and convenience of the employees and residents. The hours are often flexible and, in some cases, fees are on a sliding scale to encourage full use of the available facilities. In the case of hospital- and industry-operated programs, fees may be part of an employee benefit package implemented through the use of vouchers, direct payment to the caregivers, or a child care allowance to the employee.

Some employers offer a Dependent Care Assistance Program (DCAP) which allows employees to set aside a certain amount of their yearly pre-tax salary for child care expenses, thereby providing a substantial tax savings to the employee.

Employers are realizing they cannot meet the challenge of fulfilling employees' child care needs on their own and are reaching out to the child care community for help in managing on-site centers. Some contract with centers for a reduced fee or funded slots for employees; others prefer to contract for information and referral services in the area, but are not involved in service delivery.[12]

Profit-Making Programs (Proprietary)

Although much is written about not-for-profit programs such as Head Start, United Way centers,

[10]Stegelin, D. A. (1992). Kindergarten education: Current policy and practice. In Stacie G. Goffin and Delores A. Stegelin (eds.), *Changing kindergartens.* National Association for the Education of Young Children (NAEYC), p. 5.
[11]Report of NASBE Task Force on Early Childhood Education, *Right From the Start*, 1988. Available from: NASBE, 1012 Cameron Street, Alexandria, VA 22314 ($5.00).
[12]*Child Care Information Exchange* 87, 9/92, p. 22.

and public school programs, a large majority of the early childhood education programs in the United States are proprietary. These programs are set up to provide a service that will make a profit.

Independent Owner.   Many full- and half-day child care programs are owned and operated by an individual or a small group (partnerships or small corporations). In the case of the proprietary center, tuition is usually the only source of income, and the operators frequently have budgeting and financial problems. Although some proprietary as well as nonprofits can obtain supplementary funding from other sources, including state funds, the proprietary operators may be able to draw a salary from the tuition that is paid by families using the service. But the operators rarely make a profit over and above that because of the high cost of operating a quality program. Sometimes proprietors open more than one center in a community or region, and begin a small chain operation. Although it is difficult to make a profit from the small chain, quantity buying and shared service costs can sometimes reduce the cost per child and increase the possibility of making a profit over and above operating expenses.

Corporate Systems.   Large child care chains are operated by a parent company that develops a prototype and sets up a number of centers throughout a state or region, or across the nation and into Canada. Some of these corporations have gone public and their stock is traded on the New York Stock Exchange. These national child care chains operate under a central administration that furnishes the financial backing, and which is usually very powerful in setting the policy and controlling the program. There is often a prototype building and program, publicized by identifiable slogans, logos, brochures, and advertisements. Some corporate systems operate all centers carrying the chain name whereas others work on a franchise basis. In the latter case, an individual purchases a franchise from the parent company for a basic purchase price, then pays the company a percentage of gross intake for the ongoing use of the name and the program. In addition, the parent company supplies guidelines for fees, sample documents, brochures, advertising materials, and the like. Some of these

sample documents must be changed by center operators in order to meet local regulations and/or be in line with local practice. The parent corporation often monitors the franchised centers to maintain the company standard of quality control. Since company policy often controls the program, directors are usually expected to adopt the program as outlined by the corporate body, but they can adjust some practices based on their own philosophy. There is a misconception that most of the largest child care centers in the country are operated by for-profit corporations. The reality is that only 40 percent of the 100 largest centers are for-profit. The other 60 percent are operated by churches, employers, Head Start agencies, private individuals, or the military. A list of the largest early childhood centers, "The Exchange Top 100," can be found in Director's Resource 4–2, page 61.

Military Programs

The Department of Defense (DOD) operates child care programs at military installations across the country. Financed by a combination of government appropriations and sliding scale parent tuition fees, the programs may be full-day center-based care, part-day nursery schools, drop-in care, and, in some places, evening and weekend care.

Each of the military services (Air Force, Army, Marines and Navy) operates its own child care service, but all must follow the mandates in the Military Child Care Act of 1989. The Act addresses program funding, required training for staff, competitive pay rates for staff, and an internal inspection system. In order to meet the demand for child care services, the DOD is expanding preschool and school-aged child care options by increasing the number of programs on military installations by using existing Resource and Referral Programs to help families locate available child care, and by contracting with off-installation centers to guarantee spaces for DOD children.

Family Child Care Homes

Family child care is reminiscent of an extended family where a small group of children is cared for in the home of a child care provider.[13] Although

[13]Gordon, A., & Browne, K. W. (2000). Beginnings and beyond. (5th ed.). Albany, New York: Delmar/Thomas Learning. p. 44.

this type of child care service is most popular for infants and toddlers, these home providers also care for preschool children and offer before- and after-school care. The provider may be an employee of a system but most often operates independently, contracting directly with families who choose home care over center-based care. In some states, family child care homes must be licensed whereas in other places, they are certified by a community agency authorized to pay for children of low-income families who are in the home. Many providers join employer or community agency Information and Referral Registries that take calls from parents seeking child care. Registered family child care homes may or may not be subject to inspection by a responsible community agency. In some places, inspections are made only after a complaint has been filed.

SUMMARY

Starting a center is a challenging and exhausting undertaking. During the early planning stages, a number of concurrent activities interact with one another. The individual or group forming the nucleus of the driving force that starts a center must assess the need for a program while developing a program philosophy and determining the type of program that will meet the expressed need. Many decisions must be made concerning how needs should be assessed, what philosophy will be most representative of the thinking of the planners and the prospective director, what type of program is feasible in terms of financing, and so forth. The people who are interested in starting a center must recognize that a great deal of time and energy must be invested prior to the time when financial support is available and before a program can begin to deliver service to children and families.

Working Paper 4–1

1. What are your assumptions about growth and development?

2. How does learning or the development of knowledge come about?

3. During the early years of a child's life, what is the adult's role relative to:
   Physical development?

   Social development?

   Emotional development?

   Cognitive development?

   Language development?

   Moral development?

4. What goals do you have for the children in your care?

Working Paper 4–2

Assume you are the director of a new center. Based on your own thinking about the items listed on Working Paper 4–1 (p. 56), write a program philosophy for your new center.

Working Paper 4–3

Assume you are the director of a center that has been in operation for a number of years. The program philosophy they pass along to you to rewrite is as follows:

> The program is based on the philosophy that most children can learn the skills necessary to succeed in school, that each child learns at his or her own rate, and the success in learning will develop the child's self-image. (Program Philosophy #1, p. 52)

Expand this stated philosophy and include your own ideas based on your training and the theoretical base on which you make program decisions.

Director's Resource 4–1

Sample Needs Assessment Questionnaire

1. How many adults are there in this household? _____

2. Is there a husband in this household?   ☐ Yes   ☐ No

3. Is there a wife in this household?   ☐ Yes   ☐ No

4. If there is a wife, does she work?   ☐ Yes   ☐ No
    (a) If yes,   ☐ part time   ☐ full time

5. Are there other adults in the household?   ☐ Yes   ☐ No

6. What is the total number of children under the age of sixteen? _____

7. What is the number of children under age six? _____
    Check ages of children under six:
    ☐ Under one
    ☐ Between 1 and 2
    ☐ Between 2 and 3
    ☐ Between 3 and 4
    ☐ Between 4 and 5
    ☐ Between 5 and 6

8. Does any child in this family, younger than school age, regularly spend time away from home?
    ☐ Yes   ☐ No
    If yes, does this child have any special disabling condition?   ☐ Yes   ☐ No
    If yes, does the condition require attendance at a special school or program? ☐ Yes ☐ No

9. How many children younger than school age regularly spend time away from home? _____
    _____

10. If any child regularly spends time away from home, how many hours does he or she spend? _____

11. Is/are your child(ren) regularly cared for every day in your home by someone who does not live with you?   ☐ Yes   ☐ No

12. How many children over five regularly spend time away from home before or after school? _____

13. What are the ages of the children over five who spend time away from home before or after school? _____; _____; _____

14. For statistical purposes only, please give the total family income in this household:
    $ _____

15. If the mother is employed, what is her income? $_____

Director's Resource 4–1 (continued)

16. Approximately how much do you pay every week for the care of all your children? Circle the figure in column A. In column B, mark with an "X" how much you would be willing to pay for quality care for all of your children.

A	B	A	B
$0–25	☐	$101–125	☐
$26–50	☐	$126–150	☐
$51–75	☐	Over $150	☐
$76–100	☐		

17. Many parents have a difficult time arranging for the care of their children. Indicate what has been your experience:
☐ Easy time
☐ Not very difficult
☐ Difficult time
☐ Extremely difficult
☐ No opinion

18. If you had a choice of arrangements for the care of your child, what would your first choice be?
☐ Care in child care center for four hours or less
☐ Care in child care center for more than four hours
☐ Care by another mother or someone in her own home
☐ Care by a sitter in your own home
☐ Care in a center before and after school

19. If you could have the type of arrangement you prefer, how many days would you want your child(ren) to spend there? _____

20. Would you prefer to have your child(ren) cared for
☐ Near where your work
☐ Near where you live
☐ Other location: _____

21. Generally speaking, in selecting an ideal child care arrangement, which is more important to you? (Assume that quality is equal)
☐ Cost more important
☐ Closeness to home more important
☐ Closeness to work more important
☐ No opinion

22. If a child care center opens across the street from your office (insert home, church, factory, as appropriate), would you be likely to use it:
☐ For your infant
☐ For your toddler
☐ For your preschooler
☐ For your school-aged child(ren)

Director's Resource 4–2

The Exchange Top 40
North America's Largest For-Profit Child Care Organizations

Organization	Headquarters	CEO	Capacity*	Centers*
KinderCare Learning Centers, Inc.	Portland, OR	David Johnson	150,000	1,155
La Petite Academy	Overland Park, KS	Judith A. Rogala	100,527	749
Children's World Learning Centers	Golden, CO	Karen King	82,680	605
Bright Horizons Family Solutions, Inc.	Watertown, MA	Roger Brown	42,500	340
Childtime Learning Centers	Farmington Hills, MI	Harold Lewis	40,380	311
Knowledge Learning Corporation	San Rafael, CA	Elanna Yalow	36,126	348
Nobel Learning Communities, Inc.	Media, PA	A. "Jack" Clegg	27,500	165
Childcare Network, Inc.	Columbus, GA	James Loudermilk	12,832	97
New Horizons Child Care	Plymouth, MN	Susan Dunkley	12,140	88
The Sunshine House	Greenwood, SC	Roseann and Dennis Drew	10,983	75
Mulberry Child Care Centers	Dedham, MA	Clark Adams	10,492	84
The Children's Courtyard, Inc.	Arlington, TX	Ed Follen	10,190	58
Minnieland Private Day School	Woodbridge, VA	Jackie Leopold	8,047	74
The TesseracT Group	Scottsdale, AZ	Martha Taylor Thomas	6,500	40
Children's Friend, Inc.	Warner Robins, GA	F. Dewayne Foskey	5,284	38
Mini-Skool Early Learning Centers Inc.	Scottsdale, AZ	Douglas MacKay	5,000	30
ARAMARK Educational Resources	Golden, CO	Duane Larson	3,019	30
Rainbow Rascals Learning Centers	Lathrup Village, MI	Patrick Fenton	2,701	31
Lincoln-Marti Schools	Miami, FL	Demetrio Pérez, Jr.	2,606	20
Pinecrest Schools	Sherman Oaks, CA	Don L. Dye	2,505	12
The Phoenix Schools	Sacramento, CA	Dennis Vicars	2,492	18
Creative World Schools, Inc.	Tampa, FL	Billie McCabe	2,347	21
Stepping Stone School	Austin, TX	Rhonda Paver	2,200	11
Country Home Learning Centers	San Antonio, TX	Sharon Ford	2,000	8
Educational Concepts	Tarzana, CA	Myron Lieberman	1,770	15
Bobbie Noonan's Child Care	Frankfort, IL	Judith Nevell	1,663	13
Action Day Nurseries, Inc.	San Jose, CA	Carole Freitas	1,650	16
Crème de la Crème, Inc.	Greenwood Village, CO	Bruce T. Karpas	1,542	5
Kiddie Kare Schools Inc.	Fresno, CA	James Fisher, Jr.	1,492	10
Creative Child Care Inc. (dba Little Tyke)	Bedford, TX	Gene Little	1,452	14
Kid's Country	Snohomish, WA	Lynnda Langston	1,416	9
Tot-Time Child Development Centers	Plymouth Meeting, PA	Donna Bongarzone	1,356	10
ChildrenFirst Inc.	Boston, MA	Rosemary Jordano	1,218	25
Chappell Child Development Centers	Jacksonville, FL	Katheryne Chappell Drennon	1,139	6
Kidd's Day Care & Preschools	Fayetteville, NC	Marion Kidd	1,124	9
National Pediatric Support Services	Irvine, CA	Sheri Senter	1,047	14

National Child Care Franchising Organizations

Organization	Headquarters	CEO	Capacity**	Centers**
Tutor Time Learning Systems, Inc.	Boca Raton, FL	Alfred R. Novas/ Mark L. Schiller	44,645	228
Kids' R Kids International	Duluth, GA	Pat Vinson	17,400	87
Primrose Schools	Cartersville, GA	Jo Kirchner	15,450	83
Carousel Systems Inc.	King of Prussia, PA	Philip Schumacher	12,500	97
Kiddie Academy International, Inc.	Bel Air, MD	Michael J. Miller	7,840	60

*Total licensed capacity for all centers as of January 1, 2001. Based solely on information supplied by organizations.

**Total licensed capacity for all centers as of January 1, 2001. "Centers" includes all centers both franchised and company owned. "Capacity" is the total licensed capacity for all these centers. Based solely on information supplied by organizations.

Reprinted with permission of *Child Care Information Exchange*, P.O. Box 3249, Redmond, WA 98073-3249, 800-221-2864, www.ChildCareExchange.com.

CHAPTER 5

Licensing and Certifying

Child care center directors are responsible for understanding licensing, certification, and other regulations pertaining to provision of services for young children. Each type of regulation is developed by a governmental body and each has specific purposes. Directors must understand which regulations apply to their programs and must ensure that all requirements are fulfilled in a timely manner. They also must be prepared to pay the requisite fees. In the future, people who assume responsible roles in children's programs will probably have to deal with more and more regulatory functions. This increase in regulation is related both to the expanded use of public funds and the broader acceptance of the fact that programs for young children must not only provide care and protection for children, but also must be educationally sound. Educational accountability points to greater focus on the need for certifying or licensing the people responsible for children's programs whereas protection of children's health and safety requires licensing of centers. The term, licensing, may cause confusion since it is used to signify that a governing body is giving permission to do something. In this case, what is being permitted is operating a child care program. Later in the chapter when we discuss licensing (or certifying) teachers, what is being permitted is the opportunity to obtain a teaching position.

After programs are in compliance with the minimum standards required for local or state licensing, they can move toward higher standards and gain some form of professional recognition. Accreditation awarded by the National Academy of Early Childhood Programs of the National Association for the Education of Young Children is the most widely recognized system. Betty Caldwell is quoted in the foreword to the NAEYC Position Statement:

> Our aim has been to formulate criteria which are general enough to cover different types of settings, yet specific enough to be objectively observable. . . .

The foreword continues:

> Accreditation of early childhood programs helps teachers and directors evaluate and improve their practice and helps parents make informed decisions, but most of all, it helps the children.[1]

---

[1]National Association for the Education of Young Children. (1991). Accreditation Criteria & Procedures of the National Academy of Early Childhood Programs, Washington, D.C., p. x.

On-site directors and boards are responsible for providing the necessary inspiration and leadership to improve the center. They work to move a program from compliance with minimum licensing requirements to meeting quality performance standards. Beyond these standards lies the goal of dynamic development that continues to produce a quality educational program. Model program directors are always working to refine their programs as they move toward the goal of excellence. Since the knowledge base in child development and early childhood education is constantly growing, no program can afford to rest on its laurels.

LICENSING

Licensing of centers is required in most states and coverage varies from state to state. For example, in some states, only full-day child care programs are required to obtain a license whereas in other states, all full-day care, half-day, and home-based programs must be licensed. Depending on the type of program being planned and the geographical location of the center, it is possible that both local and state requirements will need to be met. Where federal funding is involved, there will be additional requirements. In some states, program sponsorship determines program licensing. For example, programs affiliated with public schools may be licensed by the state department of education. Your licensing agent can provide updated licensing information. The Director's Resources on page 74 contains a list of sources of information on licensing in each state.

The licensing function is a result of legislation, and its thrust is accountability for the health and safety of children. Licensing requirements are usually minimal and measurable, but they do not guarantee either quality of care or protection for the children. Licensing requirements typically include minimal educational qualifications for staff members but rarely address the educational quality of the program. The licensing function is essential and valuable, but it is often misunderstood. A license gives permission to operate rather than to indicate quality.

In most localities, the building department will review the plans and the fire, building, and

health or sanitation departments will send individual representatives to inspect the proposed space where the services for children will be offered. After initial inspection and approval, inspections and license renewals will be required on a regular basis. Directors are responsible not only for making certain that their programs are in compliance with regulations but also for being familiar with appeal and grievance procedures should conflicts regarding compliance with the regulations arise.

Licensing Regulations

Local and state licensing regulations typically cover building safety and requirements for physical space, and establish base teacher–child ratios. Although licensing regulations vary greatly from state to state, most licensing regulations include:

1. *Building safety.* Licensing regulations always include at least the minimum fire, sanitation, and building safety standards that apply to all private and public services. Fire regulations usually cover the type of building construction, ease of evacuation from the building in the event of fire, alarm systems, smoke detectors, sprinkler systems, availability of fire extinguishers, and methods of storing combustible materials. Building codes usually cover wiring, plumbing, and building construction including building materials. Health department regulations cover conditions in all areas of the building with particular attention to the bathrooms and food service operations.

When infants and/or children who are nonambulatory are enrolled in the program, the director must be sure to meet licensing requirements for those groups. Typically these requirements focus on egress in case of emergency. Usually housing these programs on the first (ground) floor is required.

2. *Physical space.* Licensing regulations usually specify the amount of space necessary for programs for infants, toddlers, and preschool children. The requirement for three- to five-year-old children is typically a minimum of 35 square feet per child of indoor space and 60 to 75 square feet of space per child outdoors. Since programs for infants and toddlers require cribs, feeding tables, and diaper changing areas, such programs require

more space per child than do programs for three- to five-year-olds. Levels and sources of light, levels of heat, sources of fresh air, fencing of outdoor areas, protection from radiators and low windows, and numbers of toilets are also included in regulations covering physical space. These standards are minimal and good programs usually exceed them. Providing more than minimal space, particularly for children who will be at the center all day, is likely to make both children and staff more comfortable.

3. *Teacher-child ratios.* Some licensing regulations include minimum teacher–child ratios. These state or local ratios vary, but are in the range of three to eight infants to one adult, four to twelve toddlers to one adult, and six to twenty preschoolers to one adult. The baseline licensing standards for child-staff ratios in child care centers in some states already meet the standards used by NAEYC, but most states are still below these significant ratios. Most regulations require that two responsible adults be on the premises at all times. The ratios are established to furnish a baseline standard for protecting the safety of children; however, group size is even more important and is also regulated by some states.

According to the National Health and Safety Performance Standards,[2] the following maximum group sizes should be maintained:

Age	Maximum Group Size
Birth–12 months	6
13–24 months	6
25–30 months	8
31–35 months	10
Three-year-olds	14
Four-year-olds	16
Five-year-olds	16
6–8 year-olds	20
9–12 year-olds	24

According to the NAEYC Accreditation Criteria, "An important determinant of the quality of a program is the way in which it is staffed. Well-organized staffing patterns facilitate individ-ualized care. Research strongly suggests that smaller group sizes and larger numbers of staff to children are related to positive outcomes for children such as increased interaction among adults, and less aggression, more cooperation among children."[3]

4. *Staff qualifications.* The teacher's training in child development and her interactions with the children are key factors in creating a quality program. In fact, NAEYC points out that "The quality of the staff is the most important determinant of the quality of an early childhood program. Research has found that staff training in child development and/or early childhood education is related to positive outcomes for children such as increased social interaction with adults, development of prosocial behaviors, and improved language and cognitive development."[4]

Although licensing regulations sometimes address staff qualifications, requirements are often minimal. Some states require that caregivers be able to read and write whereas others require at least a high school diploma for anyone who is hired as a teacher, teacher assistant, and/or aide. Most states require a director to have at least a high school diploma, and a few states require some college training which may or may not be in child development or early childhood education. Others, however, require specific training in early childhood education or attainment of the Child Development Associate credential. Professional organizations are working to upgrade the criteria for early childhood staff as one component of the effort to improve staff salaries. As this process evolves, we can expect licensing standards to continue to improve. Psychologists, nurses, doctors-on-call, and other professionals must meet the appropriate credential requirements of their respective professions.

5. *Transportation.* In centers where transportation service is provided, the service must usually meet the state motor vehicle department standards for school bus service. These standards regulate numbers of children, types of vehicles, types

[2]National Center for Education in Maternal and Child Health. *National Health and Safety Performance Standards: Guidelines for Out-of-Home Child Care Programs.* A joint collaborative project of the American Public Health Association and the American Academy of Pediatrics. Arlington, VA. 1992. p.1.
[3]Ibid., p. 39.
[4]Ibid., p. 30.

of lights on vehicles, proper identification on vehicles, use of car seats and seat belts, and appropriate licensing and insurance coverage for the vehicles and drivers. Even when it is not required, it is wise to provide drivers with training in child development and management so that time spent on the bus will be positive as well as safe for both children and drivers.

It is also advisable to have a second adult on the bus to assist in an emergency. The driver should not leave even one child on the bus while seeking help or walking a child to the door when that child's parent does not come out to meet the bus. Furthermore, some children have a difficult time leaving seat belts on. The driver, who must give full attention to the road, should not have to constantly check to ensure that all children are safely seated and belted.

6. *Other standards.* In centers serving infants, licensing usually requires detailed plans for diapering including the surface on which the baby is to be placed, a plan for disposing of soiled and wet diapers, and hand-washing by staff after each diaper change. Additional requirements for storing food, feeding babies, and for washing toys are also included.

As you review this section on licensing regulations, it should become clear that, depending on the size, location, and scope of the program for which you are responsible, you could find yourself working with local, state, and federal regulatory agencies. At times, the regulations from the various bodies are not totally compatible, and they may even be contradictory in some cases. It is your task to deal with all these regulatory agents so that your program is in compliance. If your program is not in compliance, you run the risk of having a fine imposed or of being unable to take full advantage of available funds and community resources. There is also the risk of having to delay the opening of a new program or having to close down an ongoing program because of failure to meet minimum licensing requirements.

The Licensing Process

Directors who are seeking initial licensing should allow plenty of time for the on-site visits by and conferences with inspectors from all the departments involved because the process is lengthy. It is wise to allow *at least* ninety days to complete the initial licensing process. All departments must provide clearance before the license is issued. On rare occasions, programs are permitted to continue operation when they are out of compliance because licensing specialists are trying to help provide sufficient child care in the community; but the regulatory agencies constantly monitor the work being done to bring the program into compliance with the minimum requirements. The burden is on the operator who must present data to show that the program qualifies for a license or is working toward that goal within a well-defined time line.

Since total compliance with all regulations may be expensive, it is important to have a clear understanding about essential changes before a program can operate and those changes that can be made as money becomes available. For example, the fire inspector may not allow children in the building until all required fire extinguishers are purchased, mounted appropriately, and made accessible. The health department might allow a child care program to begin before a separate sink for hand-washing is available in the food preparation area, provided that adequate hand-washing facilities are available elsewhere in the building, and that there is a double sink in the kitchen. Monies must be budgeted to move toward compliance in any areas that require further work. Therefore, the director and any board members who are involved in budget preparation should be well-informed about any aspects of the program and the physical environment that might need modification to be in compliance with licensing standards. The time allowed for total compliance with all the licensing regulations will vary greatly and may be negotiable.

The steps involved in the licensing process are as follows:

1. Request a copy of licensing requirements from the appropriate regulatory agency.
2. Ensure that the zoning authorities in the area have approved the land use; that is, does zoning allow child care at the site you have chosen? Present the zoning permit from the zoning department to the department responsible for licensing.

3. Obtain information from the licensing agent about contacting the sanitation inspector, fire inspector, building inspector, and public health office.

4. Arrange for conferences with, and on-site visits from, representatives of all necessary departments.

5. When all inspections have been completed and the inspectors have provided evidence of approval, complete the application for the license and send it, with the required fee, to the appropriate licensing agent. You may be required to submit a detailed plan for operating the center, including number of staff, daily schedule, equipment list, and center policies and procedures. You also may have to show copies of forms you will use for gathering required information such as health and emergency data.

6. On receipt of the license, post it in a conspicuous place in the child care center so that it is visible to parents.

7. Check the expiration date and establish a procedure to ensure that the renewal process will be set in motion in time to eliminate the possibility of having to interrupt the provision of services to the children or having to pay a fine.

The director, or in special cases a designated member of the board, is responsible for obtaining a license for the child care center. Renewals, although less time consuming for both the director and the licensing agents, must be taken care of on a regular basis. The cost of a state or local license itself is minimal when it is considered in light of the total budget but it is an item that must be included in the budget. Although some states do not charge a fee, others charge varying amounts, and some states base their rates on the number of children served. Some states have additional fees for special services such as review of a particular building prior to a decision to obtain that building.

The Licensing Specialist

The primary function of the licensing specialist is to ascertain whether or not a program is in compliance with the licensing regulation, and to issue, or recommend issuing, a license to those programs that meet the minimum requirements. When programs do not meet minimum requirements, the function of the licensing specialist is to provide support and to suggest resources that will help bring the programs into compliance rather than to close them. The specialist's goal is to improve services for children and families. Licensing specialists are being viewed more and more as people who provide services rather than as people who just issue licenses or close centers. In one Midwestern community, a licensing specialist noted that she actually issues licenses for the equivalent of only two months of the year, but that she is available to directors to provide resource information and support throughout the year.

Knowledge of the community combined with a thorough knowledge of the licensing regulations makes the licensing specialist a valuable resource for directors who are seeking training for staff, looking for educational program consultants, and exploring the best and least expensive ways to meet fire, health, or building regulations. The licensing specialists also may be available as a consultant when a director is petitioning to have an unusual or unrealistic restriction varied or adjusted. In situations where licensing regulations are inappropriate for children's programs, licensing specialists are available to support community efforts to have the regulations changed. Often, specialists are not in a position to initiate an action to change a very restrictive regulation. However, they may provide support and information to a group of lay or professional people who organize to bring about changes that will allow for quality service to children and, at the same time, free the programs from unrealistic restrictions. Should you find yourself confronted with a local or state regulation that seems impractical or unworkable, you may want to enlist your licensing specialist's help in making contact with other directors who feel as you do about the regulation, and form a task force to investigate the process necessary to have the regulation changed.

In one locality where all staff people were required to hold first aid certificates, center operators and licensing specialists worked together to adjust the requirement and make it more realistic, without jeopardizing the health or safety of the children. An unreasonable or outdated requirement may be included in licensing and may need to be changed, but the regulation will remain until some very pragmatic, energetic director comes along who is willing to organize the forces necessary to create change. You may find yourself interested in doing just that, with the help of other directors, related agencies, and your licensing specialist.

DIRECTOR'S CORNER

"I spend a lot of time keeping track of paperwork. I know that I have to have all the staff and child medical records as soon as a new child or staff member comes to the center. That's one of the first things I do. I also make a calendar each year that reminds me when to apply to renew our license, to get our fire inspection, and our kitchen inspection."

—Director, private not-for-profit center

You also may find yourself in a situation in which the licensing requirements have little effective protection of children. In this case, even though your center exceeds minimum standards, it is your responsibility to advocate for appropriate standards. The NAEYC Code of Ethical Conduct states in Section IV: Ethical Responsibilities to Community and Society points out our obligation to "support policies and laws that promote the well-being of children and families." Often, licensing specialists support the need for more appropriate requirements, yet their authority allows them to enforce only the written rules.

The licensing specialist also can help you work through a grievance process if you encounter a unique problem with licensing. For example, one specialist explained a situation in which the fire inspector was holding to the letter of the law by requiring that an expensive, special type of glass be installed in the windows of a center building that was not the required 30 feet from an adjacent building. The regulation requiring 30 feet is appropriate and necessary for adequate fire protection, but, in this case, the center windows were 28 feet away from an all brick, fire-resistant building separated from the center by a grassy area. There was no real hazard to the children in

this particular center. The licensing specialist provided special help to the director to expedite the grievance process and the requirement was waived for the center.

In another situation, a new all-day program was to begin for a one-year period on an experimental basis. The kitchen facility was totally inappropriate for cooking lunches for children who were to stay all day. The director, with the help of the licensing specialist, was able to obtain a temporary permit to operate the experimental program for one year by having the children bring their own lunches. Bag lunches were strictly forbidden in this particular locality under the center licensing regulations, so this particular experimental program could not have been implemented without the understanding support of the licensing specialists. It was agreed, of course, that the conditions in the center's food service area would have to meet minimum standards if the program were to be extended beyond the first experimental year, and that the bag lunches would have to be appropriately stored each day during the experimental year. The center provided information to parents about appropriate nutritional content of sack lunches.

Licensing specialists are well acquainted with many directors and teachers in the community, and they can serve as a communication bridge between centers by taking ideas and news from one center to another. For example, sharing the news about how a director in a neighboring community solved a budget problem or a staffing problem (without breaking confidentiality) can be very helpful to a director who is dealing with what seems like unsolvable problems and who is isolated from contact with colleagues facing similar problems. The specialist can assist directors who are trying to effect budget adjustments or staffing changes, but are meeting resistance from board members or influential community groups. Occasionally, for economic reasons, some board members will pressure the director to overenroll a group to increase revenue. Overenrolling is a risk because there are days when all the enrollees appear. This means that the classroom is overcrowded and understaffed on those days. It may be difficult to convince some board members that overcrowding or understaffing for a few days a month can be demoralizing for staff members and disruptive for children. In some states, overenrolling is illegal.

Although some prefer fewer government regulations, keep in mind that the quality of child care would almost certainly diminish rapidly if state regulations were reduced or eliminated. If child care center licensing were not in place, an individual could assume responsibility for large numbers of children, an unsafe condition and one that would jeopardize children's health, safety, and development.

ACCREDITATION

While licensing implies meeting minimum standards, *accreditation* implies performing at a higher level and meeting additional standards. Directors of accredited programs volunteer to be reviewed by an accrediting agency, and those programs that are accredited are deemed worthy of the trust and confidence of both the private and professional community.

Groups such as the American Montessori Society, the Association Montessori Internationale, The Child Welfare League of America, and the YMCA have various programs to ensure that their centers provide good quality child care. However, the most far-reaching effort is that of the National Academy of Early Childhood Programs, a division of the NAEYC. One facet of this professional organization's attempt to improve the quality of life for young children and their families is the accreditation system based on criteria developed over several years with input from a wide range of early childhood educators. Accreditation materials may be obtained by writing to NAEYC whose address is included in Appendix B, page 465.

DIRECTOR'S CORNER

"We were a little bit leery of going for NAEYC accreditation. It was a lot of work but the staff and parents really got interested. And when we got the letter saying we were accredited, I felt like we'd accomplished something as a team."
—Director, agency center

Since licensing is intended merely to ensure that a center meets minimum standards, engaging in the accreditation process is productive for the director, staff, parents, and ultimately for children. The self-study process may be revealing to the director since it requires reviewing all facets of the center's operation. The process also can provide opportunities for the director and staff to work together in achieving the quality they desire.

CREDENTIALING

Individuals who work in a profession may be awarded a credential indicating that they have demonstrated the capabilities necessary for successful participation in that profession. While licensing is required for an agency to operate a program, credentials are related to the educational preparation of individual staff members. Credentials may or may not be required by licensing but they are an indication that the individual has had appropriate preparation for the early childhood profession. There are several types of credentials in the field of early childhood education.

State Certification

Certification or licensing of early childhood personnel has been under discussion in many states for a number of years, and more and more states are creating prekindergarten or early childhood teaching certificates. Some states refer to the credential as a license, meaning a license to practice the profession of teaching just as a doctor, lawyer, real estate agent, or beautician may obtain a state license to practice their profession. Although the term certificate was more widely used earlier, licensing is now considered to be the base. A certificate may then be earned from the National Board for Professional Teaching Standards. Such a certificate indicates that the individual exceeds minimal requirements for teaching. This system is parallel to center licensing and center accreditation. The certificate is usually issued by the State Department of Education. In some cases, the state provides enabling legislation; that is, the certification is available but the state does not require that everyone who teaches preschool children be certified. Individual center policies may require that teachers be certified, but directors often find that they are unable to find certified teachers willing to work in child care centers at the salaries offered. Directors who require certification as a qualification for their teachers must be aware that there are many kinds of teaching certificates. Preparation for elementary or secondary teaching certificates, for example, does not include attention to most of the knowledge, skills, and attitudes necessary for those working with younger children. Therefore, these certificates are usually not good criteria for early childhood teachers.

A relatively recent initiative involves Director credentialling. A 1997 report in *Child Care Information Exchange* indicates that this type of program had begun in Wisconsin and another had taken shape under the auspices of the National Child Care Association. The Center for Career Development at Wheelock College has also pursued this goal.[5]

Child Development Associate Credential

Another type of credential is the Child Development Associate credential offered by the Council for Early Childhood Professional Recognition. Established in 1985, the Council has awarded more than 85,000 credentials to caregivers in four categories:

- Center-based preschool
- Center-based infant-toddler
- Home visitor
- Family child care

A bilingual credential is also available. This national credential is included as one of the possible qualifications for directors and/or teachers in 47 states. Candidates for the credential demonstrate their skill in six competency areas, including 13 functional areas such as advancing physical and intellectual competence (physical, cognitive, communication, creative). A combination of experience and training prepares candidates for assessment based on procedures established by the Council.[6]

Although there are fees associated with participating in this credentialling process, there are also scholarships available, and some agencies pay all or part of the fees. Contact the Council for application materials and a list of fees.

SUMMARY

The director of a child care program is responsible for initiating licensing procedures and carrying through with on-site visits from building, fire, and health inspectors. If program adjustments or building changes are necessary to bring a center into compliance with local, state, or federal regulations, the director must take steps to bring about the changes or risk a delayed opening date or denial of a license renewal. The licensing specialist is a good source of information and advice through the initial licensing process, as well as the renewal process.

Accreditation, particularly through the NAEYC National Academy of Early Childhood Programs, is an important approach to improving quality in child care centers and to involving staff in the process. Since licensing is designed to ensure that minimal standards are met, centers that have participated in the accreditation process demonstrate to parents that they are interested in exceeding minimum requirements and that they are attempting to provide high quality care for their children.

Although licensing of child care programs is mandated in most localities, few states require certification of prekindergarten teachers, a college degree-based credential. Through special training programs and after specific assessment procedures, some caregivers are qualified to receive the Child Development Associate credential.

[5]Director credentialing movement gaining momentum. *Child Care Information Exchange.* January 1997, p. 68.
[6]The information in this section is taken from Council for Early Childhood Professional Recognition, The Child Development Associate National Credentialing Program: Making a Difference for the Early Care and Education of Young Children. 1997. For further information, write to the Council at 2640 16th st. N.W., Washington, DC 20000-3575.

Working Paper 5–1

Using Your State Licensing Requirement Form

Name of state _____

1. Staff–child ratios:
    a. The staff–child ratio for infants is _____.
    b. The staff–child ratio for toddlers is _____.
    c. The staff–child ratio for three-year-olds is _____.
    d. The staff–child ratio for four-year-olds is _____.
    e. The staff–child ratio for five-year-olds is _____.
    f. The staff-child ratio for school-age children is _____.

2. Staff qualifications are:

3. Were materials understandable and easy to read? If not, give an example.

Working Paper 5–2

Early Childhood Certification

To whom did you write regarding state early childhood teacher certification or licensure?

Name: _____

Address: _____

    a.   Does the state provide certification or licensure for prekindergarten teachers?

    b.   What are the requirements for obtaining this certificate or license?

    c.   Does the state require that prekindergarten teachers have this certificate or license?

Working Paper 5–3

Licensing Specialists

1. Have you asked the licensing agent for help?

2. Has the licensing agent been helpful? In what ways?

3. What kinds of experiences have you had with:
   a. Fire inspectors?

   b. Health and /or sanitation inspectors?

   c. Building inspectors?

Director's Resource 5–1

State Child Care Licensing Agencies

ALABAMA
Department of Human Resources
Office of Day Care and Child Development
Family & Children's Services
50 Ripley Street
Montgomery, AL 36130
Phone: 334-242-9500
Fax: 334-242-0939

ALASKA
(Will refer callers to the appropriate regional regulatory office)
AK Division of Family and Youth Services
P.O. Box 110630
Juneau, AK 99811-0630
Phone: 907-465-3207
Fax: 907-465-3397 or 907-465-3190

ARIZONA
(For centers and family child care homes serving more than 5 children)
Department of Health Services
Office of Child Care Licensure
1647 East Morten, Suite 230
Phoenix, AZ 85020
Phone: 602-674-4220
Fax: 602-861-0674

ARKANSAS
Division of Child Care and Early Childhood Education
Child Care Licensing
101 East Capitol, Suite 100B
Little Rock, AR 72203-1437
Phone: 501-682-8584
Fax: 501-682-2317

CALIFORNIA
Central Operations Branch
Department of Social Services
Community Care Licensing Division
744 P Street, Mail Stop 19-50
Sacramento, CA 95814
Phone: 916-324-4031
Fax: 916-323-8352

Director's Resource 5–1 (continued)

COLORADO
Department of Human Services
Division of Child Care
1575 Sherman Street, First Floor
Denver, CO 80203-1714
Phone: 303-866-5958
Fax: 303-866-4453

CONNECTICUT
CT Department of Public Health
Child Day Care Licensing
410 Capitol Avenue
Mail Station 12DAC, P.O. Box 340308
Hartford, CT 06134-0308
Phone: 800-282-6063
Fax: 860-509-7541

DELAWARE
Department of Services for Children, Youth and Families
Office of Child Care Licensing
1825 Faulkland Road
Wilmington, DE 19805
Phone: 302-892-5800
Fax: 302-633-5112

DISTRICT OF COLUMBIA
Licensing Regulation Administration
Human Services Facility Division
614 H Street, NW, Suite 1003
Washington, DC 20001
Phone: 202-727-7226
Fax: 202-727-7780

FLORIDA
Department of Children & Families
Family Safety & Preservation
Child Care Services
1317 Winewood Blvd.
Tallahassee, FL 32399-0700
Phone: 850-487-1987
Fax: 850-488-9584

Director's Resource 5–1 (continued)

GEORGIA
Department of Human Resources
Office of Regulatory Services, Child Care Licensing Section
2 Peachtree Street, NW
32nd Floor, Room #458
Atlanta, GA 30303-3142
Phone: 404-657-5562
Fax: 404-657-8936

HAWAII
Department of Human Services
Benefit, Employment & Support Services Division
1001 Bishop Street
Pacific Tower, Suite 900
Honolulu, HI 96813
Phone: 808-586-5770
Fax: 808-586-5180

IDAHO
Department of Health & Welfare
Bureau of Family & Children's Service
450 W. State Street
P.O. Box 83720
Boise, ID 83720-0036
Phone: 208-334-5691
Fax: 208-334-6664

ILLINOIS
Department of Children & Family Services
Bureau of Licensure & Certification
406 East Monroe Street
Station 60
Springfield, IL 62701-1498
Phone: 217-785-2509
Fax: 217-524-3347

INDIANA
(For center-based child care)
IN Family & Social Services Administration
Division of Family and Children
Bureau of Child Development - Licensing Unit
402 W. Washington Street, Room 386
Indianapolis, IN 46204
Phone: 317-232-4740
Fax: 317-232-4436

Director's Resource 5–1 (continued)

IOWA [1]
(For center-based child care)
Department of Human Services
Adult, Children and Family Services
Child Day Care Unit
Hoover State Office Building, 5th Floor
Des Moines, IA 50319
Phone: 515-281-4357
Fax: 515-281-4597

IOWA [2]
(For family child care)
Department of Human Services
Adult, Children and Family Services
Child Day Care Unit
Hoover State Office Building, 5th Floor
Des Moines, IA 50319
Phone: 515-281-6074
Fax: 515-281-4597

KANSAS
Department of Health and Environment
Child Care Licensing & Registration
109 S.W. 9th
Suite 604
Topeka, KS 66612-1290
Phone: 785-296-0189
Fax: 785-296-6522

KENTUCKY
(For centers and family child care homes serving 7 or more children)
Cabinet for Health Services
Division of Licensing & Regulation
C.H.R. Building
275 East Main Street, 4E-A
Frankfort, KY 40621
Phone: 502-564-2800
Fax: 502-564-6546

LOUISIANA
Department of Social Services
Bureau of Licensing
P.O. Box 3078
Baton Rouge, LA 70821
Phone: 504-922-0015

Director's Resource 5–1 (continued)

MAINE
Day Care Licensing Unit
Maine DHS
Station 11
Augusta, ME 04333
Phone: 207-287-5060

MARYLAND
Department of Human Resources
Child Care Administration
311 W. Saratoga Street, 1st Floor
Baltimore, MD 21201
Phone: 410-767-7805

MASSACHUSETTS
Office of Child Care Services
One Ashburton Place, Room 1105
Boston, MA 02108
Phone: 617-727-8900

MICHIGAN
Department of Consumer & Industry Services
Division of Child Day Care Licensing
7109 W. Saginaw, 2nd Floor
P.O. Box 30650
Lansing, MI 48909-8150
Phone: 517-373-8300

MINNESOTA
(Refers family child care calls to counties)
Department of Human Services
Division of Licensing
444 Lafayette Road
St. Paul, MN 55155-3842
Phone: 651-296-3971

MISSISSIPPI
Department of Health
Division of Child Care
P.O. Box 1700
Jackson, MS 39215-1700
Phone: 601-576-7613
Fax: 601-576-7813

Director's Resource 5–1 (continued)

MISSOURI
Department of Health
Bureau of Child Care, Safety and Licensure
P.O. Box 570 (920 Wildwood)
Jefferson City, MO 65102
Phone: 573-751-2450

MONTANA
Department of Public Health & Human Services
Child & Family Services Division
P.O. Box 8005
Helena, MT 59604-8005
Phone: 406-444-5900

NEBRASKA
NE Department of Health and Human Services
Child Care
P.O. Box 95044
Lincoln, NE 68509-5044
Phone: 402-471-9431
Fax: 402-471-9455

NEVADA
Department of Human Resources
Division of Child and Family Services
Bureau of Child Care Licensing
3920 E. Idaho Street
Elko, NV 89801
Phone: 702-753-1237

NEW HAMPSHIRE
NH Department of Health and Human Services
Office of Program Support
Bureau of Child Care Licensing
129 Pleasant Street
Concord, NH 03301-3857
Phone: 603-271-4624

NEW JERSEY
(Refers family child care calls to counties)
Division of Youth & Family Services
Bureau of Licensing
P.O. Box 717
Trenton, NJ 08625-0717
Phone: 609-292-1018

Director's Resource 5–1 (continued)

NEW MEXICO
Child Services Unit / Licensing
PERA Building, Room 111
P.O. Drawer 5160
Santa Fe, NM 87502-5160
Phone: 505-827-4185

NEW YORK
NY State Department of Family assistance
Office of Children and Family Services
Bureau of Early Childhood Services
40 N. Pearl Street, 11-B
Albany, NY 12243-0001
Phone: 518-473-7793

NORTH CAROLINA
Division of Child Development
Regulatory Services Section
2201 Mail Service Center
Raleigh, NC 27626-2201
Phone: 919-662-4499

NORTH DAKOTA
Department of Human Services
Early Childhood Services
600 East Boulevard
State Capitol Building
Bismarck, ND 58505-0250
Phone: 701-328-2310

OHIO
(For center-based child care)
Ohio Department of Job & Family Services
30 E. Broad Street, 32nd Floor
Columbus, OH 43266-0423
Phone: 614-466-6282

OKLAHOMA
Department of Human Services
Office of Child Care
P.O. Box 25352
Oklahoma City, OK 73125
Phone: 405-521-3561

Director's Resource 5–1 (continued)

OREGON
Employment Department
Child Care Division
875 Union Street, NE
Salem, OR 97311
Phone: 503-947-1245

PENNSYLVANIA
Department of Public Welfare, Bureau of Child Day Care
Office of Children, Youth & Families
Health & Welfare Building, Room 131
P.O. Box 2675
Harrisburg, PA 17105-2675
Phone: 717-783-3856

RHODE ISLAND
Department of Children, Youth and Families
Day Care Licensing, Building 3
610 Mount Pleasant Avenue
Providence, RI 02908
Phone: 401-222-5220

SOUTH CAROLINA
Department of Social Services
Division of Child Day Care Licensing
P.O. Box 1520
Room 520
Columbia, SC 29202-1520
Phone: 803-898-7345

SOUTH DAKOTA
Department of Social Services
Child Care Services
700 Governors Drive
Pierre, SD 57501-2291
Phone: 800-227-3020

TENNESSEE
Department of Human Services
Child Care Services Unit
Citizens Plaza
400 Deadrick Street
Nashville, TN 37248-0001
Phone: 615-313-4700

Director's Resource 5–1 (continued)

TEXAS
Department of Protective and Regulatory Services
Child Care Licensing
P.O. Box 149030
M.C. E-550
Austin, TX 78714-9030
Phone: Day Care Hotline: 800-862-5252 or 512-438-3267
Fax: 512-438-3848

UTAH
Day Care Licensing
Department of Health
288 N. 1460 West
Salt Lake City, UT 84116
Phone: 801-538-6152

VERMONT
Department of Social Rehabilitation Services
Child Care Services Division
Child Care Licensing Unit
103 S. Main Street
Waterbury, VT 05671-2901
Phone: 802-241-2158 or 3110
Fax: 802-241-1220

VIRGINIA
Department of Social Services
Division of Licensing Programs
730 E. Broad Street, 7th Floor
Richmond, VA 23219-1849
Phone: 804-692-1900

WASHINGTON
Department of Social & Health Services
Office of Child Care Policy
P.O. Box 45700
Olympia, WA 98504
Phone: 800-737-0617

WEST VIRGINIA
Department of Health and Human Resources
Day Care Licensing
P.O. Box 2590
Fairmont, WV 26555-2590
Phone: 304-363-3261

Director's Resource 5–1 (continued)

WISCONSIN
Department of Health & Family Services
1 West Wilson Street
Madison, WI 53702
Phone: 608-266-1865

WYOMING
Department of Family Services
Division of Juvenile Services
Hathaway Building, Room 323
2300 Capitol Avenue
Cheyenne, WY 82002-0490
Phone: 307-777-6285
Fax: 307-777-3659

TERRITORIES

PUERTO RICO
Department of Family
Licensing Office
P.O. Box 11398
Santurce, PR 00910
Phone: 787-724-0772
Fax: 787-724-0767

VIRGIN ISLANDS
Department of Human Services
Child Care Licensing
3011 Golden Rock
Christiansted, St. Croix
U.S. Virgin Islands 00820-4355
Phone: 809-773-2323
Fax: 809-773-6121

Source: www.nccic.org/dirs/regoffic.html

CHAPTER 6

Establishing and Working with a Board

Most child care centers have a governing body that is ultimately responsible for the total program. This group is usually constituted as a policy-making body called a board of directors or a board of trustees. The center director, who is responsible to this policy-making body, implements the center program as mandated by the board. In practice, board involvement runs the gamut from heavy involvement with the center to leaving all the work to the director. In the former situation, the board carries out all the functions described in this chapter, then charges the director with full responsibility to act on decisions that the board has reached. In the latter case, the board does not question the rationale or philosophical basis for the recommendations presented by the director for board review, and gives carte blanche approval. Ideally, a board should function somewhere between these two extremes by carrying out some functions related to personnel, finance, facility, and program, and by keeping in close contact with the director who also is working on fiscal and program matters. Although some proprietary centers operate without the guidance of a governing group, the organizational structure of most agency-sponsored and public-funded programs includes a board of directors.

When the center is an arm of another agency, for example, a church-sponsored child care program, the agency board may serve as the governing board, sometimes with representation from the center. In other cases, an advisory committee for the center is formed. As the name implies, the role of the advisory committee is much less structured and the committee has less authority than a board. When child care is part of a public school system, the principal often assumes many of the director's responsibilities and a lead teacher assumes others. The actual board, then, would be the elected board of education.

When a center is to be operated as a corporation, it is a board responsibility to initiate the incorporation process. Because laws vary from state to state, an attorney should be consulted. The laws do not require that child care centers incorporate, but incorporation is desirable. The liability of the corporation is limited to the assets of the corporation; therefore, individuals holding positions within the corporation are generally protected from personal liability for acts or debts of the corporation. Many centers incorporate in order to qualify for tax-exempt status under the Internal Revenue Code. Contributions made to the center are then deductible by the donor.

To form a corporation, Articles of Incorporation must be filed with the state (usually with the Secretary of State), bylaws, also referred to as regulations or a constitution, must be adopted, and a governing body, usually called a Board of Trustees, must be formed to set policy and assume overall responsibility for the operation of the corporation. A sample form for filing Articles of Incorporation appears in Director's Resource

6–1 and sample bylaws appear in Director's Resource 6–4 on pages 97 and 102, respectively.

A corporation is owned by one or more shareholders. The shareholders elect directors to manage the affairs of the corporation, and the directors, in turn, elect officers to handle the day-to-day business of the corporation. Both federal and state laws regulate registration of stock issued to shareholders.

In the case of a not-for-profit corporation, the corporate structure is different. For example, there are no shareholders in a nonprofit corporation. Instead, there are members who elect trustees to manage the affairs of the corporation. The required number of trustees and officers varies from state to state. Once incorporated, the corporation must function in accordance with the state laws, the Articles of Incorporation, and the bylaws.

Not-for-profit corporation status does not automatically result in tax-exempt status. Based on Internal Revenue Code 501, it is still necessary for the corporation to apply to the Internal Revenue Service (IRS) for tax-exempt status and to demonstrate that the organization's purpose is educational or falls under one of the other IRS exempt categories. Department of the Treasury form 1023 must be accurately completed. This form requires a statement of the organization's sources of financial support, fund-raising programs, purpose, activities (past, present, and future), relationship to other organizations, and policies (such as nondiscrimination). This lengthy form also requires a statement of revenue and expenses, and a list of governing board members. Exemption from state and local taxes, including sales tax, is often tied to exemption from federal income tax, but application for exemption must be made to each taxing body.

Because tax law is subject to change, the director and board must keep abreast of new requirements. New directors moving in to existing centers must check to see that the documents are in order and that proper procedures are being followed.

Board membership, board duties, committee structure, and board operations vary depending on the size and type of center, and on the relationship of the center to a sponsoring or funding agency. In spite of the inevitable variation in the structure and function of center boards, you will be better equipped to assist in establishing a board

DIRECTOR'S CORNER

"The board treasurer keeps track of all the tax forms and other reports that are due. Once when we changed treasurers, we forgot to file a particular form and wound up with a big fine even though we hadn't owed any money. The board needed a lawyer on that one!"
    —Director, not-for-profit incorporated center

or to work with an existing board if you have some basic information about governing boards and how they operate.

BOARD MEMBERSHIP

Most well-planned boards consist of from ten to twenty members who are either elected or appointed to board positions. A board operates most efficiently when its size is small enough for members to know each other and feel comfortable about speaking out when issues are being discussed, yet large enough for members to cover all the committee assignments that are required to conduct business without overworking any board members. Tenure for board members is specified in the bylaws. Requirements for board membership are based on program philosophy and needs, and on state laws and sponsoring agency mandate.

Selection of Board Members

At the outset, boards may be made up entirely of appointed members, but after the bylaws are developed and incorporation is accomplished, ensuing boards are usually elected through a regulated process required by law and stated in the bylaws. When a director, a board, or a nominating committee chooses persons to be appointed or elected to a child care center board, the background and personality of the candidates, and the current board composition, must be considered.

Professionals from the fields of health, education, finance, and law are often asked to serve on child care center boards. These professionals can provide expertise in decision-making in their areas, and often volunteer time and expertise to help solve problems. For example, the physician board member may direct the board to accurate information about health practices in the center, or the accountant may help draw up the budget and prepare for an audit. A board member who can write effective proposals and has contacts with various funding sources can be a real asset. A person with knowledge of special education may support the board in its efforts to meet requirements of the Americans with Disabilities Act or may help the center staff address issues related to inclusion of children with special needs. A computer specialist also may be a valuable asset as a director ponders what type of hardware or software is best for the center. Some boards reserve a percentage of slots for parents and a teacher also may be a member, although usually a nonvoting participant.

Before people join the board, they should receive information about the center and its philosophy. If they are not in general agreement with the goals and philosophy of the center, it may be more productive for everyone if they volunteer their services elsewhere. However, openness to new ideas is critical if the center is to move ahead. Prospective board members should be informed of their responsibilities because being a board member is both a rewarding and a demanding experience. Some boards expect their members to contribute and solicit funds.

Large agencies usually provide liability coverage for board members but smaller organizations may be unable to afford this. Nonetheless, board members are usually legally liable for center operation. Prospective board members should be informed that they will need to provide their own liability coverage if that is the case. Director liability is controlled by state law and additional information on this important topic can be obtained from your insurance agent or attorney.

Terms for Board Membership

Continuity in board membership is important. Therefore, many boards elect members for a three-year term, with one-third of the members new each year. To achieve this ratio, the initial board members draw lots to determine who will hold three-, two-, and one-year terms. This time frame may not be workable for parent members who may not feel comfortable about joining the board

until their child has been at the center for a while but who may no longer be interested, if they are still board members once their child has left the center.

Although continuity is valuable, stagnation may occur when board members serve too long. Consequently, bylaws should contain a provision for a limited number of terms of board service. Provision also should be made for replacing members whose attendance is poor. When a board member resigns, an exit interview may provide insight regarding possible changes in board operation. Members who feel overworked or undervalued may choose not to complete a full term.

BOARD DUTIES

Initially, the board is responsible for drawing up the bylaws for the center's operation. Subsequently, the board makes policy decisions and provisions for the operation of the center.

Drawing Up Bylaws

Bylaws for operation of the center are written by the board and should contain:

1. name and purpose of the organization
2. composition of the board of directors including information about when and by whom its members are elected or appointed
3. officers to be elected, their duties, terms of office, and description of the procedure for elections
4. method of replacing a board member or officer when necessary
5. frequency of meetings or minimum number of meetings to be held annually
6. standing committees: their composition and duties
7. relationship of staff to board
8. rules governing the conduct of meetings
9. provisions for an annual meeting
10. procedures for amending the bylaws
11. procedures for dissolution of the corporation

Other items may be added to meet the needs of a particular board.

Bylaws should be extensive enough to meet legal requirements and to guide the board. However, when bylaws are too detailed, the board's operation is hampered. Furthermore, changes to bylaws appropriately involve detailed procedures that become burdensome if changes must be made frequently. Therefore, for example, bylaws may not list the specific month of the annual meeting or the exact number of board members.

Along with the establishment of bylaws, the board works on developing the philosophy for the center unless the philosophy has already been set by the organizers of the center. The process involved in developing a philosophy is discussed in Chapter 4.

Making Policy

After the philosophy has been established, the board sets goals for the program based on the philosophy and purpose. If goals have already been established prior to the formation of the board, the board formally adopts them. The board then informs the director and staff about the philosophy and goals that form the basis for establishing the objectives for the daily program. In some cases, a knowledgeable director can take a leadership role in guiding the board's decision-making about philosophy and goals that reflect sound theories. In any case, the board establishes policies and the director uses these policies as the basis for formulation of procedures. A *policy* is a course of action that guides future decisions. A *procedure* is a series of steps to be followed, usually in a specific order, to implement policies. It is important to have written policies for the center's major components such as personnel policies, policies relating to the children's program, and policies about parent involvement. Ensuing decisions then will be consistent because they will be based on established policy. Since the policies should not be changed without serious consideration, the board should make them general and flexible enough so that the director is able to implement them without disregarding the goals of the center, and without being required to request policy changes every time a new circumstance arises. Procedures are more detailed than the policies. Their purpose is to provide an implementation plan that is clear and

uniform. Fire drill procedures or procedures for checking out material from the storeroom are good examples. Procedures also may be written for using the building after the children leave, for using equipment in the multipurpose room or for filling a staff vacancy.

Policy decisions regarding personnel and program are ultimately subject to board approval; but in practice, they are often made by the director with official board approval a mere formality. Occasionally, a very involved, knowledgeable board will carefully scrutinize policies presented by a director, often asking for the rationale to support each policy. In some instances, staff and program policies are actually written by board members.

The type of program offered and the population served are both program policies subject to board approval. Decisions about the number and age span of children, the method of selection, and the population served are all board decisions. Examples include decisions about enrollment of children with disabilities, the question of ethnic balance, and the setting up of the program schedule to include after-school care or care for children on a part-time basis. Although these policy decisions are usually based on the director's recommendations, the board will make the final determination.

Operating the Center

The board is responsible for making provisions for the operation of the center. Major decisions in this category are:

1. selecting a director
2. providing for appropriate staff members and suitable in-service training opportunities
3. providing facilities and equipment
4. preparing or approving the budget, and overseeing the finances of the center
5. writing proposals and obtaining funding, including setting rates of tuition
6. complying with local, state, and federal laws
7. evaluating the operation of the program and the work of the director, and assisting the director in the evaluation of other staff

8. arranging for an annual audit of financial records
9. arbitrating problems between the staff and director that cannot be resolved by the director

After provisions are made for operating the program, it becomes the director's responsibility to implement the program at which point, he or she becomes accountable to the board for the total program operation.

BOARD COMMITTEES

Board work is usually done by committees. Each standing committee has a charge that is spelled out in the bylaws; when all the standing committees are in place and working, the basic board functions are carried out. As special needs arise, ad hoc board committees are appointed by the board chairperson to perform specific, short-term tasks, and report to the board. When the task has been completed, the committee is dissolved.

The board chairperson appoints members to each standing committee based on their interest and expertise, and makes an attempt to balance the membership on committees by sex, race, age, point of view, and type of skill. Some boards have special requirements for committee membership. For example, the bylaws may state that each committee must have a parent member or a community representative.

Board committees convene at intervals that correspond to meeting the demands of their workload. When a center is being formed, most committees are extremely active; however, in an ongoing program, some committees have activity peaks. For example, the building committee deals with building maintenance which is fairly routine; but if a decision is made to remodel, relocate, or build a new facility, the building committee would become very active.

Decisions about the number and types of standing committees needed to carry out the board functions are made when the bylaws are written. Some of the typical standing committees are executive, personnel, finance, building, program, and nominating.

DIRECTOR'S CORNER

"We work with a church committee of nine members and they report to the church board because the center is part of the church's mission. I'm responsible for running the program and they handle the finances. Recently we built a major addition to the building. Then I met with the building subcommittee almost every week."
—Director, not-for-profit church-sponsored center

Executive Committee

The executive committee is composed of the board's officers with the center director often serving as an ex-officio member. The executive committee advises the chairperson on actions to be taken, on changes to be made, and on committee assignments. This committee conducts board business between meetings and acts in place of the total board in emergency situations. However, it is critical that the executive committee plan far enough in advance to avoid as many "emergency" situations as possible, lest the way be opened for making important decisions without total board participation. Board members will become disgruntled and fail to contribute time or energy to board business if they find that crucial decisions are being made outside official board meetings. Whenever possible, board decisions should be made by the total board.

Personnel Committee

The personnel committee is responsible for hiring a director who will adhere to the philosophy of the center and implement the policies established by the board. To accomplish this task, the committee advertises the position, conducts the interviews, and prepares the director's contract. The personnel committee is also responsible for firing the director should that become necessary.

Personnel committee members usually assist the director in writing job descriptions, interviewing job candidates, and discussing the merits of each applicant. After these steps are completed, the hiring recommendations are made to the total board for final approval.

In small centers where there is no evaluation committee, personnel committee members may be asked to conduct the evaluation process. In this capacity, the committee determines the method of evaluation, carries out the evaluation of the director, and monitors the director's evaluation of the center staff and program.

Finance Committee

Because they prepare the budget and appropriate the funds, finance committee members must have an understanding of the program's overall operation and of the way in which the operation relates to the program philosophy. In situations where the director prepares the budget and secures the funds, the finance committee approves the budget, monitors the record keeping, and arranges for the annual audit. In some centers, the finance committee sets salary schedules and reviews bids for major purchases.

Building Committee

The responsibility for finding and maintaining a facility suitable for the type of program being offered rests with the building (or facility) committee. Prior to starting a center or establishing a new facility, the committee spends an extraordinary amount of time making decisions about purchasing, constructing, or leasing a building. The committee is responsible for locating the new facility or the construction site. Building committee members work closely with the architect when the construction or remodeling is in process, and must remember to involve the director who presumably has the most knowledge of what the center needs.

It is the building committee's responsibility to see that the building and grounds are clean, safe, and attractive. Preventive maintenance as well as emergency repairs are authorized by this committee. Although directors usually manage the details of applying for a license and arranging for necessary changes at the center to keep the program and facility in compliance with licensing standards, the building committee is the group designated by the board to monitor licensing.

Many boards also assign the building committee responsibility for the center's equipment. The director must obtain the approval of the committee on major equipment orders and the committee sanc-

tions orders after considering whether or not the suggested purchases are suitable, in both type and quantity, and are within the budget. The committee members also ascertain whether the equipment is properly stored, maintained, and inventoried.

The building committee makes long-range plans by considering such questions as the center's future building needs. It projects the type and amount of space that will be needed, and plans for ways to meet those needs. Equipment needs are considered in a similar way. Long-range planning prevents the board from suddenly finding that a major addition or repair is needed when no funds are available. Long-range planning also enables the center to stagger the purchase of equipment so that the quality and quantity are constantly maintained at a high level, and the budget is not suddenly unbalanced by the need to replace large quantities of worn-out equipment.

Program Committee

The responsibility for all center programs ultimately rests with the program committee; however, in practice, any work on the program is handled completely by the director and the staff. The children's program, the parent program, and the in-service program for staff all may be under the auspices of the program committee. The committee recommends policies to the board focusing on the enrollment and grouping of children, the hours and days of operation, and the offering of ancillary services such as health, nutrition, and social services. Some boards set up separate committees for medical services and social services if these are major components of the center's program. These separate committees are responsible for working with the director to determine what services are needed, where, and at what cost they can be obtained. The committees also may help with transportation arrangements to the medical center if required and with recruitment of volunteers to assist children and families needing special social or educational services.

Nominating Committee

The Nominating Committee's function is twofold: potential members of the board are screened by the committee, and they prepare the slate of board officers for election by the board. The process should be open and the committee should check with prospective members for permission to nominate them.

A separate committee may be set up for the orientation of new board members, or the nominating committee may serve in this capacity. Continuing the process begun at nomination, the committee makes sure that new board members understand their duties and the operating procedures of the board. New members may receive a manual containing a brief history of the center, copies of the bylaws, and explanations of all the policies and procedures applicable to the center. A binder is convenient for storing this material so that additional and replacement items such as board minutes, committee reports, and changed bylaws can be added. The binder also should contain a list of all current board and staff members' names and addresses, and the expiration date of each person's term. When a board member leaves, the manual should be updated as necessary and passed along to the new member.

From the committee descriptions, it should be obvious that the functions of the committees are interrelated, and, therefore, that communication among committees is essential. For example, the building committee must know what kind of plans the program committee is making in order to provide an appropriate facility. However, the building committee cannot choose a facility without an understanding of how much the finance committee plans to allocate for physical space. To avoid duplication of efforts, each committee's task must be clearly delineated. Sometimes a board member may be assigned to two closely related committees to facilitate communication between them. Care must be taken to divide the work of the board equitably among its members, and to see that every board member is involved in and aware of the operations of the board and of the center.

BOARD COMMUNICATION

The board shares responsibility with the director for maintaining open communication *within* the

DIRECTOR'S CORNER

Our staff seemed rather mystified about the Board—who they were and what they did. Many Board members needed to know more about the center. One of our teachers volunteered to take pictures of the staff and board members and to make a montage of the photos. Afterwards, we had an old-fashioned ice cream social, with board members serving the ice cream.

—Director, child care center

board itself and for maintaining open communication *among* the board, the sponsoring agency, the staff, and the families who use the center's services. The most successful boards are those whose members communicate effectively with the center's director and with each other. Both the board and the director have responsibilities, and it may be worthwhile to provide training in interpersonal communication for all concerned. If staff and board members both attend the training sessions, communication skills are improved, staff and board members become better acquainted with each other's values, and the outcome is a greater sense of community among those people who are responsible for the center's operation. An obvious place to start is to make sure that new board members are introduced and that continuing board members introduce themselves. Perhaps taking new board members on a tour of the facility and introducing them to the staff could be planned. When board members and staff members have developed effective communication skills, all will be expected to use the skills. Ideas will be expressed and considered openly; likewise, disagreements will be stated specifically and objectively. Board and staff members lacking these skills may be less willing to address problems directly with the result that disagreements may not be resolved and that factions may develop within the organization.

As with all good communication, communication between the board and the staff is two-way. The board informs the director of policies that have been formulated because the director is responsible for seeing that the policies are executed. The board also explains the reasons for its decisions and approaches any necessary changes in a positive way rather than in a dictatorial manner.

The director, in turn, communicates to the board any difficulties that the staff is having with the existing policies or suggests policy changes, providing the board with reasons for these changes. For example, if the director finds that there are a number of parents asking for a program for their two-year-olds, the suggestion is presented to the board, and is supported with arguments for or against the admission of two-year-olds. Facts concerning the type of services that could be provided, the facilities available, the cost of such a program, and the advisability from an educational standpoint also should be presented to the board. Considering the data and the recommendation of the director, the board makes the final decision about the admission of two-year-olds.

It is the responsibility of the board to use the director's recommendations and all other pertinent data in formulating policy. Policy decisions must be based on sound data so that they are fiscally responsible, educationally sound, and realistic. For example, a policy requiring the director to be on duty whenever the center is open may be educationally sound but will be unrealistic in practice in a child care center that operates for ten hours a day. Similarly, a board policy requiring the director to hire only well-qualified, trained teachers would make the hiring task nearly impossible if available salaries are held at the minimum wage level. Since the director is mandated to carry out board policy, the board ideally gives careful consideration to his or her recommendations to ensure that final policy is mutually agreeable and feasible.

DIRECTOR'S CORNER

"I know that our board members are really interested in our program but they aren't early childhood educators. So I have to make sure they understand the needs of the center and of our staff. I put a lot of effort into making sure key persons are well informed. Maybe I'll have lunch with the board chairperson or talk about an idea I have over coffee. You definitely don't want to surprise your chairperson with a new idea during a meeting."

—Director, agency-sponsored child care center

The board serves as the communications liaison between the center program and the sponsoring agency. The director keeps the board informed about the center's functioning by sending the board members copies of newsletters, special bulletins, and meeting notices, by reporting at board meetings, and by presenting a written report to the board at least annually. Board members may be invited when a special activity is planned at the center, and they are always welcome to visit. The board, in turn, communicates to the sponsoring agency by reporting regularly. This type of communication is two-way in that the board also receives information from the sponsoring agency concerning its expectations. For example, a community group may provide partial funding for the center with the stipulation that it be used to provide training for a staff member or for a parent program, or a church sponsor may expect preferential admissions for members' families. As long as these stipulations and expectations are compatible with the center's philosophy, they should be fulfilled.

BOARD OPERATION

When a new center is starting, the board must meet frequently, even daily, during very busy planning periods; however, in ensuing years, boards may meet monthly, quarterly, or in some cases, annually. When the board is working closely with the director and is intimately involved in policy making, monthly meetings are essential. On the other hand, if the board assigns most of the decision-making to the director, it may meet only annually to receive his or her report, approve the budget for the ensuing year, and make any adjustments in goals, policies, or procedures that seem necessary. Note how unrewarding service on such a board might be.

The board that meets frequently contributes to the operation of the center by working closely with the director and by utilizing fully the skills of all board members. The board that meets less frequently provides the director with maximum freedom to operate on day-to-day matters, although within definite guidelines. Each board must decide which alternative is more appropriate for the type of center being planned, and the director is chosen to fit into the selected method of operation.

Although each board has its own style, board meetings must be conducted according to recognized parliamentary procedures that might be covered in the bylaws. By and large, in formal organizations, a parliamentarian who is appointed or elected makes sure that business meetings are conducted according to the procedures adopted. Although too much formality may be uncomfortable for some board members, total informality leads to loose practices with disputes arising over decisions that are based on improper voting procedures or other points of order.

Reflections

Consider how you might work most effectively as a director. Would you prefer a board that left the decision-making to you and expected an annual report about what you had done? Or would you prefer to be in a situation where you had to check back with people in authority on a regular basis to get the benefit of their thinking, after which you would follow their lead as you continued your work? It would be wise to give careful consideration to your own needs and your administrative style before opening a child care center.

The board of an incorporated center is obligated, by law, to conduct its business in an organized manner and to keep accurate records of all transactions. In situations where record keeping is not required by law, it is simply good business practice to operate an agency in an orderly manner. Therefore, minutes of all board meetings, committee reports, and financial records should be kept. Copies of contracts and agreements, job descriptions, and correspondence also should be in the files.

SUMMARY

Not every center has a board of directors, but such a group must be formed as the governing body of an early childhood education center that is incorporated. When members are chosen carefully in terms of the contribution they are capable of making and willing to make, the director can receive excellent guidance from them. A well-organized board operates with a group of committees whose functions relate to the major components of the center's operation. Records of ongoing operations keep information about the functioning of the board open to everyone involved, and good communication between the board and the director produces a well-run organization. The board creates policies and the director implements those policies, but it is the ultimate responsibility of the board to see that its plans are brought to fruition.

Working Paper 6–1

Board Members Form

How many people are on the board of directors of your school district?

How did they become board members?

What are their duties?

How often do they meet?

Working Paper 6–2

Board of Trustees Form

Is there a board of trustees for your center?

How are members chosen?

How long is a member's term?

What are the duties of board members?

How often does the board meet?

Are minutes of each meeting kept?

What is the relationship between the director and the board?

Is the director a voting member of the board?

Working Paper 6–3

Bylaws Form

1. For which organization did you obtain bylaws?

2. Compared with the bylaws in the Director's Resource 6–4 (page 102):
   How are they similar in structure?

   What are the substantive differences?

   How do the differences in the documents reflect the differences in the purposes of the organizations?

Director's Resource 6–1

Sample Articles of Incorporation Form

Prescribed by
Bob Taft, Secretary of State
30 East Broad Street, 14th Floor
Columbus, Ohio 43266-0418
Form ARF (December 1990)

Approved _____
Date _____
Fee _____

ARTICLES OF INCORPORATION

(Under Chapter 1701 of the Ohio Revised Code)
Profit Corporation

The undersigned, desiring to form a corporation, for profit, under Sections 1701.01 et seq. of the Ohio Revised Code, do hereby state the following:

FIRST.   The name of said corporation shall be _____

_____ .

SECOND.   The place in Ohio where its principal office is to be located is_____

_____, _____County, Ohio.
   (city, village or township)

THIRD.   The purpose(s) for which this corporation is formed is:

Director's Resource 6–1 (continued)

FOURTH. The number of shares which the corporation is authorized to have outstanding is:
(Please state whether shares are common or preferred, and their par value, if any. Shares will be recorded as common with no par value unless otherwise indicated.)

IN WITNESS WHEREOF, we have hereunto subscribed our names, this _____ day of
_____, 19 _____.

By:_____, Incorporator

By:_____, Incorporator

By:_____, Incorporator

Print or type incorporators' names below their signatures.

INSTRUCTIONS

1. The minimum fee for filing Articles of Incorporation for a profit corporation is $75.00. If Article Fourth indicates more than 750 shares of stock authorized, please see Section 111.16 (A) of the Ohio Revised Code or contact the Secretary of State's office (614-466-3910) to determine the correct fee.

2. Articles will be returned unless accompanied by an Original Appointment of Statutory Agent. Please see Section 1701.07 of the Ohio Revised Code.

Director's Resource 6–2

Sample of Original Appointment of Statutory Agent

Prescribed by
Bob Taft, Secretary of State
30 East Broad Street, 14th Floor
Columbus, Ohio 43266-0418
Form AGO (August 1992)

ORIGINAL APPOINTMENT OF STATUTORY AGENT

The undersigned, being at least a majority of the incorporators of _____
_____, hereby appoint
(name of corporation)

_____ to be statutory agent upon whom any
(name of agent)

process, notice or demand required or permitted by statute to be served upon the corporation may
be served. The complete address of the agent is:

_____
(street address)

_____, Ohio _____.
(city)   (zip code)

NOTE: P.O. Box addresses are not acceptable.

_____
(Incorporator)

_____
(Incorporator)

_____
(Incorporator)

ACCEPTANCE OF APPOINTMENT

The undersigned, _____, named herein as the statutory agent for
_____, hereby acknowledges and accepts the
(name of corporation)

appointment of statutory agent for said corporation.

_____
Statutory Agent

INSTRUCTIONS

1) Profit and non-profit articles of incorporation must be accompanied by an original appointment of agent. R.C. 1701.07(B), 1702.06(B).

2) The statutory agent for a corporation may be (a) a natural person who is a resident of Ohio, or (b) an Ohio corporation or a foreign profit corporation licensed in Ohio which has a business address in this state and is explicitly authorized by its articles of incorporation to act as a statutory agent. R.C. 1701.07(A), 1702.06(A).

3) An original appointment of agent form must be signed by at least a majority of the incorporators of the corporation. R.C. 1701.07(B), 1702.06(B). These signatures must be the same as the signatures on the articles of incorporation.

* As of October 8, 1992, R.C. 1701.07(B) will be amended to require acknowledgement and acceptance by the appointed statutory agent.

Director's Resource 6–3

Sample Report of Use of Fictitious Name

Prescribed by
Bob Taft, Secretary of State
30 East Broad St., 14th Floor
Columbus, Ohio 43266-0418
Form NFO (September 1992)

Approved_____
Date_____
Fee $10.00

REPORT OF USE OF FICTITIOUS NAME

1. The exact fictitious name being reported is: _____

_____
(SEE INSTRUCTION # 1 ON REVERSE)

2. The user of the above name is: (check appropriate box)
☐ an individual
☐ a General Partnership
☐ a Limited Partnership; County in **Ohio**
    where certificate or application of
    limited partnership is filed is_____

☐ an Ohio corporation, charter no._____
☐ a foreign corporation incorporated in
    the state of _____
    holding Ohio license no._____
☐ an unincorporated association
(NOTE: Ohio has no provision for limited liability companies; if user is a limited liability company, please check this box.)

3. The name of the user designated in item 2 is:_____

_____

NOTE: Where the user is a partnership, the name of the partnership must appear on this line. If the registrant is a foreign corporation licensed in Ohio under an assumed name, both the assumed name and actual corporate title of such foreign corporation must appear on this line.

4. The business address of the user is:_____
                                                    (street address)

_____, _____ County, _____ _____
(City, Village or Township)   (State)   (Zip Code)

NOTE: P.O. Box addresses are not acceptable.

5. Complete only if user is a partnership:

NAMES OF ALL GENERAL PARTNERS   **COMPLETE RESIDENCE ADDRESSES**

_____   _____

_____   _____

_____   _____

_____   _____

(NOTE: Pursuant to OAG 89-081, if a general partner is a foreign (out-of-state) corporation, it must be licensed to transact business in Ohio; if a general partner is a foreign corporation licensed in Ohio under an assumed name, please note both the assumed name and the actual corporate title of such general partner.)

6. The nature of business conducted by the user under the fictitious name is:

_____

This document is signed by a corporate officer, general partner, or association member or officer, or the individual applicant.

By: _____

Title: _____

Director's Resource 6–3 (continued)

INSTRUCTIONS

Section 1329.01 of the Ohio Revised Code defines a fictitious name as "a name used in business or trade that is fictitious and that the user has not registered or is not entitled to register as a trade name."

1. The **EXACT NAME** to be reported must be provided on line 1. Words or phrases which are not part of the name being reported must **NOT** be included on this line. For example, if the user is a Delaware limited partnership, the words "a Delaware limited partnership" should be included in line 1 **ONLY** if those words are part of the name being reported and not merely descriptive of the type of business.

2. The filing fee for a fictitious name report is $10.00. Please make checks payable to the Secretary of State.

3. A fictitious name report must be renewed every five years. In addition, if the user is a partnership, the report must be renewed whenever there is a change in the listing of the general partners. The fee for renewal is $10.00.

---

30 East Broad Street, 14th Floor   **Columbus, Ohio 43266-0418**   **(614)466-3910**

Director's Resource 6–4

The Apple Tree, Inc. Bylaws
(Reprinted with permission of the Apple Tree, Inc.)

DEFINITION AND OBJECTIVE
The Apple Tree, Inc.
(A) Provides quality day care for the children of key personnel in the medical fields for the benefit of patients and the public in general.
(B) Provides day care of a racially-non-discriminatory nature. It does not discriminate against staff or students on the basis of race, color, religion, or ethnic origin.
(C) Provides education for 18-month through five-year-old children, employing accredited teachers and meeting all preschool standards of the Cincinnati Board of Health (City License), Ohio Department of Human Services (State License), and United States Department of Agriculture (Food License).

By-laws of The Apple Tree, Inc.
ARTICLE I

NAME   The name shall be The Apple Tree, Inc., founded by The Auxiliary to the Academy of Medicine of Cincinnati, Inc., hereinafter referred to as The Apple Tree.

ARTICLE II

BOARD   The Apple Tree shall be governed by a board to provide leadership and administration for The Apple Tree

ARTICLE III

OBJECT   To carry out such activities as are deemed advisable to promote the objectives of The Apple Tree.

ARTICLE IV

MEMBERS
  Section 1—   The majority of The Apple Tree Board shall be elected from members of The Auxiliary to The Academy of Medicine of Cincinnati, Inc. The remainder elected from the community-at-large.
  Section 2—   There shall not be more than fifteen (15) members of whom five (5) shall be elected each year to serve for a term of three years without compensation.

ARTICLE V

OFFICERS
  Section 1—   The Officers shall be Chairman, Vice-Chairman, Recording Secretary, Corresponding Secretary, and Treasurer, which shall comprise the Executive Committee.

Director's Resource 6–4 (continued)

Section 2— The Officers shall perform the duties prescribed for them in the parliamentary authority adopted by this Board.

Section 3— The Officers shall hold office for one year, or until their successors are elected.

ARTICLE VI

NOMINATIONS AND ELECTIONS

Section 1— A nominating committee of three shall be elected in January from the membership of The Apple Tree Board.

Section 2— The nominating committee shall recommend candidates for election to the membership of The Apple Tree Board at least one month prior to the Annual Meeting in May.

Section 3— The nominating committee shall prepare a slate containing the names of one or more members for each office to be filled.

Section 4— Nominations may be made from the floor. No names may be placed in nomination without the consent of the nominee.

Section 5— At the Annual Meeting in May, the election shall be by ballot, and a plurality shall elect. When there is no contest, the election may be by oral vote. New Board Members and Officers will assume their responsibilities in June.

Section 6— Any vacancy which may occur shall be filled for the unexpired term by a majority vote of the remaining members.

Section 7— Any officer or member of the Board may be removed therefrom by written petition of a simple majority of the Board for non-performance of duty. The petition must be presented to the Executive Committee and then acted upon by ballot by the majority of the Board.

ARTICLE VII

MEETINGS

Section 1— Meetings during the fiscal year may be held at any time or place; the number and day to be designated by the Executive Committee.

Section 2— There shall be an Annual Meeting in May.

Section 3— A Majority of the members of The Apple Tree Board shall constitute a quorum at any meeting.

ARTICLE VIII

COMMITTEES

Section 1— The Executive Committee shall meet at the discretion of the Chairman for the purpose of making recommendations to The Apply Tree Board.

Section 2— The Executive Committee, immediately following the election, shall appoint the Standing Committee chairmen who will assume their responsibilities in June.

Section 3— Each Standing Committee chairman shall perform duties for one year or until a successor is appointed.

Director's Resource 6–4 (continued)

Section 4—   The Standing Committees shall be—Admissions, By-Laws and Parliamentarian, Finance, Food, House and Grounds, Long-Range Planning, Personnel,
and Ways and Means.

Section 5—   Special Committees may be appointed by the Executive Committee.

ARTICLE IX

PARLIAMENTARY AUTHORITY   The rules contained in "Robert's Rules of Order Newly
Revised" shall govern this organization in all cases to which they are applicable and in which they are not inconsistent with these By-Laws.

ARTICLE X

AMENDMENT   These By-Laws shall be amended at any regular meeting of the organization by a two-thirds vote of those present, provided written notice of the proposed revision shall have been given each member at least ten days in
advance.

ARTICLE XI

DISSOLUTION   If deemed advisable by members of The Apple Tree Board, the organization may be dissolved pursuant to the applicable provisions of the corporation laws of the State of Ohio, and in event of dissolution all of its remaining
assets and property of any nature and description shall be paid over and
transferred to one or more corporations, trusts, community chests, funds or
foundations, preferably to one whose objectives are the same or similar to
the purpose of the organization as described in its Articles of Incorporation.

Director's Resource 6–5

Bylaws of the Lytle Park Child Development Center, Inc.

(Reprinted with permission of the Lytle Park Child Development Center, Inc.

Article I. Name.
The name of this Corporation shall be Lytle Park Child Development Center, Inc.

Article II. Not-For-Profit-Corporation.
The Corporation is a corporation as defined in Sections 1702.02 et seq., Revised Code of Ohio.

Article III. Purposes.
1. The purposes for which this Corporation is formed are:
    A. The establishment and operation of a child development center; including but not limited to: purchasing and leasing of real and personal property; hiring and firing of teaching and other personnel; and, all acts, steps, and procedures necessary, proper and incidental to the furtherance of the afore-stated purposes.
    B. The establishment of an educational environment for children ages 3 months through 5 years that promotes learning experiences which enhance cognitive and affective development.
2. No substantial part of the activities of this Corporation shall be for the purpose of carrying on propaganda, or otherwise attempting to influence legislation. None of the activities of this Corporation shall consist of participating in, or intervening in (including the publishing or distributing of statements), any political campaign on behalf of any candidate for public office.
3. No part of the net earnings of this Corporation shall inure to the benefit of any private shareholder or any individual. The property of this Corporation is irrevocably dedicated to charitable purposes and upon liquidation, dissolution or abandonment of the owner, after providing for the debts and obligation thereof, the remaining assets will not inure to the benefit of any private person but will be distributed to a non-profit fund, foundation, or corporation which is organized and operated exclusively for charitable purposes in which has established its tax-exempt status under Section 501(c)(3) and 509(a)(1), (2) or (3) of the Internal Revenue Code of 1954.

Article IV. Duration
The period during which this Corporation is to continue as a corporation is perpetual.

Article V. Address.
The area to be served by this Corporation shall be the Cincinnati, Ohio metropolitan area.
The post office address of its principal office is *, Cincinnati, Ohio.
The name and address of its registered agent is *, a natural person resident in the county in which the undersigned has its principal office, as its statutory agent upon whom any process, notice or demand required or permitted by statute to be served upon the undersigned may be served. The complete address of said statutory agent is *, Cincinnati, Hamilton County, Ohio.

Director's Resource 6–5 (continued)

Article VI.   Members.
1. Definition

    The members of this Corporation shall be the Board of Trustees and the parents of the children who are enrolled in the child development center.

2. The Classes of Members and Voting

    The Corporation shall have one class of members. Each member shall be entitled to one vote on each matter submitted to a vote of the members except as otherwise provided by law.

Article VII.   Board of Trustees.
1. The affairs of this Corporation shall be under the control of a Board of Trustees consisting of no less than nine, but no more than twelve persons, all of whom shall be volunteers and neither paid personnel of this corporation nor of any organization receiving financial support from this corporation, all of whom shall be of full age and at least one of whom shall be a citizen of the United States and a resident of the State of Ohio.
2. The Board of Trustees shall be comprised of five to seven parents whose children are enrolled in the child development center, one representative from Cincinnati Union Bethel, one representative from *, and two community members selected by the rest of the Board for their expertise in child care. Additional members might be selected for expertise in such areas as pediatric medicine, early childhood education, financial affairs, fund-raising, or marketing.
3. The members shall elect the parent representatives on the Board of Trustees for overlapping two-year terms. No person may serve more than two consecutive terms except after the absence from the Board of Trustees of one year.
4. The duties of the Board of Trustees shall be to establish the general policies of the Corporation and to manage the business and affairs of the Corporation.
5. Procedure for election of parent board members.

    Annually, the members of the Corporation will be solicited for interest in serving on the Board of Trustees by the Nominating Committee. The Nominating Committee shall present to members of the Corporation for a vote a slate of candidates from which new Board members shall be elected.

Article VIII.   Meetings, Notices, Quorum.
1. The Annual meeting of the members of this Corporation shall be held in the Spring at such place and on such day and hour as the Board of Trustees may determine.
2. Special meetings of the members for any purpose or purposes may be called pursuant to a resolution of the Board of Trustees, and shall be called by the President or Vice President/Treasurer at the request of one-third of the trustees in office, or at the written request of one-third of the members of the Corporation. Such request shall in any case state the purpose or purposes of the proposed meeting. Business transacted at all special meetings shall be confined to the subjects stated in the call and matters germane thereto.

Director's Resource 6–5 (continued)

3. Notice of any meeting of the members, annual or special, stating the time when and the place where it is to be held shall be served personally or by mail, upon each member entitled to vote at such meeting, not less than 10 or more than 30 days before the meeting.

4. The presence in person of not less than 20 members entitled to vote is requisite and shall constitute a quorum at all meetings of members for the election of trustees or for the transaction of other business except as otherwise provided by law or by these bylaws.

5. Any action by a majority of members where a quorum is present shall be the action of the membership of this Corporation.

Article IX. Meetings of Board.

1. Meetings of the Board of Trustees of this Corporation shall be held at least six times per year and additional meetings may be held on the call of the President or, if s/he is absent or unable or refuses to act, by any officer, or by any 4 trustees.

2. Notice of any meeting of the trustees, regular or special, stating the time when and the place where it is to be held shall be served personally, by telephone, or by mail, upon each trustee not less than 5 days before the meeting. Business transacted at all special meetings shall be confined to the subjects stated in the call and matters germane thereto.

3. The presence in person of not less than 5 trustees is requisite and shall constitute action by a majority of trustees where a quorum is present shall be the action of the trustees of this Corporation.

4. In addition to the powers by these bylaws expressly conferred upon them, the Board of Trustees of this Corporation may exercise such powers and do such lawful acts and things as are not by statute or by these bylaws required to be exercised by the members or officers.

Article X. Officers.

1. The officers of this Corporation who shall be elected by the Board of Trustees shall be a President and a Vice President/Treasurer, each of whom shall be members of the Board of Trustees. All officers shall hold office for one year and until their successors are elected and qualify.

2. The President, or in his/her absence, a Vice President/Treasurer selected by the Board of Trustees, shall preside at all meetings of members and of the Board of Trustees and shall perform the duties usually devolving upon a presiding officer.

3. The Vice President/Treasurer shall have the custody of all funds and securities of the Corporation and shall keep full and accurate accounts of receipts and disbursements in books belonging to the Corporation and shall deposit all moneys and other valuable effects in the name and to the credit of the Corporation in such depositories as may be designated by the Board of Trustees. S/He shall disburse the funds of the Corporation as may be ordered by the Board of Trustees, taking proper vouchers for such disbursements, and shall render to the Board of Trustees at the regular meetings of the board, or whenever they may require it, an account of all transactions and of all financial condition of the corporation.

Director's Resource 6–5 (continued)

4. The Board of Trustees may require the Vice President/Treasurer and, may at its discretion, require any other officer of this corporation, or employee of the Management Contractor, to give a bond in a sum and with one or more sureties satisfactory to the Board of Trustees, conditioned upon the faithful performance of the duties of his/her office and for the restoration to the Corporation in case of death, resignation, retirement or removal from office of all papers, vouchers, money and other property of whatever kind in his/her possession or under his/her control belonging to the Corporation.

5. The President shall ensure that minutes of meetings are taken and that records of activities are maintained in a permanent record, as legally required.

6. The Board of Trustees shall cause the financial record to be audited annually by a public account.

7. The Board of Trustees may authorize any officer(s) or agent(s) of the Corporation, in addition to the officers authorized by these by-laws, to enter into any contract or execute and deliver any instrument in the name of and on behalf of the Corporation, and such authority may be general or confined to specific instances.

Article XI.   Committees.

1. There may be an *Executive Committee* consisting of the officers and one other member of the Board of Trustees elected by the board. The Executive Committee shall have and exercise all the powers of the Board of Trustees subject to such limitation as the laws of the State of Ohio or resolutions of the Board of Trustees may impose.

2. The President shall serve as chairperson of the Executive Committee. The Executive Committee shall have power to make rules and regulations for the conduct of its business. A majority thereof shall constitute a quorum.

3. The Executive Committee shall keep regular minutes of its proceedings and report same to the Board of Trustees.

4. The President shall appoint a *Nominating Committee* of not fewer than 3 members of this Corporation to make nominations for the election of parent members and trustees. The Nominating Committee shall also nominate persons to serve as officers and as members of the Executive Committee.

5. There shall be a *Finance Committee* composed of the Vice President/Treasurer, as chairperson, and at least one other member of the board, to be appointed by the President with approval of the board and shall have power to invest and reinvest any funds of the Corporation. Their policies of investment, however, shall be subject to review by the board. The Treasurer is authorized and empowered to execute on behalf of the Corporation, when so directed by the Finance Committee, such documents as may be necessary to effectuate the sale, exchange, or transfer of securities. The Finance Committee should report to the board at regular intervals, and a complete auditor's report on the Corporation's finances should be sent annually to all officers of the board and made available to all board members. The committee shall consider the details of the budget which is prepared by the Management Contractor and presented to the board, along with the committee's recommendation, by the Vice President/Treasurer or the executive. The board, voting in official meeting, shall determine the budget for the Corporation.

Director's Resource 6–5 (continued)

6. There shall be a *Scholarship Committee* appointed by the President and approved by the board whose responsibility is to establish policies for granting reduced fees to parents. The committee also establishes procedures and reviews individual applications for such reduced fees. The Scholarship Committee should report to the board of actions at regular intervals.

7. All committee appointments shall be made as soon as possible after the election of officers or vacancies occur. Committee members shall serve for such terms as may be provided by the board.

8. The President shall from time to time appoint such standing or special committees as are authorized by the Board of Trustees. Each committee shall consist of such number of persons as the Board of Trustees deems advisable. All acts of such committees shall be subject to approval of the Board of Trustees.

9. The chairpersons of standing committees who are not already serving on the Board of Trustees shall be eligible to attend and advise at all meetings of the Board of Trustees.

Article XII.   Vacancies.

1. All vacancies in the Board of Trustees, whether caused by failure to elect, resignation, death or otherwise, may be filled by the remaining trustees, even though less than a quorum, at any stated or special meeting, or by the members at any regular or special meeting.

2. All vacancies in the Executive Committee whether caused by failure to elect, resignation, death or otherwise may be filled by the Board of Trustees at any stated or special meeting.

3. In case there is a vacancy in any office of the Corporation, whether caused by failure to elect, death, resignation or otherwise, such a vacancy may be filled by the Board of Trustees at any regular or special meeting. Such officers so elected to fill vacancies shall serve until the next annual meeting of members and until their successors are elected and qualify.

Article XIII.   Management Contract.

The Board of Trustees shall enter into a contract with an agency or individual who shall serve as the general manager of the child development center. Terms of the contract shall include responsibilities in the following areas: general, fiscal, space and equipment, staff, evaluation, enrollment, parent involvement, health, safety, children's program and community relations. Also included are provisions for insurance, term, compensation, and termination.

Article XIV.   Fiscal Year

The fiscal year of this Corporation shall be the calendar year.

Article XV.   Nondiscrimination.

The members, officers, trustees, committee members, contractors, and persons served by this Corporation shall be selected entirely on a nondiscriminatory basis with respect to age, sex, race, religion, sexual preference, and national origin.

Director's Resource 6–5 (continued)

Article XVI.   Miscellaneous Provisions.

1. Depositories. All funds of the Corporation, not otherwise, employed, shall be deposited from time to time to the credit of the Corporation in such banks, savings and loan associations, trust companies, or other depositories as the Board of Trustees may elect.
2. Checks, Drafts, Etc. All checks, drafts, or orders for the payment of money, notes, or other evidence of indebtedness issued in the name of the Corporation shall be signed by such persons and in such manner as shall from time to time be determined by resolution of the Board of Trustees. In the absence of such determination by the Board of Trustees, such instrument shall be signed by the Vice-President/Treasurer or by the President of the Corporation.
3. Investment. Any funds of the Corporation which are not needed currently for the activities of the Corporation may be invested at the discretion of the Board of Trustees.
4. Book and Records. The Corporation shall keep correct and complete book and records of accounts and shall also keep minutes of the proceedings of its members, Board of Trustees and committees having any of the authority of the Board of Trustees, and shall keep a record giving the name and addresses of the members entitled to vote. All books and records of the Corporation may be inspected by any member, or his/her agent or attorney or the general public, for any proper purpose at any reasonable time.
5. Parliamentary Procedure. All Board of Trustees and membership meetings shall be governed by *Roberts' Rules of Order* (current edition), unless contrary procedure is established by the Articles of Incorporation, these bylaws, standing rules, or by resolution of the Board of Trustees.

Article XVII.   Amendments.

The bylaws may be altered, amended, or repealed and new bylaws may be adopted by a two-thirds (2/3) majority vote of the Board of Trustees, or a majority of the voting members of the Corporation present at an Annual meeting or a duly summoned special meeting of the Trustees or members of the Corporation.

*Names and addresses deleted by author to protect the privacy of those named.

CHAPTER 7

Handling Financial Matters

The director's role as one who sets the tone for the center has already been established, but he or she must also be a pragmatist capable of dealing with all the financial obligations of running a center. The financial operation of a center should be as smooth as possible to ensure that the director can maintain control of the finances. Poor financial management leads to constant lack of funds and continuously hinders personnel as they work to achieve program goals.

The two major components of the financial plan are developing a system for managing financial resources and obtaining adequate funding. The latter will be discussed in Chapter 8.

Every center needs a long-range financial plan and a plan for the upcoming year. A money management system including both policies and procedures is essential. Although many aspects of a good early childhood education program cannot be purchased at any price, high-quality care for young children is expensive, and funds must be allocated properly to provide a developmentally sound program on which children and parents can depend. No matter how good the intentions of the staff may be, a program cannot continue to operate for long without a balanced budget.

In a new center, or one that is reorganizing, a decision must be made regarding who will be responsible for the center's financial management. Usually, the director is selected for this job, although sometimes a board member, parent (particularly in a parent co-op), or an assistant director carries all or part of the load. If there is a board with a finance committee, the staff member responsible for financial management works closely with this committee. A corporate system may have a regional or national operation of all the system's centers, and in a public school system, the finances are usually handled through the central office.

BALANCING INCOME AND EXPENSES

A major task of the director or finance committee is the preparation of a budget. The director's goal is to balance income and expenses, and in some cases, to show a profit. However, the cost of the desired early childhood education program is often higher than the total income available. The director prepares a budget by:

1. estimating how much the program will cost (based on the center's goals)
2. determining how much income will be available (see Chapter 8)
3. seeking more income to equal expenditures, adjusting expenditures to equal income, or doing both

Estimating Costs

The financial director's first task is to figure program cost. The Washington Quality Child Care Think Tank which began work in January 1996 estimates that quality child care costs $8,300 per child per year.[1] The task requires an overall understanding of the early childhood education program, its goals, and its objectives. The director determines what is needed for children in the particular community and program, then analyzes the cost of meeting these needs. If other people are preparing the budget, the director works with them in interpreting the program needs. In this planning model, some objectives may have to be postponed or omitted because of a lack of funds. Priorities should be established on the basis of the program goals, whereas the cost and the availability of funds determine the scope of the program. For example, a center may select improving salaries as a primary goal. If new playground equipment is also desirable, the decision about providing equipment in addition to improving salaries will be made based on the availability of funds.

Another question that has an impact on both program and finances is, "What is the population to be served?" "Does the program serve children from infancy through preschool age?" If so, the director will have to recognize that costs for infant programs are considerably higher than costs for preschoolers, based largely on the staff-child ratio infants need. Decisions will have to be made about holding places for children as they are ready to move up. How long can the center leave a toddler slot vacant after the toddler leaves the center or moves to a preschool classroom? The center director may realize that Baby Jones will be ready to move from the infant group to the toddler group in six weeks. Can this director afford to tell a waiting-list toddler parent that there is no room, thus forgoing six weeks of toddler income? Should the slot be filled right away, if possible, or in six weeks when Baby Jones is ready to move? Should that baby be kept in the infant room, even though she is old enough and mature enough to move to the toddler area? And, if that happens, should the Jones family pay infant tuition or the less expensive toddler tuition? Should three- and four-year-olds be in the same classroom?

Aside from the educational issues, and the pros and cons of multiage classrooms, the director may recognize that many three-year-olds need more adult assistance than do four-year-olds. Licensing may require that the ratio needed for the youngest children in the group be maintained. If so, the director will have to provide the three-year-old ratio even if the majority of children in the class are four-year-olds. Would it then be cost effective to maintain separate groups for three- and four-year-olds? Would the expected cost savings be worth sacrificing the presumed child benefits a mixed age group would provide?

Other questions might include: "How many teachers will be needed and for what hours?" "Will it be necessary to have aides? A cook? A janitor? A secretary? A bus driver?" Answers to these and dozens of additional questions should be available from the people who are responsible for designing the program. By using this method, the director keeps the goals and philosophy of the center paramount.

Some directors have difficulty with the initial phase of budgeting. Instead of starting with the goals and objectives, they start with the dollars available and attempt to determine what can be done with those dollars. Such a center is truly ruled by the budget (or by the finance director), and maintaining an educationally and financially sound program under these conditions is extremely difficult.

Although program and financial decisions may be made at the national or regional level, in a corporate system, the director of each center is responsible for implementing these decisions. The national or regional financial officer provides information about how much money is budgeted for each category; each local director then orders equipment and supplies through the main or regional office, and is responsible for generating the required tuition.

Determining the dollar amount of a budget is a major part of the overall financial plan. This figure is arrived at by listing the items needed to operate the program for a year in categories such as salaries, rent, and equipment. Next, the budget direc-

---

[1]Financing child care: The future of children. The David and Lucile Packard Foundation. Center for the Future of Children, Los Altos, CA, Summer/Fall, 1996, Appendix C, p. 173.

tor determines with as much accuracy as possible how much each of these categories will cost. The sum of the costs for each category is the amount of income needed for a year. A sample budget in Director's Resource 7–1 (page 131) provides an idea of the costs of each category and of the costs of the total program for a hypothetical center. This sample budget is not meant to be utilized in the form presented here but may be used as a guide to budget preparation. Center directors and other professional groups and organizations in each community such as gas and electric companies, kitchen equipment suppliers, toy suppliers, and business associations can furnish more specific and relevant cost information for individual centers.

Factors that will influence the total amount spent by a center and the ways in which that amount is allocated are:

1. number, ages, and special needs of children enrolled
2. teacher–to–child ratio
3. staff training
4. type and location of building
5. amount of equipment already owned or available
6. type of program and services provided
7. section of the country in which the center is located
8. general economic conditions
9. amount and type of in-kind contributions

The sum of the costs for each category is the cost of running the center for one year. Dividing this figure by the number of children to be served establishes the cost per child, a figure that can be further examined on a monthly, weekly, daily, or hourly basis. The cost of various program components such as infant or school-age programs also can be figured this way.

It is important to consider whether the center is a nonprofit organization or whether one of the goals is to make a profit. This question is sometimes a hotly debated issue among early childhood educators, many of whom feel that early childhood education centers should not be operated for profit because someone then makes money at the expense of the children. Admittedly, early childhood education costs are high and it is

Reflections

Think about the tuition that is paid by parents, particularly in regard to its relationship to the salaries that are paid by a center. Consider a situation in which a teacher's annual salary is $17,000 and the assistant teacher's annual salary is $13,000. With a total of $30,000 a year for salaries, 15 families would each pay $2,000 a year to cover these salaries alone. Unless the center has other sources of income, tuition costs also must cover costs of equipment, supplies, food, facilities, utilities, benefits, administration, and so forth. Since the last child will leave the center about ten to twelve hours after the first child has arrived, staff members will have to be present on a staggered schedule and additional help will be needed, all of which will increase salary costs. What would tuition have to be to produce a profit for the program sponsors?

difficult to make a profit. Nonetheless, if a person or group can provide a good program, meeting the needs of both children and staff while showing a profit, there is no reason to discourage such a financial plan. It is the director's responsibility to ensure that children are not short-changed in the interest of making a profit. This ethical issue may become even more challenging if the director's salary is tied to the amount of profit.

Adjusting Budget Figures

While it is relatively easy to change the budget figures on paper, chronic budgetary problems will

Reflections

It may be easier to think about the financial aspects of an educational program by looking at your own educational finances. Think about the following questions: How was your college coursework financed? If you paid tuition, what percentage of the actual cost of your education did you pay? Who financed the balance? Taxpayers? Endowments? How were other school expenses (high school and elementary school) financed?

drain staff energy from the daily operation and will remain unless the center can actually pare costs to the level of income earned.

Each expense must be analyzed with an eye toward its relative importance in the overall program. Can the equipment budget be lowered by substituting some free or inexpensive materials? Can food costs be lowered by cooperative buying? Can the consumable supply budget be reduced without a major effect on program quality?

When no cost reductions are feasible, new and current funding sources can be approached with clear documentation of the need in relation to goals. When a center's financial management is poor, the director may continue operating past this point without becoming aware that the inevitable outcome will be a poor quality program or bankruptcy.

PREPARING THE BUDGET

The following section discusses various types of budgets and the many components that go into them.

Types of Budgets

Budgets are classified in several ways. They may be based on the stage of development of the center or they may be categorized according to the stage to which the budget itself has been carried. The creation of a new center demands one kind of budget whereas the ongoing operation of a center requires a budget of a different type. Budgets also may reflect the center's accountability mechanism.

Start-Up Budgets. When a center is beginning operation, the director prepares two budgets: the start-up budget and the operating budget. The start-up budget consists of all the expenses incurred in starting the center. These expenses include initial building expenses (downpayment on the purchase of the building, the cost of building renovation, or rent deposit), the purchase of major equipment, the cost of publicizing the center, the director's salary for several months prior to the

children's attendance, the deposit on telephone service, and the utility charges during the start-up period. Salaries for any additional personnel needed to assist the director of a large center also must be provided. Total start-up costs vary widely, and when these costs are incurred, the usual sources of revenue ordinarily have not yet become available. In these cases, a special grant may be needed or the organizers of the center may arrange for a loan or invest their own funds. When a loan is obtained, the cost of the interest must be recognized as constituting a very real budgetary item.

Occasionally, suppliers will permit purchasers to defer payment for ninety days and the center can schedule purchases so that the first tuition is received before the ninety-day period ends. However, the first receipts will certainly not cover all the expenses. If receipts are due from agency or government funds, those first payments are usually made after the services have been provided. In the meantime, suppliers may charge interest on unpaid bills. Therefore, it is important to obtain as much assurance as possible that funds for start-up will be available when needed.

The United States General Accounting Office (GAO) report on child care costs found start-up costs of $8,000 to $90,000 with a median of $48,500. These costs included, in descending order of amount spent, costs for space, supplies and equipment, planning and administration, and teacher training.[2]

Operating Budget. The operating budget consists of an income and expense plan for one year, and is used when centers enroll children and begin the program annually thereafter. The center may operate on a calendar year (from January 1 to December 31) or on a fiscal year, a twelve-month period chosen for ease of relating financial matters to other operations of the center. Centers funded by agencies that operate on a fiscal year running from July 1 to June 30 find it easier to work on the same schedule as the funding agency, but many early childhood education centers choose September 1 to August 31 for their fiscal year because those dates are closely related to the start of

[2]United State General Accounting Office, *Early childhood education: What are the costs of high-quality programs?* (January 1990). Briefing report to the chairman, Committee on Labor and Human Resources, U.S. Senate.

their school year. Once a center has selected its fiscal year, no change should be made without serious reason. Planning one year's budget from January 1 to December 31 and then changing to a September–August fiscal year in the following year not only causes confusion but also may need to be justified for tax purposes.

Before hiring or purchasing can begin, the budget must be approved by the board and the funding source. At this point, conflict may arise among the board, the funding agency, and the director; each group may have varying interpretations of the center's goals and of the means for reaching these goals. Once a consensus has been reached and the budget has been approved, the budget becomes the working financial plan. The director must see that it is followed.

Analyzing Budget Categories

Most boards have a finance committee that oversees the preparation and implementation of the budget. However, even when this committee assumes major responsibility, the director is still responsible for understanding and articulating what is needed to operate the program successfully. Many board members have limited knowledge of the actual cost of child care. The director must help them develop this understanding.

DIRECTOR'S CORNER

"Our needs assessment indicated that over 100 children would use our center. Two major corporations in the neighborhood worked with us and many of their employees expressed interest in enrolling their children. We were shocked when we spent the whole first year with only nine children enrolled. Luckily, we had strong financial backing, and we have now reached capacity enrollment."
—Director, private not-for-profit center

Some centers budget by function rather than simply by category; that is, administrative costs and the costs of each aspect of the program are budgeted separately. For example, if 20 percent of the director's time is spent working directly with the children and 80 percent is spent on administration, then 20 percent of the director's salary would be allocated to the children's program salaries category and 80 percent would fall under administration. A complex center may provide and budget several separate functions such as infant program, preschool program, and after-school program. This budgeting method clearly delineates the actual cost of the children's program, and when coupled with a description of the services offered, it provides a mechanism for comparing costs with other programs and for including the value of the services provided in relation to the costs incurred. This method also provides information used in determining tuition. However, ever-changing tax laws make it essential that even small centers have the services of an accountant to guide the director in setting up fiscal systems and to provide information about new governmental requirements. An attorney may also be needed to help ensure that the center is operating within legal limits. The cost of these services must be included in the budget.

The following budget categories will provide a rough idea of the costs of early childhood education and the formats used for presenting a budget.

Salaries. In any early childhood education budget, the major component is salaries. A center can expect to spend up to 80 percent of its operating costs for personnel. This figure includes salaries and wages for full- and part-time staff members (director, teachers, cooks, janitor) and for substitutes; it also includes fringe benefits for the full-time staff. In determining the budget for salaries, the personnel policies should be consulted in regard to pay rates and fringe benefits. The salary policies may address issues such as staff member's education level, previous experience, or meritorious service. The director also must comply with the minimum wage laws, tax laws, and laws regarding employee responsibility. Other factors that may influence salaries are public school affiliation, union membership, and salary standards of the sponsoring agency. Center directors must ensure that they meet the Fair Labor Standards Act (FLSA). A number of complex issues and conflicting results of court cases make it difficult to determine who is considered a teacher for the purposes of FLSA. This determination can make a difference in whether or not an employer is required to provide overtime pay, and pay for hours spent in in-service training and parent meetings "after hours."[3]

Personnel costs to the center, over and above the salaries and wages paid to employees, consist of the percentages of these wages that are imposed as taxes by various governmental agencies that the employer may be required to pay. For example, the employer pays percentages of the employee's salary for social security, workers' compensation, and unemployment compensation. The center also incurs the bookkeeping costs that are involved with maintaining accurate records for each employee and filing reports with a variety of government agencies. Benefits such as health insurance are included in personnel costs, and provision must be made for substitute staff who work during employees' sick and vacation leave. Although benefit costs may seem expendable, they often mean the difference between a stable and a transient staff. Keep in mind that high staff turnover means additional costs for advertising, additional training time, and perhaps loss of clients. More importantly, high staff turnover has a negative effect on the quality of child care.

In addition to the benefits described above, the agency also is required to withhold certain taxes from each employee's paycheck, to accrue these funds, and to submit them to the appropriate governmental body in a timely manner with accurate records. Although these taxes are not paid by the employer, here again the cost of record keeping does contribute to the overall cost of operating the center.

Consultants. A second component of a center budget that is closely related to salaries is contract services or consultant fees. This category covers payments to people who agree to perform specified services for the center or its clients such as accountants, lawyers, doctors, dentists, social workers, psychologists, nutritionists, and educational consultants. These types of professionals could be employees of a large center or system. However, they usually serve as consultants by agreeing, for example, to give dental examinations to all children enrolled in the center or to provide workshops for teachers one day a month. When the center's staff is not well-trained, or when a broad range of services is provided for children, many consultants are needed. Although some centers do not hire consultants and most will hire only a limited number, the overall quality of the program may be increased by the services they provide.

When consultants come from out of town, their transportation, meals, and lodging may be additional costs. Sometimes, consultants are paid a per diem rate to cover meals and lodging. The current per diem rate of the federal government might be used in budgeting. Both the center and the consultant should agree in writing on all financial arrangements and performance expectations in advance of any services rendered. Under no circumstances should the director attempt to classify a staff position as a consultancy. Serious legal ramifications may result.

Plant and Equipment. The largest cost in the physical plant category is rental or mortgage payments on the facility. The costs for the maintenance of, and the repairs to, the building and grounds are also part of this budget item. When maintenance work is done on a regular basis, the costs usually will be lower in the long run. However, since it is impossible to predict all maintenance and repair needs in advance, a lump sum for this purpose should be allocated each year. A preliminary assessment of the main components of a building foundation (roof, plumbing, wiring, heating and cooling system, termite damage, and so forth) will provide a rough idea of when major repairs may be expected.

---

[3]The Child Care Law Center. The Fair Labor Standards Act and the Child Care Industry. *Child Care Information Exchange*, September 1996, pp. 82–86.

Also included in physical plant in the operating budget are utilities (heat, electricity, and water). In some cases, one or more of the utility charges may be covered in the rental fee, a point that should be fully understood and in writing before an agreement to rent is made. Some centers also may have to pay for garbage removal. When utilities are not included in the rent payments, an approximate budget figure can be obtained by checking with previous tenants or with the utility companies.

In budgeting for a new center, equipment for the office, the kitchen, and the children is a major part of the start-up budget. For a continuing center, the operating budget includes supplementary pieces as well as repair and replacement where needed. Leasing and rental charges for equipment are included here. For example, a center may rent a floor sander for a day or lease a copy machine for a year. The continuing equipment budget will be about 10 percent of the start-up equipment budget; so if the start-up equipment budget is $500 per child, the continuing equipment budget would be $50 per child per year.

Supplies.   Three types of supplies must be purchased: office and general supplies, classroom supplies, and food supplies. The first category, office and general supplies, includes items such as pencils, stationery, toilet paper, paper towels, cleansers, and brooms. Construction paper, paint, crayons, pet food, and doll clothes are included in classroom supplies. Food supplies encompass all items available for human consumption. Usually, two meals and two snacks per child per day are served in full-day centers, with one snack offered in a half-day program. In any case, sufficient food should be provided so that teachers can eat with the children. Food costs vary depending on the availability of federal food subsidies and on factors in the economy. A nutritionist engaged as a consultant can aid the director in setting up a nutritionally and financially sound food plan.

All supplies should be ordered in large quantities when that is more economical, assuming that the supplies will be used while they are still in top condition (for example, paint dries out when it is stored too long) and there is sufficient storage space. The cost of providing storage space and the possibility that plentiful supplies will be used more freely by the staff must be weighed against the savings accrued from purchasing in quantity.

Transportation.   This category may include the purchase or lease of several vans for transporting children to and from school, and on field trips. In such cases, insurance, gas, maintenance, and license fees must be budgeted. Some centers contract with a company to provide transportation for children and some may rent a bus for special occasions. Vehicles must be equipped with child safety seats or seat belts, depending on the size of the child. Other governmental regulations regarding vehicles also must be followed. Your state may require that you transport children in vehicles meeting special school bus regulations, and that drivers have special licenses. The many financial, safety, and liability issues involved lead many centers to require parents to provide the child's transportation to and from school.

Costs for staff members to travel to professional meetings, to other centers for observation, and to homes for home visits are included in the transportation category. The mileage rate for automobile travel reimbursement is usually based on the current federal government mileage rate.

Telephone.   Telephone costs can be determined by checking with the telephone company. In deciding on the number of telephones to order, consider the center's staffing pattern. For example, if a classroom staffed by one adult is located on another floor away from other classrooms, an extension phone is needed to allow that teacher to get help when necessary. Licensing requirements in some states specify where a phone is required. In any case, enough lines should be provided to enable parents and other callers to reach the center without undue delays. Call waiting is often less costly than a second line and improves accessibility for outside callers.

Getting emergency messages through immediately is a priority item, and providing staffers with access to a phone for personal calls during breaks is a benefit that recognizes their needs and helps them feel that they are respected members of the organization.

Insurance.   Insurance agents can quote rates and provide information about appropriate kinds of insurance. A center usually needs at least fire, theft, and liability insurance. A child accident policy is valuable and inexpensive. If the center has a board of directors, Directors and Officers Insurance is important. Be sure to read each policy carefully and ask questions about any items you do not understand.

Postage. Postage covers the cost of mailings to parents and prospective client families, as well as the communication needed to manage the center business. In some cases, fax or e-mail may be appropriate and less costly, but in all cases, a record of important communication should be maintained.

Billing, especially notices of overdue accounts, usually must be mailed. Some centers establish the policy that payment is due on a particular date each month and no bills are sent. Postage costs can be held down to some extent if information is distributed by sending notes home with the children, but keep in mind that these items may not always reach the parent.

Marketing. Marketing includes newspaper and telephone book advertisements, brochures and fliers, and radio or television announcements. Some agencies design a logo and use it on various products such as tee shirts, stationery, business cards, and beverage mugs. Once a center is well-established, the marketing budget may be minimal but in the initial stages, and in highly transient neighborhoods, it is an income-producing expense. All centers are wise to maintain a good public relations plan so that the community knows about and supports their work. But perhaps the best marketing tool is a satisfied customer.

Licensing. Information about licensing costs can be obtained from the licensing agent. These costs will vary according to the center's location. Other professional fees such as those for NAEYC accreditation also belong in this category.

Audit. Yearly audits are essential. They assure the board and funders that the center's financial matters are being handled properly. You should ask your accountant for a cost estimate and build that into the budget.

Miscellaneous. This category includes funds for small items that do not fall under any of the previously mentioned categories. However, attributing expenditures to a particular category provides a more accurate picture of the center's financial status and eliminates slippage in expenditures. For example, if postage and advertising were both included under miscellaneous, postage expenditures could skyrocket and not be recognized as a budgetary problem.

In-Kind Contributions. Some budget items are not received in cash and are not paid for in cash. These are called in-kind contributions and should be shown in the budget so that the true cost of operating the center is known. For example, a center may rent two 600-square-foot-rooms in a church building for $100 per month per room, which would cost the center $2,000 for a ten-month program. If the fair rental cost is at the rate of $5.00 per square foot (a total of $6,000), then the church is, in effect, contributing $4,000 to the center program.

Consultants may volunteer their services, and such services also should be shown as in-kind contributions. For example, assume that a child development specialist conducts a half-day workshop without charging the center. The specialist's contribution is valued at $200, the hypothetical per diem rate for professional services.

Sometimes, directors expect staff to volunteer to work additional hours without pay. This practice is usually inappropriate. Many teachers already spend time at home planning and preparing materials. Furthermore, staff salaries are usually alarmingly low. If staff members are expected to attend meetings and programs outside of regular work hours, these conditions should be spelled out in the job descriptions. Some centers include policies relating to staff caring for children who are center clients outside of work hours.

Budgeting for the Second and Subsequent Years

Several months prior to the end of the year, the director and members of the finance committee meet to review the budget the director has prepared for the ensuing year. For the second and subsequent budgets, the previous year's figures can serve as a guide, but the new budget figures that are based on experience and on program changes, will differ from those of the previous year. Still, the income and expenses must balance.

OTHER FINANCIAL RESPONSIBILITIES

The budget is the major tool used by the financial director for management of center finances, but balancing income and expenses is only one aspect of an overall ongoing financial system. The director has a number of continuing financial responsibilities, all of which relate ultimately to the budget.

Designing Budget Systems

Once the sources and amounts of income have been determined, these facts must be written down, along with the plan for spending, discussed earlier in this chapter. This written plan must be prepared in such a way that the people who need to read it will be able to understand it.

Small centers can use a very simple format. Centers that are publicly funded may be required to use whatever system is designated by the funding agency. Many centers use budget codes or account numbers, assigning a code number to each budget category and using separate numbers for each item within that category. For example, if the budget item equipment is coded as 110, then the subcategories might be:

111	office equipment
112	classroom equipment
113	kitchen equipment

Similarly, personnel might be coded as 510, with:

511	salaries
512	social security
513	worker's compensation

Such a system enables the financial director to record transactions according to appropriate budget categories, and to ascertain quickly now much has been spent and how much remains in a given category.

Directors of nonprofit organizations must consider several relatively new statements of financial accounting standards issued by the rule-making body of the accounting profession. These statements affect the way the center will categorize transactions in order to provide a clear picture of the center's programs and the cost of each. The new requirements also will demonstrate how re-

sources have been used and the extent to which the agency can meet its fiscal objectives.[4]

In order to have an accurate picture of the center's current financial position, accrual instead of cash accounting is essential. This means that revenues are recorded as they are incurred. By using this system, the director avoids the inaccurate picture presented when expenses are recorded only when they are paid rather than when the money is appropriated. This information is reported on a monthly cash flow report, an estimate of how much you expect to receive and spend each month. The director estimates receipts and disbursements for the year, month by month. The amount of cash expected to be on hand at the end of one month becomes the amount of cash expected to be on hand at the beginning of the following month. As actual figures become available, these are entered in the "actual" column so that monthly comparisons can be made between anticipated and actual expenses for the month and for the year to date.[5] (A sample cash flow report appears in Director's Resource 7–3, page 134.)

DIRECTOR'S CORNER

"I thought we were in good financial shape. We were showing a solid bank balance and we had full enrollment. What our cash accounting system didn't show was that we had several thousand dollars in bills which the bookkeeper hadn't paid yet. I learned that checking the cash on hand and even looking at how much we had budgeted for a category weren't necessarily appropriate ways to make decisions about what I could spend."

—Director, for-profit proprietary center

Ordering Goods and Services

With an approved budget in hand, the director or purchasing agent (or someone assigned to this role) can begin to order supplies, equipment, and services. The first step is to consult the person or people who will use the item or services. The janitor may be consulted about a waxing machine whereas the teachers should be involved in

[4]Lukaszewski, T. E., CPA. (1996). New accounting requirements for non-profits. *Child Care Information Exchange*, September, pp.35–38.
[5]Stephens, K., CPA, (1991). *Confronting your bottom line: Financial guide for child care centers*, Redmond, WA: Exchange Press Inc., 1991.

decisions about tables and chairs for the children. Both janitor and teachers could participate in selecting carpeting for the classrooms. However, when it comes to the actual ordering of the goods and services, as few people as possible—one is always preferable—should be involved.

Several methods of ordering goods and services are utilized, depending on the nature of the purchase. Major purchases are usually approved by the director, the board, or a committee. If outside funding has been received, the center's contract may require that bids be submitted for large items or for large quantities of items (such as food or paper goods). The purchaser writes out required specifications to suppliers or advertises for bids in the case of a large order. Then the purchaser examines the bids and contracts that each supplier offers. The lowest bid must be accepted unless the bidder does not meet the specifications. Specifications can refer to a description of the item in question (that is, a commercial dishwasher), to the performance of the item (with water temperature of 180 degrees), or to its delivery date (to be delivered by September 1, 2001).

Smaller purchases, or those that are routine (such as art supplies), may be ordered from a wholesaler. However, some centers require that price information on such items be obtained and that the item of appropriate quality having the lowest price be purchased. Sometimes, purchases are made with particular outlets because they allow credit but this choice will be false economy if the quality is not satisfactory.

In some large cities, several centers may band together to purchase large quantities of items at reduced prices in a plan called cooperative buying. Each center may contribute to the buyer's salary and usually must transport items from a central location to their own centers.

Making Payments

The director (or someone so designated) is responsible for making all payments. When shipments arrive, they are checked and then paid for as soon as possible within the terms of agreement. For example, if the vendor gives 30 days to pay, the center should use the money until the payment is due, but should carefully monitor bill payment so that unnecessary interest is not incurred. In cases where a discount is offered for prompt payment, that may be a wise course to follow. Before paying for any item, it is important to verify that the items received are proper in quantity and quality, and that the price on the invoice is correct.

A center should immediately establish a checking account so that payment for goods and services can be made promptly and safely. If the center is small, there may be the temptation to pay expenses directly from cash income. This practice is a major mistake because under such a plan, money can easily be lost or stolen, and errors or misunderstandings are more likely to occur. Furthermore, no audit trail of these items is available. Most centers use checking accounts and some centers require two signatures on each check (perhaps the signatures of the board treasurer and the director). In small centers or in proprietary centers, the director signs all checks. However, even more important is that there be a person other than the bookkeeper assigned to reconcile the bank balance.

When specific procedures for money management are in place, fewer errors are likely to occur. There must be a specific place to store bills and a specific time set aside for paying them. In small co-ops a parent may work at home recording transactions. In large, complex organizations, all finances may be handled through a central administrative office that may be in another city or state.

Recording Transactions

Whenever a financial transaction occurs, it should be recorded promptly on a specific form. Access to a personal computer and appropriate software makes this task relatively easy and provides clear, readily available reports which show the financial position of the center on a monthly, weekly, or even daily basis.

In fact, many directors who now use computers for record keeping wonder how they managed without them. At first, using this technology can be time consuming, particularly if you are completely unfamiliar with the way these machines work. However, once the system is set up, it takes no more time (and probably less time) to enter figures by means of a keyboard as opposed to using pencil and paper. The result is usually easier to read, may readily be converted to chart form on the computer, and can be crossreferenced. For example, you can enter into each child's record the tuition received that month from that family, and without rewriting all the amounts, query the computer for the total amount of tuition received that month.

Billing is easy. Once you have enrolled a child and entered the parent(s) names and addresses, you can direct your computer to print bills to each family customized with the specific amount owed. You may also want to add a message to each bill such as a reminder about registration for the following Autumn or an advance notice of the date of the school picnic.

Although not directly related to the center's fiscal operation, you may want lists of center children or families by child's birthdate, health checkup due date, zip code, or by class at the center. You can print out attendance (often required by funders), a task that is made even easier if the parent signs the child in and out using the computer. Clip art, or your own creative graphics add zest to notices. Remember, though, that you are directing a professional program, not a "Kutesy Korner."

Getting your payroll out on time can be much simpler with a computer. Once programmed with the hourly or monthly rates, the percentages to be withheld or deducted for various purposes, and other data to be recorded such as sick days used and available, your computer will do the calculations and print the checks. You will have a record of the transactions, make a backup disk, and keep it in a secure place.

As you work on budgets, reports to funders, cash flow statements, and any other data, you can use a password that will prevent those who do not need access to the data from viewing or modifying it. For example, a parent may not want the child's address published on the class list, or you may not want the staff to see the proposals for salary increases, until the board of directors has approved them.

Every year, hardware and software manufacturers develop new capabilities for this technology. If you are relatively new to computer usage, finding a knowledgeable board member, volunteer, or consultant to assist you is essential. Choosing computer components requires understanding how you will use your computer. Most centers cannot afford to buy a more powerful computer than they will need in the next few years, yet buying strictly on price will probably prove to be false economy. If your computer cannot run the software you need, you may wind up with not much more than an expensive typewriter.

Be aware, too, that if you are going to use a computer for communicating through e-mail, using the internet to gather information, or faxing documents, you will need a telephone line. It should be a separate line so that parents can have phone access to the center while you are using the computer. Do not forget to budget charges for the internet access.

Purchasing software can also be challenging though not as costly, of course, as the hardware. Just as you can add hardware components as you acquire the need and the funds, you also can add software packages. For instance, you may add an accounts receivable package. You may also modify or customize existing programs or purchase a basic program and create your own system.

When purchasing software, some of the items to consider are:

1. What kind of hardware is needed to run this software?
2. Can you try out the software?
3. Does it do what you need?
4. What kind of support is available and at what cost?
   - Seminars? Where and when held?
   - Phone help line?—What are the hours in your time zone?
5. Are upgrades provided?
6. How long has the company been in business?

Since both computer hardware and software are changing so rapidly, it is a good idea to check with colleagues about what has worked effectively and what they would like to add. Professional journals such as *Child Care Information Exchange* provide regular reviews. Most reputable software companies will permit you to try out the software yourself instead of watching someone else work with it and telling you about it as they go. ProCare from Professional Solutions and Kids Care from Softerware are two of the most active players in this market. However, you also may find an excellent package developed by individuals who have been or are directors, and have worked with computer programmers to design software that meets specific needs. Whether a center uses computerized records or handwritten reports, they will be timely and accurate only when timely, accurate information is recorded.

Auditing

In most businesses, including early childhood education centers, an auditor reviews the books annually. The director makes available to the auditor the financial records, whether on computer or in a ledger, the checkbook, canceled checks, receipts, and invoices. The director or bookkeeper must keep these documents in an organized manner and they must be updated regularly. Shoe boxes or laundry baskets full of invoices are totally unacceptable, and are certainly unprofessional. At the very least, such lack of organization leaves the impression that the financial transactions of the center are not accurately maintained.

"The primary purpose of an audit is to enable an independent auditor to express an opinion on the fairness of the financial statements, their compliance with *generally accepted accounting principles*, and the consistency of the application"[6] rather than to examine every transaction or to establish that each entry is valid. An annual audit not only protects the financial personnel of the center by making sure their job is being done according to procedures, but also protects the entire operation by ensuring that the use of funds is being recorded as planned.

Handling Petty Cash

The director also regulates the petty cash fund, setting the procedures for its use and maintaining sufficient cash to keep the system working effectively. This fund is usually small because serious losses by theft or carelessness may occur when large amounts are kept on hand.

There are several ways to operate the petty cash fund. Each teacher may receive a specified sum of money to spend for the classroom, or the director may allocate a certain sum per staff member, paying cash when the staff member presents an appropriate receipt. Some centers use petty cash for all unexpected small needs. The director keeps a sum of cash on hand and gives it to staff members who present legitimate requests. For example, if the cook has run out of bread, petty cash may be used to purchase a loaf or two. Petty cash should be used as little as possible to avoid obscuring substantial program expenditures under the heading petty cash. If $20 worth of food is purchased weekly with petty cash, then the item food in the budget is underrepresented. All expenditures should be recorded (or allocated) to the correct account. This can be accomplished by the bookkeeper when the user presents written receipt documentation.

Handling Salaries

Once the budget is approved, the financial director informs the personnel committee of the allocation for salaries. In a new center, the committee may then begin the employment process in accordance with the personnel policies. In continuing centers, raises should be considered.

The director keeps additional records relating to the budget category salaries. Professional staff may be paid monthly, biweekly, or weekly, but their salaries are a fixed expense regardless of the number of hours worked, as long as that individual remains on the payroll. Other staff receive wages based on number of hours worked during the pay period. Employees who are paid hourly must have some way to record the amount of time spent on the job if that is the basis on which they are paid. Some centers have employees record their working time on weekly time cards which are referred to when paychecks are prepared, or staff may sign in and out on computer. The director keeps a record of the sick days and the professional days used for all employees, including those who are salaried. Payments are made to each individual employee on the basis agreed on

[6]Gordon, T. P. (1984). When you think you need an audit: Points to consider. *Child Care Information Exchange*. October, pp. 22–24.

in the employment contract. In small centers where staff have the same schedule daily, time sheets may not be kept. In any event, the director is responsible for keeping track of hours worked, sick leave, and vacation time. Here again, entering this information into a computer database enables the fiscal officer to prepare up-to-date reports and facilitates preparation of the payroll.

The employer must obtain a federal taxpayer identification number from the IRS because before the employee is paid, the employer must make the appropriate deductions from the amount earned. These deductions may include federal, state, and local income taxes, Social Security tax, retirement, and medical insurance. Some centers, at the employee's request, deduct union dues, parking fees, or contributions to the United Way and other fundraising groups. When these categories are part of a computer program, changes in percentages or dollar amounts can be made simply and accurately. An explanation of each deduction must be provided to each employee with each pay check.

Information is available from the Internal Revenue Service regarding federal income tax. Each employee is required to file a W-4 form with the center on employment and to update it as needed. These forms, available from the Internal Revenue Service, enable the employer to determine how much tax must be withheld from each paycheck based on that employee's income and exemptions. The employer also must check with state and local governments about income taxes that may have to be withheld. The person in charge of preparing the payroll is responsible for learning what the deductions are and for seeing that they are made correctly. Your accountant can list the taxes for which your business is liable.

The director must give each employee a W-2 form by January 31 of each year, showing how much the employee earned during the previous year and how much was paid in taxes. Many employers also provide an annual summary of benefits including in-kind benefits such as meals provided by the center.

The employer serves as a collection agent, turning over to the appropriate agency the deducted money. Tax dollars are sent to the nearest Internal Revenue Service Center, to the state treasury, and to the local government treasury. For Social Security, the employer contributes an amount equal to the amount that is deducted from the employee's pay; this amount is based on a rate determined by the federal government and both the employer's and the employee's portions are sent by the employer to the Internal Revenue Service. Workers' compensation is paid entirely by the employer. This program covers payments to the employee for job-related injuries, diseases, and disabilities that occur as a result of working conditions.

The director must check with each taxing body to determine the amount of taxes to be withheld, and the time at which they must be reported and paid. Penalties and interest are charged if payments are late or inadequate, and these costs are paid by the center, not the employee. If the center provides benefits such as medical insurance or collects fees for these benefits from employees' pay, the director is responsible for making the payments at the appropriate time.

Staff members also may be on unpaid leave. Current laws require that certain leaves be available to staff for circumstances such as child rearing. The returning staff member is not guaranteed the exact job but is guaranteed employment when the legal leave concludes. Centers also may create additional opportunities for leave. In any case, accurate records must be kept of leaves requested, granted, and used and the director or designee is responsible for knowing and following related laws.

Payroll checks must be delivered to the employees at the agreed-upon time. Staff morale is lowered considerably when paychecks are not ready on the appointed day. Accuracy is essential.

Even in a small center, the magnitude of fiscal record keeping may seem overwhelming to many directors. Conceivably, the director could keep up with the day-to-day records but even a part-time assistant would be a wise investment in terms of accuracy and timeliness.

SUMMARY

To provide a good program for young children, a center must delegate the responsibility for developing and carrying out a financial plan to a competent financial director or committee. The overall plan must be carried out by a person who has knowledge of basic accounting and budgeting procedures, and an understanding of the requirements of a good program for young children.

The plan must be based on the priorities for meeting children's needs and on the available funds. The major tool used by the financial director is the budget, a plan for balancing income and expenses. The director is responsible for all other financial matters including designing budget systems, ordering goods and services, making payments, recording transactions, and preparing the new budget. An appropriate computer program can save time and money, and, if used correctly, can provide timely, accurate data in a readily accessible format.

Working Paper 7–1

List the items you would include in a start-up budget for a center preparing to serve 40 preschoolers. Indicate whether your center will be for-profit or not-for-profit, where it will be housed, and who will be responsible for implementing the start-up phase.

Working Paper 7–2

Facilities, Goods, and Services Form

List the facilities, goods, and services you would need for one year of full-day child care for 60 children. Assume that start-up equipment is already in place. List the cost of each category.

Working Paper 7–3

Insurance

1. What types of insurance are recommended for an early childhood center in your area?

2. What is the approximate cost of this coverage?

Working Paper 7–4

Cost Versus Service

Check with other early childhood education directors in your community about the cost per child per week for their centers. Find out what services are provided for this amount of money.

1. Center A:
   Cost per child per week is $_____
   Services provided:

2. Center B:
   Cost per child per week is $_____
   Services provided:

3. Center C:
   Cost per child per week is $_____
   Services provided:

Working Paper 7–5

Salary Range Form

Check with other early childhood education directors in your community about the cost per teacher per week for their centers. Find out what benefits are provided for this amount of money.

Salary	Center A	Center B	Center C	Center D

Director:

Teacher:

Assistant Teacher:

Working Paper 7–6

Cash Flow Tracking

Check with other early childhood education directors in your community about the cost per child per week for their center. Find out what services are provided for this amount of money.

Period: Year _____

	January		February		March		Total	
	Estimate	Actual	Estimate	Actual	Estimate	Actual	Estimate	Actual
1. Cash at Beginning of Period								
2. Add: Cash Received from:								
Tuition-Parents								
Dept. Human Services								
USDA								
Donations								
Community Chest								
Other sources _____								
Total Cash Received								
Total Cash Available								
3. Subtract: Cash Paid out:								
Payroll								
Supplies								
food								
educational								
office								
miscellaneous								
Insurance								
Taxes								
Employee benefits								
Other expenses								
Equipment								
Total Cash paid out								
Cash at End of Period								

Director's Resource 7–1

Sample Budget by Program

Director	$28,000
FICA, FUTA, WC	2,800
Health Insurance	2,400
Cook	9,360
FICA, FUTA, WC	900
Management Services Fee	15,000
Maintenance and Repair	7,000
Cleaning Service	9,100
Custodial Supplies	700
Insurance (Liability and Building)	3,200
Bookkeeping/Audit	11,100
Rent	16,000
Food	20,000
Education Supplies	3,500
Utilities/Phone	11,500
Office and Paper Supplies	3,000
Training/Consultants	4,000
Licenses	600
Garbage Removal	550
Payroll Service	1,440
Travel/Field Trips	1,500
Advertising	300
TOTAL	**$151,950**
Overhead Charge per Child ($151,950/73)	$2,082

INFANT EXPENSES (BASED ON A 3:1 RATIO):

Infant Primary Caregivers (3)	49,000	
Infant Aides (2)	10,600	
FICA, FUTA, WC	5,960	
Health Insurance	4,680	
Substitutes	3,170	
Vacancy (8%)	5,878	
TOTAL	$79,288	
Overhead (9 x $2082)	18,738	
TOTAL INFANT EXPENSES		$98,026
TOTAL INFANT INCOME (9 x $157 x 52)		73,476
TOTAL INFANT PROFIT/<LOSS>		($24,550)

Director's Resource 7–1 (continued)

TODDLER EXPENSES (BASED ON A 5:1 RATIO):

Toddler Head Teacher	17,500		
Toddler Assistant Teacher	13,000		
Toddler Aide	7,480		
FICA, FUTA, WC	3,700		
Health Insurance	3,120		
Substitutes	2,120		
Vacancy (8%)	5,574		
TOTAL		$52,494	
Overhead (10 x $2082)		20,820	
TOTAL TODDLER EXPENSES			$73,314
TOTAL TODDLER INCOME (10 x $134 x 52)			69,680
TODDLER PROFIT/<LOSS>			($3,834)

PRESCHOOL EXPENSES (BASED ON A 9:1 RATIO):

Head Teachers (3)	60,000		
Assistant Teachers (3)	39,600		
Preschool Aides (3)	18,900		
FICA, FUTA, WC	9,360		
Health Insurance	9,360		
Substitutes	6,340		
Vacancy (8%)	24,690		
TOTAL		$168,250	
Overhead (54 x $2082)		112,428	
TOTAL PRESCHOOL EXPENSES			$280,678
PRESCHOOL INCOME (44 x $115 x 52)		263,120	
PRESCHOOL INCOME (SUBSIDIZED) (10 x $87.50 x 52)		45,500	
TOTAL PRESCHOOL INCOME			$308,620
PRESCHOOL PROFIT/<LOSS>			$27,942
TOTAL CENTER PROFIT/<LOSS>			**($4242)**

Director's Resource 7–2

Sample Child Care Center Budget

INCOME

TUITION

Infants (8 x $145 x 51)	59,160	
Toddlers (12 x $125 x 51)	76,500	
Preschooler's (51 x $100 x 51)	260,100	
Total Gross Tuition		395,760

DISCOUNTS

Second child (6 x $10 x 51)	<3,060>	
Vacancy (3%)	<11,873>	
Total Discounts		<14,933>

OTHER INCOME

Application Fees (30 x $20)	600	
Interest on account	600	
Fund raisers	1,000	
Grant award (literacy program)	2,500	
Total Other Income		4,700
TOTAL INCOME		385,527

EXPENSES

PERSONNEL

Director	20,800	
Head Teachers (5)	83,200	
Teachers (5)	67,600	
Assistants (10 part time)	46,800	
Substitutes	2,000	
Secretary	10,400	
Custodian	6,500	
Cook	10,400	
FICA, Workers' Comp., Unemploy.	35,941	
Health Insurance (13 x $1,200)	15,600	
Total Personnel		299,241

RENT	28,800	
UTILITIES AND PHONE	15,169	
ADVERTISING	1,200	
FOOD	31,027	
OFFICE SUPPLIES	710	
CUSTODIAL SUPPLIES	780	
CLASSROOM EQUIPMENT & SUPPLIES	4,200	
C.P.A. FEES	500	
INSURANCE	3,000	
LICENSES	100	
STAFF DEVELOPMENT/TRAINING	300	
TEACHERS' PETTY CASH	500	
Total Non-personnel		86,286
TOTAL EXPENSES		385,527

Director's Resource 7–3

Sample Projected Cash Flow Statement

Period: Year 20xx	January Estimated	January Actual	February Estimated	February Actual	March Estimated	March Actual	Total Estimated	Total Actual
1. Cash at Beginning of Period	$1,430	$1,500	$1,071	$1,074	–$983	–$730	$1,518	$1,844
2. Add: Cash received from:								
Tuition-Parents	28,595	28,395	26,600	26,800	30,590	30,400	85,785	85,595
Dept. Human Services	520	507	520	520	520	494	1,560	1,521
USDA								
Donations		100		100			100	
Community Chest								
Other Sources								
Total Cash Received	$29,115	$28,902	$27,220	$27,320	$31,110	$30,894	$87,445	$87,116
Total Cash Available	30,545	30,402	28,291	28,394	30,127	30,164	88,963	88,960
3. Subtract: Cash Paid out:								
Payroll	20,400	20,400	20,400	20,400	20,400	20,400	61,200	61,200
Supplies								
food	2,800	2,753	2,600	2,614	2,800	2,817	8,200	8,184
educational	100	102	100	79	100	94	300	275
office	50	—	50	84	50	27	150	111
miscellaneous	100	20	100	123	100	131	300	274
Insurance	500	500	500	500	500	500	1,500	1,500
Taxes	—	—	—	—	—	—	—	—
Employee benefits	3,060	3,060	3,060	3,060	3,060	3,060	9,180	9,180
Other expenses								
rent	1,000	1,000	1,000	1,000	1,000	1,000	3,000	3,000
utilities	1,264	1,264	1,264	1,264	1,264	1,264	3,792	3,792
Equipment	200	229	200	—	200	305	600	534
Total Cash paid out	$29,474	$29,328	$29,274	$29,124	$29,474	$29,598	$88,222	$88,050
Cash at End of Period	$1,071	$1,074	–$983	–$730	$653	$566	$741	$910

Director's Resource 7–4

Sample Income Statement
For the Year Ended December 31, 20xx

Income Statement
For the Year Ended December 31, 20xx

Revenues

Infant Program Income	$70,500	
Toddler Program Income	64,500	
Preschool Program Income	247,120	
Federal Child Care Program	41,500	
Donations/Contributions	500	
Parent Fundraising	1,100	
Other Income	50	
Total Income		$425,270

Expenses

Salaries/Wages	267,100	
Health Benefits	19,650	
Employment Taxes and Insurance	21,840	
Management Services Fee	15,000	
Training/Consultant Fees	7,200	
Food/Beverage Supplies	21,300	
Educational Supplies	4,100	
Office & Paper Supplies	3,300	
Rent	16,000	
Payroll Service Fees	1,420	
Cleaning Service Fees	8,920	
Custodial Supplies	950	
Equipment Expense	2,800	
Utilities/Phone Expense	11,300	
Garbage Removal	650	
Advertising	850	
Travel/Field Trips	1,600	
Bookkeeping/Audit Service Fees	11,500	
Licenses	625	
Maintenance & Repair Expense	5,920	
Insurance Expense	3,200	
Total Expense		425,225
Net Income (Net Loss)		$45

Director's Resource 7–5

Sample Statement of Financial Position
As of April 30, 20XX

Assets

Cash-Operating	$7,000
Cash-Payroll	8,000
Accounts Receivable	11,200
Educational Supplies	900
Office Supplies	400
Property, Plant, and Equipment	42,000
Total Assets:	$69,500

Liabilities

Accounts Payable	$11,000	
Wages Payable	5,000	
Mortgage Payable	32,000	
Long Term Liabilities	15,000	
Total Liabilities:		63,000

Equity

Capital	6,500
Total Liabilities and Equity	$69,500

CHAPTER 8

Funding the Program

A major component of the director's responsibility is ensuring sufficient funds to establish and operate the program. Although this assignment is ongoing, peak times occur when a new program is created and when additional components are to be added to an existing program. Every director annually addresses the upcoming year's funding and experienced directors recognize the need for long-range fiscal planning.

Typically, in child care centers, the director's role is demanding in terms of time, energy, and talent. Throughout this book you have read about the wide range of expectations placed on the director. When it comes to funding, it is often wise to obtain needed assistance in one of several ways. First, the director may assign other staff to assume additional responsibilities such as organizing equipment orders or conducting inventory. Secondly, the director may enlist the aid of one or more volunteers to take on some responsibilities, thus providing time for the director to engage in fund-raising. For example, a volunteer may conduct center tours for prospective clients. An enthusiastic parent may do an excellent job of pointing out things parents are especially interested in knowing. Or a volunteer may answer the telephone one afternoon a week to provide the director with uninterrupted proposal writing time. Finally, volunteers may participate in the fund-raising process in myriad ways that will be discussed throughout the chapter.

Directors of several centers may support each other by creating a joint fund-raising plan. They may even be able to hire a fund-raising consultant to guide their efforts, particularly if they have limited knowledge of the process. In the long run, such an expense may be quite productive.

It is essential to recognize that the director alone cannot manage the entire fund-raising process. Were that the expectation, the probability of limited funds would be likely.

TYPES OF FUNDING NEEDED

Many child care centers are started by individuals or groups with limited resources and limited collateral, yet the start-up period requires major amounts of capital. Later, funding may be sought for specific equipment such as new computers or, for a new program, specialized training for staff to enable them to work with a particular aspect of curriculum. Frequently, nonprofit centers conduct an annual campaign for a variety of budgetary needs.

Start-Up Funding

Start-up capital includes the money that must be available before the program begins and that is needed to support the initial program operation until the flow of tuition and other funds is sufficient to support the ongoing program. Once a director is hired, it takes two to three months to complete the necessary preliminary planning before the program begins. Money for space, equipment, office supplies, and some staff salaries must be available during these early months before the center opens. Since programs are often underenrolled during the first few months of operation, and since checks from funding sources are sometimes delayed until the program operation is well underway, it is wise to have sufficient capital on hand at the outset to operate the program for at least six months. These operating monies cover costs for three months of planning and six months of operation and are in addition to the capital needed to finance the purchasing or remodeling of a site, and to purchase equipment and supplies for the children's program. In other words, it takes a considerable amount of money to start a program, and it is important to make careful calculations to ensure that the start-up money is adequate to cover the costs until regular operating funds become available.

Most agency-sponsored centers are nonprofit, and many are eligible to receive funding from other community or governmental agencies once there is an established, ongoing program. Some corporations that operate many centers, or very large centers, obtain funds from investors. Operators of small proprietary centers that are established for-profit or that have no sponsoring agency must invest personal capital or arrange for a loan in order to get started. Foundation money is rarely offered to proprietary centers but is reserved for serving particular populations chosen by the foundation and meeting specific foundation-determined goals.

When the community expresses great interest in getting a program started, it may be possible to promote a successful fund-raising program. However, only relatively small amounts of money can be obtained through raffles, bake sales, or paper drives. Established philanthropic groups

such as Kiwanis, Lions, various community groups, and fraternal organizations are sometimes willing to donate money to cover start-up costs such as equipment or to support a capital improvements fund-raising campaign, but like other funders, they seldom provide operating expenses.

A company may provide start-up funding for a center for its employees' children with the understanding that the director will need to secure adequate funding for operating costs from other sources, including tuition. Centers in public schools are usually funded through special government grants and the central administration may manage the budget. In the case of large chains of centers, the corporate office secures investors and funds the start-up of new centers based on their market research.

Programs that start without a sufficient funding base are in fiscal trouble from the outset. Since it is difficult to maintain a balanced budget for an early childhood education program, it is paramount to keep a balanced budget at the outset by finding enough capital to cover start-up costs.

Operating Funds

Operating funds refers to the amount needed to run the center and must include all the regular budget items described in the previous chapter. Once the facility is established and the basic equipment has been purchased, income must be adequate to ensure daily program operation. Many centers have depended heavily on tuition, government funds, and United Way moneys to provide most or all of their operating funds. An analysis of these sources for the 21st century indicates that in most cases, it is unlikely they will be sufficient to provide the quality that centers must provide.

Fund-raising for operating costs must be carefully planned in terms of the benefit to be derived from the contributors' dollars. Imagine a contribution being used to pay for rather mundane, yet certainly essential, categories such as utilities and office supplies. Such usage may not encourage the giver. The creative fund-raiser frames requests in terms of projected program accomplishments. One director in an annual fund-raising letter labeled contributions as "your opportunity to nourish the minds and bodies of 62 of our youngest children." During the preceding weeks, she had sent the local newspapers (with parental permission) pictures of several children engaged in interesting projects such as writing invitations to their parents to visit their classroom, walking to the post office to mail them, and meeting the postmaster.

In determining the amount of funds needed, a breakeven chart is useful. You and your accountant can prepare such a chart by first determining the fixed costs of operating the center such as rent, utilities, director's salary, and costs that will remain at the same level regardless of enrollment.

Next, variable costs are calculated. These are the costs for operating the program that change as children are added or subtracted. For example, when four or five children are added, the cook orders more food, more art materials are needed, and so forth.

Based on licensing requirements and center policies, when a certain enrollment is reached, an additional teacher must be employed. A simple example would be to think of a center with thirty children in which a 1:10 ratio is required. When the thirty-first child is added, the center must provide an additional teacher even though the additional tuition generated by one child will surely not pay a teacher's salary. However, if six new children are added, it may be financially feasible to have four groups of nine children. Of course, if tuition from ten children is required to pay the expenses, then the director should not add children until he or she can ensure a class of ten, or realize that money will be lost on that class.

Using the breakeven chart, the director projects the income based on the enrollment. He or she then looks for the points at which the total costs meet the income and checks to see at what enrollment levels that occurs.[1]

Tuition

When the center is largely dependent on tuition for operating funds, it will be necessary to balance the number of children to be enrolled, the amount of tuition their families can reasonably be expected to pay, and the amount of money needed to operate the program. The program will not always be fully enrolled; therefore, the budget should have at least a 3 to 8 percent vacancy rate built in. Programs just beginning may enroll only a few children for many months, necessitating close management of the initial budget and reduction of variable costs to the lowest possible level. Even some fixed costs can be reduced. For example, a director may employ one or two salaried teachers until the tuition receipts warrant the addition of more staff.

Since the salaries of most preschool teachers are unreasonably low, and since salaries comprise the biggest expenditure by far in an education budget, it is sensible to charge an amount that will provide the fairest possible salary to the staff. Therefore, the tuition rate should be based on a number of facts, including:

1. the amount needed to meet professional commitments to staff
2. the amount that is reasonable in terms of the type of program offered to families
3. the amount charged by comparable centers in the area

To assist parents or to attract clients, centers may decide to offer lower tuition when two children from the same family attend, or they may choose to offer one or more weeks' tuition free for vacation or illness. The director must balance this loss of income against the potential loss of two children or else make the initial tuition rate high enough to cover such factors. However, since these costs are variable, depending on how many two-child families are enrolled in the center at a

[1]Stephens, K., CPA, (1991). *Confronting your bottom line: Financial guide for child care centers,* Redmond, WA: Exchange Press Inc., 1991.

given time, they may add to budget instability. Holding a space for an expected infant for partial tuition has a similar budgetary effect. Giving a free vacation week may negatively affect cash flow if most parents decide to take advantage of this plan during the same week, thereby severely curtailing income. This event would be particularly damaging in a center that used the cash, rather than accrual, method of accounting.

Some centers charge tuition on a sliding scale based on the parents' ability to pay. Often, these centers receive government or agency funds to supplement tuition income. A sliding fee scale formula is prepared that takes into account the amount of income, the number of dependents, and other circumstances such as extraordinary medical bills. However, whenever a family pays less than the actual cost of care, the difference must be covered by making the top of the scale higher than the cost so that some families pay more than the cost of care, or by securing outside funds. A sample sliding fee scale appears in Director's Resource 8–1 on page 150.

Tuition charges are set by estimating what families are willing and able to pay for services and by considering what rates are charged by competing agencies in the community. Local professional organizations, or the local or state universities may have information about the amount of tuition that can be reasonably charged in a particular community. Unless a program offers something very different from that offered by nearby centers (such as NAEYC accreditation), it may be difficult to convince parents to pay significantly higher tuition for one program over another so tuition rates must be reasonably competitive. On the other hand, if tuition is lowered to attract clients, it may be difficult to cover costs and compete with other centers in offering teachers reasonable salaries and in hiring competent staff. Directors of quality centers often have to educate members of the community about the differences in program quality, and in particular, about the value of well-prepared and more costly staff.

Community Resources

Many early childhood education programs are subsidized by local charities, church groups, or by United Way funds. Church groups or other charitable sponsoring agencies typically do not provide cash to help meet the operating budget; instead, they provide in-kind contributions such as free rent, janitorial service, coverage of utility bills, volunteer help, and so forth. Should the director and the board find themselves with an unbalanced budget at the end of the year because of unforeseen problems with enrollments or unexpected expenditures, some sponsoring agencies may cover the losses. This practice is particularly prevalent in situations where one of the sponsoring agency's goals is to provide child care services to low-income members of the community. However, the director who is not managing the budget well is not likely to be "bailed out" more than once.

DIRECTOR'S CORNER

"We really couldn't charge more tuition. Parents just couldn't afford it. It means that the Board can't pay me for planning time. My contract calls for a 5 percent raise annually, but this summer the Board president said to me, 'Jeanine, we're going to have to use your raise to cover the unexpected moving expenses. There's no other way.' I know they tried hard to get other funds."
        —Teacher/director, incorporated not-for-profit center

Boards and directors may want to respond to newly identified needs and creative ideas. To meet these needs, seeking funding is almost inevitable. Occasionally, whoever funds operating costs may also fund special projects. More often, special funding must be sought. Consider the program that served Mindy, Dashawn, and Ronnie, three children with developmental delays. The teacher observed that they seemed interested in caring for classroom plants. She asked the director for gardening equipment supplies and a section of playground so that her whole class could create a garden. Mindy, Dashawn, and Ronnie were to be assigned special responsibilities. Recognizing a creative idea, the director went to a local nursery for help. Not only did the owner contribute tools and seeds, but also volunteered to help the class create the garden and joined them at circle time to discuss her job. Later, the class visited the nursery. Having been so delighted with the children's interest and the positive response from parents, several of whom later made purchases from her, the owner made a follow-up call to the director. She offered to provide a small greenhouse for the school so that the children could start plants earlier the following year. Imagine how much everyone benefitted from one idea and one director's efforts to provide funding.

United Way funds, raised through a United Appeal campaign, are available for child care services in many communities. Eligibility for these community funds will vary depending on the locale, the amount of money available, and the demands placed on that source of funding.

As the director of a program that may need community support money, you should familiarize yourself with eligibility requirements in your community so that you can plan accordingly. Often, a number of preliminary steps must be taken before a program can be presented for funding consideration. Also, some United Way agencies will not give either start-up money or operating funds to new programs. Eligibility requirements for funds typically include the following:

1. The agency must be an incorporated, voluntary, nonprofit, charitable organization, possessing tax-exempt status under Section 501 (c)(3) from the Internal Revenue Service. The agency must be licensed by the appropriate authority, carry on a needed health, welfare, or social service, and have a qualified and representative governing body that serves without compensation.
2. The agency must have, and must implement, a written policy of nondiscrimination and nonsegregation on the basis of race, ethnic origin, disabling condition, sex, or religion regarding its governing body, its employees, and the people it serves.
3. The agency must have been established and must have continued to function for a minimum of three years (number varies here) before applying for funds.
4. The agency must be willing to cooperate in the fund-raising campaign and to abide by all the policies of the United Way agency.

Once the minimum eligibility requirements have been met, the necessary steps for funding consideration must be taken by the director of the center or by a designated board member. The director is usually the only person who has all the necessary information for completing application forms and, therefore, is the one ultimately responsible for filing the numerous ongoing attendance and financial records most United Way agencies require. If a board member assumes this responsibility, the director still must provide the necessary data. Therefore, it is important that the director be familiar with the application procedures and clearly understand the ongoing reporting requirements for funded programs *before* entering into any agreements with the funding agency.

The application for funding may seem intimidating to some directors and may hinder them from applying for available funds. The process does become easier as the director gains more experience in applying and finds that many applications require similar information. Once it has been gathered, some of the data can be reused in subsequent proposals. Nonetheless, directors must be prepared to spend a great deal of time and energy on routine reporting if they expect to use outside funds.

Foundations

A foundation is a fund administered by trustees and operated under state or federal charter. Foundation funds are sometimes made available to child care centers for major equipment purchases or for a special project. Occasionally, a foundation will provide funds for building or remodeling a facility. Foundation support for a program depends on whether or not the trustees of the foundation have declared education, or more specifically early childhood education, as an area of interest.

Large philanthropic foundations such as the Ford, Carnegie, and Rockefeller Foundations have broad-ranging programs, with specific interest areas that change periodically. For example, there may be a general interest in funding innovative educational programs, but monies may be going into literacy or single-parent programs during one funding period, only to shift to programs for preschool developmentally delayed children, or innovative child care models during the next funding period. Smaller foundations may limit support to programs in a certain geographic area, or to a given problem area that may change every few years, while other special interest foundations limit support efforts to very specific interest areas that do not change.

Money from corporate foundations is available in many communities. In smaller cities, it is wise to solicit funds from small, local corporations that often have some funds set aside for use by local agencies. Frequently, the small corporate funds are controlled by corporate managers who are very sensitive to the public relations value of making a gift to the local agencies, that will, in turn, give due credit and recognition to the funder.

DIRECTOR'S CORNER

"When I write a proposal, I always try to think of something that will appeal to the proposal reader— a catchy title or an intriguing goal such as introducing preschoolers to good nutrition through 15 microwave cooking projects. In the long run, we not only meet the goal, but we still have the microwave to use for daily food preparation."
—Director, agency-sponsored not-for-profit center

When directors plan to approach a foundation for money, they must know precisely what they expect to do with the money and how they expect to do it. Their appeal for money must be tailor-made to the foundation's interest areas and all funding requests must move through the proper channels. However, personal contacts with foundation trustees or other people connected with the foundation are considered very helpful. Perhaps a member of the center's parent group or a board member has personal contacts with a foundation, or can help find the best channels to use for personal contacts.

Funds tend to flow toward challenging and interesting programs in well-run organizations rather than to needy institutions that are faltering.

Government Funding

Federal, state, and local governments all have a commitment to the care of the children of working mothers, with the federal government being the forerunner of that movement as far back as the early 1940s. Although state and local government agencies have been involved in licensing and monitoring early childhood education programs for some time, the availability of state and local money for child care for working mothers is relatively recent, when compared to federal monies available on a somewhat sporadic basis for about fifty years. Government monies typically are available for programs that serve low-income families or those that serve children with special needs. Currently, the Head Start program and the proliferation of programs for young children with various disabling conditions serve as evidence of the federal government's focus on children with special needs. California was the first state to establish an extensive network of state-supported child care centers; however, New York, Ohio, and several other states are moving to expand their state-supported systems. Although some funds are available, many children, particularly in certain areas, are underserved or receive no services.

A number of major sources of federal funding were established during the 1960s and continue to provide some basic support for child care and for children with special needs. Often, legislation involving child care is controversial. As more women work outside the home and more children grow up in single parent families, child care has taken on new political importance. Center directors need to keep informed of current and pending legislation, and make their views known to state and federal legislators who can provide up-to-date information. Local and national organizations such as the NAEYC are good sources of information on legislation related to young children. Local libraries can help you find the names of your legislators.

Some program are funded almost entirely by state or federal government tax dollars. Although one might argue that three-year-olds are just as entitled to government funds as are seven-year-olds who attend public schools, relying on tax monies to totally support a program is risky. Funding for some programs or individuals has been eliminated rather abruptly, and there is no guarantee that funds will continue from year to year. Many public elementary and secondary schools engage in additional fund-raising for aspects of the program that many consider integral parts of schooling such as music, athletics, field trips, and library books. Depending solely on government (taxpayer) dollars is unwise and unrealistic.

FUND-RAISING

Since most directors will need to be involved in annual and special fund-raising, they must establish policies and procedures regarding this responsibility. These policies and procedures can then be used to create individual funding campaigns. Step one is to find the people who will be the fund-raisers. If board of directors members have been selected in part with this activity in mind, at least some of them will be able to contribute significantly, monetarily, or in-service, to the fund-raising program. All board members should understand their responsibility to make a contribution, no matter how small, to the center. Some board members may have connections with the community or corporations who are prospects for center support. All should be willing to ask for contributions.

Preparing for Fund-Raising

Before beginning any fund-raising program, the board and director must make sure that the center has been formally chartered by the State (see Chapter 5) and has IRS exemption. Forms for the latter can be obtained from the IRS. This status permits individual donors to deduct the amount contributed to the center as a charitable contribution. Specific procedures must be followed depending on the size of the contribution and the value (if any) that the contributor receives in return such as a dinner, book, or ticket to an event. Written reports are required in these cases, and it is the director's responsibility to know and follow the law or to see that the person assigned to this task has complied. Many agencies disseminate this type of information in a special brochure.

When the contributor does not receive the proper documentation from the agency, future contributions may be jeopardized.

Whether the center retains an attorney, relies on the volunteer services of an attorney/board member, or keeps abreast of legal requirements in some other manner, the board is responsible for knowing and following the law. Professional organizations and journals are helpful in alerting directors to potential changes and to those which have been adopted. But not knowing the law is not accepted as an excuse for not following it.

Once the agency is in a position to seek contributions, the board approves the plan to conduct a fund drive. Next, the director prepares attractive and informative materials that make the case for the program's current and future operation. The information must be free of jargon and accurate rather than overblown or overly dramatic. Important points must stand out with clarity to aid the busy reader who may initially be totally unfamiliar with the center and its mission. Be sure to include the purpose of the request, the total amount being sought, and information on current funding. If the document is based on a Request for Proposals (RFP) created by a funder, the proposal must state clearly how the funds will be used and relate that information to the funder's goals. RFP guidelines must be followed closely, and meeting the funder's deadline is essential.

References. A number of reference sources are available to help you plan your fund-raising strategies and to help you target foundations, corporations, and government agencies that are likely contributors to your type of request. These include:

- AAFRC Trust for Philanthropy. *Giving USA.* 25 West 43rd Street, New York 10036.
- Council for Advancement and Support of Education. *Developing an Effective Major Gift Program.* R. Muir & J. May, eds. Suite 400, 11 Dupont Circle, Washington, DC 20036-1261, 1993.
- *Guide to U.S. Foundations, Their Trustees, Officers, and Donors.* The Foundation Center. 79 5th Ave., New York 10003-3076.
- *National Guide to Funding for Children, Youth and Families.*

- "The Philanthropy Monthly." Box 989, New Milford, CT 06776.
- *Standard & Poors. Register of Corporation, Directors and Executives.* 25 Broadway, New York, 10004.
- Stevenson, Matia. Fundraising for Early Childhood Programs, revised edition. National Association for the Education of Young Children, 1995.

Your local library will have other resources, and you will also find it helpful to conduct a computer search for books, journal articles, and requests for proposals.

Organizing Details. The director is responsible for ensuring that board members are prepared to speak knowledgeably about the agency, the funding purpose, and that they know how to ask comfortably and specifically for funds. Board members (or whoever will request contributions) should determine who will be approached, by whom, and in what time frame. Then the designated person either telephones or writes for an appointment. The latter is usually more successful and may be followed with a brief letter of confirmation. Targeting a specific amount or range for an individual or organization gift is necessary. You may receive a "no" followed by "but I can contribute a lower amount." A request for a vague amount or for a contribution may net you $100 when a specific request for $1000 may have produced that amount. Many people are uncomfortable discussing money, and even more of us cringe at the thought of asking someone else for funds. Good fund-raisers focus on the value of the contribution to the agency's clients and on providing the prospective funder an opportunity to engage in important work. The enthusiasm and sincere approach of the requester goes a long way, in most cases, toward eliciting a positive response.

Let us assume that you called on someone for funds. Whether or not the response was favorable, writing a brief thank-you letter will win friends for the agency and is common courtesy. If a contribution is made, your appreciation is certainly warranted, and if the prospective funder chose not to contribute, appreciation for the time spent with you is in order.

Reflections

Think about a time when you needed a loan from a bank, your parents, or a friend. Did you plan ahead what you would say and how you would explain your need? Did you mention the amount you needed and the purpose of the loan? How did you decide who to approach for the loan? A director who writes a proposal must answer similar questions.

Reporting to Funders

Whether the funders are organizations providing support to assist needy families, stockholders investing for profit, members of a parent co-op, school board members, or individuals who own and direct the center, every funder needs to know how the business is doing. Accurate, timely, and understandable reports are essential. The director uses the daily transaction records to prepare monthly financial reports for the funders as well as for internal use in making budgetary decisions. These reports also should be available to those staff members who choose to read them. The director may present this information at a board meeting or mail it to board members and other concerned persons. Either way, the information should be presented in clear, neat, and concise form. Computer-generated reports can be revised readily so that the most current information is available. The director must be prepared to answer questions regarding the month's operating budget and to justify the figures in the report.

Since the purpose of the report is to inform the reader, it is meaningless to present a highly technical report to a group with no background in reading such reports. On the other hand, large organizations may require that each center follow a particular reporting format. In any event, the income and expenses must be presented in such a way that the reader can easily grasp the financial situation of the center. If a report indicates the need for changes in the budget (for example, an unpredictable expense such as a furnace that must be replaced immediately), the person, or the people, who have to approve such changes can review the budget and make appropriate revisions.

The director must prepare or oversee the preparation of several types of reports.

Center Enrollment Reports. How many children are enrolled and how many are on the waiting list? If the center serves various age groups, the report should be subdivided into infants, toddlers, preschoolers, after-school care, and so on. The director also may project the number of children expected to move up to the next age group on a month-by-month basis. For example, if six children will no longer be eligible for the toddler group in March, based on the licensing rules, will there be room for them in the preschool classrooms?

Accounts Receivable. The director should receive a report at least weekly of accounts receivables. In a child care center, this figure will consist primarily of tuition owed. Repeated billing on a specific schedule (usually weekly) is essential. When friendly and specific reminders are ineffective, telephone the parent and state your expectation that the bill will be paid by a specific date. If the parent is experiencing problems, an installment plan may be worked out. Be sure to document all calls, agreements reached, and so forth, but at the same time, respect the parent's rights by keeping this information confidential. If you are unsuccessful in your collection efforts, it may be necessary to turn past due bills over to an attorney or a collection agency.[2] Even though you have planned ahead by including a factor for bad debt in the budget, serious attempts to collect are essential to maintaining your clients' understanding that these obligations are important unless the funding precludes that approach.

Budget Comparison Reports. Each month, the director prepares or receives from the bookkeeper a report showing what was spent the preceding month in each category. The report also shows budgeted spending for that month, as well as actual and budgeted spending or the year to date. The director or board can then spot cash flow problems, analyze expenditures, project remaining expenses, and revise the budget if necessary.

Balance Sheet. This document is now called Statement of Financial Position. On a monthly basis, a balance sheet should be prepared showing assets (what you own) and liabilities (what you owe).

Income Statement. An income statement must be created at the end of each year. This statement reflects the total of all revenue earned and all expenses incurred during the fiscal year. The difference between revenue and expense is net income if revenues are greater than expenses, and net loss if expenses are greater than revenues. The income statement is widely considered the most important financial statement because it is a measure of how well a business is doing at the end of the year. The statement shows whether the company has generated a profit or is incurring losses. The income statement represents the actual figures for each of your previously budgeted categories. It can be used as a tool to evaluate monies allocated to specific categories on your budget. For instance, if maintenance and repair expense was actually $7,000 for the year according to the income statement, but was budgeted at $2,500 on your operating budget, you would want to re-evaluate your budgeted figure, provided that the dollars spent for maintenance and repair were not one-time, unusual expenditures. In addition to this latter example, the income statement can be helpful for other kinds of statistical analysis.

Annual Report. At the end of the fiscal year, the director presents a final report showing the amount budgeted in each category and the amount actually spent. Up-to-date cash flow statements make it relatively easy to prepare the annual report.

A computer is an invaluable tool in preparing financial and other reports. A computer with basic word processing and spreadsheet software can be utilized for budgets, enrollment reports, budget comparison reports, cash flow statements, income statements, balance sheets, annual reports, and virtually any other financial statement that a child care program would ever need. Examples of word processing software are Microsoft Word® and Word Perfect®. Examples of spreadsheet software are Lotus 1-2-3® and Microsoft Excel®. Although all four are well-known and widely used, there are many other brands of software available for word processing and spreadsheet applications. In

---

[2]Child Care Information. (1985). Collecting Overdue Fees," *Ideas for Directors*. March, pp. 11–12.

addition to financial reporting, a computer can also be utilized for a multitude of other functions such as preparing the case for your request for funds, preparing professional correspondence with funders, and maintaining records of contacts made and responses received. When the director or a board member has the opportunity to prepare a presentation about the agency, software that supports this demonstration such as PowerPoint® can help make a good impression. Keep in mind that you will save hours of proposal preparation as you prepare materials for fund-raising. You will be able to use modifications of your basic information to meet the objectives of different funders by highlighting various aspects of your program. Not having to type everything over will lead you to value technology highly on the day the proposal is due when you are working hard to meet a deadline.

SUMMARY

Operating a good quality center requires a significant amount of funding, and dependence on tuition and government support is unlikely to provide sufficient resources. Many programs in early childhood education depend on outside funding for partial or total support. Knowledge of the sources of funding and some skill in writing proposals are important for directors who may be forced to find funds to operate their programs when tuition is not sufficient to support a high quality program. Some programs receive funds from their sponsoring agencies whereas others depend on United Way funds, grants from foundations, or government grants.

When a center operates with a board, the board makes policies about tuition, usually to balance the need to retain enrollment and the need to meet budgetary requirements. Tuition for child care programs is set based on cost of the program, parents' ability to pay, availability of other funds, and the marketplace. Board members also participate in securing funds and in creating the three- to five-year financial plan for the center.

The breakeven analysis, budget comparison report, and statement of financial position are important financial management tools for the director, and provide a clear, accurate picture for funders.

Working Paper 8–1

Funding Form

Who provides money for early childhood education in your community?

Federal government?

State government?

Community Chest or United Way?

Private individuals?

Chains or franchised centers?

Universities or colleges?

Businesses?

Proprietors?

Other?

Working Paper 8–2

Enrollment Figures

Use the figures below to determine how many children will be in each group for the next six months. If licensing requires one adult for each four infants, one for each eight toddlers, and one for each 12 preschoolers, what effect will the changing enrollment have on your budget?

February

Enrolled

Infants	10
Toddlers	16
Preschool	24

Waiting List

Infants	12
Toddlers	3
Preschool	0

Ready to Move Up

Infants to Toddlers

March	1
April	0
May	2
June	1
July	1
August	0

Toddlers to Preschool

March	0
April	1
May	0
June	2
July	0
August	0

Working Paper 8–3

Business Plan Questionnaire

Financial Analysis

1. Will you need a loan to start or expand the center? If so, approximately how much?

2. What will the loan be used for?

3. What sources will you use to obtain the loan? (Bank, Credit Union, State, City, etc.)

4. What is (are) the item(s) to be purchased and at what cost(s)?

5. Who will be supplying these items?

6. Do you have a personal savings, checking, or business account with a local bank? If so, which one, and who is your banker?

7. Have you approached them about your loan request? What was their response?

8. Do you own any assets or items of value? If so, what?

9. Would you be willing to use your personal assets as collateral against a loan to provide your center with a stable equity base?

10. Have you prepared a projected Profit and Loss Statement showing the potential revenues versus expenses of your center during your first three years of operation?

11. Will you need assistance in preparing such statements?

12. Can you provide personal tax returns for the past three years?

13. How will a loan make your business more profitable?

(Adapted from "Business Plan Questionnaire," The Ohio Department of Development, Small and Developing Business Division, Office of Management and Technical Services, Columbus, OH, 43216-0101)

Director's Resource 8–1

Sample Sliding Fee Schedule

Parent pays:	20%	30%	40%	50%	60%	70%	80%	90%
Infant	$20/wk	$30	$40	$50	$60	$70	$80	$90
Toddler	$18	$27	$36	$45	$54	$63	$72	$81
Preschooler	$16	$24	$32	$40	$48	$56	$64	$72

Director's Resource 8–2

Sample Grant Application*

Doe Learning Center Inc., is a nonprofit corporation that operates four child care centers in the greater metropolitan area. The centers provide quality child care for children ages three months through five years, and also offer school-age care at two of the sites. As a United Way agency, the centers' common goal is to work toward alleviating the current crisis of child care, as outlined in the Long Range Plan for Child Care of the United Way/Community Chest in 1992. This study shows that there is an urgent need for quality programming for children identified as having special needs. Doe Learning Center Inc. has responded to this need by operating four centers whose common goal is the inclusion of all children.

Statement of Agency Commitment

Metropolitan Learning Center (MLC) is located in the central area of the city. The program serves sixty-seven children ages three months through five years. In the summer we enroll an additional twenty children in our school-age program. Established in 1984, MCL was the first full day program in this city to be accredited by the National Association for the Education of Young Children.

Largely based on the theories of Piaget and Erikson, the center's philosophy reflects a focus on the development of the whole child and the formation of strong trusting relationships. The developmental constructivist approach holds the belief that children develop sequentially from one stage of development to another. Because of this we believe that children must be provided with opportunity that will challenge them and aid in their progression from one stage to the next. It is a necessity that learning be based on actual experience and participation. Talking without doing is largely meaningless to young children.

We believe that in order for children to grow, they must be placed in a setting that meets their basic needs. Therefore it is our utmost concern that our program provide a nurturing, comfortable environment that is specifically structured to meet the physical, emotional, and cognitive needs of each individual child.

This philosophy was the foundation for the development of the agency. Due to this commitment, the question of inclusion was never discussed; only how to do it well.

In this time of severe staff shortages in the ECE field, MLC feels fortunate to have an outstanding quality of professionals.

- four preschool head teachers—M.Ed.
- one toddler head teacher—Associate in Early Education
- two infant teachers—Bachelor Education and two infant teachers—Associate Education
- Dr. John Jones professor emeritus at the Metropolitan University has been consulting with our agency for three years. This past year Dr. Jones is working strictly at MLC coordinating our educational services.

MLC has worked extensively with the Early Childhood Education Department, Metropolitan University. The program has been a training site for the past five years, and works with an average of three to four students per quarter.

Director's Resource 8–2 (continued)

According to Washington County Child Day Care: The State of Today and Plans for 1992, "Special needs children are still at a great disadvantage. Most child care providers feel ill-equipped to serve children with developmental problems and physical disabilities." MLC has successfully integrated approximately twenty-five children identified as having special needs. One family called over sixty child care centers before finding a placement at MLC for their child with cerebral palsy. The center has served many children with a wide variety of special needs including, but not limited to: pervasive development disorder, fragile x syndrome, autism, mild mental retardation, receptive language disorder, and visual impairments, to name a few.

One of the primary goals of the organization is to meet the needs of the family, parent and child. MLC has identified its ability to meet these needs as follows:

Needs of the Child—
- placement in a program meeting the standards of developmentally appropriate practice
- Master level staff capable of identifying and working with high-risk children

Needs of the Parent—
- providing high quality care for their children
- providing quarterly parent education/training programs
- providing assistance in identifying (or working with existing) available services (i.e., early intervention) for their children.

MLC has been identified in the community as a program which will not only serve children with special needs, but give them priority on the waiting list. Metropolitan University acknowledged the endeavors of the center by placing students from the Special Education department under the guidance of our experienced staff. We have worked with many agencies in order to provide more comprehensive services to these children.

These agencies include:
- Washington County Department of Human Services
- Special Education Regional Resource Center (SERRC)
- Cerebral Palsy Services Center
- Center for Developmental Disorders
- Speech and Hearing
- Speech Pathology
- Child Advocacy Center
- Association for the Blind
- Metropolitan University—Early Childhood/Special Education Department
- Foster Grandparent Program
- The Council on Aging
- The Single Parent Center

Director's Resource 8–2 (continued)

Statement of Need

There are currently eight children enrolled in the program who have been identified as having special needs. There are several children that are integrated into the environment and are receiving services from support agencies. MLC feels confident that we can meet their needs without additional services. There are two children that pose challenges to our existing program. One child is currently enrolled in our infant program; he is twenty months old and has cerebral palsy. When we enrolled Ed, we assessed that we could meet his needs in the infant program. Though Ed is non-mobile, and non-verbal, he uses smiles, cries, and coos to communicate with his caregiver.

In order to continue serving Ed,

- we need to be able to meet the challenge of facilitating his growth through experiences with the toddlers
- we need to acquire the equipment to encourage his further development
- we need release time for his caregiver to meet with his therapist to learn how to use specialized equipment and participate in his I.E.P. meeting.

Our second child has been identified with pervasive developmental disorder, and mild characteristics of autism. Communication has been the primary barrier in the progression of Ryan's development. This aspect of his disorder carries over into other areas of his growth, including the development of self control. Ryan has been enrolled in our program for one year and within that period has gone from single word utterances to communicating in four to five word sentences. Because of this increased ability to communicate, the agency believes that a transition to the oldest preschool classroom is the next step. The goal of this move is to place Ryan in an environment of his same-age peers where he might benefit from the modeling of age-appropriate behaviors and participation in activities. Any changes in daily schedule and transition times are extremely difficult for Ryan and separation from his current classroom teacher will be a tremendous undertaking.

Our belief is that in order to best aid in this transition, MLC will need the assistance of an additional staff person for the following reasons:

- to meet the needs of Ryan during the period of transition so that classroom staff may continue to meet the needs of his peers
- to act as a facilitator, giving Ryan assistance with social interactions so that he might form relationships with his peers and staff
- to give the classroom staff opportunity to focus on forming trusting relationships with Ryan, without concern that the experiences of his peers are being limited.

Purpose of Funding/Budget
The purpose of our funding breaks into three categories; equipment, consulting/training and additional staff to decrease ratios.

Director's Resource 8–2 (continued)

Equipment

Type	*Purpose*		*Cost*
Outdoor swing	seat enables severly challenged student to enjoy the sensation of swinging		$126.95
Floor sitter	allows non-mobile child to interact with peers but have necessary support		$150.00
Button switch toy			$42.00
Jelly Bean switch toy			$42.00
Circus Truck			$27.00
Bumper Car			$25.00
Brontosaurus			$29.50
Oversized Ball	easier to manipulate than typical ball	18"	$24.35
		34"	$69.50

Consulting/Training

Topic (we would like to open these to public)

"How to adapt 'typical' equipment to meet the needs of physically challenged children"	$100.00
"How to use switch toys"	$80.00
"How to write an appropriate I.E.P. and how to make the I.E.P. meeting work for the child"	$100.00

Consulting

How to arrange the toddler environment to meet the needs of a physically challenged child	$100.00
How to encourage positive peer relationships with typical and atypical children	$50.00

Support Staff

Enrolling a physically challenged child into the infant program was within the abilities of our staff. Allowing time for this child to interact with peers of his own age, and slowly transitioning him into the toddler room will be a challenge for us. We need time for his caregiver to visit the toddler room with him, and then time for the toddler teacher to have one-on-one time for him. This cannot be done without additional staff. Any choice we make with the current staff situation will either short-change Ed, or the other children enrolled. We are requesting a part-time assistant for six months.

Cost $6,656

Having children that model age appropriate behaviors has been the most vital ingredient to Ryan's development. To continue his progress, it is imperative that he be surrounded by children exhibiting the behaviors that Ryan is striving for. As mentioned earlier any transition is very difficult for Ryan. In order to continue servicing Ryan and meet his needs by transitioning him to be with children of his own age, we will need additional staff.

We are requesting a part-time assistant for six months.   Cost $6,656

TOTAL REQUESTED $14,278.30

Director's Resource 8–2 (continued)

Expected Outcome

This grant will enable us to purchase equipment that will:
- allow physically challenged children to become more accessible to the other children by being positioned near them on the floor
- provide stimulation and encourage peer interaction
- allow isolation to lessen so that relationship with peers will increase

This grant will enable us to provide sufficient staff to
- allow challenged children to be surrounded with children of their own age providing appropriate models
- allow staff to meet the needs of our children with special needs without denying other children the attention they need
- encourage smooth transitions that encourage success with meaningful relationships with other children
- make inclusion a successful experience that will encourage staff to include additional children

This grant will provide technical assistance that will
- give the staff and management the knowledge to include these children, and additional children in the future
- encourage other early childhood programs to attend these training sessions, and build support through networking with other teachers participating in inclusion

We will be asking staff who are working with Ed and Ryan to fill out a short questionnaire before we provide additional services, and again after. We would like to see if these support services change any possible insecurities or feelings of being overwhelmed, that had previously occurred.

CHAPTER 9

Developing a Center Facility

An early childhood education program should be housed in a spacious, attractive facility that has been created or redesigned for children, and that also meets the needs of staff members and parents. The director is responsible for ensuring that appropriate space is available; therefore, space needs must be analyzed carefully for both ongoing and new programs. This job may be done in cooperation with the board building committee, or the director may assume full responsibility for analysis of space needs. These needs would then be submitted to the board for action. Corporate systems often have a prototypical design for all centers in the system, and they usually designate an employee to provide and manage the physical facilities for the system's centers. Similarly, preschool facilities in public schools are usually planned by central administration although the principal may have a major decision-making role.

ANALYZING SPACE REQUIREMENTS

In providing a suitable facility, the first task is to analyze its space needs. When a program is already in operation, this analysis is made periodically to ensure the availability of proper facilities for both present and future needs. If the center program or the enrollment change, it may be necessary to move to a different location, or add or eliminate space in the existing center. When a new center is created, or when a move is proposed, the director usually assumes major responsibility for locating appropriate facilities. All renovation, relocation, or initial facilities choices should be based on the space needs analysis.

Space needs are based on consideration for the users (children, staff, and parents), program requirements, and governmental regulations. Therefore, the director must have up-to-date information in all these areas.

The desired number of children to be enrolled will be of major importance. Very small centers may be more costly to operate whereas those which serve hundreds of children may overwhelm the child. Large centers must be carefully designed so that children do not become part of a mob; so that what the child encounters on a daily basis, in terms of facility and people, is manageable for the child.

Users' Needs

"One of the greatest challenges in designing institutions, is to transform a physical plant into a human environment. One part of the transformation has to do with discovering ways to make impersonal rooms and hallways reflect the lives of the children and adults who spend so many active hours in that space."[1] Lella Gandini, official liaison in the United States for the Administration of Early Childhood Education of the Municipality of Reggio Emilia, Italy, emphasizes the importance of recognizing the "special qualities of local life."[2] Users of an early childhood education facility fall into three groups: children, staff, and parents. An analysis of space requirements must be based on the needs of each of these types of users. Since a child care center is planned primarily to meet the needs of children, all child care facilities should be comfortable and convenient in terms of children's sizes and their developmental levels. School-aged programs require space for larger children, and must take into account the need for active play and relaxation, studying, and preparing and eating snacks. Children who spend six or seven hours in a school classroom need a change of pace, and should not feel they are in a school room before and after school. The building also must be comfortable and convenient for adult users if they are to work effectively with the children.

The primary needs planners must consider for each of these users are:

1. health and safety
2. accessibility of facilities
3. controlled traffic flow
4. personal space
5. opportunities for independence and growth
6. aesthetic character

Meeting the needs of each group of users has a cumulative and reciprocal effect since when the needs of one group are met, a step is taken toward meeting the needs of the other two groups. The dynamics of a human environment involve the impacting of each group on the others. In a well-run center, the three groups interact effectively because each is involved in the joint, sensitive process of child development.

Health and Safety. Center planners must be aware of the safety aspects above and beyond those stipulated in the licensing regulations. A hazard-free building meets the needs of staff and parents as well as children. Directors must keep abreast of environmental issues. For example, asbestos and lead paint, once considered appropriate building materials, are now not used in child care centers. Some sealed buildings in which air is recirculated may be found to be circulating poor quality air. Governmental regulations usually will determine the type of building and decorative materials such as carpeting to be used, the number and type of exits (including panic hardware and lighted exit signs), the number and location of fire extinguishers, smoke detectors and fire alarm systems, and the location of furnace and water heaters relative to the children's play area. All these regulations protect children and staff from dangers associated with fire.

Children also must be protected from such hazards as tap water that is too hot, slippery floor surfaces, unsafe or unprotected electrical outlets and wiring, and poorly lighted spaces. Covered convenience outlets or specially designed safety outlets are needed throughout the classroom for audiovisual equipment, computers, aquaria, and so forth. The director must ensure that the flooring is even, that there are no protrusions to cause falls, that stairs are provided with sturdy, low rails, and that protective screening is installed on all windows. Although the director is primarily responsible for establishing and maintaining a basic safety plan for the center, every staff member must remain alert to potential hazards, and must teach children simple safety procedures such as mopping up spilled water and reshelving toys. A Site Safety Checklist appears in Director's Resource 9–1 on page 173.

In public schools where older children use the hallways, plans for entering and exiting the building and moving about must be made to that young children experience minimal encounters with large groups of grade schoolers. Although older children can move about the building independently, additional staff may be required so that small children will have escorts when they go to the library, the office, or the restroom. Ideally, each classroom for young children should have its own adjoining bathroom.

[1]Gandini, L., (1994). Not just anywhere: Making child care centers into particular places. *Child Care Information Exchange* March, p. 48.
[2]Ibid, p. 50.

In any building, many safety practices revolve around the enforcement of center safety rules such as prohibiting children from climbing on window sills, but it is preferable to adapt the building itself so that it is a safe place for children. Placing locks on the furnace room door is less disturbing to everyone and is far safer for children than telling them that they must not enter the furnace area. Be sure, however, that security devices such as locks or gates do not block an emergency exist. Guidelines for fire safety can be obtained by consulting your local fire inspector.

For safety reasons, programs for children are usually housed on the ground-floor level of the building, even where licensing regulations do not require this location. In the event of a fire or other emergency that requires building evacuation, preschool children may become easily confused and need individual guidance to reach safety. In such situations staff members caring for infants, toddlers, and nonambulatory preschoolers will be able to remove only the one or two children they can carry. Some centers place several babies in a crib and roll the crib to safety. Therefore, stairways are dangerous obstacles to quick and safe building evacuation. It is unsafe to use elevators.

Over and above promoting the ease of evacuation, other safety considerations make ground-level facilities immediately adjacent to fenced outdoor space very advantageous. When children can go directly from their classrooms to a fenced outdoor area, the teaching staff can supervise those children who choose outdoor play and those who remain indoors, and the outdoor space is viewed as an extension of the indoor area. Fenced-in play areas prevent children from leaving the play space and prevent others from entering and damaging equipment, interfering with children's play, or leaving dangerous materials such as broken glass around the area. Some covered outdoor space provides an additional advantage because it can be used on rainy days or on very hot, sunny days.[3]

All exits from the building and the outdoor playground should be in locations where supervision of who comes and goes can be readily maintained. While the center may welcome community visitors, strangers should not be permitted to wander through the building. Similarly, children should not be able to leave unnoticed, either alone or accompanied by anyone other than authorized personnel. Panic hardware must be provided on all exit doors but they should be locked so that visitors cannot enter without being admitted. Parents and staff will probably have to be reminded that holding the door open for an arriving visitor is unwise since that person's presence in the center may be unauthorized

Accessibility of Facilities. All users must have access to the building, its program, and its materials. Many parents do not want to subject their children to long daily trips to and from the center, and they prefer a center close to home. Others will look for a center close to the workplace so that they can visit the child during the day. Location near public transportation is also desirable for staff and parents.

Access to the center is increased when people feel comfortable about entering the building; therefore, the scale of the building is another consideration. As children approach the center, they should feel that it fits them. Even a large building should have some features that indicate to the children that the building is theirs. Entranceways and the areas surrounding them can be scaled to the children's requirements so that the children are not overwhelmed by a huge, heavy door or a stairway wide enough for a regiment.

Since parents and visitors often form opinions about a program on the basis of external appearances, the grounds must be well-maintained and the building itself inviting. A building welcomes people through its scale, color, texture, and design. When the building is compatible with other buildings in the neighborhood, the center can begin to establish itself as a positive force in the community and be considered as an integral part of the total community. Understandably, a contemporary building might not be welcome in a traditional residential neighborhood.

When a child care center is housed in a building shared by other users, the center should have a separate entrance that is clearly marked so that

---

[3]For further information about playground safety see: U.S. Consumer Product Safety Commission, *A handbook for public playground safety. Volume 11: Technical guidelines for equipment and surfacing*, Washington, D.C., (n.d.).

families and visitors can find it. Entrances used by older students, agency clients, or other tenants may mean heavy traffic which may intimidate children and make supervision of their arrival and departure more difficult.

The parking area should be located near the center's entrance and should be large enough to accommodate the cars of staff, parents, and visitors. A safe walkway from parking to entry is essential since many parents will arrive with several children, diaper bag, and favorite toys.

Inside the building, there should be clear indications of where to proceed. Signs, supergraphics, or pathways incorporated in the flooring (such as tile arrows) can lead the visitor to the proper place even if no receptionist or secretary is available. A pleasant greeting from a receptionist is ideal, especially when the child and parent are called by name, but many centers are unable to afford a staff member to fill that role.

When the receptionist or secretary's office has a large glass window overlooking the entry, visual contact can be made with people as they arrive, and parents or visitors are likely to feel more comfortable about asking for assistance. In the office adjacent to the entry, the center staff can greet people and receive payments and forms from families. If parents or visitors find no one with whom to communicate when they enter the building, they may become disgruntled and leave, feeling that no one cares about their needs. Or a visitor may search out the classrooms and begin a conversation with a busy teacher, disturbing activities there and probably inviting a cursory response that is detrimental to good public relations. The entry should also be accessible to the director's office so that the director is highly visible and readily available. Furthermore, it is imperative that all visitors be screened to ensure that everyone who enters has a legitimate purpose.

In every case, the entry itself should say "welcome." The colors used in the entry should indicate that this is a place for growth and vitality; grayness and drabness do not belong here. Lighting is as important here as it is in the classrooms. The area should be bright but not harsh. Sunshine is ideal, but when that is not available, an artificially sunny area sets the tone for the real warmth that children and families can expect to experience throughout the center. Entry surfaces are also important and must be designed to withstand muddy shoes or boots and dripping umbrellas. Although the entry should be large enough to accommodate several people without being crowded, it should not be too large because such space has minimal use but still costs about as much per square foot as areas that are heavily used. Furthermore, large entranceways may overwhelm a child or intimidate an unsure parent. Some children will interpret large open spaces as an invitation to run.

The required minimum number of entrances and exits is determined by fire laws, but to determine the best locations for these doors, the planners should take into consideration the traffic patterns of people who come to the building. Teachers like to greet parents as they arrive with their children; therefore, locating the arrival point close to the classroom helps not only the parent and child but also the teacher. Similarly, when the children leave, the teacher can see the parents. Just as children should be able to reach their classrooms without walking through long, uninteresting, and perhaps frightening hallways, so should adults be able to get to their areas conveniently and without disturbing children's play. For instance, deliveries to the kitchen or other service areas should be easy to make without having to negotiate stairs and moving through the children's spaces.

Accessibility carries an additional importance for those who have disabilities. The Americans with Disabilities Act (ADA) protects them by requiring that facilities be designed so that all services can be used by all clients and employees. Entrances and exits, traffic flow patterns, and fa-

DIRECTOR'S CORNER

This morning Mrs. Adams stopped in to see me. She just wanted to let me know how much she and Ralinda missed Marion, our receptionist, who has been home with the flu for a week. She said, "Marion always calls everyone by name. She greets us with a smile and, especially on days when I'm rushing, I really enjoy the welcome."
—Director, urban center

cilities throughout the building and grounds should be designed for ease of use by the disabled. People (children included) in wheelchairs or on crutches should be able to move about comfortably, to use bathrooms, drinking fountains, and telephones, and to participate in all aspects of the center's program. Seemingly small items such as the type of faucet on sinks or the handles on cabinets can be designed to facilitate use by persons who otherwise would have to ask for assistance. The ADA requires this for centers that meet certain conditions, but even in situations where the accommodations are optional, concern for the comfort of all individuals necessitates that efforts be made to modify buildings. An Adaptive Environments Center and Barrier Free Environments Checklist for existing facilities is included in Director's Resource 9–2 on page 174. Some of the dimensions in this list, such as lavatory height, would, of course, need to be modified for children. The Child Care Law Center in San Francisco also can help with information.

Traffic Patterns.   Planners should consider the children's daily traffic patterns between indoor and outdoor spaces, as well as within those spaces. For example, children will move from classroom to multipurpose room and back, and from classroom to outdoor area and back. They may leave from the outdoor area if they are playing there when their parents arrive. A good floor plan takes into account the fact that young children should be able to go directly outdoors, preferably from their own classroom or at least with minimal walking in hallways or in areas used for other purposes.

Coat storage should be near the door where the children enter. When coats are stored in the classroom, shelving may be used to create a coat area separate from the play space.

Well-planned children's areas are designed so that teachers can supervise all areas from almost any vantage point without excessive walking. A teacher supervising in a room with an alcove may have to walk over to that area repeatedly to know what is happening there. An L-shaped outside area may be spacious, but such an area becomes impossible to supervise because as soon as children turn the corner, they are out of sight and beyond the reach of the supervising adult.

Reflections

Think about how the traffic pattern of a building you use frequently affects you. When you arrive at this building, which room do you go to first? Where is that room in relation to the door you use to enter the building? Think about the directions in which you move through the building during the day. Are there any places that could be rearranged to save you steps?

Classrooms can be arranged for variety and ease of traffic flow if areas within the room are clearly demarcated, and exits are located so that traffic does not cross through a number of areas. Block shelves are excellent room dividers that can be used to separate the block area from the housekeeping area and from the heavy traffic area, thus providing a special space for undisturbed block building. Reading and writing areas can be separated from noisy carpentry or music areas by shelves or dividers; then children can find quiet, secluded spaces for solitude and concentration. Children can work comfortably without being disturbed when traffic patterns in the classroom are taken into consideration in planning the children's space needs.

Serving meals to children further complicates the traffic flow in the center. Since preschool children usually eat in their classrooms, there is no need for a separate cafeteria. In fact, in a public school, the noise and confusion of a cafeteria is inappropriate for preschoolers and the furniture is too large to accommodate them comfortably. Preschool classrooms, therefore, must be large enough to contain tables and chairs for all the children and teachers without crowding the play space, and the kitchen should be nearby. Steps or doorways between the kitchen and the classrooms make moving food carts or carrying trays difficult, and long distances between kitchen and classrooms may mean long walks for teachers and long waits for children when something extra is needed during mealtime.

The kitchen must function primarily in relation to the classrooms and secondarily in relation to adult areas. The amount of kitchen space required varies according to the activities to be conducted. The center that uses a catering service for lunches may need very little space whereas the center in which hot lunches are prepared will require additional equipment and space. In very large centers a kitchenette may be provided for staff use, for preparation of refreshments for parent meetings, and so forth.

Licensing laws regulate the number of toilets and sinks required, but the location of the bathrooms is equally important. Children need bathrooms immediately adjacent to their classrooms, multipurpose room, and outdoor play areas so that they can get to them quickly. Each of these areas may not need a separate bathroom, but planning can include the location of one bathroom to serve two areas. Since prekindergarten boys and girls are comfortable sharing the same bathroom, doors in front of each toilet can be eliminated. However, program philosophy and the requirements of some governmental bodies now necessitate separate toilet facilities for boys and girls.

Location of adult bathroom facilities is often determined by designing a plumbing core around which the bathrooms and kitchen are built. Although a plumbing core design is economical, it may not be practical in terms of the traffic pattern and program needs because adult bathrooms must be placed appropriately to serve the people in classrooms, offices, meeting rooms, and kitchen. It is particularly important that classroom teachers have easy access to adult bathrooms while children's programs are in session.

Figure 9–1 shows the floor plan of a hypothetical child care center, but because each center should be designed to meet the needs of its clients and staff, it is not meant as a model. Several of this plan's characteristics are worth imitating, however. Note that as families arrive, the receptionist (or director) can greet them and they can then go directly to the classrooms. An observation booth is shown overlooking one classroom. When space is available, this feature may be desired for all of the children's spaces. Note, too, that each classroom has an adjoining restroom and that a multipurpose room is available for large-muscle activities.

In planning for traffic flow, the staff's daily traffic patterns also must be considered with attention focused on which areas they use in what sequence on a typical day. Figure 9–1 shows the relationship of staff members' spaces to children's spaces in one center. Teachers need a conveniently located general storage room to enable them to set up the day's activities efficiently. They must be able to move comfortably and quickly from the storage areas to the classroom, the outdoor area,

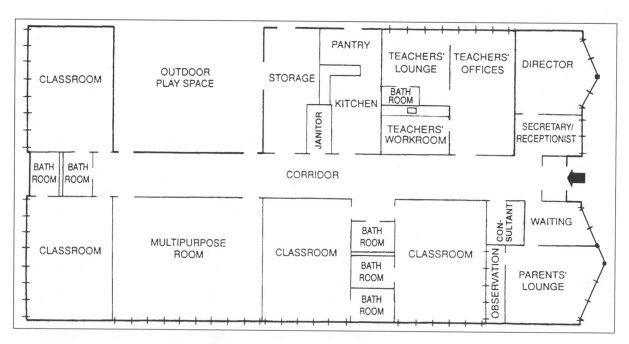

Figure 9–1   Hypothetical Center Floor Plan Showing Relation of Staff Space to Child Space

or the multipurpose room, depending on where the equipment or the supplies are needed. Teachers also need a cabinet that they keep locked for storing the solutions used to sanitize the tables and for other cleaning supplies. Sometimes, too, with proper written documentation from parents and the child's physician, a teacher will be asked to administer medication at school. Paying attention to licensing guidelines, center policies, and procedures related to these issues is essential. And, of course, teachers need coat storage that is readily accessible when they go outdoors with children.

Office space is sometimes placed close to the classrooms so that immediate additional supervision can be provided in an emergency situation; but planners may decide to place the offices farther away from the classrooms to eliminate distractions for the director, off-duty teachers, or other staff members. An intercom system can be installed to facilitate communication in emergency situations and to eliminate disturbances. The intercom or a telephone may be a necessity if a classroom or any other area used by children is isolated from direct contact with the rest of the center. For example, all classrooms may be located on the ground floor whereas the multipurpose room is a level above them. A teacher using the multipurpose room needs a phone to reach additional help if a crisis occurs.

Personal Space.   A comfortable and convenient classroom for young children includes enough space for each child to work and play without being disturbed by other activities. Thirty-five square feet per child is usually considered minimum, so a classroom for ten three-year-olds must have at least 350 square feet, meaning it measures about 18 feet by 20 feet. Fifty square feet per child is more realistic and more space should be provided whenever possible. However, extremely large classrooms are difficult to supervise and may feel overwhelming to children.

Children need cozy places where they can relax while they look at books, examine interesting objects, or daydream. These spaces should be small enough to promote a sense of privacy and intimacy, yet large enough to be shared with a friend or two. Sometimes, a loft can meet this need; it must be sturdy and have some kind of

siding to prevent objects from falling to the floor and hitting anyone below. The space under the loft can be used for storage or small group activities. In any event, the teacher must be able to supervise the area.

The classroom also must include a meeting area that is large enough for a number of children to gather for a story or special activity. Furniture can be moved for these occasions. Movable shelving and furniture facilitate such rearranging. These movable pieces also will be valued when teachers are placing cots for children's naps. Most centers do not have a separate nap room and must consider how to place cots so that children will not be too close to one another (a requirement of many licensing rules.) When cots are too close together children may find it difficult to rest. Space also must be available for cot storage.

Staff members have a variety of space needs. These include personal space for storing their belongings, bathroom facilities separate from those used by the children, and a lounge area in which to have refreshments during break times. Work space includes places in which they work with children, places in which they prepare materials for classrooms, and places in which they do paperwork or hold conferences. Work space that meets the staff members' needs assists them in performing their duties well. Some personnel have specialized work spaces (that is, maintenance staff, the cook, or the nurse). Each workplace must be of a size suitable for the activity in question. For example, full-time office staff members each need approximately 100 square feet of office space. This space should be arranged to provide for some privacy and sound control so that work can be accomplished with minimal interruption.

Parents and visitors need a comfortable lounge area in which to wait for their children or to talk with each other. Parents also need a space that is large enough for group meetings and small enough for individual conferences with a teacher or the director. Even if a whole room is not available, centers can at least provide some seating in another area. Fire laws may preclude having furniture in hallways. Facilities for observing the classrooms, while going unnoticed by the children, represent both a convenience and a learning experience for parents and visitors.

Often, employer-sponsored child care is provided near the work site. Parents will appreciate an area in the classroom where they can spend quiet time with their own children, sharing a book or puzzle. In infant centers, a private space for nursing offers a relaxing time for mother and baby.

Children who come to the center for before- and after-school care will treasure some personal space. Imagine spending 10 hours a day in a relatively small space with 30 people primarily following someone else's directions. Although many adults do spend eight hours in a work environment crowded with equipment and people, they at least have the opportunity to go out for lunch or take a short break. Children in schools are usually required to stay with their class for the entire day. After school, having some private space provides a welcome respite. Before and after school, elementary grade children also need spaces for organizing clubs and playing games, for informal sports, and for creating and carrying out their own wonderful ideas. They need adult supervision, but, at the same time, they need much more independence in organizing and reorganizing the space, perhaps decorating it so it is theirs. Since these needs are quite different from those of younger children, it is clear that they need separate spaces.

Independence.   The facility should be planned to promote the independence of both children and staff. An environment for children fosters independence and growth when it is arranged so they can make decision and solve their own problems. Such a setting has child-sized appointments including sinks, toilets, drinking fountains, and door knobs that children can reach and operate (where that is desirable), and wall decorations that are placed at the children's eye level. Planners must keep in mind that independence is equally important for children with disabilities.

A setting that encourages independence also has classroom storage that is directly accessible to children, enabling them to find and reach all the materials and equipment they use. When such storage is adequate, each piece of equipment is displayed so that the children can see it easily, can remove it from the shelf without moving other items stacked on top of it, and can return it to its proper place. Clearly marked storage space for children's personal belongings, located so that children can get to it, also will promote independence. In addition, however, storage space that is out of children's reach is also needed in each classroom so that teachers can store materials and supplies they do not want the children to obtain such as gallon jugs of glue.

Single-purpose buildings allow programming to be based on users' needs (especially those of children) rather than requiring that the program be planned based on the needs of a range of occupants. A center allows teachers to feel independent when the design of the facility enables them to plan programs for their children without constantly checking with other teachers. For example, teacher independence is curtailed when a preschool class is housed in a public elementary school where the young children must use the bathroom, lunchroom, or outdoor play space for specific time blocks because older children use these facilities at other times. Even if the children's needs suggest a deviation from this schedule, the teacher may be required to follow it. Some teachers in centers that move children from room to room for various activities find that they are not able to plan as independently if they have to direct children from the art room to the music room and then to the play room on a daily basis at a predetermined, scheduled time rather than having the children move at their own pace.

The environment that fosters independence and growth is one in which variety is apparent, offering children an appropriate number of choices. They are not overwhelmed with choices and they are not bored with the repetitive sameness in design of space. Variety in color, texture, floor level, and building materials (if not overdone) can give children a sense of vitality that can be stimulating. Noise level is another area in which variety can be appropriate. Some spaces may be set aside for noisy play whereas others are retained for quieter activities. Although acoustical ceilings, carpeted floors, and curtains all absorb sound and contribute to the auditory comfort of everyone in the center, children can still learn to use appropriate sound levels in each space and to choose their activities accordingly. Therefore, the environment leads to cooperation as well as to independence.

Aesthetic Character. An environment for children should be aesthetically pleasing to them. The factors relating to other users' needs and to program requirements can be designed so that they appeal to the children's sense of beauty. For example, it is just as easy to have an interesting painting in the classroom as it is to put up a fake window with curtains over the play sink. Both are intended to make the room more attractive. Children can enjoy a wide range of art but the value of a fake window is limited at best.

Provide as much natural light as possible while avoiding glare. Artificial lighting should be bright enough for children's activities but adjustable. Lamps that cannot be tipped over, ceiling lighting that can be controlled with dimmer switches, and area lighting all contribute to a feeling of physical and emotional well-being, and help foster productivity, relaxation and comfort.[4] Incandescent lighting and full-spectrum lighting seem more appropriate than fluorescent.[5]

Wall surfaces can provide texture and color that contribute to the room's vitality. Garish decorations or "cute" wall coverings, emblems, or cutouts contribute little to children's appreciation of beauty. Carpets replete with numbers and letters add "busyness" to the environment but provide neither aesthetics nor intellectual stimulation. Children and staff will probably be more inclined to take care of an attractive environment. It is easy to develop messy habits when the surroundings are poorly designed with inadequate facilities and unappealing spaces. It is equally easy and more satisfying for everyone to develop good habits and an appreciation of beauty when the facilities are well designed. Note that the touches a teacher adds may be inexpensive or free such as a single flower from her garden, attractively mounted pictures of the children at play, or a crystal hanging in the window to catch the light and project interesting colors and patterns throughout the room.

Having analyzed the facility requirements for a high-quality early childhood education program and the information provided by a specific needs assessment, the director can determine the center's current facility needs, and can project the building and grounds needs of the center for several years. This long-range planning is useful in enabling a center to coordinate program, facility, and financial decision-making. Whether the director is analyzing need in terms of possibly rearranging or remodeling the existing center's facilities, or of leasing or constructing a new center, the users' needs are kept in the forefront in working toward a decision about the facility.

DIRECTOR'S CORNER

"Our entire staff spend hours discussing what our ideal center would look like. We listed all the criteria for each space including details such as height and depth of classroom sinks, number of feet of shelving in the toy storage room, and type of door knobs. We couldn't have everything we wanted because of the cost, but we all felt like we had helped design our new center."
—Director, agency-sponsored center

Program Requirements

The director and building committee members must be thoroughly familiar with the early childhood education program before they attempt to evaluate an existing or proposed facility. They must understand the types of activities planned, the program goals, and the enrollment projections. For example, in contrast to a half-day program, a full-day program must provide a place for resting and eating meals. Many children who spend the entire day at a center also need room in which to seclude themselves from the group for short periods of time, a quiet place supervised by the teacher but free from the intrusion of other children.

The center's philosophy influences the type and arrangement of space. If the philosophy places heavy emphasis on parent involvement, space will be needed for meeting rooms and a lounge, and additional parking will have to be provided. The prevailing climate also affects the type of building. If children are able to be outdoors most days on a year-round basis, they will

[4]Alexander, N. (1995).Turning on the light: Thinking about lighting issues in child care. *Child Care Information Exchange*, September, pp. 65–68.
[5]Schreiber, M. E. (1996). Lighting alternatives: Considerations for child care centers. *Young Children*, May, pp. 11–13.

need more outdoor space and slightly less indoor space. On the other hand, a center located in a region with temperature extremes will put emphasis on indoor areas and will give major consideration to effective heating, ventilating, and air conditioning systems. Floor-level temperature in the children's areas is critical since children frequently play on the floor.

Planning for carpeting and tiling sections of the classroom floor should be done with activities in mind. Cleaning is facilitated when art and food activities take place on hard surfaces, and teachers will be able to focus on the children's needs rather than protecting the carpeting. A sink in the classroom is a much-used and much-desired convenience, and should also be on the tiled area.

Admission policies will have an impact on the facilities requirements. For example, centers that accept infants must provide space for infant cribs and a number of feeding tables, as well as safe places where infants can explore their environment freely. Spaces for infants and toddlers must be designed for them rather than being scaled-down versions of preschool classrooms. Ramps, wide doorways, and low light switches are necessities for children with disabilities. When planning a facility, it is mandatory to provide for children and adults with special needs so that they can be served effectively and the requirements of federal and state laws still be met.[6]

Governmental Regulations

In communities that have zoning laws, an early childhood education center that is operated for profit may be limited to locating in a business or less restrictive zone whereas a nonprofit educational facility may generally be located in any zone. Prior to signing a lease or contract to purchase property, the director must check with the local zoning board to see if usage of the particular piece of property would be in compliance with the zoning code. In some cases, a zoning variance may be allowed; that is, the director may petition to use the location for a center if it can be shown that the presence of the center will not have a neg-

ative effect on neighboring sites. Zoning ordinances also may include parking requirements. Off-street parking provisions may have to be made for center staff and visitors, including those who are disabled.

When a new facility is built or an existing building renovated or put to new use, current codes usually apply. For example, a building being used as a public school would be inspected based on the codes in existence when that building was put into use. However, if a child care center leases the space, the owner will be required to meet the current regulations. When a building is renovated or a new facility is constructed, the regulations of the Americans with Disabilities Act (ADA) must be followed. Some requirements include access by means of ramps instead of stairs, accessible restroom facilities, doors which can be opened by a person in a wheelchair, and low drinking fountains.

Other governmental regulations pertain to licensing. These are discussed in Chapter 5 and include number of square feet of space for children's use, both indoors and outdoors, fencing, exits, building materials, toilets, and hand-washing facilities. Before you purchase, lease, or renovate a building, ask your licensing agent to ensure that the facility is in compliance with governmental regulations, or can be renovated appropriately at an affordable price. There may be a charge for this consultation.

PLANNING A NEW CENTER

In planning for a new center, the director, who sometimes works along with a building committee of the board, must decide on a site early in the planning stage. The decision may be to construct a building, to buy, rent, or lease an existing building, or to locate space that would be donated by the owner on a temporary or permanent basis. Planning for a new center involves the same analysis of space requirements that is done when an ongoing program facility is assessed. The one item that stands out as being conspicuously important in decisions about planning a new center is cost.

[6]Public Law 99-457 (amending Public Law 94-142, Education of Handicapped Act) required free public education be available for all children with disabilities. Many of these children will be included in private centers as well as in public schools, making it important that all buildings be accessible to them. (See Director's Resource 7–2.)

The director who has started facilities planning with a needs assessment has applicable information about zoning, licensing, program requirements, and clients. These data, combined with the availability of a particular amount of money, are applied as criteria in the search for appropriate facilities. Some centers assess needs, locate facilities, and then mount a fund drive, anticipating that sufficient money will be obtained. The director or building committee must realistically assess the amount of money that will be available for establishing and maintaining the center facility, and the amount of money that will be required to meet the assessed need.

The building committee works closely with the budget committee to determine the amount of money needed and available for constructing, purchasing, renovating, or renting a building. Costs of real estate and construction vary widely depending on geographical location, and within a given city, vary from the inner city to the suburbs. Costs must be checked for each locale. Careful planning is essential because once construction starts, changes are costly.

Considering New Construction

Both land and building costs must be considered. The lot must be large enough for a building of the required size, for a playground of at least 75 square feet per child (groups of children may use this area at different times), and for parking for staff, parents, and visitors. The cost of the building will depend on the size of the building, the quality and elaborateness of the materials used, and the intricacy of the design. A major advantage of new construction is that the building looks like a place for children; and, if it is well-designed, it will be a place in which the program can be delivered efficiently, effectively, and with a high level of comfort for all users.

Using Existing Buildings

Costs involved with the use of an existing building are purchase price, rent, and renovation. A center may incur none, one, or all of these costs depending on the owner and on the condition of the building.

Sometimes, a church or community service organization will permit an early childhood education center to use its facilities at little or no charge. Available rooms also may be found in school buildings. This contribution is a major cost benefit to the program. Before agreeing to this use of the building, however, both the contributor and the center board should have a clear written understanding of the rights and responsibilities of each party. For example, both will need to know how liability insurance will be handled.

If funds are available, a down payment on the purchase of a lot or a building, or plans for extensive remodeling, may be made. The board must be certain that funds for monthly payments, including interest as well as principal, will be available. A bank or savings and loan company can provide information on interest rates, length of mortgage, and payment procedures; it can also explain penalties, foreclosures, and insurance requirements.

Renting

Since purchasing a building involves high initial costs, most centers rent or lease all or part of a building. Both renting and leasing involve periodic payments. Under a lease, the lessor and the lessee agree that the space will be available and paid for during a specified length of time, usually a year or more. A longer lease is preferable since moving can be expensive and clients may be lost if the center changes locations. When a space is rented, the renter may have to pay only for the period during which the space is actually used. For a nine-month nursery school program, this savings could be important and significant. Such a situation occurs primarily when renting from a church. The school's equipment may have to be moved out during the summer months or may be used by other groups as part of the rental agreement.

A lease should spell out these conditions and include items such as:

- beginning and ending dates of the lease
- whether or not the lease is renewable
- who is responsible for maintenance and repairs
  —what is included
  —who pays for it

—who provides materials, supplies, and tools

—when and what maintenance and repairs will be done

—who is responsible for compliance with building code

- who pays for utilities

For example, if the Board of Health requires the addition of a hand-washing sink (a permanent fixture), will the center or the landlord pay for the sink and its installation? The center cannot operate a program without the sink because a license will not be granted; but if the center should move, the landlord will still have the sink.

If the landlord is responsible for maintenance, can an agreement be reached that the grass is not cut during children's regular playground hours? Think about securing a written agreement about spraying for insects. Will it be done when children are present, meaning that you will have to move them to another area? Will all materials to be used be safe for areas used by children?

If the facility is shared because the landlord uses part of it or rents part of it to someone else, or because the center owns a building and rents or leases part of it to someone else, all the preceding items must be considered. In addition, the building committee or director will have to settle the matter of who has access to the building, and when they may have access. For example, if a teenage group uses the building in the evenings, will they be allowed to use the playground during the late afternoon before all the children have left? Other points to be considered are:

- who may have master keys
- who may use what equipment and supplies
- who is responsible for ordering and paying for shared equipment and supplies
- who pays the telephone bill

Other questions involve use of the center's space by other organizations or individuals when the children are not present such as during the evenings or on weekends. The use of the facilities (their own and that of others) by center staff members and the parent group during evenings, weekends, and holiday hours also must be considered.

It is easier to reach agreement on these issues before the building committee signs a lease and takes occupancy. If a lease has been signed, the center usually cannot be moved without financial penalty which means that an uncomfortable situation could exist for a number of months. When the lease clearly details the rights and responsibilities of each party, most questions can be settled amicably.

Renovating

Renovation costs also vary widely depending on the location of the building and the type of work to be done. Complex changes such as relocating plumbing, rewiring electrical circuits, or installing exits, stairways, and fire-resistant surfaces are costly. The type and amount of renovation to be done will be based on the particular licensing requirements, including fire and building codes, and on the requirements of the planned program. If the center owns the building, renovation is usually a worthwhile investment.

DIRECTOR'S CORNER

"When the renovation was initially being planned and the architects were working up the drawings, the chairperson of the committee and I went in and talked about what we would like to see happen. It seemed to break down after the initial meetings, and there were some outcomes that we were not that pleased with. Everything was ordered and half way done before I realized what was happening. There wasn't any way that we could go back and ask for change."

—Director, church nursery school

WORKING WITH OTHER PROFESSIONALS

A variety of professionals outside the field of early childhood education can be helpful in planning a space for young children. Usually, the cost of their services is relatively high on an hourly rate, but in the long run, the expertise they contribute to the center's development is often worth far more than the actual expenditure. However, checking reference and credentials before you sign an agreement with an individual or company is critical. Written agreements with each service provider are essential.

Licensing Agent

Since most programs must be licensed, the first professional that the building committee contacts is the licensing agent. This specialist often provides free services and is funded through state or local taxes. Through this agent, the committee works with other professionals in the building, sanitation, and fire departments. Community planners also may be involved, either at the governmental level or through community councils. Even though these professionals are not paid by the center, the licensing and inspection fees must be paid as required (see Chapter 5).

Architect

During the early planning stage, retaining an architect can produce positive results. An architect can evaluate a site in terms of a center's needs, or can examine an existing building and make recommendations about the renovations that are necessary for safety, efficiency, and aesthetics.

Ongoing architectural services can be contracted at an hourly rate, flat fee, or on a percentage basis. The architect should spell out clearly in a contract the services that are to be provided such as survey, site selection, design, working drawings from which a building can be built or remodeled, contractor selection, construction supervision, and/or final inspection.

An architect also will assist you in selecting materials if that is part of your contract. For instance, gypsum wallboard (which is inexpensive) is readily dented, gouged, and subject to corner damage. Sara Elizabeth Caples, an architect whose firm specializes in school facilities, recommends applying "a skim coat of 'diamond hard' plaster" to a height of four feet to increase durability."[7] If you are not familiar with building materials, this addition to your contract could save you much more than the added fee. The architect also should include the fee for services rendered in the contract, and the dates that payments are due.

When selecting an architect, choose someone with whom you feel comfortable. Many architects are unfamiliar with child care center needs, and you will want to choose one who is willing to listen to your concept and incorporate your ideas. Keep in mind, however, that architects have knowledge about design and construction which can help you attain a more attractive, more functional building within your budget. A few architects will want to put a great deal of emphasis on the exterior of the building, using such a large portion of the budget there that little money remains for finishing and furnishing. Listen to the architect with an open mind but be willing to insist on components essential to your program.

Also be sure to let the architect know what kind of a budget you are working with. You may have dreams of an elaborate center with all kinds of wonderful enhancements, but your budget may dictate that you have a much more straightforward approach. A good architect can help you get the most for your money. Figure 9–1 shows a very simple, relatively inexpensive design. Only the essential spaces are included for this hypothetical half-day program. A rectangular building is often the least expensive to build.

When the plans are complete, asking a colleague to review them with you may help uncover details you had not considered. Changes made at this stage are relatively easy; changes made once construction begins may be impossible. At the very least, they are usually quite expensive.

Generally, the architect will oversee the job, but the general contractor is responsible for scheduling subcontractors, ordering materials, and so forth. Some architects also serve as construction managers and some contractors offer building design services.

Contractor

A contractor may plan the construction or remodeling of the center's building and carry the work through to completion. Parts of the job may be subcontracted such as the electrical or plumbing work, but the contractor retains responsibility for the satisfactory and timely completion of all work. Nonetheless, the director must pay attention to the job as it moves along. Balancing frequent site visits with allowing the contractors to do their work is necessary, but asking questions when you are not

[7]Caples, S. E. (1995). Some guidelines for preschool design. *Young Children*, May, pp. 18–19.

sure about an aspect of the construction or when the work is not as promised is essential. Sometimes directors feel intimidated because they do not understand the drawings and specifications for the work. Part of the contractor's job is making sure that the work is done to the client's specifications as determined by the written contract.

Accountant

The building committee works with an accountant to determine the amount of money that can be responsibly invested in construction, purchase, or rental. The accountant also may help locate a lending agent and help the building committee find the best interest rate. Information about depreciation and taxes also may be provided. An accountant may charge an hourly rate, or a flat fee for a particular piece of work. Some centers pay an accountant a monthly retainer in exchange for whatever services are needed, including preparation for the annual audit.

Attorney

When the building committee decides to enter into a contract or sign a lease, its attorney reviews the document to ensure that the center's needs are being met and that all legal aspects have been covered. The attorney also participates in settling disputes in relation to payment, failure to perform work satisfactorily, and so forth. In a few cases, these disputes may be taken to court. In those special situations, the attorney would represent the center in court.

SUMMARY

Whether it is a brand new building or one that was constructed years ago for another purpose, the ideal early childhood education center environment is created to meet the needs of the children, the staff members, the parents, and the visitors while, at the same time, satisfying all licensing requirements. Health and safety, accessibility of facilities, traffic patterns, personal space, opportunities for independence, and aesthetic character are the guidelines for determining the design. Professional services from the architects and contractors who work with building committee members, staff members, parents, children, and other professionals, provide these aspects within the framework of the budget to create a center that is best suited for carrying out the program for which it has been designed.

Working Paper 9–1

Area Form

1. Your center has a room 20 feet by 30 feet with a two-foot by three-foot sink.
   a. How many preschool children can use the room?

   b. How many children can the room accommodate if you decide to allot 50 square feet per child?

2. What might the dimensions of the room be if you were to provide the minimum square footage required for 20 children?

3. What might the dimensions of the room be if you were to provide 50 square feet per child for 20 children?

Working Paper 9–2

Facilities Visitation Form

Record the following information for your center:

- Parking

- Exterior appearance of building and grounds

- Identifying sign

- Identifiable entrance

- Entry area

- Location of offices (director, teachers, secretary)

- Waiting room or lounge

- Adult bathrooms

- Classrooms (number, size, ease of supervision, arrangement of areas, attractiveness, neatness, noise level, temperature, relation to other areas used by children)

- Multipurpose room (size, arrangement of equipment, ease of supervision, attractiveness, temperature, noise level)

- Outdoor play area (size, fencing, arrangement of equipment, attractiveness, ease of supervision, variety of surfaces, shelter)

- Children's bathrooms in relation to classrooms, multipurpose room, and outdoor area

Director's Resource 9–1

Site Safety Checklist

1. _____Entry is inviting and easy to locate.

2. _____Exterior is neat and clean.

3. _____Playground is fenced.

4. _____Entry is visually supervised or has security device.

5. _____Lighting is right enough for each area.

6. _____All inteior areas are neat and clean.

7. _____Areas look inviting to both parents and children.

8. _____Building is scaled to child size while accommodating adults.

9. _____Floor hazards have been eliminated.

10. _____Every piece of equipment is checked daily for safety.

11. _____All medicines and toxic substances are kept in locked cabinets.

12. _____Equipment is appropriate size and type so that all children's needs are met.

13. _____Number and type of wall hangings are varied periodically.

14. _____Clutter has been eliminated.

15. (Add items specific to your own center.)

Director's Resource 9–2

Checklist for Existing Facilities

Introduction

Title III of the Americans with Disabilities Act require public accommodations to provide goods and services to people with disabilities on an equal basis with the rest of the general public. The goal is to afford every individual the opportunity to benefit from our country's business and services, and to afford our businesses and services the opportunity to benefit from the patronage of all Americans.

Prescribed by
Bob Taft, Secretary of
30 East Broad Street,
Columbus, Ohio 4326(
Form AGO (August 19

By January 26, 1992, architectural and communication barriers must be removed in public areas of existing facilities when their removal is readily achievable—in other words, easily accomplished and able to be carried out without much difficulty or expense. Public accommodations that must meet the barrier removal requirement include a broad range of establishments (both for-profit and nonprofit)—such as hotels, restaurants, theaters, museums, retail stores, private schools, banks, doctors' offices, and other places that serve the public. People who own, lease, lease out, or operate places of public accommodation in existing buildings are responsible for complying with the barrier removal requirements.

The removal of barriers can often be achieved by making simple changes to the physical environment. However, the regulations do not define exactly how much effort and expense are required for a facility to meet its obligation. This judgment must be made on a case-by-case basis, taking into consideration such factors as the size, type, and overall financial resources of the facility, and the nature and cost of the access improvements needed. These factors are described in more detail in the ADA regulations issued by the Department of Justice.

The process of determining what changes are readily achievable is not a one-time effort; access should be re-evaluated annually. Barrier removal that might be difficult to carry out now may be readily achievable later. Tax incentives are available to help absorb costs over several years.

Purpose of This Checklist

This checklist will help you identify accessibility problems and solutions in existing facilities in order to meet your obligations under the ADA.

The goal of the survey process is to plan how to make an existing facility more usable for people with disabilities. The Department of Justice recommends the development of an Implementation Plan, specifying what improvements you will make to remove barriers and when each solution will be carried out: ". . . Such a plan . . . could serve as evidence of a good faith effort to comply. . . ."

Technical Requirements

This checklist details some of the requirements found in the ADA Accessibility Guidelines (ADAAG). However, keep in mind that full compliance with ADAAG is required only for new

Director's Resource 9–2 (continued)

construction and alterations. The requirements are presented here as a guide to help you determine what may be readily achievable barrier removal for existing facilities. Whenever possible, ADAAG should be used in making readily achievable modifications. If complying with ADAAG is not readily achievable, you may undertake a modification that does not fully comply with ADAAG using less stringent standards, as long as it poses not health or safety risk.

Each state has its own regulations regarding accessibility. To ensure compliance with all codes, know your state and local codes and use the more stringent technical requirement for every modification you make; that is, the requirement that provides greater access for individuals with disabilities. The barrier removal requirement for existing facilities is new under the ADA and supersedes less stringent local or state codes.

What This Checklist Is Not

This checklist does not cover all of ADAAG's requirements; therefore, it is not for facilities undergoing new construction or alterations. In addition, it does not attempt to illustrate all possible barriers or propose all possible barrier removal solutions. ADAAG should be consulted for guidance in situations not covered here.

The checklist does not cover Title III's requirements for nondiscriminatory policies and practices and for the provision of auxiliary communication aids and services. The communication features covered are those that are structural in nature.

Priorities

This checklist is based on the four priorities recommended by the Title III regulations for planning readily achievable barrier removal projects.

Priority 1:   Accessible entrance into the facility
Priority 2:   Access to goods and services
Priority 3:   Access to rest rooms
Priority 4:   Any other measures necessary

How to Use This Checklist

✔ *Get Organized:* Establish a time frame for completing the survey. Determine how many copies of the checklist you will need to survey the whole facility. Decide who will conduct the survey. It is strongly recommended that you invite two or three additional people, including people with various disabilities and accessibility expertise, to assist in identifying barriers, developing solutions for removing these barriers, and setting priorities for implementing improvements.

✔ *Obtain Floor Plans:* It is very helpful to have the building floor plans with you while you survey. If plans are not available, use graph paper to sketch the layout of all interior and exterior spaces used by your organization. Make notes on the sketch or plan while you are surveying.

✔ *Conduct the Survey:* Bring copies of this checklist, a clipboard, a pencil or pen, and a flexible steel tape measure. With three people surveying, one person numbers key items on the floor plan to match with the field notes, taken by a second person, while the third takes measurements. Think about each space from the perspective of people with physical, hearing, visual, and cognitive disabilities, noting areas that need improvement.

Director's Resource 9–2 (continued)

✔ *Summarize Barriers and Solutions:* List barriers found and ideas for their removal. Consider the solutions listed beside each question, and add your own ideas. Consult with building contractors and equipment suppliers to estimate the costs for making the proposed modifications.

✔ *Make Decisions and Set Priorities:* Review the summary with decision makers and advisors. Decide which solutions will best eliminate barriers at a reasonable cost. Prioritize the items you decide upon and make a timeline for carrying them out. Where the removal of barriers is not readily achievable, you must consider whether there are alternative methods for providing access that are readily achievable.

✔ *Maintain Documentation:* Keep your survey, notes, summary, record of work completed, and plans for alternative methods on file.

✔ *Make Changes:* Implement changes as planned. Always refer directly to ADAAG and your state and local codes for complete technical requirements before making any access improvement. References to the applicable sections of ADAAG are listed at the beginning of each group of questions. If you need help understanding the federal, state, or local requirements, contact your Disability and Business Technical Assistance Center.

✔ *Follow Up:* Review your Implementation Plan each year to re-evaluate whether more improvements have become readily achievable.

   To obtain a copy of the ADAAG or other information from the U.S. Department of Justice, call: (202) 514-0301 Voice, (202) 514-0381 TDD, (202) 514-0383 TDD. For technical questions, contact the Architectural and Transportation Barriers Compliance Board at (800) USA-ABLE.

Questions	Possible Solutions
PRIORITY 1:	
ACCESSIBLE ENTRANCE	
People with disabilities should be able to arrive on the site, approach the building, and enter the building as freely as everyone else. At least one path of travel should be safe and accessible for everyone, including people with disabilities.	
Yes No	
Path of Travel (ADAAG 4.3, 4.4, 4.5, 4.7)	
Is there a path of travel that does not require the use of stairs? ☐ ☐	☐ Add a ramp if the path of travel is interrupted by stairs.
	☐ Add an alternative pathway on level ground.
Is the path of travel stable, firm and slip-resistant? ☐ ☐	☐ Repair uneven paving.
	☐ Fill small bumps and breaks with beveled patches.
	☐ Replace gravel with hard top.

Director's Resource 9–2 (continued)

Questions	Yes	No	Possible Solutions
Is the path at least 36 inches wide?	☐	☐	☐ Change or move landscaping, furnishings, or other features that narrow the path of travel. ☐ Widen pathway.
Can all objects protruding into the path be detected by a person with a visual disability using a cane?	☐	☐	☐ Move or remove protruding objects. ☐ Add a cane-detectable base that extends to the ground. ☐ Place a cane-detectable object on the ground underneath as a warning barrier.

In order to be detected using a cane, an object must be within 27 inches of the ground. Objects hanging or mounted overhead must be higher than 80 inches to provide clear head room. It is not necessary to remove objects that protrude less than 4 inches from the wall.

Do curbs on the pathway have curb cuts at drives, parking, and drop-offs?	☐	☐	☐ Install curb cut. ☐ Add small ramp up to curb.

Ramps (ADAAG 4.8)

Are the slopes of ramps no greater than 1:12?			☐ Lengthen ramp to decrease slope. ☐ Relocate ramp. ☐ If available space is limited, reconfigure ramp to include switchbacks.

Slope is given as a ratio of the height to the length. 1:12 means for every 12 inches along the base of the ramp, the height of one inch. For a 1:12 maximum slope, at least one foot of ramp length is needed for each inch of height.

1:12

Do all ramps longer than 6 feet have railings on both sides?	☐	☐	☐ Add railings.
Are railings sturdy, and between 34 and 38 inches high?	☐	☐	☐ Adjust height of railings. ☐ Secure handrails.
Is the width between railings at least 36 inches?	☐	☐	☐ Relocate the railings. ☐ Widen the ramp.
Are ramps non-slip?	☐	☐	☐ Add non-slip surface material.

Director's Resource 9–2 (continued)

Questions	Yes	No	Possible Solutions
Is there a 5-foot-long level landing at every 30-foot horizontal length of ramp, at the top and bottom of ramps and at switchbacks?	☐	☐	☐ Remodel or relocate ramp.
The ramp should rise no more than 30 inches between landings.	☐	☐	

Parking and Drop-off Areas (ADAAG 4.6)

Questions	Yes	No	Possible Solutions
Are an adequate number of accessible parking spaces available (8 feet wide for car plus 5-foot striped access aisle)? For guidance in determining the appropriate number to designate, the table below gives the ADAAG requirements for new construction and alterations (for lots with more than 100 spaces, refer to ADAAG):	☐	☐	☐ Reconfigure a reasonable number of spaces by repainting stripes.

Total spaces	Accessible
1 to 25	1 space
26 to 50	2 spaces
51 to 75	3 spaces
76 to 100	4 spaces

Questions	Yes	No	Possible Solutions
Are 16-foot-wide spaces, with 98 inches of vertical clearance, available for lift-equipped vans?	☐	☐	☐ Reconfigure to provide a reasonable number of van-accessible spaces.
At least one of every 8 accessible spaces must be van-accessible.			
Are the accessible spaces closest to the accessible entrance?	☐	☐	☐ Reconfigure spaces.
Are accessible spaces marked with the International Symbol of Accessibility? Are there signs reading "Van Accessible" at van spaces?	☐	☐	☐ Add signs, placed so that they are not obstructed by cars.

International Symbol of Accessibility:

Questions	Yes	No	Possible Solutions
Is there an enforcement procedure to ensure that accessible parking is used only by those who need it?	☐	☐	☐ Implement a policy to check periodically for violators and report them to the proper authorities

Director's Resource 9–2 (continued)

Questions	Yes	No	Possible Solutions

Entrance (ADAAG 4.13, 4.14)

If there are stairs at the main entrance, is there also a ramp or lift, or is there an alternative accessible entrance? ☐ ☐

☐ If it is not possible to make the main entrance accessible, create a dignified alternate accessible entrance. Make sure there is accessible parking near accessible entrances.

    Do not use a service entrance as the accessible entrance unless there is no other option.

Do all inaccessible entrances have signs indicating the location of the nearest accessible entrance? ☐ ☐

☐ Install signs at or before inaccessible entrances.

Can the alternate accessible entrance be used independently? ☐ ☐

☐ Eliminate as much as possible the need for assistance—to answer a doorbell, to operate a lift, or to put down a temporary ramp, for example.

Does the entrance door have at least 32 inches clear opening (for a double door, at least one 32-inch leaf)? ☐ ☐

☐ Widen the door.
☐ Install offset (swing-clear) hinges.

Is there at least 18 inches of clear wall space on the pull side of the door, next to the handle? ☐ ☐

☐ Remove or relocate furnishings, partitions, or other obstructions.
☐ Move door.
☐ Add power-assisted door opener.

    A person using a wheelchair needs this space to get close enough to open the door.

Is the threshold level (less than $1/4$ inch) or beveled, up to $1/2$ inch high? ☐ ☐

☐ If there is a single step with a rise of 6 inches or less, add a short ramp.
☐ If there is a high threshold, remove it or add a bevel.

Are doormats $1/2$ inch high or less, and secured to the floor at all edges? ☐ ☐

☐ Replace or remove mats.
☐ Secure mats at edges.

Is the door handle no higher than 48 inches and operable with a closed fist? ☐ ☐

☐ Replace inaccessible knob with a lever or loop handle.
☐ Retrofit with an add-on lever extension.

    The "closed fist" test for handles and controls: Try opening the door or operating the control using only one hand, held in a fist. If you can

Director's Resource 9–2 (continued)

Questions			Possible Solutions
	Yes	No	
Entrance (continued)			
do it, so can a person who has limited use of his or her hands.			
Can doors be opened without too much force (maximum is 5 lbf)?	☐	☐	☐ Adjust the door closers and oil the hinges. ☐ Install power-assisted door openers. ☐ Install lighter doors
You can use a fish scale to measure the force required to open a door. Attach the hook of the scale to the doorknob or handle. Pull on the ring end of the scale until the door opens, and read off the amount of force required. If you do not have a fish scale, you will need to judge subjectively whether the door is easy enough to open.			
If the door has a closer, does it take at least 3 seconds to close?	☐	☐	☐ Adjust door closer.
Emergency Egress (ADAAG 4.1.3 (14), 4.28)			
Do all alarms have both flashing lights and audible signals?	☐	☐	☐ Install visible and audible alarms.
Is there sufficient lighting in egress pathways such as stairs, corridors, and exits?	☐	☐	☐ Upgrade, add, or clean bulbs or fixtures.
PRIORITY 2: ACCESS TO GOODS AND SERVICES			
Ideally, the layout of the building should allow people with disabilities to obtain goods or services without special assistance. Where it is not possible to provide full accessibility, assistance or alternative service should be available upon request.			
Horizontal Circulation (ADAAG 4.3)			
Does the accessible entrance provide direct access to the main floor, lobby, or elevator?	☐	☐	☐ Add ramps or lifts. ☐ Make another entrance accessible.

Director's Resource 9–2 (continued)

Questions	Yes	No	Possible Solutions
Are all public spaces on an accessible path of travel?	☐	☐	☐ Provide access to all public spaces along an accessible path of travel.
Is the accessible route to all public spaces at least 36 inches wide?	☐	☐	☐ Move furnishings such as tables, chairs, display racks, vending machines, and counters to make more room.
Is there a 5-foot circle or a T-shaped space for a person using a wheelchair to reverse direction?	☐	☐	☐ Rearrange furnishings, displays, and equipment.

Doors (ADAAG 4.13)

Questions	Yes	No	Possible Solutions
Do doors into public spaces have at least a 32-inch clear opening?	☐	☐	☐ Install offset (swing-clear) hinges ☐ Widen doors.
On the pull side of doors, next to the handle, is there at least 18 inches of clear wall space so that a person using a wheelchair can get near to open the door?	☐	☐	☐ Reverse the door swing if it is safe to do so. ☐ Move or remove obstructing partitions.
Can doors be opened without too much force (5 lbf maximum)?	☐	☐	☐ Adjust or replace closers. ☐ Install lighter doors. ☐ Install power-assisted door openers.
Are door handles 48 inches high or less and operable with a closed fist?	☐	☐	☐ Lower handles ☐ Replace inaccessible knobs or latches with lever or loop handles. ☐ Retrofit with add-on lever extensions. ☐ Install power-assisted door openers.
Are all thresholds level (less than $1/4$ inch), or beveled, up to $1/2$ inch high?	☐	☐	☐ Remove thresholds. ☐ Add bevels to both sides.

Rooms and Spaces
(ADAAG 4.2, 4.4, 4.5, 4.30)

Questions	Yes	No	Possible Solutions
Are all aisles and pathways to all good and services at least 36 inches wide?	☐	☐	☐ Rearrange furnishings and fixtures to clear aisles.
Is there a 5-foot circle or T-shaped space for turning a wheelchair completely?	☐	☐	☐ Rearrange furnishings to clear more room.
Is carpeting low-pile, tightly woven, and securely attached along edges?	☐	☐	☐ Secure edges on all sides. ☐ Replace carpeting.

Director's Resource 9–2 (continued)

Questions	Yes	No	Possible Solutions
Rooms and Spaces (ADAAG 4.2, 4.4, 4.5, 4.30) (continued)			
In routes through public areas, are all obstacles cane-detectable (located within 27 inches of the floor or protruding less than 4 inches from the wall), or are they higher than 80 inches?	☐	☐	☐ Remove obstacles. ☐ Install furnishings, planters, or other cane-detectable barriers underneath the obstacle.
Do signs designating permanent rooms and spaces, such as rest room signs, exit signs, and room numbers, comply with the appropriate requirements for accessible signage?	☐	☐	☐ Provide signage that has raised and brailled letters, complies with finish and contrast standards, and is mounted at the correct height and location.
Controls (ADAAG 4.27)			
Are all controls that are available for use by the public (including electrical, mechanical, window, cabinet, game, and self-service controls) located at an accessible height?	☐	☐	☐ Relocate controls.
Reach ranges: The maximum height for a side reach is 54 inches; for a forward reach, 48 inches. The minimum reachable height is 15 inches.			
Are they operable with a closed fist?	☐	☐	☐ Replace controls.
Seats, Tables, and Counters (ADAAG 4.2, 4.32)			
Are the aisles between chairs or tables at least 36 inches wide?	☐	☐	☐ Rearrange chairs or tables to provide 36-inch aisles.
Are the spaces for wheelchair seating distributed throughout?	☐	☐	☐ Rearrange tables to allow room for wheelchairs in seating areas throughout the area. ☐ Remove some fixed seating.
Are the tops of tables or counters between 28 and 34 inches high?	☐	☐	☐ Lower at least a section of high tables and counters.

Director's Resource 9–2 (continued)

Questions	Yes	No	Possible Solutions

Seats, Tables, and Counters (continued)

Are knee spaces at accessible tables at least 27 inches high, 30 inches wide, and 19 inches deep? ☐ ☐ — ☐ Replace or raise tables.

Vertical Circulation (ADAAG 4.3)

Are there ramps or elevators to all levels? ☐ ☐ — ☐ Install ramps or lifts.
☐ Modify a service elevator.
☐ Relocate goods or services to an accessible area.

On each level, if there are stairs between the entrance and/or elevator and essential public areas, is there an accessible alternate route? ☐ ☐ — ☐ Post clear signs directing people along an accessible route to ramps, lifts, or elevators.

Stairs (ADAAG 4.9)

Do treads have a non-slip surface? ☐ ☐ — ☐ Add non-slip surface to treads.

Do stairs have continuous rails on both sides, with extensions beyond the top and bottom stairs? ☐ ☐ — ☐ Add or replace handrails.

Elevators (ADAAG 4.10)

Are there both visible and verbal or audible door opening/closing and floor indicators (one tone = up, two tones = down)? ☐ ☐ — ☐ Install visible and verbal or audible signals.

Are the call buttons in the hallway no higher than 42 inches? ☐ ☐ — ☐ Lower call buttons.
☐ Provide a permanently attached reach stick.

Do the controls outside and inside the cab have raised and braille lettering? ☐ ☐ — ☐ Install raised lettering and braille next to buttons.

Is there a sign on the jamb at each floor identifying the floor in raised and braille letters? ☐ ☐ — ☐ Install tactile signs to identify floor numbers, at a height of 60 inches from floor.

Is the emergency intercom usable without voice communication? ☐ ☐ — ☐ Replace communication system.

Are there braille and raised-letter instructions for the communication system? ☐ ☐ — ☐ Add simple tactile instructions.

Director's Resource 9–2 (continued)

Questions	Yes	No	Possible Solutions
Lifts (ADAAG 4,2, 4.11)			
Can the lift be used without assistance? If not, is a call button provided?	☐	☐	☐ At each stopping level, post clear in structions for use of the lift. ☐ Provide a call button.
Is there at least 30 by 48 inches of clear space for a person using a wheelchair to approach to reach the controls and use the lift?	☐	☐	☐ Rearrange furnishings and equipment to clear more space.
Are controls between 15 and 48 inches high (up to 54 inches if a side approach is possible)?	☐	☐	☐ Move controls.

PRIORITY 3: USABILITY OF REST ROOMS

When rest rooms are open to the public, they should be accessible to people with disabilities. Closing a rest room that is currently open to the public is not an allowable option.

Questions	Yes	No	Possible Solutions
Getting to the Rest Rooms (ADAAG 4.1)			
If rest rooms are available to the public, is at least one rest room (either one for each sex, or unisex) fully accessible?	☐	☐	☐ Reconfigure rest room. ☐ Combine rest rooms to create one unisex accessible rest room.
Are there signs at inaccessible rest rooms that give directions to accessible ones?	☐	☐	☐ Install accessible signs.
Doorways and Passages (ADAAG 4.2, 4.13)			
Is there tactile signage identifying rest rooms? Mount signs on the wall, on the latch side of the door. Avoid using ambiguous symbols in place of text to identify rest rooms.	☐	☐	☐ Add accessible signage, placed to the side of the door (not on the door itself). ☐ If symbols are used, add supplementary verbal signage.
Is the doorway at least 32 inches clear?	☐	☐	☐ Install offset (swing-clear) hinges. ☐ Widen the doorway.

Director's Resource 9–2 (continued)

Questions	Yes	No	Possible Solutions
Doorways and Passages (continued)			
Are doors equipped with accessible handles (operable with a closed fist), 48 inches high or less?	☐	☐	☐ Lower handles. ☐ Replace inaccessible knobs or latches with lever or loop handles. ☐ Add lever extensions. ☐ Install power-assisted door openers.
Can doors be opened easily (5 lbf maximum force)?	☐	☐	☐ Adjust or replace closers. ☐ Install lighter doors. ☐ Install power-assisted door openers.
Does the entry configuration provide adequate maneuvering space for a person using a wheelchair?	☐	☐	☐ Rearrange furnishings such as chairs and trash cans. ☐ Remove inner door if there is a vestibule with two doors. ☐ Move or remove obstructing partitions.
A person using a wheelchair needs 36 inches of clear width for forward movement, and a 5-foot diameter clear space or a T-shaped space to make turns. A minimum distance of 48 inches, clear of the door swing, is needed between the two doors of an entry vestibule.			
Is there a 36-inch-wide path to all fixtures?	☐	☐	☐ Remove obstructions.
Stalls (ADAAG 4.17)			
Is the stall door operable with a closed fist, inside and out?	☐	☐	☐ Replace inaccessible knobs with lever or loop handles. ☐ Add lever extensions.
Is there a wheelchair-accessible stall that has an area of at least 5 feet by 5 feet, clear of the door swing, OR is there a stall that is less accessible but that provides greater access than a typical stall (either 36 by 69 inches or 48 by 69 inches)?	☐	☐	☐ Move or remove partitions. ☐ Reverse the door swing if it is safe to do so.
In the accessible stall, are there grab bars behind and on the side wall nearest to the toilet?	☐	☐	☐ Add grab bars.
Is the toilet seat 17 to 19 inches high?	☐	☐	☐ Add raised seat.

Director's Resource 9–2 (continued)

Questions	Yes	No	Possible Solutions
Lavatories (ADAAG 4.19, 4.24)			
Does one lavatory have a 30-inch-wide by 48-inch-deep clear space in front? A maximum of 19 inches of the required depth may be under the lavatory.	☐	☐	☐ Rearrange furnishings. ☐ Replace lavatory. ☐ Remove or alter cabinetry to provide space underneath. Make sure hot pipes are insulated. ☐ Move a partition or wall.
Is the lavatory rim no higher than 34 inches?	☐	☐	☐ Adjust or replace lavatory.
Is there at least 29 inches from the floor to the bottom of the lavatory apron (excluding pipes)?	☐	☐	☐ Adjust or replace lavatory.
Can the faucet be operated with one closed fist?	☐	☐	☐ Replace faucet handles with paddle type.
Are soap and other dispensers and hand dryers 48 inches high or less and usable with one closed fist?	☐	☐	☐ Lower dispensers. ☐ Replace with or provide additional accessible dispensers.
Is the mirror mounted with the bottom edge of the reflecting surface 40 inches high or lower?	☐	☐	☐ Lower or tilt down the mirror. ☐ Replace with larger mirror.

PRIORITY 4: ADDITIONAL ACCESS

When amenities such as public telephones and drinking fountains are provided to the general public, they should also be accessible to people with disabilities.

Drinking Fountains (ADAAG 4.15)

Questions	Yes	No	Possible Solutions
Is there at least one fountain with clear floor space of at least 30 by 48 inches in front?	☐	☐	☐ Clear more room by rearranging or removing furnishings.
Is there one fountain with its spout no higher than 36 inches from the ground, and another with a standard height spout (or a single "hi-lo" foundation)?	☐	☐	☐ Provide cup dispensers for fountains with spouts that are too high. ☐ Provide an accessible water cooler.
Are controls mounted on the front or on the side near the front edge, and operable with one closed fist?	☐	☐	☐ Replace the controls.

Director's Resource 9–2 (continued)

Questions	Yes	No	Possible Solutions
Drinking Fountains (continued)			
Does the fountain protrude no more than 4 inches into the circulation space?	☐	☐	☐ Place a planter or other cane-detectable barrier on each side at floor level.
Telephones (ADAAG 4.30, 4.31)			
If pay or public use phones are provided, is there clear floor space of at least 30 by 48 inches in front of at least one?	☐	☐	☐ Move furnishings. ☐ Replace booth with open station.
Is the highest operable part of the phone no higher than 48 inches (up to 54 inches if a side approach is possible)?	☐	☐	☐ Lower telephone.
Does the phone protrude no more than 4 inches into the circulation space?	☐	☐	☐ Place a cane-detectable barrier on each side at floor level.
Does the phone have push-button controls?	☐	☐	☐ Contact phone company to install push-buttons.
Is the phone hearing aid compatible?	☐	☐	☐ Contact phone company to add an induction coil (T-switch).
Is the phone adapted with volume control?	☐	☐	☐ Contact phone company to add an induction coil (T-switch).
Is the phone with volume control identified with appropriate signage?	☐	☐	☐ Add signage.
Is one of the phones equipped with a text telephone (TT or TDD)?	☐	☐	☐ Install a text telephone. ☐ Have a portable text telephone available.
Is the location of the text telephone identified by accessible signage bearing the International TDD Symbol?	☐	☐	☐ Add signage.

International TDD Symbol:

CHAPTER 10

Equipping the Center

I t is challenging and rewarding to equip a center. Your personality will be reflected in the physical environment you create as you strive to meet the needs of the children and select things that enable you to set up a program congruent with your program philosophy. Although many programs are being implemented with inadequate, unsuitable materials, supplying equipment that is appropriate contributes significantly to the success of early childhood education programs, and is necessary for successful program implementation. Creating rich learning environments that are replete with abundant opportunities for children to be actively involved with age-appropriate and individually appropriate materials requires thoughtful, careful selection of classroom equipment and supplies. Also, staff members are able to do their assigned jobs more efficiently and comfortably when they work in adequately equipped environments.

Equipping a center is costly, and when mistakes are made replacements are doubly costly. Many companies charge about 30 percent of the cost of items that have been returned unless, of course, they arrived damaged. In addition, the center pays the return shipping.) Impulse buying is irresponsible when you are in charge of purchasing equipment. Therefore, plan your purchases carefully by first assessing your needs, next developing criteria for equipment selection, and finally relating needed and desired items to your budget. After selections are made, decide on ordering procedures; develop a maintenance and storage system to reduce unnecessary repairs and losses.

ESTABLISHING NEEDS

There are three major areas to equip in a child care center, and a director must determine the type and amount of equipment needed for each of these areas. The areas are:

1. Children's spaces, both indoors and outdoors
2. Adult spaces including offices, waiting rooms, conference rooms, and lounge areas
3. Service areas

Equipment includes furniture, appliances, computers, and other durable goods. Also included in the budget are supplies consisting of items which have a relatively short useful life or which are disposable.

Examples are computer disks, finger paints, food, and paper towels. The equipment and supplies budgets should provide for initial purchases, as well as for long- and short-term replacement of both basic furnishings and consumable supplies. Information about equipment and suppliers is provided in Appendix A.

Directors entering an ongoing program begin by taking inventory of what is on hand, setting up a priority system for securing new equipment, replacing worn out items, and replenishing supplies of consumable materials. Directors of new centers are confronted with the overwhelming task of equipping an entire center.

Many equipment suppliers will be happy to provide sample equipment and supplies lists. Even more valuable is the Association for Childhood Education International (ACEI) publication listing suggested purchases for various age groups from infants through school age.[1] A portion of this list appears in Director's Resources, page 213. These comprehensive lists are not intended as mandatory purchases but as guides to be adjusted and supplemented, based on the needs of particular children, staff, and families.

Children's Spaces

Program philosophy and the needs of children dictate what will be ordered for the children's spaces in the center. Most programs are set up in basic curricular areas such as art, music, science, manipulative, and pretend play, along with special spaces for math games and writing materials. All of these curricular areas require special furnishings and materials. Provisions also must be made for water and sand play, carpentry, cooking, building, and large-muscle activities. Furniture for working, resting, and eating is needed including such accessories as clocks, plants, wastebaskets, and curtains. If the director is not familiar with early childhood curriculum and the associated equipment, room arrangement, and scheduling, the center will need an education coordinator who has this knowledge and who is an experienced early childhood teacher.

Adult Spaces

Even a very small center requires some office space such as a locked file cabinet for records at the very minimum. Since adult desks are not used in classrooms for young children, some space for teachers to use as they plan their curriculum and prepare reports is essential. Furnishings that facilitate curriculum development include shelving for a teacher resource library and a work table with paper cutter, laminator, and storage for supplies such as posterboard, scissors, and markers.

When office space is provided, the basic furnishings for each occupant include two chairs, a desk, a file cabinet, and a bookshelf. A desk and cabinet can be shared by two teachers who spend most of their time in the classroom. Teachers need access to a telephone for parent contacts and for limited personal calls when they are on break. The location of the telephone should allow teachers quiet and privacy. At least one computer equipped with word processing and data management software is essential. Directors of larger centers find that a copy machine is a worthwhile investment in terms of the time and money saved in duplicating such items as newsletters, menus, and forms. Although these machines are initially expensive, they pay for themselves over time by saving staff time and enable the center to produce materials of professional quality.

The staff needs a place for meetings. When staff meetings are held after children leave, the classrooms can be used. However, it is certainly more comfortable for the adults attending meetings to have a space furnished with adult-sized chairs and tables. Comfortable furniture should be provided for use by parents who come to the center for conferences and by consultants who come to meet with staff members. Bulletin boards and coat racks are convenient accessories for adult spaces. Since some adults who come to the center have disabilities, consider the seating, other furnishings, and equipment in terms of their needs.

Some centers provide a separate lounge for parents and visitors. This area should have comfortable seating, lamps, tables, a bookshelf for pertinent reading materials, and perhaps facilities for coffee or other refreshments. Wall hangings or

[1]Moyer, J., (Ed.) (1995). *Selecting educational equipment and materials for school and home.* Association for Childhood Education International.

pictures, plants, a rug or carpet, and curtains all enhance the appearance of the space. A shelf of toys and books for visiting children indicates that the center is sensitive to children's needs.

Service Areas

Basic equipment in the bathrooms, kitchen, laundry, and janitor's closet is usually built in and, therefore, not purchased from the equipment and supplies budget. In a new facility, some appliances may be included in the equipment line. Consumables for service areas must be furnished and appliances must be replaced over time. Dishes, cutlery, cooking utensils, and serving carts must be provided in centers where lunch is served. In large centers, special appliances such as commercial dishwashers, rug shampooers, heavy-duty automatic washers and dryers, and large refrigerators and freezers are needed. The local board of health may have specific requirements about the type of kitchen equipment that must be provided.

USING SELECTION CRITERIA

Selection of all equipment should be based on a set of preestablished criteria. The primary consideration is usefulness; that is, will a specific piece of equipment meet the needs of this center in a safe manner? Other criteria are versatility, suitability, durability, ease of maintenance, attractiveness, and user preference. Some equipment for children should encourage and even necessitate cooperative play. All equipment should work the way it is supposed to, and be durable and economical. Although these criteria apply to all equipment purchases, this chapter primarily covers information about equipment that children will use.

The goals and objectives of a particular center will dictate some purchases. A center that emphasizes academic development with a special focus on mathematics and problem-solving will purchase a wide variety of materials suitable for helping children attain knowledge about math. In this case, some advanced math games will be included with the expectation that the comprehensive program in math will enable the children to enjoy these more complex materials. On the other hand, a center that emphasizes social development may concentrate more heavily on materials for pretend play and on equipment that can be used simultaneously by a number of children. Most schools will focus on these two areas equally, and only a few, if any, will exclude either area. The focal points of a program will be based on its philosophy, and will determine, in part, the types and quantity of equipment of various types to be purchased. Suitability of specific curricular materials will not be discussed here since a number of publications include this information in the context of program development.

Reflections

Think of yourself as a director who is responsible for equipment purchases. Did you realize that you would not only pore over classroom equipment and materials catalogs but also would find yourself searching through office equipment and restaurant supply catalogs? Your duties have now expanded from educator and administrator to that of purchasing agent. This responsibility probably seems like an overwhelming undertaking at the moment, since many of you have been responsible only for purchasing personal items and, in some cases, basic household equipment. You are, no doubt, beginning to realize that the role of the director has many facets and requires a wide variety of special skills.

Usefulness

The usefulness of a piece of children's equipment is measured, first, by how well it meets the developmental needs of the children in the program, and second, by whether or not the equipment can be put to multiple uses by those children.

Developmental Needs. The developmental levels, capabilities, and age range of the children enrolled influence what will be purchased. A center serving two-year-olds will need some pull toys and small climbers. Infants require special furnishings such as cribs, changing tables, and high chairs not needed by older children. Some centers use low chairs designed for feeding older infants as a safety measure. Young infants are always held during feeding. Infants also require washable, chewable toys, bibs, sheets, blankets, and disposable diapers. Parents may be asked to furnish some of those necessary items and to take responsibility for their infant's laundry.

Toddlers may need potty chairs instead of built-in toilets which are unsuitable for toilet training some children. Note that potty chairs may not be permitted by some sanitation codes. Toddlers also need toys that provide opportunities for filling and dumping, big toys that can be carried during early walking stages, and lots of duplicates so that sharing will not be necessary.

School-aged children in after-school care programs need games and crafts that are far too complex and frustrating for younger children. They also may need well-lighted working areas for homework, larger furniture in which they can sit and work comfortably, and equipment for active semiorganized sports.

Children with disabilities may require modified equipment or equipment that has been specifically designed to meet a particular need. A director who has established contact with agencies serving people with disabilities can seek their assistance in providing modifications or special equipment. The equipment should enable the child to do as much as possible independently.

Versatility. A piece of equipment that can be used in several ways is a bonus both financially and in terms of enriching the learning environment for children. Such a piece not only saves space and money but also gives children the opportunity to use their imaginations in creating different functions for one object. An example would be the large hollow blocks that can be used to make a puppet stage or a grocery store, or can serve as individual work spaces for children's small projects. A bookshelf can be both a room divider and a storage facility. Two-year-olds may find the water table to be a relaxing place for splashing while four-year-olds may be more interested in using this equipment for constructing a water maze. Many pieces of equipment may be shared by two or more classes for the same or different purposes, eliminating the purchase of duplicate materials and freeing up money for other purchases.

Some equipment can be used both indoors and outdoors, a practice that is economical and provides a wider variety of learning experiences for children. Easels, water tables, and movable climbing equipment are a few items that may be moved outside if the building and play area have been planned to facilitate such indoor-outdoor movement. When that planning has not occurred, teachers will not be able to leave the children in order to make several trips to carry equipment, and the children will not have access to those items. Perhaps a janitor, or in elementary settings, older children may be able to help set up outdoor equipment. In communities where theft is a problem, equipment must be locked away when children are not in the outdoor area.

Safety

No matter how versatile, attractive, durable, economical, and suitable a piece of equipment may be, it must be rejected if it is not safe. A climber with protruding bolts, blocks of soft wood that splinter, and tricycles that tip over easily should not be used in the center. A kitchen appliance that requires a long extension cord is a hazard to the cook and the children and should be avoided. All equipment used by the children must be of nontoxic material, and must not have sharp or pointed edges. Safety is maintained by staff members who make a point of being constantly alert to the condition and the arrangement of the equipment that is placed in the learning environment.[2]

However, a safety issue may be inadvertently overlooked. Realizing that lead paint has been banned for consumer use for many years, directors may not realize the lead hazard lurking in playground equipment. Commercial users can still coat products with paint containing lead and children need consume only small quantities on a regular basis to create a harmful lead level. Even the surface under the equipment may contain

[2]Wortham, S. C., & Frost, J. L., (Eds.). (1991). *Playgrounds for young children: American survey and perspectives*, Reston, VA: American Alliance for Health, Physical Education, Recreation and Dance.

lead. Having a trained inspector check a playground periodically for lead and other hazards is a wise investment.[3]

Suitability

Some equipment must be provided in several sizes to meet the needs of each user. For example, the secretary must have a standard adult-sized chair, but chairs for children are usually 10, 12, and 14 inches high, depending on the child's age and height. Children's chairs that are so large that seated children cannot put their feet on the floor are not suitable for those users. Children's chairs should also have a wide base to they will not tip.

Stereotypes. Equipment must be chosen with the understanding that it may be used equally by all children. Staff members who plan curricula in a stereotyped way will need special guidance on this point so that boys are not relegated to playing with blocks and trucks, and girls are not always expected to dress dolls and play quiet table games. People with disabilities should be depicted in books, puzzles, and classroom displays, and they should be shown participating in a variety of activities. Classroom materials should reflect many cultures and depict a variety of roles being chosen by members of various cultures and of both sexes. For example, dolls of many races should be available. The play figures that are used as block accessories should include female postal workers and black doctors. Books, music, foods, and posters should be carefully selected to avoid any stereotyping, and to depict the culturally pluralistic society in which the children live. This principle applies even when the school serves only one race, a situation which may occur when students all come from a segregated neighborhood.

Special Needs. In determining the suitability of equipment, you must consider children with disabilities. Children who cannot walk, for example, may need easels and water tables that can be used while they sit in a chair or a wheelchair. Sometimes, such equipment is very low to enable children who are sitting on the floor to use it. In selecting the equipment, you should consider the height of the chair or wheelchair that is used and the length of the children's arms; in this way you can determine the optimum height of the working space for a particular child.

If children are crawling in body casts or in leg braces, they need comfortable floor surfaces. Wheeled equipment such as a sturdy wagon or a special buggy with seat belts will make it possible for children with physical disabilities to enjoy tours around the center neighborhood with the rest of the class. Other children may need an augmentative communication system so that they can interact with staff and children.

Reflections

Think about your previous experiences with individuals with disabilities. Have you had enough experience to be aware of their special needs? If you have a friend or relative with a lifelong disability, imagine what his or her special needs might have been during the preschool years. Now consider yourself responsible for equipping an environment that is suitable for that child as well as for a group of typically developing children. What special provisions would have to be made for your friend or relative with special needs?

Children with hearing impairments need ample visual cues such as pictures attached to storage areas so that they can tell where equipment belongs, even though they cannot hear the teacher's directions. Children with visual impairments need some toys that vary in terms of weight, texture, and sound. Balls with a bell inside and storage containers covered with different materials (for example, velvet on a container of beads or corduroy on a box holding small blocks) are especially appropriate for these children. When children who do not have disabilities use these same materials, they may develop greater insights into the experience of children with disabilities.

In purchasing equipment for a center, the director will need to know, in general, the lifestyles

[3]Aronson, M.D., S., (1997). Lead paint poisoning from playground equipment. *Child Care Information Exchange*, January, pp. 79–81.

of the families and the learning styles and interests of individual children. Children must be provided with enough ordinary, simple equipment so that they need not be bombarded nine hours a day with novelty. A balance of the familiar with the novel creates a learning environment that is neither overstimulating nor boring; the proper balance may be different in full-day child care centers than it is in half-day programs.

Ease of Maintenance

Ease of maintenance should also be a consideration when choosing equipment. Sinks, toilets, and drinking fountains that must be cleaned daily and table tops that must be washed several times each day should be extremely simple to clean. The surfaces should be smooth and all areas easy to reach. Small pieces that are hard to clean around may cause problems and harbor dirt and germs. Equipment parts that are cleaned separately such as high chair trays should be easy to remove and replace. Some plastic chairs have surfaces that are slightly roughened or ridged, and although the surface feels relatively smooth to the hand, there are actually shallow indentations that attract and hold dirt. It is almost impossible to wipe or even scrub these chairs so that they look clean. This type of furniture may be slightly less expensive than other furniture, but maintenance problems outweigh the possible savings.

Outdoor equipment that must be repainted frequently should be designed so that it can be sanded and painted easily. Places that are difficult to reach are a nuisance, and surfaces that catch and hold rain increase the need for maintenance. Equipment that will rust or rot easily should not be purchased for outdoor use.

Attractiveness

Child care center equipment should be well designed and aesthetically attractive. Most parents and teachers would like their children to appreciate beauty, and one of the best ways to help children acquire this appreciation is to surround them with beauty. An attractive environment also carries the subtle message that children, families, and staff who enter the setting are appreciated and

that great care is taken to make their environment beautiful. A material that is aesthetically appealing need not be expensive. In fact, it is often the ability of the director or teacher to find beauty in nature that provides the most attractive places for children. A colorful tablecloth on the housekeeping area table with a small vase of wildflowers in the center makes that classroom area attractive and inviting. A large square of interesting gift-wrapping paper or a square yard of fabric serves as an attractive and inexpensive wall hanging.

Reflections

Think about the times you have cleaned classroom equipment or your own items at home. Which pieces of equipment were difficult or time consuming to clean? Why? Could this difficulty have been avoided in any way? How?

When equipment is made for the classroom, it should be prepared with special attention to its visual appeal. A math game, for example, can be made using well-designed stickers or beautiful pictures cut from duplicate copies of magazines instead of using cartoon-like gimmicky stickers or drawings. The cardboard should be cut evenly, and laminated or covered with a plastic coating instead of being presented to children with rough, crooked edges. Preparing beautiful materials takes a little longer and may require initial costs that are somewhat higher, but the product is worth the investment. It is the director's job to help staff and children value quality rather than quantity, and appreciate the beauty in the objects around them.

Teacher Preference

Sometimes, teacher preference determines the type of equipment ordered. One teacher may choose to buy many books whereas another depends heavily on the library; one sees an autoharp as a necessity but another finds this instrument encumbering. One teacher may choose a guinea pig as the ideal classroom pet, another prefers fish, and still another considers all pets to require an inordinate amount of the teacher's time. As long as these teacher preferences do not mitigate against appropriate classroom practice, they are legitimate and should be honored if at all possible. When budgeting constraints or other equipment needs make it impossible to fill all teachers' requests, the director must notify teachers that their preferences are under consideration and that plans are being made to fill all requests as soon as possible. The teacher who wants an autoharp may have to wait until next year's budget provides it, and meanwhile, the director can support that teacher by informing the staff of planned equipment purchases. Each teacher's preferences deserve careful consideration because each teacher will ultimately set the stage for learning through the use of the center's equipment. Of course, the director will have to intervene if a teacher chooses to order inappropriate items such as games with very small pieces for toddlers or workbooks for preschoolers.

DIRECTOR'S CORNER

"Our Board is meeting today to discuss how to spend the $400 they earned by selling coupon books. They asked each teacher to keep a wish list on hand. When the order comes in, we have a celebration, with the Board and staff gathering to open the cartons."
 —Director, agency-sponsored child care center

WORKING WITHIN A BUDGET

There are many things to consider when working within the constraints of a budget. The following are but a few of these.

Durability and Economy

Durability and economy often go hand in hand. The climbing apparatus that costs three times as much as a competitor's product is worth the original investment if it lasts three times as long or is safer and sturdier. When more durable items are purchased, the center is not faced with the problem of replacement as often, and considerable shipping costs are saved, particularly with large pieces of equipment. Price and durability are not always perfectly correlated, but it is safe to say

that inexpensive tricycles appropriate for home use are inappropriate for group use. When used at a center, the standard equipment that is used at home will be in the repair shop far sooner and more frequently than the sturdier, more expensive equipment that is designed for school use. Keep this fact in mind when well-meaning board members want to donate items their children have outgrown rather than including sufficient dollars in the equipment budget.

In child care center kitchens, many adults and occasionally children use the equipment. This heavy usage (and perhaps misuse), coupled with lack of care, may lead to the need for earlier replacement. Refrigerator and freezer doors are opened frequently and are often left standing open while children take out ice cubes or put in trays of sloshing jello. Dishwashers may be improperly loaded or overloaded, and sinks are sometimes scoured with rough scouring pads or abrasive powders. It is important to provide heavy-duty kitchen equipment because equipment made for home use will require costly service calls when it is subjected to the hard use it will inevitably get in a center. A prepaid maintenance agreement may be a cost-effective way to manage equipment repairs. Furthermore, instructions on how to use equipment may be posted on each item and a short in-service session may be helpful.

In setting up a new center, the director can expect to spend $6,000–$12,000 per classroom on equipment. The variance is due to the number of children in each classroom and the quality of the items purchased. A typical budget for manipulatives (puzzles, table toys, and small blocks) for a center of about 75 children is about $2,000, assuming that the items are centrally stored so that teachers can share them. To reduce this cost, directors often search for free materials and supplies. However, the director may then have to pick up the items or enlist a volunteer for this service.

ORDERING EQUIPMENT

Decisions about what, when, and where to buy equipment are usually left to the director. At the very least, directors are consulted and they have considerable control over what is bought with the money that is budgeted for equipment and supplies.

Equipment Requisition

Directors usually develop an equipment request procedure. Staff members notify the director, in writing, of the type of equipment that is needed or desired, provide additional information such as the rationale to support the need, give the name of a possible vendor, and provide an estimated purchase price. All of these data are helpful when final purchase decisions are made. Some centers use purchase orders or requisition forms which are nothing more than request forms that can be sent to vendors with a duplicate retained for center records (see Director's Resource 10–1). Even though this request procedure is formal and perhaps cumbersome, it puts the purchase of equipment on a business-like basis and gives each staff member an equal opportunity to bid for the equipment dollars in the budget.

In corporate systems, requisitions are processed through a central purchasing agent and shipments are made directly to the center from the manufacturer. The central office handles all the orders and saves money through collective, quantity buying and through careful selection of suppliers. This approach cuts costs but limits the options for those staff members selecting equipment. Public school programs usually have specific purchasing procedures to follow, requisitioning their supplies through the principal or through a supervisor responsible for the preschool or after-school programs.

In centers where directors are fully responsible for receiving staff requests and placing orders, they check requests against the established selection criteria and the budget allowance before completing order forms. All order forms should include quantity, price, catalog order number (if available), and name or description of each item. When making final decisions on purchases, make certain that careful consideration is given to possible savings through bulk buying. For example, newsprint for painting can be bought from some vendors for as much as $2 less per ream when bought in 48-ream packages. Economies realized through bulk buying are practical only if adequate storage space is available for the unused materials.

Equipment costs also can be reduced in non-profit centers by applying for tax-exempt status. When orders are sent to suppliers, the center will not be charged a sales tax if the order includes the center's tax-exempt number.

Some centers have provisions for teachers to purchase specified dollar amounts without permission, and within a given time period. For example, a teacher may receive $100 to spend for the classroom each year in addition to the centerwide purchases which the director makes. In some cases, the purchase is made and the teacher is reimbursed on presentation of the receipt to the board treasurer or the director. The practice of giving teachers some petty cash to spend for classroom materials gives them some freedom to provide for special program needs, and more importantly, communicates trust in their ability to make appropriate choices for their children.

Reflections

Assume that your classroom is stocked with basic equipment for your fifteen four-year-old children. You have received $100 from petty cash. Think about how you might spend your allocation.

Purchase Time Line

Equipment purchasing occurs in three different time frames: start-up, supplementary, and replacement.

First, there must be a major start-up equipment purchase when a center is opened so that all the basic aspects of the program can function with appropriate equipment. This phase is obviously the most expensive of the three, but extensive purchases at this point are absolutely essential because it is unfair to children and staff to operate a program without basic equipment. To save money, some secondhand, borrowed, or homemade equipment can be used, keeping in mind the criteria described earlier. There is no formula that can tell a director exactly what must be provided, but the staff will need equipment of the type, quantity, and quality that will allow them to focus on the children and their needs rather than on the equipment or the lack thereof. Children in a classroom with inappropriate or inadequate equipment will be likely to engage in inappropriate behavior as they seek to create something interesting to do.

The second phase of equipment purchasing is the supplementary phase that provides for additional equipment purchases throughout the year. When supplementary equipment purchases are spaced throughout a program year, both children and staff members enjoy greater variety and a change of pace. Furthermore, teachers can adjust equipment requests to meet the needs of particular children such as a child with special needs who enrolls mid-year and requires a chair with particular supports, a prone board, or a walker. Although outside funding may be available for some of these larger items for an individual child's use, teachers still need to consider books with large print, puzzles with large knobs, or writing tools that have been adapted for easier handling.

The third, or replacement phase, helps maintain a constant supply of equipment that is in good repair and allows for adjustments in available equipment and materials as program needs change or as new items come on the market. For example, a few years ago, all African-American dolls had Caucasian hairstyles and facial features, but newer dolls have features that match the ethnic group being represented. Vinyl records were the major source of recorded music for children, followed by audiotapes, and now compact discs. Similarly, film strips have been replaced by videos. At the same time, the 50th anniversary edition of the much loved children's book, *Goodnight Moon*,[4] reminds us that new isn't always better.

The budget also should include enough money for emergency replacements. Although careful usage combined with a maintenance plan minimizes the need for emergency replacements, unexpected breakage or loss is sure to occur. When a copier repair is too costly, it is sometimes more economical to buy or lease a new model than to repair the old one.

Sources of Equipment

Much equipment for early childhood education centers is purchased from catalogs. If the dealers are reliable, this arrangement is satisfactory. It is wise to check with other directors, professional organizations, or the Better Business Bureau to determine the suitability of making purchases from a particular company. Among the advantages of purchasing by catalog are the wide variety of merchandise that is often available and the lowering of costs with the bypassing of the retailer. On the other hand, shipping costs may be charged and return of unsatisfactory merchandise may be cumbersome. It is helpful to have a supply of catalogs available to the staff. Most companies will be pleased to put your center on their mailing list. Appendix A lists equipment suppliers.

Equipment purchased from local retail outlets can be seen and tried out and has obvious advantages; but most retail outlets cater to home users and carry a limited stock of classroom equipment. If a local outlet has access to a manufacturer of school equipment, it may be possible to order from a catalog through a local retailer. A buying co-op is another equipment source that is worth investigating because group buying can be very economical. In this system, the co-op group buys in quantity at a wholesale price and sells items to co-op members at just enough above cost to pay the co-op operating expenses.

Exhibit areas at state or national early childhood conferences provide great opportunities to view a huge range of products for early childhood classrooms and to talk with the vendors. Keep in mind that their goal is to sell their products, but a careful shopper can garner a wealth of information, and sometimes a special price. Particularly at the end of the exhibit hours, vendors would just as soon give you a discount, as ship materials back to their home base. Remember also that conference sponsors rarely endorse products being displayed, and conferees are responsible for using their own good judgment because what is available is not always appropriate for early childhood education.

Toy libraries are popular equipment sources in some areas. A center director or teacher may borrow anything from a puzzle to a complete set of housekeeping equipment, just as one borrows library books. Sometimes, a group of center directors finds it worthwhile to help establish a toy library for their mutual benefit and it is especially helpful to have toy-lending programs that furnish materials for special needs children. Occasionally, toy-lending or toy-sharing systems are set up by community organizations to make equipment available to centers and to parents.

Secondhand shops, discount stores, antique shops, and garage or yard sales frequently are excellent sources of equipment or raw materials for pieces needed by the center. The buyer may discover a garlic press that can provide an interesting physical knowledge experience for children. With imagination and effort, large ice cream cans can become storage places for musical instruments or some other equipment that demands a number of relatively small, easily accessible spaces. Perhaps a used desk or file cabinet for the center office can be located. When such discoveries need to be put into finished, usable, and attractive form, it is sometimes possible to enlist the help of the parent group, a high-school vocational class, or a senior citizens' organization whose members enjoy repairing and painting. In some regions, high-school woodworking, metal working classes, or Junior Achievement groups make new equipment and sell it to centers at reasonable prices.

Another way to obtain equipment is to solicit the help of parents, teachers, board members, or residents of the community in equipment-making parties. This activity enhances the feeling of community in the center's program. Child care center staff members often take advantage of the children's naptime to make classroom materials. Encouraging staff members to make some materials is important because few centers have unlimited resources and commercial equipment cannot always be suitably adapted to meet individual children's needs.

Gifts of equipment are usually welcome, but their suitability must be measured against the same criteria employed for equipment purchases. A gift, such as a toy gun, in a center where pretend gun play is discouraged, or the gift of an animal that induces allergic reactions in some children must be refused graciously.

MANAGING EQUIPMENT

Even before equipment is delivered to the center, the director must consider how it will be man-

aged. All equipment must be checked and inventoried on delivery, and before it is stored or put into use, a maintenance plan should be set up to minimize repair and replacement needs.

Checking and Inventorying Equipment

When equipment is received, it must be checked against the order to ascertain whether or not it corresponds with the order in terms of quantity, size, color, and so forth. It is also important to make certain that only the items actually received are listed on both the order and the packing slip, and that prices are correct. If discrepancies are found, the vendor must be notified immediately. It is wise to keep original packing materials in case any equipment needs to be returned.

Most center directors keep a record of at least the major items purchased, and some directors keep a running account of all small items and consumables as well. An inventory of purchases can be recorded as items are unpacked by listing each item on computer or a file card, noting the description, supplier, price, date of purchase, and location in which the item is to be used. Some directors mark equipment with the name of the center, with an inventory number, or with an identifying number so that if a center owns five identical record players, each is individually identifiable. In public schools, the usual practice is to put the room number on each piece of equipment. The labeling practice is helpful when pieces are sent out for repair, when school buildings are cleaned during vacation periods, or when items are stolen. Valuable equipment should be insured. When equipment is added or removed from the center, the inventory should be updated.

An accurate record of equipment will always be available when the inventory is updated regularly. Director's Resource 10–2 shows a suggested inventory form. A backup disk of the inventory should be kept in a safe place, in a fire-resistant file cabinet or other storage unit if possible, so that losses can be reported accurately in the event of fire or theft. Computer inventories should be backed up and disks should be safely stored. Furthermore, an ongoing, updated inventory minimizes the work of taking an annual inventory which is usually necessary for insurance purposes, for annual reporting to the board, sponsoring, or funding agency, or for reporting to a corporate central office that must have an accurate annual inventory to determine the assets of the corporation. Updated inventories also give directors a clear picture of what is available in the center, and help pinpoint center areas or types of equipment that are incurring heavy damage. This information is useful in determining how much and when to reorder, and in making decisions about changing vendors or brands of equipment ordered. Information about persistent damage in certain areas should lead to a careful examination of the storage and maintenance system.

After the equipment is checked in and inventoried, the director must notify the staff that the new equipment is available for use. No doubt everyone will know when a new climbing tower arrives or when a new microwave oven is available, but if twelve new puzzles are placed on the shelves or a fresh supply of felt markers is stored, it could be weeks before all teachers in a large center discover the new materials.

Maintaining and Storing Equipment

As soon as equipment is placed in the center, the job of maintenance begins. For instance, an untreated wooden climber that is placed outdoors in a rainy area is doomed to rot. It will need immediate treatment, followed by periodic coatings of a penetrating nontoxic stain if it is to withstand weathering. Carpeting under an easel will become stained with paint unless additional floor covering such as a rubber or plastic mat is placed on top of the carpet under the easel.

Equipment used by the children must be checked daily and removed if it is in need of repair, even if immediate replacement is impossible. Children need attractive, usable equipment, and should not be subjected to the frustration of trying to make sense out of broken or incomplete classroom materials. Puzzles with missing pieces, tricycles with broken pedals, or books with torn or defaced pages should not be left in the classroom.

Storage of equipment is also directly related to its maintenance. It is easy to return equipment after it has been used when each piece has a specific, clearly delineated storage space. The space,

whether in a storage room or on a classroom shelf, must be large enough so that the object does not have to be jammed into place and perhaps damaged. And the space must be accessible to staff members (and in many cases, to children) to ensure that it will be used for storage purposes. When storage spaces are inconveniently located relative to the areas in which the equipment is used, items may be moved from temporary place to temporary place until eventually, many parts are lost or broken or everyone has difficulty locating the misplaced items. Each center must work out a method for storing certain equipment and supplies that are used daily and must remain in the classroom; other supplies should be designated for return to a central area. Storage also must be provided for items such as tricycles that are used daily but must be protected from weather and theft. Additional storage is needed for items that are purchased in quantity for long-range use such as paper towels and paint.

When a large number of people have access to the central supply storage areas, there is some tendency for each person to assume that someone else will maintain order and cleanliness in the area. Therefore, many of the users feel little or no responsibility for maintaining the area. When this happens, some users return materials in a haphazard way, fail to place them on the correct shelves, or return them in poor condition. Other staff members become irritated when they try to find what they need and have to cope with a messy storage area. These frustrations lead to conflict and a breakdown in positive staff relationships. Sometimes, this problem can be avoided by assigning each teacher the responsibility for maintaining a specific storage area such as for art materials, outdoor equipment, or books and records for a given length of time. In other centers, periodic work sessions are scheduled to involve the entire staff in cleaning and straightening central storage areas. Some centers institute a system for checking equipment in and out of the storage room that is similar to the practice conducted in a library. A few centers keep all the equipment in classrooms either on shelves available to the children or in closed cabinets available to the teacher, but this practice is expensive because it requires duplication.

In whatever way equipment is stored, its placement should be neat and easy to find so that children and teachers alike will be encouraged to maintain some degree of order in their attractive environment. The director's job is to establish and follow routines that lead to the easy accessibility of all equipment to everyone. These routines make putting things away far less burdensome for both teachers and children. Orderliness does not have to be an obsession; rather, it is an appropriate way to manage a large variety of equipment which is used in a number of ways by a wide range of people.

SUMMARY

Appropriate equipment allows the staff to focus on the essentials of their work as they provide an excellent early childhood program. Initial purchases are made when a center opens, and additional items for children's and adults' spaces and for service areas are purchased to supplement and replace this equipment. Most centers acquire equipment from a variety of sources, but all equipment should be considered in terms of its usefulness, durability, economy, ease of maintenance, attractiveness, teacher preference, and safety. Once equipment is made available, it must be properly maintained and stored. A plan for use and care of equipment must be developed for both children and staff as a component of the center's program.

Director's Resource 10–1

Sample Purchase Order Form

**REQUISITION/PURCHASE ORDER
THE CHILDREN'S CENTER**

To: _____

_____

_____

Catalog No.	Description	Quantity	Price	Total

Ship to:
The Children's Center
1099 Main Street
Centerville, CA 00000–0000

Account charged: _____

Approved by: _____

Date ordered: _____

Date received: _____

Director's Resource 10–2

Sample Inventory Form

INVENTORY FORM					
Date Purchased	Description	Identifying Number	Source	Price	Location in Center

Director's Resource 10–3

Suggested Equipment and Materials
Suggested Order of Acquisition

Essential Items—A   **Extensions—B**

Note: Items, quantities and priorities suggested on the following pages of this section are to be thought of as guides rather than inventories.

SUGGESTED ITEMS	QUANTITIES A	B	SUGGESTED ITEMS	QUANTITIES A	B
I BASIC ENVIRONMENTAL EQUIPMENT			Sand table (see Psycho-Motor Development)		
Bookcase for children's books, on casters, 1 or 2 slanted shelves on top	1		Shed, outdoor, with cupboards, for storage of maintenance supplies and items such as hollow blocks, vehicles, sand-box toys, art materials, etc., rain and vandal-proof	1	
Bookshelf, for adult books, up high	1				
Bulletin boards, portable	2				
Cabinets:			Shelf unit, for blocks, so individual sizes and shapes can be easily seen, chosen and put back by children and adults	1	
Movable, sturdy, with adjustable shelves for storage of curriculum materials, cleaning supplies, foods, etc.	4		Sinks:		
			Indoor, with counter space	1	
Movable, sturdy, with rigid shelves, child height for self-help equipment and displays	2		Outdoor, with counter space		1
			Smoke alarms	X	
Chairs:			Step-stool	1	
Adult size:			Stove	1	
Desk	1		Tables:		
Folding, for meetings	10	20	Adult size, seating 4, folding	1	
Rocking	1		Child size:		
Child size, stackable, lightweight but sturdy, 1 per child, several for staff and visitors	30		Seating, 4–8, same height, so can be combined, 18" to 20" high	4	
			Seating 8–10 children and adults, for outdoor use	1–2	
Chalkboard, portable, with chalk and erasers	1		Serving cart	1	
Clock, wall	1		Trash cans, with lids, large	2	
Counter or shelf for preparation of craft materials and food	2		Trays, storage, non-toxic, impact resistant/lids	X	
Cubbies, indoor, wood, with bottom shelf, hooks above and 1 or 2 shelves at the top, 1 per child	20		Wastebasket, large with lid	1	
			Wastebaskets for recyclable items	X	
Drinking fountain, child height	1				
Filing cabinet, 2–4 drawers	1		II GENERAL MAINTENANCE, INDOOR/OUTDOOR		
Fire extinguishers	X		Broom, push, heavy duty for outside	1	
Laundromat (See Housekeeping Supplies—Cleaning)			Buckets, 1 metal, 1 plastic, flat bottom, large	2	
Peg board with pegs for storage/ display	1		Electrical extension cord and plug, heavy duty	1	
Pillows	4		Hardware kit: nails, nuts, bolts, sandpaper, screws, staples, washers, etc.	1	
Plants	X	X	Iron, electric	1	
Refrigerator	1		Ironing board	1	
Rugs, if room not carpeted, indoor/ outdoor, approx. 9' x 12'	1	1	Plunger	1	

Director's Resource 10–3 (continued)

SUGGESTED ITEMS	QUANTITIES A	B	SUGGESTED ITEMS	QUANTITIES A	B
Rakes:			Gauze pads, sterile, boxes	4	
Garden	1		Gloves, latex, for use when in contact		
Leaf	1		with all body fluids	X	
Rope, 4' to 8'	1		Hypoallergenic adhesive tape	2	
Shovel or spade	1		Ice pack	1	
Tool box	X		Medicine glass	1	
Trash bins	1		Red Cross first aid manual	1	
Twine, cone	1		Rubbing alcohol, bottle	1	
			Safety pins, pkg.	1	
III HOUSEKEEPING SUPPLIES			Thermometer strips	3	
Brooms:			Tweezers	1	
Push	1		Flashlight	1	
Regular	1		Handkerchiefs, paper, small hospital		
Cleansers:			size, boxes	18	
Disinfectants	X		Rugs, plastic covered foam mats or cots		
Glass cleaner, can	1		for resting, 27" x 48", or towels from		
Scouring powder, cans	12		home	24	
Cloths, cleaning	6		Towels, paper, junior size, pkg. of 150	10	
Dishpan	2		Food preparation and service:		
Drying rack, folding	1		Food and cooking are considered part		
Dust pan with brush	X		of the education program for children		
Garbage bags/ties	X		and adults, as well as serving		
Garbage can with lid	1		nutritional needs. Health standards		
Mops:			and regulations must be observed.		
Dust	1		Items are suggested only for schools		
Wet	1		that serve hot meals daily.		
Soap:			Blender	1	
Bar, doz.	3		Bottle opener	2	
Liquid, qt.	3		Bowls:		
Powder, box	3		Serving, unbreakable, assorted sizes	3	
Sponges, several sizes	6		Soup/cereal, plastic	30	
Strainer, sink	1		Sugar	2	
Toilet paper, carton of 3,000 sheets	5		Bowl scrapers, various sizes	2	
Towels:			Cake pans, unbreakable	4	
Bath, each child brings own	X	X	Canisters, or other food containers,		
Dish	12		with lids	6	
Hand	12		Can openers:		
Paper, case of 3,000	6		Electric	1	
Vacuum cleaner, if floor is carpeted		1	Hand	1	
Vacuum cleaner bags, as needed		X	Colander	1	
			Cookie:		
IV HEALTH AND SAFETY			Cutter, assorted sizes, special shapes		
First aid supplies:			for holidays	12	
Cotton blankets, one per child	24		Decorator	1	
First aid cabinet stocked in accord-			Sheets	4	
ance with individual school regula-			Corn popper, hand or electric	1	
tions or with the following items:			Cups, paper, flat bottom, box of 100, 5 oz.	6	
Antiseptic soap (Phisoderm™)	2		Cutlery:		
Bandages, plastic strips, boxes	6		Forks:		
Eye bath	1		Heavy plastic, reusable, for		
Gauze, sterile, boxes	4		special events	60	

Director's Resource 10–3 (continued)

SUGGESTED ITEMS	QUANTITIES A	B	SUGGESTED ITEMS	QUANTITIES A	B
Long handled	2		Salad bowl and servers	1	
Salad, stainless steel, for children			Salt shakers, incl. one for stove	4	
and adults	36		Sauce pans, 1 qt., 4 qt., 6 qt., with lids	4	
Serving	3		Sieves:		
Knives:			Large	1	
Bread	1		Small	1	
Butcher	1		Spatulas, assorted sizes	3	
Dinner, heavy plastic, reusable, for			Storage containers:		
special events	60		Freezer	2	
Paring	2		Refrigerator	4	
Stainless steel, for children and			Tablecloths, plastic, to be used for meals		
adults	12–20		or cooking activities, one for each table	X	
Spoons:			Table mats, plastic, if desired	24	
Cooking, with long handles,			Teakettle	1	
unbreakable	3		Tongs	1	
Serving	6		Trays, assorted sizes	6	
Soup, stainless steel	6		Vegetable peeler	1	
Teaspoons, stainless steel	36				
Double boiler	2		V AUDIOVISUAL EQUIPMENT		
Egg beater, hand	1		CD and cassette recorder/ player, dual		
Electric mixer	1		cassette decks, separate speaker with		
Flour sifter	1		3' extension cord, auto-reset		
Fry pans:			tape counter	X	
Electric	1		CDs	X	
Regular, 6", 8", 10", 12"	1		Filmstrip projector	1	
Funnels:			Filmstrips (access to)	X	
Large	1		Movie and sound projector, (access to)	X	
Small	1		Projection screen	X	
Glasses, unbreakable:			Record player	X	
Large, 10 oz.	6		Records	X	
Small, 6 oz.	24–36		Tape recorder	1	
Hot pads	4		Tapes or cassettes for listening and		
Hot plate, electric stove, if full day	1		recording	4	
Ladles	2				
Measures:			VI PSYCHO-MOTOR DEVELOPMENT		
Bowls, nesting set, unbreakable	3		Balls, rubber, assorted sizes (10)	X	
Cups, unbreakable, sets	2		Barrels	1	
Spoons, sets	2		Bars for hanging	2	
Napkins, paper, buy in quantity	X		Bean bags	20	
Oven, portable, if no stove available	1		Boards:		
Pie pans, unbreakable	6		Cleated, 1'–6'	1	
Pitchers, unbreakable:			Plain, 6'–8'	3	
Cream	1		Resilient, for jumping	2	
Pt. size	4		Bowling pins set	X	
1–2 qt. size	4		Boxes, large, wooden	2	
Plates:			Climbing structures: old tires, empty		
Dessert, paper	48		electrical reels, concrete culvert units	2	
Dinner, heavy plastic	36		Crates, packing boxes	1	
Dinner, paper	36		Crawl-through tunnel or cubes, large	1	1
Serving, assorted sizes	4		Dollies, hand	1	
Pot holders	4		Folding mats, anti-bacterial, anti-		
Rolling pins, additional ones for			fungal, reinforced seams to place		
children's use	2		at the end of the indoor slide, etc.	5	

Director's Resource 10–3 (continued)

SUGGESTED ITEMS	QUANTITIES A	B	SUGGESTED ITEMS	QUANTITIES A	B
Hoops, 18" to 24" in diameter	20		Shape or sorting box with interchangeable panels	1	
Hose, length as needed	1		Sound cylinders, approx. 3" high, 2" diameter, set of 5	2	
Ladder, lightweight, sturdy for children, 4' to 6'	1		Tactile materials: sandpaper, cloth, wood, metal, sponge, rocks, etc., in container	X	
Net, cargo, for climbing		1			
Pails, assorted sizes, for outdoor play	3		Taste materials: sugar, flour, salt, fruit juices, etc., in plastic containers with removable lids	X	
Parachute, sturdy, 6' diameter, hand-held strap	X		Water table with water toys	X	
Pulleys	1				
Rakes	2				
Recordings, suggesting gross and fine muscle activities	4		**VIII BUILDING AND CONSTRUCTION**		
Ribbon sticks for ribbon dance	20		Blocks:		
Rocking boat	1		Hollow	30	
Rope, 6' to 8' length	1		Parquetry, set	2	
Sandbox frame with sand (water faucet and hose nearby)	1		Table, choose from cube, interlocking, nesting, regular small sets in variety of materials: wood, plastic, rubber	3	
Sand toys, variety	X		Unit, full school set (protected floor space and appropriate shelving important)	150	
Shovels, small but sturdy	4				
Spades	2		Boards, small, flat 24"–36" long, to use with blocks	4	
Swing set, double with canvas or rubber seats	1		Building sets: (choose from such as the following in school size sets of sufficient quantities to satisfy needs)		
Trampoline, rubber, attached to climbing structure, low enough for children's safety	1		Crystal Climber	1	
Wheel toys:			Giant tinker toys	2	
Tricycles	2		Lego	2	
Tricycle trailers	1		Lincoln Logs	1	
Wagons	2		Rig-a-jig	1	
Wheelbarrow	1		Rising Towers	1	
			Tinker toys	1	
VII PERCEPTUAL DEVELOPMENT			Carpentry: (all tools real, not toy)		
Bead laces	12		Bench	1	
Beads, wooden, 1/2" cubes and assorted shapes, box of 1,000	1		Bits, 1/4", 1/2' and 3/4'	1	
Counting rods, sets	2		Block plane	2	
Dressing frames	4		Boiled linseed oil	2	
Games, matching:			Brace, adult size, $1^1/_2$ lbs.	1	
Block: attribute, design, domino, number, property, etc.	4		Brushes	5	
Card: animals, geometric shapes, flowers, vehicles, etc.	4		Clamps, vise or c-clamps	6	
Frame: bingo and lotto type with birds, flowers, food, clothing, zoo animals, etc.	4		Coping saw, wooden handle	1	
			Coping saw blades	1	
Lacing toys	X		Crowbars	3	
Linking toys	X		Goggles (eye protection), adult and child-sized	X	
Magnetic board, 18" x 36"	1		Hammers, 7–13 oz., flat head with claws	2	
Magnetized figures, 50 items, set	1				
Mechanical board: bolts, nuts, locks, etc.	1		Hand drill and drill sets	1	
Nest of rings or boxes, 6 to 8 items	1		Hinges, 1" and 2" with screws	X	
Olfactory materials: spices, foods, greenery, etc. in plastic bottles with perforated, tightly sealed lids	X		Measuring rod, tape, ruler, one of each	3	

Director's Resource 10–3 (continued)

SUGGESTED ITEMS	QUANTITIES A	B	SUGGESTED ITEMS	QUANTITIES A	B
Nails, assorted sizes, 1/2″ to 2″, some very long, lbs.	5		IX CREATIVE ARTS		
Nuts and bolts, assorted, box	1		Aprons, plastic or cloth, homemade	10	
Pliers	1		Beads, and other objects for stringing	500	
Sandpaper, medium grit, pkg.	1		Brushes, glue, 1/2–1″ thickness handle length, 6″–9″	2	
Saws, crosscut, 14″ blade, 18″ blade, 8 teeth per inch	2		Brushes, paint 1/2–1″ thickness handle length, 6″–9″	12	
Screwdrivers, 8″, 12″, regular and Phillips	2		Brush holders	2	
Screws, steel, flat head, assorted sizes, box of 50	2		Cans, cookie cutters, for cutting dough, assorted sizes	4	
Washers, assorted sizes, box	1		Chalk:		
Cloth, yds.	2		Assorted colors, large box	2	
Corks, supply accumulated	X		White, box	1	
Foam rubber pieces, supply accumulated	X		Clay, gray and red, lbs. each	25	
Glue, tubes	1		Cloth:		
Lumber:			Burlap and/or heavy weight mesh for stitchery, yds.	2	
Assorted shapes and sizes, soft, scrounged (often available from lumber yard disposal bins and carpentry shops) 50–75 pieces	X		Old sheeting to paint/draw on, supply accumulated	X	
Assorted sizes, rough measure footage, 30′–60′, purchased	1	1	Plastic drape, one for each table	X	
Sand/water play materials, all unbreakable:			Clothespins, for hanging art work	48	
Brushes, large	3		Coffee filters, box of 100	1	
Containers, wide variety	6		Collage materials, scrounged, such as pieces of cloth, paper, leather, plastic, old greeting cards, buttons, Styrofoam, yarn, ribbon, sequins, glitter, beads, etc., supply accumulated	X	
Dishes, variety	4		Containers:		
Dishpans	1		For clay, plastic with lid	2	
Floating toys and objects	4		For collage materials: old boxes, baskets, jars, etc., supply accumulated	X	
Funnels, assorted sizes	2		For paint: small cans, cut down cartons, plastic, with lids	10	
Hose, small pieces, can be scrounged	2		Cookie cutter, for use with play dough	12	
Measuring sets:			Corks for painting	6	
Cups	2		Cotton balls, bags	4	
Spoons	2		Crayon holders	2	
Molds, assorted	3		Crayons, jumbo, assorted colors, boxes	10	
Pitchers	1		Drying rack for art materials, if needed	1	
Scoops	4		Easels, double adjustable	2	
Sieves	2		Fabric scraps (assorted box)	1	
Sand/water table or tray	1		Garlic presses for use with clay	2	
Straws, plastic, pkg.	1		Hole puncher	1	
Tongue depressors or craft sticks, pkg. of 1,000	1		Kiln (access to)	X	
Toothpicks, colored box	1		Knives, plastic (box of 25)	1	
Vehicles:			Knives, table, for use with clay and dough (can be old)	6	
Construction, large, sturdy, variety	3		Looms, handmade out of cardboard, paper plates, wood and nails, f or simple weaving	2	
Transportation, unbreakable, in various sizes	6				
Wheels, wooden disks	6				

Director's Resource 10–3 (continued)

SUGGESTED ITEMS	QUANTITIES A	B	SUGGESTED ITEMS	QUANTITIES A	B
Marking pens, non-toxic	6		Rolling pins for play dough	4	
Masking tape, roll	4		Salt, for cooking and making play		
Natural items for collage and painting			dough, boxes	2	
(e.g., acorns, corks, dried flowers,			Sand:		
herbs, leaves, feathers, seeds, etc.)	X		Indoor sandbox, white, fine (lbs.)		
Newspapers	X		or cornmeal or sawdust in		
Paint:			comparable amounts	200	
Finger, commercial, pts.	6		Outdoor sandbox, coarse, lbs.	800	
Finger (make as needed out of starch,			For painting, lbs.	2	
water, tempera and soap flakes)	X		Scissors:		
Liquid tempera, assorted colors, qts.	10		Double handled training, child-size	2	
Powdered tempera, assorted			Rounded, left-handed, child-size	8	
colors, boxes	6		Semi-pointed, right-handed, child-size	8	
Watercolors, boxes with brush	2		Shears, pair, adult-size	1	
Paint jars, plastic with lids	16		Scotch tape, rolls	4	
Paper:			Sponges, to be cut into pieces approx.		
Brown, wrapping, 15 lb. roll with			1" x 2" x 2" for painting	2	
dispenser	1		Spray bottles	5	
Construction, colored, 9" x 12",			Squeeze bottles, supply accumulated	X	
pkg. of 50 sheets	20		Staple remover	1	
Construction, colored, 12" x 18"			Stapler, adult-size	2	
pkg. of 50 sheets	8		Stapler, child-size	4	
Manila for drawing, 12" x 18", reams	8		Staples, box	2	
Mural paper, white, roll	1		Starch for mixing finger paint, boxes	2	
News, unprinted, 18" x 24", pkg.	15		Straws for blow painting (box)	1	
Poster, colored, 9" x 12",			Tape, Mystic, cloth with plastic finish,		
pkg. of 100 sheets	20		3" wide x 108", roll	1	
Poster, colored, 12" x 18",			Water color markers, non-toxic, water		
pkg. of 100 sheets	4		soluble, pkg.	3	
Tagboard, medium weight,			Wax	1	
24" x 36", sheets	10		Wheat paste, lbs.	1	
Tissue, 20" x 30", pkg. of 24 sheets	4		Wood pieces for collage and		
Paper bags, approx. 8" x 14"	20		construction, scrounged, supply		
Paper brads of fasteners, boxes	2		accumulated	X	
Paper clips, box of 100	4		Yarn for collage, stitchery and weaving,		
Paper cutter, 12" blade	1		scrounged and balls	4	
Paste, semi-liquid, gal.	2				
Paste jars, 2" diameter, 1 1/2" deep,			X DRAMATIC PLAY		
with covers	10		Animal:		
Pastesticks, hardwood, pkg. of 500	1		Figures, small, plastic/rubber, a		
Pencils, soft, thick lead, without erasers	12		variety, in quantity for use with		
Pencil sharpener	1		blocks and sand/water play	16	
Pie tins or other containers, for children			Puppets, assorted	6	
to use in mixing paint	6		Stuffed animals	4	
Pins, safety, medium size, box of 100	1		Camping:		
Pipe cleaners, assorted colors, pkgs.	2		Backpack, from surplus store	1	
Plasticine, single color, lbs.	5		Lantern		1
Play dough, can be made or purchased,			Pup tent		1
as needed	X		Sleeping bag		1
Printing materials for play dough, clay			Utensils	4	
and paint, assorted kinds: cut			Doctor/Nurse:		
vegetables, spools, blocks, etc.,			Bandages, kit	1	
supply accumulated	X		Clip board and pencils	2	

Director's Resource 10–3 (continued)

SUGGESTED ITEMS	QUANTITIES		SUGGESTED ITEMS	QUANTITIES	
	A	B		A	B
Cot	2		removable	1	
Instruments:			Doll house dolls: families, multiethnic,		
Sphygmomanometer for blood			multicultural, bendable preferred,		
pressure	1		to use also with blocks, vehicles,		
Stethoscope	1		sand/water play	4	
Mirrors	1		Dolls, baby boy, girl, multiethnic,		
Mask	1		multicultural, unbreakable, washable	X	
Grooming-toilet articles, male and			Dress-up properties, male and female:		
female: comb, hair brush, hair rollers,			aprons, belts, billfolds, blouses, boots,		
hand mirror, nail brush, manual razor			uniforms, dresses, hats, hose, overalls,		
without blades and/or electric razor			jackets, jewelry, pants, purses, scarves,		
with plug off, shampoo bottles, hair			shawls, shoes, skirts, suitcase, ties,		
spray bottles, shaving brush, soap	X		watches, wigs, supply accumulated	X	
Home management and family living:			Furniture for playhouse area, sturdy,		
Bathing and cleaning:			unbreakable:		
Broom, child size	1		Bed and mattress, big enough for		
Dishcloth	2		child to curl up on	1	
Dry mop	1		Chairs:		
Dustpan	1		High chair with tray	1	
Iron, wood or plastic	1		Rocking	1	
Ironing board	1		Straight	4	
Pail	1		Curtains, as desired	X	
Soap flakes, sample boxes	1		Dresser or chest	1	
Towels:			Mirror, full-length, child height	1	
Bath	1		Refrigerator	1	
Dish	2		Sink	1	
Hand	2		Sofa	1	
Washcloths	2		Stove	1	
Wet mop, 30" handle	1		Table, to seat four children	1	
Cooking and eating equipment, real,			Telephone	1	
unbreakable:			T.V. frame, scrounged	1	
Baby bottle	2		Office and school:		
Cutlery: forks, knives, spoons, place			Attache case, scrounged	1	
settings	4		Computer monitor/keyboard		
Dishes: bowls, cups, saucers,			(scrounged)	1	
small glasses, plates, plate settings	4		Paper pads	2	
Food containers, empty	X		Paper trays	2	
Food, pretend	X		Pencils and erasers	2	
Utensils: cake pan, colander, frying			Typewriter, scrounged	1	
pan, kettle, ladle, large spoon,			Waste baskets	2	
measuring cups and spoons, mixing			Playhouse, outdoor	1	
bowls, pie pan, sauce pan, sieve,			Puppets, family, hand or finger	4	
toaster (each)	2		Repair and yard work:		
Doll equipment:			Carpentry apron	1	
Baby bottles	2		Paintbrushes	X	
Bed	1		Paint cans containing colored soapsuds	3	
Buggy and stroller	1		Sewing materials: buttons, cloth		
Clothes, assorted, male, female, baby,			pieces, decorations (pieces of lace,		
older, various fastenings	12		ribbon, beads), large needles,		
Dishes, place settings	2		rounded scissors, thread, yarn,		
Doll house, open on sides, top			scrounged	X	

Director's Resource 10–3 (continued)

SUGGESTED ITEMS	QUANTITIES A	B	SUGGESTED ITEMS	QUANTITIES A	B
Transportation/Occupations: buy and scrounge			Maracas	4	
			Piano	1	
Dress-up clothes: hats, uniforms, tools for a variety of occupations, such as bakers, bus drivers, carpenters, divers, engineers, fire fighters, air pilots, police officers, sailors, taxi drivers, train engineers, postal workers, construction workers	X		Recorder, wind instrument	1	
			Sticks, rhythm, flat/fluted sets	12	
			Tambourines	2	
			Triangles	1	
			Ukulele	1	
			Wind chimes	1	
			Wood blocks	2	
Model sets: airport, camper, fire station, garage, space center, etc., with proportioned buildings, figures, furnishings, tools, vehicles	4		Xylophone	2	
People figures, proportioned, plastic, rubber, wood, representing a variety of workers	6		**XII LANGUAGE ARTS**		
Puppets, representing different workers	4		Alphabet letters, movable, sandpaper, tactile, in several sizes	300	
Traffic signs for air terminals, highways, railroad crossings, waterways	5		Books:		
Note: Additional dramatic play centers such as the following could also be provided based upon the children's needs and experiences: animal hospital, bakery, dentist office, farm, fire station, flower shop, gas station, grocery, hair salon, laundromat, pizza restaurant, police station, post office, repair shop, etc. Materials for the above can be easily scrounged by parents, teachers and community friends.			Permanent collection of 30 or more, and circulating collection borrowed from library. Choose high quality children's books, look for multicultural, multiethnic, non-sexist content.	X	
			Topics to include:		
			Animals		
			Child activities		
			Community		
			Fairy tales		
			Fantasies		
			Holidays		
			Mother Goose		
			Seasonal		
			Sensitive topics—adoption, divorce, illness		
			Easy to read books	X	
XI MUSIC			Picture books, including alphabet books and dictionaries	X	
Autoharp	1		Poetry to read aloud	X	
Cassettes	X		Resource books on such topics as biological science, community, crafts, cultures, family, geography, holidays, physical sciences, space science	X	
CDs	X				
Cassette player for children to handle	X				
Claves	6		Camera for snapshots of children, etc.	1	
Dancing clothes: scarves, skirts, streamers, supply accumulated	X		Chalkboards, portable, with chalk and erasers	1	
Guiro tone block	1		Chart paper, large, for experiences	2	
Guiro with scraper	1		Computer (for exploration)	1	
Rhythm instruments:			Felt board	1	
Bells, variety: ankle, cow, wrist, melody set, supply accumulated	X		Felt board pieces: alphabet, stories, animals, familiar objects, etc., pkg. of 50 items	1	
Castanets	2		Games, simple, such as lotto and other picture games	4	
Drums, variety: snare, tom-tom, etc.	2				
Guitar	1		Notebooks for dictated stories	3	
Kazoo	2		Perception cards, set	1	
Keyboard, can be homemade	2				

Director's Resource 10–3 (continued)

SUGGESTED ITEMS	QUANTITIES A	B	SUGGESTED ITEMS	QUANTITIES A	B
Puzzles, wooden, 9 to 16 pieces	8		Tubing, 3' length	1	
Typewriter, primary	1		Windmills for water and sand	4	
			Animal foods that are appropriate for below	X	
XIII MATHEMATICS			Animals: Follow all public health and		
Counters, unbreakable: animals, beads, blocks, buttons, cards, color chips, nails, napkins, marbles, sticks, etc.	X		safety laws and regulations, provide adequate food, medical care, shelter. Choose from:		
Food to cut and divide	X		Baby chicks		
Geometric figures, wooden, 3" units, approx. 6 items, set	1		Ducks		
Matching sets	X		Fish		
Measuring equipment, English and Metric:			Gerbils (when permitted law)		
Dry units	4		Guinea pigs		
Liquid units	4		Hamsters		
Rulers	2		Mice		
Tape	1		Parakeets		
Thermometers:			Rabbits		
Hand manipulated model	1		Snails		
Indoor/Outdoor	1		Snakes		
Money, play, homemade	X		Sponges, living		
Number games	4		Aquarium	1	
Numerals, tactile in variety of sizes and materials	20		Books dealing with science concepts	X	
Objects: any in environment to examine their properties, likenesses and differences	X		Eggs and incubator	4–6	
			Food and gardening: Use of food in science is essential to a child's experiencing the changes of state in matter.		
Peg boards, 12" x 12"	4		Children's cookbook	1	
Pegs, hardwood, 1/8" diameter, 2" long, box of 1,000	1		Containers: bottles, cartons, flower boxes, flower pots, jars, etc., supply accumulated	X	
Shapes, basic sets, tactile, unbreakable, variety of sizes and materials, supply accumulated	X		Cotton, box	1	
			Dirt box or dirt plot	1	
Sorting containers, unbreakable: baskets, boxes, cans, glasses	3		Fertilizer, lbs.	5	
Timers, buy or scrounge, as needed for curriculum:			Food: Natural foods, fruits, nuts, vegetables	X	
Calendars	2		Packaged mixes and processed foods, pkg.	4	
Clocks:			Raw ingredients: flour, salt, soda, spices, sugar, etc., in tightly covered containers, one for each item	X	
Alarm, hand-wound	1				
Electric, wall	1		Garden tools, child size: hoe, rake, spade, set	1	
Watch	1		Plants, cultivated and wild	X	
Weights, English and Metric:			Seeds, collected from nature and purchased, supply accumulated	X	
Bathroom scale	1		Stakes and string or wire fencing	X	
Kitchen scale	1		Terrarium	1	
			Watering cans or hoses	2	
XIV SCIENCE			Grow chart, height, weight	1	
Air experiments: (obtain as needed each year)			Light and heat:		
Balloons	6		Electricity: batteries, bulbs, buzzers, simple circuits, supply accumulated	X	
Bubble pipes	20				
Squeeze bottles, supply accumulated	X				
Straws	24				

Director's Resource 10–3 (continued)

SUGGESTED ITEMS	QUANTITIES A	B	SUGGESTED ITEMS	QUANTITIES A	B
Magnifying glasses, hand	2		cleaners, etc., supply accumulated	X	
Magnifying glasses on stand	1		Wheels	4	
Mirrors, unbreakable	2		Minerals: rocks, stones, etc.	X	
Prisms, assorted	2				
Liquids and supplies:			XV OFFICE SUPPLIES AND RECORD KEEPING		
Liquids:					
Ice	X		Bulletin board	1	
Oil, $1/2$ pt. can	1		Calendar	1	
Other liquids	X		Correction fluid for typewriter (bottle)	1	
Supplies:			Diskettes for computer	X	
Containers, plastic, supply			Diskette tray	1	
accumulated	X		Fax machine (access to)	1	
Kettle	1		File cabinet	1	
Medicine dropper	2		Index cards	X	
Paper:			Key organizer	1	
Blotting, odds and ends	X		Manila envelopes, 2 sizes	36	
Filter, pkg.	1		Manila folders	36	
Sponges	2		Marking pens, several colors	4	
Sprayer	1		Message pads	10	
Squeeze bottles, supply accumulated	X		Microcomputer	1	
Squirt bottles, for spraying, supply			Paper clips, 2 sizes, boxes	2	
accumulated	X		Paper hole puncher	1	
Mechanics and physics:			Pencils, boxes	6	
Inclined planes	1		Pens (boxes)	5	
Magnets, variety of shapes and sizes,			Photocopier (access to)	1	
and things to try to pick up	2		Rubber bands, assorted sizes, boxes	4	
Picture collection: animals, plants,			Scissors	2	
geography, astronomy,			Stationery, letterhead and plain, 2 sizes,		
machines, etc.	X		quire of each	10	
Siphon	1		Thumbtacks, boxes	8	
Soda bottles for experiments	X		Writing paper tablets, ruled and		
Take-apart equipment (donated): old			unruled, in several sizes	8	
clocks, typewriters, vacuum			Yardstick	1	

Director's Resource 10–3 (continued)

Suggested Educational Equipment and Materials for:

An Infant/Toddler Group
6–8 Children—Ages 0–3
Suggested Order of Acquistion

SUGGESTED ITEMS	QUANTITIES A	B	SUGGESTED ITEMS	QUANTITIES A	B
Diapers, disposable and unscented (if not provided by parents or if diaper service is not used), pkg. of 1 doz.	400		Furniture: stove, table, sink, cupboard, bed, baby carriage, high chair, shopping cart	4	
Dishwasher (See Basic Environmental Equipment)			Housekeeping: (child-sized) broom, dustpan, one each		2
Hamper for soiled clothes	1		Housekeeping: pots, pans, spoons and other kitchen utensils, multiethnic	4	
Smocks, infant	4		Playhouse, child-sized, dividers or low screen		1
Sprays:			Large muscle activity toys:		
Air freshener, cans	2		Balls, various sizes, 3", 6", 12", 20" diameter, rubber or plastic	4	
Disinfectant, cans	4		Blocks, large foam, plastic or cardboard	10	6
Towelettes, disposable, as needed	X		Pounding peg board and mallet	2	
Towels:			Pull toys, commercial or teacher-made	4	
Bath size	12		Push toys	4	
Fingertip size	18		Riding toys, propelled by arms or feet		3
Trash cans (See Basic Environmental Equipment)			Rocking horse		1
Washcloths	18		Throw toys: Bean bags, textured foam balls, yarn balls	4	
Washer and dryer (See Basic Environmental Equipment)			Wagon, small	1	
Wastebaskets (See Basic Environmental Equipment)			Sand play: (can be used with materials)		
			Cups, spoons, plastic bottles and other measuring devices	6	
IV GROSS MOTOR EQUIPMENT (Indoor/Outdoor)			Dump and fill containers: bowls, cans, pails, measuring cups and spoons, sieve, funnel, scoop, sand shovel	10	
Apparatus:			Indoor sandbox or table approximately 24" x 24" x 5", filled with sand	1	
Boxes of various sizes for climbing	5				
Crawl-throughs: oil drum, lined barrels, cardboard tubing, perception box	1		Outdoor sandbox with cover	1	
Indoor stair and slide combination	1		Umbrella or other shade	1	
Pads to place under climbing and sliding apparatus	2		Water play:		
Rocking boat	1		Container: plastic bathtub, dishpan or water table	1	
Tumbling mat	1		Dump and fill containers: bowls, cans, bottles, pails, watering cans, pitchers	10	
Wading pool		1	Manipulative materials: corks, floating tub toys, soap, sponge, sprinkler bottle, lotion dispenser, bottle, funnels	X	X
Walking boards—planks slightly raised at one or both ends	1	1			
Dramatic play:			Vinyl sheet to place under water container	1	
Dishes, soft, unbreakable	12				
Dolls, soft, unbreakable, washable, multiethnic, with Velcro® clothes	4				
Foods, unbreakable plastic, multiethnic	2				

Director's Resource 10–3 (continued)

SUGGESTED ITEMS	QUANTITIES A	B	SUGGESTED ITEMS	QUANTITIES A	B
V MANIPULATIVES			Poke boxes (shallow boxes with hand holes on lid through which infant can touch variety of textures)	1	1
Infant:			Texture ball (cloth ball covered with textures such as velvet, fur, cotton, sandpaper, etc.)	1	1
Clutch balls, large with finger holds in soft materials	2		Texture glove made from a variety of materials, to be worn by an adult		1
Infant gyms, floor model	2		Wall hangings, textured and touchable	1	1
Rattles, securely enclosed, pleasing to the ear, including measuring spoons on a ring, spools in a box, sound makers contrived from juice cans and large plastic beads	4		Warm and cold materials: hot cereal, ice cubes, etc.	X	X
Squeeze toys, soft washable	4		Visual materials:		
Teething toys, durable	6	4	Color paddles, set		1
Toys to wear:			Mirrors, unbreakable, hand held	2	
Bell bracelets, securely made with a strip of elastic and a small bell	4		Mobiles, brightly colored	2	1
Colorful wrist and ankle bands	4		Pictures, laminated or covered with clear contact paper, multiethnic	X	X
Foot sock with a smiling face	4				
Toddler:			VII COGNITIVE		
Beads, jumbo, plastic, set	1		Aquarium with fish		1
Duplos®, set	1		Bird feeding shelf		1
Peg board, giant plastic, set	1		Blocks, unit set of foam or plastic	1	
Pop-up toys	2		Books on numbers		2
Mazes, commercial beads on wire tracks	1	1	Coffee cans, empty, with clothes pins to be clipped on the rim	4	
Vehicles, plastic	2	2	Counting cubes and disks, large enough not to be swallowed	100	
			Floating and sinking objects	6	
VI SENSORY PERCEPTION			Form boards	2	1
Listening materials:			Gear turning toys, wood or plastic	2	
Bell blocks, wood, with bell inside each block, set of five	1		Hardware fixture board with workable parts: hinges, door bolts, knockers, knobs, etc.	1	
Bell bracelets	6		Locks and attached keys, large	2	
Chimes, wind		2	Magnetic board and accessories	1	
Mobiles, musical		2	Magnifier on tripod		1
Music boxes, pull-a-cord or wind-up	1	1	Nature objects: autumn leaves, snow, flowers, fruits, nuts	X	X
Paper to rattle and tear	X	X	Nesting toys, commercial and teacher-made	4	2
Records and tapes, children's music, classical, multiethnic, bilingual	X	X	Number puzzles	X	
Smelling materials:			Number sorters		2
Fresh flowers	X	X	Nuts and bolts, large, wood or plastic, set	1	
Spices, sealed, in plastic bottles with perforated lids, set	1		Plants, living, non-toxic	X	X
Tasting materials:			Puzzles, variety, some with handled pieces	6	6
Foods, new and familiar in identical containers, for identification games	X	X	Shells and rocks, wide assortment, set of 8–10	1	
Foods for tasting: fruits, vegetables, breadstuffs, cereals	X	X	Stacking toys, commercial and teacher-made	4	2
Touching and feeling materials:					
Cuddle toys, animals, dolls	5	2			
Flannel covering for babies' bottles to encourage feeling while feeding		3			

Director's Resource 10–3 (continued)

SUGGESTED ITEMS	QUANTITIES A	B	SUGGESTED ITEMS	QUANTITIES A	B
Sorting toys, commercial and teacher-made	4	2	Play dough for modeling (cooked and uncooked recipes)	X	X
Terrarium with plant and amphibian life		1	Poster paint: red, yellow, blue, white, black, brown, quart each	1	1
VIII CREATIVE			Soap suds, colored, made with vegetable coloring	X	X
Music			Natural objects: flowers, plants, rocks, shells, wood	X	X
Autoharp		1	Paper:		
Bells, melody, hand and wrist, set	1		Assorted colors for mounting display materials, pkg.	4	4
Chimes, set	1		Assorted sizes, shapes and colors	X	X
Instruments: multiethnic			Computer print-out, recycled	X	X
Drums			Magazines, recycled	X	X
Bongo	2		Newsprint, pkg. of 100 sheets	3	3
Handcrafted drums, such as coffee can with plastic lid or innertube top, oatmeal box with lid glued on	4		Wallpaper, samples	X	X
Maracas	2		Movement and pretend play		
Rhythm sticks, pair	2		Dramatic play props (See Gross Motor Equipment)		
Tambourines	2		Hats, washable	X	X
Xylophone	1		Scarves and ribbons, as movement props	X	X
Record player	1		Telephones	2	
Songbooks:					
Nursery rhymes	1		IX COMMUNICATION		
Traditional, multiethnic selections	2	1	Books:		
Tape recorders, adult and child	2		Cloth and paper, with squeeze and feel pictures, various sizes and shapes	10	2
Tapes and records: multiethnic			Nursery rhyme books	2	
Blank cassettes	2	2	Story, to read to children, plus access to library books, include multiethnic	10	10
Musical: listening, activity	4	2	Discussion pictures about foods, health, safety, science, social learning, everyday objects, some laminated	X	X
Narrative: talking stories and poems	4	2			
Sounds: animals, city noises, farm noises	1		Feel box (use small box with child hand-size hole, fill with objects child can feel, take out, talk about and put back)	1	
Art			Flannel board	1	
Accessories:			Flannel board accessories: animals, numerals, letters, geometric shapes, multiethnic people	18	6
Brushes, large for water painting and painting with color	5		Language games involving identifying, sorting, matching	4	
Crayon holders	2		Puppetry, familiar figures:		
Easel	1		Hand puppets, multiethnic	4	
Smocks (use old shirts worn backwards or aprons)	X	X	Homemade puppets, stick, sack, cloth	4	
Tray, plastic for finger painting	2		Screen or stage behind which puppets can operate	1	1
Illustrations of pleasing line, form, color, such as designs on wallpaper samples, gift wrap, wall decorations mounted fabrics, calendar photographs and drawings	X	X			
Media:					
Chalk, soft, white for chalkboard or paper, white, chubby sticks, box	1				
Crayons, large assorted colors, box	2	2			
Markers, washable, non-toxic, assorted colors including multiethnic skin tones, box	2	2			

Director's Resource 10–3 (continued)

SUGGESTED ITEMS	QUANTITIES		SUGGESTED ITEMS	QUANTITIES	
	A	B		A	B
X RECORD KEEPING			File cards, 6" x 4" or to fit available		
Attendance record sheets, weekly	52		file drawers, pkg. of 100	5	
Booklets, to record children's			Health and general information		
verbalizations	8		reporting sheets	X	X
Budgeting record book	1		Portfolios of children's work	12	
Card file for anecdotal records	1		Progress reporting sheets on specific		
Daily "communication with parent"			behaviors	12	
forms	250		Teacher planning book	1	

Director's Resource 10–3 (continued)

Suggested Order of Acquistion
An Infant/Toddler Group

Essential Items—A			Extensions—B		
	QUANTITIES			QUANTITIES	
SUGGESTED ITEMS	A	B	SUGGESTED ITEMS	A	B
I BASIC ENVIRONMENTAL EQUIPMENT			Serving cart	1	
			Shelves:		
Box, wooden or plastic on rollers with handles		1	High, closed for toys and supplies not in use	1	
Bulletin boards, staff and parent	2		Low, open, for children's toys and supplies	2	
Cabinet, closed and locking for storing adult supplies out of children's reach, such as first aid or cleaning supplies	1		Storage bins on rollers for outdoor toys	1	
			Tables:		
Carpet or other resilient floor covering	X		Changing table at adult height	1	
Chairs:			Adult height for food preparation	1	
Adult-sized:			Child height	2	
Comfortable	1		Toilet facilities:		
Rocking	2		Dressing table	1	
Child-sized:			Sink, tub, or plastic tub for bathing	2	
High	3		Lavatories	2	
Rocking	1		Toilet seat	1	
Stackable	6		Training chairs	3	
Clock, wall hung	1		Tote tubs for play materials	6	4
Clothes rack for drying clothes		1	Trash cans, covered	2	
Cots or mats for resting	4		Vacuum cleaner	1	
Cribs, one per infant	X		Washer and dryer	1	
Cubbies or tubs for personal belongings	8		Wastebaskets, covered	3	
Cushions, washable, plastic	4	1	Window coverings as needed	X	
Dishwasher	1		Work station on wheels, for adults	1	
Electrical outlet covers, as needed	X				
Feeding and play table	1		II HOUSEKEEPING EQUIPMENT AND SUPPLIES		
File cabinet	1		Brooms:		
Front pack, for carrying young infant	1	1	Adult size, straight & push, one each	2	
Hamper for soiled clothes (See Health Materials)			Child size, straight	2	
Infant bounce seat (floor model, not mobile)	1		Brushes:		
			Bottle	2	2
Infant stroller	1	1	Counter	1	
Infant swing	2		Hand	2	
Microwave oven		1	Cleaners, scouring powders, cans	3	
Mirror, unbreakable:			Dishpan	2	
Horizontally mounted at floor level	1		Dishtowels	6	3
Vertically mounted at child's eye level	1		Dishwasher (See Basic Environmental Equipment)		
Photocopier, access to	X		Disinfectants, bottles, replace as needed	X	X
Playpen or similar structure to allow young infants protection from and visual access to older infants and toddlers	1		Dustcloths, replace as needed	X	X
			Dust mop	2	
			Hand held portable vacuum	1	
Portacrib	2		Heating and serving dishes	4	2
Refrigerator	1		Soap, liquid hand and dishwasher, as needed	X	X
Safety gate	1		Sponges	3	
Screens, low sturdy folding panels for use as area dividers	2		Towels, paper, case of 3,000	2	

Director's Resource 10–3 (continued)

SUGGESTED ITEMS	QUANTITIES A	B	SUGGESTED ITEMS	QUANTITIES A	B
Trays	4		Tweezers	1	
Vacuum cleaner (See Basic Environmental Equipment)			Food service:		
			Bibs, disposable dental, used with clips	300	
Washer and dryer (See Basic Environmental Equipment)			Bottles, spare:		
			4 ounce	2	
Wastebaskets (See Basic Environmental Equipment)			8 ounce	2	
			Bowls, plates, cups, glasses, unbreakable sets	12	
III HEALTH AND SAFETY MATERIALS			Flatware:		
First aid and toilet supplies:			Forks, juvenile	6	
Bandages, adhesive, boxes	2		Knives, juvenile	2	
Butterfly bandages, boxes	1		Paper cups	200	
Calamine lotion	1		Paper napkins, packages of 100	5	
Cotton, sterilized, boxes	2		Place settings, adult	6	
Cotton tip swabs, boxes	4		Spoons, juvenile	12	
Eye bath	1		Spoons, serving	4	
Gauze, sterilized, boxes	2		Toddler trainer cup, two handled	4	
Gauze, sterilized, pads	2		Resting facilities:		
Gloves, disposable	X		Blankets	12	
Ice pack	2		Cots (See Basic Environmental Equipment)		
Lotion, nonallergenic	3		Cribs (See Basic Environmental Equipment)		
Medicine dropper	1				
Nonallergenic adhesive tape, rolls	2		Mattress pads, assorted sizes	18	
Paper towels, package	25		Sheets:		
Petroleum jelly	3		Cotton, assorted sizes, patterns and colors	18	
Powder, talcum, cans	8				
Ointment, antiseptic	1		Rubber, assorted sizes	12	
Red Cross first aid manual	1		Sanitation:		
Rubbing alcohol	1		Diaper changing pads, vinyl	6	
Scissors	1		Diaper changing paper rolls, hygienic	X	
Soap, antiseptic	3				
Temperature strips	X				
Tissue:					
Facial	18				
Toilet	25				

CHAPTER 11

Staffing the Center

The basic tools used in developing plans and procedures for hiring the child care center staff are written personnel policies and job descriptions. On the surface, these documents and procedures appear to be easily drawn and delineated; at a more subtle level, they reflect the philosophy of the overall program as it focuses on individuals and their worth as human beings. As policies and procedures are adjusted and changed, they will reflect the ability of responsible administrators in the organization to make optimum use of available human resources.

An analysis of each center's purposes and manner of operating will determine the broad policy areas to be covered in the personnel policies. The center that employs large numbers of professional and ancillary staff may have policies with separate sections for each category of employees and other personnel including substitutes, resource teachers, and other support staff. In all cases, every policy statement should contain an affirmative action section that verifies the center's intent to adhere strictly to acceptance of all personnel regardless of race, age, sex, creed, national origin, sexual preference, or disability.[1]

DESIGNING PERSONNEL POLICIES

The following section discusses in detail the many components that make up a center's personnel policy.

Purpose

The need of the personnel for security and confidence in their daily job performance should be balanced with the center's need to function effectively in the establishment of carefully conceived personnel policies. When staff members are unsure about their rights and responsibilities, some may tend to probe and test to determine where the limits lie. The dissension among staff members that ensues drains energy from child care. On the other hand, the staff members who know what is expected of them can recognize how their assigned roles fit into the overall organizational structure, and can, therefore, function more comfortably in those roles. Administrators also can function more assuredly when there is little doubt

---

[1]For information regarding employment discrimination and affirmative action issues and questions, contact: Public Information Unit, Equal Employment Opportunity Commission (EEOC), 1801 L Street, N.W., Washington, D.C. 20507 (202-663-4700, 800-669-3362 (publications only), 800-669-4000 (connects to caller's state office).

about policies because questions can be handled by referring to policies rather than by involving individual personalities. When the rights and responsibilities of each staff member are understood by the entire staff, friction is eliminated and negotiations can be conducted between members.

Inclusive personnel policies tailored to a specific child care operation, whether it is staffed by few or by many, serve two purposes. First, they reduce procedural errors and free administrators from unnecessary involvement in resolution. Second, they reduce anxiety by helping each staff member to understand expectations and move, independently *and* as part of the team, toward efficient operation of the program.

DIRECTOR'S CORNER

"During my new staff orientation program, I sit down with each new employee and read through the Personnel Policies, leaving time for questions and discussion. I give special attention to the section on holidays, sick days, personal days, and vacation time. It helps me feel comfortable that this new staff person has at least looked at the Personnel Policies once, and not just put the document in a file or on her night table to read later when she has more time."

—Director, private not-for-profit center

A written statement of the personnel policies and procedures should be given to each employee at the beginning of the term of employment. These policies will set the parameters within which the total staff will function. There may be situations in which a new employee may require time on the job before fully understanding all that is written in the policy statement; nonetheless, distribution of the written policy to everyone is a tacit statement on the part of administrators that communication is open, and that there are no secret or hidden agreements or rules at any level in the staff hierarchy. The administrator should make a point of checking periodically with employees to ascertain whether or not the policies are understood. Although these policies must be tailored to the needs of each program, the samples in Director's Resources on page 247 will serve as a guideline for their preparation.

Source

Since the task of writing personnel policies is complex and the sphere of their influence is extensive, the decision about who writes them requires careful consideration. They must be precise, well-written, inclusive, and take into account the best interests of staff, children, and families. The interest of the sponsoring group, whether it be to make a profit or not, deserves consideration as well. For example, a one-year probationary period for a new teacher may be agreeable to a sponsoring agency and provide good protection for a new staff member, but it could turn out to be devastating for the children if a newly-hired individual clearly demonstrates a lack of skills in the classroom. In turn, the reputation and income of the sponsoring group could suffer. Therefore, those who are responsible for writing the policies must have both an understanding of the scope of the program and insight into the vested interests of all involved.

Depending on the size and the organizational structure of a center, the personnel policies might be prepared by the hired director of a community-sponsored center, an owner of a proprietary center, a personnel director of a center sponsored by an industry, or of a national child care chain. Existing public school personnel policies for teachers or, in some cases, for civil service employees, will often be applicable in public school-sponsored programs.

The more usual practice in child care settings is to have policies drawn by a subcommittee or a standing personnel committee of the policy-making board. The bylaws, as drawn up by the policy board, should contain the mechanism for creating a personnel committee and detail the manner in which the membership of that committee will be selected. The center director should serve on the committee and represent the staff's interest. Other members of the committee might be parents, people from the community, and representatives of licensing and/or certifying groups who would, in each case, represent a special-interest group. See Chapter 6 for the establishment of a policy board, standing committees, and so on.

Inclusions

In general, personnel policies cover all matters relating to employment, and include job responsibilities, tables of organization, schedules of reimbursement for services, evaluation and grievance procedures, and description of the steps necessary to change the policies themselves. They must conform to union requirements, where applicable, and to all regulations which apply to employment practices. For example, as of July, 1992, employers with 25 (this number is 15 as of July, 1994) employees or more, must comply with the Americans with Disabilities Act which covers nondiscrimination practices related to recruitment, advertising, tenure, layoff, leave, fringe benefits, and all other employment related activities.[2] Since many of these elements are included in the personnel policies, it is important to understand the implications of the ADA for you and your staff to ensure compliance with these regulations, as well as protection for your program. Personnel policies spell out specifically the rights of employees and what they may expect from the employer; therefore, they should include the following items.

Career Ladder.   Developing the career ladder for a center is a challenge to the director and/or the board. Each center must develop its own version of a career ladder after reviewing the roles and responsibilities of each staff position, budget limitations, and the professional goals of the center. The career ladder clearly defines education and experience as well as corresponding salaries and benefits for every step in the hierarchy.[3]

Contract.   The contract is usually a bilateral agreement, signed by both parties, that mutually binds the employee and the employer to acquire certain rights from each other. In this case, the employee agrees to provide a service (as defined by the appropriate job description) and the employer agrees to reimburse the employee for the service at a given rate for a specific length of time. Those employers who have an "at-will" policy do not use employment contracts. The samples shown in Figures 11–1 and 11–2 show forms that include some of the alternative features of a contract.

Employment at Will.   Employment at will is operative in most states unless you have contracted with an employee and your contract says something other than that the employee is an employee at will. When the personnel policies state that employees are employees at will, it means either the employer or the employee may terminate the employment relationship for any reason or without reason. The sample Personnel Policies in Director's Resource on page 247 provides exact wording for those who choose to use the employment at will provision. But that being the case, it is important to use caution in wording the Staff Handbook so nothing in that document can be viewed by the court as a contract. Since employment law is changing all over the country and regulations vary state by state, it is wise to consult an attorney on these employment-related questions and issues.

Job Description.   The job description is a detailed outline of what is expected from the person who fills a specific job opening including director, head teacher, teacher assistant, cook, custodian, and so on. Job descriptions are discussed in greater detail later in this chapter.

Salary Ranges.   Salary range for each position on the career ladder should be indicated clearly. Salary will then be based on the training, experience, and years of service that the person brings to the particular position. Details about overtime pay, merit pay, raises, vacation pay, pay for holidays, sick leave, or professional days should be detailed under salary and salary range.

Each state may have its own laws regulating minimum wage and overtime pay, but all state regulations must be compatible with the federal Fair Labor Standards Act (FLSA). There is considerable controversy over whether or not child care staff are covered by the FLSA. The Child Care Law Center can provide information on the current status of the issues around how the FLSA affects child care employees in different states.[4]

Staff and Fringe Benefits.   Staff and fringe benefits available to employees must be clearly stated in the personnel policies. Retirement plans, health insurance, educational opportunities for

[2]*The Americans with disabilities act: Questions and answers*, U.S. Equal Employment Opportunity Commission, July 1991, p.1.
[3]Bloom, P. J., Sheerer M., & Butz, J. (1991). *Blueprint for action.* Distributed by Gryphon House, Inc., pp. 135–142 for a detailed discussion of career ladders.
[4]Child Care Law Center, 22 Second Street, 5th Floor, San Francisco, CA 94105.

```
Employee's Name _____

Employee's Position _____

From _____  to _____
        (appropriate date)              (appropriate date)


The Mountview Child Development Center Board agrees to the following:
(1)  Salary $ _____ per _____
(2)  Proportional benefits including Blue Cross/Blue Shield, retirement
     benefits as described in Personnel Policies for this position, sick
     leave as described in Personnel Policies, provide up to $75.00 per
     year for additional training and/or education (at the discretion of
     the Director).

The Employee agrees to the following:
(1)  Fulfill the responsibilities of the job based on the Job Description
     for this position.
(2)  Give at least two weeks notice if a change in employment is anticipated.




                        _____
                        Director - Mountview Child Development Center


                        _____
                        Board Chairman - Mountview Child Development
                                        Center


                        _____
                        Employee's Signature

Date _____
```

Figure 11–1   Mountview Child Development Center Employment Contract

12 Park Place -- telephone 231-7642

Date _____

Dear Ms. Smith,

After interviewing several candidates for the teacher position at
our nursery school, it is the decision of the Personnel Committee that
you meet the qualifications for the position. Therefore, you are invited to become a staff member at the Park Lutheran Church Nursery School
for the year beginning September, _____, and ending _____.

Your beginning salary has been set at $_____, subject to
annual increases in accordance with the Personnel Policy. Your working hours will be from _____ to _____ Monday through Friday,,
subject to exceptions in accordance with the Personnel Policies.

If these terms are to your satisfaction, and if you have read the
Personnel Policies and agree to abide by the terms therein, please sign
and date both copies of this agreement and return them to us. One copy
will be sent back to you after our signature has been added.

Sincerely,

Albert J. Jones, Chairperson
Personnel Committee

Accepted _____   Date _____
         Director

         _____   Date _____
         Chairperson - Personnel Committee

Approved _____   Date _____
         Ms. Jeanne Smith - Teacher

Figure 11–2   Park Lutheran Church Nursery School Employment Contract

personal or professional staff-development, re-duced tuition for family members, Social Security, Workmen's Compensation, liability coverage while working in the center with children, and any other items that might be covered under staff and fringe benefits should be included.

Health and Safety Measures.   A health ex-amination for all staff members is required in most centers. In many localities, the law requires the health examination of center administrators who are viewed as being ultimately responsible for the health and safety of the children in the cen-ter. Those who work with children should be free of any infectious disease, whether or not there is a local certifying or licensing group responsible for monitoring health regulations. It is also recom-mended that child care staff be advised to update their immunizations because intimate contacts with children puts them at risk for contracting a variety of infectious diseases. Furthermore, since the work is often physically demanding, the ex-amination protects members of the staff by explor-ing their health limitations and reminding them to follow basic healthful practices such as getting ad-equate rest and proper food.

Child abuse and other child safety issues are a major concern among child care professionals. Therefore, there is an increasing trend to seek ways to certify that employees do not use drugs and have no criminal record. Some states and/or government-funded programs require that pros-pective staff be screened for one or more of these. Employers with more than 15 employees must comply with the 1992 ADA when dealing with em-ployment issues. Employers must avoid job related discrimination based on an employees' disability, but ". . . may prohibit use, or working under the influence of, alcohol or illegal drugs as well as smoking in the workplace."[5] The problem of AIDS is causing concern as well. In some states, this dis-ease is treated as a disability, and employers may not ask candidates about it on applications or dur-ing the prehiring process. The sample form in Figure 11–3 which covers the criminal record issue will serve as a guide for obtaining information from staff members as well as job candidates about some sensitive areas of inquiry. If there are ques-

tions about the legality of making inquiries of this nature, contact the Equal Employment Opportunity Commission (EEOC) or seek legal counsel.

Personnel policies should state clearly that professional staff must submit certified copies of credentials, and that personal and professional references furnished by all new employees will be contacted before job offers are made.

Daily Hours and Employment Period.   The daily schedule and the total employment period should be stated in the personnel policies. Careful scheduling of personnel is critical for effective and efficient operation of all centers. This schedule should be stated in the personnel policies and reit-erated in each contract or letter of employment, if these are used. Daily hours will not exactly coin-cide with the hours the children are present in the center, nor will they be the same for each staff member. Obviously, some staff members must ar-rive before children do, to prepare the learning en-vironment. Furthermore, large child care centers will need extra staff to cover peak hours. For ex-ample, if school-aged children come to the center before and after school or for lunch, the staffing needs will be increased during those hours. A key staff member must be present late in the day to chat with people who pick up the children near closing time. When all children have gone, the center must be in order for the early arrivals on the following day; therefore, some of the staff must stay beyond the time that all children leave.

The complexity of the staffing plan and the format used to lay out the plan in an understand-able way will vary. The major consideration is to set it up so it provides sufficient coverage to meet the licensing requirements, where applicable, guarantee safety of children, and adequate staff to maintain high standards of quality throughout each day. In planning the staffing patterns, direc-tors must keep in mind the concerns about child abuse in child care centers and take prevention precautions. Schedule at least two caregivers to be present at all times, particularly early and late in the day, and during nap and toileting routines. This will not only protect children, but also staff should one member be unjustly accused of abuse.[6] The sample staffing plans in Director's Resources

[5]*Young children*. National Association for the Education of Young Children. July 1992, p. 19.
[6]*Child Care Information Exchange: The Directors' Magazine*, 60, March 1988, p. 11.

For use by Head Start Agencies to comply with 45 CRF Part 1301, Subpart D, Head Start Grants Administration, Personnel Policies, Section 1301.31(c) and (d).

Name of Prospective Employee:_____

Federal policies now require that Head Start agencies require all prospective employees to sign a declaration prior to employment which lists:

1. All pending and prior criminal arrests and charges related to child sexual abuse and their disposition;
2. Convictions related to other forms of child abuse and/or neglect; and
3. All convictions of violent felonies.

The declarations may exclude:

- Any offense, other than any offense related to child abuse and/or child sexual abuse or violent felonies committed before the prospective employee's 18th birthday, which was finally adjudicated in a juvenile court or under a youth offender law;
- Any conviction for which the record has been expunged under Federal or State law; and
- Any conviction set aside under the Federal youth Corrections Act or similar State Authority.

Note that individuals who declare, through this form, that they have been arrested, charged with or convicted of any of the offenses listed above are not automatically disqualified from being hired. Head Start agencies must review each case to assess the relevance of an arrest, charge or conviction to a hiring decision.

Please provide your signature on the appropriate category below:

I *have not been* arrested, charged and/or convicted on one or more of the three types of offenses listed above.

_____   _____
Signature   Date

OR

I *have been* arrested, charged and/or convicted on one or more of the three types of offenses listed above.

If so, please attach information listing the offense(s), the date(s) of the arrest, charge and/or conviction, and other relevant information.

_____   _____
Signature   Date

IMPORTANT:
Each Head Start agency must take necessary steps to assure the confidentiality of this form.

Figure 11–3   Sample Declaration Form for Prospective Employees in Head Start Programs

11–4, 11–5, and 11–6 on pages 279, 280, and 281, respectively, will serve as guidelines for setting up staffing patterns in single program centers (infant programs) and in multiple program centers. Use of graphing, listing by staff member, listing by room, or listing by program are a few of the ways to record a staffing pattern so it is clear to those who are interested in it including staff, board members, licensing agents, and especially parents.

In addition to information on staffing plans, the policy statement should also indicate methods for obtaining tenure if that is a possibility within the system.

Relief Periods. A planned system of daily relief periods should be stated. The policy on rest periods may be flexible or carefully scheduled, but in either case, the policy should be clearly stated and include the designated space where staff may take breaks. Staff must know that it is acceptable to need to be away from the children for a time each day, and that it is acceptable to go to the bathroom now and then, although some administrators fail to provide that option. In half-day nursery schools, it is rare to find a set policy on rest periods due to the short time span of concentrated effort required by staff members. On the other hand, in child care programs in which a teacher may work an eight- or nine-hour day that includes having lunch with children, it is essential to provide time to rest and be away from the children. Some centers prefer to have some staff members work a split shift to provide time for rest, shopping, or study at midday. This serves to reduce costs at a time of low need.

Vacations, Holidays, and Sick Leave. A statement on vacations and holidays should appear in the personnel policies. Specific details about lead time for vacation applications, and the length and timing of vacations is advisable for larger, year-round centers. But smaller centers in session only during the typical school year may not require the same specificity in their policy. However, both large and small centers observe certain holidays. These holidays will vary depending on the religious and ethnic orientation of the staff and/or the children served, the agency with which the school is affiliated (church, public school, and so on), and the community mores. All employees should know exactly which holidays will be observed by closing the center.

Sick days and personal days, maternity leave and child-rearing leave for either parent, and special leave days for jury duty or voting should be included in the personnel policies. It is also wise to cover details like unused leave days, the necessity for documenting illness, and policies around closing due to bad weather. Some employers allow "earned time" over and above holidays, and each employee decides how and when to take that time. This flexible earned time plan may make it difficult for a director who must find substitutes and it could be detrimental to the well-being of the children. A variation on this plan is to give one Friday or Monday off each month to each staff person, thereby guaranteeing one long weekend a month. Staff members decide when they want their long weekend, and in a large center, the director can hire a regular substitute to work every Monday and Friday which gives greater continuity to the program for the children.

The center's plan for hiring substitutes for each staff position during vacation periods, special holidays, and sick days must be clearly spelled out. The policy should state that all health, safety and training qualifications for staff also apply to substitutes. Maintaining a substitute file which includes all the necessary personnel information and payroll paperwork on available persons will make it easier to find substitutes on short notice. A plan for hiring substitutes avoids confusion when emergencies occur and also facilitates budget planning for these special needs.

Meeting Schedules. Scheduled staff meetings, parent meetings, and board meetings should be listed in the personnel policies. Most programs, regardless of size, have a series of meetings at various levels to gather individuals together to discuss plans and mutual concerns. In some cases, only selected personnel are expected to attend meetings. The personnel policies should state which meetings each employee is expected to attend and the frequency of such meetings, as well as those meetings that are open to any interested staff member. Whether or not there will be reimbursement or comp-time for attending meetings outside the working day should be made clear.

Probationary Periods. Many programs include probationary periods after initial employment to allow an adjustment period for both adults and children in the program. A director may be appointed on an "acting" basis for as long as a year. The time period must be long enough for the new employee to demonstrate competency in a given position but not so long that valuable aspects of the program can be undermined by an incompetent individual.

Teacher competency can be validated in a three- to six-month period by an experienced director who operates under a clearly defined philosophy of education, and evaluates with an experienced eye. Since the teacher works directly with the children, and any incompetence could have direct detrimental effects on them, the probationary period for teachers should be carefully delineated and clearly understood at the time of employment. This practice protects the welfare of the children and is more equitable for the teachers in the long run because they come into a new role with a clear understanding of the time allowed for initial review and evaluation.

Evaluation and Grievance Procedures. Evaluative review of personnel should be scheduled on a regular basis. Evaluation and grievance procedures are included in the personnel policies (see Figure 11–4). These procedures should be made available to all center personnel. Ideally, they will include details about who evaluates whom, when the periodic evaluation will take place, what techniques or instruments will be used in the evaluation, who makes the decision on whether or not the criteria are met, and what the consequences are of not meeting the stated criteria.

Not meeting stated criteria could mean no recommendation for a raise, no opportunity for advancing to a higher level position, or termination. When there are other actions that could cause dismissal such as use of corporal punishment, these should be in writing. In some situations there may be no recourse once a decision to deny a raise or to terminate an employee has been made. Although that may seem unfair, it is better to state it at the outset than to deal with all the negative feeling generated by the decision when an employee is unaware that there is no way to appeal it.

Evaluation Forms. Staff members are entitled to know evaluation procedures as well as evaluation criteria. Therefore, evaluation forms for all staff positions should be part of personnel poli-

cies. Teaching staff is usually evaluated by the director who, in turn, may be evaluated by the Personnel Committee of the board, or by the Personnel Director in cases where centers are part of a larger organization. Other support staff may be reviewed and evaluated by the director or by other designated staff. The Sample Teacher Evaluation Form in the Director's Resource on page 289 provides a prototype for other evaluation forms needed. Although there may be some overlap in areas covered by the evaluation forms such as physical and mental health, ability to work well with other adults, and personal attributes such as enthusiasm or a sense of humor, some are unique to a given position. For example, the cook must be able to manage time well in order to have meals ready for serving at a given hour whereas a teacher must adjust the daily schedule based on the changing needs of children. Knowledge of evaluation criteria helps build a sense of trust and partnership between staff to be evaluated and the evaluator who is either the director or another staff member. See Chapter 15 for more information on evaluation.

Organizational Chart. An organizational chart that is part of the personnel policies and is made available to all members of the staff can clarify lines of communication and responsibility for everyone in the center. For a newcomer, even a very simple organizational pattern may be difficult to see unless it is presented in a diagram or flow chart. Figure 11–5 shows two sample organizational charts. An organizational chart enables an employee to determine how each position meshes with other positions in the center. This information, coupled with complete job descriptions, evaluation procedures and forms, and open staff communication leaves little doubt about expectations, areas of responsibility, and who will be the evaluator for each position.

Amending and Changing the Policies. The personnel policies should contain a section that details the procedure for amending the policies. The amending procedure presumably parallels the one that was used initially for developing the policies and that is stated in the bylaws, but the policy-making body may now be expanded to include staff members or parents who were not available during the initial stages of development. As the

EVALUATION AND GRIEVANCE PROCEDURES

1. Frequency of Evaluation
   Performance evaluations will be made twice during the probationary period for every new staff member -- at the midpoint and the end of the probationary period -- and annually thereafter. It is the responsibility of the Personnel Committee to evaluate the work of the Director and the responsibility of the Director to evaluate all members of the staff. All evaluations will be shared with the employee and then become part of the employee's file.

2. Purpose of Evaluation
   The primary purpose of the annual evaluation is to create a mutual understanding between the Director and each member of the staff of what is expected and how they both view the best way to move toward fulfilling those expectations.

   Annual evaluations will be used as a basis for continued employment, horizontal or vertical movement on the career ladder, salary increments in cases where the job description allows for merit raises, and demotion or dismissal.

3. Basis for the Evaluation
   Staff members will be evaluated on knowledge of the job as described in the job description, quality of skill demonstrated in fulfilling the job, interest and initiative, dependability, personal and professional growth, attendance and punctuality, and ability to work effectively in cooperation with other staff members.

   Evaluation forms for each staff position in the Center are included in these Personnel Policies.

4. Evaluation Procedure
   Each staff member will be notified as to when his/her evaluation will take place. The evaluation will be discussed with the staff member, at which time the staff member will be given the opportunity to express his/her disagreement or agreement with the evaluation. The outcome of this discussion will become part of the staff member's record.

5. Review of Grievances
   The staff member who wishes to present a grievance must present it first to the Director. Failing to reach settlement with the Director, the staff member may submit to the Chairperson of the Personnel Committee a written statement of the situation, requesting that the grievance be reviewed by the Personnel Committee. The Personnel Committee will review the grievance and report with recommendations to the Board of Directors for action.

Figure 11–4   Townville Child Development Center (a United Way Agency) Evaluation and Grievance Procedures

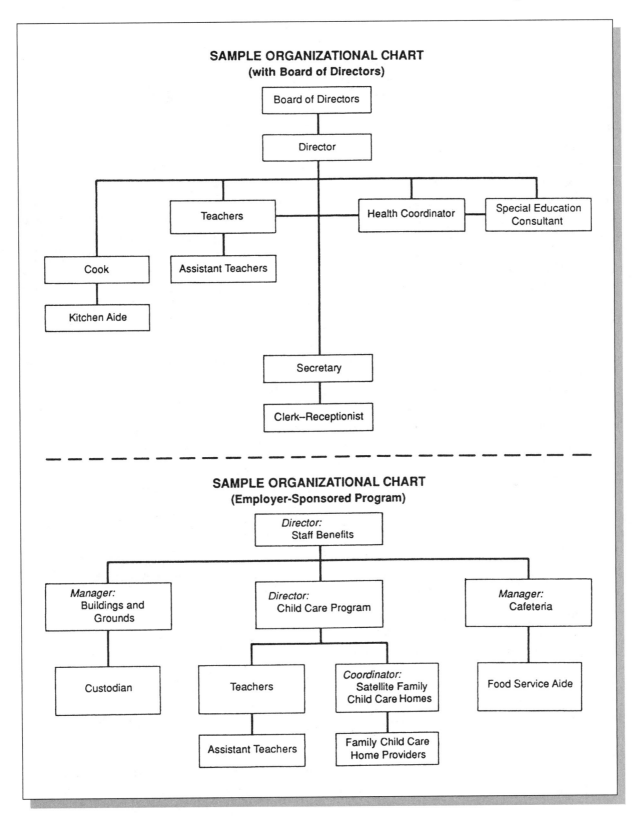

Figure 11–5   Sample Organizational Charts

center undergoes its regular evaluation period, the personnel policies should also be checked to determine whether or not changes are needed. The board can then follow the amendment procedures when it becomes necessary to make changes. Once a change has been adopted, the board's duty is to inform all personnel of the changes and the director is charged with implementing the new policy.

Clearly, small private centers will not use all the preceding items in their personnel policies; however, large, complex organizations will undoubtedly include all of these and more. Policies must be drawn and shaped to the unique needs of each center, and they must be constantly evaluated and changed to meet the ever-changing and growing needs of the program for which they are written.

DRAWING UP JOB DESCRIPTIONS

One mechanism for reducing conflict and uncertainty for staff members is to provide a clear definition of the role of each member on staff. Each role requires a thorough description so that no matter who fills the role, the same basic job will be done. The description must be written to clarify expectations, yet retain the personal freedom of all staff members to follow through in the performance of their roles according to their own unique style. Well-written job descriptions provide a framework within which an individual can function creatively while performing the tasks required for the program. Detailed descriptions of required knowledge, skills, and physical abilities are important because subsequent performance evaluations are based on the job description. Sample job descriptions included in the Personnel Policies and others that are not provide guidelines for writing descriptions for various staff positions including full-time and part-time professionals and support staff for both agency-sponsored and proprietary child care centers, as well as public school preschools. Job descriptions usually cover at least the following:

- job title
- person to whom responsible
- people for whom responsible
- qualifications (education, experience, personal health, physical abilities, and so forth)

- duties and responsibilities
- salary schedule
- work schedule

Job descriptions should be reviewed on a regular basis to determine whether changes are necessary. Such periodic review is useful because you will have to deal with changing rules or regulations governing practices such as the recent ADA and adjust the policies as role expectations at different levels shift and change when new personnel bring changing talents and skills to a staff. For example, menu planning and shopping may be part of a director's job description, but a new cook who has been trained to plan meals may take over those functions. Job descriptions for both the director and the cook can be adjusted accordingly, allowing staff members to perform at their highest creative level.

Reflections

Think of yourself as a new teacher and remember the uncertainty and accompanying anxiety you felt when you did not have a clear understanding of what was expected of you. How did you feel when you were unsure about who was to set up the snack or who was to straighten up the storage room? How did you manage when you were not sure about who to call when you knew you would be late because you had missed the bus? How did you react to criticism when you did not put all the blocks on the shelf while another adult had the children outside and you had not been informed that you should do that? Can you remember how energy-draining these experiences were and how they interfered with your creative work with children? A carefully written job description for your position might have helped you have a clearer understanding of your role.

Initial writing of job descriptions is only the first step in an ongoing process. This process requires expertise in using information from the program evaluation, and an ability to adjust to changing and growing strengths of personnel in order to make efficient use of available talent for a more effective program. Individual staff members might assist in updating job descriptions, and with input from the director, these might become part of the evaluation and review process.

Recruiting

Once the job descriptions have been written, the major hiring procedure begins. In fact, in many large centers or in programs with a board, the first task assigned to a new director is to initiate staff-recruitment procedures. Each center should establish and follow some general procedures regarding advertising, interviewing, and selecting employees to use during initial hiring in a new center, and in filling vacant staff positions for an ongoing program.

Advertising for new staff is usually the director's responsibility. However, in some public schools and in corporate settings, the personnel office may set up school district or company advertisements that cover available positions throughout the organization. If the center program is ongoing, the director should notify cur-

rent staff members, board members, and parents about job openings as they become available. People in the organization may choose to apply for the new job or they may know qualified individuals who would like to apply. For employees to learn of openings in their own center from an outside source is disconcerting and it exemplifies poor communication within the center.

Affirmative action statements must be included when advertising for center personnel. Advertising should appear in a range of publications to make the information available to diverse segments of the population. Figure 11–6 shows examples of advertisements. Local professional organizations that publish classified ads in their newsletters are good places to advertise for classroom staff, as are high schools, colleges, or universities that have child care training programs. Ads also may be placed in national professional journals if there is sufficient time to meet publication deadlines and to wait until the circulation date. Some colleges and vocational high schools maintain placement services, and some hold placement

---

Sample Classified Advertisement for the *Waynesburg Chronicle*

Teacher Assistant in a Child Care Center. Responsibilities include assisting the classroom teacher in the planning and implementation of the daily program for children, assisting in the family involvement aspect of the program and taking responsibility for some designated record keeping. Must have an Associate Degree in Early Childhood Education or equivalent. Experience preferred. Job available immediately. Send written resume to P.O. Box 320, Waynesburg, Iowa 36103. Our employees know about this opening. We are an Equal Opportunity Employer.

Sample Classified Advertisement for the Local Association for the Education of Young Children Newsletter

Director wanted for the Community Head Start Center. Responsibilities include hiring and supervision of entire staff for a program serving 75 children, record keeping, proposal writing, working with Center staff, Community Action agency, parents, and other community agencies. Applicant must have a Master's Degree in Early Childhood Education with some training in at least one of the following: social work, special education, administration. Three years administration

experience required—Head Start teaching experience preferred. Send resume to Community Head Start Center, 352 Ninth St., Sioux City, Iowa. Deadline for applications, July 1. We are an Equal Opportunity Employer.

Sample Classified Advertisement for *The New York Times*

Nursery School Teacher wanted for suburban church-affiliated nursery school. Responsibilities include planning and implementing an age-appropriate developmental type nursery school program for a group of 15 three- and four-year-old children. Bachelor's Degree required—nursery school teacher experience preferred. Write for application to Ms. D. L. Jones, Director, Upper Plains Christian Church, 130 Meadows Place, Upper Plains, New York 11112, or call (713) 431-6037 Monday through Thursday from 1:00 to 3:00 P.M. We are an Equal Opportunity Employer.

Sample Classified Advertisement for the *Parkville Times*

Cook wanted for child care center at outskirts of town. Responsibilities include preparing snacks and lunch for 65 preschool children, cleaning kitchen appliances and cupboards, and making weekly shopping list. Experience preferred. Please send resume to, P.O. Box 932, Parkville, VA 23221. Equal Opportunity Employer.

Figure 11–6   Sample Advertisements

conferences so that employers can interview applicants. Notices of job openings can also be posted on community bulletin boards and in community papers that reach special segments of the population such as the African-American or Native American community, or non-English speaking groups.

The classified section of newspapers is frequently used for advertising, but the result may be large numbers of unqualified applicants who then must be screened before interviewing can begin. Nevertheless, when a position must be filled quickly, advertising in both small community weekly newspapers and large city daily newspapers is helpful because information is quickly disseminated to large numbers of people.

Personnel ads should include enough information to minimize the number of applications from completely unqualified persons but should not be so narrowly written that qualified persons fail to apply. If you are expected to write the advertising copy, you must be completely familiar with all the qualifications that are essential for performance of the job. Careful review of the job description is a good way to become familiar with the desired qualifications for potential candidates. Each advertisement should include the job title, a brief job description, the essential qualifications required, the method of applying (telephone, letter, application blank), and the name of the person to contact with a telephone number and/or address. Starting date, working hours, starting pay, fringe benefits, and goals of the organization may also be included.

Advertisements that clearly state all nonnegotiable items will eliminate practically all unqualified applicants. On the other hand, negotiable items stated equivocally tend to attract a more diverse pool of candidates from which to choose. For example, "experience necessary" is much more restrictive than "experience preferred." If experience is a nonnegotiable qualification, then say, "experience necessary." However, if the position could be filled by a person with good training and a variety of life experiences that may or may not have been with children, then say "experience preferred." The latter phrase appeals to a broader population and will increase the number of applicants.

The director should be cautious about luring people into the field by presenting a glowing picture of life in a child care center. Hiring staff members under false pretenses can quickly lead to job dissatisfaction. Rapid staff turnover disrupts program continuity and is hard on the families and children who must constantly establish new relationships. Therefore, an advertisement that lists the required job qualifications in specific and realistic terms increases the probability of getting the best match between applicants and available positions, and reduces turnover.

Careful consideration must be given to the best method for receiving applications. If the need is urgent and immediate, it may be necessary to accept applications by telephone. This option means that a new employee can be found quickly because an interview can be scheduled moments after the ad appears; but it also means that current staff members may have to spend hours on the telephone that detracts from their work with the children, and puts them in the position of answering questions from people who are not seriously interested in the job.

Listing a post office box number in an ad places fewer demands on the director and the staff because potential candidates do not know the identity of the center and are unable to call. On the other hand, qualified people may decide not to apply if they are unsure of the source of the ad. Others may feel that they could be applying to the center in which they work, another reason for notifying all employees of every opening. In fact, occasionally ads read, "Our employees know about this advertisement."

Allowing applicants to apply in person can be very inconvenient and is inappropriate for some positions. Unless the center has its own personnel director, or one that is affiliated with a sponsoring agency such as public school, having applicants appear at the door during the hours in which children are present is awkward. However, this problem can be handled by setting specific hours during which interviews may be scheduled. In neighborhoods where many people do not have telephones, and where letter-writing is difficult for some adults, it may be appropriate to have people apply in person. If the job does not entail making written reports such as in the case of a cook or a housekeeper, then the ability to communicate effectively in writing may not be a criterion for selection and there is no need to see a resume or written application. On the other hand, in the case of a teacher, teacher assistant, or special education resource teacher, writing skills are important. For these positions, a written response to an advertisement provides helpful data for initial screening of applicants, and should be made mandatory before an interview is scheduled.

The advertiser will also have to decide whether to have the candidates request an application form or send a resume. If a secretary is available to answer requests for application blanks, the process can be speeded up. If the director will be distracted from work by recording the name and address of applicants and mailing out applications, it is wiser to have candidates mail in resumes and fill in a formal application when they are interviewed. The application forms in Figures 11–7 and 11–8 show how applications are adjusted depending on availability of a resume from the applicant.

When all the applications have been collected, they must be screened to eliminate obvious unsuitable candidates. If no suitable candidates have applied, and attempts to recruit staff from other centers has failed, the advertising and application process is reopened. The director or the chairperson of the personnel committee usually screens the applications for those that meet the job requirements, particularly in the areas of education, health, or experience, and then interviews can be arranged. Interviewers should not be burdened with candidates who have no qualifications for the job. Therefore, the careful writing of the ads to interested qualified candidates and the initial screening process to eliminate totally unqualified candidates are both important steps in the recruiting process.

Applications that are received from people who are not subsequently called for an interview should be retained so that affirmative action procedures can be completed where that is a requirement. A record must be kept listing the reasons why any applicant was not interviewed, and they should receive written notification that they will not be interviewed. Applicants who are called for an interview should be advised to bring identification to prove citizenship. A candidate who is not a United States citizen will be required to prove eligibility to work in this country. In order to be in compliance with the Immigration Reform and Control Act of 1986, every person hired must complete Form I-9, available from the Immigration and Naturalization Service (INS). A copy of Form I-9 can be found in Director's Resource 11–10 on page 243.

Interviewing

Interviewing is essential, and should not be eliminated no matter how urgent the need for obtaining a staff member may seem. Even though a candidate can make an excellent impression during an interview, then turn out to be an ineffective staff member, interviewing will provide insights that cannot be gleaned from written applications or resumes, and will facilitate judicious hiring decisions in the majority of cases. The relative amount of time spent interviewing can be extremely profitable when compared with the amount of time that might otherwise be spent solving personnel problems because a poor candidate was hastily selected. The person or group responsible for staffing the center must decide who will interview the candidates and develop the plan for the interview.

Interviewers. While applications are being collected and screened, decisions must be made about who will interview the viable candidates. In a very small program, the director may take full responsibility for all interviewing or may do it with the help of one or more of the following:

- staff person
- member of the board
- community person
- other professional (social worker, special educator, physician, school principal)
- people responsible to the new employee

In most programs, the interviews are conducted by committees, often by the personnel committee.

The composition of the interview committee may be previously established by the board, as in the case of the personnel committee; or the committee can be set up by the director to pertain

SAMPLE APPLICATION FORM

(Suggested for use when no resume is on file)

Application for Employment

Jewish Community Nursery School -- Fairmount, Pennsylvania

Name of Applicant _____
                   Last   First   Middle or Maiden

Address _____ Zip _____

Telephone _____Social Security No._____

Birthdate_____

Citizenship: USA_____   Other_____

RECORD OF EDUCATION

School	Name and Address of School	Years Attended		Check Last Year Completed	List Diploma or Degree
		From	To		
High				1 2 3 4	
College				1 2 3 4	
Other (Specify)				1 2 3 4	

Figure 11–7   Sample Application Form (no resume)

List below all present and past employment, beginning with your most recent

Name and Address of Employer	From		To		Describe in detail the work you did	Weekly Starting Salary	Weekly Last Salary	Reason for Leaving	Name of Supervisor
	Mo.	Yr.	Mo.	Yr.					

List all professional and community organizations with which you are affiliated. (Indicate if you hold office in the organization)

_____

_____

Write your educational philosophy.

What do you feel most qualifies you for this position?

What are your professional goals?

List names and addresses of three references.

1.

2.

3.

Figure 11–7   (continued)

```
              SAMPLE APPLICATION FORM

     (Suggested for use when a resume  is available)

              Application for Position

              University Day Care Center

          Ogden University, Ogden City, Michigan


Name of Applicant_____
                   Last         First        Middle or Maiden

Address  _____

         _____Telephone_____

Birthdate _____Social Security No._____

Title of position for which you are applying._____

What do you feel best qualifies you for this position?_____

_____

_____

Would you be willing to continue your education by taking

college courses or in-service training if recommended to do

that?

_____

_____

What satisfaction do you expect to receive from this position?

_____

_____

List three references (Preferably one former employer, one

former teacher and one community person).

1.

2.

3.
```

Figure 11–8   Sample Application Form (resume on file)

specifically to the job being filled. For example, when there is an opening for a teacher, the committee might be composed of the director, a teacher, and a parent. Community people could be included as well as people from other professions such as community health or special education. There might be more than one person from a given category, but if the committee is too large, its effectiveness will diminish. It can be difficult for large numbers of people to interview a given candidate at one time, and the procedure can be very threatening for the candidate. Nonetheless, it is best if the committee is representative of the center staff with whom the person will work, of the families who use the center, and of the people who represent the sponsoring agency if all who have a vested interest in the position to be filled are to be represented.

Although the committee make-up may vary, depending on the type of center and on the position to be filled, both the committee members and the candidates must be aware that the organizational structure of the center takes precedence in making hiring decisions. For example, if a janitor is being hired, it may be appropriate to have the teachers express a preference for the candidate who would be most able to meet their needs for classroom maintenance. However, if the person who becomes janitor is going to be responsible to the center director, then the director's opinion must weigh heavily in the final hiring decision.

A major exception to this hiring and interviewing procedure is in public school-sponsored programs where hiring is based on established school district policies. Public school union contracts often dictate hiring policies and procedures. In most cases, the personnel office will handle advertising, interviewing, and hiring. Involving teachers or parents in the process is unlikely. This could result in a team that will have to spend time building a workable partnership and working through possible philosophical differences.

Preparation for the Interview. Just as candidates should come to the interview prepared to express their strengths, weaknesses, goals, expectations, and past experiences, so the interviewers

should be prepared for each interview. Their questions should reflect a thorough knowledge of the center, its program, its staff, and the clients served by the program. Interviewers should be familiar with the information in the candidate's resume, application form, and reference letters, and they should look for evidence of warmth, good-natured calmness, and ease of relating to others. As Greenberg notes, it is important to select caregivers who have "the right stuff" to start with because "you can teach people to conform to certain schedules, perform specific acts, use assorted tips and techniques—but you cannot develop an entirely different character, personality, and self-esteem in a staff person."[7] An interview is conducted most productively when all parties are well-prepared and when the environment has been set up for a meaningful dialogue between interviewers and interviewee.

Interviewer Information. Each interviewer should be totally familiar with the job description for the vacant position, and should have copies of the candidate's application and references. A letter or questionnaire that has been prepared in advance for submission to all listed references will provide comparable data for all candidates and make it easier for reference people to respond. If reference letters are not received promptly, the candidate may be asked to contact the reference person, and sometimes it is necessary to proceed with interviewing before information has been received from all references. Although it is important to have written information from the candidate's references, a follow-up call to discuss the written responses can provide valuable information (see sample reference letter in Figure 11–9).

Interview Plan. Interviewers must plan the type of interview they will conduct. Sometimes, a predetermined list of questions is developed so that all candidates will respond to the same questions. This procedure provides uniform data but is somewhat inflexible and may not elicit the most useful data from each candidate. At other times, questions are developed as the interview progresses. This spontaneous procedure is more likely to give rise to potentially constructive data

[7]Greenberg, P. (1990). *Character development: Encouraging self-esteem and self-discipline in infants, toddlers and two-year olds*, NAEYC, p. 5.

TO: Mr. L. N. Davidson
      University Court - Rm 416
      Midtown University
      Midtown, KY   35231

FROM: Mr. John Wilkins, Director
      Midtown Child Development Center
      414 Main Street
      Midtown, KY   35213

_____ has given us your name as
a reference. We are interested in having any information from you about this
applicant which will help us in hiring the best person available for an
assistant teacher position on our staff. Your cooperation is greatly appreciated.

In your opinion, what is this applicant's ability in each of the following
areas?

Working with other staff members

Working with young children

Working with families from the inner city

Capacity for personal and professional growth

Ability to evaluate self

In what capacity did you know this applicant?

How long have you known this applicant?

Comments:

                                        Signature _____

                                        Title   _____

                                        Date   _____

Figure 11–9   Sample Reference Letter

but requires more skill on the part of the interviewers.

The person who develops the questions should keep in mind the parameters of the job description and understand the requirements of Title VII of the 1964 Civil Rights Act and the ADA. There must be a "business necessity" for all questions asked during the interview. Questions to avoid include ". . . date of birth or age, marital status, spouse's occupation, pregnancy issues and number of children, child-care arrangements, religious affiliation, membership in organizations (except pertaining to the position) . . . union memberships and disabilities."[8] The first question should be open-ended and require more than a simple yes or no answer. Furthermore, it should focus on previous jobs, education, hobbies, or any other subject matter with which the candidate is familiar. This technique puts the candidate at ease and creates an environment for more focused probing later in the interview. For example, the interviewer might say, "I see in your resume that you have worked for Head Start in California. What were the aspects of that job that you liked best?" Or, "I see you studied at Wheelock in Boston. Tell us about that program." From these questions, it is possible to cull out material that can be examined at greater depth. "You said you enjoyed working with the Parent Policy Committee in California. What did you do with that group that you see as applicable to this job?"

Interviewers can learn a great deal about the ways in which a teacher candidate would fit into their center's program by posing hypothetical situations and asking questions such as, "What would you do if a child kicked you?" Or, "How would you work with a toddler who is not yet talking?" This type of question can produce ideas about curriculum, classroom management, parent involvement, staff relations, and understanding of the development of young children. Certainly, the questions should relate to the job for which the person is applying. For example, a prospective cook might be asked, "What would you do if sandwiches were on today's menu and the bread delivery had not been made by 10:00 A.M.?" A list of sample questions in Director's Resource 11–3 on page 263 can give you some ideas for questioning both degreed and nondegreed job candidates.

Interview Setting.   Before the interview, careful thought must be given to the setting. Will the candidate be as comfortable as possible? Will everyone be able to see and hear everyone else? Is the seating arrangement comfortable and planned so that desks or large tables do not separate the candidate from the interviewers? Is the interviewing room free of distractions? Has the time of the interview been appropriately chosen so that everyone can focus on the interview rather than on the next appointment? Is adequate time available for developing rapport and exploring details of the answers to the questions? Has provision been made to offer water or some refreshments to the candidate? When the goal is to make applicants feel welcome and at ease, the interview setting becomes a matter of central concern. Indeed, the interviewers are revealing to the candidate a major part of the center philosophy as they create an accepting environment for an interview, and are more likely to obtain an accurate picture when the candidate is at ease.

Reflections

Can you recall your first job interview? If so, you may be able to remember some of your reactions during that interview. Were you put at ease when you entered the room? Were you introduced to everyone before the questioning began? Did you feel the interviewers had prepared for the session by reviewing your resume and credentials? Were you given time to ask questions? How did they close the interview? As you think about being interviewed and recall the stress you experienced, you will increase your sensitivity to an applicant's feelings.

The director sets the nonverbal tone for the interview by being relaxed and friendly. It is important to sit back, smile, and maintain an open posture with arms down in the lap and body facing the candidate.

[8]Decker C. A., & Decker, J. R. (1997). *Planning and administering early childhood programs,* Merrill/Prentice-Hall, p. 107.

The Interview.   At the beginning of the interview, candidates should be given some idea about its length and should be informed that there will be a time at the end to ask questions. Interviewers should be prepared to present information about the program's philosophy, the job, and the center and should clearly and honestly answer the applicant's questions. The interviewers should maintain eye contact and let the applicant do most of the talking. They should refer to the personnel policies and clarify thoroughly the expectations that are held regarding performance standards for the position.

The interviewers should look for an applicant who plans to stay with the center for a number of years because staff stability provides continuity for children and nurtures a sense of community at the center. Nonetheless, caution should be used about requesting any information in sensitive areas such as those mentioned earlier. It is recommended that employment records be limited to that information relevant to employment decisions, and that disclosures of that information to third parties be strictly limited where not authorized by the candidate or employee. It is advisable that child care centers develop a written policy and procedure concerning this issue. Also, since federal law provides only a portion of the employment discrimination picture, and many states have their own discrimination laws, it is wise to consult an attorney regarding applicable state laws for your center.[9]

Interviewers should obtain as much information as possible during the interview, but note-taking or discussing the candidate's qualifications should be done after the interview. Some discussion about the candidate within the groups is useful, and reaching a consensus serves a worthwhile purpose. Discussion provides the opportunity for interviewers to share their impression of the candidate as they draw on each other's perceptions. Confidentiality is a critical issue, and all committee members must understand that information on candidates and any committee discussion must be kept confidential.

Teaching Interview.   Observing a teacher or assistant teacher candidate in a classroom setting provides the committee with additional data on classroom presence and skills with children. Some candidates are able to give you all you want to hear in an interview, but when you observe them with children, it becomes obvious that they are not comfortable with children. It is unfair to have the regular classroom teacher leave a new person alone in the classroom because of the anxiety that would be produced in both the candidate and the children, but a great deal can be learned by observing a prospective teacher read a story to a few children or join a small group for snacks. Asking to see sample lesson plans, resource files, or picture files also provides useful information to the interview committee. Some centers select candidates from the substitute list in which case the center staff will have worked with the candidate before the interview.

SELECTING THE EMPLOYEE

When interviewing is completed, the person or committee responsible for selecting the employee uses material such as the personnel policies and the job description, combined with all the information from the interview and the observation, to reach a final decision. All data are weighed and balanced until the best match among job description, current staff composition, and candidate qualifications is obtained. It is also important to review the nondiscrimination prohibitions in this decision-making process, especially if you have an applicant with a disability. An employer is not required to give preference to a qualified applicant with a disability over other applicants, but may not consider the disabled candidate unqualified if that person can perform the "essential functions" of the job.[10] It may be helpful to have a second interview with selected candidates from the pool who seem best qualified for the position in order to further narrow the choice. The procedure for making a decision should be clear to all interviewers. Will the director ultimately choose the employee? Will the director present two or three names to the board and have the board make the decision? Will the board make the decision or will the committee rule by majority vote? Generally,

[9]Consult an attorney or contact EEOC if you are uncertain about what may be asked in an interview.
[10]Ibid. *The Americans with disabilities act: Questions and answers,* pp. 2, 3.

the director will make the decision, taking into account the recommendations of the interviewing committee. Final approval from the board is sometimes part of the hiring policy.

The selected candidate should be notified of the job offer by the director or the chairperson of the committee. On acceptance, the new employee may be asked to sign a contract stating the salary and the length of time covered by the contract, provided the Personnel Policies do not state that all employees are employees at will (see the sample contracts in Figures 11–1 and 11–2). The job description is usually referred to in the written contract. Both the employer and the employee retain copies of this document. Immediately after the new employee has been informed of the job and has accepted it, all other interviewees are informed of the selection, thanked for their interest, and told that their resumes will be kept on file if another vacancy should occur.

ORIENTING THE EMPLOYEE

The director is responsible for introducing the new employee to the work environment. The new person will need to know where to find work space, what storage facilities and materials are available, and what schedule is to be followed. A tour of the building and introductions to all other staff members, either during the tour or at a staff meeting shortly thereafter, are essential to the orientation procedure. The person who conducts the tour and makes the introductions sets the tone for the employee's future interpersonal relationships with the other staff members. Each staff member has an obligation to become involved with making the new employee's transition to the staff position as smooth and satisfying as possible.

The new employee also should be introduced to the parents at the earliest possible time. Some directors notify parents of staff additions or changes by mail; others use their bulletin boards or newsletters; still others introduce the new member informally as the occasion arises or at a regularly scheduled meeting.

During the initial weeks of employment, it is important for the director to check with the new

staff member to answer any questions and make a conscious effort to build a positive relationship. At the same time, the director can continue to reiterate expectations and expand on ways to follow and implement the program philosophy. A carefully planned staff orientation program can promote better staff relationships and reduce staff turnover.

DIRECTOR'S CORNER

"We do a five day orientation for each new staff person before we finalize the hiring process. The prospective employee is paid for those hours of classroom participation, meetings with me, joint reading of Do's and Don'ts in the classroom, etc. It's well worth the time and money, and has helped us make good hiring decisions."
—Director, private not-for-profit center

Sometimes, it is difficult for the director to be available to the new teacher often enough. It can be helpful to establish a mentor program or assign a staff member to watch over the new staff person. Mentors can help new staff with basic orientation questions like where to find and file various forms, as well as introduce them to all staff including support persons like the van driver and the custodian. Mentors also can provide information about the special capabilities of other staff such as planning effective group times, general planning and carrying out smooth transitions, or making challenging math games. A mentoring system assists the director with orientation of new staff and enriches and enhances the self-esteem of the mentor.[11]

It also helps if the director leaves a note in the teacher's box asking questions like, "What went well today?" or "What did I miss today in your room that you would like to share with me?" The director also might leave a message about being available the next day at nap time, or a plan to stop in before lunch to see how things are going. These steps help make the new teacher feel that the director really is available to give support and help.

Some directors prepare handbooks and provide a copy for each employee. In corporate cen-

---

[11]*Child Care Information Exchange: The Director's Magazine*, 102, March/April 1995, p. 66.

ters, the parent firm may prepare a handbook for use in all centers, whether franchised or run by the corporation. Guidelines in this handbook may even detail how many children should be permitted in blocks or dramatic play at any given time, or exactly how the daily cleaning is to be done by the classroom teachers. However, handbooks are rarely that detailed. More often, they include items like:

- philosophy of the center
- bylaws of the board (if applicable)
- personnel policies
- policies and procedures for the children's program
- copies of forms used by the center
- information about the community the center serves
- information about the staff (job titles, home addresses, telephone numbers, and so forth)

A handbook is useful because it gives everyone a common reference point and provides new employees with materials that familiarize them with the center.

Reflections

Perhaps you can recall your first day as a new student or an employee in a child care center. How did you feel on that first day? What else do you wish you had known about the center or the program? Do you recall what it was like not to know where the extra paper towels were kept or how awkward it was when you could not find the easel paper? As you recall those feelings, consider what you would tell a new teacher in your center if you were responsible for orienting the new employees.

SUMMARY

The staffing process in a child care center is based on the personnel policies and job descriptions that define the staffing requirement to operate the center's program. Decisions about the content of advertisements, interview questions and procedures, and final hiring should be based on specific job requirements that are detailed in the job descriptions. Interviewing may be done individually or in a group, and should be a time for two-way communication between the candidates and the representatives of all aspects of the center's programs. Questioning should focus on the requirements of the position and the candidate's potential for fulfilling those requirements. The purpose of the entire process is to provide the employer with the information necessary for selecting the best available person for each staff position.

Working Paper 11–1

Job Description

Write the qualifications for a cook in a Head Start center. Write an advertisement for the position of cook.

Cook

Schedule: Monday through Friday—7:30 a.m. to 3:30 p.m.

Responsible to the Head Start Director.

Responsible for:
1. Safe preparation of all food (breakfast, lunch, and snacks).
2. Requisition appropriate amounts of foodstuffs based on designated menus.
3. Check food deliveries against orders.
4. Store foods appropriately, before preparation, in refrigerator, freezer, bins, cupboards, etc.
5. Prepare all foods using methods that maintain food value and freshness.
6. Follow menus, recipes, or other directives furnished by Head start nutrition consultant.
7. Record amounts of food used daily and maintain an inventory of staples on hand.
8. Wash and sterilize dishes and all utensils according to sanitarian's directions.
9. Clean appliances and storage areas according to a designated schedule.
10. Supervise assistant cook.

Qualifications:

Working Paper 11–2

Interview Summary

Candidate Qualifications for Infant/Toddler Assistant Teacher

Education:

Experience with children:

Other relevant experience:

Ability to express ideas verbally:

Congruence of philosophy to that of the center:

General appearance:

Evidence of ability to work as part of the teaching team:

Other comments:

Director's Resource 11–1

Sample Application Form

Application for Employment

Jewish Community Nursery School -- Fairmount, Pennsylvania

Name of Applicant _____

Last   First   Middle or Maiden

Address _____ Zip _____

Telephone _____ Social Security No._____

Birthdate_____

Citizenship: USA_____   Other_____

RECORD OF EDUCATION

School	Name and Address of School	Years Attended		Check Last Year Completed	List Diploma or Degree
		From	To		
High				1 2 3 4	
College				1 2 3 4	
Other (Specify)				1 2 3 4	

Director's Resource 11–1 (continued)

List below all present and past employment, beginning with your most recent

Name and Address of Employer	From		To		Describe in detail the work you did	Weekly Starting Salary	Weekly Last Salary	Reason for Leaving	Name of Supervisor
	Mo.	Yr.	Mo.	Yr.					

List all professional and community organizations with which you are affiliated. (Indicate if you hold office in the organization)

_____

_____

Write your educational philosophy.

What do you feel most qualifies you for this position?

What are your professional goals?

List names and addresses of three references.

1.

2.

3.

Director's Resource 11–2

Sample Personnel Policy and Procedures—Roark Learning Centers

Roark Learning Center, Inc.* Personnel Policies, Benefits, and Job Descriptions

General Policies

I. INTRODUCTION

This employee handbook is presented for informational purposes only, and can be changed at any time by the company with or without notice. This handbook is not an employment contract, expressed or implied. Company employees are employees at will and either the employee or the company can terminate the employment relationship at any time, for any reason, or without reason. No supervisor, or any other representative or employee of the company, other than the Executive Director, has the authority to enter into an agreement (written or oral) with an employee that is contrary to the foregoing.

II. ADMINISTRATION OF PERSONNEL POLICIES

It is the responsibility of the Director and the Board of Roark Learning Center, Inc. to review and submit revisions of the Personnel Policies each year. Any additions to and/or deletions from the policies must be approved by the Board before going into effect.

III. EQUAL EMPLOYMENT OPPORTUNITY

Roark Learning Center, Inc. recognizes our employees as one of our greatest assets. We are committed to providing equal employment opportunities for all, without regard to race, color, religion, national origin, age, sex, disability, and/or sexual orientation.

These opportunities include, but are not limited to, recruitment, hiring, training and promotion, compensation, benefits, and all other terms and conditions of employment.

IV. COMPENSATION

Compensation is to be set for each employee according to agreement among the employee, Director, and the Board. Compensation will be based upon abilities, training, length of service, education, experience, and job responsibilities. Increases to compensation will be based on the performance, professional growth, responsibilities of the employee, the company's financial ability, and upon agreement between the Director and the Board.

Questions concerning your compensation or pay should be directed to your supervisor.

V. HOURS OF WORK

Teachers' hours will be set upon hiring. Schedules will change according to enrollment, and all teachers are required to sign in and out each day. No staff member will be guaranteed a specific shift. If a teacher should be late for any reason, he/she must call the center to notify staff as early as possible. Teachers are required to attend all staff meetings and expected to attend parents' meetings when scheduled, and any activities to improve parent–teacher relations. When staff meetings are scheduled after shift hours, staff will be compensated for this time.

*Reprinted by permission of Roark Learning Center, Inc.

Director's Resource 11–2 (continued)

VI. RECRUITMENT

Applications are always to be accepted and filed. The Center works with the University of Cincinnati and local vocational schools to provide placements for students in teacher training programs. When a position becomes available within the corporation, staff are notified and can be considered for the position if qualified.

VII. RESIGNATION

If you choose to resign from the Center, it is requested that you submit a written two-week notice.

VIII. PROFESSIONAL DEVELOPMENT

Regardless of their previous education or experience, employees will be expected to continue studies of and training in early childhood education practices in order to keep abreast of new developments in the field. This continued study and training may take place on the employee's own time outside of regular working hours, and as recommended by the Director. Methods employed may include, but are not limited to: in-service training classes at the Center, attendance at a recommended professional conference or meeting, membership in a professional organization and attendance at their monthly meetings, enrollment in pertinent courses offered by local colleges and universities.

A. *Child Development Training*

Each non-degree (ece) staff person must complete a minimum of 15 hours of child development training each year. Each degreed staff person must complete a total of six hours of training, four of which will be child development topics. These requirements may be waived by the Director if the staff person is taking a university credit course of one to three hours.

B. *City and State Requirements*

Within the first three months of employment each staff person must complete first aid, communicable diseases, and child abuse training to comply with city and state standards. This training for all staff will be paid for by the Center. Staff members must attend all training for which they are registered. If a staff member misses a training session, they must reimburse the Center for the cost of the training.

C. *Inservice Training*

Two days each year, typically on Good Friday and the Friday after Thanksgiving, the Center will be closed for inservice training. The inservice days will consist of training and individual time for planning, goal setting, etc. Every staff person must attend. If someone misses due to illness they must make this time up on a Saturday and replacement training will be at their own expense. This inservice must be made up within 30 days of it being offered/scheduled.

IX. SUPERVISION AND PROBLEM RESOLUTION

An Open Door philosophy is an essential part of maintaining open communications and a positive work environment. We are interested in knowing our employees' ideas, questions, suggestions, problems and concerns.

Director's Resource 11–2 (continued)

In most instances, your immediate supervisor is the person best qualified to solve a problem or answer a question and you are encouraged to communicate your concerns and suggestions to them.

However, there may be times when you wish to discuss a concern or problem with someone other than your immediate supervisor. You are encouraged to bring these matters to any other member of management.

Following is a listing of the reporting relationship within our organization:
- Board of Directors
- President of the Board
- Executive Director
- Director
- Assistant Director
- Educational Coordinator
- Head Teacher
- Assistant Teacher
- Teacher's Aide

X. DRESS CODE
All staff are encouraged to wear comfortable clothing. A professional appearance must be maintained at all times. The following should be observed:
- jeans should be in good condition
- no halter or tube tops
- good hygiene (clean hair, clothes, etc.)
- hiking shorts or sun dresses are appropriate summer wear

XI. CONFIDENTIALITY POLICY
Records of all children are confidential and only staff and referral agencies may have access. A file may not leave the Director's office without approval. A staff member may be dismissed for discussing children outside of the school, staff or referral agencies.

XII. CHILDREN AND CLOSING
It is the closing staff's responsibility to confirm that all children have been picked up before leaving the building. Two staff members must always be present when a child is in the Center. In the event that a child is not picked up at the closing of the Center, the remaining staff will follow these guidelines:
A. If attempts to reach parent at work and home are unsuccessful, call emergency contact number.
B. If attempts to contact emergency contacts are unsuccessful, contact the director immediately.
C. YOU ARE A PROFESSIONAL: AT NO TIME MAY YOU TRANSPORT A CHILD OR LEAVE A CHILD UNATTENDED.

Director's Resource 11–2 (continued)

XIII. CLASSROOM EXPENSES

The following conditions must be met for staff to receive reimbursement for any expenses for classroom activities:
- approval is granted by the Director or Assistant Director.
- a written receipt must be submitted.

XIV. NO SMOKING

In an effort to provide a healthy, comfortable, smoke-free environment for all of our employees and children, smoking in all of our facilities is prohibited.

XV. DRUGS AND ALCOHOL

The possession, sale, distribution or use of illegal drugs and the possession, sale, use or being under the apparent influence of alcohol or other intoxicants while on work time or on company property, is strictly prohibited.

XVI. PERSONAL PROPERTY

The center cannot assume responsibility for any staff member's personal property. It is encouraged that staff do not bring personal belongings to the Center.

XVII. TUITION PAYMENTS

Only management staff may accept tuition payments. No cash will remain on site.

Employee Benefits

I. VACATION

The eligibility for paid vacation is based on the status of employment and length of continuous service.

Upon hiring, each full-time (40 hour/week) employee will receive two vacation days to be used in their first year of employment. Upon hiring, each full-time employee will accrue one vacation day for every 52 days worked to be used in the following year. After one year of employment vacation days are accrued at one for every 37 days worked, also to be used in following years. Vacation days must be used each year or be forfeited. The following chart outlines how vacation days are accrued for full-time employees:

Period	Vacation Days
0–12 months	2 days
after 1st anniversary	5 days
after 2nd anniversary and on	7 days

Part-time employees are entitled to two vacation days per year after their first full year of service. Management personnel are entitled to vacation that will accrue at a rate of one day every 26 days worked.

Requests for vacation time must be approved in advance by the director, who will take into consideration the employees' length of service. No deductions from pay will be made for vacation or holiday closings.

Director's Resource 11–2 (continued)

II. HOLIDAYS

All employees are paid for the following holidays: New Year's Day, Memorial Day, July 4th, Labor Day, Thanksgiving, and Christmas Eve and Christmas Day, when these days fall on a regular work day (Monday through Friday).

III. PERSONAL DAYS

After 30 days of employment, each full-time (40 hours/week) employee will receive one personal day each month. These days will be scheduled by the Director or scheduled no more than three months before, and no less than one before. The Center reserves the right under special circumstances to reschedule personal days. These days are not accrued vacation, and none will be due to staff who resign or are terminated. A staff person may save up to three personal days per year to be used as vacation. They must be used within the same year.

IV. SICK DAYS

Upon hiring, each full-time (40 hours/week) staff person immediately receives two sick days, and will then start accruing sick days for their first year of employment. Sick days are accrued at a rate of one sick day for every 52 days worked, with a maximum of five sick days per year. These must be used within the calendar year as sick days or vacation days.

V. BREAKS

Breaks will be offered to staff if coverage of duties/responsibilities is available. Breaks may not be taken at the end of a schedule or accrued as vacation.

VI. OVERVIEW OF TIME OFF

Benefit	Full-time	Part-time
Vacation: First year	2	0
Vacation: Second year	5	2
Vacation: 3+ years	7	2
Personal days	12	0
Sick days	5	0
Holidays	7	7

VII. INSURANCE BENEFIT

All employees will be covered by Social Security, Workmen's Compensation, and State Unemployment. Each full-time (40 hours) employee will also receive a $35,000 life insurance policy. A single policy group health insurance program has been established that each full-time employee may take part in. After two months of employment, the Center will pay 100% of the health insurance premium for each full-time employee.

Maternity Leave/Medical Disability

An employee's position and benefits will remain in effect three months from the final day of work during a disability or maternity leave. Employees must have a disability statement from their physician in order to be eligible for disability leave.

Director's Resource 11–2 (continued)

The employee is responsible for covering the full cost of insurance benefits while on a personal leave of absence.

VIII. TUITION REDUCTION

Center employees may be granted a reduced tuition rate as follows:

All full-time employees: $^1/_3$ tuition reduction

Reduced tuition slots are limited based upon available accommodations and management's discretion.

IX. PERSONAL LEAVE

Unpaid personal leaves may be granted at the Director's discretion, based on the staffing needs of any center. Leaves in excess of 90 days during any 12-month period are not permitted. The employee is responsible for covering the full cost of insurance benefits while on a personal leave of absence.

Director's Resource 11–2 (continued)

Job Description
Director

PERSONNEL ADMINISTRATION
1. Insures the development and periodic review of a wage and administration program that insures similar remuneration for similar responsibility, education and experience.
2. Insures the adherence of agency personnel policies and practices.
3. Insures program compliance with federal, state, and local laws and regulations covering equal opportunity employment.

SUPERVISION
1. Develops supervisory standards for the program. Insures adherence to the standards.
2. Supervises directly the teachers and educational coordinator. Makes recommendations for salary adjustments, dismissals, and promotions for employees in the program.
3. Supervises the development of in-service training programs for the staff.

PUBLIC RELATIONS
1. Develops an atmosphere of support for the program within the geographic program area of the community.
2. Maintains liaison with community agencies, organization and ethnic groups.
3. Assists colleges and universities in teacher training and internship programs.
4. Acts as a resource person of other township, state and federal programs.
5. Makes speeches; writes articles; assists in the development of brochures and news releases.

GENERAL
1. Shapes the programs; leads; coordinates; makes decisions; develops and maintains a quality early childhood program.

REPORTING RELATIONSHIP
1. Reports to the Executive Director
2. The director will build the organizational chart to reflect the professional staff and size of the program she/he administers.

LIMITS OF AUTHORITY
1. Must have prior commitments
   a. to set program policy
   b. to set fiscal policy
   c. to add/delete programs
2. May take action but must inform
   a. when re-organizing the program's administrative structure
   b. when revising wage and salaries
   c. when terminating employees
   d. when hiring employees that are not consistent with the educational requirements

Director's Resource 11–2 (continued)

3. May take action without informing
   a. when insuring preparation of procedure statements and manual
   b. when insuring the development of the programs; staffing plans; licensing requirements
   c. when developing supervisory standards, supervising staff; insuring the development of in-service training programs
   d. when developing a public relations image for the agency; acting as a resource person; making speeches; writing articles
   e. when leading; coordinating; making decisions; developing and maintaining a quality agency

JOB REQUIREMENTS
1. Knowledge of children's physical, emotion and, developmental patterns
2. Knowledge of general learning theories and curriculum development, with an emphasis on Jean Piaget, Erik Erikson and the constructivist approach
3. Demonstrated ability to administer a program and budget
4. Demonstrated professional skills in the areas of curriculum planning; in-service training; program goal setting; federal, state and city funding sources; and establishing procedures for evaluating the progress of individual children
5. Demonstrated ability to discern when enrolled children may need special medical or psychological services
6. Demonstrated ability in accessing outside agencies for referral and consultation
7. Ability to delegate authority judiciously
8. Articulate in making prepared and extemporaneous talks
9. Evidence of emotional maturity and stability
10. Highly demonstrated personal integrity

EDUCATIONAL REQUIREMENTS
   A Master's or Bachelor's degree in Early Childhood Education; experience as a preschool teacher, preferably NAEYC accredited; experience supervising support staff and teaching assistants; knowledge in the field of budget management.

Job Description
Head Teacher—Infants

The person selected for this position will be responsible for the care and supervision of the three infants assigned to her/his pod. She/he is directly responsible for working closely with assistant infant teachers to ensure that continuity of care is maintained throughout the infant's entire day at the Center. However, because infant care requires that caregivers work as a team, she/he will also be responsible for aiding in the care and supervision of all the infants in the program.

QUALIFICATIONS
The person selected for this position must be at least 18 years of age and have a strong desire to work with children. This person must have a warm, nurturing, and friendly personality, be sensitive to the feelings and needs of others, be able to relate well with children and be willing to fulfill her/his responsibilities in accordance with the Center's philosophy. Because infant care requires a team approach, this person must have a mature attitude that allows her/him to communicate effectively, problem solve and anticipate the needs of her/his fellow workers. An educational background in early childhood is preferred.

RESPONSIBILITIES
The head teacher is responsible for:
1. Being the communications liaison between the Center and the parents. All pertinent information about the Center should be relayed through the head teacher and/or directly through the Program Coordinator or Director.
2. Implementing the infant's schedule in accordance with the parents established schedule.
3. Ensuring that assistant infant teacher is kept informed on a daily basis of any changes in the babies' schedules.
4. Reporting daily events, changes in schedule, feeding times, food amounts, infant's health and sleeping habits to the aides so that continuity of care is maintained. (This can best be accomplished through the completion of end-of-shift report form.)
5. Completion of Daily Report Sheet during the course of her shift. This includes writing a general note about the infant's day.
6. Completion of monthly planning sheet. (This will be completed with aid of Program Coordinator.)
7. Completion of weekly anecdotal record sheet.
8. Arranging and planning for an environment that best meets the individual infant's developmental needs. This includes planning art and sensory activities along with providing variety of toys and gross motor equipment. Toys and equipment should be rotated approximately every two weeks.
9. Directly overseeing assistant infant teachers. Your role in the classroom is to act as a role model to assistants, to interject. When inappropriate behavior may cause immediate harm, report to program coordinator or director inappropriate behaviors or general observations made about assistant. Your input is vital part of staff evaluation.

Director's Resource 11–2 (continued)

10. Completion of Infant Competency Profile Assessment Form. These should be completed preferably every three months, but at least every six months.
11. Holding Parent Conferences. These should be held in conjunction with completion of the assessment form. These conferences are established so that you and the parents can meet together to establish goals for their infants.
12. Contributing equally in the housekeeping tasks of the infant area.
13. Being a competent member of the infant care team. This entails maintaining open communication between fellow team members, contributing equally in daily routine tasks, and being aware of the overall needs of the infant program, and coming to lack others' aid as needed.
14. Attending all staff meetings, parent meetings, and other mandatory or required in-services.
15. Maintaining confidentiality of children, parents, and fellow staff members.
16. Dressing appropriately in accordance with the Center's established dress code policy.
17. Maintaining professional attitude and loyalty to the school at all times.
18. Lastly, you are responsible for knowing the policies of the program in regards to
    a. communicable disease and exclusion of sick children
    b. first aid and medical emergency
    c. fire evacuation
    d. tornado and severe weather evacuation
    e. child abuse reporting
    f. discipline
    g. termination

Director's Resource 11–2 (continued)

Job Description
Assistant Infant Teacher

The person selected for this position will be responsible for the care and supervision of the three infants assigned to his/her* pod. She is directly responsible for working with the head teacher of that pod in order to insure continuity of care for the infants. However, because infant care does require the caregivers to work as a team, she will also be responsible for aiding in the care and supervision of all the infants in the program.

QUALIFICATIONS

The person selected for this position must be at least 18 years of age and have a strong desire to work with children. This person must have a warm, nurturing, and friendly personality, be sensitive to the feelings and needs of others, be able to relate well with children, and be willing to fulfill her responsibilities in accordance with the Center's philosophy. She must be willing to be a working member of the team to ensure that the children are cared for in a warm, safe, and nurturing environment. Background in early childhood education or experience in working with infants is preferred.

RESPONSIBILITIES

1. You are expected to arrive at work at the scheduled time. If unable to come to work at the specified time, you are expected to contact your supervisor as soon as you know so that arrangements can be made for a substitute.
2. You are responsible for knowing the policies of the program in regards to:
   a. communicable disease and exclusion of sick children
   b. first aid and medical emergency
   c. fire evacuation
   d. tornado and severe weather evacuation
   e. child abuse reporting
   f. discipline
   g. termination
3. You are expected to dress appropriately in compliance with the Center's dress code policy.
4. You are responsible for signing in and out on a daily basis. The bookkeeper will only pay you for the hours for which you have signed in.
5. Upon arrival, at the beginning of your shift, you are expected to get a report on your children from the head teacher of your assigned pod. A sample of the report is included in the orientation manual.
6. You are responsible for aiding head teachers in the completion of their work, so they can leave on a timely basis.
7. You are expected to keep open communication between head teacher, parents, supervisor, director, and other team members.
8. You are responsible for equally aiding in the completion of the closing procedures. These include
   a. washing toys every day
   b. taking out garbage from infant area and activity room

Director's Resource 11–2 (continued)

c. vacuuming activity room
d. vacuuming pods if necessary
e. straightening pods and beds in pods
f. mopping activity room floor and infant floor if needed
g. straightening toy shelves in activity room
h. turning out lights
i. turning off heaters/fans/air conditioner

9. Most importantly, you are accountable for your three children during the course of your shift. This includes
    a. relaying information to parents about infant's day
    b. giving specific information to parents from head teacher and/or from the parents to the head teacher as the need arises
    c. charting on infants for all diaper changes, feeding, naps. This is very important information. To the parents, if it is not charted, then it was not done. At times, you may also be responsible for writing a general note about the infant's day. If the head teacher doesn't write this, then you should either remind them to do this or you should complete it yourself.

10. Attend all staff meetings, parent conferences and recommended required training programs.

11. Maintain professional attitude and loyalty to the school at all times.

12. Maintain confidentiality of the children and their parents. Failure to do this can result in termination of employments.

13. While you are primarily responsible for your three assigned babies, the infant teachers work as a team. This requires that you are also responsible for ensuring that each infant is well cared for in a safe and nurturing environment.

14. Several times a week, a head teacher will leave the classroom when you arrive at 2:00 P.M., so that she can work on assessment forms and planning. You are then responsible for the supervision of those children in her absence.

15. Lastly, because you are a vital member of the infant caregiving team, your input is very valuable. We expect for you to contribute any observations made during your time spent with the infants. These can be written as anecdotal records, verbally transmitted to the head teacher and/or stated during staff meetings.

Director's Resource 11–2 (continued)

Job Description
Assistant Teacher—Preschool

QUALIFICATIONS

A person applying for this position must be at least 18 years of age, in the process of becoming professionally prepared to be a teacher of young children, and meet the requirements of the city and state licensing agencies. This person must have a warm and friendly personality, be sensitive to the feelings and needs of others, and be able to relate well to children. In addition he/she must be willing to fulfill his/her responsibilities in accordance with the Center's educational philosophy.

RESPONSIBILITIES

- Assisting in planning and implementing the daily program under the direction of the head teacher
- Assisting in planning and preparing the learning environment, setting up interest centers, and preparing needed materials and supplies
- Supervising the classroom when the teacher is out of the room
- Helping with the general housekeeping tasks
- Assisting the teacher in any other appropriate way
- Maintaining professional attitudes and loyalty to the program at all times
- Treating all of the children with dignity and respect
- Attending all staff meetings and recommended training programs and conferences
- Participating in professional organizations that work toward the improvement of early childhood education

Director's Resource 11–2 (continued)

Job Description
Cook

Responsible to the Director

Requirements: previous experience cooking for large groups and be able to demonstrate knowledge of basic math.

The person hired to prepare meals will be able to:
- work cooperatively with teaching staff, communicate with, and be sensitive to children and their needs
- read and follow directions successfully
- finish projects promptly
- be able to prepare alternates in menu planning in the event of an emergency
- list food proportions
- prepare morning breakfast, lunch, and afternoon snacks
- prepare all meals according to USDA requirements
- discuss any changes that might be made in menus and food purchases
- keep the kitchen clean at all times (mop floors, clean refrigerator, freezer, stove, cabinets and food storage areas)
- put dishes away neatly and keep inventory of dishes and utensils
- purchase all food from local stores and prepare food order
- encourage good health habits and nutrition with children when cooking
- answer the telephone according to the standards of the Center
- call the night before if ill

Director's Resource 11–3

Sample Personnel Policies and Job Descriptions—U.C. Child Care Inc.

**U.C. Child Care, Inc.
Personnel Policies
Issued April, 1986
Revised: May, 1996**

Neither this personnel policy nor any of the information contained herein shall be construed to be an employment contract.

I. GENERAL INFORMATION
    A. PROGRAM STORY

Quality child care has been a growing concern of many constituencies in our society over the past two decades. This has been due in part to the tremendous increase in the number of women who are entering the working world, or returning to colleges to complete their education. The latter reason caused various student organizations and other interested persons at the University of Cincinnati to advocate for a child care program at this institution; that would meet the needs of busy parents for flexible scheduling, a convenient location, and a quality program.

In 1973, an evening child care program was established and in 1975 the program was expanded to include a day program. Due to the lack of steady enrollments, the evening program was discontinued in 1977. The day program, however, continued to grow and the demand for this service increased. In 1975, the Child Care Program relocated to the St. John's Unitarian Church (320 Resor Avenue). Relocation permitted the program to expand its license capacity from 13 to 20 children. The Center's hours were also expanded. The program continued to grow and in 1983 the license capacity was raised from 20 to 29. In 1987, a second center was opened at the First Unitarian Church (536 Linton Street), and is licensed to serve 15 toddlers and 30 preschoolers.

In 1991, the Resort Avenue program was closed due to a decision made by the members of St. John's Unitarian Church to renovate the space for their use. In response, the University of Cincinnati purchased a building at 3310 Ruther Avenue to house the displaced child care program. Also in 1991, the former U-Kids Child Care Cooperative, which merged with U.C. Child Care Center, was closed in 1994 and moved into our expanded Ruther Avenue Center.

All of our programs have excellent ethnic and racial representation including children of African, African-American, Asian, Middle Eastern, and Hispanic cultures. They are licensed by the State of Ohio Department of Human Services and the Cincinnati Board of Health. The laws and rules governing child day care operations are available at the centers for review upon request. The Center's licenses are posted in the entries.

Director's Resource 11–3 (continued)

B. EDUCATIONAL PHILOSOPHY

The educational program and philosophy of the U.C. Child Care Program is based on meeting the developmental needs of each child. The program is based on an environment that fosters cognitive as well as physical, emotional, and social development. The program design fosters the belief that quality preschool education involves constant interaction among the environment, the child, the teacher, and the parent. Our goal is to provide a warm, happy, and secure environment in which children can grow and learn.

Under the guidance of child development specialists, children engage in a variety of activities, which offer opportunities to construct knowledge. The classroom and curriculum are designed to allow for children's experimentation, and exploration in many areas including creative activities, dramatic play, art, music, sensorimotor skills, the community, and the environment. Skills involving language, number concepts, and science are included in the programming.

Children in the child care program are encouraged to develop skills in self-direction, and the ability to make choices and decisions. Behavioral limits are imposed in manners which preserve the child's self-respect, and help the child grow in self-control. The program is carefully planned to balance freedom with direction in order to meet group needs as well as individual needs.

C. EDUCATIONAL MISSION

1. To provide a comprehensive early childhood education program and day care service for young children, the curriculum shall be designed to enhance the total development of each child in ways which respect and promote cultural diversity, and a healthy self-concept;

2. To establish a flexibly scheduled day care service designed primarily to meet the needs of the University student, but also serving faculty and staff of the University of Cincinnati as space permits;

3. To provide parents with the opportunity to retain responsibility for their young children during such programs through a parent volunteer program support system;

4. To demonstrate the feasibility of such facilities located in proximity to the parents' places of work, as opposed to their homes;

5. To serve as a model and an agent for change in the improvement and expansion of similar services in the community;

6. To receive contributions or grants from any and all sources, either for the foregoing purposes, or to distribute funds to organizations that qualify as exempt organizations under 501(c)(3) of the Internal Revenue Code of 1954, or the corresponding provisions of any subsequent federal tax laws.

D. PROGRAM ADMINISTRATION

Currently the U.C. Child Care Center, Inc. is a non-profit day care agency. The Executive Director is responsible for its daily operation and the implementation of policies established by its Board of Trustees. The Program Directors, if any, are responsible for overseeing the day-to-day operations of the Centers.

Director's Resource 11–3 (continued)

In addition to salaried teachers and aides, students from the College of Education use the program to gain practical experience. These students are afforded an excellent learning opportunity in a unique child care setting. Parents also work, on a volunteer basis, and are a most welcomed addition to the staff.

II. AFFIRMATIVE ACTION POLICY AND PLAN
(This Plan was approved by U.C. Child Care Center, Inc. Board of Trustees, October 1, 1985 and revised May 1996.)

A Primary goal of the Center is to promote a diverse work force that will enrich the children's experiences. The importance of developing and implementing non-discriminatory and affirmative action employment policies is well understood by the members of the Board of Trustees, Administration, and employees of the U.C. Child Care Center, Inc. This plan is set forth in order to facilitate the creation and implementation of sound affirmative action policies and procedures.

A. *Non-Discrimination*

U.C. Child Care Center, Inc. shall not discriminate against any employee or applicant for reasons of race, creed, marital status, color, age, gender, sex-orientation, religion, national origin, physical or mental disability, or status as a disabled veteran or veteran of the Vietnam era.

B. *Implementation*

The responsibility for implementing affirmative action policies and procedures is placed with the Executive Director. However, all employees share responsibility for promoting and implementing the spirit of the policies.

C. *Filling of Vacancies*

Recruitment and Appointment of Employees

Recruitment to fill vacancies will be conducted to assure no adverse impact on employment opportunities because of race, creed, marital status, color, age, gender, sex-orientation, religion, national origin, physical or mental disability, or status as a disabled veteran or veteran of the Vietnam era. All current employees, and parents of children served by the U.C. Child Center, Inc. will be appropriately notified of employment opportunities. Positions will be advertised in applicable public places to attract a diverse work force.

a) Qualification for professional (program) and administrative (clerical) positions will be reviewed when vacancies occur to ensure that no artificial barriers exist which may limit the pool of candidates. The Center's application form for employment and job interview procedures also will be reviewed and evaluated on a timely basis.

b) In filling vacancies, consideration will be given first to present employees who qualify for promotion. A job description and salary information will be posted for no less than ten (10) working days prior to application deadlines.

D. *Audit, Report and Evaluation*

The U.C. Child Care Center, Inc. will comply with any statistical reports that are required by law. Additionally the Center will maintain the following statistics.

Director's Resource 11–3 (continued)

1. Staffing breakdown by race, gender, and other affirmative action categories;
2. Promotions by job classification showing race, gender, or other criteria;
3. Termination by job classification showing race, gender, and reason for termination;
4. Employee participation in staff development or training programs;
5. A copy of all employment applications or resumes received will be kept for a minimum of two years from the date the position is filled.

E. *Review of Personnel Policies, Job Descriptions and Wage Administration*
   A checklist for compliance will be utilized to insure current review of personnel policies, job descriptions, and wages to ensure that they are non-discriminatory.

F. *Training Program*
   All employees will be encouraged to take advantage of training programs, which will provide opportunities to upgrade their skills to qualify for promotion to more responsible positions, as they become available.

G. *Administrative Responsibility*
   The Executive Director, or designee, will be responsible for evaluating the progress of the Affirmative Action Program, and make timely reports to the U.C. Child Care Center, Inc. Board of Trustees.

H. *Board of Directors*
   The U.C. Child Care Center, Inc. Board of Trustees shall make timely determinations of the adequacy of the agency voluntary Affirmative Action Policy, and Plan by standards of review based on Section 713 (b)(1) of Title VII of the Civil Rights Act of 1964.

I. *Dissemination of Policy*
   Dissemination of the Voluntary Affirmative Action Policy as set forth in this Article II of this agency will be communicated through appropriate means to inform members of the Board of Trustees, Administration and employees.
   1. This voluntary Affirmative Action Policy and Plan is included in agency personnel policies; a copy will be sent to each employee, or others requesting it, and will be discussed in employee orientation, training, and management meetings.
   2. A copy of the Policy and Plan will be given to each new employee, and is available upon request to job applicants, community residents, and other persons.

III. HARASSMENT/SEXUAL HARASSMENT
   Consistent with its legal and ethical obligations, the U.C. Child Care, Inc. prohibits staff harassment based upon race, color, gender, age, religion, national ancestry, disability, sexual orientation, marital status, parental status, source of income, military discharge status, or any other protected status. This prohibition includes, of course, sexual harassment. The U.C. Child Care, Inc. will take strong disciplinary steps, up to and including discharge, against any person who engages in conduct which violates this policy.

A. *Definition of Harassment/Sexual Harassment*
   Harassment consists of unwelcome statements or action based on gender, race, age, religion, national origin, handicap, sexual orientation or other protected group sta-

Director's Resource 11–3 (continued)

tus that are sufficiently severe or pervasive so as to unreasonably interfere with an individual's work performance or create an intimidating, hostile or offensive working environment.

Sexual harassment includes unwelcome sexual advances, requests for sexual favors, and other such verbal or physical conduct of a sexual nature. It exists where a co-worker or superior exercises or threatens to exercise his or her authority to affect the job, duties, earnings, or career of another person working at the U.C. Child Care Inc. (including prospective staffers), in order to obtain a sexual favor. It also exists when unwelcome conduct of a sexual nature is sufficiently severe or pervasive so as to unreasonably interfere with an individual's work performance or creates an intimidating, hostile, or offensive working environment.

B. *Reporting Policy for Harassment/Sexual Harassment*
Everyone at U.C. Child Care Inc. is responsible for assuring that our work place is free from all forms of prohibited harassment. Any person who has a complaint of prohibited harassment by anyone at the U.C. Child Care Inc. including superiors and co-workers, is strongly urged to bring the problem to the attention of the Executive Director of the U.C. Child Care, Inc. Complaints may be raised with the Executive Director, Program Directors, and/or the Board of Trustees.

The U.C. Child Care, Inc. prohibits retaliation against anyone for having raised such a complaint in good faith. Complaints will be investigated and handled as confidentially as possible in the manner described as follows.

C. *Procedure For Handling Complaints Of Prohibitive Harassment*
Complaints of prohibited harassment will be investigated as promptly as possible. The allegations of the complaint, and the identity of the persons involved shall be maintained on a confidential basis; subject to the need to conduct a full and impartial investigation, remedy violations, monitor compliance, and administer the policy.

The investigation will include, but will not be limited to, discussion with the complaining party, the complained-of party, and witnesses. Where appropriate, a report shall be forwarded to the Board of Trustees with recommendations concerning remedial action, if necessary. The Board of Trustees shall review the recommendation and any additional submission by either party, determine the appropriate corrective action, if any, notify the complained-of party and the complaining party of its decision, and implement that decision.

IV. RESPONSIBILITY FOR PERSONNEL ADMINISTRATION
  A. *Board of Trustees:* The determination of personnel policies and practices is a function of the Board of Trustees of U.C. Child Care, Inc. The execution of these policies and practices is a function of the Executive Director, who is appointed by the Board. The selection and employment of all additional employees shall be the responsibility of the Executive Director.
  B. *Selection of Personnel:* In the selection of staff personnel, equal opportunity employment shall be afforded to all qualified persons without regard to race, religion, color, gender, age, national origin, or marital status, as well as without regard to any social

Director's Resource 11–3 (continued)

or political affiliation. The Affirmative Action Plan set forth in Article II shall be positively implemented to assure equal-opportunity recruitment, hiring, and upgrading of staff. All staff positions shall include job descriptions clearly detailing the qualifications, duties, responsibilities, and supervisory relationships. All staff personnel shall be evaluated at least once a year.

C. *Change and Revisions of Personnel Policies:* These policies will be reviewed annually, and updated if necessary by the Executive Director and the Personnel Committee. Any changes must be submitted to, and approved by, the Board of Trustees.

D. All personnel are required to sign the form verifying receipt of these policies. The form is the last page of these policies. This form must be signed and in the personnel files prior to receipt of the first paycheck.

V. EMPLOYMENT PROCEDURES

A. The Board of Trustees is responsible for interviewing prospective candidates for the position of Executive Director of U.C. Child Care, Inc. The Executive Director of the agency in turn is responsible for the employment of staff.

B. There will be current job descriptions and salary ranges for every position in the agency. These job descriptions will include detailed information on the duties and responsibilities, qualifications and supervisory relationships. They will be used with prospective workers as the basis of detailed discussion in considering employment. All vacant positions will be filled within a reasonable time after the position is advertised and interviews conducted.

C. *Job Applications:* Each job applicant must submit in writing a complete job application. In most cases U.C. Child Care, Inc. will require an applicant to submit a complete personal resume.

D. *References:* References, in writing, concerning education and work experience of applicants will be requested. The letters of reference should contain a brief description of the agency's function, and a description of the job that was performed by the prospective employee.

E. Appointment to a position should always be on the basis of personal interview with the applicant and the person or persons responsible for hiring.

F. *Promotion and Transfer:* In filling vacancies, consideration shall be given first to present members of the staff with sufficient qualifications to justify promotion or transfer. In the event several employees apply for the same job, the selection shall be at the discretion of the Executive Director.

G. *Orientation:* An orientation program will be provided for all new employees.

H. After successful completion of the required probationary period before an employee becomes a member of the staff, the employee will be provided with a written documentation detailing his/her hourly rate, the job title, effective date of employment and certain policies/procedures which the prospective employee agrees to abide by. A copy of Personnel Policies and Board Policies related to employment will also be given to each employee. A copy of administrative/office procedures may also be given. The employee will receive a copy of his/her job description.

Director's Resource 11–3 (continued)

Upon acceptance of a position with U.C. Child Care, Inc., the employee thereby agrees to accept the above-mentioned policies and to abide by them.

VI. EMPLOYMENT STATUS:
   A. *Regular Full-Time:* An employee working a minimum of 40 hours weekly.
   B. *Regular Part-Time:* An employee working less than 40 hours weekly.
   C. *Temporary Employee:* An employee hired for a designated period of time, and given an appointment with a specified ending date, including without limitation, students enrolled at U.C. and who are assigned to the U.C. Child Care Center, Inc.
   D. *Probationary Period Prospective Employees:* An employee must successfully complete the required probationary period before becoming a member of the staff. Time spent during the probationary period will be credited toward calculating length of service. The probationary period is six (6) months. During the probationary period, the prospective employee may be terminated at any time at the discretion of the Executive Director. Absence from work, for any cause, during the probationary period is deductible from salary.
   E. *Probationary Period (Promotion or Requested Transfer):* When a staff member assumes a new position, either by promotion or requested transfer, the terms of probation as stated in Section V.H. will apply, with the exception that sick and vacation leave may be used. An employee applying for a promotion or transfer should be aware that the agency does not guarantee that he/she may return to his/her former position.

VII. WORKING CONDITIONS
   A. Performance Evaluation
      1. All evaluations shall be based on the employee's job description and specification for the designated position. The written performance evaluation for a regular employee shall occur on an annual basis.
      2. A performance evaluation process shall consist of the following steps:
         a) The employee's supervisor completes a written, signed evaluation. This evaluation includes a section with advice on ways to improve performance and recommendations for training. The staff member is expected to act on this advice and demonstrate efforts to improve and refine performance. Performance improvement will be monitored and evaluated on a regular basis.
         b) The contents of the evaluation are reviewed in a personal conference with the employee; the employee's immediate supervisor; and the Executive Director.
         c) Each participant in the evaluation review should sign the evaluation report to indicate that he/she has read it.
         d) If any party disagrees with the report, that individual can exercise the right to include on the report the nature or basis of the disagreement, and may request a conference with the Executive Director.
         e) The Executive Director shall then review and sign all evaluations.
   B. *Health Examinations:* Health examinations and tuberculosis tests are required by State and/or City Health Departments. The employee will bear this expense.

Director's Resource 11–3 (continued)

C. *On-the-Job-Injuries:* Any Employee sustaining an injury on the job shall report the incident immediately to his/her supervisor so that proper medical attention may be given if needed. The Executive Director should be informed, and a written report forwarded to the Executive Director within 48 hours. An employee may be eligible for Workers' Compensation according to current State law.

D. *Personnel Records:* Confidential personnel records of each employee will be maintained in a locked file at U.C. Child Care, Inc. These records will include at least the, job application, resume, changes in wages, administrative actions affecting employees, performance evaluation reports, three personal references, conviction statement(s) where applicable, record of Police Check, record of medical examination, High School or College Diploma, and record of training. An employee may examine records in his/her personnel file. An employee may not remove any material from his/her file without the written approval of the Executive Director.

E. *Theft of Property:* Employees are discouraged from bringing personal property to work. Adequate cabinet space will be provided so that purses, etc. can be locked up. In the event of a theft, the agency cannot be responsible for personal property that may be stolen. Employees are advised against having payroll checks cashed during working hours.

F. *Dress Code:* All staff members are expected to dress neatly and in a manner appropriate for their specific assignment.

G. *Security:* Staff members will be held responsible for the equipment, supplies, confidential materials, cash or checks, and other items of value entrusted to them, and they should take proper precautions to prevent the loss of these items. At the close of the work day, each staff member will lock all confidential files and cabinets in his/her care. The center may request employees to be bonded if deemed appropriate.

VIII. STAFF DEVELOPMENT

A. *Introduction*

Each employee of U.C. Child Care, Inc. has the responsibility to take advantage of development and training programs that will contribute to his/her improvement of job performance. Although opportunities may be provided by the agency, the employee has the obligation to search out opportunities on his/her own initiative. This is especially applicable in meeting minimum qualifications for a specific job. All teaching staff will be required to attend training in First Aid (6 hrs), Communicable Disease (6 hrs), Child Abuse (6 hrs), and CPR (6 hrs).

B. *Purpose of the Policy on Staff Development*

Career development occurs through academic study, and by such other means that will contribute to future service to the agency. Participation in staff development programs shall not conflict with performance of regular duties. Payment of fees and tuition for conferences, educational courses, or other training experiences shall be made by U.C. Child Care Inc., when recommended by the supervisor, approved by the Executive Director, and when such plans are:

Director's Resource 11–3 (continued)

1. Within budgetary constraints.
2. Complementary to agency purposes and programs.
3. Deemed to be a needed benefit to the individual's career.
4. Submitted in advance for approval to the Executive Director.

C. *Tuition Reimbursement*
1. Regular full-time employees who have been employed one year or more, will be eligible to request tuition reimbursement for one work-related course per quarter if approved by the Executive Director.
2. Any request for time off and/or tuition reimbursement for long term or degree programs may be approved on an individual basis and will require:
    a) A clear statement of program objectives;
    b) types of courses to be taken
    c) length of time to complete degree or long-term program;
    d) availability of funds.

IX. STANDARD WORK WEEK AND SCHEDULE
A. *Standard Work Week:* A regular, full-time appointment will reflect the number of weeks per quarter specified at the beginning of an academic year. The standard work week will be 40 hours. This does not include a lunch period. The lunch period should not exceed one-half ($1/2$) hour daily. U.C. Child Care, Inc. will be open from 7:30 A.M. until 5:30 P.M., Monday through Friday (Linton) and 7:00 A.M. until 6:00 P.M., Monday through Friday (Ruther).
B. *Working Additional Hours:* Employees may occasionally be required to work additional hours or to attend a function during the evenings or on a Saturday. If this occurs, the Supervisor may schedule time off that same week on an hour-for-hour basis.

   When the hours worked per week exceed the equivalent of forty hours per week, employees will receive overtime pay as provided by wage and hour laws.
C. *Compensation for Hours Worked Beyond the Standard Work Week:* All hours worked beyond the standard work week must receive written approval in advance from the Executive Director. To receive compensation, the prior written approval must be attached to the time period. It is the employee's responsibility to secure the prior written approval.
D. *Exceptions:* Overtime pay will not be given either for voluntary attendance at workshops and training or for State and City Licensing mandated training, e.g., First Aid, CPR, etc. (Section 785.31, Title 29, Part 785, Fair Labor Standards Act.) However, time off for additional hours spent in such training may be granted by the Executive Director.
E. *Time Records:* Daily attendance records, including time records, vacation, sick leave, etc., must be maintained and forwarded to the Program Director's office at the end of each pay period. The time record must be current before the employee receives his/her pay for the period. The employee is required to record "time in and out" for the lunch period.

Director's Resource 11–3 (continued)

X. EMPLOYEE BENEFITS

The agency will extend the following fringe benefits:

A. *Group Health Insurance Plan:* The center will provide the cost of single enrollment in a group health insurance plan, or an equivalent cash amount for all full-time employees who have completed their probationary periods. Part-time employees are eligible for their choice of half of this paid benefit after they complete their probationary periods.

B. *Pension Plan:* Employees may contribute to a 403(b) tax-deferred annuity. Contributions are deducted from the participant's pay on a before-tax basis.

C. *Social Security:* The U.C. Child Care, Inc. provides Social Security benefits which are required by law.

D. *Workers' Compensation:* The U.C. Child Care, Inc. provides workers' compensation for all employees, regardless of employee status.

E. *Liability Insurance:* U.C. Child Care, Inc. is covered by general liability insurance. Employees are included as additional insureds, should they be named in a liability suit against U.C. Child Care, Inc.

F. *Holidays*

1. The following holidays are granted, with pay, to all regular full-time, probationary, and part-time (on a prorated basis) employees: Martin Luther King Day, Memorial Day, Independence Day, Labor Day, Thanksgiving Day, Christmas Day and New Year's Day.

2. If any of these holidays fall on Sunday, the following Monday will be considered the holiday. If any holidays fall on Saturday, the preceding Friday will be considered the holiday.

3. Employees must work the day preceding the holiday and the day following the holiday in order to receive pay for the holiday unless the employee has requested those days and had them approved by the Program Director.

G. *Vacation Accrued Leave:* Vacation leave is accrued as follows: Full-time staff: Five days per year; after three years of service, ten days per year; after eight years of service, 15 days per year. Part-time employees accrue on a prorated basis. Temporary employees do not accrue vacation.

H. *Use of Vacation Leave and Personal Leave:*

1. When scheduling vacation time, all employees must plan in advance, giving full consideration to the work load and staff obligations. Vacation requests shall be submitted in writing one month in advance for approval by the Program Director; the judgement of the Program Director shall be final, if vacation requests cannot be honored because of work load or staff obligations.

   At the discretion of the Executive Director, employees may be permitted to carry over vacation up to three (3) weeks. This carry-over must be used before the expiration of the next calendar year.

2. When a holiday falls on what is normally a workday during an employee's vacation period, the holiday shall not be counted as a vacation day.

Director's Resource 11–3 (continued)

3. Employees are not entitled to be paid for unearned vacation time upon termination of their employment.
4. Employees are encouraged to use accrued vacation time during the quarter breaks.
5. It may happen that day care service is not needed by enrollees during the week between Christmas and New Years. In this event, the Center will be closed. Work days which fall in this period, except December 25 and January 1, shall be charged against the employee's accumulated vacation time or at the employee's option, it will be considered as leave without pay.

I. *Sick Leave.*

Accrual Rates:

1. Regular full-time employees are entitled to two (2) days sick leave per quarter. Regular part-time employees accrue the equivalent of one (1) day per quarter. Temporary employees do not accrue sick leave. Sick days may not accrue beyond the end of a year.
2. *Illness of Family Members:* This involves cases of illness of a member of the family, i.e., Spouse, Child, Father or Mother when circumstances make it necessary for the employee to be at home to attend the sick person or otherwise attend to matters related to the illness. Payment up to two (2) days absence for this reason will be deducted from earned sick leave, if any is available. Request for absence beyond a period of two (2) days must be referred to the Executive Director.
3. *Evidence Required for Payment of Sick Leave:* If absence due to illness exceeds five (5) consecutive work days, the employee must present a physician's statement upon returning to work. Failure to present such evidence may result in loss of pay.
4. *Sick Leave:* On-the-Job Injuries: If any employee has loss of time due to a work-related injury, the employee may use accrued sick leave if Worker's Compensation benefits are not applicable (e.g., lost time benefits are allowed when the employee loses eight (8) or more calendar days from work).

XI. LEAVES OF ABSENCE

A. *Medical Leave of Absence*

1. When the medical condition of an employee precludes the employee from performing his/her regular responsibilities, the employee may request a medical leave of absence. The request for the medical leave must be accompanied by a physician's statement certifying the employee's medical condition. An employee may use accrued sick leave time to cover the leave period.

Request for medical leaves are to be submitted for approval to the Executive Director.

2. The Executive Director may also require that an employee undergo a physical examination in the event that it appears that he/she should be placed on medical leave.

Director's Resource 11–3 (continued)

3. The position of the employee may be filled on a temporary basis for the first six (6) months of the medical leave. However, the employee has no guarantee to a position if the medical leave extends beyond six (6) months.

4. If an employee takes time off for medical reasons, but does not have accrued sick leave available, the employee must present a physician's statement. If no statement is presented, the disciplinary process will be initiated. (See Section XIII, B.)

B. *Bereavement Leave:* Regular employees, full-time and part-time, shall be allowed up to three (3) days of bereavement leave to be charged to sick days, in the event of death of a member of the "immediate" family (i.e., Spouse, Child, Father, Mother, Brother, Sister, Father-in-Law, Mother-in-Law, Grandparents). Request for exception to the above must be directed to the Executive Director.

C. *Education Leave:* Request for education leave and time off for courses, seminars and institutes for more than two (2) weeks or ten (10) work days, with or without pay, must be approved in advance by the Executive Director.

D. *Military Leave:* Staff members called to military duty, or otherwise engaged in military service are protected as provided by existing Federal and State Laws for job protection.

E. *Other Leaves of Absence:* Any other situation is open for discussion and must be approved by the Executive Director. All such leaves of absence are considered to be leaves without pay.

F. *Employee Benefits During Leaves of Absence*

1. If an employee is on a leave of absence with pay (e.g., a Medical Leave of Absence using accrued sick leave time), the employee continues to earn all benefits at the same rate as specified for employees on active duty.

2. If an employee is on a leave of absence without pay, the employee does not earn any benefits other than the center paying its prorated share of the Group Health benefit for the first month of the employee's leave. If the employee wishes to retain health insurance for subsequent months, the employee must reimburse the center for the full cost of the health insurance.

XII. EMPLOYEE WORK RULES

Policy

The following regulations constitute the work rules of the U.C. Child Care Center, Inc. Inappropriate Behavior, as described within these regulations, "are prohibited" and shall result in disciplinary action up to and including immediate discharge.

1. Discourteous or disrespectful treatment (including use of profanity or physical or verbal threats) of children, parents, visitors, and other employees.

2. Failure to maintain a clean, neat, professional appearance.

3. Failure to keep work area neat and clean, and to plan and implement an age appropriate curriculum and program as determined by the Program Director, as well as NAEYC guidelines.

Director's Resource 11–3 (continued)

4. Unauthorized discussion of information pertaining to children, parents, or other employees with friends, relatives, the general public or the news media.

5. Possession of intoxicants (alcohol or drugs), while on center property. (Being under the influence of intoxicants (alcohol or drugs) while on the job.

6. Hindering or limiting normal operations. Interfering with another employee's work.

7. Abuse, destruction, neglect, or loss of center property.

8. Illegal conduct.

9. Violating any U.C. Child Care Center, Inc. policies and encouraging or inciting others to do the same.

10. Incompetency.

11. Insubordination: refusal of an employee to follow instructions, or perform designated work where such instructions or work normally and properly are required of an employee.

12. Dishonesty or theft.

13. Neglect of duty.

14. Use of U.C. Child Care Center, Inc. telephones for personal calls without authorization (except in the case of a dire emergency). Charging personal calls including long distance, directory assistance, cellular phone calls to the U.C. Child Care Center, Inc.

15. Abuse of sick leave. Failure to comply with sick leave notification policies. Repeated tardiness, or absence without authorized leave.

16. Falsification of records.

17. Failure of employees to report to their assigned classroom at the beginning of their work period. Leaving work prior to the end of their work period.

18. Sleeping on the job.

19. Having unauthorized visitor during work hours without permission (including former employees, relatives, friends).

20. Smoking in unauthorized areas.

21. Violating State of Ohio Day Care Licensing Regulations and/or City Board of Health Regulation.

22. Failure to report an accident involving an on-the-job injury or damage to center property.

23. Soliciting, collecting money, or circulating petitions on U.C. Child Care Center property without written permission of Executive Director.

24. Transporting children to or from the center without written permission from the Executive Director.

25. Any other deviation from normal and accepted behavior of a U.C. Child Care Center employee.

26. Care for children served by U.C. Child Center, Inc., outside of the U.C. Child Care Center, Inc. facility.

27. Failure to abide by the policies of the U.C. Child Care Center, Inc.

28. Failure to abide by the procedures and policies as outlined in the Employee Handbook.

Director's Resource 11–3 (continued)

XIII. SEPARATION OF STAFF
   A. *Resignation:* Employees are expected to give at least one (1) month's written notice prior to resignation to the Executive Director.
   B. *Retirement:* Employees eligible for retirement shall give no less than three (3) months' notice to the Executive Director.
   C. *Reduction of Staff*
      1. Whenever it becomes necessary to reduce staff, terminations will be made with consideration for staffing requirements and personnel qualifications. The ultimate decision will rest with the Executive Director. Staff will be given two (2) weeks' written notice and paid for that time.
   D. *Dismissal* is also a type of "staff separation" (See Section XIII, E.)
   E. *Termination Process and Keys:* The employee must return all keys and/or other center property.

XIV. DISCIPLINARY ACTION
   A. Introduction
      The disciplinary process may be initiated at the discretion of the Program Director for the following reasons: Unsatisfactory Performance, Excessive Absence, failure to abide by the Employee Work Rules (Section XII, 1–28), or other infractions of rules, policies, performance expectations, and Handbook Procedures.
      1. *Unsatisfactory Performance:* Determination of Unsatisfactory Performance is at the discretion of the Program Director and/or the Executive Director, and will be based on the Performance Evaluation (VII, 2) and the degree to which the employee improves performance, based on the advice and recommendations made subsequent to the evaluation process.
      2. *Excessive Absence:* The disciplinary process will be initiated when an employee demonstrates a pattern of absence for reasons other than approved vacation periods. Patterns of absence include, but are not limited to:
      One or more days' absence per month for four successive months. Two or more days' absence per month, for three successive months.
   B. *Disciplinary Process*
      1. The supervisor informs the employee in writing of an action or actions, which do not meet requirements of the job, and/or which interfere with the performance of required duties.
      2. If there is no satisfactory improvement, the supervisor submits a written statement of warning to the employee. The statement includes expectations regarding performance, and the time period in which the improvement is to be made.
      3. If performance continues to be unsatisfactory, the employee may be placed on probation.
   C. *Probationary Period for Disciplinary Reasons*
      1. When the performance of an employee continues to be unsatisfactory after the disciplinary process warnings, the supervisor shall have a conference with the employee detailing the unsatisfactory performance. During the conference, a

Director's Resource 11–3 (continued)

probationary period will be established during which time the employee will be given the opportunity to improve his/her performance. There will be a weekly supervisory conference, the results of which are to be written and co-signed by the supervisor and employee.

2. The probationary period will be not less than one (1) month, but not more than three (3) months, for administrative and program personnel; not less than two (2) weeks, but not more than one (1) month, for other staff workers.

3. If, at the end of the specified probationary period, the Executive Director determines that acceptable standards have not been met, then the notice of dismissal shall be given.

D. *Suspension:* When an employee is accused of serious misconduct or of a crime, the Executive Director may temporarily suspend the employee without pay while the Executive Director ascertains the facts necessary to make a definite decision. The following procedures shall be followed:

1. Within ten (10) working days of the suspension, the employee shall be notified of the date and time of the hearing.

2. The employee has the right to present evidence in his/her behalf, and to be represented by legal counsel at his/her own expense.

3. During the hearing, the suspended employee may cross examine any witness(es) who testify against him/her at the hearing.

4. No employee will be suspended for more than sixty (60) days before a decision is made.

5. Wages retroactive to the date of suspension will be paid, should the findings result in the employee's favor.

E. *Dismissal:* The Executive Director has the right to dismiss an employee for Misconduct, Absence Without Notice, Excessive Absence, Unsatisfactory Performance, and Failure to Abide by Employee Work Rules.

1. *Misconduct:* Connotes a serious behavior problem. It has broad interpretation, but would indicate a major problem such as, but not limited to theft, acts of a totally unprofessional nature, evidence of the use of drugs or alcohol on the job, falsification of records, unauthorized use of agency equipment for non-agency related business, a criminal offense, etc. Action: The Executive Director shall submit a written notice of dismissal to the employee. No prior notice is required.

2. Absence Without Notice or Excessive Absence: The following situations make an employee eligible for immediate dismissal:

    a) Absence from work for two (2) days or more without notifying supervisor.

    b) Failure to report back from vacation or leave of absence as scheduled without prior authorization from the supervisor.

    c) Excessive Absence as described in XIV, A, 2.

3. Unsatisfactory Performance as described in VII, 2, a.

4. Care of Children Served by U.C. Child Care, Inc., outside of the Center. (See Paragraph XVI, G for "Grounds for Dismissal.")

Director's Resource 11–3 (continued)

F. *Right to Appeal Dismissal:* An employee dismissed for any of the above reasons has the right to make a written appeal to the Executive Director.

XV. USE OF PERSONALLY OWNED VEHICLES
A. Use of Non-Agency Owned Vehicles for Work-related Purposes:
1. Employees are prohibited from transporting children of U.C. Child Care Center, Inc.
2. Employees who use their own vehicles for work-related purposes (other than transportation to and from their job site), must carry liability insurance, including bodily injury and medical payments coverage.
3. Employees should be aware that U.C. Child Care, Inc's liability coverage on non-agency owned vehicles IS EXCESS OVER ANY OTHER VALID or COLLECTIBLE INSURANCE.
4. Each employee expecting to use his/her vehicle for center business, must submit proof of automobile insurance coverage to the Executive Director.

XVI. PRIVACY AND CONFIDENTIALITY
It is the professional responsibility of every employee of U.C. Child Care, Inc. to maintain the client's right to a relationship of mutual trust; to privacy and confidentiality; and to responsible use of information.

The collection and sharing of information or data shall only be related to the professional services function to be performed, with the client informed as to its necessity and use.

No information shall be released without the prior knowledge and informed consent of the client, except where the client cannot be responsible, or others may be seriously jeopardized.

The employee must avoid any action that violates or diminishes the civil and legal rights of clients with regard to privacy and confidentiality.

XVII. MISCELLANEOUS
A. *Nepotism:* In order to avoid any semblance of Nepotism (i.e., favoritism shown to a relative on a basis of relationship), an employee shall not be hired or supervised by a blood or legal relative.
B. *Policy Regarding the Acceptance of Gifts:* The Center recognizes that at times, clients may want to express their gratitude to an individual employee or worker with a gift. On the other hand, employees must be aware that unscrupulous individuals may attempt to bribe them by offering them gifts or money. In no cases may money be accepted by an individual employee. If an individual wishes to give money, it must be given to the center. When an employee feels that an individual is offering a gift in good faith, he/she may accept it, and should report acceptance of the gift to his/her supervisor. If on the other hand, an employee feels a gift is being offered as a bribe, this should be reported to the Executive Director.
C. *Policy Regarding Stipends and Honoraria:* When Staff are offered an honorarium or a stipend for speaking engagements or other consultative efforts, the employees may retain such compensation.

Director's Resource 11–3 (continued)

D. *Acting as Representative of the Center*
1. Employees may accept appointment to a Board of Directors or another policy-making body as a representative of the center, only upon the recommendation of the Executive Director. Care should be taken to avoid any conflict of interest situation.
2. Employees shall refrain from soliciting money, goods, or services in the name of the Center unless specifically asked to do so by the Executive Director. An accurate accounting of funds is to be made to the Executive Director. Employees may not solicit other U.C. Child Care Center, Inc. employees, or parents during working hours.
3. Employees may not hold in trust, any funds which belong to individual clients or client groups. Any exception must be approved by the Executive Director, and will be made only if a workable mechanism of accountability can be arranged.
4. Employees should refrain from making statements of public record or of a public relations nature on behalf of the Center to the press, news media, persons or agencies, unless the content of the statement has been approved by the Executive Director.

E. *Jury Duty*
1. The center's position in this matter is that an employee should serve when called for jury duty, as matter of good citizenship, unless there are pressing business reasons which make it seem necessary to request to be excused from such duty.

F. *Care of Children Served by the U.C. Child Care Center, Inc., Outside the Center:*
Employees may not accept employment, whether compensated or not, whether directly or indirectly employed, for the care of children served by the U.C. Child Care Center, Inc., at any location not operated by U.C. Child Care Center, Inc. Such employment shall result in the immediate dismissal of the employee.

XVIII. GRIEVANCE POLICY/PROCEDURE
A. The employee may present any grievance or appeal in writing to the Executive Director. The Executive Director will answer the employee in writing within five (5) working days.
B. If not resolved, the employee may present his/her grievance or appeal, in writing to the Executive Director. The Executive Director will answer the employee in writing within five (5) working days.
   The Personnel Committee may take final action, or refer the matter to the U.C. Child Care Board of Directors.
   The employee may request, in writing, a personal appearance before the Personnel committee.
C. The right of appeal is terminated by resignation.
D. If an employee desires to present an appeal as a result of termination of employment, the appeal must be presented within five (5) working days of the termination

Director's Resource 11–3 (continued)

notice. The appeal must be in writing and submitted to the Executive Director. If the appeal is not resolved, follow procedure B. above.

E. The failure of an employee to follow grievance procedures terminates the right of appeal, and termination is final.

Approved by Board of Trustees: 00/00/00

Director's Resource 11–4

Interview Questions*

Degreed Candidate

1. Tell us about your past experiences in this field—both your previous work experience and/or your practicum placements.
2. Of all the theories and ideas you studied in school, what had the greatest impact on you with regards to discipline in the classroom?
3. How do you think children learn? Give an example of how you would set up an experience for learning about a simple machine like an inclined plane or a pulley.
4. What would you do when an irate parent approaches you about an incident (such as biting in the classroom)? How would you handle that?
5. How would you handle problem solving in the classroom? For example, if two children are arguing over a basket of Legos, each saying she had it first, what would you do?
6. Choose an area of the curriculum (ex. science, math, music, etc.). Tell us how you would set it up.
7. How do you view your role as a preschool teacher?
8. What would you strive for in a parent/caregiver relationship?
9. What do you see as strong points in our program? Weak points?
10. How do you feel about themes when planning a curriculum?
11. How do you feel separation issues should be handled? For example, a child comes in with a special toy from home, and he is very reluctant to have Mom leave him. How might you handle that situation?
12. What are your long-term professional goals?
13. Since consistency is important in every program, how do you feel about committing to one year here?

Non-Degreed Candidate

1. Tell us about your experience in the field of early childhood education, as well as any other work experience you have had.
2. What do you see as your particular strengths which would apply to a position like this?
3. What are your professional goals? Would you be willing to attend some training sessions in the fall?
4. How would you handle an irate parent who approaches you at the end of the day when the teacher has gone?
5. If two children are arguing over Legos, each saying she had them first, what would you do?
6. What do you see as your role in the classroom?
7. What do you think the purpose of child care should be?
8. How would you handle a situation where a child has just knocked down another child's block building?
9. How do you think discipline is different from punishment?
10. What did you see during your tour of our center which you particularly liked? What were some of your questions as you toured the classroom?
11. What special skills and abilities do you feel you can bring to our program?

*Adapted and used by permission from Roark Learning Centers, Cincinnati, OH.

Director's Resource 11–5

Sample Staffing Plan—Infant Program

The sample staffing schedule offered here can be used to staff a small program or an individual class in a larger program. Guidelines for its use in programs with varying numbers of children follow. This schedule assumes a 1:3 adult-child ratio, for twelve infants.

Schedule for One Classroom of 12 Infants

B = paid rest break of 15 minutes   Lunch = unpaid lunch break of 30 minutes
. . . = 15-minute intervals (i.e., 8:15, 8:30, 8:45)

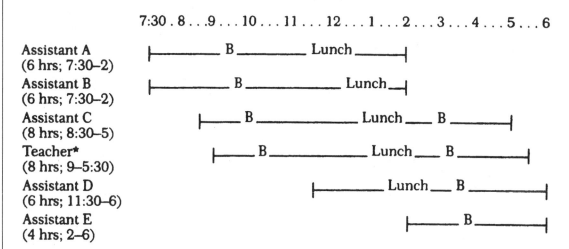

* These 8 teacher hours may be covered by more than one qualified teacher.
Note: This schedule shows child care staff only. Hours for administration and housekeeper or other maintenance personn
not included.

Gordon, L. Staffing schedules. (1988). In A. Godwin & L. Schrag (co-chairs). *Setting up for infant care: Guidelines for centers and family day care homes.* NAEYC, p. 50.

Director's Resource 11–6

Sample Staffing Plan (One Week)

M 11/11 **FALL**

2 10 YOUNG INFANTS 11 +1
4 10
8 10   6:00 - 2:30   Jeannie
       7:30 - 4:00   Pam
       8:30 - 5:00 Judy ~~Angie~~
       9:30 - 6:00   Lisa B.
       7:30-9:30 & 12:30-6:30 Kathy O'L.

1 9   OLDER INFANTS 9
2 11
6 11   7:00 - 10:30   Jill
       7:30 - 4:00   Mattie
       8:00 - 4:30   Karen M.
       9:30 - 6:00   Michelle
       12:30 - 5:30   Roxanne

1 10 YOUNG TODDLERS 12
6 11   7:00-7:30 & 8:30-9 Terry
9 12   6:00 - 2:30   Kathy O'R.
       7:30 - 4:00   Colette
       8:00 - 5:30   Julie
       9:30 - 6:00   Lisa M.

3 8   OLDER TODDLERS 8 +1
4 8   7:30 - 8:00   Terry
7 8   6:00 - 3:00 Robyn ~~Mary~~
       8:00 - 4:30   Stephanie
       9:00 to 5:30 Amy E ~~Robyn~~

       2:00 - 6:00 Yolanda

10 44 PRESCHOOL 49+0+1
15 45   8:00 - 8:30   Terry
26 47   6:30 - 3:00   Wendy 13
        7:00 - 3:30   Andrea
        7:30 - 4:00   Yvonne
        8:00 - 4:30   Joanie 13
        8:30 - 5:00   Dee Dee
        9:00 - 5:30   Amy W. 9+0+1
        9:30 - 6:00   Michele 14
        9:30 - 6:00   Debbie
        11:30- 12:30 Amy E to cover Mentor

KITCHEN

       6:45 - 3:15   Cheryl
       10:00 - 6:30   Jean

N/O 5/9

MAC
Angie
Mary L
Consuelo
~~1) Colette~~
~~2) Karen M.~~
~~3) Yolanda~~
~~4) Joanie~~

Andrea
Mentor
11:30 -
12:30

CLOSE   7:30

FLOATERS	Monday	Tuesday	Wednesday	Thursday	Friday
Amy E.	9-5³				
Consuelo	~				
Deborah	5³-7³				
Jill	7-10³				
Judy B.	8³-5				
Kathy O'L.	7³-9³ & 12³-6³				
Randall	~				
Roxanne	12³-5³				
Shelly	5³-8				
Terry	6³-3				
Trisha	~				
Yolanda	2-6				
Jenny	~				

Night Owls: I/T Adam-7³   Garrett -6:5   T/P   Annie-6:5   Jarrell-7
                              Jacob -6:5   Brady-6:5   Jeremy-7³
                              Anna - 6³   Laura-6³   Lisa-7³
                              Morgan - 7³   Phaethon-6³
                                                   Andrew-7
                                                   Shirley-7

Reprinted by permission Children's for Children, Children's Hospital Medical Center, Cincinnati, Ohio.

Director's Resource 11–6 (continued)

T 11/12 **FALL**

1	8	YOUNG INFANTS 8 + 2 + 1 co-op		2 9	OLDER INFANTS 11 + 2 COOP

```
1   8   YOUNG INFANTS 8 + 2 + 1 co-op          2   9   OLDER INFANTS  11 + 2 COOP
3   8   6:30 - 1:30      Jeannie               4  11
7   8   7:30 - 4:00      Pam                    7  11   7:00 -           Jill
        8:30 - 4:00 Judy Angie                         7:30 - 4:00      Mattie
        9:30 - 6:00      Lisa B.                        8:00 - 4:30      Karen M.
       12:30 - 6:30      Kathy O'L.                     9:30 - 6:00      Michelle
                                                        9:00 - 5:30      Amy E


0  12   YOUNG TODDLERS 14
5  13   8:00 - 9:00      Terry                  4   9   OLDER TODDLERS 10 + 2
8  14   6:15 - 2:15      Kathy O'R.             6   9   7:00 - 8:00      Terry
        7:30 - 4:00      Colette                9  10   6:30 - 3:00      Mary
        8:30 - 5:00      Julie                          8:00 - 4:30      Stephanie
        9:30 - 6:00      Lisa M.                         9:00 - 5:30     Robyn
        2:00 - 8:00      Jenny                          2:00 - 6:00      Yolanda


9  49   PRESCHOOL
22 51   6:15 - 2:15      Wendy 15               KITCHEN
32 52   7:00 - 3:30      Andrea
        7:15 - 3:15      Yvonne                  6:45 - 3:15     Cheryl      Angie
        7:15 - 4:15      Joanie 14              10:00 - 6:30     Jean        MAC
        8:00 - 4:30      Dee Dee
        8:30 - 5:00      Amy W. 12+1
        9:30 - 6:00      Michele 13
        9:30 - 6:00      Debbie                 N/O 4/8
        4:00 - 8:00      Trisha
```

CLOSE   8:00

FLOATERS	Monday	Tuesday	Wednesday	Thursday	Friday
Amy E.		9 –5^3			
Consuelo		∼			
Deborah		∼			
Jill		7 – 11			
Judy B.		7^3–4			
Kathy O'L.		12^3 6^3			
Randall		∼			
Roxanne		∼			
Shelly		∼			
Terry		6^3–3			
Trisha		4–8			
Yolanda		2–6			
Jenny		2–8			

Night Owls: I/T   Garrett –6^{15} T/P   Anne –6^{15} Jarrell –7
                              Anna – 6^3 Brady –6^{15} Allison –8
                              Chloe– 6^3 Laura– 6^3
                              Morgan –7   Phaethon –6^3
                                                            Andrew –7
                                                            Shirley –7

Director's Resource 11–6 (continued)

W ¹¹/₁₃ **FALL**

<table>
<tr><td>2 8</td><td colspan="3">YOUNG INFANTS 9</td></tr>
<tr><td>4 8</td><td></td><td></td><td></td></tr>
<tr><td>7 8</td><td>6:30 - 7:30</td><td></td><td>Jeannie</td></tr>
<tr><td></td><td>7:30 - 4:00</td><td></td><td>Pam</td></tr>
<tr><td></td><td>8:30 - 4:00</td><td>Angie <s>Angie</s></td><td></td></tr>
<tr><td></td><td>9:30 - 6:00</td><td></td><td>Lisa B.</td></tr>
<tr><td></td><td>12:30 - 6:30</td><td></td><td>Kathy O'L.</td></tr>
</table>

<table>
<tr><td>1 7</td><td colspan="3">OLDER INFANTS 9</td></tr>
<tr><td>2 9</td><td></td><td></td><td></td></tr>
<tr><td>6 9</td><td>7:00 - 11:00</td><td></td><td>Jill</td></tr>
<tr><td></td><td>7:30 - 4:00</td><td></td><td>Mattie</td></tr>
<tr><td></td><td>8:00 - 4:30</td><td></td><td>Karen M.</td></tr>
<tr><td></td><td>9:30 - 6:00</td><td></td><td>Michelle</td></tr>
<tr><td></td><td>1:00 - 3:00</td><td></td><td>Amy E</td></tr>
<tr><td></td><td>4:00 - 8:00</td><td></td><td>Trisha</td></tr>
</table>

<table>
<tr><td>0 9</td><td colspan="3">YOUNG TODDLERS 12+1</td></tr>
<tr><td>3 10</td><td></td><td></td><td></td></tr>
<tr><td>6 11</td><td>6:30 - 3:00</td><td></td><td>Kathy O'R.</td></tr>
<tr><td></td><td>7:30 - 4:00</td><td></td><td>Colette</td></tr>
<tr><td></td><td>9:00 - 5:30</td><td></td><td>Julie</td></tr>
<tr><td></td><td>9:30 - 6:00</td><td></td><td>Lisa M.</td></tr>
</table>

<table>
<tr><td>5 9</td><td colspan="3">OLDER TODDLERS 10</td></tr>
<tr><td>6 9</td><td></td><td></td><td></td></tr>
<tr><td>9 10</td><td>6:30 - 3:00</td><td></td><td>Mary</td></tr>
<tr><td></td><td>9:00 - 3:30</td><td></td><td>Stephanie</td></tr>
<tr><td></td><td>8:45 - 5:15</td><td></td><td>Robyn</td></tr>
<tr><td></td><td>2:00 - 6:00</td><td></td><td>Yolanda</td></tr>
</table>

<table>
<tr><td>10 46</td><td colspan="3">PRESCHOOL 52</td></tr>
<tr><td>15 50</td><td></td><td></td><td></td></tr>
<tr><td>29 50</td><td>6:30 - 3:00</td><td></td><td>Wendy 12</td></tr>
<tr><td></td><td>7:00 - 3:30</td><td><s>Michele Andrea</s></td><td></td></tr>
<tr><td></td><td>7:30 - 4:00</td><td></td><td>Yvonne</td></tr>
<tr><td></td><td>8:00 - 4:30</td><td></td><td>Joanie 13</td></tr>
<tr><td></td><td>8:30 - 3:30</td><td></td><td>Dee Dee</td></tr>
<tr><td></td><td>9:00 - 5:30</td><td></td><td>Amy W. 14</td></tr>
<tr><td></td><td>8:00 - 6:00</td><td>Andrea <s>Michele</s> 13</td><td></td></tr>
<tr><td></td><td>9:30 - 6:00</td><td></td><td>Debbie</td></tr>
<tr><td></td><td colspan="3">8:30-1 & 3-5 Amy E</td></tr>
</table>

KITCHEN

6:45 - 3:15   Cheryl
10:00 - 6:30   Jean

N/O ³/₇

Angie
DeeDee lvs 3:3
Andrea Mentor
in at 1:00

Accreditation
Meeting
9³-12³ For
DeeDee
Judy
Kathy O'
MAC
Chris

CLOSE   8:00

FLOATERS	Monday	Tuesday	Wednesday	Thursday	Friday
Amy E.			8³-5		
Consuelo			~		
Deborah			5³ 8		
Jill			7-11		
Judy B.			7³ 4		
Kathy O'L.			12³-6		
Randall			~		
Roxanne			~		
Shelly			~		
Terry			6³-3		
Trisha			4-8		
Yolanda			2-6		
Jenny			~		

Night Owls: I/T   Garrett -6¹⁵   T/P   Annie -6¹⁵   Shirley-7
                          Anna- 6³   Brady-6¹⁵   Jarrell-7
                          Morgan-8   Laura-6³
                                                         Phaethon -6³
                                                         Andrew-7

Director's Resource 11–6 (continued)

H 11/14 **FALL**

2 10   YOUNG INFANTS 11 + 1
5 10   8:00 - 8:30   MAC If Needed
9 10   6:00 - 3:30   Jeannie
       7:30 - 4:00   Pam
       8:30 - 4:00 Judy ~~Angie~~
       9:30 - 6:00   Lisa B.
       12:30 - 6:30   Kathy O'L.
       1:00 - 4:30   Amy E

1 8   OLDER INFANTS 11 + 1
3 10 7:00 - 9:30   Jill
7 11 7:30 - 4:00   Mattie
      8:00 - 4:30   Karen M.
      9:30 - 6:00   Michelle
      12:30 - 5:30   Roxanne
      4:30 - 6:00   Amy E

1 12   YOUNG TODDLERS 13 + 2
7 13   7:00 - 9:00   Terry
11 13 6:00 - 2:30   Kathy O'R.
       7:30 - 4:00   Colette
       8:30 - 5:00   Julie
       9:30 - 6:00   Lisa M.
       2:00 - 8:00   Jenny
Cover { 9:30 - 1:00 Amy E
for   { 9:45 - 11:30 Jill 11:30-12:30 Roxanne
PT6   { 10:00 - 12:30 Kathy O'L

6 9   OLDER TODDLERS 10 + 2
7 9   6:30 - 7:00   Terry if needed
9 10 6:30 - 3:00   Mary
      8:00 - 3:30   Stephanie
      9:00 - 5:30   Robyn
      2:00 - 6:00   Yolanda

PRESCHOOL 54 + 1 + 2

10 45   6:30 - 3:00   Wendy 14
15 48   7:00 - 3:30   Andrea
29 50   7:30 - 4:00   Yvonne
        8:00 - 4:30   Joanie 15 to + 2
        8:00 - 4:30   Dee Dee
        9:00 - 5:30   Amy W. 11 + 1
        9:30 - 6:00   Michele 14
        9:30 - 6:00   Debbie
        4:00 - 8:00   Randall

KITCHEN

     6:45 - 3:15   Cheryl
     10:00 - 6:30   Jean

N/O 8/11

Angie
Mary N.
Andrea Mentors
        11:30-12:30
Alligator Mini MTG
        10 - 12³
    Jill 10 - 11³
    Amy E 9³-1
    Kathy O'L 10 - 12³
    Roxanne 11³
           12:30

CLOSE   8:00

FLOATERS	Monday	Tuesday	Wednesday	Thursday	Friday
Amy E.				9³-6	
Consuelo				～	
Deborah				～	
Jill				7-11³	
Judy B.				7³-4	
Kathy O'L.				12³-6³	
Randall				4-8	
Roxanne				11³-5³	
Snelly				～	
Terry				6³-3	
Trisha				～	
Yolanda				2-6	
Jenny				2-8	

Night Owls: I/T Tyler-6³   Jacob-6⁵   T/P   Joseph-6⁵   Jarrell
               Adam-7³   Anna- 6³   Jack- 6⁵   Jeremy-7³
                               Morgan-7   Laura- 6³   Maria-7³
                               Jimmy -7³   Phaethon-6³ Allison-8
                               Garrett-8   Andrew -7   Brady-8
                               Christopher-8   Shirley-7

Director's Resource 11–6 (continued)

FALL

		YOUNG INFANTS 10+1		
1	10			
4	10	7:30 – 9:30		
8	10	6:30 – 7:30	Jeannie	
		7:30 – 4:00	Pam	
		9:00 – 5:30	~~Judy~~ ~~Angie~~	
		9:30 – 6:00	Lisa B.	
		12:30 – 2:45	~~Yolanda~~ ~~Kathy O'L.~~	
		1:00 – 6:00	Amy E	

		OLDER INFANTS 12		
1	9			
3	12	7:00 – 11:00	Jill	
7	12	7:30 – 4:00	Mattie	
		8:00 – 4:30	Karen M.	
		9:30 – 6:00	Michelle	
		12:30 – 6:30	Roxanne	
		1:00 – 5:30	Jenny	
		11:00 – 12:30	Amy E.	

		YOUNG TODDLERS 10+2		
1	8			
5	9	6:30 – 3:00	Kathy O'R.	
5	10	8:00 – 9:00 MAC ~~Colette~~		
		9:00 – 5:30	Julie	
		9:30 – 6:00	Lisa M.	

		OLDER TODDLERS 11		
4	6			
6	10			
10	11	6:35 – 2:45	Mary	
		9:00 – 3:30	Stephanie	
		9:00 – 5:30	Robyn	
		2:45 – 6:00	Yolanda	

		PRESCHOOL 43+1		
9	39			
14	42	6:30 – 3:00	Wendy	10
24	42	7:00 – 3:30 ~~Michele~~ Andrea		
		7:30 – 4:00	Yvonne	
		8:00 – 4:30	Joanie	11
		8:30 – 5:00	Dee Dee	
		9:00 – 5:30	~~Amy H.~~	9+1
		9:30 – 6:00	~~Andrea~~ Michele	13
		9:30 – 6:00	Debbie	
		4:30 – 5:30	Consuelo	
		9:30 – 1:00	Amy E.	

KITCHEN

6:45 – 3:15	Cheryl
10:00 – 6:30	Jean

N/O 5/6

Angie
Kathy O'L
1) Amy W.
2) Pam lvs 1:00
3) Colette
Andrea Mentors
7:30   in at 1:00

CLOSE

FLOATERS	Monday	Tuesday	Wednesday	Thursday	Friday
Amy E.					9^3-6
Consuelo					4^3-7^3
Deborah					~
Jill					7–11
Judy B.					9-5^3
Kathy O'L.					~
Randall					~
Roxanne					12^3-6^3
Shelly					5^3-7^3
Terry					6^3-3
Trisha					~
Yolanda					2–6
Jenny					~

Night Owls: I/T

Garrett – $6^{.5}$
Anna – 6^3
Morgan – 7
Chloe – 7^3
John – 7^3

T/P

Brady – 6^3
Laura – 6^3
Phaethon – 6^3
Andrew – 7
Shirley – 7
Jarrell – 7

Director's Resource 11–7

Sample Staffing Plan—Multiple Program B
Staff Plan by Staff Member

Title	How Many	Schedule	Recommended Salary	Total Yearly
Director/Administrator	1	MWF 7:30 A.M.– TTH 12:00 P.M.	$11.00/hr $22,880.00/yr	$22,880.00
Head Teachers	5	7:30–3:00 P.M. 30-min break between 12:00–1:30 P.M.	$8.50/hr $17,680.00/yr	$88,400.00
Teachers	5	11:00–7:00 P.M. 30-min. break between 1:00–2:30 P.M.	$7.00/hr $14,560.00/yr	$72,800.00
Morning Assistants	5	7:30–12:30 P.M. 15-min. break between 11:00–12:00 P.M.	$5.00/hr $6,500.00/yr	$32,500.00
Afternoon Assistants	5	12:30–7:00 P.M. 15-min. break between 2:30–3:00 P.M.	$5.00/hr $8,450.00/yr	$42,250.00
Secretary/Bookkeeper	1	9:00–5:30 1-hr. lunch	$6.00/hr $10,400/yr	$12,480.00
Custodian	1	5:00–10:00 P.M. Mon.–Thur. 5 hrs. on Sat. 15-min. break	$5.00/hr $6,500/yr	$6,500
Cook	1	7:30–3:00 P.M. 30-min. lunch	$5.00/hr $10,400/yr	$10,400
Total Yearly Salaries:				$288,210.00

(Reprinted by permission of Tara Schnicke and Brigid Nally)

Director's Resource 11–7 (continued)

Staff Plan by Classroom

Classroom	No. of Children	Staff/Child Ratio
Infants	8	required: 5:1
		maximum: 8:3
Rm:101		minimum: 8:2
Toddlers	11	required: 7:1
		max: 11:3
Rm:201		min.: 11:2
3-Year-Olds	17	required: 12:1
		max.: 17:3
Rm:202		min.: 17:2
3-and 4-Year-Olds	17	required: 12:1
		max.: 17:3
Rm:203		min.: 17:2
4-Year-Olds	17	required: 14:1
		max.: 14:3
Rm:204		min.: 14:2

Each classroom will be staffed as follows:

1 Head Teacher	7:30–3:00 P.M.
1 Teacher	11:00–7:00 P.M.
1 Assistant	7:30–12:30 P.M.
1 Assistant	12:30–7:00 P.M.

This flexible schedule allows ample time for classroom planning in the morning and evening when the ratios will be low because most children arrive at the center between 8:00–9:00 A.M. and leave between 5:00–6:00 P.M.. Nap time is when team planning and communication takes place.

Director's Resource 11–7 (continued)

Additional Comments about Staffing

—Breaks must maintain staff/child ratio at all times.

—Flexibility in scheduling breaks is necessary to meet the immediate needs of the class-rooms.

—Short restroom breaks, or emergency phone calls could be arranged as needed, as long as ratio is maintained.

—Staff schedules are designed for enhancing staff communications, and for meeting the needs of the children.

—Swing scheduling for directors are designed to encourage and maintain communication with all staff members, family members, board, and community contacts.

—It is the teacher's responsibility to take care of housekeeping emergencies during the day.

—The cook is solely responsible for cleaning the kitchen, other than the clean-up after the afternoon snack, which is the teacher's responsibility.

—One morning snack, one afternoon snack, and one full meal will be provided each day.

—Encourage male applicants for all positions to balance male–female models.

—Parent(s)/surrogate(s) provide transportation.

—Tuition $95/week for infants and $85/week for all others.

—80 percent of tuition income goes for salaries.

Director's Resource 11–8

Sample Evaluation Form (Teaching Staff)

COMMUNITY DAY CARE ASSOCIATION

NAME: _____ DATE: _____

CENTER: _____ DIRECTOR: _____

EVALUATION OF TEACHER

Indicate evaluation by using numbers 1 through 5:5 meaning high, appropriate, or very good; 3 average; and 1 low, inappropriate, or poor in that particular characteristic.

PERSONAL QUALITIES
1. _____Friendly, warm.
2. _____Appearance: dress, posture.
3. _____Speech and voice: Clear and well modulated.
4. _____Tact and courtesy: Observes social conventions; tolerant and considerate of others.
5. _____Displays a sense of humor.
6. _____Dependable.
7. _____Self-confident.
8. _____Enthusiastic about teaching.
9. _____Expresses a desire to learn.
10. _____Ability to evaluate self.
11. _____Profits by criticism.

ASSUMING RESPONSIBILITIES
12. _____Is independent in assuming responsibility.
13. _____Adjusts temperature, light, and ventilation.
14. _____Achieves efficient and satisfactory arrangement of playroom and play yard.
15. _____Is flexible in planning program for children.
16. _____Plans activities to enrich the lives of children according to their level of development.
17. _____Overall planning for program activities.
18. _____Daily preparation for program activities.
19. _____Discusses pertinent problems with director.

WORKING WITH CHILDREN
20. _____Creates a warm and accepting environment.
21. _____Likes children, shows a real enjoyment of them.
22. _____Recognizes when children are happy and relaxed.
23. _____Enjoys humorous incidents with children. Seems to enjoy laughing with them.
24. _____Understands children on their own level.
25. _____Accepts each child as he is.

Director's Resource 11–8 (continued)

26. _____Recognizes that each child is a sensitive, thinking individual and treats him accordingly.
27. _____Shows awareness of progress or lack of it in a child's behavior.
28. _____Relates easily to children.
29. _____Impartial in dealing with children.
30. _____Aware of differing moods of children, adjusts standards for them at times when they are fatigued, irritated, overstimulated, etc.
31. _____Is imaginative and creative.
33. _____Is resourceful in a practical way, has common sense.
34. _____Uses positive approach.
35. _____Helps children accept limitations.
36. _____Makes suggestions without antagonizing.
37. _____Does not overstimulate or cause tension in children.
38. _____Removes distracting influences.
39. _____Alert to total group, even when dealing with a part of it.
40. _____Remains controlled in startling or difficult situations.
41. _____Encourages and guides the expression of feelings.
42. _____Assists children in gaining confidence.
43. _____Treats the child's possessions and projects with care.
44. _____Gives children opportunity for manipulating various kinds of creative materials.
45. _____Explains relations between a child's individual rights and group rights.
46. _____Provides guidance of children in group relationships.
47. _____Provides guidance of activities according to group needs and interests.
48. _____Provides guidance of children in developing motor coordination.
49. _____Provides guidance in music experiences.
50. _____Provides guidance in story and language experiences.
51. _____Provides guidance in science experiences.
52. _____Provides guidance in use of creative materials.
53. _____Provides guidance in toileting routine.
54. _____Provides guidance in resting.
55. _____Provides guidance in eating experiences.

WORKING WITH ADULTS
56. _____Is interested in people, thinks in terms of helping them rather than criticizing.
57. _____Cooperates well with adults.
58. _____Is considerate of activities of other adults.
59. _____Welcomes new ideas, flexibility as shown by willingness to consider new ideas.
60. _____Maintains high standards of professional ethics in regard to children and staff.
61. _____Realizes that situations cannot always be handled in the home as they are at school.
62. _____Attitude in working with parents is cooperative.

Director's Resource 11–8 (continued)

SPECIFIC STRENGTH OF TEACHER:

SPECIFIC LIMITATIONS OF TEACHER:

OTHER COMMENTS:

Director's Resource 11–9

Sample Job Description—Special Education Consultant

Title: Special-Education Consultant

Responsible to: Center Director

Responsibilities: The special-education consultant is responsible for assisting the director and the professional staff in identifying, evaluating, locating special services for and working with special needs children and their families who are enrolled in the program. Duties include the following:

1. Participate on the team involved in screening, selecting, and placing the disabled children in this program.
2. Assist the staff in identification of disabled children during the process of screening and assessment.
3. Provide special education services when deemed appropriate, after the initial information gathering process.
4. Act as case manager for each identified disabled child.
5. Participate in the I.E.P. team process; the in-house staffings, the multi-disciplinary team conferences with the parents, and the implementation of the I.E.P. when necessary.
6. Assist the Director with referral sources, connections to public and private agencies, as well as the public school system.
7. Participate in quarterly staffings on each enrolled disabled child.
8. Be available to the teaching staff on an "as needed" basis for consultation and problem-solving regarding the disabled children in the classrooms.
9. Facilitate the referral of identified disabled children, through the development of a systematic procedure for documenting services to disabled children in the area of screening, assessment, diagnosis, placement, and referral.
10. Provide or arrange for appropriate special-education-related inservices as deemed necessary after consultation with the director.

Qualifications: A Master's degree in Early Childhood Special Education or equivalent and some classroom experience with both disabled and non-disabled preschool children. Some experience using screening and assessment tools and knowledge of agencies providing special education services.

Work Schedule: Five hours per week on a schedule worked out with the director and based upon staff and family needs. Total hours not to exceed 20 hours per month.

Salary Schedule: Range $20.00 to $30.00 per hour based upon training and experience.

Director's Resource 11–10

Sample Job Description—Public School Instructor II and Instructor I
Public Schools Civil Service Personnel Branch
Position Description

TITLE
Instructor II

PILOT PROGRAM
Constructivist Preschool Pilot Program at Social and Academic Skills Demonstration Schools.

RESPONSIBLE TO
School Principal; in collaboration with Constructivist Pilot Program Supervisor, and/or Project Coordinator

SUPERVISES
Instructor Assistant, volunteers and/or student teachers

REQUIREMENTS
1. Minimum—Bachelor in Child Development or Early Childhood Education from accredited college; some teaching experience with preschool children; ability to communicate articulate knowledge of child development with a focus on constructivist theory; must demonstrate ability to implement a constructivist's approach to teaching young children; must have good oral and written communication skills.
2. Must have the results of the annual physical and Mantoux TB test on file at the center before the first day of school for children.
3. Must have transportation available in order to make required home visits and other parent or community contacts.
4. Must be able to relate well to adults and children and work effectively with another adult in a classroom situation.
5. Must be available for evening meetings when scheduled.
6. Must have a current First Aid Certificate from the American Red Cross on file at school.

PERFORMANCE RESPONSIBILITIES
1. Be responsible for a reasonable amount of processing with Instructor Assistant on a regularly scheduled basis.
2. Plan and evaluate the ongoing classroom program with Instructor Assistant on a weekly basis.
3. Evaluate Instructor Assistant according to the method chosen by the school system.
4. Confer with Constructivist Pilot Program Supervisor and Instructor Assistant on a regularly scheduled basis.

(Reprint by permission of Cincinnati Youth Collaborative)

Director's Resource 11–10 (continued)

CHILDREN

1. Plan, execute, and maintain a file of weekly educational plans for classroom activities for children. Plans are posted for parents' review. These must be based on constructivist theory.

2. Set up and maintain a safe, attractive, developmentally appropriate classroom environment for children—one which encourages autonomy, creativity, and particularly individual and group problem-solving.

3. Conduct ongoing observations of the children enrolled in the classroom, and maintain anecdotal records in order to assess each child's construction of knowledge and overall developmental progress.

4. Develop and facilitate activities which will promote the healthy social, emotional, intellectual and physical development of each child, allowing the child to feel accepted and free to express feelings.

5. Maintain accurate, up-to-date records—a. Pupil folders, attendance, referrals, progress reports; b. Inventories of equipment and materials.

6. Supervise serving of breakfasts, snack, and lunch.

Director's Resource 11–10 (continued)

Public Schools Civil Service Personnel Branch
Position Description

TITLE
Instructor Assistant I

PILOT PROGRAM
Constructivist Pilot Preschool Program at Social and Academic Skills Demonstration Schools.

RESPONSIBLE TO
Principal and/or designee (i.e. Preschool Instructor).

REQUIREMENTS
1. MINIMUM—Associates Degree in Child Development or Early Childhood Education from an accredited college. Some teaching experience preferred.
2. Must have the ability to communicate, articulate, and demonstrate a sensitivity toward and nurturing of children.
3. Must have a current school medical form, tuberculin test results, and verification of degree/certificate on file at the school.
4. Must have or obtain a current First Aid Certificate from the American Red Cross on file at the School.
5. Must have good written and oral communication skills.
6. Must be available for occasional evening meetings/activities when scheduled.
7. Must follow directions and work independently.

RESPONSIBILITIES
1. Cooperate with and assist Instructor in implementing a constructivist approach to teaching young children.
2. Assist Instructor in setting up and maintaining an orderly, safe, healthy, nurturing environment for young children.
3. Prepare and implement, with teacher's guidance, appropriate curriculum activities (i.e. art, music, cooking, etc.) with individual children and small groups. As guided by Instructor, supervise children as they manage clothing, toileting, eating, etc.
4. Maintain a communicative relationship with young children in the expression of needs and feelings which will foster the development of positive self concepts.
5. Assist Instructor and/or assume responsibility for cleanup of activities and total classroom environment.
6. Assist Instructor in maintaining storage of classroom equipment in a safe and orderly manner.
7. Perform clerical duties relative to the classroom as directed by the Instructor to include but not be limited to such items as assisting parents with forms; documenting attendance, putting children's names on notes.
8. Make community contacts by assisting with recruitment as needed; making parent contacts as directed by Instructor.

Director's Resource 11–10 (continued)

9. Plan and discuss the ongoing classroom program with Instructor on a regular basis.
10. Confer with Constructivist Pilot Program Supervisor and Instructor on a regular basis.
11. Attend and participate in in-service to further develop a constructivist knowledge base.
12. Observe and adhere to school policies and to the Ohio Association for the Education of Young Children's Code of Ethics.

Director's Resource 11–11

U.S. Department of Justice
Immigration and Naturalization Service

OMB No. 1115-0136
Employment Eligibility Verification

Please read instructions carefully before completing this form. The instructions must be available during completion of this form. **ANTI-DISCRIMINATION NOTICE.** It is illegal to discriminate against work eligible individuals. Employers CANNOT specify which document(s) they will accept from an employee. The refusal to hire an individual because of a future expiration date may also constitute illegal discrimination.

Section 1. Employee Information and Verification. To be completed and signed by employee at the time employment begins

Print Name: Last	First	Middle Initial	Maiden Name

Address (Street Name and Number)		Apt. #	Date of Birth (month/day/year)

City	State	Zip Code	Social Security #

I am aware that federal law provides for imprisonment and/or fines for false statements or use of false documents in connection with the completion of this form.

I attest, under penalty of perjury, that I am (check one of the following):
☐ A citizen or national of the United States
☐ A Lawful Permanent Resident (Alien # A _____)
☐ An alien authorized to work until ____/____/____
(Alien # or Admission # _____)

Employee's Signature	Date (month/day/year)

Preparer and/or Translator Certification. (To be completed and signed if Section 1 is prepared by a person other than the employee.) I attest, under penalty of perjury, that I have assisted in the completion of this form and that to the best of my knowledge the information is true and correct.

Preparer's/Translator's Signature	Print Name

Address (Street Name and Number, City, State, Zip Code)	Date (month/day/year)

Section 2. Employer Review and Verification. To be completed and signed by employer. Examine one document from List A OR examine one document from List B and one from List C as listed on the reverse of this form and record the title, number and expiration date, if any, of the document(s)

List A	OR	List B	AND	List C
Document title: _____		_____		_____
Issuing authority: _____		_____		_____
Document #: _____		_____		_____
Expiration Date (if any): ___/___/___		___/___/___		___/___/___
Document #: _____				
Expiration Date (if any): ___/___/___				

CERTIFICATION - I attest, under penalty of perjury, that I have examined the document(s) presented by the above-named employee, that the above-listed document(s) appear to be genuine and to relate to the employee named, that the employee began employment on (month/day/year) ___/___/___ and that to the best of my knowledge the employee is eligible to work in the United States. (State employment agencies may omit the date the employee began employment).

Signature of Employer or Authorized Representative	Print Name	Title

Business or Organization Name	Address (Street Name and Number, City, State, Zip Code)	Date (month/day/year)

Section 3. Updating and Reverification. To be completed and signed by employer

New Name (if applicable)	B. Date of rehire (month/day/year) (if applicable)

If employee's previous grant of work authorization has expired, provide the information below for the document that establishes current employment eligibility.

Document Title: _____ Document #: _____ Expiration Date (if any): ___/___/___

I attest, under penalty of perjury, that to the best of my knowledge, this employee is eligible to work in the United States, and if the employee presented document(s), the document(s) I have examined appear to be genuine and to relate to the individual.

Signature of Employer or Authorized Representative	Date (month/day/year)

Form I-9 (Rev. 11-21-91) N

Director's Resource 11–11 (continued)

LISTS OF ACCEPTABLE DOCUMENTS

LIST A

Documents that Establish Both Identity and Employment Eligibility

1. U.S. Passport (unexpired or expired)

2. Certificate of U.S. Citizenship (INS Form N-560 or N-561)

3. Certificate of Naturalization (INS Form N-550 or N-570)

4. Unexpired foreign passport, with I-551 stamp or attached INS Form I-94 indicating unexpired employment authorization

5. Alien Registration Receipt Card with photograph (INS Form I-151 or I-551)

6. Unexpired Temporary Resident Card (INS Form I-688)

7. Unexpired Employment Authorization Card (INS Form I-688A)

8. Unexpired Reentry Permit (INS Form I-327)

9. Unexpired Refugee Travel Document (INS Form I-571)

10. Unexpired Employment Authorization Document issued by the INS which contains a photograph (INS Form I-688B)

OR

LIST B

Documents that Establish Identity

1. Driver's license or ID card issued by a state or outlying possession of the United States provided it contains a photograph or information such as name, date of birth, sex, height, eye color, and address

2. ID card issued by federal, state, or local government agencies or entities provided it contains a photograph or information such as name, date of birth, sex, height, eye color, and address

3. School ID card with a photograph

4. Voter's registration card

5. U.S. Military card or draft record

6. Military dependent's ID card

7. U.S. Coast Guard Merchant Mariner Card

8. Native American tribal document

9. Driver's license issued by a Canadian government authority

For persons under age 18 who are unable to present a document listed above:

10. School record or report card

11. Clinic, doctor, or hospital record

12. Day-care or nursery school record

AND

LIST C

Documents that Establish Employment Eligibility

1. U.S. social security card issued by the Social Security Administration (other than a card stating it is not valid for employment)

2. Certification of Birth Abroad issued by the Department of State (Form FS-545 or Form DS-1350)

3. Original or certified copy of a birth certificate issued by a state, county, municipal authority or outlying possession of the United States bearing an official seal

4. Native American tribal document

5. U.S. Citizen ID Card (INS Form I-197)

6. ID Card for use of Resident Citizen in the United States (INS Form I-179)

7. Unexpired employment authorization document issued by the INS (other than those listed under List A)

Illustrations of many of these documents appear In Part 8 of the Handbook for Employers (M-274)

Form I-9 (Rev. 11-21-91) N

FPI-RBK

CHAPTER 12

Publicizing the Center and Selecting the Children

An important part of the director's job, in both new and ongoing programs, is publicizing the center. Decisions about the total population of children to be served by the center will determine the nature of the publicity that is written, as well as the audience to whom it is addressed. Publicity is not only related to recruitment and selection of children but also is integrally related to the center's public relations program.

PUBLICITY

Publicizing a program can be done through newspaper, magazine, or journal advertising, radio or television advertising, fliers or posters, and neighborhood papers or church bulletins. The director's first task is to decide where to direct the major thrust of the advertising.

Where and How to Advertise

The direction that the publicity takes should be based on the consideration of which families need to be reached in order to recruit children and promote the program. Obviously, young families are the first to come to mind since most programs are set up to serve children from infancy to five years of age or primary school-aged children in before- and after-school programs. However, there are other considerations. If program survival depends on tuition, the target population is clearly limited to those who can afford to pay for the service. On the other hand, if outside funding sources exist, it will be necessary to increase the scope of the publicity effort so that a greater portion of the potential clientele can be reached. Whether or not the program will serve families within walking distance of the center or will draw from a broader geographical area by transporting children from rural areas, surrounding suburbs, or nearby businesses will affect the publicity effort. Likewise, the program sponsorship and program location will exert an influence in this regard. For example, sometimes program sponsors limit the population to be served to university families, poverty-level families, children of hospital personnel, children of families who are employed in a particular factory or office complex, children of club or church members, and so forth.

All these factors and others that you may have thought about will enter into the decision about where and how to publicize the center. Newspaper ads and radio announcements reach a wide audience whereas a more limited population is reached through direct mailing of brochures or circulars, display of window placards, door-to-door solicitation, and advertisements in local papers, church bulletins, and military newsletters.

As a director, it behooves you to take advantage of opportunities to invite reporters to the center to do newspaper or television pieces on your center. If you are affiliated with a large business or hospital, their public relations staff may help you. Television and newspaper reporters are interested in what is new at your center. If there is a new infant room opening, or you have a new custom-designed playground, reporters and cameramen will come to you. Other newsworthy items might be a new teacher who signs for deaf, installation of a ramp to accommodate children and adults with disabilities, or the use of senior citizen volunteers in the preschool classrooms.

Taking your message to the local lodge or church gathering, PTA groups, or community meetings where it will reach parents whose busy lives may limit the time spent reading publications or listening to radio or television, is still another way to publicize the program. Taking slides or videotapes to these meetings to show what children and teachers do in child care centers will enrich your presentation.

It is important to get your message out to companies in the community, as well as to individuals and community groups. The first wave of companies interested in addressing the child care needs of their employees typically were attracted to setting up on-site child care centers. Recently, however, companies are more inclined to look to existing community child care centers where they can purchase slots, buy priority status, or negotiate for corporate group rates for their employees. Developing a professional presentation which is designed for use with corporate clients and timely follow-up with appropriate contacts within the corporation will enhance your chances of attracting corporate clients.[1]

It is important to consider various ways to publicize your program, but do not underestimate the value of "word-of-mouth" from parents who are enthusiastic about the quality of your program. Nothing sells a program better than offering a high quality program which is worthy of accreditation and led by well-trained, qualified early childhood teachers.

Advertising Materials

The choice of words and the photographs used in the printed materials distributed by the center should reflect a subtle message of concern and appreciation for children, and should express the philosophy behind the center's program. These materials project the image of the center, and should reflect your professionalism.[2]

DIRECTOR'S CORNER

"The thing we had the most success with when we opened our second center was the newspaper piece about using the "pod" concept for our infant program. It not only helped our infant enrollment, but it helped fill all the groups in that center. That notion about the "pod" bringing together the richness of group care and the individualized nurturance of home was very appealing—it seemed to give parents a solid idea to hold onto. It was the best public relations piece we ever had."

—Director, independent not-for-profit center

The content and appearance of brochures or fliers make a statement to parents. The words should be informative and spell out the philosophy of the center's program. The photographs or some creative, clever artwork should convey, in less obvious ways, the fact that the staff of the center is professional and creative. The message for parents should be clear: any child who is sent to this center will share in that professionalism and creativity. When unsolicited letters from parents are available, using statements from those letters in brochures or publicity releases is an excellent way to get your message across. Every detail of any mailing piece to be used for initial advertising

[1]Duncan S., & Thornton, D. (1993). Marketing your center's services to employers. *Child Care Information Exchange: The Director's Magazine,* January, pp. 53–56.
[2]Tiger, F. (1995).The art of brochure. *Child Care Information Exchange: The Director's Magazine,* 102, March/April, p. 24.

or in response to inquiries about the program should be carefully scrutinized.

Brochures. The director is responsible for the preparation and the mailing of brochures, but other staff members, as well as parents, can contribute to the effort by providing artistic talents, access to a printer they know about, or some other expertise. When a brochure is prepared, two major considerations are cost and content.

Costs vary depending on number, length, quality of paper, use of color, and use of photographs. Therefore, it is wise to discuss ideas for the brochure with a printer as soon as possible. Costs increase when the professionally done brochure includes photos or a logo which requires artwork, but it is these unique features that may be precisely what attracts the attention of prospective clients. Money spent on an attractive brochure may be a good investment. Using a single color on heavy weight, standard size paper will give a look of high quality yet keep the costs down.

If the brochure is to be used over a long period of time, it is wise to avoid using items that are subject to change such as the school calendar or the fee schedule. These variable items can be detailed in a short insert. The brochure itself should contain information that remains constant from year to year. The following list includes some of the more stable items typically included in a brochure:

- name, address, and telephone number of the center
- a map showing location of the center
- description of the program
- sponsorship of the program
- enrollment procedures and children served (ages, developmentally disabled, and so forth)
- licensing and/or accreditation status of the center

It is important to include the hours, days, and months for the program. The stability of the operational schedule will determine whether such information should go into the brochure itself or be part of the insert.

Public Relations

The center's image is an important consideration in all aspects of the public information and public relations efforts. The appearance of the physical setting and the behavior of personnel in that setting are fundamental factors in creating good public relations and sound relationships with the children and with their parents. These factors are what convey professionalism and concern about children and families. The director should serve as a model and encourage the staff to be mindful of their role as community advocates for children. Parents entering the building should see an interior prepared for use by children. Furthermore, parents should be greeted by a warm, caring person who expresses interest in them and in their children. When parents or others telephone the center, the person who answers must be pleasant, tactful, and knowledgeable.

An open house for parents who have made inquiries or have responded to your marketing efforts is a good way to expand the public relations program for the center. Remember to invite current parents, current staff members, and board members to these social events. An open house affords an opportunity for the staff to have an informal meeting with others who are interested in the center's activities. In the case of a new program, publicizing the open house can be part of the initial efforts at promotion. In the case of ongoing programs, staff and board members also will reap benefits from this kind of gathering because it provides a time for interaction and communication among adults who have common concerns and share an interest in the children attending the program.

When the center is opened for visitors, the environment should be prepared just as it would be for the children. In this way, you can demonstrate how a well-planned environment should look, and provide an opportunity for parents to participate and use available materials. What better way to give parents a feeling for what happens each day than to have them use the materials in the classrooms! In addition, slides, a scrapbook of photos, or a videotape of children actively participating in the classroom can give parents further insights into what a quality program can offer their children.

Planning for the open house should be done by people who understand the lifestyles and expectations of the clients who are likely to show interest in the event. Careful and sensitive planning regarding the time of the event and the level of informality communicates to members of the community that the people at the center understand and care about them and their children.

Reflections

Think about your center. You are sitting outside in the parking lot as parents arrive. Is the building inviting? Does it really welcome children and families? Now imagine yourself inside the building. Do adults stoop down and extend a friendly welcome to the children? Are parents recognized and called by name? As you walk further into the building, how does it look? What sounds do you hear? How does it smell? The impressions you are reliving are the same parents and children experience each day they enter that center.

SELECTING THE CHILDREN

Ultimately, the director is responsible for the decisions about which children will be admitted to the program. The teachers often are called on to assist in this decision, and sometimes a standing committee authorized by the board is asked to make policy or give advice. An Admissions and Recruitment Committee might be charged with policy-making decisions about the population to be served. There are also decisions about the admission of children with disabilities and about the grouping of children.

Other factors, such as readiness of the child, needs of the child and family, and age of the child may enter into the final selection. There are pressures to admit all applicants when enrollment is not full. However, it is always important for the director to exercise good professional judgment about which children to admit, basing admission decisions on what is in the best interest of the child. The number of children to be served by the program will be determined by the size of the space, as well as the number of adults available for the children's programs. In many areas, criteria set by licensing regulations must be satisfied (see Chapter 5).

Readiness of Children and Families

The Director or a member of the professional staff must assess the child's readiness to enter the program. It is essential that this assessment be made with the participation of the family. In some situations, the age of the child is the only consideration, but that is clearly a tenuous criterion if it is the only one used in deciding whether or not a child can manage a group experience in a particular center. Indeed, it is analogous to the idea of judging a book by its cover. Chronological age is only one factor among many that will determine whether or not a child will be able to move into a program and profit from the experience. Other determinants are the emotional, social, and intellectual development of the child, and, of course, the child's health.

This is not to suggest that a child who does not meet some arbitrary standard or norm should be rejected on that basis alone, unless licensing regulations prohibit admission of children before a certain age. What it does mean is that the professionals at the center must decide if the available staff and the particular program offerings at the center can be adapted to provide the most enriching experience for a particular child. In other words, can this program provide what this child needs to develop to his or her fullest potential? If there is any doubt in the minds of either the members of the family or the director, careful consideration should be given to a number of questions. Can the program be adjusted to accommodate this child? Is there another program with a different focus that would provide a better match for this child and the lifestyle of this family? Is it better for the child and the family to consider waiting a while longer before placing the child in the center so that all will be more prepared for an initial separation, even though the family is seeking placement for the child so the parents can work? What other arrangements can be made for the care of the child?

What about the child who must be placed in full-day care to meet a family need that is both urgent and imminent? Perhaps there is some financial crisis, some tragedy, or illness that makes it impossible to keep the child at home. That need must be heard. However, an experienced person with a strong sense of professional integrity would certainly avoid admitting a child to a program if the program, as it is currently set up, could be potentially damaging to the child. In special cases, a child could be accepted on a trial basis, or alternatives such as a family child care home or a qualified baby sitter might be recommended for the child. In any case, as director, you must remember that your decisions are affecting the lives of children and families who are looking to you for help in the decision-making process. Your task is to provide help that is educationally and professionally sound.

There is also another side to the issue. Not only must the child be ready for the separation and the group environment, but the family, and most importantly the primary caregiver, also must be ready to leave the child. Members of the professional staff at the center may have excellent skills when it comes to adapting the learning environment to each child, regardless of the child's age or level of readiness. However, coping with the reluctant parent is another problem that may be much more difficult to manage. For this very reason, the assessment of readiness and the final decision on admission must be a cooperative effort between a member of the professional staff and the family. Interviews, visits to the home and to the center, and careful observation of the child in the context of the family are all helpful in making a final admission decision.

Admission of Children With Disabilities

The general question of readiness applies to all children and families seeking admission, whether the children are atypical or normal. The critical questions in each case are the same:

- Will the child's needs be met?
- Will the family's needs be met?
- Will the program meet the needs of both the child and the family without interfering with meeting the needs of all the other children and families involved in the program?

In 1986, Congress enacted Public Law 99-457, amending the Education of Handicapped Act (EHA, PL 94-142). The reauthorization of both PL 94-142 and PL 99-457 came in 1990 with the passage of PL 101-479, Individuals with Disabilities Education Act, known by the acronym IDEA. The law requires that states provide a free appropriate public education to all children with disabilities, ages three to five years. States that fail to comply will no longer receive any EHA funding for preschoolers. The new law also mandates that states develop a state plan for expansion and improvement of early intervention programs for children with disabilities birth through age two, and there is a provision whereby funding is available to extend intervention programs to at-risk infants and toddlers as well. Knowledge of the ADA is also important as directors review requests for admission of children with disabilities. Centers are prohibited from denying admission to a child simply because of a disability unless such admission would fundamentally "alter the nature of the program," or would be an "undue burden" on the program.[3] As we move into the 21st century, directors in early childhood education programs must be prepared to cope with the challenge of providing quality inclusion environments for increasing numbers of preschool children with disabilities.

Directors are faced with the issue of applying the critical question of readiness, as stated above, when considering admission of children with special needs and also must have knowledge of the laws related to these special children. It is helpful for them to know how the law applies to infants, toddlers, and preschoolers, and to understand how preschools and child care centers are likely to fit into the scheme of services for atypical children. They also should know what role they and their staff can play as part of the interdisciplinary, interagency team effort to give these children the benefit of quality early childhood education experiences.

Provisions of PL 99-457.[4] PL 99-457 extends all rights and due process protection of PL 94-142 to children with disabilities ages three to five. Therefore, preschool children with special needs

---

[3]*Child Care Information Exchange: The Director's Magazine*, 106, November/December, 1995, p. 81.
[4]Most of the information in this section is taken from K. Eileen Allen K. E. & Schwartz, I. S. (1996). *The exceptional child: Inclusion in early childhood education* (3rd edition), Demar.

are ensured free public education in a least restrictive environment based on an Individualized Education Program (IEP) developed by a team that includes the child's parents. The programs are to be administered through state or local education agencies (LEA) that may contract with other service providers to offer a range of service models. The designated state agency is ultimately responsible for monitoring overall services and use of the federal funds. Other sources of funding such as Medicaid or Maternal and Child Health also must be utilized when the children are eligible, and the new funds are to supplement but not supplant these existing sources. Thus, the new funds may be used in addition to but not instead of existing sources of funding. States are not required to report the number of children served by a disability category, thereby eliminating the necessity to categorically label these children because of data collection requirements.

PL 99-457 also establishes a state grant program for infants and toddlers with disabilities, ages birth to three years, for the purpose of providing early intervention for all eligible children. This part of the law, known as *discretionary legislation*, says that states may serve this age group, but are not required to do so. The exception is for those states which serve nondisabled infants and toddlers; they must serve those disabled in that age group. The governor of each state is to designate a lead agency in the state to administer the program. That agency will develop eligibility criteria. The law allows but does not require extension of services to those babies viewed as at-risk for developmental delay based on medical or environmental factors, in addition to identified infants with disabilities. A case manager, sometimes called a service coordinator, must be designated for each child. That person, who is the liaison between agencies and services needed, is also responsible for the development of the Individualized Family Service Plan (IFSP) which must have evidence of multidisciplinary input and include information about the child's level of development, the family's strengths and needs as these relate to the child, the specific intervention services planned, and the projected outcomes for the child and the family. The IFSP is somewhat comparable to the IEP required for the three to five population.

Role of Child Care Centers. The law allows for variation in length of day, as well as range and variety of programs, which means part-time or full-time home-based or center-based services can be utilized. This is likely to lead to more inclusion models as state and local agencies contract with half-day and full-day child care programs in order to expand the continuum of services to include more center-based care in integrated settings. Now that the values of early childhood education programs are sufficiently high and demand public notice, state education agencies, which have almost unlimited discretion to choose program models, see that these programs offer viable alternatives to the current typical public school categorical model. In many public school models, children with disabilities may be in a separate wing of the regular school building, and the only time they share space with normal children is on the playground or at lunch. A major exception to this is Head Start when located in public schools; 10 percent of classroom slots must be reserved for children with disabilities.

The vast majority of unserved atypical children who come into programs under the new law are mildly disabled because most severely disabled already receive services and are not likely to be included in preschools or child care centers. However, based on ADA, you must consider each applicant on a case-by-case basis, and may not exclude a child merely because of a severe disabling condition. If your program could include the child by making reasonable accommodations in the environment, you are expected to do that. However, you need not make changes that put an undue burden on the resources readily available at your center.[5]

The law requires that these identified special needs children be in a "least restrictive environment" (LRE). Legally, this means that every effort must be made to maintain developmentally disabled children with their peers in a regular educational setting, and when placements are made away from normal peers, the state bears the burden of proof to demonstrate that the integrated

[5]Ibid. *Child Care Information Exchange: The Director's Magazine*, pp. 81–84.

setting is not appropriate.[6] In practice, the least restrictive environment is one which facilitates opportunities to function and grow optimally in all areas of development. Directors of centers with inclusion models are responsible for providing such an environment for children with disabilities who are admitted and funded under the new law. Children must share the pedagogical and social environment, and teachers must be specifically trained to facilitate interaction among and between normal children and those who are developmentally disabled.

Although there is evidence that significant benefits accrue to special needs children who participate in groups with normal peers, these benefits are not the result of merely being in the same classroom. The factors that determine how well children with special needs do in an inclusion environment depends on the quality of the program, and the presence of a teacher who has developed specific intervention plans that support interaction between, and among the atypical and their normal peers.[7]

When available staff do not have sufficient time or background to provide the special support for children with special needs in the classroom, it may be possible to reach out to the community for additional help. Volunteers from parent groups, senior citizens, service organizations, or students from early childhood or special education programs can help in the classroom. Special training for volunteers and the staff can be arranged through special educators at the local school or university, or from other community agencies.

Including children who have been identified with special needs is a challenge for both the teaching staff and the director. However, because so many resources are available to them and their families, it can work out to benefit everyone involved. The more vexing challenges are those you face when a new child enters the program, and, soon after admission, begins to manifest social/emotional problems through disruptive emotional outbursts in the classroom. In these cases, neither the director nor the teaching staff has had a chance to prepare themselves or the children for this new student. It becomes stressful and time consuming to work with this new family, and to provide the necessary support for the troubled child and the classroom teacher. In these situations, directors are pulled in many directions: sometimes struggling with a screaming angry child, sometimes talking with hostile, defensive, or bewildered parents, sometimes taking time after hours to give support to an exhausted teacher. These are the times when directors must call on all their professional skills to help the child, the family, and the teacher cope and eventually move forward toward resolution.

DIRECTOR'S CORNER

"When I put a special needs child in a classroom I always talk at length with the teacher, telling her how I feel she can make it work—how I understand that it's important for all of us and for this child to really find ways to integrate this child into this group. It's very important for a staff member to tell me when she thinks it isn't working. I have to be able to confirm that it's not working both for the group and for the child, but I must also be able to tell her that there are ways to make it work, if that, indeed, is the case, and help her find those ways."

—Director, independent not-for-profit center

Role of the Director in an Interdisciplinary/Interagency Effort

"Cooperation among education agencies, social service agencies, Head Start, and private providers will be crucial, especially if much greater numbers of children are to be served in the least restrictive environment."[8] Directors conversant in the law and its implications for child care programs will be able to respond more knowledgeably to professionals from related agencies who make inquiries

[6]Smith, B. J., & Strain, P. S. (1988). Early childhood special education in the next decade: Implementing and expanding PL 99-457. *Topics in early childhood special education* (TECSE), Vol. 8(1), 1988, pp. 37–47.
[7]Ibid., Allen, p. 9.
[8]Barrett, S. W. (1988). The economies of preschool special education under public law 99-457," *Topics in early childhood special education*, Vol. 8(1), p. 22.

about placements for children with special needs. These directors may be called on to make decisions about whether or not their programs can meet the needs of the selected special needs children, to serve on interdisciplinary teams where IEPs are developed and referral decisions are made, and to support their teachers who will be working with special educators, therapists, and the children's families. If the children are to benefit from what early childhood educators have to offer, turf-guarding must be set aside and they must assertively advocate developmentally appropriate practice using the expertise they bring to the interdisciplinary and interagency team.

In order to facilitate communication between and among members of interdisciplinary teams and to support their work, directors must understand how and why inclusion works, and what makes it work or prevents it from working. That often means directors must learn more about children with special needs through additional training and reading to prepare themselves for coaching classroom staff and for working with an interdisciplinary team. When members of the interdisciplinary team view each other as colleagues, all of whom bring special skills and training to the situation, and when they keep in mind that their common goal is to provide the best environment for the children, they can work together to that end.

SUMMARY

Publicity about the center must be drafted for and directed to the population that the program is designed to serve. Successful recruitment of children and families will depend on the content and dissemination of the publicity about the program, as well as on the total public relations effort. The written materials advertising the center must be carefully planned to attract the families to be served; any other efforts or activities to publicize the center deserve considerable thought and attention as well. After the families have indicated their interest, it is the responsibility of the professional staff to select children for the program, taking into account the readiness of the children and the capacity of the program to serve their needs and those of their families. The mandate to provide services for three- to five-year-old children with disabilities continues to have far-reaching implications for early childhood programs into the 21st century. It will influence the selection of children to be enrolled and effect the dynamics within classrooms.

Working Paper 12–1

Evaluation Form

Talk with a peer who heads a nearby early childhood care center and collect some of that center's printed materials. Describe what the director said and explain how the printed materials reflect each of the following categories.

1. Ages served and groupings of children.

2. Availability of service in terms of hours, days of the week, time of the year, and so on.

3. Suitability of writing level, layout, and photos for the target population.

4. Clarity about what the program is like as to the philosophy and goals mentioned in the printed material, and how these match what you were told.

Working Paper 12–2

Group Ideas

Discuss with peers or your staff the following issues related to PL 99-457. Record the group's responses to each issue.

1. How will an early childhood director determine if a program is indeed the least-restrictive environment for a specific developmentally disabled child?
   - What factors must be considered in the determination?
   - Where can the director go for help?

2. What are some of the strategies early childhood education professionals can use to communicate to other professionals such as special educators, physicians, psychologists, social workers, and the like about "developmentally appropriate practice" and its importance for all children?

3. What are the major things early childhood educators need to learn from special educators?

4. What are some of the specific classroom strategies a director can share with the teaching staff that will facilitate interaction between and among atypical children and their typically developing peers?

CHAPTER 13

Grouping and Enrolling the Children

D ecisions about grouping the children must be reached before making the group assignments and pursuing all the subsequent steps in the enrollment procedure. Decisions about group size, ages of children, and composition of the groups must be made before the children can be assigned. Once assignments have been made, teachers can contact families and initiate the enrollment process. Although the degree of flexibility around grouping in ongoing child care programs is more limited than in preschools, even there, the cyclical nature of demand usually follows the public school year, thereby giving rise to numerous grouping decisions for newcomers in the fall.

GROUPING THE CHILDREN

A number of factors are considered in dealing with the complex question of how children should be appropriately grouped. The size of groups is determined by a variety of factors including the physical space available, the licensing requirements, the number of staff members, and the program philosophy. Appropriate group size has a positive influence on both children and teachers.[1] Other factors that relate to the grouping of the children are the needs and skills of the staff, the needs of the children, the question of chronological age grouping versus vertical (sometimes called family) grouping, the number of special needs children to be enrolled, and the nature of their disabilities.

Total Number of Children

To a large extent, the number of children available, and the size of the physical space determine the total number of children in a center. If it is a new program, once the needs assessment in the community has been completed (Chapter 4) and the facility has been selected (Chapter 9), the final decision about the total number of children in the center must be made. Often, this decision is simply to take all children available. However, when the requests for service are overwhelming, or when the available space cannot accommodate large numbers of children, the director and/or the board may want to limit the enrollment.

---

[1]Decker, C. A., & Decker, J. R. (1997). *Planning and administering early childhood programs*, Merrill/Prentice-Hall, p. 238.

Centers for young children must radiate a feeling of intimacy and warmth. Little children often feel frightened and uncomfortable about entering a large, forbidding building. The noise, the inevitable confusion, and the motion created by many people concentrated in one area can provoke anxiety in young children. It is difficult to maintain an inviting, comfortable atmosphere for small children when buildings are very large, and when children are moved through crowded play yards, hallways, or receiving areas before they reach their room and their teacher.

Since the atmosphere in large public school buildings can be overwhelming for very young children, it is important for early childhood professionals and public school people to give special attention to the selection of the classroom and play yard space for the preschool children. Partnerships between early childhood educators and public school personnel can result in site selection for public school-sponsored programs which may be in a separate wing of the building or in a facility completely separate from the school building. Greater stability and insulation from political attack and protection from sudden economic shifts may be some of the advantages of funneling preschool and day care services into public school sponsorship.[2] However, early childhood educators must guard the safety and well-being of the children when site selection for these programs is under discussion.

Space and Group Size

Group size varies according to the licensing regulations, and how the available space is organized. Licensing regulations often limit the number of children in a room and usually dictate the adult-child ratio for children of different ages as well. Since space requirements and adult-child ratio standards in the licensing regulations are, for the most part, based on the knowledge of experienced professionals, it is wise to follow a standard of small groups with low teacher-child ratios.[3]

DIRECTOR'S CORNER

"I had to go down the hall and upstairs when I wanted to take the children to the gym for large muscle activities. I always tried to avoid having them in the halls of the school building when the older children were moving in and out of the auditorium or the lunchroom. It was very confusing for the preschoolers to be taken through the long lines of older children—especially if remarks were made like, 'make room for the baby group' by the children or the elementary teachers."

—Director, cooperative preschool in a public school building

The organization or plan of the available space affects the size of the groups that can be accommodated. When bathrooms are two floors down or when outside areas are not directly adjacent to the classroom, groups must be smaller to be manageable during the transition periods when children move from one place to another. If fenced-in play areas outside can be reached directly from the classroom, the total space can be supervised more easily; this means a larger group could be assigned to the space.

Reflections

Can you recall how you felt as a first-year high school student when you initially entered your big high school building? Were you afraid and anxious? How did it feel to be the youngest or the smallest in the whole school? Did you feel that you might not be able to find your room or your locker? Did you ever have nightmares about forgetting your schedule or losing your most important notebook? If you can recall any of those feelings, perhaps you can begin to relate to the young child who leaves a familiar home environment and enters a large, strange, crowded place called a child care center or school.

---

[2]Shaker, A. (1988). Public school day care." *Report on preschool programs*, Feb. 17.
[3]Accreditation Criteria and Procedures of the National Academy of Early Childhood Programs, NAEYC, 1834 Connecticut Ave. N.W., Washington, D.C., 1991, p. 41.

When space is adequate to accommodate large numbers of young children, some directors and teachers find creative ways to use dividers, draperies, or movable partitions to break the space into smaller units. Even where available space would accommodate larger groups, smaller groups are viewed as optimal.[4]

Skills of Staff and Group Size

In deciding on the size of groups, the director must consider the skill level of the staff and factor that into the decision about how many children should be assigned to each classroom. The staff for each group must be available to provide frequent personal contact, promote age-appropriate and meaningful learning experiences, create a nurturing environment using effective classroom management strategies, and respond immediately to all emergencies.

Needs of Children and Group Size

It is beyond the scope of this book to discuss the policy of making group size or placement decisions on the basis of differing individual family and child needs, even though every director must consider such needs carefully. However, some basic considerations apply to all children.

The needs of children will vary depending on their experiences, their level of development in all areas, and their ages. However, it is generally agreed that very young children in their first group experience find it most satisfying to relate to a constant adult. After the initial shift in attachment from the primary caregiver (usually the mother) to a constant adult at the center, the child begins to branch out, and relate to other adults and other children in the group. This natural progression suggests that the child's first experience should be in a small, intimate group with a constant adult. The children in this group may be the same chronological age or they may range over a year or two in age. Volunteers, student teachers, or parent helpers may rotate through the classroom, but the one primary constant caregiver becomes the trusted adult figure to whom children can turn when they need caring and attention.

[4]Ibid., NAEYC. 1991, p. 41.
[5]Ibid., Decker & Decker. 1997, p. 240.

Reflections

Think about your first practicum experience in a classroom. Think about how many children you were able to manage at one time. Could you comfortably work with five children? If you were asked to work with ten children without a second person to help, would you still feel that you could practice effective management skills? What adult-child ratio and total group size is most comfortable for you, keeping in mind your philosophy of early childhood education?

For young children spending the full day in a center, it is wise to consider small, intimate grouping patterns. Since children in full-day programs spend practically all of their waking hours in the center, it becomes a surrogate home for them. Young children who must deal with all the stimulation and interpersonal relationships of a large group for an extended period of time may be exhausted at the end of their long day. Small groups in a carefully planned space provide time and space for the child to be alone, to establish close relationships with just one or two children, or to spend time alone with just one adult. Quiet and intimacy in a comfortable setting with a few people more closely resembles the home environment, and can soften the institutional atmosphere that prevails in many large centers.

Chronological versus Vertical Age Grouping. There is no consensus on one best grouping practice. Although there has been some movement toward greater homogeneity in classrooms for young children that usually results from chronological age grouping, there is a resurgence of interest in multiage or vertical grouping.[5] Program philosophy may dictate the preferred approach to grouping the children. However, unless licensing regulates how children should be grouped, the way classrooms are organized within the program is left to the discretion of the director and the professional staff.

Chronological Grouping. Grouping by age has traditionally been a more popular practice in early childhood programs than vertical grouping. It involves grouping based solely on the basis of age—three- and four-years-olds are in different groups and toddlers are separated from infants. When children are grouped chronologically, there is little discussion about which group a given child will join. The director's task is simplified because in accepting the center program, parents accept the fact that their three-year-old will be in Group 1 and their four-year-old will be in Group 2. There will be ranges of ability and behavior within an age group due to individual differences, but the child's exposure to differences is inevitably lessened when chronological grouping is used. Therefore, the child's opportunity to develop a broad appreciation for diversity is abated. On the other hand, there are advantages to age grouping such as simplifying the planning of the learning environment and making classroom management less troublesome. The less experienced teacher may find both of these factors very helpful.

Reflections

Think about the progression of your feelings when you spent an entire day in large, crowded classrooms, a busy, noisy cafeteria, community bathrooms, and noisy student centers. Consider those long days when you found no privacy, no place to be alone and talk to a friend about a problem or listen to music, either by yourself or with a special person. If you can think how you felt, you will develop greater insight into how a child feels when placed in a large group for a full-day program. The lack of intimacy and warmth in an institutional setting creates both anxiety and fatigue.

Chronological age grouping is based on the assumption that children of the same age are within the same range in ability and level of development. Because children of the same age are not homogeneous, many programs go to multiage grouping where children advance at their own rate through individualized programming. Multi-

age grouping allows for children's uneven development and provides an environment in which younger children engage in more interactive and complex types of play with older children who are easily accessible.[6]

Vertical Grouping. Vertical grouping, or family grouping as it is sometimes called, involves placing children of different ages in the same group; the children in any one group may range in age as much as two to three years. This multiage grouping more closely resembles one that would occur in a family; hence the label family grouping. Depending on licensing requirements, infants and sometimes even toddlers must be kept in separate groups. When vertical grouping is the pattern, decisions about the size and the composition of each group, as well as the number of adults needed for each one, become more complex. The broad age range also complicates managing the children and planning their learning environment.

Sometimes parents object to having their two-year-old with older children who may be viewed by the toddler's parents as being loud and rough. These parents are concerned about the safety of their toddler and sometimes fear that their young child will be unable to cope in a group covering a wide age range. However, many of these parents can be helped to see that a young child in a multiage group has more opportunity to learn from older children in the group, and that every child has a chance to teach the other group members. Peer teaching and learning has intrinsic value because it enhances a child's sense of mastery and worth and facilitates cooperation and appreciation of others. For example, two-year-olds may not be as efficient as five-year-olds about putting equipment back on the shelf, but the total concentration they give to an activity like water play and the sense of ability they show in exploring this material may help their more controlled three- or five-year-old counterparts try splashing in the water. The director must cope with the dubious parents and with teachers who are reaching out for support as they work with a broad age range. However, sometimes the advantages of multiage grouping such as peer modeling and peer tutoring are outweighed by the

[6]Katz, L. G., Evangelow, D., &. Hartman, J. A. (1990). *The case for mixed-age grouping in early education*. National Association for the Education of Young Children, pp. 7, 15.

challenges of planning for the age span, and equipping and managing the classroom. Directors become coaches and sources of support for staff as they try to meet these challenges.

Inclusion of Children with Special Needs

When children with special needs are included in the group, the size and composition of the group must be adjusted accordingly to ensure that enough adults will be available to respond to their needs. Consider which group can offer something to the child with a disability, as well as what that child can offer to the group. Unless the child is truly integrated into the group, each offering something to the other, there is a risk that the child with the disability will be ignored and become an isolate, therefore, not in the least restrictive environment. The least restrictive ruling is not necessarily a mandate to enroll all children with a disability into regular programs; however, the advantages of inclusion for both nondisabled children and children with developmental disabilities are numerous and well-documented.[7] Social competence and the ability to maintain higher levels of play is enhanced for children with disabilities who have the opportunity to interact with normally developing peers in inclusive classrooms. At the same time, their language and cognitive gains are comparable to their peers in self-contained special education classrooms. On the other hand, children without disabilities in inclusive classrooms become more accepting of others who are different, and become more comfortable with those differences.

There is no ideal disabled/normal ratio, and recommendations range from at least two or more to an even balance (50–50), to more disabled than nondisabled, sometimes called "reverse mainstreaming" where nondisabled make up no more than one-third of the enrollment.[8] "The best ratio of special needs to nonspecial needs children is the one with which teachers, administrators, and parents are most comfortable. Variables which must be considered include the severity of the disabling conditions of the special needs children in the group; the characteristics of the nondisabled children, how they will try to explain and understand the disabilities of their peers, and the expertise of the available adults who are to work with the inclusive group.[9]

Multiage groups are advantageous for children with special needs because they provide peer models with a broad range of skills and abilities. The atypical child is exposed to the peer model who has higher level skills or abilities, but will also have a chance to develop friendships with younger children who may be more compatible developmentally.

Decisions about group size or group patterns will affect program planning, child and teacher behaviors, group atmosphere, and ultimately the experiences of both teacher and child in the learning environment. An inclusive program must consider the uniqueness of every child and family in the classroom, and how each child's strengths and needs will be addressed.[10] Therefore, grouping the children is a complex issue that has far-reaching results.

ENROLLING THE CHILDREN

Filling out forms, interviewing parents, and visiting back and forth between home and school are the major components of the enrollment procedure. The director is responsible for developing forms that will provide the center staff members with the information they need about the families and the children. The director also manages the planning and timing of this procedure; however, these plans must be discussed with staff members who will be required to carry them out.

Information on Families and Children

The director must first determine what information is needed from each family, then develop a plan for obtaining it. Forms and interviews can be

[7]Allen, K. E. (1996). *The exceptional child: Inclusion in early childhood education.* Delmar, p. 14.
[8]Ibid., Allen, 1996, p. 2.
[9]Taylor, B. J. (1997). *Early childhood program management: People and procedures.* Merrill (Prentice-Hall), p. 77.
[10]Ibid., Allen, 1996, p. 2.

used for this purpose, and it is up to the director to design the forms and develop the plan for interviews or conferences. The ultimate goal is to assemble the necessary information for each child and family, and to make it available to selected adults at the center who will be responsible for the child and the family.

The following list includes the type of preenrollment information that is typically obtained from the family. Note that all the information is important to efficient business operation of the center, to the health and safety of the children, or to the better understanding of the child and the family:

- name of the child (including nickname)
- names of family members and ages of siblings
- names of other members of the household and their relationship to the child
- home address and telephone number
- name, address, and telephone number of employer(s) of parent(s)
- arrangement for payment of fees
- transportation plans for the child (including how the child will be transported and by whom)
- medical history and record of a recent physical examination of the child by a physician
- social/emotional history of the child
- name, address, and telephone number of the child's physician or clinic
- emergency medical treatment authorization
- name, address, and telephone number of a person (outside the family) to contact in an emergency if a member of the family cannot be reached
- permission to participate in the total school program (field trips, photos, videotaping, research, and so on)

In order to ensure that you have all the information and signed releases required to satisfy licensing and to cover liability questions, contact your local licensing agent and consult an attorney.

Forms

A number of sample forms included in Director's Resources at the end of this chapter demonstrate various ways in which the information listed above can be recorded. These are only sample forms and cannot be used in the exact format presented, but they can provide a basis for developing appropriate forms to meet the specific needs of each center. For example, the director of a small cooperative nursery school does not need all the data on family income that is required by Head Start or publicly funded programs, but needs details on family schedules to plan for parent participation.

Public school-sponsored programs may or may not require family income information but will require a Medicaid number for those children entitled to the benefits of that program. They also may need a birth certificate to validate the age of the child.

Because there is so much variation among programs about information required on children and families, directors must develop forms which meet the specific need of the program.

In the case of child care centers and preschools, applications for admission are mailed to interested families in response to their initial inquiry about the center. In fact, sometimes the application is enclosed in a brochure or is actually part of it. On receipt of the applications, the director can begin to arrange the groups based on whatever guidelines have been adopted for grouping the children. If selection and grouping of the children requires more subjective data than can be gleaned from the application form or any other written information that has been collected prior to admission, the director can arrange to talk with the parent(s).

After most of the children have been admitted and assigned to groups, those who have not yet been placed are held for deferred enrollment, or, in the case of ongoing programs, put on a waiting list. If a child is rejected for reasons other than full enrollment, the reasons should be discussed with the family to avoid any misunderstandings that could quickly undermine the public relations efforts of the center staff and impair communication between the staff and potential clients from the community.

Confidentiality

Information on families and children recorded on forms or obtained by staff members during interviews or home visits is confidential and *must not* be released to unauthorized persons without parental consent. Furthermore, a federal law provides that any public or private educational institution which is the recipient of federal funds made available under any federal program administered by the United States Department of Education must give parents access to their children's educational records. Since all information in the files must remain available to parents, it is important that staff members use discretion when recording information in a child's permanent record. Parents should be informed of what information will be kept confidential and what will be available to teaching staff, office staff, and other support staff. Parents decide how much detail they are willing to release. They realize that emergency telephone numbers and authorized persons to pick up the child will be needed by all teaching and office staff. However, they may choose to have medical histories and income information available only to the director and the lead teacher.[11]

Records and other confidential information should not be disclosed to anyone other than center personnel without written consent of the parent or guardian unless its disclosure is necessary to protect the health or safety of the child. Written parental consent is required in order to pass information on to the public school by any preschool or Head Start program. As a general rule, parental consent should be obtained except in emergency cases, or where it appears that the parent is a threat to the child.[12] Centers that receive funds from government sources should be familiar with any regulations or guidelines on confidentiality and privacy that are tied to the funding source.

Intake Procedures

The director decides which staff members will be involved in each step of the intake procedure but it is imperative that the child's teacher be actively involved throughout. The adult who will work directly with the child must interact with the child and the family to begin to establish feelings of mu-

tual trust among the child, the family, and the teacher.

Parents often feel guilty and apprehensive about placing children in a child care program. A carefully planned intake process that provides frequent opportunities to talk with the teacher, the director, and the social services staff (if available) can help the parents cope with their feelings. At the same time, young children are upset when they are first separated from their parents and family. They feel frightened and lonely; therefore, their transition to a new physical and social environment must be made gradually and accompanied by continuous support from family members. For the mental health of both the parents and children, the sequences followed in the intake process should be arranged so that everyone involved will be able to cope successfully with the separation experience. Four steps are commonly employed in introducing the family and the child to the center program and to the teacher. They are discussed here because it is the director's responsibility to ensure that this careful intake procedure is implemented.

1. Initial Interview with Parents. The purpose of an initial interview is to get acquainted with the parent(s), answer their questions about the center program, communicate what will be expected of them, take them on a tour of the center, and familiarize them with the forms that must be filled in before their child can be admitted. It may be useful to go over the family information, the child's social history, the medical history, the emergency information record, and the various release and permission forms during the interview to answer questions about any confusing items. The informality and friendliness of this first personal contact will set the tone for all future contacts. Since this is precisely the time to establish the foundation for mutual trust among director, teacher, parent, and child, it is important that these interviews be conducted in a nonthreatening manner.

Scheduling the interview must be done at the convenience of the family. Even though the teacher or the office staff may do the interview scheduling, it is essential that the director monitor

[11]Ibid., Taylor, 1997, p. 339.
[12]III(B)(4) The Family Educational Rights and Privacy Act (Buckley Amendment), 1974 Education Amendments, sec. 513,88 Stat. 571,20 U.W. C.A. Sec. 1232g (Supp. 1875).

it to ensure that families are not unduly inconvenienced. Careful consideration of family needs indicates that the center staff is sensitive to individual lifestyles and family preferences. When parents work, evenings or weekends may be best for interviews. Center staff members must also consider the transportation problems for some families, the availability of babysitters, and the schedules of other children in the family.

2. Home Visit with the Family.   A home visit may be the next step in the intake procedure. The director should describe the purpose of home visits to the staff and go over a home visit report with them before family appointments are made (Sample Home Visit Report, Director's Resource 13–1). The purpose is not to evaluate the home but to gather information that will enable the staff to have a better understanding of the child. Trust between the parent(s) and the staff will be destroyed and communication impaired if the family interprets the purpose of these home visits as evaluative. Observing a family at home will help the teacher understand the family lifestyle and the family attitudes toward the child.

DIRECTOR'S CORNER

"We are fairly firm with parents about spending some time here with their child because we know, from experience, that even a child who comes in with apparent ease may have a problem two months hence, which harks back to skipping the gradual transition into the group. Even if a parent can spend only 15 minutes in the morning with a child for a week or two, we accept that and make it clear we expect it. My staff is sold on the importance of gradual separation and will even come in 15 or 30 minutes early—before we open—to give a new child time in the classroom with both the parent and the teacher present."

—Director, independent not-for-profit center

3. Initial Visit to the Center.   The scheduling of the initial visit to the center should be arranged by the director and the staff before home visits begin so that information about visiting the center can be given to parents during the home visit.

This initial visit to the classroom must be planned to help the child make that first big step from home and the trusted caregiver to the center and a new caring adult. The visit should last from 30 to 45 minutes, and terminate before the child is tired or bored. Although the teacher is clearly responsible for working with the child and the accompanying adult during this visit, it is important for the director to be available to greet the newcomers and answer any questions that might arise. It provides a perfect opportunity for the director and the parent(s) to get to know each other better, and is a good time to give the parent a copy of the Parent Handbook (see Chapter 16 for further discussion of the Parent Handbook).

4. Phasing-in the Children.   The first three intake steps described above can be implemented in all types of center-based programs. The scheduling of each step should be adjusted to individual family needs (obviously much more difficult for working parents). In fact, the scheduling of these steps may seem to be somewhat unrealistic for full-day child care programs but can be accomplished through creative planning. Implementing the intake procedures in child care programs could involve evenings, early mornings, or weekends. The director must, therefore, work out the scheduling with the staff, and may give comp time or extra compensation for overtime.

The phasing-in or staggered-entrance procedure will, of necessity, be very different in ongoing child care programs than in programs that are just starting or those that are based on the typical school calendar.[13]

Arranging for the staggered entrance of a group of twelve to fifteen children at the beginning of the year poses a complex scheduling problem, but it is an essential step in the orientation process. Since scheduling is very involved, it is important for the director and staff to consult with parents about convenient times for them to come and stay with their child. Successful implementation of the plan depends on staff and family commitment to it.

In public school-sponsored programs where there is no precedent for gradual intake of new children, early childhood staff will have to meet

[13]For discussion of staggered entrance, see Read, K., Gardner, P., & Mahler, B. (1993). *Early childhood programs: Human relationships and learning* (9th edition), Harcourt, Brace Jovanovich.

with administrators and building principals to explain the importance of this procedure for the well-being of children and families. Because early childhood programs in public schools are considered part of the elementary school and are accredited with the elementary school in the local school district, they are usually expected to provide a given number of instructional days to maximize the amount of state funds they receive. Developmentally appropriate practices like phasing-in children is often one of the first issues that creates conflict between developmental early childhood educators and the academic/school readiness elementary educators.

In full-day child care programs, the major problem is to find a trusted adult to stay with the child until all persons involved feel comfortable about the child being at the center every day for the full day. When a family needs full-day care for a child, both parents are usually working or the child is a member of a one-parent family. In these special cases, a grandparent or other member of the extended family may be the best person to provide the emotional support that is necessary for the child during the phasing-in-period.

If there is any question among staff members about the importance of the gradual orientation program for the child, the family, and the success of the total program, it is up to the director to help everyone understand that this process represents the next logical step in developing mutual trust within the teacher-child-family unit. Orienting children is usually exciting and productive for the teacher, but it is also time consuming and energy-draining. The process can only be successful if the entire staff understands its relevance to the total program and recognizes it as being consistent with developmentally appropriate practice.

SUMMARY

Most of the decisions about grouping the children appropriately are made by the director who must consider the unique needs of the children, space available, licensing regulations about ratios, and group size. Policy decisions about chronological or multiage grouping must be made before children are assigned to groups. Skills and experience of staff, ages of children, and the numbers and types of children with special needs selected for admission are all factors that will effect where children will be assigned.

Enrolling the children involves filling out forms, interviewing parents, making home visits, and gradually phasing-in the children. Although the staggered-enrollment procedure is complex and time consuming, it is a critical step in the process of building trust between the school, the child, and the family.

Working Paper 13–1

Develop a Staggered Enrollment Plan

- Enroll 12 children over a period of eight days.
- The plan is for a half-day preschool which meets from 9:00 A.M. to 11:30 A.M. daily.
- Remember to have children come for shorter hours, in small groups, and gradually move toward having all children together for the full 2½ hours on the ninth day of school.
- Fill in the time-slots with the child's number—1, 2, 3 . . . 12.
- Time slots can be adjusted to suit your plan.

Week 1	Monday—1	Tuesday—2	Wednesday—3	Thursday—4	Friday—5
9:00					
9:30					
10:00					
10:30					
11:00					
11:30					

Week 2	Monday—6	Tuesday—7	Wednesday—8	Thursday—9	Friday
9:00				Children 1–12	Children 1–12
9:30					
10:00					
10:30					
11:00					
11:30				↓	↓

Director's Resource 13–1

Sample Home Visit/Parent Contact Report

Center _____

Type of Program _____

  1. Name of interviewer _____ Title _____

  2. Child's name _____

  3. Parent or guardian _____

  4. Address _____

  5. Date and time of visit or meeting _____

  6. Purpose of visit or meeting_____

_____

_____

  7. Specific action taken as result of visit or meeting _____

_____

_____

_____

_____

_____

  8. Observations and comments _____

_____

_____

_____

_____

_____

_____

Director's Resource 13–2

Sample Child Care Application Form (requesting income information)

For office use only
District Status: _____
Income Status: _____
Priority Status: _____
Date Application Received: _____
Date Eligible for Entrance: _____
Enrollment Age: _____

Child's Name: _____ Date of Birth: _____ Sex: _____
Race, Nationality, or Ethnic Group: _____
Address: _____ Phone: _____

Mother's Name: _____ Date of Birth: _____ SS # _____
Father's Name: _____ Date of Birth: _____ SS # _____
Child lives with _____

Children attend the center-based program four (4) half days per week; they eat lunch and snack at the center. Transportation is provided for handicapped or special needs children.

Do you wish to apply for center-based program? Yes ____ No ____
        Session preferred A.M. ____   8:45 – 11:45
                           P.M. ____   12:45 – 3:45

Children and families in the home-based program are visited once per week in the home and are transported to the center on Friday for a group experience. The home-based teacher will assist parents in creating a home environment to promote children's growth and development. This program is in the morning only.

Do you wish to apply for home-based program? Yes ____ No ____

∗ ∗

Family Income   Family Size:
   $_____ per week $ _____ per month $ _____ per year

Source of Reimbursement or Services (Circle "Yes" or "No" for each source)
   YES   NO   EPSDT/Medicaid (Latest certification #): _____
   YES   NO   Federal, State or Local Agency: _____
   YES   NO   In-kind Provider: _____
   YES   NO   Insurance: _____
                I.D. #: _____
   YES   NO   WIC
   YES   NO   Food Stamps

Does this child or any of your family members have a disability or special need? Describe: _____
_____

How well does your child speak and understand English? _____
_____

How did you obtain information about this program? _____
_____

Director's Resource 13–3

Sample Application—No Information Requested
Walnut Corner Children's Center Preregistration Form

CHILD'S FAMILY INFORMATION

Child's Name_____   Name Used_____

Date of Birth, or Expected Date of Birth _____

Child's Address_____

Father/Guardian Name _____   Mother/Guardian Name _____

Home Address_____   Home Address_____

_____   _____

Employer_____   Employer_____

Address_____   Address_____

_____   _____

Business Phone_____   Business Phone_____

REQUESTED DAYS OF ATTENDANCE

Days: M   T   W   TH   F   Hours: _____ AM _____ PM

Requested Start Date:_____

HOW DID YOU LEARN ABOUT WALNUT CORNER CHILDREN'S CENTER?

Personal Referral/If so, who? _____

Newspaper_____   Radio_____   Other _____

Thank you for this information

PLEASE INCLUDE THE NON-REFUNDABLE $25 REGISTRATION FEE WITH THIS FORM.

THIS FEE WILL SECURE YOUR CHILD'S NAME ON OUR WAITING LIST.

(Reprinted by permission Walnut Corner Children's Center)

Director's Resource 13–4

Sample Student Enrollment Form

SAMPLE STUDENT ENROLLMENT FORM
(Public School-Sponsored Program)
S T U D E N T   E N R O L L M E N T   F O R M
(MUST BE RETAINED IN STUDENT'S CUMULATIVE RECORD)

DO NOT WRITE IN THIS BOX
Assigned to: Gr____ Hr____
SDF sent to Census_____
Type a new CR_____
CR in office file_____
CR requested_____
Health Record Yes____ No____
Rec'd 4 part SDF_____

Name of school student is entering_____ Grade Entering*_____ Special Ed_____

Name_____
Student's Legal Name (as listed on Birth Certificate)

Circle
Sex: Male Female

Circle
Race: Black White Other

Address_____ Apt No._____ Zip Code_____ Phone No._____

Place of Birth_____ Date of Birth_____
          City   State   County   Mo   Da   Yr

Check one of the Birth Verifications listed below:

Birth
Certificate No._____

Baptismal
Certificate_____

Physician's Record_____

Passport_____

IMMUNIZATION DATA:	DPT	Polio	Measles	Rubella	Mumps

	Name	Place of Birth		Deceased (Date)
		State	County	
Father:				
Mother:				
Step-Parent:				
Guardian:				

SOCIAL RECORD

	Occupation	Place of Employment	Business Phone No.
Father's Occupation			
Mother's Occupation			

If Family Is Supported
By Another Source Indicate:

Names of Brothers & Sisters - School of Attendance	Still in School	
	Pre-School	

Circle one:
Family Status
of Parents: Married   Single   Divorced   Separated   Remarried

Student is living with_____ Relationship_____

LANGUAGE OTHER THAN ENGLISH SPOKEN IN HOME:_____

Did student attend this school last year?

____YES

____NO Name of school_____ Address_____

☐ YES – PRIVACY REQUESTED: If this box is checked no information pertaining to this student will be released to any person or institution (including colleges or universities) without your written approval.

☐ NO – PRIVACY IS NOT REQUESTED

Parent/Guardian's Signature_____

Date:_____

In case of emergency, call_____ _____ _____
                        Name   Relationship   Phone No.

NAME
Last
First
Middle
STUDENT NUMBER
SOCIAL SECURITY NO.

Director's Resource 13–5

Sample Developmental History
Arlitt Child Development Center* Developmental History

Child's Name _____   How you want your child's name written in the classroom _____

Address _____ Zip _____ Phone _____

Birth Date _____ Place of Birth _____ Race _____

Sex _____

I. THE CHILD'S FAMILY

Parents or Guardians

A. Name _____ Birthdate _____

Education (include highest grade completed or degrees) _____

_____

Occupation _____ Usual working hours _____

Work phone _____

B. Name _____ Birthdate _____

Education (include highest grade completed or degrees) _____

_____

Occupation _____ Usual working hours _____

Work phone _____

Status of Parents (check):   Living together _____   Living apart _____

Child lives with _____

If parents work or are students, who keeps the child in their absence? Check one:

grandparent _____   other relative _____   friend _____   paid sitter _____   other _____

Other children in the family: (list in order of birth)

Name	Sex	Birthdate	What grade if in school

Sisters or brothers who attended Arlitt _____

Additional members of household (give number) _____

Friends _____   Others _____

Boarders _____   Relatives _____

(indicate relationship)

What part do these other persons have in the care of your child? _____

_____

Has your child been separated from his parents for long periods of time and, if so why? _____

_____

*Reprinted by permission of Arlitt Child Development Center University of Cincinnati

Director's Resource 13–5 (continued)

Have you moved frequently? _____

What language is usually spoken at home? _____

(If more than one, what other language(s) are spoken? _____

II. DEVELOPMENT IN EARLY CHILDHOOD

Comment on the health of the mother during pregnancy _____

Comment on the health of your child during delivery and infancy _____

_____

When did your child walk? _____	When did your child talk? _____
Is your child adopted? _____	Does he/she know it? _____
Does your child have bladder control? _____	Child's terminology _____
Does your child have bowel control? _____	Child's terminology _____

_____ Does your child need reminding about going to the

bathroom? _____ Does your child usually take a nap? _____ At what time? _____ Describe any special

needs, handicaps, or health problems _____

Does your child have any difficulty saying what he/she wants or do you have any trouble understanding

his/her speech? _____

III. HEALTH RECORD

Immunization Record. Enter month/day/year of each immunization.

DPT: 1 _____   2 _____   3 _____   4 _____   *5 _____

Polio: 1 _____   2 _____   3 _____   *4 _____

Measles, mumps, rubella—usually combined as MMR _____

If separate, measles _____   mumps _____   rubella _____

*The 5th DPT and 4th polio are normally administered just prior to kindergarten.

1. List all allergies and any special precautions and treatment indicated for these allergies:

_____

_____

2. List any medications (food supplements, modified diets or fluoride supplements currently being administered to the child):

_____

_____

3. List any chronic physical problems and any history of hospitalization:

_____

_____

4. List any diseases, serious illnesses, or operations the child has had:

_____

_____

5. List any accidents the child has had:

_____

6. Has your child ever had ear/hearing examination or treatment? _____

When? _____   By whom? _____

Results: _____

Director's Resource 13–5 (continued)

7. Has your child ever had vision examination or treatment? _____

When? _____ By whom? _____

Results: _____

IV. EATING HABITS
Dietary Habits

1. What foods does your child especially like? _____
   _____

2. Are there any foods your child dislikes? _____
   _____

	Yes	No	12. About how often does your child eat a food from each of the following groups?	Approximate Number of Times a Week (circle the number(s) nearest to parent's answer)
3. Does your child take vitamins and mineral supplements? (a) If "yes," what kind are they?			(a) Milk, cheese, yogurt	0* 1* 2* 3 4 5 6 7 7+
(b) Do they contain iron? (c) Do they contain fluoride? (d) Were they prescribed?			(b) Meat, poultry, fish, eggs, or dried beans/peas, peanut butter	0* 1* 2* 3 4 5 6 7 7+
4. Is there any food your child should not eat for medical, religious, or personal reasons?	*		(c) Rice, grits, bread, cereal, tortillas	0* 1* 2* 3 4 5 6 7 7+
5. Is your child on a special diet? (a) What kind?_____	•		(d) Greens, carrots, broccoli, winter squash, pumpkin, sweet potatoes	0* 1* 2 3 4 5 6 7 7+
6. Has there been a big change in your child's appetite in the last month?	*			
7. Does your child take a bottle?	*		(e) Oranges, grape-fruit, tomatoes (fruit/juice)	0* 1* 2* 3 4 5 6 7 7+
8. Does your child eat or chew things that aren't food?	*		(f) Other fruits and vegetables	0* 1* 2 3 4 5 6 7 7+
9. Does your child have trouble chewing or swallowing?	*		(g) Oil, butter, margarine, lard	0* 1* 2 3 4 5 6 7 7+*
10. Does your child often have: (a) Diarrhea? (b) Constipation?	* *		(h) Cakes, cookies, sodas, fruit drinks, candy	0 1 2 3 4 5 6 7 7+*
11. Do you have any concerns about what your child eats?	*			

*Starred answers may require follow-up. Explain details or give additional comments here.

V. PLAY AND SOCIAL EXPERIENCES
Has your child participated in any group experiences? _____
Where? _____
Did your child enjoy it? _____
Do other playmates visit the child? _____
Does your child visit other playmates in their homes? _____
How does your child relate to other children? _____
Does your child prefer to play alone? _____ With other children? _____
Does your child have any imaginary playmates? _____ Explain. _____
_____
Does your child have any pets? _____
What are your child's favorite toys and/or activities? _____
_____
What is your child's favorite TV program? _____

Director's Resource 13–5 (continued)

How long does your child watch TV each day? _____

What are your child's favorite books? _____

How many times a week is your child read to? _____

Is there anything else about your child's play or playmates that the school should know? _____

_____

VI. DISCIPLINE

In most circumstances, do you consider your child easily managed, fairly easy to manage, or difficult
to manage? _____

What concerns do you presently have about your child? _____

_____

How are these concerns dealt with? _____

_____

VII. PARENTS' IMPRESSIONS AND ATTITUDES

From your point of view, what were the events that seemed to have had the greatest impact on your child
(moving, births, deaths, severe illness of family members, divorce)? _____

_____

In what ways would you like to see your child develop during the school year? _____

_____

_____

_____

VIII. ADDITIONAL INFORMATION

_____

_____

_____

School Year   Date   Signature

_____   _____   _____

_____   _____   _____

_____   _____   _____

_____   _____   _____

Director's Resource 13–6

Sample Personal History—Your Child's Development

Date: _____

CHILD'S NAME: _____   NICKNAME: _____

ADDRESS: _____ ZIP: _____   PHONE: _____

DATE OF BIRTH: _____ PLACE OF BIRTH: _____   RACE: _____

I. THE CHILD'S FAMILY   SEX: _____
   Parents or Guardians
   A. Name: _____   BIRTHDATE: _____
      Education (Include highest grade completed or degrees): _____
      _____
      Occupation: _____   Usual working hours: _____
                                     Work phone: _____

   B. Name: _____   BIRTHDATE: _____
      Education (Include highest grade completed or degrees): _____
      _____
      Occupation: _____   Usual working hours: _____
                                     Work phone: _____

   Status of Parents (Check):   Living Together _____   Living Apart _____
   Child lives with _____
   If parents work or are students, who keeps the child in their absence?

   Circle one: Grandparent   Other Relative   Friend   Paid Sitter   Other

   Other children in the family: (List in order of birth)

Name	Sex	Birthdate	What Grade if in School

   Additional members of household (give number):
      Friends _____   Others _____
      Boarders _____   Relatives _____
                                    (Indicate relationships)

   What part do these other persons have in the care of your child? _____
   _____
   Has your child been separated from his parents for long periods of time, and, if so
   why? _____
   Have you moved frequently? _____
   What language is usually spoken at home? _____
   (If more than one, what other language(s) are spoken?) _____

   C. Income _____ (per month) _____ (per year)
   D. Medical card number _____ (parent)
          Child's number _____

Director's Resource 13–6 (continued)

II. DEVELOPMENT IN EARLY CHILDHOOD

Comment on the health of the mother during pregnancy. _____
Comment on the health of your child during delivery and infancy. _____
_____
When did your child walk? _____   When did your child talk? _____
Is your child adopted? _____   Does he/she know it? _____
Does your child have bladder control? _____   Child's Terminology _____
Does your child have bowel control? _____   Child's Terminology _____
Does your child need help when going to the bathroom? _____
Does your child need reminding about going to the bathroom? _____
Does your child usually take a nap? _____   At what time? _____
Describe any special needs, handicaps, or health problems. _____
_____
Does your child have any difficulty saying what he/she wants or do you have any
trouble understanding his/her speech? _____

III. EATING HABITS

What is your child's general attitude towards eating? _____
What foods does your child especially like? _____
For which meal is your child most hungry? _____
Does the child feed himself entirely? _____
Does your child dislike any food in particular? _____
Is your child on a special diet? _____
Does your child take a bottle? _____
Does your child eat or chew things that are not food? Explain: _____
_____
Do you have any concerns about your child's eating habits? Explain: _____
_____
Is there any food your child should not eat for medical, religious, or personal
reasons? _____

IV. PLAY AND SOCIAL EXPERIENCES

Has your child participated in any group experiences? _____
Where? _____
Did your child enjoy it? _____
Do other playmates visit the child? _____
Does your child visit other playmates in their homes? _____
How does your child relate to other children? _____
Does your child prefer to play alone? _____   With other children? _____
Does your child worry a lot or is he/she very afraid of anything? _____
_____
What causes worry or fear? _____
Does your child have any imaginary playmates? _____   Explain: _____
_____
Does your child have any pets? _____
What are your child's favorite toys and/or activities? _____
_____

Director's Resource 13–6 (continued)

What is your child's favorite TV program? _____
How long does your child watch TV each day? _____
What are your child's favorite books? _____
How many times a week is your child read to? _____
Is there anything else about your child's play or playmates which the school should
know? _____
_____

V. DISCIPLINE

In most circumstances, do you consider your child easily managed, fairly easy to
manage, or difficult to manage? _____
What concerns do you presently have about your child? _____
_____
How are these concerns dealt with? _____
_____

VI. PARENT'S IMPRESSIONS AND ATTITUDES

From your point of view, what were the events which seemed to have had the greatest
impact on your child (moving, births, deaths, severe illness of family members,
divorce)? _____
_____
How would you describe your child at the present time? What changes have you seen
in your child during the past year? _____
_____
Does your child have any behavior characteristics which you hope will change?
Please describe. _____
_____
In what ways would you like to see your child develop during the school year? _____
_____
_____
_____
_____
_____
_____

_____
Signature(s) of person/persons filling out this
questionnaire

(Adapted from Arlitt Child Development Center form)

Director's Resource 13–7

Sample Child's Medical Statement

Enrollment Date _____

DAY CARE CENTER/PRE-SCHOOL CERTIFICATE OF MEDICAL EXAMINATION
TO BE COMPLETED BY FAMILY PHYSICIAN OR CLINIC

This is to certify that _____ _____
                                    Child's Name   Birthdate

Child of: _____ _____ _____
                     Mother   Address   Phone

_____ _____ _____
          Father   Address   Phone

was examined by me on _____, and based upon his/her medical
                                  Date of Examination

history and physical condition at the time of this examination, is free from apparent
communicable disease and is in suitable condition for enrollment in a child day care
facility; and has had the immunizations required by Section 3313.671 of the Revised
Code for admission to school, or has had the immunizations required by the State
Department of Health for infants and toddlers, or is to be exempted from these requirements for medical reasons.

Tuberculin Test
(within last year
for new enrollee)   Date _____ Type of Test _____ Results _____

DPT Series and
Boosters Dates   1st _____ 2nd _____ 3rd _____ 4th _____ *5th _____

Oral Polio
Series Dates: 1st _____ 2nd _____ 3rd _____ *4th _____

          *The 5th DPT and 4th polio are normally administered
           just prior to kindergarten.

Measles (Rubeola,
10-day)   Date: _____

Rubella (3 day)   Date: _____

Mumps   Date: _____   (Hib vaccine is required
                                                         for children ages 2 yrs.
Haemophilus b Polysac-   through 4 yrs.)
charide (Hib)   Date: _____

Is able to participate in all regular activities except: _____

_____

REMARKS: _____

Physician's Signature: _____ Date _____

Clinic Name: _____ Phone _____

Office Location: _____

City, State, Zip: _____

PARENT SHOULD RETAIN THIS SHEET WHEN CHILD WITHDRAWS FROM CENTER

Director's Resource 13–8

Sample Emergency Information Record

Child's Name_____

Home Address_____ Home Phone_____

_____
Father's name/Husband   Place of Employment   Bus. Phone
(or guardian)

_____
Mother's name/Wife   Place of Employment   Bus. Phone
(or guardian)

Please fill in information below so that the school may act more effectively in event of illness or injury to the child.

EMERGENCY: Person to be called if parent (husband or wife) cannot be reached.

_____
Name   Address   Phone

_____   _____
Date   Parent's Signature (or guardian)

Director's Resource 13–9

Sample Permission Form

While your child is enrolled in this program, he/she will be involved in a number of special activities for which we need your permission. Please read the following information carefully. You are encouraged to ask questions about anything which is unclear to you. You, of course, have the option of withdrawing permission at any time.

_____

(Child's Name)

(Please circle your choice)

A. I DO   DO NOT give my permission for my child to go on walks with the classroom teacher and class in the nearby neighborhood.

B. I DO   DO NOT give my permission for my child to be screened for speech and language.

C. I DO   DO NOT give my permission for my child to be screened for hearing.

D. I DO   DO NOT give my permission for my child to be screened for specific educational needs.

E. From time to time photographs of our preschool program will be made for educational and publicity purposes. These pictures will be representative of the enriching experiences offered your child during the year.

   I DO   DO NOT give my permission for my child to be photographed for use in educational, nonprofit publications/presentations intended to further the cause of public education. This permission is applicable for current, as well as, future project use.

As part of this program, your child's records may be included in research which evaluates the value of the program. In all cases, the confidentiality of individual children's records is maintained.

_____

Parent's Signature

_____

Date

(Reprinted by permission of the Cincinnati Youth Collaborative.)

Director's Resource 13–10

Sample Transportation and Attendance Release Form
Escort Form
Transportation of Children To & From School*

1. Child's Name: _____ Teacher: _____

   Parent Signature: _____ Date: _____

2. I authorize these people to assume responsibility for my child to and from school.

   _____

   _____

   _____

   _____

   _____

   _____

   If someone other than myself or these people are going to bring or pick up my child I will send a note or phone the school office 556-3802.

3. My child carpools with these children on these days.

   Child's Name   *Days*

   _____   _____

   _____   _____

   _____   _____

   _____   _____

   _____   _____

*It is our policy not to send a child home with anyone other than the parent without written permission.
(Reprinted by permission Cincinnati Youth Collaborative)

CHAPTER 14

Managing the Food and Health and Safety Programs

The director is ultimately responsible for the center's food service, and health and safety programs despite the fact that the components of these programs may be the immediate responsibility of assigned staff members. In large programs, a nutritionist and/or food service coordinator and a cook may have full responsibility for the center's food service, but the director should be knowledgeable about the program and is accountable to the board, the funding agencies, and the center's families. Similarly, a social service or health coordinator may plan and implement the health and safety program, but again the accountability for the program lies with the director. Directors of small programs often have full responsibility for both planning and implementing the food service and health and safety programs. Since you, as a director, will be expected to supervise and monitor these programs, or in small centers, to fully implement them, you must be informed about the elements of the food service and health and safety programs, and about the importance of these programs to the children and families in your center.

FOOD SERVICE PROGRAMS

The total food service program, whether limited to mid-morning snack, or consisting of a two- or three-meal-a-day program, is important because nutrition affects the mental functioning and physical well-being of the child, and because nutritional habits and attitudes toward eating are established during the early years. Providing variety in food choices, the style of serving the food, and establishing an appropriate emotional atmosphere for mealtime are foremost considerations whether the children's meals and snacks are catered, served from frozen prepackaged microwave dinners, come from public school or company cafeterias, or are completely prepared from start to finish in the center's kitchen. In some programs, children bring "brown bag" lunches, a practice that can be a boon to your budget and provide an opportunity to help parents learn more about good nutrition. All brown bag lunches must be dated and properly labeled. They must be refrigerated and all leftover foods discarded, not sent home in the child's lunch box. Nutritious foods selected appropriately from the Food Guide Pyramid Food Groups (see page 337) should be offered daily, using variations in serving styles such as self-help and group snacks, family-style and cafeteria-style meals, picnics, bag lunches, and more casual food service for special occasions.

It should be understood that the adults in the classroom sit down with the children when food is served, that the adults eat the same food that is served to the children, and that the adults take charge of creating pleasant conversation among the entire group during snack time or mealtime. Conversation can focus on food, on what children have been doing or expect to do later in the day, or on any topic that is of interest to most children. An accepting adult who avoids having children wait to be served, who encourages but does not demand tasting new foods, who uses utensils appropriately and suggests that children try to manipulate their own small forks or spoons, and who avoids associating unpleasantness or punishment with food, is demonstrating healthy habits and attitudes toward eating.

For the young infant, a caring familiar adult who is unrushed is important during feeding time. Infants should be held while taking a bottle but encouraged to begin to hold it for self-feeding as voluntary control progresses. Staff must be reminded not to prop up bottles for infants because of the dangers of choking or falling asleep with milk or juice in the mouth, detrimental to healthy gums and teeth as well as possible increase in ear infections. In addition, for their emotional and social well-being, it is critical that babies be held and cuddled while being fed.

Older infants benefit from sitting in adapted chairs near the table with older toddlers and preschoolers whenever possible. They can often enjoy finger foods with the toddlers and participate in the pleasant atmosphere of eating time. Since choking may be a problem for babies who are beginning to feed themselves, a caregiver must be close by at all times. Foods should be cut in bite-sized pieces, be of proper consistency, and, at the very beginning, be offered one piece at a time. Make sure the cook and the caregivers in the program know that some foods are likely to cause choking in young children. There are high-risk foods often implicated in choking. Ninety percent of all fatal chokings occur in children under age four. Therefore, it is wise to avoid foods like hot dogs (sliced into rounds), whole grapes, hard candy, nuts, seeds, raw peas, dried fruits, pretzels, chips, peanuts, popcorn, marshmallows, spoon-fuls of peanut butter, pieces of raw carrot, and chunks of meat larger than what can be swallowed whole.[1] It is also essential for children to sit down while eating or drinking to further avoid the dangers of choking.

Since directors are responsible for all aspects of the food service program, they must monitor and supervise the atmosphere, and the health and safety features of mealtimes. They also must oversee the planning, buying, and preparation of food, and provide opportunities for in-service training to the food service staff members and other adults who work with the children during snack and mealtime.

Menu Planning

The proportion of the total daily food requirement provided by the center depends on the total number of hours the child spends in the center. Licensing regulations vary but general guidelines are as follows:

- Children in care eight hours or less shall be offered at least one meal and two snacks or two meals and one snack.
- Children in care for nine hours or more shall be offered at least two meals and two snacks, or one meal and three snacks.
- A nutritious snack shall be offered to all children in mid-morning and in mid-afternoon.
- Children shall be offered food at intervals of not less than two hours and not more than three hours apart unless the child is asleep.[2]

Infants in group care have very different needs, and must have individualized eating schedules with carefully prepared formulas and special diets.

In 1992, the United States Department of Agriculture (USDA) presented the Food Guide Pyramid to replace the Basic Four as a guide for making daily food choices. The Food Guide Pyramid includes the food groups listed below:

[1]From: *Caring for our children: National health and safety performance standards: Guidelines for out-of-home child care programs,* Copyright 1992 The American Public Health Assoc. and the American Academy of Pediatrics, p. 125.
[2]*Caring for our children: National health and safety performance standards: Guidelines for out-of-home child care programs,* Copyright 1992. The American Public Health Assoc. and the American Academy of Pediatrics, p. 115. Reprinted with permission.

Food Guide Pyramid
A Guide to Daily Food Choices

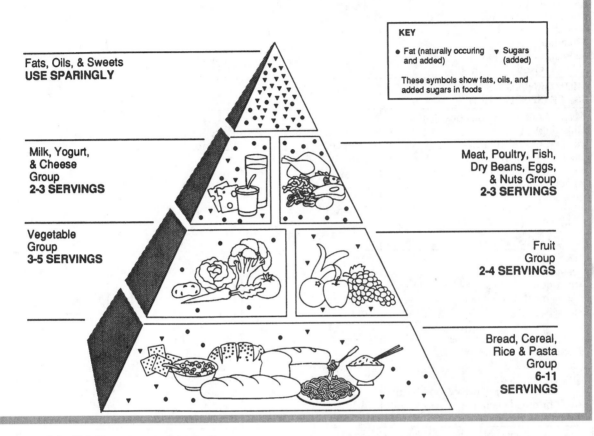

Fats, Oils, & Sweets
USE SPARINGLY

KEY
● Fat (naturally occuring   ▼ Sugars
  and added)   (added)

These symbols show fats, oils, and added sugars in foods

Milk, Yogurt, & Cheese Group
2-3 SERVINGS

Meat, Poultry, Fish, Dry Beans, Eggs, & Nuts Group
2-3 SERVINGS

Vegetable Group
3-5 SERVINGS

Fruit Group
2-4 SERVINGS

Bread, Cereal, Rice & Pasta Group
6-11 SERVINGS

Courtesy of the U.S. Department of Agriculture.

- the Bread, Cereal, Rice, and Pasta Group
- the Vegetable Group
- the Fruit Group
- the Milk, Yogurt, and Cheese Group
- the Meat, Poultry, Fish, Dry Beans, Eggs, and Nuts Group
- the Fats, Oils, and Sweets Group[3]

Nutritious meals and snacks must be based on an appropriate selection from these Food Guide Pyramid Groups. It is important to check local licensing standards for additional details on nutrition requirements. For centers involved in the USDA Child and Adult Care Food Program, nutritional standards for meal and snack serving sizes for children, birth through age 12 can be found in Figure 14–1.

Reflections

Think about your earliest recollections of eating with the family or with a teacher. Do you recall being pressured about table manners, finishing your main course before dessert, and tasting new foods that you disliked? Can you recall how you felt at those times? What emotions did you feel? How did you feel about the adults who made demands on you? How did you feel about eating and mealtime when you were put under pressure to eat too much or eat foods you disliked? What are your present attitudes about eating and about unfamiliar foods? Can you relate these present attitudes to your earlier experiences with eating and sampling new foods?

[3]Marotz, L. et al. (2001). *Health, safety, and nutrition for the young child* (5th edition), Delmar, p. 304.

BREAKFAST	Children 1 and 2 years	Children 3 through 5 years	Children 6 through 12 years
Milk, fluid	$1/2$ cup	$3/4$ cup	1 cup
Juice or fruit or vegetable	$1/4$ cup	$1/2$ cup	$1/2$ cup
Bread and/or cereal, enriched or whole grain			
Bread or	$1/2$ slice	$1/2$ slice	1 slice
Cereal: Cold, dry or	$1/4$ cup (1)	$1/3$ cup (2)	$3/4$ cup (3)
Hot cooked	$1/4$ cup	$1/4$ cup	$1/2$ cup
MIDMORNING OR MIDAFTERNOON SNACK (SUPPLEMENT)			
(Select 2 of these 4 component(s))			
Milk, fluid	$1/2$ cup	$1/2$ cup	1 cup
Meat or meat alternate (4)	$1/2$ ounce	$1/2$ ounce	1 ounce
Juice or fruit or vegetable	$1/2$ cup	$1/2$ cup	$3/4$ cup
Bread and/or cereal, enriched or whole grain			
Bread or	$1/2$ slice	$1/2$ slice	1 slice
Cereal: Cold, dry or	$1/4$ cup (1)	$1/3$ cup (2)	$3/4$ cup (3)
Hot cooked	$1/4$ cup	$1/4$ cup	$1/2$ cup
LUNCH OR SUPPER			
Milk, fluid	1/2 cup	3/4 cup	1 cup
Meat or meat alternate			
Meat, poultry, or fish, cooked (lean meat without bone)	1 ounce	$1 1/2$ ounces	2 ounces
Cheese	1 ounce	$1 1/2$ ounces	2 ounces
Egg	1	1	1
Cooked dry beans and peas	$1/4$ cup	3/8 cup	$1/2$ cup
Peanut butter or other nut or seed butters	2 tablespoons	3 tablespoons	4 tablespoons
Nuts and/or seeds	1/2 ounce (5)	3/4 ounce (5)	1 ounce (5)
Vegetable and/or fruit two or more to total	$1/4$ cup	$1/2$ cup	$3/4$ cup
Bread or bread alternate, enriched or whole grain	$1/2$ slice	$1/2$ slice	1 slice

(1) $1/4$ cup (volume) or $1/3$ ounce (weight), whichever is less.
(2) $1/3$ cup (volume) or $1/2$ ounce (weight), whichever is less.
(3) $3/4$ cup (volume) or 1 ounce (weight), whichever is less.
(4) Yogurt may be used as a meat/meat alternate in the snack only. You may serve 4 ounces (weight) or $1/2$ cup (volume) of plain, or sweetened and flavored yogurt to fulfill the equivalent of 1 ounce of the meat/meat alternate component. For younger children, 2 ounces (weight) or $1/4$ cup (volume) may fulfill the equivalent of $1/2$ ounces of the meat/meat alternate requirement.
(5) This portion can meet only one-half of the total serving of the meat/meat alternate requirement for lunch or supper. Nuts or seeds must be combined with another meat/meat alternate to fulfill the requirement. For determining combinations, 1 ounce of nuts or seeds is equal to 1 ounce of cooked lean meat, poultry or fish.

Figure 14–1   Child and Adult Care Food Program Meal Pattern for Children

Every precaution must be taken to ensure that children with food allergies or other conditions requiring a special diet will be served only those foods on their prescribed diet. Both the cook and all classroom staff must be alerted to these special dietary requirements, and both the director and the staff must know the emergency procedures to follow in the event a particular child should have an allergic reaction. For some special diet cases, parents may choose to send food for the child. It is important that these packed lunches be properly refrigerated until served, *not* shared with other children. Any food from home must be labeled showing the child's name and date.

Nutritional considerations in meal planning for young children are necessary but not sufficient to guarantee that children will be adequately nourished. Children's appetites and food preferences also must be taken into consideration when meals are planned. Three- and four-year-old children tend to have small, unpredictable appetites, and they are prone to food sprees. Their foods must be neither too hot nor too cold, not too spicy or gluey, and it is best if they are cut into bite-sized manageable portions. Variation in texture, color, and flavor are also important considerations in planning children's meals. Every effort should be made to limit use of salt and sugar. Serving certain ethnic foods will provide wider variation for all the children, and will make available familiar foods to the children from specific ethnic groups represented in the classroom. It is always a good idea to introduce a new food along with old familiar favorites.

Further considerations that affect menu planning are the availability of equipment and utensils, and the preparation time for each menu item when all foods are prepared in the center kitchen. It is virtually impossible to prepare hot breads, an oven-cooked main dish, and a baked dessert for one meal if only one oven is available. Also, the number and sizes of pots and pans must be checked when menus are planned to ensure that there is an adequate supply of equipment of an appropriate size to prepare the foods for a particular meal. Preparation time is another factor that influences meal planning. Meals that require too much last-minute preparation create problems for the cook which, in turn, could delay the serving time. Hungry children who are forced to wait for their food become impatient and restless, and teachers must then find ways to help them cope with these unnecessary delays.

Meals and menu planning can be systematized and simplified by using meal planning guides, standardized recipes, and sample menus. A number of government booklets and other menu planning guides are useful in planning four to six weeks of basic menus. Menu changes based on the availability of seasonal or plentiful foods can be made on a weekly basis, but beyond those minor changes, basic menu patterns can be repeated every four to six weeks.

Teachers often have helpful suggestions about changes in the basic menu patterns. Some lunches include too many items that are difficult for children to manage or time consuming to serve. For example, soup, banana sections which have to be peeled, and bread slices to be buttered is a menu both difficult to serve and a problem for children to manage. If the cook has a way to get input from the teachers, menu adjustments can be made easily.

Inviting the cook to lunch with the children provides an opportunity for him or her to hear comments from the children about the food and to observe how well they manage the foods served. It also gives the cook a chance to feel more a part of the total center program instead of being the person who spends all day in the kitchen and away from the children.

Since parents are often interested in what children have been served for snacks and/or for breakfast and lunch, it is helpful to post weekly menus or publish them regularly in the parent newsletter. Posting menus helps the parents plan for a child's meals at home and serves as a model for parents who may be inexperienced with planning balanced family meals.

An interesting feature to add to the menu posting area is a pictorial menu for the children. The cook, another staff member, or an interested parent may be willing to collect food pictures and post each day's snack and/or lunch on an eye-level bulletin board for children to "read." It creates interest among the children who then look forward to a dish they especially enjoy and it becomes part of the center's nutrition program.

Food Buying

Careful menu planning reduces cost and waste, and provides a clear-cut basis for setting up shopping lists for daily, weekly, and monthly food buying. Whether meals are catered, partially prepared from prepackaged meals especially designed for children, or fully prepared in the center kitchen, the food budget will affect both meal planning and food purchasing. Quantity buying and cooperative buying arrangements among a group of centers sometimes results in lower prices, but also might limit choices, increase the pressure to purchase foods of lesser quality, and create storage problems when quantity purchases exceed the available storage space. Therefore, although price is an important consideration, quality, available storage space, and the food preferences of the children must be taken into consideration when food purchasing decisions are made.

Catered meal service requires practically no shopping time, no storage space, and very little time selecting foods and developing the shopping lists. It also eliminates the need for a complete meal preparation space and a full-time cook. But the service may be more expensive than when meals are prepared at the center. It could also turn out to be less satisfying to the children and is likely to give the director less control over the entire food service entity.

The prepackaged frozen meals that are prepared in conduction or microwave ovens are expensive conveniences. This type of food service requires large freezers and special ovens, yet requires neither a full-time cook nor complete meal preparation space. The director must select carefully so the choices are appropriate for young children and there is variety in the menu. Fresh foods and beverages must be bought daily or weekly as needed if prepackaged meals are used.

Using company or public school cafeterias requires planning with the cafeteria manager and staff. Foods brought from cafeterias serving adults or older children are sometimes served in containers or in portions which are difficult for young children to manage. A whole hamburger, a large strip of dill pickle, catsup in a sealed foil container, and milk in a sealed carton are all difficult for young children to handle. But since that is standard public school cafeteria fare, you may find no other choices for your children. Also, cafeteria service customarily means self-help and carrying trays, and that is out of the question for young children. It is important to develop clear-cut guidelines for portion sizes, family style service, and alternative menus so you can work with the cafeteria food service staff to find ways to make appropriate adjustments for young children.

DIRECTOR'S CORNER

"One of the things I learned quickly when I started to work with this program in the public school was to become friendly with the cafeteria manager. Now she cuts the hamburgers in quarters, sends pickle slices instead of those huge strips of dill pickles, and includes a sharp knife for my use when there are apples to be cored and sliced or oranges to be quartered."

—Director, public school preschool

Meals prepared at the center mean that the center must have a complete meal preparation space which meets all licensing requirements and employ a full-time cook if it is a full-day child care program. Preferably, the cook will have planning and buying skills. If not, then a staff person (sometimes the director) will plan and purchase the foods in consultation with the cook. Planning purchases, doing the shopping, and checking deliveries are all time consuming; however, total meal preparation at the center allows for greater variation in foods served and more involvement of the children in shopping, preparation, and serving. It also guarantees that items on the menu will be prepared and served with young children in mind.

*USDA Child and Adult Care Food Program.** Some centers serve children who are eligible for free or reduced-price meals from the USDA Child and Adults Care Food Program (CACFP). Although some programs may have a designated staff person or the cook do some of the paperwork in order to receive the USDA reimbursement, in most cases the director does the necessary paperwork, or at least is responsible for making sure it is done correctly.

Eligibility of children for free or reduced-price meals is based on family income. Income levels for family eligibility and reimbursement rates for providers is adjusted annually. Therefore, in order to determine which families in your center are eligible and what the reimbursement rate will be for those meals, contact the USDA Public Information Office at (703) 305-2276, or contact a regional office (see Figure 14–2).

An Income Eligibility Application (see Figure 14–3) must be on file for every child who receives meals under the USDA Child and Adults Care Food Program. These forms must be kept on file for at least three years to ensure that they will be available at the time your agency undergoes a Verification Review. It is essential that the information on the forms be complete and accurate to avoid the possibility of penalties should errors be discovered at the time of the review.

Providers who fit into one of the categories listed below may receive USDA reimbursement for eligible children enrolled.

*Note: The USDA forms vary from state to state. The samples included here may not be like those used in your state. Check with your local office.

Mid-Atlantic Regional Office
Mercer Corporate Park
300 Corporate Blvd.
Robbinsville, NJ 08691-1598
609-259-5025

*Delaware, District of Columbia, Maryland,
New Jersey, Pennsylvania, Puerto Rico,
Virginia, Virgin Islands,West Virginia*

Midwest Regional Office
77 West Jackson Blvd., 20th Floor
Chicago, IL 60604-3507
312-353-6664

*Illinois, Indiana, Michigan, Minnesota,
Ohio, Wisconsin*

Mountain Plains Regional Office
1244 Speer Blvd., Suite 903
Denver, CO 80204-3581
303-844-0300

*Colorado, Iowa, Kansas, Missouri, Nebraska,
North Dakota, South Dakota, Utah, Wyoming*

Western Regional Office
550 Kearney Street, Room 400
San Francisco, CA 94108-2518
415-705-1310

*Alaska, Arizona, California, Hawaii, Idaho, Nevada,
Oregon, Washington, Guam Trust Territories,
Commonwealth of the Northern Mariana Islands,
American Samoa*

Northeast Regional Office
10 Causeway Street, Room 501
Boston, MA 02222-1069
617-565-6370

*Connecticut, Maine, Massachusetts, New Hampshire,
New York, Rhode Island, Vermont*

Southeast Regional Office
61 Forsyth Street, SW, Room 8T36
Atlanta, GA 30303-3415
404-562-1800

*Alabama, Florida, Georgia, Kentucky, Mississippi,
North Carolina, South Carolina, Tennessee*

Southwest Regional Office
1100 Commerce Street, Room 5-A-6
Dallas, TX 75242-9980
214-290-9800

Arkansas, Louisiana, New Mexico, Oklahoma, Texas

Figure 14–2   Food and Consumer Service Regional Offices Information

Eligible providers are:

- nonresidential public or private not-for-profit child care and ADC* centers
- profit making child care centers that receive Title XX compensation for at least 25 percent of the children attending
- Head Start programs
- settlement houses and recreation programs
- family child care homes (if they participate in the CACFP under a sponsoring organization that has tax-exempt status)

All participating agencies must serve meals that meet the standards for the Special Food Service Program for Infants, Preschool Age, and School Age Children which are covered in Figure 14–4. Following these guidelines ensures well-balanced meals. However, some recommended serving sizes may be overwhelming for young children if put on the plate all at one time.

The USDA Child and Adult Care Food Program requires extensive paperwork which must be done accurately and on a regular basis. A Claim for Reimbursement form (see sample in Figure 14–5) and a Monthly Financial Report (Figure 14–6) must be filed monthly with the State Division of School Food Service reporting data on:

- attendance
- number of meals served
- cost of food calculated on the basis of information obtained from a monthly food inventory
- labor and purchased service costs
- income from reduced-lunch fees and other sources

*Temporary Assistance for Needy Families (TANF) replaces Aid to Dependent Children (ADC) on documents and literature after the 1996 Welfare Reform.

INSTRUCTIONS: To apply for free and reduced-price meals, complete the following information, including signature and return this application to the center. *Part 1* is to be completed by All households. *Part 2* is to be used only for a child receiving Aid to Families with Dependent Children (AFDC) or for a child living in a household receiving Food Stamp benefits. *Part 3* is only for children not receiving Food Stamp benefits or AFDC benefits. * **Asterisk items must be filled in for each part you complete.** Additional instructions are on the back of this form. If you need help, call _____.
FORM MUST BE UPDATED ON ANNUAL BASIS AND IS VALID FOR ONLY 12 MONTHS INCLUDING MONTH SIGNED.

PART 1 - Print information for all children participating in CACFP.

* NAME	AGE	BIRTHDATE
1		
2		
3		
4		

PART 2 - List each child's Food Stamp or AFDC case number, if any.

* FOOD STAMP NUMBER	* AFDC NUMBER

PART 3 - HOUSEHOLD MEMBERS AND MONTHLY INCOME: For children NOT receiving FOOD STAMPS OR AFDC

* HOUSEHOLD MEMBERS — List names of all household members	Gross MONTHLY Earnings (Before Deductions) Job 1	Job 2	MONTHLY Welfare Payments, Child Support, Alimony	MONTHLY Payments, Retirement, Social Security	Any Other MONTHLY Income
1	$	$	$	$	$
2	$	$	$	$	$
3	$	$	$	$	$
4	$	$	$	$	$
5	$	$	$	$	$

PART 4 - FOSTER CHILD: Check here if the child is a foster child._____ List the child's monthly personal use income. Enter "0" if the child has no personal use income. Personal Use Income $_____

PART 5 - SIGNATURE AND SOCIAL SECURITY NUMBER: I certify that the above information is true and correct and that all income is reported. I understand that this information is being given for receipt of federal funds; that program officials may verify the information on the application; and that deliberate misrepresentation of the information may subject me to prosecution under applicable state and federal criminal laws.

*
_____   _____
SIGNATURE OF ADULT HOUSEHOLD MEMBER   SOCIAL SECURITY NUMBER (Required only for Part 3)

Print Name_____ Daytime Telephone Number_____ Work Telephone Number_____

Street/Apt._____ City/Zip/County_____ Date_____

PART 6 - RACIAL/ETHNIC IDENTITY: Please check the racial/ethnic identity of your child(ren). You are not required to answer this question.
White, not Hispanic _____ Black, not Hispanic _____ Hispanic _____ Asian/Pacific Islander _____ American Indian/Alaskan Native _____

Privacy Act Statement: Section 9 of the National School Lunch Act requires that, unless your child's food stamp or AFDC number is provided, you must include the Social Security Number of the adult household member signing the application or indicate that the household member does not have a Social Security Number. Provision of a Social Security Number is not mandatory, but if a Social Security Number is not given or an indication is not made that the signer does not have such a number, the application cannot be approved. The Social Security Number may be used to identify the household member in carrying out efforts to verify the correctness of information stated on the application. These verification efforts may be carried out though program reviews, audits, and investigations and may include contacting employers to determine income, contacting a food stamp or welfare office to determine current certification for receipt of food stamps or AFDC benefits, contacting the State Employment Security Office to determine the amount of benefits received and checking the documentation produced by household members to prove the amount of income received. These efforts may result in a loss or reduction of benefits, administrative claims or legal actions if incorrect information is reported.

FOR SPONSOR USE ONLY

TOTAL HOUSEHOLD SIZE: _____   TOTAL MONTHLY INCOME, ALL SOURCES: $_____

CHECK ONE: FREE _____   REDUCED _____   NOT ELIGIBLE (PAID) _____

SIGNATURE OF SPONSOR'S DETERMINING OFFICIAL:_____ DATE_____

EDU 0157   CACFP 008   6/96

Figure 14–3   Sample Application for Free and Reduced Price Meals

To apply for free and reduced price meals, complete the application using the instructions for your type of household.

PART 1 - CHILD INFORMATION: ALL HOUSEHOLDS COMPLETE THIS PART.
- (a) Print the name of the child(ren) for whom you are applying. Children from the same household (except foster children) may be listed on the same application.
- (b) List their age and birthday.

PART 2 - HOUSEHOLDS GETTING FOOD STAMPS OR AFDC: COMPLETE THIS PART AND PART 5 - If a child is a member of a food stamp household or AFDC assistance unit, the child is automatically eligible to receive free CACFP benefits subject to application completion.
- (a) List a current food stamp or AFDC case number for each child.
- (b) Sign the application in PART 5. An adult household member must sign.

SKIP PART 3 - Do <u>not</u> list names of household members or income if you list a food stamp or AFDC case number for each child.

PART 3 - ALL OTHER HOUSEHOLDS: COMPLETE THIS PART AND PART 5
- (a) Write the names of everyone living in your household, whether they receive income or not. Include yourself, the childr(ren) you are applying for, all other children, your spouse, grandparents, and other related and unrelated people in your household. Use another piece of paper if you need more space.
- (b) Write the amount of income each household member received the previous month, before taxes or anything else is taken out, and where it came from, such as earnings, welfare, pensions, and other income. If any amount during the previous month was more or less than usual, write that person's usual monthly income.
- (c) An adult household member must sign the application and give his/her social security number in PART 5.

PART 4 - HOUSEHOLDS WITH A FOSTER CHILD: COMPLETE THIS PART AND PART 5 - In certain cases, meals served to foster children may be reimbursed regardless of the foster family's income. If you wish to apply for a foster child living with you complete the application as if for a family of one since a foster child is the legal responsibility of a welfare agency or court. Complete a separate application for each foster child.
- (a) List the foster child's monthly "personal use" income. Write "0" if the foster child does not receive "**personal use**" income.
- (b) An adult member of the foster home must sign the application in PART 5.
- (c) A social security number is not needed for the foster child's application.
  "Personal use" income is: (1) money given by the welfare office identified by category for the child's personal use, such as for clothing, school fees, and allowances; and (2) all other money the child receives, such as money from his/her family and money from the child's full-time or regular part-time jobs.

PART 5 - SIGNATURE AND SOCIAL SECURITY NUMBER: ALL HOUSEHOLDS COMPLETE THIS PART
- (1) All applications must have the signature of an adult household member.
- (2) An application that lists monthly income must have the social security number of the adult who signs. If the adult does not have a social security number, write "none" or something else to show that the adult does not have a social security number. If you listed a food stamp or AFDC number for each child or if you are applying for a foster child, a social security number is not needed.

PART 6 - RACIAL/ETHNIC IDENTITY
  Complete the racial/ethnic identity question if you wish. You are not required to answer this question to be eligible to get free or reduced price meals. This information is collected to make sure that everyone is treated fairly and will be kept confidential. No child will be discriminated against because of race, color, national origin, sex, age, or disability.

NON-DISCRIMINATION: This facility is operated in accordance with USDA policy which does not permit discrimination because of race, color, national origin, sex, age or disability. Any person who believes that he or she has been discriminated against in any USDA related activity should write immediately to the Secretary of Agriculture, Washington D.C., 20250.

INCOME ELIGIBILITY GUIDELINES
Guidelines to be effective from July 1, 1996 through June 30, 1997

Households with incomes less than or equal to the values below are eligible for free or reduced meal benefits.

Household Size	Year	Month	Week
1	$14,319	1,194	276
2	$19,166	1,598	369
3	$24,013	2,002	462
4	$28,860	2,405	555
5	$33,707	2,809	649
6	$38,554	3,213	742
7	$43,401	3,617	835
8	$48,248	4,021	928
EACH ADDITIONAL HOUSEHOLD MEMBER ADD.	$ 4,847	404	94

Figure 14-3 (continued)

	Infants Birth through 3 months	Infants 4 through 7 months	Infants 8 through 11 months
BREAKFAST	4–6 fl. oz formula (1)	4–8 fl. oz. formula (1) or breast milk (5) 0–3 Tbsp. infant cereal (2) (optional)	6–8 fl. oz. formula (1) breast milk (5), or whole milk. 2–4 Tbsp. infant cereal (2) 1–4 Tbsp. fruit and/ or vegetable.
LUNCH OR SUPPER	4–6 fl. oz formula (1)	4–8 fl. oz. formula (1) or breast milk (5) 0–3 Tbsp. infant cereal (2) (optional) 0–3 Tbsp. fruit and/or vegetable (optional)	6–8 fl. oz. formula (1) breast milk (5), or whole milk. 2–4 Tbsp. infant cereal (2) and/or 1–4 Tbsp. meat, fish, poultry, egg yolk, or cooked dry beans or peas or 1/2 to 2 oz. cheese or 1–4 oz. cottage cheese, cheese food or cheese spread 1–4 Tbsp. fruit and/or vegetable
SUPPLEMENT	4–6 fl. oz. formula (1)	4–6 fl. oz. formula (1)	2–4 fl. oz. formula (1) breast milk (5), whole milk, or fruit juice (3). 0–1/2 slice bread or 0–2 crackers (optional) (4).

Figure 14–4   Child and Adult Care Food Program Meal Pattern for Infants

(1) Shall be iron-fortified infant formula

(2) Shall be iron-fortified dry infant cereal

(3) Shall be full-strength fruit juice

(4) Shall be from whole-grain or enriched meal or flour

(5) Breast milk provided by the infant's mother may be served in place of formula from birth through 11 months. Meals containing only breast milk are not reimbursable. Meals containing breast milk served to infants four months or older may be claimed when the other meal component(s) is supplied by the child care facility

To complete these claim forms, you must have accurate attendance records, invoices or cash tapes and receipts for all food and some nonfood purchases, and financial records on all cash received from those families who pay full or reduced-lunch costs.

Even when there is an extra person on staff to do the USDA paperwork, data collection for the reports and preparation of the Verification Review involves the director, cook, and teaching staff.

Each program is subject to a Verification Review by the state agency every three years. The purpose of the review is to determine that all the income eligibility forms since the last review have been filled out correctly, that each family is properly classified as free, reduced, or paid, and that the figures reported to the state on the monthly claim forms are accurate. When the CACFP consultant comes to the center to do the Verification Review, you must provide the following:

- all income eligibility forms
- attendance records

- enrollment forms (to confirm that children listed as eligible for reimbursement are enrolled)

In addition to reviewing records on children, the consultant also will review administrative records. For that review you must provide:

- record of meal counts
- menus
- monthly food inventories
- documentation of food and supply costs
- documentation of labor costs
- documentation of Title XX enrollments if it is a proprietary center

Complicated you say! Yes, indeed, very complicated. As a director, it is essential that you understand the USDA program so you can do the paperwork if it is part of your job description, or delegate the responsibility and coach those who are doing the detailed record keeping and reporting.

■ CACFP 006   Mark Reflex® by NCS MM105158-2   321   ED01 ■ ■ Printed in U.S.A.

DEPARTMENT OF EDUCATION
DIVISION OF CHILD NUTRITION SERVICES

CHILD AND ADULT CARE FOOD PROGRAM CLAIM FOR REIMBURSEMENT

October 1, 1996 Through September 30, 1997

DARKEN ONE PROGRAM TYPE:

Child Care (Non-Profit)   Head Start

For Profit (Child)   OSH

Adult Care

DARKEN ONE CIRCLE:

Original Claim

Revised Claim

PLEASE READ
INSTRUCTIONS ON
REVERSE SIDE

• DO NOT FOLD OR STAPLE FORM •

ENTER SPONSOR IRN

FILL IN REPORT MONTH

○ Oct.
○ Nov.
○ Dec.
○ Jan.
○ Feb.
○ March
○ April
○ May
○ June
○ July
○ Aug.
○ Sept.

A Number of Operating Days

SPONSORING AGENCY

ADDRESS   CITY   ZIP

(   )   –

COUNTY   PHONE

I CERTIFY that to the best of my knowledge this claim is correct in all respects, that records are available to support this claim, that it is in accordance with the terms of existing agreement(s), and that payment, therefore, has not been received. I recognize that I will be fully responsible for any excess amounts which may result from erroneous or neglectful reporting.

SIGNATURE OF AUTHORIZED REPRESENTATIVE   TITLE   DATE

PROGRAM PARTICIPANTS

B Average Daily Attendance

C Number of Sites

Eligible Number of Meals Served

D Breakfasts   **E** Lunches   **F** Suppers

Eligible Supplements Served

G AM   **H** PM   **I** Evening

PROGRAM ADULTS (Nonparticipants)

Number of Meals Served

J Breakfasts   **K** Lunches   **L** Suppers

Supplements

M AM   **N** PM   **O** Evening

Enrollment by Income Category

P Free   **Q** Reduced   **R** Paid

Figure 14–5   Child and Adult Care Food Program Claim Reimbursement

General: To receive federal assistance for meal service, each program must report month-end counts on a claim for reimbursement. The claim covers operations for one calendar month only. Claims are processed once each week.

Special Note: If this is a revised claim, darken the bubble and complete only the items needing changes. Leave all other items blank. Original or revised claims received more than 60 days after the end of a reporting month will not be processed for reimbursement.

To Fill Out the Form: Failure to follow directions will cause delay in processing the claim for payment.

1. Use a No. 2 lead pencil. The sponsoring agency name and address may be typed if the typing does not overlap into the reporting areas.
2. Write the numbers in the rectangles above the numbered bubbles. ───▶ Pay attention to the commas.
3. Darken the corresponding bubble below each number. ───▶
4. Clearly erase any response that is changed. Completely darken the bubble for each number you mark.

Special Instructions for Items A through R:

A **Operating Days:**   Enter the total number of days food service was provided for participants in the claim month.

B **Average Daily Attendance:** Compute by adding daily attendance for each day of the month and dividing the total by the number of operating days in the month.

C **Number of Sites:**   Enter the number of sites approved for CACFP benefits operating during the claim month.

D Eligible Number of Meals and Supplements Served (to participants)
E Enter the total number of breakfasts,
F lunches, suppers, a.m., p.m., and evening supplements
G served to enrolled participants attending the child care,
H adult care, or outside-school-hours care centers during
I the claim month.

J Program staff/others (non-participants):
K Enter the total number of breakfasts, lunches, suppers,
L a.m., p.m., and evening supplements served to adults who
M perform labor required to support the program such as
N menu planning; preparing, serving and clean-up; on-site
O recordkeeping, supervision of participants at meals.

P Enrollment by Income Category: ZERO OR GREATER MUST BE DARKENED FOR P, Q, AND R FOR THE FORM
Q TO BE ACCEPTED. Enter the number of enrolled participants classified as free, reduced or paid. Each person
R classified as FREE or REDUCED must have on file with the sponsor a correct Income Eligibility Application. Anyone without an Income Eligibility Application or whose household income is above the qualifying income eligibility guidelines is categorized as paid.

Forward the ORIGINAL and ONE COPY of the claim for reimbursement to the Ohio Department of Education, Division of Child Nutrition Services, Child and Adult Care Food Program, 65 South Front Street, Room 715, Columbus, Ohio 43215-4183. A copy is to be retained by the submitting agency for a permanent record. All CACFP records must be retained for three past fiscal years plus the current year.

Figure 14–5   (continued)

Department of Education
Division of Child Nutrition Services

October 1, 1996 through September 30, 1997

PLEASE READ INSTRUCTIONS ON REVERSE SIDE

• DO NOT FOLD OR STAPLE FORM •

SPONSORING AGENCY

ADDRESS

CITY, STATE, ZIP

COUNTY   PHONE

DARKEN ONE CIRCLE:
○ Original Claim
○ Revised Claim

ENTER SPONSOR IRN

FILL IN REPORT MONTH
○ Oct.
○ Nov.
○ Dec.
○ Jan.
○ Feb.
○ March
○ April
○ May
○ June
○ July
○ Aug.
○ Sept.

A Number of Operating Days

B FOOD

C NON-FOOD SUPPLIES

D PROGRAM ADMINISTRATION

E PROGRAM LABOR

F PURCHASED SERVICES

G DEPRECIATION FOOD SERVICE EQUIPMENT

H TOTAL FOOD INCOME RECEIVED

I TOTAL MONTHLY EXPENSE

I hereby certify that to the best of my belief and knowledge, this financial report is correct in all respects, that records are on file in support of it, and that it is in accordance with the terms of the existing Child and Adult Care Food Program Agreement.

SIGNATURE OF AUTHORIZED REPRESENTATIVE

TITLE   DATE

Figure 14–6   Child and Adult Care Food Program Monthly Financial Report

Instructions

General: To receive federal assistance for meal service, each program must report food related expenses and income each month. This financial report of expenses and income is to be sent to the state agency with the corresponding monthly claim. The claim will not be processed for payment until a monthly financial report is received.

Original and revised claims postmarked more than 60 days after the end of a reporting month will not be processed for reimbursement (unless adjustment is downward).

Be sure the sponsoring agency name and address is the same as the sponsor name and address on the Child and Adult Care Food Program (CACFP) Application.

Revised Report: Darken this bubble when a revision needs to be made to the information that was submitted on the original report. Complete only the items in A through I needing changes; leave all other items blank.

To fill out the Form:
Failure to follow directions will cause delay in processing the claim for payment.
1. Use a No. 2 lead pencil.
2. Write the numbers in the rectangles above the numbered bubbles.
   Pay attention to the commas and decimal point.
3. Darken the corresponding bubble below each number.
4. Clearly erase any response that is changed.
   Completely darken the bubble for each number you mark.

Special Instructions for Items A through I:

A. Operating Days: Enter the total number of days food service was provided to participants for the claim month.

B. Food Costs: Enter total costs for food including delivery and transportation of food. Monthly beginning and ending inventory values must be added to and subtracted from food costs reported.

C. Non-Food Supplies: Enter total cost of food service related supplies such as paper cups, trays, plates, napkins, straws, etc. and expendable, nondepreciable equipment (items costing less than $500.00). Monthly beginning and ending inventory values must be added to and subtracted from non-food costs.

D. Program Administrative Costs: Enter cost of salary and fringes of administrative personnel, supplies, printing, training, contracted services, occupancy, travel, and communications when clearly related to administration of food service.

E. Program Labor Costs: Enter cost of salary and fringes of food service personnel and staff time spent in serving, supervising, or cleaning-up meal service.
Note: Payroll records are required to document personnel costs. Personnel not assigned full-time to food service may be reported based upon a time study covering only time spent on the CACFP.

F. Purchased Services: Enter total costs for rental of food service facilities and equipment, repairs of food service equipment, and utilities cleaning, pest control, etc. when clearly related to food service. Costs must be prorated if CACFP activities account for only a partial percent of total use.

G. Depreciation of Food Service Equipment: Enter total depreciation costs recorded for tax purposes, or enter depreciation costs of food service equipment items with acquisition costs over $500. Compute by dividing the acquisition cost by the years of life expectancy for each item.

H. Total Food Income Received: Enter total income received from food sales, paying guests, parents, or from catering food to other programs. Do not include monies received from CACFP reimbursement.

I. Total Monthly Expense: Enter total expenses by adding items B through G and subtracting H.

Forward the original and one copy of the monthly financial report to the Ohio Department of Education, Division of Child Nutrition Services, Child and Adult Care Food Program, 65 South Front Street, Room 715, Columbus, Ohio 43215-4183. A copy should be retained by the submitting agency for a permanent record. All CACFP records must be retained for three past fiscal years plus the current year.

Figure 14–6   (continued)

Food Storage

Storing food requires careful planning so that sufficient quantities of food items are conveniently accessible to the preparation area and storage areas, and containers are sanitary and chilled. The available shelf space and containers must be appropriate to accommodate the packaged size of the food items as they are delivered from the supplier. All food items should be stored separately from nonfood items, and food storage rooms should be dry, relatively cool (60° F to 70° F), and free from insect or rodent infestation. Commodities should be stored in tightly covered, labeled metal or heavy plastic containers that are at least six inches above the floor level to permit air circulation and to protect them from dirt. Dating containers ensures food supplies will be used in the order received.

Perishable foods must be stored at temperatures that prevent spoilage. Refrigerator temperature must be 40° F or lower; freezer temperature should be at 0° F or lower. Shelf space should allow for air circulation around the refrigerated foods, and thermometers in the warmest sections of refrigerators and freezers should be checked daily.

Food Preparation

Cooks must follow recipes in meal preparation and adhere to directions about cooking times and temperatures, proper techniques, and temperatures for holding prepared foods, and proper methods for storing and using leftovers. Sanitation in the food preparation area is of utmost importance. The food service staff must follow sanitary food-handling practices, and maintain good personal hygiene while handling foods and cleaning food preparation equipment and utensils. Even though there may be a nutritionist or other staff member responsible for the total food service program in the center, it is advisable for you, as director, to make periodic checks on the food preparation techniques and the sanitation practices of the cook as food is prepared and served to the children. It often becomes the director's responsibility to coach the cook when correct preparation procedures are not being followed.

Sanitation guidelines are available from your local health department or your state or local licensing agent. The licensing regulations at all levels include clearly stated sanitation requirements related to food preparation in child care centers. A local health department staff member or your center licensing agent are excellent resources for helping interpret and implement the sanitation regulations applicable in your area.

Resources

The following list includes places to go for printed material and for consultation on the center's nutrition component. These resources can supply copies of laws, regulations, and guidelines in response to questions regarding nutrition and health.

- public health nutritionists in state or local health departments, or the county extension agency
- nutritionists in local dairy councils or comprehensive health centers
- USDA extension home economists
- home economists in nearby high schools or universities
- members of local home economics associations
- dietitians in local hospitals

THE HEALTH AND SAFETY PROGRAM

The center staff members are responsible for the health and safety of the children while they are at the center; therefore, directors must be knowledgeable about health and safety regulations as stipulated in the licensing regulations, staff liability in cases of accidents at school, and procedures for protection from and reporting of communicable disease and child abuse. Although some large centers may have a health consultant on staff, in most places, the director is the designated individual responsible for the health program.

The health services provided through the child care center may range from no service at all to comprehensive service including regular physicals, dental checkups, and treatment, vision screening, hearing screening, and mental health services. The scope of the health services program depends on the program's health policies set by the funding agent, the socioeconomic status of the families, the family expectations, and the licensing regulations. All centers should maintain up-to-date health and immunization records on the children whether or not direct health services are provided.

Health Records for Children and Staff

Children's health records should cover information up to the time of registration plus any new health or medical information received while the child is in the program. Formats for these records vary and may be set by local health departments (see sample in Director's Resources 13–5 and 13–7 on pages 323 and 330, respectively). The information provided, in addition to the basic demographics like name, birth date, parents names, and so forth, should include medical and developmental information, and must be completed and signed by the child's health care provider. The medical report on the child should include:[4]

- records of the child's immunizations
- description of any disability, sensory impairment, developmental variation, seizure disorder, emotional or behavioral disturbance that may affect adaptation to child care
- assessment of the child's growth based on height, weight, head circumference (percentile for these if the child is younger than 24 months)
- results of screenings—vision, hearing, dental, nutrition, developmental, tuberculosis, hemoglobin, urine, lead, and so forth
- dates of significant communicable diseases (for example, chicken pox)
- prescribed medications including information on recognizing and reporting potential side effects

- description of current acute or chronic health problems under or needing treatment
- description of serious injuries sustained by the child in the past
- special instructions for the caregiver

It is preferable to have the child's medical report on file prior to or on admission, but imperative that it be completed within six weeks after admission or as required by licensing laws. These records should be updated every six months for children under two years and every year for children ages two to six years.

The above listing of items that should be in the medical report indicates a dental screening should be included. An authorized health care provider often does the dental screening on children under age three, at which time the child should visit a dentist. If the earlier dental screenings reveal special oral/dental problems, the child should see a dentist immediately.

Staff medical records that follow the licensing requirements must be on file at the center. Even when not required by licensing, there should be a medical record on every adult who has regular contact with the children including substitutes, volunteers, practicum students, cooks, and van drivers. The staff records should include a physical assessment and an evaluation of the emotional fitness of those who are to care for the children. The staff health appraisal should include:[5]

- health history
- physical exam
- vision and hearing screening
- tuberculosis (TB) screening by the Mantoux (intracutaneous) method
- a review of immunizations (measles, mumps, rubella, diphtheria, tetanus, polio)
- a review of occupational health concerns
- assessment of need for immunizations against influenza, pneumococcus, and hepatitis B
- assessment of orthopedic, psychological, neurological, or sensory limitations, and communicable diseases that may impair a staff member's ability to perform the job

[4]Ibid., pp. 331–332. Reprinted by permission.
[5]Ibid., p. 36. Reprinted by permission.

Unless licensing regulations require more frequent updating of staff health records, it is recommended this be done every two years. Although new cases of tuberculosis have been falling, incidence varies so it is wise to consult your local health authorities to determine the frequency of repeat TB testing.

Currently, there are no screening or self-appraisal tools to identify specific health conditions that may seriously impair a caregiver's ability to provide safe and healthy experiences for children. However, there are some obvious things which a director can assess. For example, can the teacher do the following:[6]

- move to supervise and assist the children?
- lift children, equipment, and supplies?
- sit on the floor and on child-size chairs?
- practice frequent hand-washing?
- eat the same food served to the children?
- hear and see the playground at a distance?

Communicable Diseases

Cases of communicable diseases at the child care center must be reported to all center families and to the local health authorities. The usual children's diseases, as well as cases of meningitis, scarlet fever, infectious hepatitis, and head lice must be reported so that necessary precautions can be taken immediately. It is important that pregnant staff members consult their physician about precautions related to exposure to communicable diseases at the workplace.

Directors and some of the teaching staff should have training in communicable diseases to enable them to recognize symptoms and make decisions about exclusion of children from the group. Communicable disease training is available in most communities through the Red Cross or the local Health Department. Licensing usually requires updated communicable disease training for classroom staff. Every center should provide easy access to a Communicable Disease Chart (see Director's Resource on page 370) for staff who must recognize

symptoms and make exclusion decisions. The most important measure in preventing the spread of disease in child care centers is hand-washing, not only after toileting or diapering, but also after nose-blowing or helping a child with a runny nose or cough, and before handling dishes or serving food. Sanitizing surfaces after diapering on tables before using for eating also will help cut down on the spread of disease. Cleanliness is the major contributing factor to effective disease control in child care environments.

Staff members responsible for giving first aid to children and those likely to come in contact with blood or body fluids should have special training in dealing with blood-borne pathogens such as HIV or hepatitis B. These employees should also be offered hepatitis B vaccine, and the director should maintain records of immunizations as well as exposure incidents.[7]

The spread of disease also is minimized through precautionary measures for handling situations where children become ill during the day and when children are ill on arrival. A written policy regarding management of sick children must be conveyed to parents when children are enrolled. Since very few centers have facilities to care for a sick child who must be separated from the other children, the usual practice is to call the parent or a designated adult to come for the child. In the meantime, the child is usually removed from the classroom, and under adult supervision, rests or plays quietly. Often, the director is the only staff person who has a schedule flexible enough to allow time to stay with the sick child. An extra cot and a few toys for use while waiting to be picked up by a parent is standard equipment in many directors' offices.

Exclusion Policy. Exclusion policies must be made clear to parents and to the child care staff. If the purpose of excluding an ill child is to prevent the spread of infection to others in the group, it is important to specify which types of illnesses require exclusion. This list should include infectious diarrhea and vomiting, untreated conjunctivitis, impetigo, ringworm, head lice, and scabies.[8] Most

[6]Ibid., 136. Reprinted by permission.
[7]Aronson, S. S., MD. (1992). OSHA requires employers to give hepatitis B immunization and protection to first aiders," *Child Care Information Exchange, The Director's Magazine*, November, p. 55.
[8]Aronson, S. S., MD. (1982). Exclusion criteria for ill children in child care," *Child Care Information Exchange, The Director's Magazine*, May, p. 14.

centers develop special policies and procedures for excluding ill children so that all staff members and parents are aware of the specific criteria for exclusion. A rise in body temperature is common in young children, and may or may not be a symptom of a contagious or serious illness. Nonetheless, most centers have strict policies about exclusion of children with a fever. Guidelines for when a child should be checked by a physician are:

- an oral temperature of 101° F or greater who also has behavior changes or other signs or symptoms of illness
- a rectal temperature of 102° F or greater who also has behavior changes or other signs or symptoms of illness
- an axillary (armpit) temperature of 100° F or greater who also has behavior changes or other signs or symptoms of illness
- an aural (in the ear) temperature that corresponds to 102° F rectal or 101° F oral[9]

When the policy is clear, it helps both parents and staff make decisions about when to exclude children from the group. Programs which have staffed facilities to care for mildly ill children can have more liberal exclusion policies than those with no staff or space for these children to receive the extra rest and supervision they require.

Although there is an ever-increasing amount of information on the risks posed by children infected with HIV (a viral infection which can lead to AIDS) attending child care programs, evidence is inconclusive at this time. Since new information about HIV/AIDS is constantly being generated, stay in touch with local health authorities or the Centers for Disease Control for updated information and guidance. If a child infected with HIV applies for admission, the public health department and the child's physician can help determine if it is safe for the child to be in a group situation. They also will provide help in determining whether the presence of this child exposes other children and adults to undo risk.

Despite concerns among child care professionals about this question, few centers will be confronted with this difficult decision due to the small number of children infected with HIV/AIDS. The overwhelming majority of children in this country who are infected acquired the HIV virus from their mother during pregnancy.[10] The primary risk of admitting children with AIDS is that these children run a greater risk of contracting illnesses and infections from the other children because their immune systems are not functioning properly. These infections pose a serious threat to the child's life.[11] The current information regarding HIV and the hepatitis B virus is that neither is easily transmitted in school or child care environment, or through casual contact such as touching, hugging, eating together, or sharing bathrooms. However, many centers are choosing to have a written policy on HIV and hepatitis B in order to protect the rights of an infected child and the other children in the center.

The Centers for Disease Control recommend that HIV-positive children only be excluded from group child care settings if they have open sores, uncontrollable nosebleeds, bloody diarrhea, or are at high risk for exposing others to blood-contaminated body fluids.[12] To obtain updated information on this question or others involving infectious diseases, contact the Centers for Disease Control.[13]

Sick Child Care.   As more children under five require some type of care outside the home, there is the consequent increase in the need for sick child care. The first alternative is to have the child remain at home with a caring parent whose employer allows time off for that purpose. Being at home may be the best alternative but it is not always the most realistic. That means child care professionals, with the help of health professionals, are beginning to develop alternative sick child care models.

Sick children might be accommodated in:

- a sick bay at the center called a Get Well Room

[9]*Preparing for illness: A joint responsibility for parents and caregivers*, PA Chapter American Academy of Pediatrics 1996, p. 3.
[10]Kendrick A. S., Kaufman, R., & Messenger K. P. (Eds.). (1995). *Healthy young children: A manual for programs.* National Association for the Education of Young Children, p. 249.
[11]Ibid., Marotz, et al, p. 140.
[12]Ibid., Marotz, et al, p. 140.
[13]Center for Disease Control, Atlanta, Georgia 30333, (404)329-3091.

- a center in a separate building which might be the cooperative venture of several child care programs
- a center in a wing of a hospital or on hospital grounds that is available to the general public
- a "satellite" system of family child care homes linked to a child care center
- the child's own home under the supervision of a trained person sent from the center or local health agency

"Deciding how to meet sick children's needs and parents' needs for child care is often difficult. Isolation and exclusion is not necessary for many illnesses. A balance must be struck between the needs of the child, the other children in the group, and an arrangement made that does not strain the staffing resources of the day care program."[14] Since children with AIDS are extremely vulnerable to infection from other children, it is probably unwise to have them in a sick child care facility where they would be exposed to other sick children.

DIRECTOR'S CORNER

"I'm very interested in sick child care because of my background in nursing, and I know how much kids need Mom or Dad when they are sick! I also know there is a critical need for sick child care for those cases where job pressures force parents to get to work, even when their baby is sick. My dream is to develop a satellite family child care home system which will use our center as a base."
—Director, proprietary not-for-profit center

Disaster Plan

Although licensing regulations do not always require disaster plans, it is important to plan for building evacuation in the event of fire and to detail additional measures to be taken during tornadoes, earthquakes, smog alerts, floods, sudden loss of heat or air conditioning, or any other major emergency or disaster. The director must instruct all staff members on the best ways to evacuate the premises and the safe places to shelter children in weather or civil defense emergencies. It is important to practice all emergency procedures with staff so they are conditioned to respond and less

likely to panic. An evacuation plan should be posted in every classroom (see Figure 14–7). Fire emergency plans must include alternative exit routes and evacuation drills should be held regularly so children become familiar with this routine. Parents must be informed, in advance, about alternative shelters so they know the whereabouts of their children during emergencies.

Daily attendance records and information needed to reach parents must be maintained in a convenient location and removed from the building by the designated adults as part of the evacuation procedure. The "chain of command" regarding who will call for emergency fire or police help, who will secure the building and make a final check that everyone is out, how the building will be secured, and who will contact the parents must all be arranged in advance and communicated to staff by the director. Fire alarms, fire extinguishers, smoke detectors, and emergency exit lights should be checked regularly to ensure they are in working order.

Supplies stored in emergency evacuation areas and to be taken to the alternative shelter include:

- first aid kit
- blankets
- food and water
- battery operated radio
- flashlight
- children's books, crayons, paper, and so on.

Fire, earthquake, and tornado plans and drills are important, but keep in mind that there are many other disasters that can impact the child care center in addition to those requiring building evacuation. Rehearsals for building evacuation are a necessity, but how will the staff respond when a sleeping child stops breathing, when an angry noncustodial parent appears with a gun, or an inebrious person harasses departing parents and children? There are resources in most communities to call on for help as you develop emergency plans for a vast array of possible emergencies and train the staff to deal with unexpected events. Invite local law enforcement personnel, health professionals, Red Cross, legal aid, and social service people to assist you with developing procedures and providing staff training.

[14]Deitch, S. R., MD. (Ed.), (1987). *Health in daycare: a manual for professionals*. American Academy of Pediatrics. (AAP), p. 16.

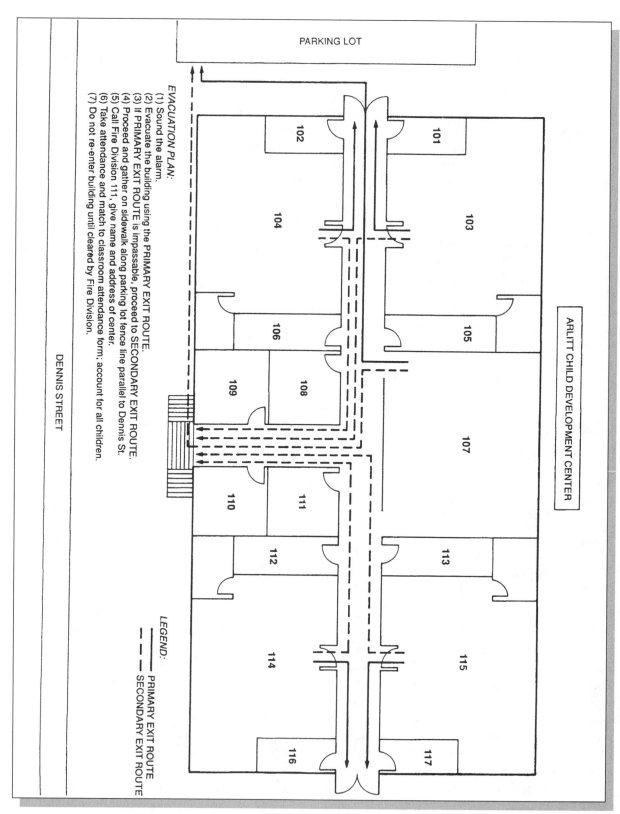

Figure 14–7   Sample Evacuation Plan

General suggestions to keep in mind when you write emergency plans are included in Figure 14–8, Suggestions for Code Blue Design.

Directors' responsibilities do not end with plan development, training, and rehearsing staff on procedures, then carrying out the plan when a real disaster strikes. They also must deal with the follow-up for parents and children, and deal with the press. After a crisis such as a fire, shooting, the death of a child at the center, or an allegation of child abuse, it is critical that accurate information be presented to families and the public through the press. Although this responsibility usually falls to the director, it is wise to consider who else might serve as a spokesperson. A carefully selected and knowledgeable spokesperson who is savvy about handling the press can help protect the center and its families when serious emergencies or damaging allegations arise. Choices for spokesperson may be:[15]

- the center's lawyer
- the director of public relations or human resources if it is an employer-sponsored center

- a priest, rabbi, or minister if the center has a religious affiliation
- a board member or other volunteer who has a vested interest in the center, is respected in the community, and is trained in public relations

All staff must be trained to deflect media questions to the spokesperson or director, and to answer informal questions from parents and others by quoting center written policy, or by referring these inquiries to the director.

To obtain more information on the best methods to provide protection in particular areas, contact local health and fire department officials, building inspectors, the Environmental Protection Agency (EPA), or the Occupational Safety and Health Administration (OSHA). Also, make sure all foreseeable issues are covered by various insurance policies.

Emergency Health and Accident Plan

An emergency health plan is usually developed by the director with input from board members,

---

Suggestions for Code Blue Design

Review the organization chart and the chain of command. Each time the director leaves the building, it should be clear who is in charge.

Make it a priority that no adult is left alone in the building. In cases where this is necessary, program a phone and teach one of the older children to use it to call for help if something happens to the caregiver.

Assume the program loses power—how will communication be maintained? Is there a back-up lighting system? A cellular phone? A laptop computer?

Get to know the press in the area over positive issues first! Invite them to the center, refer positive information to them on a regular basis, put announcements in their calendars, etc. so that their first encounter with the center is not over an emergency.

Train the receptionist or designate someone to answer the phone who is unflappable and will deliver a succinct message to all callers.

Make it clear that all staff will stay at the center until the Code Blue is over. Ask other staff to come in to help.

Update code Blue materials every September when new information peaks.

Reassure staff and board that this planning is preventative—it will probably not be needed, but if it is, every attempt has been made to minimize the damage.

From: Copeland, M. L. (1996). Code blue! Establishing a child care emergency plan. CCIE, 107, p. 18. Reprinted with permission from *Child Care Information Exchange*, P.O. Box 2890, Redmond, WA 98073, 1-800-221-2864.

Figure 14–8   Suggestions for Code Blue Design

---

[15]Copeland, M. L. (1996). Code blue! Establishing a child care emergency plan. *Child Care Information Exchange: The Director's Magazine*, 107, January/February, p. 19.

staff members, and families. It should include the step-by-step procedures to be followed when a child is injured at the center. The purpose of the plan is to provide the center staff with a detailed set of instructions to follow when giving an injured or sick child the best and quickest treatment, notifying the family, and filling out the necessary papers for maximum liability and insurance protection for both staff and family. See Figure 14–9 for a sample emergency medical plan.

If the child must be taken away from the center for emergency care, the caregiver must stay with that child until the parent arrives or accompanies the child to the hospital. A signed consent form from parents that gives detailed information on where the child should be taken for emergency treatment and permission to transport the child for emergency treatment should be in each child's

folder (see Sample Child Care Emergency Contact Form in Figure 14–10). Since the parent cannot give informed consent in advance for emergency treatment because the nature of the injury is not known, it is essential that parents understand that the center must know their whereabouts or that of another responsible adult at all times. It is suggested that the telephone numbers on the child's emergency record, including those for the child's usual source of health care, be updated several times a year.

The director, as well as some members of the teaching staff, should have first aid training including cardiopulmonary resuscitation (CPR) so that preliminary emergency treatment can begin before professional help arrives and minor injuries will be handled correctly. An injury report must be filled out any time a child is hurt, and it should be

---

Procedures for Medical Emergencies

1. Each classroom teacher shall assume responsibility for care in any emergency which occurs on school property.
2. Assistant teachers or volunteers should contact the classroom teacher in case of emergency. If the teacher is not available, contact should be made with another classroom teacher in the building or the director.
3. If, in the judgment of the teacher, the injury needs medical attention, the director will call the parent of the child. If the parent cannot be reached, the director will call the emergency number on the Emergency Information Record.
4. If the injury requires immediate emergency treatment, call for medical assistance and transportation to the Emergency Room of the hospital authorized by the parent. Ambulance number is _____. The classroom teacher will accompany the child to the hospital and the director will call the parent.

Staff Instructions for Ill Children

1. If a child should become ill after arrival at school, contact the parent to come and take the child home. If parents cannot be reached, the director will call the emergency number on the Emergency Information Record.
2. If no transportation is available, provisions will be made for the child to remain at school until the regular departure time. The child will be removed from the classroom and will be cared for in the director's office.

Additional Instructions for Staff

1. An accident report must be filled out for any injury requiring medical attention. The report is to be filled out by the teacher and given to the director to be placed in the office health file with a copy in the child's file.
2. Any incident or injury occurring at school which appears to be upsetting or traumatic to the child shall be related to the parent by the teacher.
3. The center maintains a $25.00 deductible insurance policy on each child. If injuries sustained by a child incur costs above this amount, the parent should be told to contact the director for appropriate insurance forms for coverage.

(Adapted from Arlitt Child Development Center form.)

Figure 14–9   Sample Emergency Medical Plan

Emergency Contact Information

Child's Name _____ Date of Birth _____

Address _____ Home Phone _____

Mother's Name _____ Business Phone _____

Father's Name _____ Business Phone _____

Name of other person to be contacted in case of an emergency:

1. _____ Address _____

Relationship (sitter, relative, friend, etc.) _____ Phone _____

2. _____ Address _____

Relationship (sitter, relative, friend, etc.) _____ Phone _____

Authorization is hereby given for the Child Development Center Staff to release the above named child to the following persons, provided proper identification is first established (list all names of authorized persons, including immediate family):

1. _____ Relation: _____

2. _____ Relation: _____

3. _____ Relation: _____

Physician to be called in an emergency:

1. _____ Phone _____ or _____

2. _____ Phone _____ or _____

I, the undersigned, authorize the staff of the Child Development Center to take what emergency medical measures are deemed necessary for the care and protection of my child enrolled in the Child Development Center program.

_____
(Signature of Parent or Guardian/date)

Signature witnessed by:
(Notary)

_____
(Signature of Parent or Guardian/date)

The above statement sworn before me on:

_____

_____

Figure 14–10 Sample Child Care Emergency Contact Form

filed in a central location with a copy in the child's file (see Figure 14–11). It is essential to follow the accident plans, have staff properly trained to deal with injuries, and fill out injury reports for the safety and well-being of children and the protection of staff. Directors and board members must understand that taking all these precautions may not completely protect the staff from liability. Therefore, the center should carry accident insurance on the children and have liability coverage for the staff as an additional precautionary measure. It is wise to consult an attorney and your insurance agent about what constitutes adequate coverage.

Child Abuse

Directors must be vigilant and take steps to prevent the possibility of abuse on the premises, recognize signs of abuse on children who come to the program, and make certain suspected cases of abuse are properly reported.

Prevention on the Premises. Precautions must be taken to prevent both physical and sexual abuse on the premises. Physical abuse occurs most often when adults are stressed; further, the abusive act is unplanned and explosive, and usually occurs when other adults are not around. Sexual

Name of Child _____ Birth Date _____

Parent Name _____

Address _____ Phone Number _____

Usual Source of Health Care _____

Date of Injury _____ Time _____ Age _____ Sex _____

Type of Injury (circle) Bite Broken Bone Bruise Burn Choking Cut Eye Injury Foreign Body
Head Injury Poisoning Scrape Sliver Sprain Sting
Other _____

Location Where Injury Occurred _____
e.g., child care room, bathroom, hall, playground, large-muscle room,
bus, car, walk

Type of Equipment Involved _____

How Injury Happened (details of who, what, when, how): _____

_____

_____

_____

_____

Type of Treatment Required _____
e.g, first aid only in day care, visit to doctor's office or clinic, emergency
room, hospitalized, sutures, cast, bandage, medication given

Signature of Person Filling out the Report _____

Signatures of Witnesses _____

Name of Medical Professional Consulted _____

Date _____ Time _____ Advice _____

Figure 14–11   Sample Injury Report Form

abuse, on the other hand, although it also occurs when other adults are not around, is frequently planned ahead, and these pedophiles may even seek employment in child care centers to gain access to children. In the latter case, careful preemployment screening, use of criminal record checks, and fingerprinting may provide helpful information but how effective these expensive measures really are is still unknown.[16]

Since abuse of all types usually occurs when other adults are not around, the preventive measures mentioned in connection with staffing patterns (Chapter 11), developing the facility (Chapter 9), and making it clear to everyone that parents may visit at any time should help eliminate the possibility of abuse occurring in your center.

Recognizing and Reporting Abuse. All directors and members of the teaching staff in child care programs should have some training in recognizing the physical and behavioral signs of abuse, whether or not licensing requires it. In most states, professionals involved with children are required to report suspected cases of abuse. When mandated to report suspicion of abuse, those reporting

[16]Ibid., AAP, p. 48.

are not required to prove their allegations. Nonetheless, reports should be made carefully because much harm can come to children and families when the accusations are unfounded. The director should be notified of all suspected cases of abuse and review the case with the staff member who has found evidence of abuse before the case is reported to the authorities. In most states, information is given to law enforcement agencies or child protective agencies. Familiarity with state laws and local rules for reporting is essential for all child care directors.

SUMMARY

Directors are responsible for overseeing the food service and health and safety programs in the child care center. Although a designated staff person and the center cook may plan menus, order food, and prepare meals, the director is accountable to both the center families and the sponsoring or funding agency for the quality of the food service program.

Monitoring the health program and implementing plans to care for children who are injured or sick is also part of the director's responsibility. It is important to have written policies and reporting procedures for all emergencies, and rehearsal for various emergency procedures. Plans for caring for sick children with specific exclusion guidelines are helpful. It also is important to take preventive precautions regarding child abuse in the center and to make certain that suspected cases of abuse are detected and reported.

Working Paper 14–1

Food Reimbursement Allowances

	Free	*Reduced*
Breakfast	___per child	___per child
Lunch/Dinner	___per child	___per child
Snack	___per child	___per child
(Supplements)		

Fill in the above grid with information from your regional USDA office, a local daycare center, or a Head Start program. Use this information to complete Working Paper 14–2.

Working Paper 14–2

Number of Meals Served

Date	Breakfast		Lunch/Dinner		Snack	
	Free	Reduced	Free	Reduced	Free	Reduce
3	12	2	21	3	21	3
4	13	2	20	3	20	3
5	11	1	18	2	19	2
6	15	1	18	2	19	2
7	15	2	18	1	18	1
10	12	1	17	1	18	1
11	14	2	21	1	20	1
12	15	1	20	2	20	2
13	15	2	18	3	18	3
14	13	2	18	3	18	3
17	12	2	19	2	19	2
18	11	2	19	1	19	2
19	13	1	18	3	19	3
20	13	1	17	3	19	3
21	14	2	19	3	18	3
24	13	2	19	2	19	2
25	14	1	18	3	18	3
26	15	1	18	2	18	2
27	16	0	19	3	19	3
28	14	2	18	3	18	3
31	14	2	20	3	20	2
TOTAL						

Using the information from Working Paper 14–1 on reimbursement amounts for free and reduced meals, and the information from the chart Number of Meals Served, fill in the following table.

Breakfast	number of free meals x rate =	_____
	number of reduced meals x reduced rate =	_____
Lunch/Dinner	number of free meals x free rate =	_____
	number of reduced meals x reduced rate +	_____
Snack	number of free meals x free rate =	_____
(Supplement)	number of reduced meals x reduced rate =	_____
	Total claim for reimbursement	_____

Working Paper 14–3

Emergency Telephone Numbers

Record the following emergency telephone numbers and contact person where that information is requested.

- General emergency number (e.g., 911)   _____

- Police   _____

- Fire   _____

- Ambulance   _____

- Poison Control Center   _____

- Health Department   _____

Contact Person

- Report Child Abuse   _____

_____

Agency

_____

Contact Person

Director's Resource 14–1

Communicable and Acut Illness: Identification

Communicable Illness	Signs and Symptoms	Infectious Agent	Methods of Transmission	Incubation Period	Length of Communicability	Control Measures
AIRBORNE TRANSMITTED ILLNESS						
Chickenpox	Slight fever, irritability, coldlike symptoms. Red rash that develops blisterlike head, scabs later. Most abundant on covered parts of body, e.g., chest, back, neck, forearm.	Virus	Airborne through contact with secretions from the respiratory tract. Transmission from contact with blisters less common.	2–3 weeks after exposure	2–3 days prior to the onset of symptoms until 5–6 days after first eruptions. Scabs are not contagious.	Specific control measures: (1) Exclusion of sick children, (2) Practice good personal hygiene, especially careful handwashing. Children can return to group care when all blisters have formed a dry scab (approximately 1 week). Immunization is now available.
Common Cold	Highly contagious infection of the upper respiratory tract accompanied by slight fever, chills, runny nose, fatigue, muscle and headaches. Onset may be sudden.	Virus	Airborne through contact with secretions from the respiratory tract, e.g., coughs, sneezes, eating utensils, etc.	12–72 hours	About 1 day before onset of symptoms to 2–3 days after acute illness.	Prevention through education and good personal hygiene. Avoid exposure. Exclude first day or two. Antibiotics not effective against viruses. Avoid aspirin products (possible link to Reye's Syndrome). Watch for complications, e.g., earaches, bronchitis, croup, pneumonia.
Fifth's disease	Appearance of bright red rash on face, especially cheeks.	Virus	Airborne contact with secretions from the nose/mouth of infected person.	4–14 days	Prior to appearance of rash; probably not after rash develops.	Don't need to exclude children once rash appears. Frequent handwashing; frequent washing/disinfecting of toys/surfaces. Use care when handling tissues/nasal secretions.

Director's Resource 14–1 (continued)

Communicable Illness	Signs and Symptoms	Infectious Agent	Methods of Transmission	Incubation Period	Length of Communicability	Control Measures
Haemophilus influenza Type b	An acute respiratory infection; frequently causes meningitis. Other complications include pneumonia, epiglottitis, arthritis, infection of the bloodstream and conjunctivitis.	Bacteria	Airborne via secretions of the respiratory tract (nose, throat). Persons can also be carriers with or without symptoms.	2–4 days	Throughout acute phase; as long as organism is present. Noncommunicable 36–48 hours after treatment with antibiotics.	Identify and exclude sick children. Treatment with antibiotics 3–4 days before returning to group care. Notify parents of exposed children to contact their physician. Immunize children. Practice good handwashing techniques; sanitize contaminated objects.
Measles (Rubeola)	Fever, cough, runny nose, eyes sensitive to light. Dark red blotchy rash that often begins on the face and neck, then spreads over the entire body. Highly communicable.	Virus	Airborne through coughs, sneezes and contact with contaminated articles.	8–13 days; rash develops approximately 14 days after exposure	From beginning of symptoms until 4 days after rash appears.	Most effective control method is immunization. Good personal hygiene, especially handwashing and covering coughs. Exclude child for at least 4 days after rash appears.
Meningitis	Sudden onset of fever, stiff neck, headache, irritability and vomiting; gradual loss of consciousness, seizures, and death.	Bacteria	Airborne through coughs, nasal secretions; direct contact with saliva/nasal discharges	Varies with the infecting organism; 2–4 days average	Throughout acute phase; noncommunicable after antibiotic treatment	Encourage immunization for Exclude child from care until medical treatment is completed. Use Universal Precautions when handling saliva/nasal secretions, frequent handwashing, and disinfecting of toys/surfaces.
Mononucleosis	Characteristic symptoms include sore throat, intermittent fever, fatigue, and enlarged lymph glands in the neck. May also be accompanied by headache and enlarged liver or spleen.	Virus	Airborne; also direct contact with saliva of an infected person.	2–4 weeks for children; 4–6 weeks for adults	Unknown. Organisms may be present in oral secretions for as long as one year following illness.	None known. Child should be kept home until over the acute phase (6–10 days). Use frequent handwashing and careful disposal of tissues after coughing or blowing nose.
Mumps	Sudden onset of fever with swelling of the salivary glands.	Virus	Airborne through coughs and sneezes; direct contact with oral secretions of infected persons.	12–26 days	6–7 days prior to the onset of symptoms until swelling in the salivary glands is gone (7–9 days).	Immunization provides permanent protection. Peak incidence is in winter and spring. Exclude children from school or group settings until all symptoms have disappeared.

Director's Resource 14–1 (continued)

Communicable Illness	Signs and Symptoms	Infectious Agent	Methods of Transmission	Incubation Period	Length of Communicability	Control Measures
Roseola Infantum (6–24 mo.)	Most common in the spring and fall. Fever rises abruptly (102°–105°F) and lasts 3–4 days; loss of appetite, listlessness, runny nose, rash on trunk, arms, and neck lasting 1–2 days.	Virus	Person to person; method unknown.	10–15 days	1–2 days before onset to several days following fading of the rash.	Exclude from school or group care until rash and fever are gone.
Rubella (German Measles)	Mild fever; rash begins on face and neck and rarely lasts more than 3 days. May have arthritis-like discomfort and swelling in joints.	Virus	Airborne through contact with respiratory secretions, e.g., coughs, sneezes.	4–21 days	From one week prior to 5 days following onset of the rash.	Immunization offers permanent protection. Children must be excluded from school for at least 7 days after appearance of rash.
Streptococcal Infections (strep throat, scarlatina, rheumatic fever)	Sudden onset. High fever accompanied by sore, red throat; may also have nausea, vomiting, headache, white patches on tonsils, and enlarged glands. Development of a rash depends on the infectious organism.	Bacteria	Airborne via droplets from coughs or sneezes. May also be transmitted by food and raw milk.	1–4 days	Throughout the illness and for approximately 10 days afterward, unless treated with antibiotics. Medical treatment eliminates communicability within 36 hours. Can develop rheumatic fever or become a carrier if not treated.	Exclude child with symptoms. Antibiotic treatment is essential. Avoid crowding in classrooms. Practice frequent handwashing, educating children, and careful supervision of food handlers.
Tuberculosis	Many people have no symptoms. Active disease causes productive cough, weight loss, fatigue, loss of appetite, chills, night sweats.	Bacteria	Airborne via coughs or sneezes.	2–3 months	As long as disease is untreated; usually noncontagious after 2–3 weeks on medication.	TB skin testing, especially babies and young children, if there has been contact with an infected person. Seek prompt diagnosis and treatment if experiencing symptoms; complete drug therapy. Cover coughs/sneezes. Practice good handwashing.

Director's Resource 14–1 (continued)

Communicable Illness	Signs and Symptoms	Infectious Agent	Methods of Transmission	Incubation Period	Length of Communicability	Control Measures
BLOOD-BORNE TRANSMITTED ILLNESSES						
Acquired Immuno-deficiency Syndrome (AIDS)	Flu-like symptoms, including fatigue, weight loss, enlarged lymph glands, persistent cough, fever, and diarrhea.	Virus	Children acquire virus when born to infected mothers from contam-inated blood transfusions and possibly from breast milk of infected mothers. Adults acquire the virus via sexual transmission, contaminated drug needles, and blood transfusions.	6 weeks to 8 years	Lifetime	Exclude children 0–5 years if they have open lesions, uncontrollable nosebleeds, bloody diarrhea, or are at high risk for exposing others to blood-contaminated body fluids. Use Universal Precautions when handling body fluids, including good handwashing techniques. Seal contaminated items, e.g., diapers, paper towels in plastic bags. Disinfect surfaces with bleach/water solution (1:10) or other disinfectant.
Hepatitis B	Slow onset; loss of appetite, nausea, vomiting, abdominal pain, and jaundice. May also be asymptomatic.	Virus	Through contact with blood/body fluids containing blood.	45–180 days; average 60–80 days	Varies; come persons are lifetime carriers.	Immunization is preferable. Use Universal Precautions when handling any blood/body fluids; use frequent handwashing.
CONTACT (direct and indirect) TRANSMITTED ILLNESSES						
Conjunctivitis (Pinkeye)	Redness of the white portion (conjunctiva) of the eye and inner eyelid, swelling of the lids, yellow discharge from eyes and itching	Bacteria or virus	Direct contact with discharge from eyes or upper respiratory tract of an infected person; through contaminated fingers and objects, e.g., tissues, washcloths, towels.	1–3 days	Throughout active infection; several days up to 2–3 weeks.	Antibiotic treatment. Exclude child for 24 hours after medication is started. Frequent handwashing and disinfection of toys/surfaces is necessary.
Cytomegalo-virus (CMV)	Often no symptoms in children under 2 years; sore throat, fever, fatigue in older children. High risk of fetal damage if mother is infected during pregnancy.	Virus	Person to person contact with body fluids, e.g., saliva, blood, urine, breast milk, in utero.	Unknown; may be 4–8 weeks	Virus present (in saliva, urine) for months following infection.	No need to exclude children. Always wash hands after changing diapers or contact with saliva. Avoid kissing children's mouths or sharing eating utensils. Practice careful handwashing with children; wash/disinfect toys and surfaces frequently.

Director's Resource 14–1 (continued)

Communicable Illness	Signs and Symptoms	Infectious Agent	Methods of Transmission	Incubation Period	Length of Communicability	Control Measures
Hand, Foot, and Mouth Disease	Affects children under 10 years. Onset of fever, followed by blistered sores in the mouth/cheeks; 1–2 days later raised rash appears on palms of hands and soles of feet.	Virus	Person to person through direct contact with saliva, nasal discharge, or feces.	3–6 days	7–10 days	Exclude sick children for several days. Practice frequent handwashing, especially after changing diapers. Clean/disinfect surfaces.
Herpes simplex (Cold sores)	Clear blisters develop on face, lips, and other body parts that crust and heal within a few days.	Virus	Direct contact with saliva, on hands, or sexual contact.	Up to 2 weeks	Virus remains in saliva for as long as 7 weeks following recovery.	No specific control. Frequent handwashing. Child does not have to be excluded from school.
Impetigo	Infection of the skin forming crusty, moist lesions usually on the face, ears, and around the nose. Highly contagious. Common among children.	Bacteria	Direct contact with discharge from sores; indirect contact with contaminated articles of clothing, tissues, etc.	2–5 days; may be as long as 10 days	Until lesions are healed.	Exclusions from group settings until lesions have been treated with antibiotics for 24–48 hours. Cover areas with bandage until treated.
Lice (head)	Lice are seldom visible to the naked eye. White nits (eggs) are visible on hair shafts. The most obvious symptom is itching of the scalp, especially behind the ears and at the base of the neck.	Head louse	Direct contact with infected persons or with their personal articles, e.g., hats hair brushes, combs, orclothing. Lice can survive for 2–3 weeks on bedding, carpet, furniture, car seats, clothing, etc.	Nits hatch in 1 week and reach maturity within 8–10 days	While lice remain alive on infested persons or clothing; until nits have been destroyed.	Infested children should be excluded from group settings until treated. Hair should be washed with a special medicated shampoo and rinsed with a vinegar/water solution (any concentration will work) to ease removal of all nits (using a fine-toothed comb). Heat from a hair dryer also helps destroy eggs. All friends and family should be carefully checked. Thoroughly clean child's environment; vacuum carpets/upholstery, wash/dry or dry clean bedding, clothing, hair brushes. Seal nonwashable items in plastic bag for 2 weeks.

Director's Resource 14–1 (continued)

Communicable Illness	Signs and Symptoms	Infectious Agent	Methods of Transmission	Incubation Period	Length of Communicability	Control Measures
Ringworm	An infection of the scalp, skin, or nails. Causes flat, spreading, oval-shaped lesions that may become dry and scaly or moist and crusted. When it is present on the feet it is commonly called athlete's foot. Infected nails may become discolored, brittle, or chalky or they may disintegrate.	Fungus	Direct or indirect contact with infected persons, their personal items, showers, swimming pools, theater seats, etc. Dogs and cats may also be infected and transmit it to children and adults.	4–10 days, (unknown for athlete's foot)	As long as lesions are present.	Exclude children from gyms, pools, or activities where they are likely to expose others. May return to group care following medical treatment with a fungicidal ointment. All shared areas, such as pools and showers should be thoroughly cleansed with a fungicide.
Rocky Mountain Spotted Fever	Onset usually abrupt; fever (101°–104°F); joint and muscle pain, severe nausea and vomiting, and white coating on tongue. Rash appears on 2nd to 5th day over forehead, wrist, and ankles; later covers entire body. Can be fatal if untreated.	Bacteria	Indirect transmission; tick bite.	2–14 days; average 7 days	Not contagious from person to person.	Prompt removal of ticks; not all ticks cause illness. Administration of antibiotics. Use insect repellent on clothes when outdoors.
Scabies	Characteristic burrows or linear tunnels under the skin, especially between the fingers and around the wrists, elbows, waist, thighs, and buttocks. Causes intense itching.	Parasite	Direct contact with an infected person.	Several days to 2–4 weeks	Until all mites and eggs are destroyed.	Children should be excluded from school or group care until treated. Affected persons should bathe with prescribed soap and carefully launder all bedding and clothing. All contacts of the infected person should be notified.
Tetanus	Muscular spasms and stiffness, especially in the muscles around the neck and mouth. Can lead to convulsions, inability to breathe, and death.	Bacteria	Indirect: organisms live in soil and dust; enter body through wounds, especially puncture-type injuries, burns, and unnoticed cuts.	4 days to 2 weeks	Not contagious.	Immunization every 8–10 years affords complete protection.

Director's Resource 14–1 (continued)

Communicable Illness	Signs and Symptoms	Infectious Agent	Methods of Transmission	Incubation Period	Length of Communicability	Control Measures
FECAL/ORAL TRANSMITTED ILLNESSES						
Dysentery (Shigellosis)	Sudden onset of vomiting; diarrhea, may be accompanied by high fever, headache, abdominal pain. Stools may contain blood, pus or mucus. Can be fatal in young children	Bacteria	Fecal-oral transmission via contaminated objects or indirectly through ingestion of contaminated food or water and via flies.	1–7 days	Variable; may last up to 4 weeks or longer in the carrier state.	Exclude child during acute illness. Careful handwashing after bowel movements. Proper disposal of human feces; control of flies. Strict adherence to sanitary procedures for food preparation.
E. coli	Diarrhea, often bloody	Bacteria	Spread through contaminated food, dirty hands	3–4 days; can be as long as 10 days	For duration of diarrhea; usually several days.	Exclude infected children until no diarrhea; practice frequent handwashing, especially after toileting and before preparing food.
Encephalitis	Sudden onset of headache, high fever, convulsions, vomiting, confusion, neck and back stiffness, tremors, and coma.	Virus	Indirect spread by bites from disease-carrying mosquitoes; in some areas transmitted by tick bites.	5–15 days	Man is not contagious	Spraying of mosquito breeding areas and use of insect repellents; public education.
Giardiasis	Many persons are asymptomatic. Typical symptoms include chronic diarrhea, abdominal cramping, bloating, pale and foul-smelling stools, weight loss, and fatigue.	Parasite (protozoa)	Fecal-oral transmission; through contact with infected stool (e.g., diaper changes, helping child with soiled underwear), poor handwashing, passed from hands to mouth (toys, food). Also transmitted through contaminated water sources.	7–10 days average; can be as long as 5–25 days	As long as parasite is present in the stool.	Exclude children until diarrhea ends. Scrupulous handwashing before eating, preparing food, and after using the bathroom. Maintain sanitary conditions in bathroom areas.
Hepatitis (Infectious; Type A)	Fever, fatigue, loss of appetite, nausea, abdominal pain (in region of liver). Illness may be accompanied by yellowing of the skin and eyeballs (jaundice) in adults, but not always in children. Acute onset.	Virus	Fecal-oral route. Also spread via contaminated food, water, milk, and objects.	10–50 days (average range 25–30 days)	7–10 days prior to onset of symptoms to not more than 7 days after onset of jaundice.	Exclude from group settings a minimum of 1 week following onset. Special attention to careful handwashing after going to the bathroom and before eating is critical following an outbreak. Report disease incidents to public health authorities. Immunoglobulin (IG) recommended for protection of close contacts.

Director's Resource 14–1 (continued)

Communicable Illness	Signs and Symptoms	Infectious Agent	Methods of Transmission	Incubation Period	Length of Communicability	Control Measures
Pinworms	Irritability, and itching of the rectal area. Common among young children. Some children have no symptoms.	Parasite; not contagious from animals.	Infectious eggs are transferred from person to person by contaminated hands (oral-fecal route). Indirectly spread by contaminated bedding, food, clothing, swimming pool.	Life cycle of the worm is 3–6 weeks; persons can also reinfect themselves.	2–8 weeks or as long as a source of infection remains present.	Infected children must be excluded from school until treated with medication; may return after initial dose. All infected and noninfected family members must be treated at one time. Frequent handwashing is essential; discourage nail biting or sucking of fingers. Daily baths and change of linen are necessary. Disinfect school toilet seats at least once a day. Vacuum carpeted areas daily. Eggs are also destroyed when exposed to temperatures over 132°F. Education and good personal hygiene are vital to control.
Salmonellosis	Abdominal pain and cramping, sudden fever, severe diarrhea (may contain blood), nausea and vomiting lasts 5–7 days.	Bacteria	Fecal-oral transmission via dirty hands. Also contaminated food (especially improperly cooked poultry, milk, eggs) water supplies and infected animals.	12–36 hours	Throughout acute illness; may remain a carrier for months.	Attempt to identify source. Exclude children/adults with diarrhea; may return when symptoms end. Carriers should not handle or prepare food until stool cultures are negative. Practice good handwashing and sanitizing procedures.

Evaluating Center Components

E valuation is an ongoing process. An evaluation can take the form of an analysis of a person's behavior, of an administrative procedure, or of some other component of an early childhood education program in terms of its usefulness or worth. Once an early childhood education program has
been planned, the evaluation of that program should be designed immediately because continuation of
an ineffective aspect of the program is fruitless and frequently expensive. Inappropriate staff behavior
may be detrimental to children's development or to staff relations. Desirable behavior, on the other hand,
should be recognized and encouraged as a result of the evaluation process.

Evaluation that is planned during the early stages of program development facilitates the assessment
and notifies everyone from the start how the evaluation process will be conducted. The evaluator uses the
goals statement that was prepared prior to the opening of the center as the basis for making judgments
about what is valuable in the program. The objectives that grow from the goals also are helpful guidelines
in assessing the center's program and the performance of individuals affiliated with that program.

Assuming that the director has worked to create a "we" feeling described in Chapter 2, evaluation
also will take on a collaborative tone. Rather than being threatening or punitive, evaluation will be a way
to note and celebrate progress. Whether the evaluation is focused on the center, the staff, or the children,
participants can work together to assess current conditions and decide on goals. Then, they can support
each other in reaching those goals.

EVALUATORS

The director usually conducts staff evaluations although a committee of the center's board may be involved. In some centers, staff members evaluate other employees whom they supervise (for instance,
teachers evaluate their aides) or employees evaluate all fellow employees whose jobs are related.
Therefore, teachers may evaluate each other, aides and teachers may evaluate each other, and everyone
working under the director may evaluate and be evaluated by him or her. It is unlikely, however, to find
auxiliary staff evaluating teaching staff because the decision about who does the evaluating is based on
how the assigned jobs relate to one another. In other words, the maintenance staff would not evaluate the
teaching staff even though teachers might be asked to evaluate the janitor's work in relation to their role.

Often, parents are asked to give their opinions about the center, its personnel, and its operation to enable the center staff to understand how people directly affected by the program feel about it. In corporate

systems, a national or regional staff member may plan and conduct some or all of the evaluation. When funds are received from a governmental or private agency, an employee of that agency may be assigned to perform an evaluation. When public schools operate preschool or child care programs, the principal is usually responsible for evaluating the staff.

PURPOSE OF EVALUATION

Since the major purpose of evaluation is to determine whether the center's goals are being met, the evaluators need to know what these goals are before gathering data. In effect, the evaluators must know who the clients are, what their needs are, and which of these needs the center is attempting to meet. In a community where the local high school is expressing concern about the high number of dropouts due to pregnancy, a center director may decide to work with the school system to assess how many students could return to school if care were provided for their infants and toddlers. Together, the center and the school may be able to obtain funding to provide this service. In such a situation, particularly if tax dollars are to be used, community education would be important since many taxpayers might believe that the program would cause teen pregnancy instead of preventing school dropouts.

A further purpose of evaluation is to determine how effective the program is in meeting the needs of clients, and how efficient it is in terms of cost, time, and energy. Are needs met to the satisfaction of the center and of the clients? Are they partially met or not met at all? More important, are significantly more teen parents returning to and staying in school when their babies received child care? Even if needs are met, could the same job have been done for less money or by using less time or energy? Funding agencies, board members, and clients expect documentation that the center is doing what it has agreed to do. An evaluation provides the data for such documentation, and possibly the basis for further research.

A final reason for evaluation is the need to have a solid basis for future planning. The director uses the data from the current evaluation to deter-

mine the strengths and weaknesses of the program, and to adapt the plan for the following year appropriately to correct any deficiencies or to respond to newly perceived needs. For example, if one of the goals of the center is to provide an education program for all parents but the data show that only 10 percent of the parents participated, then the director needs to determine whether the goal is inappropriate or whether the method of achieving it is not meeting the needs of the clients. If a thorough evaluation has been done, the director will have information from parents regarding how they felt about the program and why they did or did not attend. The information can then be used to plan changes in next year's program, or to ascertain that this community does not need parent education from this center.

It would be easy to arrive at the conclusion that parents in the preceding example do not want or need parent education. But the director has to consider other factors such as:

- Have parents been involved in the planning so that they feel as though they are part of the program?
- Is there another parent education program already established in the community that is meeting these parents' needs?
- Is the timing, format, or content inappropriate for these parents?
- Has there been a breakdown in communication so that parents do not feel welcome or comfortable about coming?
- Are there other, more pressing matters confronting the parents?
- Are there ancillary problems, such as babysitting or transportation?

Since one or more of these factors may have had a major effect on parent participation, the director should address them to make sure that the evaluation is accurate.

EVALUATION PRINCIPLES

Evaluation plans should be based on certain principles that reduce anxiety and increase cooperation among the individuals being evaluated.

1. The evaluation process is open; that is, the people or groups being evaluated know about the evaluation process in advance and have access to their own evaluation data. Furthermore, the people being evaluated have an opportunity to give input into their own evaluation.

2. Evaluation relates directly to program goals and objectives.

3. Each person being evaluated knows why, when, where, how, and by whom the evaluation is to be done.

4. Evaluation is conducted on an individual basis; however, for reporting purposes, the results are compiled and group data instead of individual data are presented.

5. The individual's evaluation is a confidential matter and is accessible only to those who need to know such as an employee's supervisor or a child's teacher.

6. Evaluation is built into the program so that it occurs on a regular basis.

An early childhood education evaluation plan involves three components: staff, child, and total program evaluation. A plan for each of these components includes delineating who will evaluate what, how, and when the evaluation will be conducted, and for what purposes a particular evaluation is being done.

Staff Evaluation

Staff evaluation is a natural outgrowth of supervision, one of the basic duties of the director. Every staff member should be evaluated on a regular basis according to the procedure included in the policies and procedures manual.

Reflections

Think about the people who evaluate you. Who are they? Why do they evaluate you? Do all these people see you in the same way? If not, why do some of them evaluate you in different ways? What is the purpose of their evaluation?

DIRECTOR'S CORNER

"The steering committee conducts an annual parent survey. One parent gathers all the information and then gives each classroom a printout of what the parents in their room specifically said. The parents' names aren't included though. Parents seem willing to write things that they might not take time to say in person and it's been real helpful to the staff to get this kind of feedback."
—Director, agency-sponsored child care center

Staff evaluation is conducted to enable the director and staff members to analyze what the staff member is doing well, and in what areas growth and change could occur. This type of evaluation provides information to the funding agency and the board about how employees spend their time; it also validates the work of the employees.

The first form of evaluation is employee selection. In assessing an applicant's ability to work well with other employees, the director must be cautious, avoiding the selection of only those people who fit a mold. A successful choice is based on a careful evaluation of credentials and behavior rather than on an overgeneralization of positive or negative traits. For example, a candidate who answers an early question to the interviewer's liking may be regarded as being highly qualified although he or she may actually be poorly skilled in working with young children. On the other hand, the candidate with an unusual style of clothing may be considered initially as being incompetent when, in reality, that person might work quite well with young children. The director should avoid hiring only those applicants who are similar to current employees, yet must consider whether or not the qualifications of a particular candidate will combine well with those of current employees to provide the total staff strength that is needed to meet center goals. In any case, the most important criterion is: "Is this the best person available to do the job?"

Ongoing evaluation of staff members begins when they accept a position. At this time, the director and the new staff member go over the job description together carefully and make adjustments as needed to fit the circumstances, writing these changes (if any) into the job description. A comprehensive evaluation is based on this job description. The director makes it clear to employees from the beginning that they will be evaluated. However, another important component to be discussed with the employee is the support that will be provided to assist new staff members as they become acclimated to a new role. This support is particularly helpful for first-year teachers. The director informs each employee about why, when, where, and by whom the evaluation will be done, and outlines the basis for the evaluation and the method to be used. Sometimes, a new employee is evaluated after a two- or three-month probationary period. If the employee's work is found to be satisfactory at this time, the employee and director then plan together for further growth by writing out what the employee expects to do prior to the next evaluation. In this initial step in the evaluation cycle, the employee writes out goals and brings them to a meeting with the director at which time both must agree on their importance and reasonableness. The goals must relate to the job description, and the subsequent evaluation is based on the mutually agreed-on objectives.

For example, if one of the teacher's goals is to maintain a more orderly classroom, that teacher's procedural plan may include teaching the children to return things to the proper shelf, rearranging the classroom, or working with the classroom aide to develop a mutually agreeable plan for keeping materials in order. Sometimes, the director gives help at this stage, either by assisting the employee in finding ways of meeting an objective, or by designating areas in which specific objectives should be defined. The primary goal at this step is to draw up a workable plan that the staff member can follow and that will enhance the overall program.

Next, the director and employee decide how data will be gathered. Will the director observe? Will parents be asked for their opinions? Will the teacher be asked to engage in a self-evaluation process? Will teachers observe each other? Will children's behavior be used as a criterion? Again, both director and staff member reach agreement on what is the best plan to use. Some centers use checklists or rating scales. These tools are most useful in large centers in which a number of staff are working on comparable skills such as fostering a relaxed classroom atmosphere or preparing appropriate classroom materials.

The objectives and evaluation format together are called a work plan which is the formative component of staff evaluation. Once the plan has been written, the director and the staff member each receive a copy for reference as they work to achieve the objectives and evaluate the progress that is made. They plan a specific time period for the next meeting, in one month, at the end of the semester, or whatever length of time fits their needs.

The director's role in staff evaluation is to observe and analyze the work of a staff person, encourage the development of that person's strengths, and look for ways to promote growth in weaker areas. If the weak areas considerably outweigh the strong, then the director must terminate the employment of that individual because the director's role (except in special cases) is to promote growth rather than provide on-the-job training. The staff member's role is to work out the details of meeting the agreed-on goals and to implement these plans.

Some directors observe each teacher weekly, biweekly, or monthly and have an informal conference after making the observation. The director may take notes during the observation or write notes afterward, but any notes should be shared with the teacher because they are useful in helping to fulfill the specific objectives that have been set. It is sometimes easy to pick out and focus on the weak spots in a teacher's style that leaves the teacher feeling incompetent. Other directors concentrate only on the positive aspects and are unable to address problem areas. The teacher who is aware of a problem knows that the director is not providing appropriate guidance; the teacher who is unaware of a problem receives unofficial sanction of the behavior when the director ignores it. In either case, some of the center's objectives are not met and the observation and informal conference times are nonproductive. (See chapter 11 for a sample observation tool.)

Some directors make video or audio tapes of teachers, and review them with that teacher afterward. The advantage is that both are viewing the same situation during the conference. The disadvantage is that taping is intimidating to some staff. Of course, the tapes are confidential and the subject's permission must be obtained if they are to be shown to others.

When the agreed-on observations have been completed and other assessments have been made, the director meets with the staff member for a comprehensive evaluation of the work that is based on the work plan set up earlier. The staff member may bring a self-evaluation in a form that is preselected by the director to be completed by the employee, in a narrative form that is written by the employee, or in an unwritten form such as thoughts the employee has planned to discuss with the director. During the conference, a work plan, including the objectives and an evaluation format, is drawn up again for the next evaluation cycle, and the director summarizes the staff person's evaluation for the previous cycle in a dated, written form. The staff member may add written comments if desired. Then both the staff member and the director sign the evaluation form and the new work plan. Although this process is somewhat formal, the director's evaluation role becomes businesslike as well as personal if it is followed. (A sample staff evaluation form is included in Director's Resource on page 404.)

In all staff evaluation situations, a professional approach must be taken. Such an approach conveys to each staff member the importance of the role and of that person's performance. Because this may seem difficult in the informal child care setting, the director may want to discuss with the staff what an important professional responsibility evaluation and planning should be.

Arranging unhurried, uninterrupted time and space for evaluation sessions is essential. Such procedures may seem superfluous in the majority of situations. However, establishing the pattern sets the stage for the occasional difficult evaluation conference, and should make it easier to proceed in a professional manner in those instances. Careful and thoughtful evaluation also sends a message to all staff that their work is indeed serious, and can leave them feeling positive about what they have accomplished as well as ready to work toward continued development.

A similar evaluation process is followed for the director, and the board is usually responsible for its implementation. In a multisite corporate system, a regional representative may conduct the director's

evaluation. Since the staff members in a well-run center may feel close to one another and consider the director a personal friend, it is wise to maintain structure in the evaluation process to allow everyone to be as objective as possible. Parents' perspectives on the director's performance are significant and may be gathered in a survey.

Since the director is responsible for the overall quality of the center, logical evaluation focuses on reaching quality indicators. These include low staff turnover, low rates of staff absenteeism, high occupancy rates by clients, and sufficient resources in terms of teacher salary and classroom equipment and supplies.[1] When these criteria are being met, evaluators must surely show their appreciation in a variety of ways including, but not limited to, increased remuneration.

As director credentialling becomes more available, the board may want to require the credential as part of the evaluation. Currently, the credential is gaining in popularity as a way to improve center quality and to market the center to families.

EVALUATION OF CHILDREN

Because the major goals of an early childhood education center revolve around the development of children, the evaluation most commonly thought of and most frequently used is that of children's behavior. A number of techniques for conducting this process are available, but they must be examined carefully.

Since young children develop rapidly, it is important that the progress they make in their normal development is not attributed solely to the center's program. Many other conditions affect the child's development including parental behavior, cultural background, nutrition, and general health. Any one of these variables or combinations of them can affect the child's development positively or negatively, just as the center's program may have a positive or negative influence. The child's total development is a result of the interaction of many factors that makes it almost impossible to evaluate the influence of one variable such as a specific child care or nursery school experience.

[1]Neugebauer, R. (1996). Out of the box ideas for director evaluation—Part 1. *Child Care Information Exchange.* May, pp. 87–89.

Reflections

Think about your own feelings the last time you were evaluated. Were your feelings positive? Negative? Mixed? How did the evaluator influence these feelings? What was the behavior of an evaluator who helped you feel positive? Can you recall the behavior of an evaluator who left you feeling incompetent?

One way to obtain a measure of the effect of the center's program is to assess the children who participate in the program and a control group of children who do not. However, most centers do not have a control group available and they do not have the time or funds for such assessment. Another way to evaluate children is to look at norms for similar children and compare the behaviors of the center children with them. However, as previously stated, the children's performances may or may not be the result of their attendance at the center.

Keeping in mind the preceding restrictions, the director, in consultation with teachers and sometimes with an educational testing consultant, organizes an evaluation plan for children to assess whether or not the center's goals have been met for children. In general, the center's goal should be that each child develop in all areas. Therefore, information about the child at the beginning of the program is needed as a benchmark for assessing progress at future dates. There are several ways to collect these data.

Teacher Observations. Throughout the year, the teacher may keep anecdotal and running records on each child. These notes, recorded on file cards or in a log book, are summarized by the teacher at the end of the year. Bentzen,[2] Boehm and Weinberg,[3] and Genishi[4] are among the authors who describe general guidelines for observing children. The teacher notes the changes in developmental level and the specific objectives that the child has met. Using this method, the teacher is able to make statements about each child individually, placing emphasis on what the child's needs were as based on initial observations, and how the needs were met. This method uses subjective data provided by the teacher, and is valuable only if the teacher is a skilled observer and collects data regularly. In a center that is minimally staffed, use of this method may be difficult. However, NAEYC, in a brochure on testing young children, states, "The systematic observations of trained teachers and other professionals, in conjunction with information obtained from parents and other family members, are the best sources of information."[5]

Checklist. The director may find or create a checklist that names the behaviors toward which the center's objectives are aimed. Then the teacher merely checks whether or not the child exhibits the listed behavior. A question arises when the child sometimes does the task and sometimes does not, either because the task is just being learned, because the child chooses not to do it, or because no opportunity is made available. For example, an item might be "Buttons own coat." The child who does this occasionally may be in the process of learning and may not be ready to struggle with buttons on some days; or the child may be asking the teacher for help because he or she needs attention rather than help.

Rating Scales. The director may create or locate a rating scale that lists the behaviors hoped for in the center's objectives. The rating scale alleviates the problem created by a checklist by providing a way for teachers to qualify their answers. The teacher rates each child at the beginning and end of the school year, and perhaps more frequently. The rating may be based on numbers, for example,

Speaks clearly enough for a stranger to understand.

1   2   3   4   5

[2]Bentzen, W. (2001). *Seeing young children: A guide to observing and recording behavior.* 4th edition. Albany, NY: Delmar.
[3]Boehm, A. E., & Weinberg, R. A. (1987). *The classroom observer: Developing observation skills in early childhood settings,* 2nd edition. Teachers College.
[4]Genishi, C., ED. (1992). *Ways of assessing children and curriculum: Stories of rarly childhood practice.* Teachers College.
[5]National Association for the Education of Young Children. (1988). *Testing of young children: Concerns and cautions,* Washington, D.C.: # 582.

with an explanation of whether 1 or 5 is high.

The rating may involve descriptive words such as:

Participates in group activities:

> never
>
> seldom
>
> occasionally
>
> usually
>
> always

See Director's Resource for a sample rating scale on page 400. The problems with rating scales are that each teacher may interpret the categories differently, and most teachers are reluctant to use the two ends of the scale (1 and 5, or never and always). Such scales, however, can be useful in pointing out general strengths and weaknesses in any child's development, and in the functioning of the group. Rating scales are relatively quick to complete and the teacher can do them when the children are not present.

Both checklists and rating scales are suitable for use if they are viewed as a particular teacher's assessment of an individual child instead of a comparison of one child or class with another. In reporting data from checklists and rating scales, the director may comment on how many children recognize their name in print, or play cooperatively in a group of two or more children. But this information must be placed in proper context by pointing out the children's ages, and other factors that may influence the data. In any case, group data of this sort should be deemphasized.

Standardized Tests. NAEYC has published an informative brochure entitled, Testing of Young Children: Concerns and Cautions. Because "(m)ass standardized testing of young children is potentially harmful to children educationally,"[6] it is important that directors become familiar with the issues. The NAEYC brochure describes types of standardized tests and appropriate uses, and explains why standardized testing is inappropriate for young children. According to NAEYC, "Standardized testing seldom provides information beyond what teachers and parents already know."[7]

Portfolios. One type of record keeping tool that can provide valuable information about each child is the portfolio. Some teachers use a two-part system with one folder in a locked cabinet, and a second folder in the classroom readily accessible to the child. Folder one contains forms and information from families, the teachers written observations such as anecdotal records, notes on plans for that child, progress reports, medical reports, and reports from previous teachers, agencies, or consultants who have worked with the child. This information is confidential and should be available to only those who have a legitimate right to it. The second folder provides the child with an opportunity to save products which she or he created. The teacher may add photos, videos, and audiotapes although the availability of these records depends on the center's budget and the time available to teachers to prepare them. Periodically, the records must be sorted and decisions made about what is to be retained since the record is intended to follow the child throughout school years. The child should participate in deciding what is to be retained and the family, too, may want to be involved. Some records, however, must be retained by school policy or by law. See Nilsen, 1997, for other ideas about portfolios.[8]

Other Observers. The director may observe a particular child when a teacher has concerns about that child. Sometimes, an outside observer such as the director or a consultant brings a more objective analysis, or may see factors in the environment or even in the teacher's behavior that appear to be influencing the child's behavior. After collecting data, the observer confers with the teacher, and together they design a plan for working with the child. When an individual child is being evaluated to an extent beyond the center's regularly scheduled observation plan, parental permission must be obtained, and parental participation in planning is preferable and sometimes required by law.

When a child with identified special needs is enrolled, the director, with written parental permission, contacts agencies familiar with the child

---

[6]Ibid.

[7]Ibid.

[8]Nilsen, B. A. (2001). *Week by week: Plans for observing and recording young children.* 2nd edition, Delmar.

to obtain previous evaluations. The director and representatives of other agencies also may meet to share information that would be useful in working with the child and family.

Reporting a child's behavior to parents is usually handled in a conference (see Chapter 16). Written information may be provided, but the use of checklists and rating scales for this purpose is often misleading. Parents may misunderstand the significance of this type of written report, and categorize their child as a success or a failure. A more appropriate written evaluation for parents is a narrative report that describes the child's strengths and progress at school, and discusses areas in which the child has difficulty.[9] The teacher also may confer with parents about ways to help the child to continue progressing toward future educational goals.

Parents have the right to review information from their child's folder at any time. In some cases, they feel that it is damaging to the child to have certain information passed along to the next teacher. In other cases, they are eager for the new teacher to understand as much as possible about their child immediately, so that the child does not have to endure a time period in which the teacher is discovering a hearing loss or some other condition for which an instructional plan should be designed. In any case, the teacher and parent discuss available information about the child, and to-gether determine which data should be sent forward to the next teacher.

Total Program Evaluation

The program goals of the center and the program itself are designed to meet the particular needs for which the center was established. Consequently, at evaluation time, the needs, goals, and program are evaluated.

At regular intervals, the community's needs must be assessed so that the center can plan for current and future populations. The methodology for conducting a community needs assessment is discussed in Chapter 4. Since goals are closely tied to the philosophy of the center program, they change slowly. Nonetheless, they should be examined periodically, perhaps every few years, to determine whether or not they are still applicable. Because the objectives are more directly related to the individuals served at a given time, they may change more rapidly than the goals; therefore, the objectives should be examined annually prior to the start of a new school year.

In addition, the director or the board may prepare checklists or rating scales for the evaluation of the program that can be distributed to staff members, parents, and community representatives. Or these people may be asked to provide evaluations of the program in written or oral form. Board members and funding agency representatives may contribute to the evaluation by reviewing aspects of the overall program such as the physical environment, curriculum, parent program, ancillary services, and board operations. They also may evaluate the staff performance in general rather than on individual terms. Periodically, perhaps every few years, the policies and procedures manual, the job descriptions, and the board bylaws are reviewed. Even the evaluation plans and procedures are evaluated!

A widely used center evaluation tool is the Early Childhood Environment Rating Scale.[10] Seven areas are covered in separate subscales. These include personal care routines, furnishings and display for children, language-reasoning ex-

Reflections

Think about report card day when you were in elementary school. Can you recall any of your feelings about receiving a report card? If the experience was not always a good one for you, who could have made the experience different? You? The teacher? Your parents? Other children? When you consider what you will include in a child's folder, try to remember your own grade school days. Think about the effects that the inclusion of data about your behavior may have had on your relationships with teachers and your parents.

[9]Horm-Wingerd, D. (1992). Reporting children's development: The narrative report. *Dimensions of early childhood, 21* (1), Fall..
[10]Harms, T., & Clifford, R. M. (1980). *Early childhood environment rating scale.* New York: Teachers College.

periences, fine- and gross-motor activities, creative activities, social development, and adult needs. After observing, the rater circles the appropriate category from 1 (inadequate) to 7 (excellent). Each subscale total rating is plotted on a profile sheet. Center staff then can decide in which areas they wish to make improvements. Profiles produced at different points in time can be used to determine changes in the center's program during that time period. Similar scales have been produced for rating infant/toddler programs and family child care. Instructional guides for observers are available in print and on videocassette.

Perhaps the most important evaluation a director can conduct is to look at quality of work life. Jorde-Bloom points out that high staff turnover rate, stress, and burnout soon affect commitment to the profession. When staff experience these tensions, it becomes impossible for directors to maintain high quality programs.[11]

Jorde-Bloom recommends, therefore, that the director examine ten dimensions necessary to create a professional climate. Among these are supervisor support, opportunities for professional growth, and amount of staff autonomy in decision-making. She further recommends surveying the staff, then using the resulting data to plan changes.[12] Another form of staff survey is included in the NAEYC center accreditation package. Werner suggests a climate survey of from 30 to 80 items. Using a scale of 1 to 5 such as "poor" to "outstanding" or "strongly disagree" to "strongly agree," the survey might consist of a series of positive statements that relate to job satisfaction.[13]

Staff surveys are usually anonymous, although in large centers, individuals may be asked to indicate age, job type, race, level of education completed, and/or any other category that will provide productive information. The purpose is to use the data for revising administrative practice and planning realistic changes in the center. Items that are obviously unattainable should not be included. For instance, one would not list: "The cen-

ter shall allow monthly unpaid mental health days" if such a policy would not be workable.

Many center directors and staff members are aware that they need to check the quality of their relations with parents, children, and staff members from a variety of cultures. Although it was not designed specifically for child care centers, the Cultural Competence Self-Assessment Instrument[14] may help directors provide leadership in analyzing areas of strength and areas where improvement is needed. This publication includes sections entitled Valuing Diversity, Documents Checklist, Governance, Administration, Program and Policy Development, Service Delivery, Clients, and Interpreting Your Results.

DIRECTOR'S CORNER

"We decided as a staff to do more fun things together. This past year hasn't been much fun because everybody has been putting in overtime since we had two teachers on maternity leave. The steering committee gave us some money from a fund-raiser and we're meeting next week to decide how to have fun together with it. It's a real morale booster."
    —Director, agency-sponsored child care center

Accreditation

One of the most professional ways to evaluate the center is to use the National Academy of Early Childhood Programs Center Accreditation Process. This process was designed by NAEYC based on input from thousands of early childhood professionals from all over the United States. The goal is to improve the quality of care and education afforded young children. Some directors may decide not to get involved because their centers are not perfect or because the process seems too complicated. In many communities, directors' support groups are springing up to encourage directors, to answer their questions, and to dispel myths. In

[11] Jorde-Bloom, P. (1988). *A great place to work: Improving conditions for staff in young children's programs*. Washington, D.C.: National Association for the Education of Young Children.
[12]Ibid.
[13]Child Welfare League of America, (1993). *Cultural competence self-assessment instrument*. Washington, D.C.
[14]Werner, S. (1996). Need a barometer for assessing the climate of your center?" *Child Care Information Exchange*, May, pp. 29–31.

some cases, these groups have obtained funding from community agencies or business groups to provide technical assistance to centers that recognize the need to improve their programs.

Materials for the accreditation process may be obtained from NAEYC. Most directors find that when they take the time to read through the Guide to Accreditation, the steps they need to take are all laid out for them, and the procedures no longer seem intimidating. The director's role is to obtain the support of the board and the staff by letting them know what is expected, and that they will be engaging in a worthwhile team effort. Sharing the accreditation materials with confidence, and being open to addressing staff members' questions and concerns, will help everyone get started willingly.

The next step is to begin a self-study. Letting parents know that the center is engaging in this process, and that their ideas and participation are essential, contributes to the collaborative nature of the work.

NAEYC provides classroom observation booklets for each classroom. The lead teacher and the director, education coordinator, or some other appropriate person observe in the classroom and respond to the items in the booklet. Some centers also ask that a parent observe each classroom and respond to each item. The advantage here is that many parents get involved, their ideas are recognized, and they learn a great deal about the daily program. Every parent is asked to complete a questionnaire evaluating the program and each staff member evaluates the total program using the staff questionnaire.

Together, the participants review the data and determine a plan of action. The director's role is to help staff and parents identify strengths and weaknesses, to celebrate the strengths, and to determine how to rectify the weaknesses. The director must be cognizant of defensiveness on the part of some staff members and support them as they accept the fact that some changes will be needed. Everyone involved may feel stressed as change is discussed. Here again, the director must listen to concerns and help the group decide about how to address them. Making changes is less stressful when the group feels ownership. Some changes may be out of the question, often because of the finances involved. This does not necessarily mean that the center cannot become accredited but the program report will have to describe how the staff has designed an appropriate alternate approach. In many cases, the staff will have to set priorities and create a schedule for working on various components within a certain time frame. Trying to tackle everything at once can be overwhelming and counterproductive.

NAEYC points out that in some cases, the self-study is as far as a center wants to go. However, it is not necessary that a center be perfect. "Accreditation is awarded for substantial compliance with the Criteria."[15]

If the decision is to proceed toward accreditation, the director prepares the Program Description that includes:

1. The Center Profile (the way in which the program is staffed and organized)
2. Results of the Classroom Observations
3. Information about administrative practices

This information is recorded on forms NAEYC provides and the *Guide* provides help. The NAEYC 800 number is also a great support system. Once you mail the completed program description to the Academy, you can expect to hear from them within 30 days in order to schedule a validation visit.

Your validator will be a volunteer early childhood professional. She or he will have participated in validator training, recognizes the importance of following the procedures carefully, and is committed to maintaining confidentiality. You and the Academy representative will agree on a date for his or her visit. You will have one or two validators for one or two days, based on the size of your program. The validator's role, as the name implies, is to validate the accuracy of the materials that have been submitted to the Academy. Validators work to ensure that everything they write is accurate. The director reviews the validator's work before it is submitted to the Academy, and is encouraged to comment on any area where the

[15]National Academy of Early Childhood Programs. (1991). *Guide to accreditation by the national academy of early childhood programs: Self-study, validation, accreditation* (revised edition). Washington, D.C.: National Association for the Education of Young Children, pp. 81–98.

program description and the validator's rating differ. Both the director and the validator sign the visit form and all materials are mailed immediately to the Academy.

Summarizing Data

The director is responsible for summarizing the data that is collected from all aspects of the evaluation process showing the progress (or regression) since the last evaluation instead of focusing solely on the present performance level. The summary should provide a clear data picture for the reader, and should reflect accurately the facts, ideas, and opinions provided by those who participated. A comment that occurs frequently should receive more weight in the summary than an item that seldom appears in the data, no matter how striking or impressive that item appears. Furthermore, no new information should appear in the summary.

The summary is written, dated, and signed by the summarizer, and should include a listing of sources used in its compilation. Some data may appear in graph or chart form, particularly if this format makes it easier to understand or more likely to be read. Appropriate computer software makes this task much easier.

Analyzing and Using the Data

The director or a designated committee uses the summary to cull out information. For example, in analyzing enrollment records, the dropout rate of children whose transportation is provided by the school may be compared with the dropout rate of those children who travel to school by some other means.

In examining this information, it is necessary to keep other factors constant. For example, if all the children receiving transportation are from low-income families and if some, or all, of the other children are from middle-income families, the dropout rate might be more closely related to income level than to mode of transportation. To clarify the situation, additional data would be needed.

Once the data have been analyzed, the director prepares a report for the funding agency, the board, and the other people or groups to whom the center is responsible. This type of report is usually prepared annually, although interim reports may be compiled. The report should be clearly expressed, easily comprehensible, and professional in appearance. Using a computer simplifies this task and enhances the results.

Each board member receives a copy of the annual report, one or more copies are submitted to each funding agency that is involved, and one or more copies are filed at the center. The narrative may be enhanced and clarified by the addition of appropriate graphs, charts, or tables. A pie chart showing the use of the director's time, for example, can be more effective than a lengthy narrative that contains the same information. Graphs and charts can be computer-generated and add an extra professional touch to a report. The fact that the report is read by people from a variety of backgrounds should be considered.

Usually, by the time the report for a given year is complete and is in the hands of board members, the planning process for the new year has been completed and put into operation. The annual report is then used primarily for future planning. The board looks at the report that includes the director's recommendations to determine the areas that need modification. For example, if there is a high rate of turnover among the teaching staff, the board looks further to see if the cause can be determined from the evaluation data. Perhaps the salaries at this center are much lower than those of other centers in the community, or perhaps the physical environment is poor. Decisions for change are based on available evidence that grows out of the total evaluation process.

SUMMARY

From the center's inception, an evaluation plan is an essential component of the total program. The purpose of the plan is to determine the value of the center's operation, to evaluate the individuals within it through an analysis of the progress and functioning of the staff, the children, the overall program, and to provide a basis for future planning. The evaluation process is open and ongoing, and relates to the goals and objectives of the center. The process includes collecting, summarizing, analyzing, and using data according to a prespecified plan that lets everyone involved know by whom, how, when, where, and why evaluation is being done.

Working Paper 15–1

Evaluation Response Form

Ask a peer about the evaluation plan used in his or her center. Based on your discussion with this person, write your responses to the various categories below.

1. Who conducts evaluations?

2. When is the evaluation done?

3. Where does the evaluation occur? (classrooms, director's office, parents' homes)

4. Describe the evaluation procedures for each of the following components:

   • Staff

   • Children

   • General program

Working Paper 15–2

Rating Sale for Evaluating Director Form

List at least five items on which a director could be evaluated. Include the format you would use to indicate the level of performance.

Director's Resource 15–1

Sample Preschool Child Assessment Form

CHILD ASSESSMENT (1st child)

Child's Name _____ Birth date _____

School _____ Teacher _____

Form completed by _____ Date _____

Note: These items are listed to give a sense of long-range goals. Preschool children are not expected to accomplish all of them.

	Consistent	Frequent	Beginning	Not yet
1. Comments on numbers and numerical relationships	_____	_____	_____	_____
2. Rote counts to _____	_____	_____	_____	_____
3. Counts sometimes using double counting or skipping items	_____	_____	_____	_____
4. Counts in 1 to 1 correspondence	_____	_____	_____	_____
5. Recognizes last number counted as total quantity	_____	_____	_____	_____
6. Compares quantities globally (more)	_____	_____	_____	_____
7. Compares quantities globally (less)	_____	_____	_____	_____

Director's Resource 15–1 (continued)

CHILD ASSESSMENT (2nd child)

Child's Name _____ Birth date _____

School _____ Teacher _____

Form completed by _____ Date _____

Note: These items are listed to give a sense of long-range goals. Preschool children are not expected to accomplish all of them.

	Consistent	Frequent	Beginning	Not yet
1. Comments on numbers and numerical relationships	_____	_____	_____	_____
2. Rote counts to _____	_____	_____	_____	_____
3. Counts sometimes using double counting or skipping items	_____	_____	_____	_____
4. Counts in 1 to 1 correspondence	_____	_____	_____	_____
5. Recognizes last number counted as total quantity	_____	_____	_____	_____
6. Compares quantities globally (more)	_____	_____	_____	_____
7. Compares quantities globally (less)	_____	_____	_____	_____

Director's Resource 15–2

Sample Child Evaluation Form for a Montessori Program

Name _____ Month/Year _____ Age _____

I. Personal Characteristics

Self Concept: Independence:

Order: Concentration:

Imagination/Creativity: Listening Skills:

II. Physical Characteristics

Height _____ Weight _____ Dominance: Right _____ Left _____ Not established _____

Body and Spatial Concepts: Large-motor Skills:

Small Muscle Skills: Hand-Eye Coordination:

III. Social Characteristics

Types of Social Interaction (individual,   Closest Friends and Type of Relationship:
small circle, universal, mixture, etc.):

Concern and Care for Others   Outdoor Environment Play:

Director's Resource 15–2 (continued)

IV. Activities, Skills, and Concepts

Everyday Living

Manipulative: Care of Self:

Care of Environment: Sequence of Activity:

Sensorial

Size Discrimination: Color:

Form: Auditory, Tactile, etc.:

Math

Number-Numeral Concept, 0–10:   Decimal System:

Teens/Tens: Operations:

Language

Vocabulary/Self-expression: Visual Matching/Classification:

Story Comprehension: Letter Sounds/Phonetic Skills

Writing: Function of Words:

Science:

Art:

Geography:

V. Parent Contacts: Date and Topics Discussed

(Reprinted by permission of Xavier University Montessori Teacher Education Program.)

Director's Resource 15–3

Sample Teachers Evaluation Form
Xavier University Montessori Teacher Education Program

Evaluation of Xavier University Montessori Lab School Teachers

Name of Teacher_____ Position_____

Level of Teaching: _____Preprimary _____Elementary. (Check one)

Director_____

Date_____   Scale: S = Satisfactory Performance
                                                NI = Needs Improvement

1. Maintains an aesthetically beautiful and intellectually stimulating environment. Includes daily clean up, repair of materials, making new materials, and clean personal appearance.
   1. S_____ NI_____   3. S_____ NI_____
   2. S_____ NI_____   4. S_____ NI_____

Comments:_____

_____

2. Develops each child's maximum potential in four areas: physical, emotional, intellectual, social
   a. Fosters warm, relaxed, non-threatening atmosphere in classroom   S_____ NI_____
   b. Develops warm relationship with each child   S_____ NI_____
   c. Acquires knowledge of background of each child   S_____ NI_____
   d. Continually evaluates each child in each area; introduces new
      activities to foster growth in all areas   S_____ NI_____
   e. Maintains record of child's progress   S_____ NI_____

Comments:_____

_____

3. Communicates as needed with parents for the purpose of fostering the development of the total child.
   a. Schedules conferences on regular basis   S_____ NI_____
   b. Holds unscheduled meetings, as needed, for exchanging
      pertinent information   S_____ NI_____
   c. Programs and participates in workshops and training sessions   S_____ NI_____

Comments:_____

Director's Resource 15–3 (continued)

4. Engages in frequent communication with staff for purpose of improving classroom operation and understanding of each child.
   a. Communicates frequently with appropriate staff to facilitate operation of classroom within above framework, including daily communication with assistants   S_____   NI_____
   b. Trains assistants and classroom volunteers, and interns, if present   S_____   NI_____
   c. Participates in staff meetings   S_____   NI_____

Comments:_____

_____

5. Assumes responsibility for furthering teaching skills.   S_____   NI_____

Comments:_____

_____

6. Constantly evaluates each of the above tasks to strengthen weak areas in order to improve development of each child.   S_____   NI_____

Comments:_____

_____

General Work Habits:

Responsibility and Dependability: Consider willingness to accept responsibility, time spent on assigned duties and follow-through on work.

S_____   NI_____   Comments:_____

_____

Stability and Adaptability: Consider ability to adjust to changes in job conditions, assignments, and schedules; receptiveness to constructive criticism; stability under pressure; calmness during crisis.

S_____   NI_____   Comments:_____

_____

Initiative: Consider how well teacher begins an assignment and recognizes the best way of doing it.

S_____   NI_____   Comments:_____

_____

Ability to analyze situation, develop options, form opinion and act: Consider ability to analyze facts and solve problems; estimate and foresee results of decisions, and ability to take action and make firm decisions.

S_____   NI_____   Comments:_____

_____

Director's Resource 15–3 (continued)

Proficiency: Consider effective use of time, quantity of acceptable work actually accomplished, necessity of follow-up.

S_____   NI_____ Comments:_____

_____

Cost Control: Consider ways to control costs without reducing efficiency.

S_____   NI_____ Comments:_____

_____

Has the teacher been counseled about his or her performance? _____Yes_____No

Date of Counseling since last appraisal:
(Attach signed written description of counseling)

APPRAISAL REVIEW

After teacher and Director have jointly reviewed this appraisal, each should sign below to acknowledge that appraisal has been reviewed and discussed.

Space is provided below each signature for comments.

Teacher's Signature_____Date_____
  Comments:

Director's Signature_____Date_____
  Comments:

Director's Resource 15–4

Sample Child Evaluation Form

Use different color for each assessment. Record date in that color.

CHILD EVALUATION

Child's Name:_____ Birth Date:_____

School:_____ Teacher:_____

Form completed by:_____

Date:_____   Date:_____   Date:_____

General Autonomy

	consistent	frequent	beginning	not yet	comments
A. Initiative					
1. Develops and pursues own ideas in activities	____	____	____	____	____
2. Expands ideas of others	____	____	____	____	____
B. Self-confidence					
1. Assured in expressing ideas and convictions	____	____	____	____	____
2. Copes well with new experiences	____	____	____	____	____
3. Manifests general feeling of self-satisfaction	____	____	____	____	____
4. Verbalizes feelings	____	____	____	____	____
C. Independence					
1. Cares for self (bathroom, dressing)	____	____	____	____	____
2. Chooses activities	____	____	____	____	____
3. Separates comfortably from parent	____	____	____	____	____
4. Seeks attention, help and recognition when appropriate	____	____	____	____	____
D. Responsibility					
1. Cares for materials	____	____	____	____	____
2. Cleans up (with minimal prompting)	____	____	____	____	____
3. Keeps up with own belongings	____	____	____	____	____
E. Appears psychologically engaged in child-selected activity	____	____	____	____	____

Sociomoral Development

	consistent	frequent	beginning	not yet	comments
A. Responsibility					
1. Can verbalize classroom guidelines	____	____	____	____	____
2. Adheres to classroom guidelines	____	____	____	____	____
*3. Participates in setting classroom guidelines	____	____	____	____	____
*4. Participates in enforcing classroom guidelines	____	____	____	____	____
*5. Initiates or participates in a discussion of classroom problems	____	____	____	____	____
6. Facilitates and participates in classroom routine (by anticipating transitions, etc.)	____	____	____	____	____

*Asterisk indicates that it would not be expected until at least four years.

Director's Resource 15–4 (continued)

	consistent	frequent	beginning	not yet	comments

B. Cooperation
*1. Uses appropriate assertive behavior and language to resolve conflicts
*2. Takes up for others' rights and attempts to help others in conflict situations
3. Channels feelings of anger, frustration, etc. in appropriate ways
4. Generates game rules
*5. Follows game rules agreed upon by players
*6. Considers others' point of view
*7. Discusses moral dilemmas (extra guests, enough cookies for class)
*8. Takes turns
9. Invites others to participate in activities
10. Responds to invitations to participate in activities
*11. Recognizes rights of others (may not act on)
*12. Channels competitive impulses in cooperative direction (enjoys the process and accepts the outcome)

C. Relating to Group
1. Calls children and adults by name
2. Identifies which children are absent
3. Notices others' needs (such as getting tissue for another)
4. Interested in doing things for group (such as preparing snack)
5. Spontaneously expresses caring for others (solutions when another is hurt)
6. Shows interest in what others at grouptime say
7. Participates in voting process

Cognitive Development
A. Writing
1. Writes using personal cursive
2. Writes pseudoletters
*3. Copies letter and numbers
*4. Writes own name
*5. Writes other words
*6. Writes from left to right
*7. Experiments with conventions of writing (such as writing from right to left)
*8. Asks for models (how to write a letter or word or how to spell a word)
9. Uses writing with intention of communicating
10. Asks to dictate messages

B. Reading
1. Enjoys stories
2. Requests stories
3. Holds book properly and turns pages
4. Pretends to read
5. Distinguishes between print and picture
6. Recognizes first letter of own name
7. Recognizes own name in print

Director's Resource 15–4 (continued)

	consistent	frequent	beginning	not yet	comments
8. Recognizes printed names of other children	____	____	____	____	____
9. Recognizes meanings of signs	____	____	____	____	____
10. Matches words in print	____	____	____	____	____
*11. Knows what a word is	____	____	____	____	____
12. Recognizes letters	____	____	____	____	____
13. Reads own writing	____	____	____	____	____
14. Attempts voice print pairing	____	____	____	____	____
*15. Generates rhyming words	____	____	____	____	____
*16. Generates words that begin alike	____	____	____	____	____
17. Knows one reads from left to right, front to back, and top to bottom	____	____	____	____	____
*18. Reads predictable books	____	____	____	____	____

C. Language
  1. Spoken

	consistent	frequent	beginning	not yet	comments
a. Speaks clearly enough for a stranger to understand	____	____	____	____	____
b. Modulates tone of voice based on situation	____	____	____	____	____

  2. Understood Language

	consistent	frequent	beginning	not yet	comments
a. Responds appropriately to questions including who, what, when, and how	____	____	____	____	____
b. Responds appropriately to why questions	____	____	____	____	____
c. Carries on meaningful conversations	____	____	____	____	____
d. Stays on topic in group discussion	____	____	____	____	____

Cognitive Dispositions

A. Autonomy

	consistent	frequent	beginning	not yet	comments
1. Generates several alternatives in play situations	____	____	____	____	____
2. Has "wonderful ideas" (thinks of new ideas in relation to objects and activities)	____	____	____	____	____

B. Physical Knowledge

	consistent	frequent	beginning	not yet	comments
1. Experiments with objects (water, sand, art media, pendulum, and other mechanical apparatus)	____	____	____	____	____
2. Makes and verifies predictions (such as water will come out hole in side of container	____	____	____	____	____
3. Notices effects of actions on objects	____	____	____	____	____
4. Notices changes in objects	____	____	____	____	____

C. Logico-Mathematical Knowledge

	consistent	frequent	beginning	not yet	comments
1. Comments on number and numerical relationships	____	____	____	____	____
2. Rote counts to_____	____	____	____	____	____
3. Counts sometimes using double counting or skipping items	____	____	____	____	____
4. Counts in 1 to 1 correspondence	____	____	____	____	____
5. Recognizes last number counted as total quantity	____	____	____	____	____
6. Compares quantities globally (more)	____	____	____	____	____
7. Compares quantities globally (less)	____	____	____	____	____
8. Compares quantities globally (as much as, etc.)	____	____	____	____	____
9. Reasons about addition and subtraction in classroom situations	____	____	____	____	____
10. Compares quantities numerically (5 is more than 3)	____	____	____	____	____
*11. Identifies numerals	____	____	____	____	____
12. Thinks about spatial relationships					
a. Follows path on game board	____	____	____	____	____

Director's Resource 15–4 (continued)

	consistent	frequent	beginning	not yet	comments
1. Own path	___	___	___	___	___
2. Commmon path (straight)	___	___	___	___	___
3. Curved path	___	___	___	___	___
b. Reasons about spatial problems (as in aiming at target)	___	___	___	___	___
c. Reasons about body fitting in space	___	___	___	___	___
d. Uses prepositions such as in, on, over, etc. appropriately	___	___	___	___	___
*e. Uses "first" appropriately	___	___	___	___	___
*f. Uses "last" appropriately	___	___	___	___	___
*g. Uses "middle" appropriately	___	___	___	___	___
*h. Uses "second" appropriately	___	___	___	___	___
*i. Uses "in between" appropriately	___	___	___	___	___
3. Reasons about classes and relations					
a. Groups objects according to similarities and differences in games and other classroom situations	___	___	___	___	___
*b. Conceptualizes part/whole relations in sets of objects (as in card games with suits)	___	___	___	___	___
4. Temporal reasoning					
a. Knows order of classroom routine	___	___	___	___	___
b. Refers to clock to monitor routines	___	___	___	___	___
*c. Understands "today"	___	___	___	___	___
*d. Understands "tomorrow"	___	___	___	___	___
*e. Understands "yesterday"	___	___	___	___	___
*f. Global understanding of past and future ("a long time ago," "a long time from now," etc.)	___	___	___	___	___
g. Knows order of events in familiar stories	___	___	___	___	___
5. Patterns					
a. Recognizes patterns	___	___	___	___	___
b. Matches patterns	___	___	___	___	___
c. Creates patterns	___	___	___	___	___
d. Extends patterns	___	___	___	___	___
6. Constructs matching sets	___	___	___	___	___
a. 1–3	___	___	___	___	___
b. 4–6	___	___	___	___	___
*c. 7–12	___	___	___	___	___
7. Makes count–cardinal transitions	___	___	___	___	___

(This form was drawn from previous work of Rhetade Vries and of Brenda Hieronymus and Sally Moomaw.)

CHAPTER 16

Working with Parents, Volunteers, and the Community

"The job of the child care center director is one that calls for enormous skill, particularly in working with parents. It is being a professional who simultaneously creates a friendly atmosphere yet retains an appropriate distance; an expert who builds competence in others, who is understanding, empathetic, yet at times firm. Most important is the role of the model—whose words or way of handling a sad, tired or exuberant child are inspiring to parents."[1] Developing a first-class program for children is the primary goal of the child care center administrator, but many centers have a secondary focus on special programming for parents that requires the director to assume an additional major role as leader of the parent program or as supervisor of the staff members that are responsible for the parent program. Work with volunteers and community organizations or agencies is also an integral part of the total center program that falls within the director's purview in some centers.

PARENT PROGRAM

Although center directors are not always responsible for the total planning and implementation of all aspects of the parent program, they are held accountable for the program. Classroom staff members or someone designated as a parent coordinator may assume some responsibility for parts of the program, but directors monitor the work, train those who are working with the parents, supervise the program, and serve as a resource for both the staff and the parents.

A positive attitude toward parents and what they can contribute to the center program must be demonstrated by the director. There are a number of reasons why parents may be hesitant about coming to the child care center or preschool program. They may feel threatened by the idea that the teacher is very knowledgeable about children and are fearful that their child-rearing practices will be criticized. Some parents, particularly from impoverished backgrounds, may feel inhibited around the school environment because of their limited or unsuccessful school experiences.[2] It is also difficult for parents who have other special problems such as having a child with a disability, being a potential abuser, a single parent, or one who is unable to read or write. Staff behavior and the atmosphere at the center must communicate to parents that each parent is valued as an individual and that each is highly regarded as the

[1]Galinsky, E. (1984). How to work with working parents," *Child Care Information Exchange*, June, p.4.
[2]Decker C., & Decker, J. R. (1997). *Planning and administering early childhood programs* (6th edition). Merrill, an imprint of Prentice-Hall, p. 317.

child's first teacher and as someone who knows a great deal about the child. All parents should be aware that they are welcome to come as frequently (or as infrequently) as they wish.

Any number of things can communicate this feeling of acceptance and trust to parents although some are more tangible than others. A parent-receiving area is the place where parents establish their first impressions of the center. It should be a well-defined space where parents and center staff exchange information. It should be orderly and aesthetically attractive, with some adult chairs and evidence that it is an adult space, yet it should communicate the fact that the center is for children. Parent bulletin boards should contain information about the center, highlight interesting articles, and display a calendar of coming events. Pamphlets and journals on child-rearing, toy selection, nutrition, and how to make play dough or fingerpaint can be made available in the parent-receiving area. A parent and child book lending library or toy lending library might be located nearby. Sometimes, interested parents are asked to manage the entire lending program.

Some centers choose to offer families a few ancillary services including take-out meals or dry cleaning pick-up. When James Hymes originally presented this idea, he was responding to a need during World War II when mothers worked seven days a week, many did not drive, or had limited gasoline supply if they did drive. Although few present-day parents work day or night shifts seven days a week, many find themselves using time-saving measures that help them meet their family's needs. These "family friendly" offerings can help ease some of the nagging stresses on young parents. If you choose to offer these "extras" to your families, you must consider the space and staffing requirements, as well as costs to you and your staff in time and energy. All related expenses should then be factored into your cost per child.

The less tangible things that make parents feel welcome include the manner in which their calls are handled by the staff member who answers the telephone or the greeting they receive from the van driver who picks up their child each day. Parents' feelings about the center program and staff also are substantially influenced by their first contacts with their child's teacher or the center director. Since it is very difficult to perceive what is having the most significant impact on the parents' reactions to a center program, directors have to be alert to any number of subtle factors that may be influencing parental attitudes and feelings.

The success of the entire parent program depends on the feelings of trust that must be built between the center staff and the children and families who use the center. Such trust begins to develop at the first contact and will continue to grow as it is nurtured by center staff.

The parent program can be divided into three categories: parent contacts, parent education, and parent involvement. Clearly, these three aspects of the parent program overlap; however, they are separated here for the purposes of discussion.

Parent Contacts

Parent contacts range from the most informal arrival or departure greetings to formalized interviews, regularly scheduled conferences, and special conferences when problems are encountered. Whatever the occasion, contacts with parents can be useful channels for communication. It is through these contacts that the center staff members communicate to parents that they have important information to share with one another and that they have a very special mutual concern for a child whom they both value. Details of initial interviews and intake procedures were discussed in Chapter 13. When staff members are not fully prepared to handle initial contacts with parents, in-service training time should be devoted to discussion or role playing of parent interviews and intake procedures. See Chapter 3 for the discussion of in-service training.

It is important to plan regularly scheduled parent conferences where parents and teachers meet at mutually agreed-on times and places to discuss the child. It may take several scheduled conferences and unscheduled calls, or casual contacts before a teacher can be successful in creating a totally relaxed environment in which both parent and teacher can comfortably discuss the child. When a good relationship exists, the scheduled conference is a time when parents and teachers can discuss the child's progress, present their concerns and their satisfaction about the child's progress, and develop a plan to follow both at home and at school that will stimulate the child to progress further. In the interval between scheduled conferences, casual telephone calls and informal contacts at the center are excellent ways to converse about how the plan for the child is working.

DIRECTOR'S CORNER

"I make it clear at my very first meeting with a prospective parent that we are open to parents visiting at any time. Our parents understand that even before admission to the program, they can come by to observe in our classrooms as they are weighing the pros and cons of sending their child to this center. It's the first step on the road to building a trusting relationship between all of us here at the center and the families that are with us."

—Director, independent not-for-profit center

Preconference planning sheets can be useful tools in planning parent conferences. Depending on the parent population being served, you, as a

director, may have both the parents and the teachers complete a preconference planning sheet (see the sample in Figure 16–1). Experienced teachers can plan the conference based on information from their notes and observations of the child, the information supplied by the parent, and their knowledge of the characteristics of an effective parent conference. The director should provide some coaching for inexperienced staff before they conference with parents.

After the preconference planning sheet has been developed, it can be used as a basis for outlining the conference itself. Items on the conference outline might include:

- greeting and stating the plan for this conference
- sharing a positive experience the child had within the past couple of days
- asking parents how things are at home and actively listening to their responses
- showing work samples from the child's portfolio and discussing developmental

Child's Name:_____

Parent(s) Name:_____

Date and Time of Conference:_____

   Above is the date and time of your parent/teacher conference. Please call the office and reschedule if the assigned time is not convenient.
   I look forward to talking with you about your child. Some of the things I have planned to share with you are:

   I am specifically interested in finding out about the areas of interest or concern which you would like to discuss with me. Please use the space below to tell me what those things are.

   Please return this to my box in the office at least a week before the scheduled conference. Thank you very much.

Figure 16–1   Sample Preconference Planning Sheet

expectation in various areas represented in the samples (for example, art and writing)

- sharing anecdotes that will focus discussion on the child's strengths, as well as those areas for potential growth such as math concepts, social interactions, self-help and independence, and self-control
- asking the parents to share what they would like to see happening for their child in the classroom during the ensuing months
- developing a plan that will facilitate the child's progress toward the agreed-on goals and expectations discussed during this conference
- closing with consensus on when the next conference should be held and making sure the door is left open for ongoing dialogue

It is important that parent conferences start and end on a positive note, and that incidents or samples of work be used to make specific points about the child's progress. Parents must be given time to express concerns and teachers should practice their best listening skills. Just as early childhood professionals build trust with children by listening to concerns and reflecting those feelings, they also build trust with parents by practicing those same listening skills. Putting parents at ease and avoiding arousing anxiety will enhance the quality of the relationship during the conference and will carry over to the daily interactions with parents as well.

Special conferences are sometimes necessary when either parents or teachers have a need to discuss particular concerns about a child or the center program. The special conferences are likely to produce anxiety for everyone because they are most often called when a problem arises. Sometimes, the director is asked to sit in on a special conference to give support to both teacher and parent, and to help clarify what is being said and heard. The teacher may have a conference with the director prior to a particularly difficult parent conference so that they both have a clear understanding of the problem to be discussed. The teacher also may ask the director to recommend the best way to present a problem, and to offer some suggestions on how to handle the parents' questions and reactions during the conference. Sometimes, these special conferences include other specialists or consultants from referral agencies such as a mental health center or a speech and hearing center. Both the teacher and the director should be well-prepared for special conferences because they will be expected to make a knowledgeable contribution to the discussion about the child. In some cases, they will have to provide support for the parent who may feel tense and threatened.

Uninterrupted time and a comfortable space are essential for successful parent conferences. Timing is important; the time of day or evening that is chosen must suit both the staff members and the parents so that no one feels pressured or rushed. The time allotted must be long enough to discuss matters thoroughly, but not so long that the discussion becomes tedious. Both parents should be encouraged to attend conferences, and, in cases of divorce, teachers may be expected to arrange a conference with each parent separately. Both teacher and parents leave a successful conference feeling that they have accomplished their goals. In addition, parents should go away with an awareness that their child is valued and appreciated. Finally, it is critical that parents have complete confidence that confidentiality will be maintained. The parent-teacher trust relationship will be seriously damaged if a parent should learn from some outside source that shared information about the family or the child was not kept confidential.

A postconference review will help teachers evaluate the quality of their participation. The following checklist will help them focus on their responses during the conference. Directors may want to review the following questions with their teachers after their encounters with parents.[3]

1. Did you give the parents a chance to talk about their concerns?
2. Did you remain an acceptant listener?
3. When you made comments, did you talk in terms of the parents' feelings instead of what they were doing?

---

[3]Adapted from Hewes, D., & Hartman, B. (1988). *Early childhood education: A workbook for administrators*, p. 105.

4. Were you able to restrain yourself from giving advice?

5. Did you remember that suggestions are usually nothing more than advice under a different guise?

6. If you did offer suggestions, did you give more than one so the parents have options?

7. Did the parents do most of the talking?

8. Were you able to restate to the parent the feelings just expressed?

9. Did you listen? Furthermore, did you listen because you really cared?

Parent Feedback

Parents' viewpoints and suggestions can be solicited by using a parent rating scale with items addressing center ambience, childrens' program, and the center communication network. Many questions can be addressed during a parent-teacher conference where parents can respond to family-specific inquiries such as, "Are your needs for information on your child's daily activity being met?" Or, "What are the best times for me to call you when I have questions about how Betsy is handling the arrival of the new baby?" But written evaluations or rating scales with items which may draw parents' attention to features of your high-quality service give parents an opportunity to ponder and reflect on their reactions to the center. The parent rating scale (Figure 16–2) is a sample of indicators for a 1–4 rating scale and a short list of appropriate scale items. It is yet another way to let

DIRECTOR'S CORNER

"I realize now that I really have to keep in touch with what parents are thinking about our program and how they see us. Last year we had two or three families leave our program, and I wasn't really sure why they were making a move. When I contacted several of them, I realized that they were feeling the quality of our program was not what they had come to expect from us. Of course, I acted on that immediately, but I also developed a rating scale for parents to complete, so they could let us know how we're doing."

—Director, suburban for-profit center

parents know that you are interested in hearing from them and that you are eager to partner with them to provide the richest possible experiences for their child.

Parent Education

Typically, the parent education program is designed to improve parenting skills or to interpret the center program to the parent group. In some centers, there are more ambitious goals for the parent education program including education on consumerism, nutrition, stress management, and time management. Some centers even provide vocational education programs or special remedial classes to help parents complete high school or take the General Education Development test (GED).[4]

Planning parent education programs is the responsibility of the director, but the planning group should include parent representatives. Format and content must reflect the needs and interests of the parents, and be adjusted to the level of education and previous training of the parent population. Centers that serve families from diverse educational, cultural, and socioeconomic backgrounds should present a wide variety of choices from which the parents can select the programs best suited to their needs.

Activities in the parent education program may be as informal as casual classroom observations followed by one-to-one or small-group discussions with a staff member, or as formal as a planned lecture, workshop, panel discussion, or seminar. The planned activities should meet the parents' needs in terms of timing, content, and presentation strategy. Casual classroom observations are particularly helpful to parents who are curious about how their child's behavior compares with that of peers. For example, a mother who feels great concern about the explosive yelling and unacceptable language of her preschool son may feel reassured when she observes other four-year-olds who are also noisy and explosive. It is also helpful for that mother to discuss these erratic outbursts with a staff member who can interpret the behavior in terms of expected behaviors at this developmental stage. Group

---

[4]A successful score on the General Education Development test leads to a High School Equivalency Certificate.

Dear Parents:

Please rate your child's child development center experience on each of the items listed below. Use the following numeric scale.

4—very satisfied   2—somewhat dissatisfied
3—somewhat satisfied   1—very dissatisfied

Your rating, keeping your own child in mind:

(   )   1.   Amount and quality of warmth and understanding received?

(   )   2.   Amount of individual attention given?

(   )   3.   Amount of planning and effort teachers invest in the program?

(   )   4.   Amount and diversity of experiences and materials available?

(   )   5.   Amount of activities fostering creativity?

(   )   6.   Amount of activities enriching intellectual ability?

(   )   7.   Amount of activities enriching language development?

(   )   8.   Amount of activities encouraging your child's social development—making friends, being with children, etc.?

(   )   9.   Amount of activities enhancing motor skills such as running, climbing, throwing, catching, and the like?

(   ) 10.   Amount of activities helping your child feel good about himself or herself?

(   ) 11.   The amount of encouragement given for your child to take care of himself or herself and become more independent?

(   ) 12.   Number of children in the class?

(   ) 13.   Number of adults helping in the class?

(   ) 14.   Amount of space available in the classroom and play yard?

(   ) 15.   Amount, type, and quality of equipment in the yard?

(   ) 16.   Communication network for keeping parents informed?

(   ) 17.   Opportunity you have had to visit the classroom or teacher?

(   ) 18.   Your child's overall progress this year?

(   ) 19.   Write below or on the back of this page your concerns that do not seem to be covered in the questions above.

Figure 16–2   Parents' Program Rating Sheet[5]

discussions, lectures, films, videotapes, or workshops that are offered by center staff members or by outside consultants are all useful tools for providing parents with information on child rearing, child development, or topics related to parental problems and concerns.

Topics of interest and concern to parents range from specific questions like, "What do I do about my child who awakens at 4:30 A.M. every day and wants to get up?" to broader issues facing employed parents who struggle with the stresses of job, home, and family. Programs should focus on building parents' sense of expertise. In planning parent education programs, consider emphasis on empowering parents to explore ways to cope with their concerns and issues about parenting.

Directors are responsible for ensuring that parent education programs and parent meetings

[5]Hildebrand V., & Hearron, P. F. (1997). *Management of child development centers* (4th edition). Merrill/Prentice-Hall. Reprinted by permission of Prentice-Hall, Inc., Upper Saddle River, NJ.

are both timely and responsive to the parents' interests and concerns. A designated parent educator may select some of the topics for parent meetings, but when parents are involved in planning parent meetings, the topics are more likely to be relevant to parents' interests.[6]

Parent meetings are usually considered part of the total parent education program. The frequency of scheduled parent meetings varies widely from program to program. Some programs offer monthly meetings whereas others have as few as one or two meetings a year. The first meeting of the year for a preschool on the typical public school calendar is often devoted to the parent groups, introducing the staff, and taking parents through a typical day at school by using slides or classroom visitation. The format for all parent meetings should include time for questions and informal socialization. Regular parent meetings are a good way to create a parent support group that can be mobilized to act as a strong political force when threats to child care programs arise in your community.

Parent Involvement

Parent conferences and parent education are, indeed, parent involvement, but the parent involvement concept implies a more extensive parental commitment than participation in parent conferences or in selected parts of the parent education program. Although parents should be encouraged to become involved, they also should have the option to remain uninvolved. It is an imposition on the parents' right to choose if they are made to feel that they must become involved in the center program. If, however, the program is a co-op, then by definition it requires full parent participation.

The purpose of a parent involvement program is to get parents active in planning, implementing, and evaluating the total program. In comprehensive child care programs, parents serve on advisory and policy boards, participate in all aspects of program planning and classroom activity, take part in the evaluation of staff and program, and participate in budget and personnel decisions.

Parents sometimes enjoy working regularly in the classroom or helping with children's parties or field trips, and some center programs depend on the help that parents can provide. Before parents participate in any aspect of the children's program, they should know something about classroom ground rules, routines, and what to expect of the children. The mother who comes to read to the children may need some help on how to include children other than her own in a small, informal, shared reading experience. The father who takes a morning off to come and read to the children may be disappointed when only three or four children are interested enough to stay for more than one book. He must be helped to understand that children have choices and that they are free to choose not to participate. It is also helpful if he knows the ground rules about deciding who chooses books to be read, and techniques for helping children wait to have their choice read. Parents who work in the classroom on a regular basis should participate in a more extensive orientation program and be assigned specific tasks when they come to the center. Both parents and volunteers can attend the same orientation sessions.

There are innumerable ways for parents to be involved in the center program other than direct classroom participation. They can do clerical work, repair or make equipment, take responsibility for the lending library, babysit during conference periods or committee meetings, or drive carpools. If they have special talents or interests in fund-raising, they can serve as a resource for the center board or the director. If they have special language skills, they can provide priceless service in bilingual programs. There are also many opportunities for parents to serve in a variety of ways on the board, on advisory committees, or on any number of standing or ad hoc committees (see Chapter 6 for the discussion of the composition of the center board and of the committee structure).

Clearly, when the director is committed to a parent involvement program and that attitude prevails throughout the center, it is possible to find a special place for every parent to participate, provided that the parent has the time and interest to become involved. However, it is important for the director to be sensitive to individual family situations. Employed parents who are unable to be involved with center activities must be reassured that they are free to choose not to participate. A successful parent involvement program does require some management; therefore, the center staff must feel a commitment to the program to give it the time and attention it requires.

PREPARING A PARENT HANDBOOK

A handbook for parents is a convenient way to communicate basic program information and should be distributed to all families at some point in the enrollment procedure. Since the contents may change from year to year and vary from program to program, directors will have to use some general guidelines for developing a handbook, then adapt those to their specific program. Some items such as program philosophy or grouping children may or may not be part of the publicity brochure, but could be repeated in the handbook. As a director, you will have to decide what information parents need to know and the best way to convey it to them. If a handbook seems too overwhelming for the particular parent population in your program, consider putting an item or two on colorful single sheets to be handed out over a period of several weeks after admission to the program.

The suggested list of items that follows is not exhaustive but provides useful guidelines for developing a parents' handbook (see Sample Parent Handbooks in Director's Resource on page 426).

- names of center staff members, and information about when and how to reach them
- brief statement of the program philosophy
- outline of the daily program and an explanation of how it fits the program philosophy
- fees and arrangements for payment including details about reimbursement possibilities and credit for absences
- carpool and/or transportation arrangements (if transportation is not provided, indicate that fact and state what information you need to have about the family's transportation arrangements for the child)

- expected arrival and pick-up times and procedures
- center policy on health and safety precautions to be taken by the family and the center staff to ensure the health and safety of children (state your policy about bringing medication to the center, children coming to the center when symptoms of illness are apparent, cover the procedures used by the center staff when a child becomes ill at school, and so on)
- explanation of liability and medical insurance carried by and/or available through the center
- sample menus for snacks and/or meals, and any expectations the staff may have about eating
- services the center staff will offer to children and families such as opportunities for having conferences, special medical or psychological services or referrals, discussion groups, group meetings, and so on
- center discipline policy
- requests for help from parents, whether for time spent in the classroom, help on field trips, clerical help, making materials for the classroom, and so on
- summary of scheduled events at the center and what families may do at the center to celebrate holidays and birthdays, making the policies reflect the program philosophy (include what to send, what to expect the child to bring home, which holidays will be celebrated, and so on)
- expectations about the child's use of transition objects while getting adjusted to the center, and policies about bringing other items or food from home, making clear how these policies are developed to meet the needs of children and to reflect the program philosophy
- description of the legal obligations of center staff to report any evidence of child abuse

This list provides guidelines for developing a handbook that ultimately must be fashioned to fit your program and your parent population. In writing material for a handbook, it is important to consider content, format, length, and, most important, style of writing. Should the style be scholarly or chatty, formal or informal, general or detailed? Answers to these questions can best be found by giving careful consideration to the families being served by the program.

The parent handbook is a useful tool to acquaint parents initially with the center program and to help them understand what to expect. However, it must be supplemented with other written and verbal communications to keep them abreast of center events and the progress of their children.

Some directors send parents a chatty newsletter describing special events that are being planned for children or families. It is important for parents to know that one family brought their new baby to visit the classroom, or that a symphony musician came to show the children a slide trombone. Such information will help parents understand a child's questions and any ideas that are expressed at home. Newsletters can keep parents informed about the centers' progress, program philosophy, special programs, and future plans. It can include a monthly calendar, information about fund-raisers, updates of staff changes, and activities. Including a profile of a staff person, another parent, or a center volunteer is a sure way to generate readership and enthusiasm about your newsletter. News items from each classroom are always welcome, especially if childrens' names are mentioned. Parents will search the pages to find a mention of their child or their child's teacher. Best of all, parents are eager to read the "Director's Message" which is a must for each issue. Remember, the director sets the "feeling tone" for the center, and the tone of a "Director's Message" communicates that to parents.[7]

Other ways to communicate with parents include meetings, regularly scheduled parent conferences, and telephone calls to tell parents about happy experiences that their children had at school. Center staff must take advantage of every opportunity to communicate with the family, to share ideas about the child, and to strengthen the basic trust in the relationship.

VOLUNTEER PROGRAM

Volunteers are welcomed in most early childhood education centers and the volunteer program is usually managed by the center director. Occasionally, a member of the center staff other than the director or a volunteer who is willing to undertake the coordinating responsibilities manages the volunteer activities. The coordinating function includes recruiting, orienting, and scheduling the volunteers. Other aspects of the volunteer program such as planning activities for volunteers and handling the supervision and record keeping responsibilities connected with a volunteer program, must be delegated or performed by the director.

Volunteer Recruitment

Recruiting volunteers is time consuming and often frustrating, but there are individuals in every community who are potential volunteers. Finding those people who have both the time and the interest in serving a child care center may present a problem at the outset; however, a program that provides both challenge and appropriate incentives soon will build up a roster of available volunteers who come regularly.

Available sources for recruiting volunteers will vary, depending on the size of the community and the demands of other agencies in the community. Larger cities have organized volunteer bureaus, Junior Leagues, universities with student volunteer programs, and any number of philanthropic groups that can supply volunteers. Church groups, high schools, senior citizen groups, and business groups are other sources that can be found and approached in both large urban communities or small rural areas. The volunteers must feel that they are welcome and needed; in addition, they must feel a sense of personal regard for their efforts.

Volunteer Orientation

Participation in the volunteer orientation program should be a requirement for every person who chooses to give time to the center program.

---

[7]Jones, R. (1996). Producing a school newsletter parents will read," *Child Care Information Exchange: The Director's Magazine*, 107, January/February, pp. 91–93.

Although it may seem presumptuous to insist that volunteers participate in orientation, it is essential that they become completely familiar with the operation of the center and that they have a clear understanding of how their services fit into the total service offered by the center program. Furthermore, the volunteers usually recognize that a center staff that will take the time to plan and carry through a meaningful and helpful orientation program for them also will value their involvement in the center program.

Orientation meetings should provide volunteers with a staff directory and introduction to as many staff members as possible. The director should talk about the organizational structure of the agency, the goals and objectives of the center program, and the importance of volunteer help in meeting those goals and objectives. Further, licensing standards and health requirements for volunteers must be explained. That will clarify what is expected of them regarding immunizations, health examination, and classroom health and safety procedures, and help them understand the rationale for restrictions on their participation. For example, in most places, a volunteer may not be alone at any time with a group of children because of licensing and insurance requirements. When the rationale for that ruling is understood, volunteers are less likely to be offended when told they may not take the children on a walk or drive them the few blocks to the park.

Confidentiality is an issue for everyone at the center including the volunteers. It is wonderful to have volunteers who become ambassadors for the program in the community, but it is essential that they adhere to a strict policy of absolute confidentiality. Volunteers who share their general enthusiasm about working with the children or doing other work for the center can be a great asset, but talking about specific children, families, or teachers can be very damaging to your program.

Other details that should be covered at the orientation meeting include sign-in and sign-out procedures for volunteers, and where they should call if they expect to be absent. The record keeping is necessary because many publicly-funded centers must report volunteer hours, and some private agencies often choose to keep records and reward volunteers based on their hours of service.

Volunteer Activities

Volunteers can do most things that parents do in a center program, and they often have more free time than working parents or parents with young families. Volunteers, like parents, must be made to feel welcome; and like parents they must leave with a sense of satisfaction and a feeling that their services are needed and appreciated. Since they do not have the reward of seeing the joy their own children experience by having them participate in the program, it is doubly important for the center staff to make them feel welcome, to define their task for them, and to let them know how highly their service is regarded. Volunteers will continue to serve only in situations where they feel needed.

Reflections

Think about your own volunteer activities. Perhaps you tutored young students or worked in a program for children with disabilities. What motivated you to be there at the scheduled time? Did you look for excuses not to go? If not, why not? How did you feel about yourself after you spent time volunteering? What rewards did you receive?

ORGANIZATIONS AND AGENCIES

In addition to working with parents and volunteers, the director is responsible for involvement with professional organizations, referral agencies, and the community in which the center is located. In each case, the amount of time and degree of involvement varies according to the type of center and the director's individual style.

Professional Organizations

Directors frequently join one or more local, regional, and national professional organizations. Sometimes, the board encourages and assists them by paying their dues. A list of professional organizations is presented in Appendix B. Through these memberships, directors can accomplish several goals.

First, directors can obtain information and make contacts that may be personally and professionally helpful. Therefore, they may select organizations that focus on development of administrative skills, presentation of research data, and provision of information about legislation and funding. Through contacts at group meetings, the director may meet potential staff members although "pirating" staff from other centers should certainly be avoided. Directors also may see professional organizations as providing a forum for their ideas, a place where they can speak before a group and discuss their concerns with other professionals. They may volunteer to hold meetings at their centers, thereby providing opportunities for others in the field to see different early childhood education facilities.

When directors join a professional organization, the organization is enhanced because the directors have had a number of years of education and experience, and carry some influence in the community. As a result of their having belonged to these organizations or similar groups for a number of years, they have expertise that can help move the group forward and give guidance to newer, less experienced members.

Directors may join professional organizations to become part of a group that effects change. Legislators who will not listen to an individual's recommendations on teacher-child ratios may be persuaded by an organization's stand, and directors can have input through their membership.

In some communities, directors form support groups because they need a forum to discuss problems unique to their particular position. They can share information and ideas, and work out cooperative plans for staff training. With the increased, widespread focus on child care, national support groups are forming to provide hotlines, consultation services, and management retreats.

When they join organizations, directors serve as models for staff members. In some cases, the staff profits more directly from the organization than the director, but staff members put off joining, or may even be hesitant about attending meetings if they do not know other members. Directors can provide an incentive by offering to accompany teachers to the first meeting and by notifying staff members of upcoming meetings. Directors may work out a plan for released time from center duties that staff members can use for participation in the work of professional organizations. They also may provide staff meeting time for members who have attended sessions to share their information.

For similar reasons, directors should attend (and facilitate staff members' attending) lectures, courses, and conferences that are related to early childhood education. Directors also have the responsibility for reading current books and periodicals, and for occasionally passing these materials on to staff members. A list of periodicals appears in Appendix C. Most staff members will respond positively to an article from the director that is marked to indicate a personal application such as "This article addresses an interest of yours, new ways of teaching math concepts." Or, "Have you seen the reviews of these new multiethnic books? Which ones should we order?" This personal touch encourages the staff member to read the article and perhaps discuss it further with the director. When the director has provided a model of this behavior, staff members may begin to circulate articles or books that they have found to be worthwhile.

Referral Agencies

Directors contact referral agencies and advise staff members to use special services when appropriate. Directors also help staff members delineate the boundaries of their own professional expertise and recognize those circumstances under which an opinion obtained from another type of professional could be useful.

The job of relating to referral agencies begins with the collection of a list of services that are available in the surrounding community. In some areas, a booklet is published that contains the names of all the social service agencies, their addresses, telephone numbers, hours, charges, what services are provided and to whom, and whether or not a referral from a physician or caseworker is required. Some communities add other kinds of information such as lists of recreation centers, churches, schools, and government agencies and officials. If this type of directory is not available, a center director can develop a referral list. Writing the data on file cards provides a convenient reference that can be updated easily.

After determining which agencies provide services related to the clients' needs, directors should attempt to make personal contact with as many of these agencies as possible. This contact can be accomplished by visiting the agency, by attending programs sponsored by the agency, and by meeting their staff members at professional meetings. Later, when the need for services from such an organization exists, it will be easier for the director to make contacts with the people who are already known. The director is also in a good position to explain the nature of the services provided by these agencies to the center staff and to parents, when that is necessary.

DIRECTOR'S CORNER

"When I first became a director one of the things I had trouble finding out about was the whole referral network, and I realize that takes time and comes with experience. You have to know the agencies, how they work, and the particular people to contact before you can help your teachers or your families with referrals. I always feel better when I can call a specific person whom I have already met."

—Director, YMCA-sponsored center

In addition to working with the staff in referring children and families for care and treatment, directors make use of agencies in other ways. For example, agencies usually have personnel and material resources available for in-service training or parent meetings. Some agencies in the community such as Community Coordinated Child Care (4Cs) provide consultation and technical assistance. A range of services may be available from other types of agencies such as the public library which usually offers storytellers, films, and teachers' collections of books.

If the center's program includes the provision of medical, dental, and mental health services to children, the director may be able to provide these services, at low cost and with convenience in scheduling, through agency contacts. For example, arrangements can be made for a physician to come to the center to do routine physical checkups so that children do not have to endure long trips, boring waiting rooms, and frightening strange buildings. The director who is well acquainted with physicians, psychologists, speech therapists,

and social workers is able to depend on their services, but is sensitive to the needs and limitations under which they operate. It is important that directors establish reciprocal relationships with these professionals by being open to accepting children referred to the center by them and their agencies.

WORK WITH THE COMMUNITY

The director explains the center to the community, and in turn, explains the community to the staff. This function requires familiarity with the community in which the center is located. If some or all of the children who attend the center live in other communities, the director should become informed about those areas as well.

In publicizing the center to the community, the director uses public relations and communications techniques that were covered in Chapter 12. These include news releases, open houses, and tours of the center. The effective use of the interpersonal skills that were discussed in Chapter 2 is particularly appropriate when working with the community. Certainly, the appearance and maintenance of the center's building and grounds also can have an influence on the relationship with the community.

Sometimes, individual members of the community become interested in the center and its work through the director's efforts. For example, the owner of a lumber yard may agree to provide scrap lumber for the children's woodworking projects, or a printer will offer to save all the paper ends from print jobs for the children's use. If the director and staff have met the local grocer and other shopkeepers, these business people may be far more responsive to the children when they visit on field trips or when they walk by as they explore the area with classmates.

Directors help their staff members understand the community by encouraging involvement in community activity and by providing information about life in the community. Obtaining a knowledge of the historical background of the area, and the cultural or ethnic groups that live there, will increase staff awareness of the needs of families who come to the center. The director is responsible for making center staff members sensitive to the customs, language, and values of the people they serve. Frequently, staff members live in other communities and represent different cultural or ethnic groups. It is impossible for staff members to work effectively with children and parents from a culture about which they have no knowledge.

When the director has done a good job of understanding the community, and when all the pertinent information is conveyed to the staff, everyone at the center gains an appreciation of the community from which a strong working relationship can emerge. The center's team of staff, parents, and children working together can be expanded to incorporate community members as well.

SUMMARY

The director works with, or is accountable for, the parent program. A major aspect of this role is helping staff members establish effective parent relationships. The parent program includes parent contacts, parent education, parent involvement, and places emphasis on the participation of the individual parent to the degree that is appropriate and comfortable for him or her. Directors are also involved in recruiting and orienting volunteers, and in providing recognition for their services. In addition, they work closely with professional organizations, referral agencies, and members of the community. Part of their role involves setting an example for staff members of an appropriate amount of professional involvement, and training them in the techniques of working with a variety of resources. Directors also provide information to staff members, and give them opportunities to make use of the services that professional organizations, referral agencies, and the community at large have to offer.

Working Paper 16–1

Volunteer Tasks Form

List specific tasks a volunteer could be assigned to do in each of the classroom areas or activities listed below. Think beyond supervising children. Consider care and development of materials, enriching the area, or making it more aesthetically pleasing.

Dramatic play (expand beyond house-type play)

Carpentry

Literature/library area

Writing center

Lunchtime

Naptime

Working Paper 16–2

Parent Conference

Think about the items in this checklist. If your role was that of director or parent, respond to the questions in terms of your perception of how well the teacher handled the conference. Give more than yes or no answers. Document your answers with examples from the conference.

Did you give the parent time to talk about his or her concerns?

Were you a receptive listener?

When you made comments, did you talk in terms of the parents' feelings?

Were you able to restrain yourself from giving advice?

Did the parent do most of the talking?

What was accomplished during the conference?

Director's Resource 16–1

Sample Handbook

Handbook
for
Families, Visitors, Volunteers
& Other Friends of Young Children

Children's for Children
The employer-sponsored child care center of
The Children's Hospital Medical Center

3255 Burnet Avenue
Cincinnati, Ohio 45229
(513) 559-4999

Director's Resource 16–1 (continued)

CHILDREN'S FOR CHILDREN

the employer-sponsored child care center of
The Children's Hospital Medical Center

HANDBOOK FOR
FAMILIES, VISITORS, VOLUNTEERS
AND
OTHER FRIENDS OF YOUNG CHILDREN

CHILDREN'S FOR CHILDREN

3333 Burnet Avenue
Cincinnati, Ohio 45229
(513) 559–4999

Walter J. Flynn
Vice-President
Human Resources
559–4753

Chris Stafford
Manager
Child Care
559–4055

Accredited by the
National Academy of Early
Childhood Programs (NAEYC)

Director's Resource 16–1 (continued)

TABLE OF CONTENTS

Director's Resource 16–1 (continued)

Hello!

I bring you a warm welcome to **Children's for Children**, the child development center of the Children's Hospital Medical Center. Founded in 1987, the child care center is one of Cincinnati's largest, loveliest, and liveliest child care facilities. I like to think of **Children's for Children** as a place that children and adults consider their second home ... a place where they are accepted and loved ... a place where laughter and play are cherished ... a place where children's rhythms are caught and given warm response.

I hold special pride in the center's professional staff. Selected for their knowledge of child development as well as their strong interpersonal skills, they are the strength of our program. When visiting **Children's for Children**, please take time to listen, to watch, and to learn from this unique group. You will be enriched.

It is my role and the role of my staff to not only facilitate the learning of children, parents, and one another, but also to work as enablers to the important work of our outstanding hospital medical center. We are pleased to embrace these roles.

Sincerely,

Chris Stafford
Chris Stafford
Manager

Philosophically Speaking

Childhood is a time like no other. It's a time for exploring . . . for creating . . . for discovering about oneself . . . for meeting the world . . . for learning how to learn . . . for being accepted "just the way I am." It's a time for blossoming and being cherished . . . a time for being allowed the time to be a child.

Our child care center administrators and caregivers are committed to the belief that children have achieved . . . that is, they CAN DO a lot. It is the role of the caregivers to build upon those things that children are able to do. We believe that most of life's learning—including how to learn—occurs in the first five years of life. Since each child learns at her own pace, our staff will look to her to determine the next stage of development. This "can do" approach is the basis of our philosophy for the center. This "can do" viewpoint allows our society's precious future to become confident and to enjoy successes in an atmosphere of respect, warmth, and love.

Time and again, research is showing us that THE main component of sound, quality child care is the trained, sensitive adult who is the caregiver. Through careful selection of a staff trained in early childhood development who value, respect, and sensitively respond to the unique needs that children hold, we feel that children will best learn. The time that they are away from Mommy and Daddy must be a blossoming time.

We respect parents as the most significant providers of care and nurturance. We are pleased to serve as extended family members.

Director's Resource 16–1 (continued)

An Overview of Our Services

Child care centers are special places. A center becomes even more special when it is created to serve a unique population. So it is at Children's Hospital Medical center (CHMC). Our on-site child care center, **Children's for Children**, Provides services primarily to the children of hospital personnel in a convenient setting for the seven affiliated institutions of CHMC. Our center is the most comprehensive in Cincinnati. The hours extend until 8 P.M., with weekday holiday care available. We offer full day service for children over 3 months of age through preschool age. Partial day service is only provided to children enrolled before June 3, 1996.

Our center is accredited by the National Academy of Early Childhood Programs (NAEYC); we have also been successfully evaluated by Comprehensive Community Child Care on several occasions.

Research shows us that the most important component of quality child care is the choice of staff. We pride ourselves on our selection of caregivers whose special sensitivity to children is unmatched. Our caregivers are nurturing, positive in nature, understand children's needs, and are specially trained. The center's administrative team carefully evaluates staff performance to assure that the children are provided age-appropriate experiences in an accepting, warm environment.

Our services stretch beyond child care to support the whole family. Families using the center receive daily communications on their child's day, prompt attention to any concerns, and parent-teacher conferences at least twice a year. Families gather several times a year for social events. A Child Care Support Committee includes parents and is an important resource to the center. A center newsletter offers classroom news, parenting tips, and a calendar of coming events.

Director's Resource 16–1 (continued)

A Brown Bag series is offered throughout the year to any CHMC employee. Topics focus on issues related to issues facing today's families.

The center does not discriminate in the enrollment of children or selection of staff or volunteers upon the basis of race, color, creed, age, religion, sex, national origin, handicap, or status as a veteran.

Persons desiring to be employees, to register their children, or to apply for tuition assistance must follow the established procedures.

Director's Resource 16–1 (continued)

Collaborating for Children

It is to the benefit of our children, families, and staff to collaborate with an extensive network of agencies and individuals.

Resources held by the affiliated institutions of Children's Hospital Medical Center are used by the professional staff of this center. All these groups focus on the healthy development of children, on providing the family ultimate support, and on advocating for safe environments for young ones.

The center is licensed to operate by both the Ohio Department of Human Services and by the City of Cincinnati. Licenses are posted in the first floor lobby. We are also licensed for food service operation with documentation displayed in the kitchen. Our compliance with all licensing requirements is monitored regularly. Licenses are renewed in a timely manner. To receive a copy of current state day care laws and rules, contact the Ohio Department of Human Services' office, (614) 466-3822. Our compliance reports/evaluations from the health, building, and fire departments are also available from ODHS. To report any suspected violation of the state law, please contact the local Department of Human Services' office, 852-3296. City regulations and compliance reports are available from the Cincinnati Department of Health, 352-3115. All state and city rules are also available at the center.

Employees of **Children's for Children** have advocated and testified on numerous occasions to strengthen the city and state laws to their current level. We are pleased to cooperate in the important role of protecting children.

Director's Resource 16–1 (continued)

We are members of the Comprehensive Community Child Care (4C). Individual staff members belong to various professional groups, such as the National Association for the Education of Young Children (NAEYC). We uphold the Ohio AEYC Code of Ethics.

Students from community colleges and universities may be assigned to the center to complete their teaching internships. In addition, student nurses and medical residents/fellows may come to observe healthy children at play.

Doctoral, corporate, or other research is conducted at the center with parental permission only. On occasion, we have the opportunity to participate in consumer research (toy design firms, etc.). Sometimes we have assisted with research projects of CHMC. No research is completed without the approval of the Center's Support Committee Research Review Subcommittee.

Our staff also joins hands with hospital, community, and parent volunteers. All volunteers are carefully screened and trained for their "jobs" by the center's administrators and lead teachers. We request physical statements to be on file for volunteers who interact with our children. Classroom or field trip volunteers are to support the staff, but are never left in charge of the children.

Parent orientations are held prior to a child's first day. Families are encouraged to visit the center frequently before the day of admission. The center staff and families begin building a collaborative relationship early.

Director's Resource 16–1 (continued)

Discipline

Children at our center will not receive physical punishment. Children who have conflicts or problems with others while at our center will be encouraged to verbalize their angers and concerns. Even infants without verbal skills will hear their caregivers describing problems, solutions and logical consequences. The role of the adult at school is to be a helper to positive problem solving. Our staff members guide rather than punish.

Children whose behavior endangers others will be supervised away from other children. The child then will process the problem with a staff member and any other concerned parties. Staff rarely use "time out" unless a child is emotionally out of control, and needs a private time to regain composure. Verbal processing is our preferred technique.

Discipline, i.e., guidance, will always be positive, productive, and immediate when behavior is inappropriate. Many of the staff members have had extensive course work in Dr. Thomas Gordon's Teacher Effectiveness Training (TET) and utilize TET techniques in assisting children with problems.

No child will be humiliated, shamed, frightened, or subjected to verbal or physical abuse by staff or by parents on the premises or during field trips.

Director's Resource 16–1 (continued)

Our Staff

We select our staff carefully in order to provide the best possible care and education for the children. The manager has a minimum of a bachelor's degree in early childhood education and experience as a center administrator. An assistant manager is a master teacher of children and adults. An administrator oversees the food program and facility. The services coordinator II supports the smooth operation of the center. Lead teachers have degrees in early childhood education and experience as teachers of young children. Teachers I & II have special training as well as demonstrated competence with young children. They must have a high school diploma, and most have graduated from vocational school programs or universities with degrees in early childhood. Our menu is carefully prepared on-site by our cooking staff.

We employ people who are warm and nurturing, who understand child development, who can apply their knowledge in the classroom, and who respect each child as an individual. We seek employees who value working as a team with parents, colleagues, and volunteers.

Each staff person has on file three written references from previous employers and/or supervisors. We require a police record check, a physical examination, and drug screening.

Continuing education is an important part of working at **Children's for Children**. Each staff person attends training in first aid, communicable disease recognition, child abuse prevention and recognition, child development, and teaching methods.

All staff members are supervised by the center administrators who report to the vice-president of Human Resources.

Parent Involvement

Teachers meet with individual parents to review each child's progress throughout the year. Conferences may be scheduled at any time. Parents of our children receive daily written information regarding their child.

Parents may serve on the Center's Support Committee and its subcommittees to help guarantee a setting designed to reflect the needs of today's families.

If parents have concerns or need assistance with problems related to the child development center, they may discuss the issue, if applicable, with the staff involved. If they are not satisfied, they may discuss their concerns with either child care administrator.

Rosters of names and telephone numbers of parents, custodians, or guardians of children attending the center are available. The rosters will not include the name and telephone numbers of any parent, custodian, or guardian who requests not to be included.

Social and educational events are held throughout the year to encourage interactions between staff and families.

Director's Resource 16–1 (continued)

Center Operations

We are open for operation between the hours of 6:30 A.M. and 8 P.M., Monday through Friday. We ask that parents with fluctuating schedules inform us in a timely manner. Schedules are due the Monday prior to the week of service. To run a smooth operation, we appreciate cooperation in this regard. Our staff schedules will "go with the flow."

We are authorized to serve a licensed capacity of:

Infants (3 months–18 months)	35
Toddlers (18 months–36 months)	34
Preschoolers (36 months–60 months)	59
Schoolagers (60 months–8 years)	3

We maintain these child/adult ratios and class sizes:

Young infants	4:1 licensed for groups no larger than 12
Older infants	4:1 licensed for groups no larger than 12
Young toddlers	5:1 licensed for groups no larger than 14
Older toddlers	5:1 licensed for groups no larger than 14
Preschoolers	10:1 licensed for groups no larger than 20
Schoolagers	15:1 licensed for groups no larger than 20

The center may be open on CHMC holidays if parents must work. A survey to determine the need is taken a few weeks prior to the holiday.

Director's Resource 16–1 (continued)

Our financial policies are provided to parents enrolling their children. These policies are periodically reviewed and revised. A summary of these policies is found on page 33 of this handbook.

Our services are offered to CHMC employee families only. If a family is enrolled and then leaves CHMC, ninety days of service may be used after the date of termination. Assistance in locating new child care may be obtained by calling 4C, 221-0033.

Director's Resource 16–1 (continued)

Typical Daytime Schedule

Although each classrooms' daily schedule varies, activities alternate between quiet and active, free play, and total group experiences. Daily lesson plans are posted in classrooms of the five oldest groups of children. Infant schedules are at the baby's preference. An example of a daily schedule for older groups is:

6:30–8:00	arrival, warm greeting, play with parents, free play with friends
8:00–8:30	wash hands, breakfast
8:30–8:45	wash table space, brush teeth, transition to outdoors
8:45–9:30	outdoor play
9:30–9:50	language or music activities in whole group
9:50–10:00	transition to free play
10:00–11:15	self-selection in all learning areas
11:15–11:30	preparation for lunch, wash hands
11:30–12:15	lunch in small groups
12:15–12:30	wash hands, brush teeth, toileting
12:30–2:30	soft music, back rubs, naptime
2:30–3:00	toileting, wash hands, snack, some departures and second shift arrivals

Director's Resource 16–1 (continued)

3:00–3:45	self-selected activities
3:45–4:15	outdoor play
4:15–4:45	group time (songs, stories)
4:45–5:45	free choice of activities or muscle room
5:45	transition to evening program
6:00	dinner

Typical Nighttime Schedule

The "Night Owls" are children who stay for dinner and beyond. Our staff plans special activities for these children who are in "family" groupings. An example of an evening schedule is:

6:00–6:30 P.M.	dinner is served
6:30–7:00	self selection of activities in all learning areas
7:00–8:00	muscle room or outdoors

Director's Resource 16–1 (continued)

What to Bring From Home
(Please check with classroom staff as well)

Infants:
- baby food, labeled with child's name and dated
- formula, labeled and dated
- baby bottles, labeled and dated
- pacifiers, labeled
- favorite soft crib toy or crib mobile
- disposable diapers, labeled on box or cloth diapers with pail
- blankets, labeled
- 1 or 2 changes of clothes, labeled
- security items
- photo of family

Toddlers:
- pacifiers, labeled
- naptime toy
- blanket and pillow, labeled
- disposable diapers, labeled on box or cloth diapers with pail
- 1 or 2 changes of clothes, labeled
- sweater or jacket, labeled
- security items
- toothbrush, labeled
- toothpaste, labeled
- comb or pick
- photo of family

Preschoolers:
- naptime toy
- blanket and pillow, labeled
- 1 change of clothes, labeled
- sweater or jacket, labeled
- toothbrush, labeled
- toothpaste, labeled
- comb or pick
- security items, labeled
- photo of family

Director's Resource 16–1 (continued)

What Not To Bring From Home

(please check with classroom staff as well)

toys of violence

candy

chewing gum

"jellies", sandals

anything unlabeled

a frown

Director's Resource 16–1 (continued)

The Infant Program

Our program for infants sets its pace around the needs and unique differences of each child. Our younger infants have a "primary" caregiver who centers her day around the schedules of those for whom she cares. This care, while meeting basic needs for food, diapering and adequate rest, goes beyond that. This keen observer plans and enhances the interactions and activities the infant's behavior is identifying.

Routines are the curriculum for an infant's day. Every moment of a young child's day offers opportunities for learning. The skilled educator catches these moments and helps each baby establish trust, discover and feel good about herself, tackle a motor task, realize the power of language, and begin to understand this strange new world from many angles. This is accomplished as each teacher keys into the verbal and nonverbal messages the child is sending.

An infant teacher, with the education and understanding of early childhood development, knows that rich verbal interactions with children help them to understand that language is a tool for identifying and expressing their needs, ideas, and feelings in later life. Each of our caregivers accepts that infants developmentally need to explore the world through mouthing and touching and allows for this, viewing it as a valuable learning experience. This teacher is alert to the need for proper sanitation measures and follows them consistently and conscientiously. As the trained adult looks at the environment, she views it from the child's eye and creates a cozy, inviting, and stimulating place for children. She understands that what is made available for children to use depends on who the children are and what their needs are developmentally. This might necessitate frequent rotation of toys to "keep up" with a growing child, or prompt a teacher to make a toy that focuses on the child's interest or need.

Director's Resource 16–1 (continued)

Infants need to view the world from many angles, and are allowed that experience. This includes crawling, being carried, stroller rides, outdoor play, climbing, and rocking so that various perspectives are gained. Diaper changing, feeding, and other routines are viewed as vital times for communication, self discovery, and socializing. They are encouraged to master feeding themselves despite the messiness that accompanies this activity. While being supportive of infants in their quest for competence, our teachers look to the parents as the best resource in working with their children. Early childhood educators view themselves as professionals with children and with parents.

Director's Resource 16–1 (continued)

The Toddler Program

In providing a program for toddlers, our teachers understand that these children learn with their whole bodies. They learn more by doing than by being told. Toddlers discover their world on a physical level, so it is expected that they will prefer walking, climbing, carrying objects, dumping, or dropping objects to sitting, picking up toys, or playing only in a designated space. These large muscle activities are the legitimate activity of toddlerhood.

In planning for toddlers, our educators are prepared to be flexible and spontaneous. Because they are active explorers, toddlers are eager to try new things and use materials in different ways. Our understanding teachers will go with the cues of the child and view that as learning, extending it even if it isn't part of the day's planned curriculum.

Toddlers are working on becoming autonomous. The educated teacher respects this and allows opportunities for the child to be responsible and to make choices. This teacher also understands why certain behaviors must be limited, and sets limits that are fair and consistent. Expectations for behaviors are developmentally appropriate and allow the child to be challenged yet to feel support from the teacher. Consequently, frustration is kept to a minimum and the child's dignity and self-concept remain intact.

Our teachers, with patience, warmth and respect, redirect toddlers to help guide them toward controlling their impulses and behaviors. The teacher draws more attention to a child's appropriate behavior than to the inappropriate because she understands that toddlers will act in the way that draws the most attention. Constant testing and expression of opposition are viewed as the child's development of a healthy sense of self. The teacher accepts this and offers positively worded directions to avoid getting into power struggles. The teacher views herself as a model for how she wants the children to develop. She does this in her verbal interactions, because she understands that toddlers lack the skills to cope with frustrating situations and might act out in a physical way without her guidance.

Director's Resource 16–1 (continued)

The teacher recognizes that routine times are important moments to help children learn about themselves and others. An early childhood educator views play as valuable, and facilitates this so that children stay interested and move from simple to more complex aspects of their play. The classroom includes materials for children to engage in imaginative play, appropriate art experiences for creative exploration, various manipulatives to develop cognitive and physical skills, as well as building blocks, music, and books. The environment allows for the children to choose activities and respects their need for ample time to use and reuse activities, because repeated experiences foster competence. The setting is stimulating and inviting. It offers comfortable spaces for privacy and for interacting in small groups. Children's art is displayed proudly and respected for what it is. The little ones are encouraged by a knowing adult to care for the belongings and the environment in ways they can handle. The teacher creates and adapts the environment and activities to meet the children's changing needs from day to day.

Director's Resource 16–1 (continued)

The Preschooler Program

Preschoolers are usually most responsive to activities in which they are involved in a "hands-on" manner. Our teachers accept that and design their classroom spaces with "learning stations" at which children can freely choose whether to participate or not and for how long. Our quality staff rotate and add materials frequently to maintain and extend the child's interest. Often our teachers create their own games and materials if commercial ones do not offer the challenge needed, or do not reflect the interests of the children. Young children seem to learn best when trained teachers build on the interests and abilities of the children. This reflects the currently recognized theory that endorses non-pressured, child-centered activities guided by an adult with a solid child development base and strong problem-solving skills. In such a program, parents truly become partners with the professional staff. Information or discoveries about the child's development are mutually shared, resulting in a program tailored to the individual child.

The preschool curriculum includes activities centering on communication, science, math, social studies, music, art, large and small motor development. An enrichment program that includes field trips and visitors is offered. Dramatic play opportunities reinforce learning of practical life experiences.

LANGUAGE/COMMUNICATION—The whole language approach is our model. This is one in which children are exposed to print and language that is integrated into each activity center. Thomas Gordon's communication system is mastered by staff to facilitate problem solving and language building.

SCIENCE—Open-ended questions by the trained teacher help the children learn how to question . . . how to be thinkers. Hands-on activities include using simple machines, sensory table play, plant and animal life. Nutrition awareness and weekly cooking activities are offered.

Director's Resource 16–1 (continued)

MATH—Activities include concepts of introductory geometry, seriation, classification, sets, number, quantity, length, weight, use of simple graphs, simple addition/subtraction (more/less), and money.

SOCIAL STUDIES—Learning about the "world around us" is the focus of this curriculum area. Field trips and studies of occupations are included.

MUSIC—Exposure to and involvement with simple rhythm instruments and autoharps is part of our music program. Rhythms are also "practiced" by the learning of songs and finger plays. Guest musicians visit the children to give exposure to a variety of sound and diverse musical styles. Tone, volume, and pitch awareness is part of the music curriculum.

ART—Exploratory, sensory art activities help the child experience a variety of media. Collages and creating mobiles are offered. Paints, chalk, pencils, paper, markers, glue, paste, and play dough are all available in a "free choice" activity center for the children to use as they wish.

Director's Resource 16–1 (continued)

LARGE MOTOR—Movement activities including free dance, parachute handling, climbing, crawling, running, and balancing are just a small part of the large motor program. The large muscle room is available daily.

SMALL MOTOR—From the handling of simple tools to completing pegboards, children are continually offered opportunities to develop their smaller muscles, an important prerequisite for writing.

FIELD TRIPS—Occasional trips are taken by the two oldest groups to nearby places such as the Art Museum, the Zoo, and the Museum of Natural History. Periodic walks to Levine Park, adjacent to the Medial College, are taken. Field trip fees are occasionally requested. Parents may ask the manager about field trip fee assistance. Our desire is to have all preschool children participate in trips.

VISITORS—Classroom visitors might describe a career or hobby. They could include SPCA and zoo representatives with animals or parents describing hobbies.

DRAMATIC PLAY—From "playing house" to being a cashier in a pretend grocery store to repairing cardboard automobiles in a child-sized garage, the children are able to practice role that productive adults hold.

Director's Resource 16–1 (continued)

Health

Our center operates for well children and staff only. Children who are mildly ill (e.g., minor cold symptoms) may remain at the center only with an Administrator's approval. Children should be fully able to participate in all activities, including outdoor play. Parents should provide appropriate changes of clothing so children do not become either chilled or overheated. Snow pants and boots are needed for snowy days. Swimsuits are needed for toasty days. Light sweaters or jackets should be made available, as well. "Jellies", "flip-flops", and sandals are not appropriate for wear at school. Sun screens or diaper area lotions may be applied by staff, with the written permission of the parent on a center-supplied form.

Children with symptoms of communicable disease remain with a staff member until the parent or designated representative arrives for the child. We make every effort to reach the parents when a child is ill, but after 30 minutes we will contact the emergency contacts indicated by the parents.

We will not serve children with:

- a fever of 101° F or above, axillary

- a fever of 100° F–100.9° F, axillary, if combined with another sign of illness

- a skin rash that has not been identified by a phone call or in writing from a physician who has seen the rash

- diarrhea and/or vomiting two or more times in a day

- evidence of head lice or other parasites

- severe coughing

Director's Resource 16–1 (continued)

- rapid or difficult breathing

- yellowish skin or eyes

- conjunctivitis

- unusually dark urine and/or gray or white stool

- sore throat or difficulty swallowing

- stiff neck

- infected skin patches

- pain of which the child complains and interferes with normal activity

- evidence of infection

- excessive fatigue

- a moist or open cold sore

Children may be readmitted:

A. with a physician's statement that the child is free from communicable disease, and that returning poses no risk to the child or others.

OR

B. if visibly free from communicable disease, fever free without benefit of fever reducing medications for 24 hours, and free of vomiting/diarrhea for 24 hours while on a normal diet.

Director's Resource 16–1 (continued)

The center retains the right to continue to exclude a child despite a physician's statement if that statement contradicts the center's policies. When any youngster in a child's class has a communicable disease, parents are informed in writing within 24 hours.

Staff with symptoms of illness will remain away from the center.

Our staff members have special training in recognizing communicable diseases. The staff rely on their training, as well as the disease chart posted in the staff sign-in area to determine indicated diseases. We follow strict hand-washing and disinfection procedures. The disinfectant policy is posted in the classroom and reviewed with any adult working in that space.

Medication is given only if parents sign a center-supplied permission form. Prescription medication must have a prescription label with the child's name and date on it. Medical samples and over-the-counter oral medicines MUST have a written note from the doctor as well as a parent-signed form. Permission forms must be renewed every six months. Chapstick, sun screen, diaper rash medications, and modified diets do not require a physician's signature, but do need a parent's written instructions and permission. Such items must be labeled, given to a teacher, and taken home daily.

If a child's diet must be modified for health reasons, a physician's written explanation is required. If a child's diet is modified for cultural or religious reasons, the parent is asked to put the request in writing, and may be asked to help provide supplemental foods.

Director's Resource 16–1 (continued)

Nutrition

We provide nutritionally balanced snacks, meals, and cooking activities. Menus are posted in each classroom and copies are made available on Friday afternoons for the coming week. We encourage the children to have a "hello" bite, that is—to try a taste of everything. We limit sugars and prefer birthday celebrations sent by parents to be raisins or other fruits, yogurt-sicles or juice-sicles, or other nutritious alternatives to cake and ice cream.

We provide approximately two-thirds of the child's daily nutritional needs. Seconds are offered to the children. Adults eat seated with the children, except the infant staff. Mealtimes are relaxed times, rich with conversation and fellowship. Parents may join us for lunch or dinner if the cooks are aware by 9:30 A.M. Cost of lunch or dinner is $3 per adult except staff, for whom meals are provided.

Director's Resource 16–1 (continued)

Safety

We ask that parents closely supervise their children in the driveway, lobbies, and elsewhere in the center. It is recommended that children exit from cars on the curb side of the driveway, and be offered a hand to hold. When departing from the center, please resist having the children run to the car while the parent signs them out. Sticking together seems to be a reasonable safety request. When going to the classroom, the family is asked to stay together. Sending the child on the elevator while the adult uses the stairs (or vice versa) is a safety concern. Likewise, older children should accompany parents to infant rooms, and not be left in a lobby. So much could happen in a moment or two, and we request your cooperation.

Children must be signed in and <u>out</u> each day in the front lobby. This is extremely important since this list is used to check attendance during emergency drills or events. Children are released only to persons for whom the staff has written permission from the parents. Parents should provide us with the social security number of any person designated to pick up a child. We will ask to see photo identification.

No child is ever left alone or unsupervised. At arrival, parents are expected to help the child settle into play, which may require ten minutes or so. Parents complete a portion of the daily report form before departing for work or training. Parents are permitted access to all parts of the center at any time, including nap times and preadmission tours or observations. Parents may request key cards for building entry from the services coordinator II.

There is always immediate access to a phone at the center. Telephones are located in the entry, all offices, and in most classrooms. A security phone is on the playground.

Aerosol sprays are not used when children are present. Smoking is not permitted in the building.

Maintenance is provided by the Marriott's Environmental Services department. Most cleaning is done after 6 P.M.

Admittance to the building is by a buzzer/doorbell at the driveway entrance. All doors are locked at all times for security. Doors are easily opened from the inside in case of emergency. Parents have keys (access cards) for immediate entry through the front door or via the Pavilion building.

The center is monitored indoors and outdoors by camera surveillance.

All center employees are required under Section 2151.421 of the Ohio Revised Code to report any suspicion of child abuse or child neglect. All staff have training to recognize signs of neglect and abuse.

Preschool children are well prepared for trips through relevant classroom activities and conversations. Parents must sign a permission form for each trip. This form includes the child's name, date and destination of trip, as well as parent signature and date signed. The ratios maintained on trips do vary according to the means of travel, destination and the "personality" of the class. For example, a ratio of 6:1 may be determined for a trip to the firehouse but 1:1 may be more appropriate for the heliport. Parents are always informed of ratios on the permission form.

Director's Resource 16–1 (continued)

A lack of adequate staff and chaperones to meet the stated ratio will cause the trips to be postponed.

Ratios for walking trips also differ from those within the building. Infants and young toddlers limit their walks to the hospital grounds, avoiding the Erkenbrecher/Burnet corner. The older toddlers traverse the CHMC grounds and, on occasion, walk to Levine Park on Bethesda Avenue. The ratios for infant/toddler outings are:

Infants in strollers: 3:1

Infants on foot: 2:1

Toddlers in strollers: 4:1

Toddlers on foot: 3:1

Preschoolers who walk on the hospital grounds or to Levine park meet these ratios:

Oldest three classes: 7:1

Youngest class: 6:1

A minimum of two paid staff are part of each field trip or walk.

Transportation for trips is provided by public transit. A staff person trained in first aid goes on all trips, taking a complete first aid kit and emergency permission forms for each child. Children wear tags that include the center's name, address, and phone number.

Director's Resource 16–1 (continued)

Emergencies

Monthly emergency drills are held at varying times and documented by the Security Office. The following procedures are rehearsed:

FIRE:—Staff members remain calm and reassure the children. The person noting the fire sounds the alarm and calls the fire department, 8877. Staff members escort second floor children to the nearest safe exit and congregate on the grassy area near the Pavilion Building and South Garage. First floor children walk to the Pavilion's back entrance (the "circle" drive). The infants are placed in a single crib and wheeled outdoors. The staff takes attendance which is compared to the daily sign-in sheets. The administrators check classrooms, bathrooms, kitchen, playground, and all other areas. Plans for evacuation are posted in each classroom. Elevators are not used for evacuation.

WEATHER ALERT:—CHMC's Security Office alerts us to dangerous weather concerns. In addition, the center owns a weather monitor. The staff members remain calm and reassure children. Children are escorted to the inner hallway near the first floor elevator, as free as possible from flying window glass. Staff may bring books or manipulative games for the children. Parents who arrive to take their children are strongly encouraged to remain at the center until the weather alert has been lifted.

ACCIDENT:—First aid boxes are kept in the offices of the manager the office coordinator, as well as in the preschool wing. Emergency numbers for children and volunteers are filed in the first floor lobby file cabinets; for staff in an assistant manager's office. All staff have first aid and CPR training. In a serious emergency, the life squad, CHMC transport team or hospital security is

Director's Resource 16–1 (continued)

notified as well as the parents and an administrator. When going for treatment, the <u>child's complete file</u> and injury report form (if applicable) is taken. This contains a summary of the child's medical history, as well as medical emergency permission forms. Children not requiring treatment or observation remain supervised, and reassured that their friend is being well cared for. Any incident or accident, including the administration of Syrup of Ipecac, or the emergency transportation of a child, that occurs on the center premises will be reported to the parent in written form.

Emergency closings occur when weather is so severe that the Mayor issues a travel ban, if there are problems with our physical plant, or if the Board of Health orders closure for disease control. Each of these instances is highly unlikely.

Director's Resource 16–1 (continued)

Emergency Transportation

The center obtains written emergency transportation authorization from each parent or guardian before the child begins attending the program. We will not accept any children whose parents or guardians refuse to grant permission for emergency transportation.

If a child is injured and needs treatment immediately, the center will call the lifesquad, CHMC transport team, or hospital security for assistance transporting the child. A staff member will go to the hospital with the child, and will take the child's records. The parents will be called to meet the child and staff person at the hospital. The staff person remains at the hospital until the parent arrives or longer if possible.

Director's Resource 16–1 (continued)

Financial Information

Fees are determined by the manager and the vice-president of Human Resources. The rates are based on those charged by programs of similar quality and do not meet the actual cost of care that we provide. CHMC generously subsidizes our program.

We offer full day service for children over 3 months of age through preschool age. Partial day service is only provided to children enrolled before June 3, 1996. A full day is 5–11 hours in length and a partial day is 5 or less hours. A two week deposit is required by the child's first day. This is credited to the child's last two weeks at the center. Fees vary according to amount of time that children are scheduled and the ratio of the group the child enjoys. Tuition is due on the Friday prior to service.

No sick or vacation allowances are made.

There are miscellaneous fees for late tuition, insufficient funds, use exceeding 11 hours, occasional field trips, and additional meals.

Parents receive the financial policies prior to enrollment. The services coordinator II is available to clarify policies of a financial nature.

Director's Resource 16–1 (continued)

Closing Statement

Children's for Children is designed for the unique needs of the Children's Hospital Medical Center. We hope that visitors and participants will sense that we have created a home away from home. We appreciate feedback from any visitor or family member. We are pleased to elaborate on any facets of our program. Tours are available by prior arrangement to small groups of persons wishing to see quality programming for children.

Thank you for your continuing interest in quality child care in our community.

Revised 6/96

Partial List: Sources of Early Childhood Materials, Equipment, and Supplies

ABC School Supply
3312 N. Berkeley Lake Road
Duluth, GA 30096
800-669-4222

African American Images
Chicago, IL 60643–1105
773-445-0322

Childcraft Education Corp.
P.O. Box 3239
Lancaster, PA 17603
800-631–5652

Child Life Play Specialties, Inc.
55 Whitney Street,
Holliston, MA 01746
800-467–9464

Child Plus Software
750 Hammond Drive
Building 10, Suite 300
Atlanta, GA 30328
404-252–6674

Children's Press
Grolier Publishing Co.
Sherman Turnpike, P.O. Box 1796
Danbury, CT 06816
800-621–1115

Clarion Books
Division of Houghton-Mifflin
222 Berkeley Street
Boston, MA 02116
617-351-3000

Community Playthings
P.O. Box 901, Route 213
Rifton, NY 12471
800-777-4244

U.S. Toy Company
Constructive Playthings
13201 Arrington Road
Grandview, MO 64030–1117
800-841–6478

Creative Educational Materials
14650 28 Avenue N
Plymouth, MN 55447
800-888–2343

Developmental Learning
    Materials (DLM)
One DLM Park
Allen, TX 75002

Delmar, a Thomson Learning
    company
3 Columbia Circle, Box 15015
Albany, NY 12212–5015
518-464–3500
800-998–7498

Didax Educational Resources, Inc.
395 Main Street
Rowley, MA 01969
800-458–0024

Gryphon House, Inc.
P.O. Box 207
Beltsville, MD 20704–0207
800-638–0928

John R. Green
411 W. 6th Street
Covington, KY 41011
800-354–9737

Harcourt School Publishers
6277 Sea Harbor Drive
Orlando, FL 32887
800-225–5425

Harper Collins Children's Books
10 E. 53rd Street
New York, NY 10022–5299
212-207–7000

Holcomb's Educational Materials
P.O. Box 94636
Cleveland, OH 44101
216-341–3000 Ohio
800-362–9907 or other
800-321–2543

Houghton-Mifflin Publishers
222 Berkeley Street
Boston, MA 02116
617-351–5000

Johnson & Johnson Consumer
    Products, Inc.
Johnson & Johnson Place
New Brunswick, NJ 08933
800-526–3967

Kaplan School Supply, Corp.
P.O. Box 609
Lewisville, NC 27023
800-334–2014

Little, Brown & Co.
Time and Life Building
1271 Avenue of Americas
New York, NY 10020
800-343–9204

Micro Revisions, Inc.
5301 Hollister, Suite 170
Houston, TX 77040
713-690–6676

Mulberry Hill Park, Inc.
2710 S. Washington Street
Englewood, CO 80110
303-781–8974

New Horizons
P.O. Box 863
Lake Forest, IL 60045
708-295–2968

Penguin USA (Lodester Books)
375 Hudson Street
New York, NY 10014–3657
212-366–2000

Picture Book Studio/Simon &
    Schuster
12310 Avenue of the Americas
New York, NY 10020

Playtime Equipment and School
    Supply, Inc.
5310 North 99th Street, Suite 2
Omaha, NE 68134
800-28–TEACH

SofterWare, Inc.
540 Pennsylvania Avenue, Suite
    200
Fort Washington, PA 19034
215-628–0400
800-220–4111

The Little Tikes Co.
2180 Barlow Road
Hudson, OH 44236–9984
800-321–0183

Private Advantage Center
Management Software for
    Macintosh Computer
Mt. Taylor Programs
716 Collegeview, Suite B
Santa Rosa, CA 95404
800-238–7015

Teachers College Press
Columbia University
New York, NY 10027
800-575–6566

Things From Bell, Inc.
    S+S Worldwide
P.O. Box 513
Colchester, CT 06415
800-543–1458

Redleaf Press
450 N. Syndicate, Suite 5
St. Paul, MN 55104–4125
800-423–8309

Toys to Grow On/Lakeshore
    Learning Materials
2695 E. Dominguez Street
P.O. Box 17
Long Beach, CA 90801
800-542–8338

Willow Tree Publications
P.O. Box 428
Naperville, IL 60566–9725
800-453–7148

Partial List: Early Childhood Professional Organizations and Information Sources

Administration for Children and
  Families
370 L'Enfant Promenade, S.W.
Washington, D.C. 20447
202-670–6782

Administration for Children,
  Youth and Families (ACYF)
Head Start Division
330 C Street SW, Room 2212
Washington, D.C. 20047
202-205–8572
www.acf.dhhs.gov

American Academy of Pediatrics
141 Northwest Point Boulevard
Elk Grove Village, IL 60007–0927
800-433–9016
847-228–5005
www.aap.org

American Association for Gifted
  Children—Duke University
Box 90270
Durham, NC 27708-0270
919-783–6152

American Association of Families
  and Consumer Sciences
1555 King Street
Alexandria, VA 22314
703-706–4600
www.aafcs.org

American Association of School
  Administrators
1801 N. Moore Street
Arlington, VA 22209
703-528–0700
www.aasa.org

American Council on Education
  (ACE)
1 Dupont Circle, NW, Suite 800
Washington, D.C. 20036
202-939–9300
www.acenet.edu

American Educational Research
  Association (AERA)
1230 17th Street, NW
Washington, D.C. 20036–3078
202-223–9485
www.aera.net

American Federation of
  Teachers (AFT)
555 New Jersey Avenue, NW
Washington, D.C. 20001
202-879–4400
www.aft.org

American Montessori Society
  (AMS)
281 Park Avenue S, 6th Floor
New York, NY 10010
212-358–1250

American Medical Association
515 N. State Street
Chicago, IL 60610
800-621–8335
www.ama-assa.org

American Speech, Language and
  Hearing Association
10801 Rockville Pike
Rockville, MD 20852
800-638–8255
www.asha.org

Appalachian Regional
  Commission
1666 Connecticut Avenue, NW,
  7th Floor
Washington, D.C. 20009
202-884–7799
www.arc.gov

Association for Childhood
  Education International (ACEI)
1790 Georgia Avenue, Suite 215
Olney, MD 20832
800-423–3563
www.acei.org

Association for Library Service
  to Children
American Library Association
50 E. Huron Street
Chicago, IL 60611
312-944–6780
www.ala.org

Association Montessori
    Internationale, USA
410 Alexander Street
Rochester, NY 14607
716-461–5920

Association for Supervision and
    Curriculum Development
    (ASCD)
1703 N. Beauregard Street
Alexandria, VA 22311
703-578–9600

California Child Care Resource
    and Referral Agency
111 New Montgomery
San Francisco, CA 94105
415-882–0234
www.rrnetwork.org

Center for Career Development
    in Early Care and Education
Center for Parenting Studies
Wheelock College
200 The Riverway
Boston, MA 02215–4176
617-879–2214

Centers for Disease Control &
    Prevention
1600 Clifton Rd. N.E.
Atlanta, GA 30333
404-639–3286
www.cdc.gov

Center for Early Childhood
    Leadership
National Louis University
1000 Capitol Drive
Wheeling, IL 60090-7201
703-305–2276
www.nl.edu/cec/

Child Care in Health Care (for-
    merly National Association of
    Hospital Affiliated Child Care
    Programs)
1100 South 105 Street
Edwardsville, KS 66111
913-676–2088 (w)
913-441–4065 (CCHC)

Child Care Information
    Exchange
P.O. Box 2890
Redmond, WA 98073–2890
800-221–2864
www.ccie.com

Child Care Law Center
973 Market Street, Suite 550
San Francisco, CA 94103
415-495–5498
www.childcarelaw.org

Child Welfare League of
    America (CWLA)
440 1st Street, NW, Suite 310
Washington, D.C. 20001–2085
202-638–2952
www.cwla.org

Children's Defense Fund
25 E. Street, NW
Washington, D.C. 20001
202-628–8787
www.childrensdefense.org

Council for Early Childhood
    Professional Recognition
    (CDA)
2640 16th Street, NW
Washington, D.C. 20009–3573
800-424–4310
202-265–9090
www.edcouncil.org

Council for Exceptional Children
    (CEC)
1110 N. Glebe Road, Suite 300
Arlington, VA 22201-5704
www.cec.sped.org

Council for Indian Education
1240 Burlington Avenue
Billings, MT 59102

Early Childhood Directors
    Association
450 North Syndicate, Suite 80
Saint Paul, MN 55104
763–603–5853

Education Development Center
    (EDC)
55 Chapel Street
Newton, MA 02458

Education Funding Research
    Council
4301 N. Fairfax Suite 875
Arlington, VA 22203
703-528–1000

ERIC Clearinghouse on Elemen-
    tary and Early Childhood
    Education (ERIC/EECE)
University of Illinois, Children's
    Research Center
51 Gerty Drive
Champaign, IL 61820–7469
800-583–4135
217-333–1386
www.ericeece.org

ERIC Clearinghouse on Dis-
    abilities and Gifted Education
Council for Exceptional Children
1110 N. Glebe Road, Suite 3000
Arlington, VA 22201-5704
703-264–9474
800-328–0272
www.ericec.org

ERIC Clearinghouse on Teaching
    and Teacher Education
1307 New York Avenue, NW,
    Suite 300
Washington, D.C. 20005-4781
202-293–2450
800-822–9229
www.ericsp.org

Forum for Early Childhood
    Organization and Leadership
    Development
Henry W. Bloch School of Busi-
    ness and Public Administration
University of Missouri—Kansas
    City
5100 Rockhill Road
Kansas City, MO 64110-2499
http://bsbpa.umkc.edu/mwcal//

Handicapped Children's Early
  Education Program (HCEEP)
Office of Special Education and
  Rehabilitation Services
U.S. Department of Education
600 Independence Avenue, SW
Washington, DC 20202

Head Start—Johnson and John-
  son Management Fellows
  Program
University of California, Los
  Angeles
110 Westwood Plaza
Box 951481
Los Angeles, CA 90095
www.anderson.ucla.edu/

High/Scope Educational
  Research Foundation
600 N. River Street
Ypsilanti, MI 48198–2898
734-485–2000
800-407–7377
www.highscope.org

International Child Resource
  Institute
1581 Leroy Avenue
Berkeley, CA 94708
510-644–1000
www.icrichild.org

International Reading Association
800 Barksdale Road
P.O. Box 8139
Newark, DE 19714–8139
302-731–1600
www.ira.org

Leadership Development
  Program
Bank Street College of Education
210 West 112th Street
New York, NY 10025
www.bnkst.edu

National Academy of Early
  Childhood Programs NAEYC
1509 16th Street, NW
Washington, D.C. 20036
800-424–2460

National Association of Child
  Care Resource and Referral
  Agencies
1319 F Street NW, Suite 810
Washington, DC 20004
202-393–5501
www.naccrra.org

National Association for the
  Education of Young Children
  (NAEYC)
1509 16th Street, NW
Washington, D.C. 20036
202-232–8777
800-424–2460
www.naeyc.org

National Association of
  Elementary School Principals
1615 Duke Street
Alexandria, VA 22314–3483
703-684–3345
800-386-2371
www.naesp.org

National Association of State
  Boards of Education
277 S. Washington Street,
  Suite 100
Alexandria, VA 22314
703-684–4000
www.nasbe.org

National Black Child
  Development Institute
  (NBCDI)
1101 15th Street, NW, Suite 900
Washington, D.C. 20005
202-833–2220
www.nbcdi.org

National Center for Education in
  Maternal and Child Health
2000 15th Street, North Suite 701
Arlington, VA 22201–2617

National Child Care Association
  (NCCA)
1016 Rosser Street
Conyers, GA 30012
800-543–7161
www.nccanet.org

National Child Labor Committee
275 7th Avenue, 15th Floor
New York, NY 10001
212-292-3821

National Coalition for Campus
  Children's Centers
11 E. Hubbard, Suite 5A
Chicago, IL 60611
800-813-8207
www.supuschildren.org

National Council of Jewish
  Women (NCJW)
Center for the Child
53 W. 23rd Street, 6th Floor
New York, NY 10010
800-829-6259

National Education Association
  (NEA)
1201 16th Street, NW
Washington, D.C. 20036
202-833-4000

National Head Start Association
1651 Prince Street
Alexandria, VA 22314
703-739-0875
www.nhsa.org

National Institute of Child Health
  and Human Development
NIH Building 31, Room 2A32
31 Center Drive
Bethesda, MD 20892
301-496–5133

North American Montessori
  Teachers Association
  (NAMTA)
13693 Butternut Road
Burton, OH 44021
www.montessori-namta.org

Parent Cooperative Preschools
  International, U.S. Office
National Business Center
1401 New York Avenue, NW
Washington, D.C. 20005
800-636-6222

Puerto Rican Association for
    Community Affairs
853 Broadway, 5th Floor
New York, NY 10003
212-673–7320

Save the Children Federation
54 Wilton Road
Westport, CT 06880
www.savethechild.org

School-Age Child Care Project
Wellesley College
Center for Research on Women
106 Central Street
Wellesley, MA 02481
781-283-2547

Society for Research in Child
    Development (SRCD)
University of Michigan
505 E. Huron, Suite 301
Ann Arbor, MI 48104
734-998-6578

Southern Early Childhood
    Association (SECA)
P.O. Box 55930
Little Rock, AR 72215-5930
800-305–7322
www.southernearlychildhood.org

Superintendent of Documents
Government Printing Office
Washington, D.C. 20402–9325
202-512–1800

The Children's Book Council, Inc.
12 W. 37th Street
New York, NY 10018
212-966–1990
www.cbcbooks.org

The Feminist Press
at The City University of New
    York
365 Fifth Avenue, 5th Floor
New York, NY 10116
212-817-7915

U.S. Consumer Product Safety
    Commission
Washington, D.C. 20207
301-505–0580
800-638-CPSC
www.cpsc.gov

U.S. Department of Agriculture
14th & Independence Avenue,
    SW
Washington, D.C. 20250
202-720-2791
www.usda.gov

U.S. Department of Education
400 Maryland Avenue, SW
Washington, D.C. 20202
800-USA–LEARN

U.S. National Committee of OMEP
World Organization for Early
    Childhood Education
1314 G Street, NW
Washington, D.C. 20005–3105
800-424–4310

Work/Family Directions, Inc.
200 Talcott Avenue West
Watertown, MA 02472
617-673-3100
www.wfd.com

Work and Family Life
    Studies\Research Division
Bank Street College
610 W. 112th Street
New York, NY 10025
212-875–4400

Zero to Three—National Center
    for Infants, Toddlers and
    Families
2000 M Street, NW, Suite 2000
Washington, DC 20036
202-638–1144
www.zerotothree.org

Partial List: Early Childhood Periodicals and Media

Periodicals

Access Child Care: News and Information on the Americans With Disabilities Act
Disability Resource Group, Inc.
8 East Long Street
Columbus, OH 43215–2914

Beginnings
Exchange Press, Inc.
P.O. Box 2890
Redmond, WA 98073–2890
800-221–2864

Byte
BYTE Publications, Inc.
70 Main Street
Peterborough, NH 03458
603-924–9281

The Black Child Advocate
National Black Child
    Development Institute
101 18th Street, NW, Suite 900
Washington, D.C. 20005
202-833–2220

CCI&R Issues (Child Care Information and Referral)
Child Care Resources and
    Referral Network
2116 Campus Drive S.E.
Rochester, MN 55904

CDF Reports and Child Watch Updates
Children's Defense Fund
25 E. Street, NW
Washington, D.C. 20001
202-628–8787

Campus Child Care News
National Coalition for Campus
    Child Care, Inc.
11 E. Hubbard, Suite 5A
Chicago, IL 60611
800-813–8207

Center for Parent Education Newsletter
81 Wyman Street, No. 6
Waban, MA 02168–1519
617-964–2442

Child Care Information Exchange
P.O. Box 2890
Redmond, WA 98073–2890
800-221–2864
www.ccie.com

Child Care Quarterly
Day Care And Early Education
Human Sciences Press
233 Spring Street
New York, NY 10013
212-620–8000
800-221–9369

Child Development
Society for Research in Child
    Development
University of Michigan
505 E. Huron, Suite 301
Anne Arbor, MI 48104
734-998–6578

Child Health Alert
P.O. Box 338
Newton Highlands, MA 02161
617-237–3310

Child Health Talk
National Black Child
    Development Institute, Inc.
1023 15th Street, NW, Suite 600
Washington, D.C. 20005
202-387–1281

Childhood Education
Association for Childhood
    Education International
17904 Georgis Avenue, Suite 215
Wheaton, MD 20832
800-423–3563

Children Today
Office of Human Development
    Services
P.O. Box 371954
Pittsburgh, PA 15250–7954
202-783–3238

Children's Voice
Child Welfare League of America
440 First Street, NW, Suite 310
Washington, D.C. 20001–2085
202-638–2952

*Competence: News for CDA
    Community*
Council for Early Childhood
    Professional Recognition
2640 16th Street, NW
Washington, D.C. 20009-3573
800-424–4310

Council News and Views
Council for Early Childhood
    Professional Recognition
2640 16th Street, NW
Washington, D.C. 20009–3573
800-424–4310

Day Care and Early Education
Human Sciences Press, Inc.
233 Spring Street
New York, NY 10013–1587
212-620–8000

Dimensions
SECA
P.O. Box 56130
Little Rock, AR 72215–6130
501-663–0353

Early Childhood Research Quarterly
Ablex Publishing Corporation
355 Chestnut Street
Norwood, NJ 07648–2090
201-767–8450 or 8455

Education Week
4301 Connecticut Avenue, NW,
    Suite 432
Washington, D.C. 20077–6796
202-364–4114

ERIC/EECE Newsletter
ERIC Clearinghouse on Elemen-
    tary and Early Childhood
    Education
Children's Research Center
51 Gerty Drive
Champaign, IL 61820–7469
217-333–1386
800-583–4135

Exceptional Children
Council for Exceptional Children
1110 N. Glebe Road, Suite 3000
Arlington, VA 22201-5704
(888) 232-7733

Food and Nutrition
Superintendent of Documents
U.S. Government Printing Office
Washington, D.C. 20402–9325
202-783–3238

Growing Child
22 North Second Street
P.O. Box 620
Lafayette, IN 47902–0620
317-423–2624

Growing Child Research Review
22 N. Second Street, P.O. Box 620
Lafayette, IN 47902–1100
317-423–2624

InfoWorld
InfoWorld
155 Bovet Road, Suite 800
San Mateo, CA 94402
415-572–7341

Journal of Child Care Administration
Prakken Publications
P.O. Box 8623
Ann Arbor, MI 48107–9942

MacWorld
501 2nd Street, 5th Floor
San Francisco, CA 94107
415-243–0505

PC Magazine
Ziff-Davis Publishing Co.
1 Park Avenue, 4th Floor
New York, NY 10016
212-503–5100

PC World
PCW Communications, Inc.
501 2nd Street, Suite 600
San Francisco, CA 94107
415-243–0500

Report on Preschool Programs
951 Pershing Drive
Silver Springs, MD 20910–4464
301-587–6300
800-274–6737

Resource
High-Scope Educational
    Research Foundation
600 N. River Street
Ypsilanti, MI 48198–2890
734-485–2000
800-407-7377

School Age Notes
P.O. Box 40205
Nashville, TN 37204
615-242–8464

Software Digest Ratings Report
60025 Ridge Pike, Building D
Conshohochen, PA 19428
610-941–9600
800-328–2776

*Teaching Pre K–8: The Professional
    Magazine for Teachers*
Early Years, Inc.
325 Post Road W.
Westport, CT 06880

The Well-Centered Child
P.O. Box 428
Naperville, IL 60566–9725
800-453–7148

Young Children
National Association for the
    Education of Young Children
1509 16th Street, NW
Washington, D.C. 20036
800-424–2460

Zero to Three
Zero to Three—National Center
    for Infants, Toddlers and
    Families
2000 M Street, NW
Washington, D.C. 20036
202-638–1144
800-899–4301 (publications only)

Media

C&J Videos
3127 Davenport Avenue
Saginaw, MI 48609
517-790–5911
Video-Cassettes:
*What Does It Look Like?
    Developmentally Appropriate
    Learner-Centered Classrooms in
    Public Schools—1994*
*The Challenge: Quality Public
    School Programs for Four Year
    Olds—1996*

CRM/McGraw-Hill Films
P.O. Box 641
Del Mar, CA 92014
619-453–5000
Video-cassettes:
*Communicating Non-Defensively:
    Don't Take It Personally*
*Communications: The Nonverbal
    Agenda*
Decisions
A New Look at Motivation
*Performance Appraisal: The Human
    Dynamics*
Verbal Communication
Power of Listening

National Association for the
    Education of Young Children
1509 16th Street, NW
Washington, D.C. 20036–1426
800-424–2460
Video-Cassettes:
*Cultivating Roots—Home/School
    Partnerships—1996*
*Seeds of Change—Leadership and
    Staff Development—1996*
*Celebrating Early Childhood
    Teachers—1986*
Partnerships With Parents—1989
Quality Family Child Care—1993
*The Early Childhood Program: A
    Place to Learn and Grow: (7 pro-
    gram series)—1996*
*Places to Grow—The Learning
    Environment—1996*
*Safe Active Play: A Guide to
    Avoiding Play Area Hazards
    Caring For Our Children—1997*

National Institute of Child Care
    Management
The Mount Community Center
751 South 8th Street
Atcheson, KS 66002
913-367–2936
Audio-Cassettes:
*Creating Harmony in Your
    Center—1994*
*Interviewing Strategies: Moving
    From Survival to Success—1995*
*Supervising Your Child Care Staff
    Effectively—1994*
*Success As An Effective Director—
    1994*

Teachers College Press
Teachers College—Columbia
    University
New York, NY 10027
800-575–6566
Video-Cassettes:
*Video Observations for The Early
    Childhood Ratings Scale
    (ECERS)—1992*

The National Association for the Education of Young Children Code of Ethical Conduct

PREAMBLE

NAEYC recognizes that many daily decisions required of those who work with young children are of a moral and ethical nature. The NAEYC Code of Ethical Conduct offers guidelines for responsible behavior and sets forth a common basis for resolving the principal ethical dilemmas encountered in early childhood education. The primary focus is on daily practice with children and their families in programs for children from birth to eight years of age: infant/toddler programs, preschools, child-care centers, family daycare homes, kindergartens, and primary classrooms. Many of the provisions also apply to specialists who do not work directly with children, including program administrators, parent educators, college professors, and child-care licensing specialists.

Standards of ethical behavior in early childhood education are based on commitment to core childhood education deeply rooted in the history of our field. We have committed ourselves to:

- Appreciating childhood as a unique and valuable stage of the human life cycle
- Basing our work with children on knowledge of child development

- Appreciating and supporting the close ties between the child and family
- Recognizing that children are best understood in the context of family, culture, and society
- Respecting the dignity, worth, and uniqueness of each individual (child, family member, and colleague)
- Helping children and adults achieve their full potential in the context of relationships that are based on trust, respect, and positive regard

The Code sets forth a conception of our professional responsibilities in four sections, each addressing an arena of professional relationships: (1) children, (2) families, (3) colleagues, and (4) community and society. Each section includes an introduction to the primary responsibilities of the early childhood practitioner in that arena, a set of ideals pointing in the direction of exemplary professional practice, and a set of principles defining practices that are required, prohibited, and permitted.

The ideals reflect the aspirations of practitioners. The principles are intended to guide conduct and assist practitioners in resolving ethical dilemmas encountered in the field. There is not necessarily a

This Code of Ethical Conduct and Statement of Commitment was prepared under the auspices of the Ethics Commission of the National Association for the Education of Young Children. The Commission members were Stephanie Feeney (Chairperson), Bettye Caldwell, Sally Cartwright, Carrie Cheek, Josué Cruz, Jr., Anne G. Dorsey, Dorothy M. Hill, Lilian G. Katz, Pam Mattick, Shirley A. Norris, and Sue Spayth Riley.
Reprinted with permission from the National Association for the Education of Young Children.

corresponding principle for each ideal. Both ideals and principles are intended to direct practitioners to those questions which, when responsibly answered, will provide the basis for conscientious decision making. While the Code provides specific direction for addressing some ethical dilemmas, many others will require the practitioner to combine the guidance of the Code with sound professional judgment.

The ideals and principles in this Code present a shared conception of professional responsibility that affirms our commitment to the core values of our field. The Code publicly acknowledges the responsibilities that we in the field have assumed and in so doing supports ethical behavior in our work. Practitioners who face ethical dilemmas are urged to seek guidance in the applicable parts of this Code and in the spirit that informs the whole.

SECTION I: ETHICAL RESPONSIBILITIES TO CHILDREN

Childhood is a unique and valuable stage in the life cycle. Our paramount responsibility is to provide safe, healthy, nurturing, and responsive settings for children. We are committed to supporting children's development by cherishing individual differences, by helping them learn to live and work cooperatively, and by promoting their self-esteem and resiliency.

Ideals

I–1.1—To be familiar with the knowledge base of early childhood education and to keep current through continuing education and in-service training.

I–1.2—To base program practices upon current knowledge in the field of child development and related disciplines and upon particular knowledge of each child.

I–1.3—To recognize and respect the uniqueness and the potential of each child.

I–1.4—To appreciate the special vulnerability of children.

I–1.5—To create and maintain safe and healthy settings that foster children's social, emotional, intellectual, and physical development and that respect their dignity and their contributions.

I–1.6—To support the right of each child to play and learn in inclusive early childhood programs to the fullest extent consistent with the best interests of all involved. Usually, children with disabilities should be served in the same programs they would have attended if they did not have disabilities.

Principles

P–1.1—Above all, we shall not harm children. We shall not participate in practices that are disrespectful, degrading, dangerous, exploitative, intimidating, psychologically damaging, or physically harmful to children. *This principle has precedence over all others in this Code.*

P–1.2—We shall not participate in practices that discriminate against children by denying benefits, giving special advantages, or excluding them from programs or activities on the basis of their race, religion, gender, national origin, ability or the status, behavior, or beliefs of their parents. (This principle does not apply to programs that have a lawful mandate to provide services to a particular population of children.)

P–1.3—We shall involve all of those with relevant knowledge (including staff and parents) in decisions concerning a child.

P–1.4—When, after appropriate efforts have been made with a child, the family, and appropriate specialists if needed, the child still does not appear to be benefiting from a program, we shall communicate our concern to the family in a positive way and offer them assistance in finding a more suitable setting.

P–1.5—We shall be familiar with the symptoms of child abuse, including verbal or emotional abuse, and neglect and know community procedures for addressing them.

P–1.6—When we have evidence of child abuse or neglect, we shall report the evidence to the appropriate community agency and follow up to ensure that appropriate action has been taken. When possible, parents will be informed that the referral has been made.

P–1.7—When another person tells us of their suspicion that a child is being abused or neglected but we lack evidence, we shall assist that person in taking appropriate action to protect the child.

P–1.8—When a child protective agency fails to provide adequate protection for abused or neglected children, we acknowledge a collective ethical responsibility to work toward improvement of these services.

SECTION II: ETHICAL RESPONSIBILITIES TO FAMILIES

Almost all children grow up in families. Families are of primary importance in children's development. (The term *family* may include others, besides parents, who are responsibly involved with the child.) Because the family and the early childhood educator have a common interest in the child's welfare, we acknowledge a primary responsibility to bring about collaboration between the home and school in ways that enhance the child's development.

Ideals

I–2.1—To develop relationships of mutual trust with the families we serve.

I–2.2—To acknowledge and build upon strengths and competencies as we support families in their task of nurturing children.

I–2.3—To respect the dignity of each family and its culture, language, customs, and beliefs.

I–2.4—To respect families' child-rearing values and their right to make decisions for their children.

I–2.5—To interpret each child's progress to parents within the framework of a developmental perspective and to help families understand and appreciate the value of developmentally appropriate early childhood practices.

I–2.6—To help family members improve their understanding of their children and to enhance their skills as parents.

I–2.7—To participate in building support networks for families by providing them with opportunities to interact with program staff and families, and other community resources.

Principles

P–2.1—We shall not deny family members access to their child's classroom or program setting.

P–2.2—We shall inform families of program philosophy, policies, and personnel qualifications, and explain why we teach as we do—in accordance with our ethical responsibilities to children (see Section I).

P–2.3—We shall inform families of and, when appropriate, involve them in policy decisions.

P–2.4—We shall involve families in significant decisions affecting their child.

P–2.5—We shall inform the family of accidents involving their child, of risks such as exposures to contagious disease that may result in infection, and of occurrences that might result in emotional stress.

P–2.6 Families shall be fully informed of any proposed research projects involving their children and shall have the opportunity to give or withhold consent without penalty. We shall not permit or participate in research that could in any way hinder the education or development of the children in our programs.

P–2.7—We shall not engage in or support exploitation of families. We shall not use our relationship with a family for private advantage or personal gain, or enter into relationships with family members that might impair our effectiveness in working with children.

P–2.8—We shall develop written policies for the protection of confidentiality and the disclosure of children's records. The policy documents shall be made available to all program personnel and families. Disclosure of children's records beyond family members, program personnel, and consultants having an obligation of confidentiality shall require familial consent (except in cases of abuse or neglect).

P–2.9—We shall maintain confidentiality and shall respect the family's right to privacy, refraining from disclosure of confidential information and intrusion into family life. However, when we are concerned about a child's welfare, it is permissible to reveal confidential information to agencies and individuals who may be able to act in the child's interest.

P–2.10—In cases where family members are in conflict we shall work openly, sharing our observations of the child, to help all parties involved make informed decisions. We shall refrain from becoming an advocate for one party.

P–2.11—We shall be familiar with and appropriately use community resources and professional services that support families. After a referral has been made, we shall follow up to ensure that services have been adequately provided.

SECTION III: ETHICAL RESPONSIBILITIES TO COLLEAGUES

In a caring, cooperative workplace, human dignity is respected, professional satisfaction is promoted, and positive relationships are modeled. Our primary responsibility in this arena is to establish and maintain settings and relationships that support productive work and meet professional needs.

A—Responsibilities to Co-Workers
Ideals

I–3A.1—To establish and maintain relationships of trust and cooperation with co-workers.

I–3A.2—To share resources and information with co-workers.

I–3A.3—To support co-workers in meeting their professional needs and in their professional development.

I–3A.4—To accord co-workers due recognition of professional achievement.

Principles

P–3A.1—When we have concern about the professional behavior of a co-worker, we shall first let that person know of our concern in a way that is respectful of cultural diversity among staff and attempt to resolve the matter collegially.

P–3A.2—We shall exercise care in expressing views regarding the personal attributes of professional conduct of co-workers. Statements should be based on firsthand knowledge and relevant to the interests of children and programs.

B—Responsibilities to Employers
Ideals

I–3B.1—To assist the program in providing the highest quality of service.

I–3B.2—To maintain loyalty to the program and uphold its reputation

Principles

P–3B.1—When we do not agree with program policies, we shall first attempt to effect change through constructive action with the organization.

P–3B.2—We shall speak or act on behalf of an organization only when authorized. We shall take care to note when we are speaking for the organization and when we are expressing a personal judgment.

C—Responsibilities to Employees
Ideals

I–3C.1—To promote policies and working conditions that foster competence, well-being, and self-esteem in staff members.

I–3C.2—To create a climate of trust and candor that will enable staff to speak and act in the best interests of children, families, and the field of early childhood education.

I–3C.3—To strive to secure an adequate livelihood for those who work with or on behalf of young children.

Principles

P–3C.1—In decisions concerning children and programs, we shall appropriately utilize the training, experience, and expertise of staff members.

P–3C.2—We shall provide staff members with working conditions that permit them to carry out their responsibilities, timely and non-threatening evaluation procedures, written grievance procedures, constructive feedback, and opportunities for continuing professional development and advancement.

P–3C.3—We shall develop and maintain comprehensive written personnel policies that define program standards and, when applicable, that specify the extent to which employees are accountable for their conduct outside the workplace. These policies shall be given to new staff members and shall be available for review by all staff members.

P–3C.4—Employees who do not meet program standards shall be informed of areas of concern and, when possible, assisted in improving their performance.

P–3C.5—Employees who are dismissed shall be informed of the reasons for their termination. When a dismissal is for cause, justification must be based on evidence of inadequate or inappropriate behavior that is accurately documented, current, and available for the employee to review.

P–3C.6—In making evaluations and recommendations, judgments shall be based on fact and relevant to the interests of children and programs.

P–3C.7—Hiring and promotion shall be based solely on a person's record of accomplishment and ability to carry out the responsibilities of the position.

P–3C.8—In hiring, promotion, and provision of training, we shall not participate in any form of discrimination based on race, religion, gender, national origin, culture, disability, age, or sexual preference. We shall be familiar with laws and regulations that pertain to employment discrimination.

SECTION IV: ETHICAL RESPONSIBILITIES TO COMMUNITY AND SOCIETY

Early childhood programs operate within a context of an immediate community made up of families and other institutions concerned with children's welfare. Our responsibilities to the community are to provide programs that meet its needs and to cooperate with agencies and professions that share responsibility for children. Because the larger society has a measure of responsibility for the welfare and protection of children, and because of our specialized expertise in child development, we acknowledge an obligation to serve as a voice for children everywhere.

Ideals

I–4.1—To provide the community with high-quality, culturally sensitive programs and services.

I–4.2—To promote cooperation among agencies and interdisciplinary collaboration among professions concerned with the welfare of young children, their families, and their teachers.

I–4.3—To work, through education, research, and advocacy, toward an environmentally safe world in which all children are adequately fed, sheltered, and nurtured.

I–4.4—To work, through education, research, and advocacy, toward a society in which all young children have access to quality programs.

I–4.5—To promote knowledge and understanding of young children and their needs. To work toward greater social acknowledgment of children's rights and greater social acceptance of responsibility for their well-being.

I–4.6—To support policies and laws that promote the well-being of children and families. To oppose those that impair their well-being. To participate in developing those that are needed. To cooperate with other individuals and groups in these efforts.

I–4.7—To further the professional development of the field of early childhood education and to strengthen its commitment to realizing its core values as reflected in this Code.

Principles

P–4.1—We shall communicate openly and truthfully about the nature and extent of services that we provide.

P–4.2—We shall not accept or continue to work in positions for which we are personally unsuited or professionally unqualified. We shall not offer services that we do not have the competence, qualifications, or resources to provide.

P–4.3—We shall be objective and accurate in reporting the knowledge upon which we base our program practices.

P–4.4—We shall cooperate with other professionals who work with children and their families.

P–4.5—We shall not hire or recommend for employment any person who is unsuited for a position with respect to competence, qualifications, or character.

P–4.6—We shall report the unethical or incompetent behavior of a colleague to a supervisor when informal resolution is not effective.

P–4.7—We shall be familiar with laws and regulations that serve to protect the children in our programs

P–4.8—We shall not participate in practices which are in violation of laws and regulations that protect children in our programs.

P–4.9—When we have evidence that an early childhood program is violating laws or regulations protecting children, we shall report it to persons responsible for the program. If compliance is not accomplished within a reasonable time, we will report the violation to appropriate authorities who can be expected to remedy the situation.

P–4.10—When we have evidence that an agency or professional charged with providing services to children, families, or teachers is failing to meet its obligations, we acknowledge a collective ethical responsibility to report the problem to appropriate authorities or to the public.

P–4.11—When a program violates or requires its employees to violate this Code, it is permissible, after fair assessment of the evidence, to disclose the identity of that program.

Director's Library[1]

Leading People

Early Childhood Directors Association, *S.O.S. Kit for Directors*. St. Paul, MN: Resources for Child Caring (distributed by Toys'n Things Press), 1987.

Practical answers to directors' most frequently encountered problems in supervising, organizing, and supporting staff.

Gordon, *Thomas. Leadership Effectiveness Training* (LET). Putnam 1984.

The basic skills for effective interpersonal communication, including active listening, "I" messages, and no-lose problem solving are covered. These skills are analogues to those covered in Gordon's Teacher Effectiveness Training and Parent Effectiveness Training.

Jones, Elizabeth. *Teaching Adults. An Active Learning Approach* NAEYC, 1986.

Although this is a story based on the author's experience as a teacher of child development in a university setting, the notions about building trusting relationships, empowering learners, and trusting the learners' potential have implications for parent education, staff development and in-service training.

McGregor, Douglas. *The Human Side of Enterprise.* New York: McGraw-Hill, 1985.

A management classic. This 25th anniversary printing makes a persuasive case for abandoning traditional authoritarian leadership approaches and focusing instead on employees' abilities to direct their own performance.

Steinmetz, Lawrence L. *Managing the Marginal and Unsatisfactory Performer* (2nd ed.). Reading, MA: Addison-Wesley, 1985.

An in-depth look at the supervision of difficult workers. This book looks at the issue both from theoretical (motivational and personality theories) and practical (identification, appraisal, supervision, counseling, and severance) perspectives.

Working with Staff, Board, Community, and Parents

Caruso, J. J. and M. T. Faucett, *Supervision in Early Childhood Education: A Developmental Perspective.* New York: Teachers College Press, 1986.

This book addresses supervisory issues pertinent to personnel in both public and private settings. The focus of this book is staff development, and it is both descriptive and practical.

Greenman, J. T. and R. W. Fuqua (eds). *Making Day Care Better: Training, Evaluation and the Process of Change.* New York: Teachers College Press, 1986.

Descriptions of the current status of the child care field and recommendations on how to promote positive changes. Issues dealt with include environments, caregivers, marketing, evaluation, regulation, training, consultation and information and referral.

Jones, Elizabeth (ed.). *Growing Teachers: Partnerships in Staff Development.* NAEYC, 1993.

This book applies a constructivist model for staff development. It describes activities which

[1]Adapted with permission from *Child Care Information Exchange*, P.O. Box 2890, Redmond, WA 98073

are open in design; where philosophy and process are defined, but not outcomes. Using these approaches, teachers are expected to participate actively in the construction of knowledge about their work, and about how they can grow professionally.

Jorde-Bloom, P., Marilyn Sheerer, and Joan Britz. *Blueprint for Action: Achieving Center-Based Change through Staff Development.* New Horizons Press (distributed by Gryphon House, Inc.), 1991.

This book does not offer "quick fixes" or prescriptions for improving relationships in a center. Rather it offers a comprehensive method for analyzing program components, which will help with diagnosing organizational problems and in selecting ways to implement and evaluate progress.

Jorde-Bloom, P. A. *A Great Place to Work: Improving Conditions for Staff in Young Children's Programs.* NAEYC, 1988.

Directors concerned about retaining qualified staff will find this book helpful. It provides information on the kind of environments that are conducive to professional and personal fulfillment.

National Association for the Education of Young Children (NAEYC), *Family-Friendly Communication for Early Childhood Programs*, Debora Diffily and Kathy Morrison, (eds), 1996.

This practical resource for directors includes samples of messages to include in Newsletters for parents. Each item is designed so it can be photocopied and included in your correspondence to parents. No permission is required to use the material. The messages, written for lay persons, address the many facets of developmentally appropriate practice.

National Directory of Children, Youth & Families Services (9th edition). P.O. Box 1837, Longmont, CO 80502–1837, 1994.

This is a current and up-to-date resource to State, County and Federal agencies and services for children, youth and families. It includes names, addresses, phone numbers, and fax numbers for all agencies and services listed.

Stonehouse, Anne, *How Does It Feel?*, Child Care Information Exchange, 1995.

This book aims to help child care staff get a clearer idea of how child care feels to a parent.

Because it is so important for all staff to understand the importance of seeing the child in the context of the family, this booklet is one a director must share with the teaching staff.

Warger, Cynthia (ed.). *A Resource Guide to Public School Early Childhood Programs.* Alexandria, VA: Association for Supervision and Curriculum Development (ASCD), 1988.

The purpose of this collection of articles is to address issues and concerns that surround decisions that administrators and teachers must make regarding preschools in public schools. Discussion of appropriate practice and concerns about pressures on young children is followed by descriptions of nineteen programs in public schools.

Watkins, Kathleen P. and Lucius Durant, Jr. *Preschool Directors Staff Development Handbook.* West Nyack, N.Y.: The Center for Applied Research in Education, 1987.

This guide provides practical techniques and materials for improving staff development and in-service training. It includes material on leadership styles, and also discusses the use of staff development as a means of motivating change.

Financial Management Fund-Raising and Marketing

American Appraisal Associates, Inc. *Appraisal of an Operating Day-Care Center: Real Estate Valuation Guide.* 525 E. Michigan Street, P.O. Box 664, Milwaukee, WI 53201, 1986.

This booklet is designed to facilitate the appraisal of the real estate, equipment and the operation itself of a child care center. There is discussion of three valuation approaches—the cost approach, the income approach, and the market data approach.

Children's Defense Fund. *An Advocate's Guide to Fund Raising.* Children's Defense Fund Publications, 1990.

This booklet covers the basics of how to raise money from foundations, corporations, and individuals.

Finn, Matia. *Fundraising for Early Childhood Programs: Getting Started and Getting Results.* Washington, DC: NAEYC, 1982.

This booklet describes techniques used by nonprofit institutions to raise money by contacting sources of support including individual donors, corporations, foundations, and government. It also includes a section on proposal writing and an updated bibliography.

Gross, Malvern, and William Warshauer. *Financial and Accounting Guide for Nonprofit Organizations.* New York: John Wiley and Sons, 1995.

Comprehensive, well-written resource. Detailed advice on cash, accrual, and fund accounting; financial statements; budgeting; internal control; tax requirements; and bookkeeping.

Morgan, Gwen. *Managing the Day Care Dollars: A Financial Handbook.* (Rev. Ed.) Cambridge, MA.: Steam Press, 1992.

A practical guide to financial management in the child care setting. Addresses budgeting, accounting, financial statements, and meeting insurance needs.

National Governors' Association. *Taking Care: State Developments in Child Care.* Center for Policy Research, Washington, DC.

This report summarizes state funding resources for child care services as states begin to implement the federally mandated Family Support Act. Citing evidence from a recent survey, the report suggests that states will continue to expand their role as regulators, system builders, and employers in support of child care assistance for families.

On-Target Marketing: Promotion Strategies for Child Care Centers, Child Care Information Exchange, 1996.

A compilation of articles which first appeared in Child Care Information Exchange: The Director's Magazine. Very helpful articles on courting the press, advertising your center, and handling parents' visits to your center.

Young, Joyce. *Fundraising for Non-Profit Groups.* Seattle, WA: Self-Counsel Press, 1981.

A practical fundraising guide with ideas on developing strategies, approaching corporations, foundations, and government agencies; direct mail solicitation; and fundraising in small communities.

Children with Special Needs

Allen, K. Eileen, and Ilene S. Schwartz. *The Exceptional Child: Inclusion in Childhood Education* (3d ed.). Delmar, 2001.

Although this book focuses on mainstreaming special needs children, emphasis is on teachers having a thorough knowledge of normal growth and development as a major avenue for creating developmentally appropriate programs for children who are "at risk" or have developmental problems.

Child Care Law Center. *Caring for Children with Special Needs: The American's With Disabilities Act and Child Care.* ADA Series, 1993.

A well-written booklet which discusses admitting and accommodating special needs children plus a discussion of liability and record-keeping issues when children with disabilities are enrolled. The booklet contains an extensive list of resources for center directors.

Caring for Children with Special Needs: The Americans with Disabilities Act, Child Care Law Center.

This 44 page booklet covers questions and issues about admitting children with disabilities, what are viewed as "reasonable accommodations" for these children, and who will cover the extra costs of inclusion.

Meisels, Samuel J. and Sally Provence. *Screening and Assessment: Guidelines for Identifying Young Disabled and Developmentally Vulnerable Children and Their Families.* Zero to Three/National Center for Clinical Infant Programs, 1989.

These guidelines identify and assess children who should participate in programs related to the infant-toddler and preschool components of the Individuals with Disabilities Education Act. It focuses on the rationale, core components, and guidelines for establishing a system of screening and assessing children with disabilities and those who are developmentally vulnerable, birth through age five.

Miller, Regina, *The Developmentally Appropriate Inclusive Classroom in Early Education*, Delmar, 1996.

An exploration of the role of developmentally appropriate curriculum and practice in the inclusive classroom, through the implementation of an integrated thematic curriculum. This book features the application of theory to practice by drawing upon practical situations from classroom practice.

Rab, Victoria Y. and Karen I. Wood, *Child Care and the ADA*, Bookes, 1995.

In clear and practical terms, this book offers information and support needed by early childhood educators to effectively implement inclusive programs, and make them work. It is a guide to professionals as they make plans to include children with disabilities.

Health, Safety, and Sick Child Care

American Academy of Pediatrics. *Report of the Committee on Infectious Diseases* (20th edition). 1986.

This manual and subsequent updated policies from AAP provide specific criteria for exclusion of children with infectious diseases from child care centers.

Child Welfare League of America. *Serving Children With HIV Infection in Child Day Care: A Guide for Center-Based and Family Day Care Providers.* 1991.

This book presents a straightforward and reassuring approach to working with HIV-infected children and their families. It provides information on how to safeguard children, families, and staff while meeting the needs of HIV infected children.

Model Child Care Health Policies, PA Chapter, American Academy of Pediatrics, Bryn Mawr, PA., 1993.

These model health policies are written for any type of child care facility. The book includes sections on care of ill children, sanitation and hygiene, evacuation drills and plans, food handling and feeding policies, etc. It also includes some emergency plans and medication policies.

Marotz, Lynn R., Jeanettia M. Rush, and Marie Z. Cross, *Health, Safety and Nutrition* (5d ed.). Delmar, 2001.

This up-to-date, comprehensive text covers the essential aspects of health, safety, and nutrition for young children. It includes material on infant nutrition, AIDS, and sanitary procedures in group care facilities.

National Association for the Education of Young Children. *Healthy Young Children: A Manual for Programs.* Abby Shapiro Kendrick, Roxanne Kaufman, & Katherine P. Messenger (eds.), 1988.

This excellent manual is a reference and resource guide to help you meet your health and safety responsibilities. The information reflects the current research and recommendations from experts in both health and early childhood education.

National Center for Prevention Services. *Immunization: National Resource Directory: Informational and Educational Materials for Health Care Professionals and the General Public.* U.S. Department of Health and Human Services, Centers for Disease Control, 1993.

This directory contains names, addresses and phone numbers for organizations which distribute informational and educational materials on immunizations.

National Maternal and Child Health Clearinghouse, *National Health and Safety Performance Standards: Guidelines for Out-of-Home Child Care Programs*, National Center for Education in Maternal and Child Health, Arlington, VA., 1992.

This huge volume presents a set of health standards which can be applied to child care programs across the country. This set of standards was jointly developed by the American Public Health Association and the American Academy of Pediatrics.

Work/Family Directions. *A Little Bit Under the Weather: A Look at Care for Mildly Ill Children.* 1986.

A comprehensive coverage of the need for sick child care and how it is viewed by child care professionals, families, employers, medical professionals, and the child.

Infant/Toddler Care

Godwin, Annabelle and Lorraine Schrag. *Setting Up for Infant Care: Guidelines for Centers and Family Day Care Homes.* Washington, DC: NAEYC, 1988.

This collection of articles by practitioners describes quality care for infants and toddlers, and includes examples of kinds of equipment, personnel practices, uses of time and space, health and safety practices, and budget information for both center-based and family day care home infant/toddler care.

Greenberg, Polly. *Character Development: Encouraging Self-Esteem and Self-Discipline in Infants, Toddlers, and Two-Year-Olds.* NAEYC, 1991.

The twelve essays in this book examine what infants and toddlers need and how care can fill those needs in a high quality, respectful way.

Weiser, Margaret G., *Infant/Toddler Care and Education*, (2nd Ed.), Merrill, 1991.

This author uses the term "educaring", following the lead of Magda Gerber and Bettye Caldwell who also use this term, which so aptly describes what infant/toddler caregivers do. The text covers development, curriculum, health and safety, and the environment. A helpful resource for centers which provide infant/toddler care.

Evaluation

Bredekamp, S. and T. Rosegrant (eds.). *Reaching Potentials: Appropriate Curriculum and Assessment for Young Children*, Vol. 1. NAEYC, 1992.

This book presents guidelines for curriculum and assessment practices which will make it more likely for both teachers and children to reach their potentials.

Harms, T., Cryer, D., & Clifford, R. Early *Childhood Environmental Rating Scale*. Teachers College Press, 1234 Amsterdam Avenue New York, NY 10027

There are 4 Harms, Cryer & Clifford Rating Scales. They are:

Infant/Toddler Environment Rating Scale (ITERS)

Early Childhood Environment Rating Scale (ECERS)

School-Age Care Environment Rating Scale (SACERS)

Family Daycare Rating Scale (FDCRS)

These easy-to-use evaluation instruments answer many questions about the adequacy of early childhood settings. The ratings cover issues such as space, care routines, language, reasoning skills, social development, and adult needs.

Jorde-Bloom, Paula. *Improving the Quality of Work Life: A Guide for Enhancing Organizational Climate in the Early Childhood Setting*. Early Childhood Professional Development Project, National College of Education, 2840 Sheridan Road, Evanston, IL 60201, 1986.

After an overview of the concept of organizational climate as it relates to the quality of work life in the early childhood setting, an assessment tool for measuring organizational climate is provided. Helpful suggestions for how a cen-

ter director can improve the overall quality of work life are also included.

Planning Spaces

Greenman, Jim. *Caring Spaces, Learning Places: Children's Environments that Work*. Redmond, WA: Exchange Press, 1988.

This is a helpful guide to planning spaces for young children. It is full of ideas and observations, as well as problems and solutions for those responsible for planning spaces for child care.

Vergeront, Jeanne. *Places and Spaces for Preschool and Primary (Indoors) and Places and Spaces for Preschool and Primary (Outdoors)*. National Association for the Education of Young Children, 1987 and 1988.

These two booklets can be a handy reference on indoor and outdoor spaces for directors who need something to share with parents, board members or funders.

Program Management

Child Welfare League of America. *Guide for Establishing and Operating Day Care Centers for Young Children*. Revised 1991.

This booklet provides a brief and concise overview of essential information in the areas of licensing, budgeting, housing and equipping, staffing, and dealing with health and safety issues for those who are responsible for operating a child care center.

Program Development, Curriculum, and Guidance

Boyer, E. L. *Ready to Learn: A Mandate for the Nation*. The Carnegie Foundation for the Advancement of Teaching, 1991.

This report is about all the nation's children and how we can be sure that all of them are ready for school.

Bredekamp, Sue and C. Coppel (eds). *Developmentally Appropriate Practice in Early Childhood Programs* Washington, D.C.: NAEYC, 1997.

This book is intended to explain the position of NAEYC on what is developmentally appropriate practice birth through age eight. It will help teachers, directors, parents, and board members better understand sound practice which should reverse the current trend toward a narrow focus on academics for young children.

Cohen, Dorothy H. and Virginia Stern, with Nancy Balaban. *Observing and Recording the Behavior of Young Children* (3rd ed.). New York: Teachers College Press, 1983.

A classic text for learning about children through observation. It includes material applicable to infants and toddlers and children with special needs.

Feeney, Stephanie, et al. *Who Am I In the Lives of Children?* (5th ed.). Merrill (an imprint of Macmillan), 1995.

A particular strength of this book is the practical discussion of guidelines, strategies, and suggestions for coping with many of the troublesome parts of teaching. These authors are primarily concerned with the development of thoughtful teachers.

Gordon, Ann Miles and Kathryn Williams Browne. *Beginnings and Beyond: Foundations in Early Childhood Education* (5th edition). Albany, N.Y.: Delmar, 2001.

A comprehensive text covering many of the traditional questions which are of interest to early childhood educators including: What Is The Field of Early Childhood? Who Is the Young Child? Who Are the Teachers of the Young Child? What Is the Setting? What Is Being Taught? and How Do We Teach for Tomorrow?

Hendrick, Joanne. *The Whole Child: Developmental Education for Early Years* (6th ed.). Merrill 1996.

This excellent book assumes that the function of education is to care for the whole child. Recommendations for curriculum are based on the assumption that children develop in stages, and that teachers can assist growth by offering age-appropriate and challenging classroom experiences.

Jones, E. and J. Nimmo, *Emergent Curriculum*, NAEYC, 1994.

This practical book emphasizes that planning needs to emerge from the daily life of children, and must be based on their interests. The "emergent curriculum" concept implies a harmonious combination of planning and spontaneity, and both of these come to life in this book.

Kamii, Constance, M. Manning, G. Manning (eds.). *Early Literacy: A Constructivist Foundation for Whole Language.* NAEYC, 1991.

The purpose of this book is to consider early literacy education and whole-language from the perspective of constructivist theory and research. It is meant to enable whole-language advocates to improve upon their beliefs and practices about how children acquire knowledge.

Koralek, D. G., et al, *The What, Why and How of High-Quality Early Childhood Education: A Guide for the On-Site Supervisor*, NAEYC, 1993.

This guide for on-site supervision was designed as a practical tool for trainers and supervisors in early childhood education programs. It is useful for many persons in supervisory situations including educational coordinators for Head Start, curriculum specialists in military child care, directors of private child care centers, and family child care training specialists.

Miller, D. F., *Positive Child Guidance*, (2nd ed.), Delmar, 1996.

Child guidance is a challenging process of finding ways to help children become responsible, cooperative members of their group. This book is for caregivers who spend a great deal of time helping children become self-disciplined members of society. It is intended as a road map to guide adults, as they work to meet the individual needs of children from infancy through early childhood.

Moomaw, S. *More Than Singing*, Redleaf Press, 1997.

This book, which includes a cassette recording, offers a wealth of wonderful musical experiences which teachers can plan, even though they may not be trained musicians. Teachers will learn to make resonant, inexpensive instruments as well as gain knowledge about how to select songs and rhythm activities, and coordinate these with their whole language curriculum.

Moomaw, S. and B. Hieronymous, *More Than Magnets*, Redleaf Press, 1997.

The science curriculum in early childhood classrooms has typically consisted of a classroom "display", usually with a plant/animal focus, or teacher-directed experiments. This book offers a comprehensive, developmentally appropriate approach to science education with young children, with special attention to physics and math. It has more than 100 activities that engage children in interactive science explorations, in many areas of the classroom.

Moomaw, S. and B. Hieronymous, *More Than Counting: Whole Math Activities for Preschool and Kindergarten*, Redleaf Press, 1995.

An excellent resource for use with teachers and parents as they come to understand the "whole math" curriculum based on the constructivist model of cognitive development. The math games and materials described here in detail are not just additions to enrich the curriculum, they are the math curriculum for preschool and kindergarten.

National Association for the Education of Young Children, *Reaching Potentials: Appropriate Curriculum and Assessment of Young Children, (Vol. 1)*, Sue Bredekamp and T. Rosegrant, (eds.), 1992.

This volume includes the thoughts of many contributors who address reaching potentials for special needs, minority, and linguistically diverse children through anti-bias curriculum. There is also discussion of developmentally appropriate curriculum with a framework for how to apply developmentally appropriate practice.

National Association for the Education of Young Children, *Reaching Potentials: Transforming Early Childhood Curriculum and Assessment (Vol. 2)*, Bredekamp, Sue, and T. Rosegrant, (eds) 1995.

This second volume focuses on how to reach potentials through transforming specific areas of the curriculum, including math, science, social studies, visual arts, music and language, and literacy.

Phillips, D. A. (ed.). *Quality in Child Care: What Does Research Tell Us?* NAEYC, 1987.

The research reported in this volume reflects the full range of quality child care available. Together, the contributions to this monograph illustrate the value of pursuing answers to the question, "What is high quality child care?" if we are ever to make this goal a reality for children.

Read, Katherine, Pat Gardner, and Barbara Mahler. *Early Childhood Programs: Human Relations and Learning* (9th ed.). Harcourt, Brace, Jovanovich, 1993.

No director's library should be without this time tested book now in its ninth edition. Play is emphasized as the most important mode of

learning for young children, and there is a major focus on understanding and guiding children's personality development. The authors point out the importance of a trusting, close relationship between the child and the teacher.

Teachers College Press, *Valuing Quality in Early Childhood Services: New Approaches to Defining Quality*, Peter Moss and Alan Moss (Eds.), 1994.

The chapters in this book which include contributions from eighteen experts on early childhood services, fall into three main areas of discussion relevant to the question of quality in early childhood services. These areas are: (1) ways to define quality, (2) researching quality, and (3) examples of processes and structures which support the development of a new inclusionary model for quality.

Diversity/Anti-Biased Curriculum

Child Welfare League of America. *Cultural Competence Self-Assessment Instrument.* 1993.

This self-assessment instrument will assist an agency in identifying strengths and weaknesses in its' response to a culturally diverse staff and client population, and will enable the agency to develop action steps for specific management and/or service delivery changes to progress toward the goal of cultural competence.

Derman-Sparks, L. and the A.B.C. Task Force. *Anti-Bias Curriculum: Tools for Empowering Young Children.* NAEYC, 1989.

Teachers can use principles and methodology from this book to create an anti-bias curriculum in relation to the specific groups of children and families in their settings.

Kendall, Frances E., *Diversity In The Classroom: New Approaches to the Education of Young Children*, Teachers College Press, 1996.

This new edition builds on the theory presented in the earlier edition, and also incorporates the perspectives of Michael Cole, Howard Gardner, and Lev Vygotsky. The author addresses many aspects of anti-bias education, focusing particularly on the teacher's role as a change agent.

Gonzalez-Mena, J. *Multicultural Issues in Child Care.* Mayfield, 1993.

This booklet is a companion to Louise Derman-Sparks' Anti-Bias Curriculum (see above). This author takes off from where Derman-Sparks stopped. Derman-Sparks' focus is on an anti-bias approach to preschool curriculum; the focus here is on an anti-bias approach to cultural information, adult relations, and conflicts in goals, values, expectations, and child-rearing practices.

Neugebauer, B. (ed.). *Alike and Different: Exploring Our Humanity with Young Children* (Revised Edition). NAEYC, 1992.

This is a collection of essays which will help teachers integrate children with special needs and children from diverse backgrounds, and make programs better for everyone.

Saracho, O. N. and B. Spodek (eds.). *Understanding the Multicultural Experience in Early Childhood Education.* NAEYC, 1983.

This book incorporates the contributions of professionals concerned with the education of children from various cultural and ethnic groups. It presents different interpretations of the functions and consequences of early childhood education, and its impact upon people of different cultural groups.

Tobin, J. J., et al. *Preschool in Three Cultures.* Yale University Press, 1991.

This book explains Japanese, Chinese and American preschools from both insiders' and outsiders' points of view. It ends with a comparative discussion of the ways people from each of the three countries conceptualize the purpose of preschools.

Funding

Annual Register of Grant Support. Bowker, R. R. (ed.). 1997.

A comprehensive guide to various types of grant support, both governmental and private.

Getting a Grant: How to Write Successful Proposals. 1990.

A general guide to writing proposals for funding.

National Databook, 7th edition, 2 volumes. 1983.

A listing of grantmaking foundations in the United States. Chiefly of use in seeking grants for groups or projects.

The Foundation Directory. 1993.

Nonprofit, non-governmental organizations with resources of one million or more, or those making grants of $500,000 or more per year. Covers both grants to individual grant seekers and grants to organizations. Excellent index by subject field.

The Foundation Grants Index. 1993.

Funding interests of major foundations by subject area, geographic focus, types of support, and types of organizations which received grants in the past.

Computer Information

A to Z: The Early Childhood Educator's Guide to the Internet, by ERIC/EECE Publications, 1997.

This guide is a basic primer and tool for finding and using resources on the Internet that are of interest to early childhood educators. The guide cites resources accessible by various Internet tools, (Telnet, Gopher, World Wide Web browsers, news groups, electronic discussion lists, etc.); produced by various organizations and institutions in the field of education.

It is arranged by broad subject areas and has subject, organizational, geographic, and personnel indexes.

Index